Cook on Costs
2003

ABOUT THE AUTHOR

Judge Michael Cook is unique in the realm of legal remuneration. Before his appointment as a circuit judge he broadcast frequently on radio and TV. He has been the Secretary and President of the London Solicitors Litigation Association, of which he is proud to be an honorary member, and a founder member of both Holborn and Westminster Law Societies. On behalf of the Law Society he negotiated with the Lord Chancellor's Department about levels of remuneration and costs reforms over many years. He also sat regularly as an assessor with High Court judges on reviews of taxation (now assessments) and advised and represented many firms of solicitors on costs problems, appearing as advocate in several leading costs cases. He is now the general editor of *Butterworths Costs Service* and of *The Litigation Letter*, a contributor to *Cordery on Solicitors*, a member of the SCCO Costs Practitioners Group, lectures on costs for the Judicial Studies Board, chairs the IBC annual costs seminar and is the Honorary President of the Association of Law Costs Draftsmen. He is currently a member of the Civil Justice Council's working party on predictable costs and Costs Forum.

Cook on Costs 2003

A guide to legal remuneration in civil contentious and non-contentious business

Michael J Cook

Butterworths
A member of the LexisNexis Group

Members of the LexisNexis Group worldwide

United Kingdom	LexisNexis Butterworths Tolley, a Division of Reed Elsevier (UK) Ltd, Halsbury House, 35 Chancery Lane, LONDON, WC2A 1EL, and 4 Hill Street, EDINBURGH EH2 3JZ
Argentina	LexisNexis Argentina, BUENOS AIRES
Australia	LexisNexis Butterworths, CHATSWOOD, New South Wales
Austria	LexisNexis Verlag ARD Orac GmbH & Co KG, VIENNA
Canada	LexisNexis Butterworths, MARKHAM, Ontario
Chile	LexisNexis Chile Ltda, SANTIAGO DE CHILE
Czech Republic	Nakladatelství Orac sro, PRAGUE
France	Editions du Juris-Classeur SA, PARIS
Hong Kong	LexisNexis Butterworths, HONG KONG
Hungary	HVG-Orac, BUDAPEST
India	LexisNexis Butterworths, NEW DELHI
Ireland	Butterworths (Ireland) Ltd, DUBLIN
Italy	Giuffrè Editore, MILAN
Malaysia	Malayan Law Journal Sdn Bhd, KUALA LUMPUR
New Zealand	LexisNexis Butterworths, WELLINGTON
Poland	Wydawnictwo Prawnicze LexisNexis, WARSAW
Singapore	LexisNexis Butterworths, SINGAPORE
South Africa	LexisNexis Butterworths, DURBAN
Switzerland	Stämpfli Verlag AG, BERNE
USA	LexisNexis, DAYTON, Ohio

A CIP Catalogue record for this book is available from the British Library.

First edition 1991
Second edition 1995
Third edition 1998
First annual edition 2000

ISBN 0 406 95862 9

Typeset by Columns Design Ltd, Reading, Berks
Printed in Great Britain by Clays Ltd, Bungay, Suffolk

PREFACE

For many years I was asked why I was interested in such a boring subject as legal costs. No longer. Lord Justice May has described them as being the biggest problem of all in civil litigation, while the Master of the Rolls refers to what he calls the 'costs industry' and to the satellite litigation arising out of conditional fee agreements involving many who would not otherwise have become involved in the rather specialised area of costs. Certainly the Court of Appeal with its decision in *Callery v Gray* last year and *Halloran v Delaney* this year, has more than justified the decision to produce *Cook on Costs* annually. I only wish they would not leave their ground-breaking judgments until just after I have delivered my manuscript to the publishers!

Apart from the headline hitters, there have been many developments during the past 12 months in most areas of contentious and non-contentious costs, including wasted costs, litigants in person and a decision, which is being appealed, that in probate work it may no longer be appropriate for a solicitor's charges to be based both on value and the number of hours spent.

I am again grateful to my colleagues on *Butterworths Costs Service*, Nicholas Bacon, Harry Birks and David Chalk, for their respective contributions to the chapters on state funding, detailed assessment and conditional fee agreements. Perhaps the work should now be re-titled *Cook and Co on Costs*.

Finally, a word of thanks to those readers who have drawn attention to errors and misprints and generally made helpful suggestions. All contributions are gratefully received. Two prize misprints in the last edition were a reference to me acting for many 'forms' of solicitors and the heading of CPR Rule 44.12 as 'Cases where costs orders deemed to have been mad'. Both were beyond the help of spell-check.

The law is stated as at 1 November 2002.

Michael Cook
Burwood Park
November 2002

FOREWORD TO THE FIRST ANNUAL EDITION

For litigation practitioners, the issue of costs used to be a relative afterthought. However, over the last decade the pendulum has swung to the point where the funding of litigation – whether the case can be funded and who pays what to whom at the end – has become a new and essential skill for litigators everywhere.

Fortunately *Cook on Costs* has been there in recent years to help the profession steer its way through the costs maze. But even Michael Cook, whose authorship on this complex subject has always kept us up-to-date, has appreciated that the current pace of change is so fast that an annual edition is now required. So that is what he has produced in the first annual edition of *Cook on Costs*. This is an indispensable text for every solicitor, whose own understanding of costs and the funding of litigation by conditional fees, the state or otherwise, is essential to the overriding need to ensure that costs issues are fully explained to and understood by the client.

Like my predecessor, Phillip Ely, who wrote the foreword to the excellent first edition, I am delighted to commend to all firms the timely arrival of *Cook on Costs 2000*.

Michael Napier
President
The Law Society

FOREWORD TO THE FIRST EDITION

It is my privilege as President of the Law Society to commend Michael Cook's very practical guide to all aspects of solicitors' costs (other than criminal costs).

He modestly suggests that the book does not contain any facts and figures that cannot be found elsewhere. Recognising the ultimate and total dependence of solicitors on the costs which they receive, he presents all those facts and figures with clarity borne of experience. This book adds to the major contribution which Michael Cook has already made to the profession on this vital topic.

It is also a clear response to the need for a definitive and manageable guide to an area which requires such practical and positive skills.

I hope that it will find a place in every solicitor's office.

October 1991

P T Ely
President
The Law Society

PREFACE TO THE FIRST EDITION

When the publishers asked me to write a preface I cavilled on the two grounds that no-one reads prefaces and they serve no useful purpose. I was told that the purpose is to explain the aims and intention of the work; in other words, why I have written the book and why you should read it. Fair enough. My late partner, Lionel Cranfield, at the end of some heavy litigation used to say, 'Now we come to the interesting part – the costs!'. In the quarter of a century since Lionel was killed in the hunting field, the profession has become increasingly aware that money is the life-blood of a solicitor's practice, but I continue to be perplexed that, in spite of this realisation, most solicitors and their clients lose out financially because of the profession's basic lack of understanding and interest in all aspects of costs. In a College of Law survey of the areas of skills on which solicitors wished the Law Society's new Legal Practice course to be based, costs did not even appear in the list.

And that is why I have written this book. It does not contain any facts and figures you cannot find elsewhere – apart from it being illustrated from my collection of unreported cases – but I have tried to write about costs in an interesting, coherent and digestible way. My aim in writing the book is therefore to impart to you the understanding of, and enthusiasm for, costs that Lionel Cranfield aroused in me all those years ago.

I much appreciate the kindness of Philip Ely in writing a foreword to the book in his year as President of the Law Society. I am seriously indebted to my old friend Master Michael Devonshire of the Supreme Court Taxing Office for reading the manuscript of the book and making many useful suggestions on the condition that I did not mention his name.

The law is stated as at 1 October 1991.

Michael Cook
Limpsfield
October 1991

ACKNOWLEDGMENTS

Many of the unreported cases first appeared in *The Litigation Letter* and are reproduced with the kind permission of the publishers, Informa plc.

Extracts from the various Law Society publications and Legal Services Commission material are reproduced with the kind permission of the Law Society and Legal Services Commission.

CONTENTS

PART II BETWEEN THE PARTIES

TABLE OF STATUTES

*References in the right-hand column are to page number. Page references printed in **bold** type indicate where the Act is set out in part or in full.*

TABLE OF STATUTORY INSTRUMENTS

*References in the right-hand column are to page number. Page references printed in **bold** type indicate where the statutory instrument is set out in part or in full.*

TABLE OF CIVIL PROCEDURE RULES

*References in the right-hand column are to page number. Page references printed in **bold** type indicate where the CPR is set out in part or in full.*

TABLE OF PRACTICE DIRECTIONS SUPPLEMENTARY TO CPR

*References in the right-hand column are to page number. Page references printed in **bold** type indicate where the Section is set out in part or in full.*

TABLE OF NON-STATUTORY PROVISIONS

*References in the right-hand column are to page number. Page references printed in **bold** type indicate where the provisions are set out in part or in full.*

TABLE OF CASES

C

D

H

I

N

O

S

Part I

Solicitor and client

CHAPTER 1

THE RETAINER

1. A CAUTIONARY TALE

Let us start with a story. It arose when I was sitting as Chairman of the Solicitors' Disciplinary Tribunal, so it is a horror story. The applicant, in person, complained that the respondent had been guilty of conduct unbefitting a solicitor. The applicant's wife wished to sue her former employers, HM Government, over pension rights. In his search for justice on behalf of his wife, the applicant had been to no fewer than 22 firms of solicitors in London – a circumstance he regarded as reflecting criticism on the legal profession and not on himself. The respondent was his twenty-third solicitor. The respondent agreed to instruct counsel to see the applicant in conference and thereafter to give his opinion in writing. The applicant paid the respondent £150 on account of costs. The conference was a disaster. It lasted for over three hours and broke up in confusion. There was no doubt that it was agreed that the applicant would provide counsel with further papers through his solicitor. On receipt of the further papers, the solicitor rendered a bill to the applicant for £450 plus £250 counsel's fees, requesting immediate payment together with a further sum of £2,000 generally on account of costs before he would deliver the papers to counsel. The client demurred. He wrote to the solicitor saying that the sum of £150 that he had paid was an all-in fee. When he heard nothing he wrote to the solicitor with detailed complaints and enquiries, to which he again received no reply. The solicitor issued a writ against the applicant and his wife for his and counsel's fees. He obtained summary judgment. On appeal the judgment was set aside and the action transferred to the county court. In the middle of the trial before the judge in the county court the applicant sought an adjournment, which unlikely request was granted only upon the condition that the applicant paid the full amount of money claimed into court. He failed to do this and judgment was entered once again. Although the applicant again appealed, the Court of Appeal refused leave to appeal. The solicitor issued a bankruptcy petition. On the hearing of the petition the applicant disputed the judgment on which the petition was based, but again he failed. He and his wife were adjudicated bankrupt. The applicant reported the solicitor to the Professional Purposes Committee (as it then was) of the Law Society, who declined to take any action. He then applied personally to the Solicitors' Disciplinary Tribunal, who held there was no prima facie case against the solicitor. The applicant appealed from that decision to the Court of Appeal who said that on his version of events there was a case for the solicitor to answer and directed the Disciplinary Tribunal to hear the application. That is where I came in. I am not going to tell you what happened because that is not the point of the story. The point I wish to make is that in my opinion that solicitor was not entitled to render a bill at all and therefore there should have been no writ, no judgment and no bankruptcy. When you have read this chapter I hope you will agree with me.

2. A CONTRACT

The giving of instructions by a client to a solicitor constitutes the solicitor's retainer by the client. It is a contract. It creates the solicitor's right to be paid. The rights and liabilities of the parties are governed by the ordinary law of contract, but the relationship is also subject to the special statutory provisions which govern contracts between a solicitor and his client. It is an implied term of the contract that the client will pay the solicitor's charges and disbursements. The retainer need not be in writing but, if the true construction of an arrangement is that the solicitor's costs are guaranteed by a third party, then, of course, the requirement that a guarantee must be in writing applies to the arrangement between the solicitor and the third party.

Where there is a difference between a solicitor and his client on the question of an oral retainer, the word of the client is to be preferred to the word of the solicitor, or, at any rate more weight is to be given to it. The reason is plain. It is because the client is ignorant and the solicitor is, or should be, learned. If the solicitor does not take the precaution of getting a written retainer, he has only himself to thank for being at variance with his client over it and must take the consequences. The onus is on the solicitor to establish the terms of the retainer and in the absence of persuasive evidence the court should prefer the client's version. (*Fereidooni v Pettman Smith* (SCCO Case No 6 of 2001 18 July).)

3. TERMINATION OF THE RETAINER

(a) Other than by the solicitor

(i) The client may terminate a retainer at any time for any reason.
(ii) The retainer may also be terminated by the effluxion of time if it was for a fixed period, or by the death, bankruptcy or insanity of the solicitor or the client (or both!), or if its continuance becomes unlawful.

Paragraph 24.04 of the Law Society's *Guide to the Professional Conduct of Solicitors 1999* suggests that where the client suffers insanity, a solicitor should contact the relatives, the Public Trust Office or the Official Solicitor.

(b) By the solicitor

(i) For good cause

There is an implied term that the solicitor may terminate the retainer upon reasonable notice for good cause, such as a failure to provide funds for disbursements or give adequate instructions; the client requiring the solicitor to behave unlawfully or unethically, obstructing the solicitor, or preventing him from dealing with the matter and where there is a serious breakdown in confidence between them.

Paragraph 12.03 of the Law Society's *Guide* reads: 'A solicitor must not act or continue to act in circumstances where the client cannot be represented with competence or diligence'. The commentary suggests that this would apply where a solicitor has insufficient time, experience or skill to deal with the instructions. Although it would be unethical for the solicitor to continue to act in these circumstances it would not be a 'good cause' for terminating the retainer and the solicitor would be in breach of it, thereby disentitling him to any payment for work done (see section 4, 'An Entire Contract', below) and he would be liable for any damage the client may suffer as a result of the termination.

(ii) Under the Solicitors Act 1974, s 65(2)

In respect of contentious costs only, the Law Society secured in the Solicitors Act 1974, s 65(2) an important concession for solicitors. Where a solicitor requests a client to pay a reasonable sum of money on account of costs incurred and to be incurred in respect of contentious business and the client fails to make that payment within a reasonable time, this shall be a good cause upon which the solicitor may, on giving reasonable notice to the client, terminate the retainer.

4. AN ENTIRE CONTRACT

A retainer is normally an entire contract under which the solicitor is to do certain work for the client and under the law of contract in the absence of agreement, or a request from the client for a final bill, he cannot seek any remuneration until that work has been completed or the retainer has been terminated in some other way. Subject to the provisions of the Solicitors Act 1974, s 65(2) (above) in respect of contentious business, and to any special agreement entered into with a client covering contentious or non-contentious business, a solicitor is not entitled to any payment on account of his costs other than disbursements. If the solicitor wrongfully terminates the retainer he is not entitled to any payment at all for the work he has done, either on a quantum meruit or any other basis (*Wild v Simpson* [1919] 2 KB 544, CA). A more recent example was *Wong v Vizards (a firm)* [1997] 2 Costs LR 46, QBD, where solicitors declined to represent their client at a hearing unless he made a substantial payment on account of a disputed bill. He declined to pay and it was held that because the amount claimed by the solicitors was unreasonable they had wrongfully terminated the retainer and were therefore not entitled to any payment on a quantum meruit for the work they had done in preparation for the hearing.

5. INTERIM BILLS

Even though the Solicitors Act 1974, s 65(2) is limited to contentious business, solicitors have always been free to agree the terms of their retainer with their clients in respect of both non-contentious and contentious business. It is only in recent years that solicitors have realised what has long been appreciated in every other walk of life, both in this country and abroad, that without stage payments by the client the entire burden of financing the work falls upon he who is doing it. Litigation in particular can be protracted, complicated and lingering, as can some non-contentious work. An agreement with a client that the firm will render interim bills at monthly, three-monthly or six-monthly intervals will transform a firm's cash flow. I know that there are problems in preparing detailed interim bills during the currency of an active matter, but any basic system of time recording and costing will enable simple interim bills to be produced based on time spent and hourly rates. Any anomalies or inequities can be rectified in the final bill. The clients will be grateful. Solicitors live in fear of offending their clients with requests for payments on account of costs and disbursements, but it is nothing compared with the fear of the clients of the ever-growing size of an unknown bill which they know they will inevitably receive. Clients welcome knowing the amount of costs they have incurred to date, even if it may mean them crying 'Halt!' before any more costs are incurred; they will also welcome the opportunity of making stage payments. Furthermore, clients appreciate that a solicitor who is efficient in the conduct of his own affairs is likely to be no less efficient in looking after theirs.

There are two kinds of interim bill, and the difference between them is crucial.

(a) Interim statute bills

(i) Self-contained final bills

These are called statute bills because they comply with all the requirements of the Solicitors Act 1974 (see p 27) and result in all the consequences which flow from such compliance – the solicitor can enforce payment by suing the client, the client can obtain an order for a detailed assessment and the various time limits relating to the client's rights to a detailed assessment run from the date of their delivery. Although they are interim bills they are also final bills in respect of the work covered by them. There can be no subsequent adjustment in the light of the outcome of the business. They are complete self-contained bills of costs to date. Interim statute bills during the currency of the retainer can arise in only two ways: by natural break or agreement.

(ii) Natural break

There is authority for the rendering of an interim statute bill at a natural break in protracted litigation. There is, however, little authority for identifying what is a natural break. In *Chamberlain v Boodle and King* [1982] 3 All ER 188, CA, Lord Denning said: 'It is a question of fact whether there are natural breaks in the work done by a solicitor so that each portion of it can and should be treated as a separate and distinct part in itself, capable of and rightly being charged separately and taxed separately'. In that case the Court of Appeal held that there had been no natural breaks justifying treating a series of accounts rendered during litigation as final accounts and that they should accordingly be treated as one bill all of which could be taxed. (The case is also memorable for the plaintiff being a gentleman who lived in New Orleans, rejoicing in the name of Bartlett Beardslee Chamberlain III.) The Council of the Law Society's advice is not to rely on the 'natural break' principle as a ground for delivering an interim statute bill except in the clearest circumstances.

(iii) Agreement

> 'Before a solicitor is entitled to require a bill to be treated as a complete self-contained bill of costs to date, he must make it plain to the client expressly or by implication that that is the purpose of his sending in that bill for that amount at that time. Then of course one looks to see what the client's reaction is. If the client's reaction is to pay the bill in its entirety without demur, it is not difficult to infer an agreement that the bill is to be treated as a self-contained bill of costs to date.'

That was how Lord Justice Roskill put it in *Davidsons v Jones-Fenleigh* (1980) 124 Sol Jo 204, CA. In that case the court found that each of four bills delivered was complete and final in its own right and that the time for taxing three of them had expired. In *Abedi v Penningtons (a firm)* [2000] NLJR 465, CA the solicitors did not agree with their client that they could deliver interim bills and there were no natural breaks in the litigation, but the solicitors did in fact deliver bills on a monthly basis, each purporting to be a final bill for the period in question, even though they were for a round figure. The client at first paid regularly but then stopped leaving five bills unpaid and four bills partially paid. The client then alleged that she had been overcharged and sought a detailed assessment under the Solicitors Act. She was so long out of time in making her application that if the bills were treated as final bills she was not entitled to have them assessed under the Act. The Court of Appeal upheld the award of summary judgment to the solicitors on the grounds that the possibility of interim bills being payable could arise by virtue of an inferred as well as an express agreement. The client, far from disputing the bills, had paid them regularly and had promised to pay the outstanding bills. The case was distinguished from *Re Romer & Haslam* [1893] 2 QB 286, CA because in that case the solicitors had never asked for payment of any of their bills, but merely asked for and took payment on account.

In *Adams v Mackinnes* (SCCO No 13 of 2001) the retainer commenced in 1990 with a client care letter, no copy of which survived. In August 1994 the solicitor sent a further client care letter, which was available, stating they would apply an uplift for care and conduct but probably not until the end of the action, when they could decide what mark-up was merited. However, they did not change the format of their bills until May 1996, when they bore a prominent message that the bill was an interim bill. Prior to then the bills were drawn in a way which made them look like final bills. They set out exactly what work had been done, the rate being charged and the period covered by the bill, and each carried a notice informing the client of his rights to detailed assessment under the Solicitors Act. In these circumstances the solicitors were not entitled to any uplift for care and conduct prior to their client care letter of August 1994. It was not mentioned in the short report, but on the face of it, it would be arguable that the format of the bills until May 1996 resulted in them being final bills on which no mark-up could subsequently be claimed.

The Law Society advises practitioners to make it expressly clear in their Terms of Business letter that they propose to deliver interim statute bills in the event of protracted work.

(b) Interim bills on account

(i) Request for payment on account

We have seen that the Solicitors Act 1974, s 65(2) provides that in respect of contentious business a solicitor may request the client to pay a reasonable sum on account of costs and that the refusal or failure to make such a payment shall be deemed to be a good cause whereby the solicitor may, upon giving reasonable notice to the client, withdraw from the retainer. It is vital to differentiate between a request for payment under s 65(2), which is usually known as a 'bill on account', and an interim statute bill, particularly as both are often described as 'interim' bills.

(ii) Not enforceable by action

A bill on account is really nothing more than a request for payment on account in fancy dress. Not being a statute bill it cannot be sued upon by the solicitor, the client cannot apply for a detailed assessment of it and, of course, the time limits for applying for a detailed assessment (see p 44) do not run. In *Palomo SA v Turner & Co* [2000] 1 WLR 37, CA, five bills rendered during the course of litigation had been headed 'on account of charges and disbursements incurred or to be incurred'. It was held these could not be construed as final or statute bills in respect of the work covered by them, and accordingly the time limits for applying for a detailed assessment under the Solicitors Act had not started to run. If the client does not pay a bill on account the solicitor should give him the 'reasonable notice' required by s 65(2), that unless payment is made within a stipulated (reasonable) time, the solicitor will withdraw from the retainer. If the client regards the amount requested on account as excessive he can invite the solicitor to render a statute bill which he may then have assessed. If the solicitor fails to render a statute bill the client can obtain an order from the court that he should do so, pursuant to the Solicitors Act 1974, s 68.

(iii) May be increased

One advantage to the solicitor of rendering a bill on account is that it need not be the final quantification of all the work included in it, but is merely the minimum amount of his charges to date. It also avoids the risk of limiting any between-the-parties costs recoverable in respect of this period to the amount of the bill on account on the indemnity principle (see p 173) and any risk of appearing to charge by results. For this reason it is important to make it clear to the client that the bill on account is simply a request for payment on account of the statute bill which will be delivered later. Wording on the following lines will achieve this:

> 'There is statutory provision for various discretionary factors to be taken into account when calculating solicitors' fees, some of which cannot be assessed until all the work is completed; these will be taken into account in our final bill when we shall be able to make an overall evaluation of the matter.'

The position is also covered in the precedent terms of business letter at p 23.

(iv) Payable into the office account

A bill on account constitutes a written intimation to the client of the amount of costs incurred to date and therefore entitles a solicitor to transfer from his client account into his office account money received from the client in accordance with the Solicitors' Accounts Rules 1991. Such a transfer is restricted to the amount of costs already incurred and must not cover anticipated future costs. A bill on account must therefore be restricted to costs incurred. Any request for money on account of future costs must, in respect of contentious business, comply with the requirements of the Solicitors Act 1974, s 65(2) and in respect of non-contentious costs must be pursuant to an agreement with the client.

6. THE SIX HURDLES

We can now see where the solicitor in the story at the beginning of this chapter went wrong. The business had not been completed, the retainer had not been terminated, there had been no agreement that a statute bill could be delivered and there was no natural break – they were in mid-conference. Even on the solicitor's own version – rejecting the suggestion he had agreed an all-in fee of £150 – this 'bill' was at best a request for payment on account pursuant to the Solicitors Act 1974, s 65(2). Before the solicitor could issue a writ there had to be six stages:

(a) A request for a reasonable amount on account.
(b) Failure to pay that amount.
(c) Reasonable notice by the solicitor of his intention to terminate the retainer.
(d) Termination of the retainer.
(e) Delivery of a statute bill.
(f) The expiration of one month (see p 60).

The solicitor got over none of these hurdles. Even assuming (1) the request for a further payment was reasonable (the Tribunal found that it was not), (2) that this was contentious business and (3) the client had failed to pay the amount requested, the solicitor had not given notice of his intention to terminate the retainer, had not in fact terminated it and was not entitled to deliver a statute bill. You will be relieved to know that the Tribunal did not regard the improper delivery of the account as amounting to professional misconduct – not only did the solicitor think he was entitled to do so, a Queen's Bench master, a High Court judge, a county court judge, a bankruptcy registrar and the Court of Appeal (twice) saw nothing wrong with it either. I told you it was a horror story.

7. POSTSCRIPT

For the client there was a semi-happy ending. The solicitor's insurers settled the claim for £200,000 and £50,000 costs, but it was three years after the death of his wife.

CHAPTER 2

AGREEMENTS WITH CLIENTS

1. NON-CONTENTIOUS BUSINESS AGREEMENTS

The Solicitors Act 1974, s 57 as amended by the Courts and Legal Services Act 1990, s 98, provides that a solicitor and his client may before, after or in the course of non-contentious business, make an agreement as to the solicitor's remuneration in respect of that business. It must be in writing and be signed by the client or his agent. It must show all the terms of the bargain (*Chamberlain v Boodle and King* [1982] 3 All ER 188, CA). It is a binding contract if all of these conditions are satisfied but s 57(5) provides that if the solicitor relies on it and the client objects to it as being unfair or unreasonable, a costs officer may enquire into the facts and certify them to the court. If from that certificate it appears to the court that the agreement should be set aside, or the amount payable under it reduced, the court may so order. The court may also give such consequential directions as it thinks fit, such as directing that an itemised bill be delivered and assessed (*Rutter v Sheridan-Young* [1958] 2 All ER 13, CA). Although the court requires only prima facie evidence of unfairness or unreasonableness in order to intervene, in the opinion of Mustill J in *Walton v Egan* [1982] QB 1232 'from a practical point of view the agreement of the client is the strongest evidence that the agreement is reasonable'. Section 57(2) enacts that the agreement may provide for remuneration by a gross sum or by a commission or percentage or by a salary or otherwise. An important amendment introduced by the Courts and Legal Services Act, s 98 permits an agreement to be by reference to an hourly rate. The amendment provides that if, on the assessment of any costs, an agreement by reference to an hourly rate is relied on by the solicitor and the client objects to the amount of the costs (but is not alleging that the agreement is unfair or unreasonable), then the amount of the hourly rate will be binding on the client but the costs officer may enquire into (a) the number of hours worked by the solicitor, and (b) whether the number of hours worked by him or her was excessive. The agreement may include all or any disbursements made by the solicitor in respect of searches, plans, travelling, postage, fees or other matters.

2. CONTENTIOUS BUSINESS AGREEMENTS

(a) Solicitors Act 1974, s 59

A solicitor may make an agreement with his client as to his remuneration in respect of any contentious business before, after or during doing the work pursuant to the Solicitors Act 1974, s 59(1). As with non-contentious business agreements, it must be in writing, signed by the client or his agent and show all the terms of the bargain. Also as with non-contentious business agreements the Courts and Legal Services Act 1990 permits a contentious business agreement to be by reference to an hourly rate. This means, unlike where work is to be done for a fixed sum, the client is not able to calculate how much he is being asked to pay, because neither he nor anyone else knows how long the litigation will last.

The agreement must not give the solicitor any interest in the proceedings; ie it must not be champertous or on a contingency basis. It may, however, contain a conditional fee agreement stipulating for payment only in the event of success (with or without a fee uplift), provided it complies with the rules and regulations relating to conditional fee agreements (see Chapter 42). The effect of a contentious business agreement is to preclude a detailed assessment of the costs as between the solicitor and the client except in respect of agreements by reference to hourly rates when the same provisions apply as for non-contentious business agreements. The agreement itself does not give a cause of action. Before a solicitor can rely on it he must apply to the court for leave to enforce the agreement, equally, the client may apply to the court to set it aside (Solicitors Act 1974, s 61(1)). Where the agreement relates to an action the client may also apply under s 61(3) to a costs judge or district judge who may either allow the agreement or require the opinion of the court to be taken on it. Both applications are made under CPR Part 8. The outcome will depend on whether or not the court is of the opinion that the agreement is fair and reasonable. Applications in respect of bills less than £25,000 must be made in the county court (Courts and Legal Services Act 1990, s 3). An application may be made at any time before the bill is paid, before or after the work has been done. The Solicitors Act 1974, s 61(5), provides that the court may re-open the agreement within 12 months of payment or longer if there are special circumstances.

(b) Precedent application under Solicitors Act 1974, s 61(1)

CLAIM FORM N208 CPR PART 8

Details of claim

1. A declaration that the written agreement entered into between the applicants and the respondent on [date], a copy of which is attached, is a valid contentious business agreement within the meaning of the Solicitors Act 1974, s 59.
2. A declaration that the agreement is valid in all respects and may be enforced.
3. Such order or orders for further or other relief as may be necessary for the enforcement of the agreement.
4. The respondent may be ordered to pay the applicants' costs of and incidental to this application.
5. The grounds for this application are:
   (a) the agreement is a valid contentious business agreement within the meaning of s 59 of the Act;
   (b) the business described or referred to in the agreement has been properly and fully done by the applicants for the respondent;
   (c) the respondent, despite demands made upon him by the applicants, has refused or failed to pay the amount due under the agreement;
   (d) the agreement should therefore be enforced.

Statement of truth

(c) CPR Rule 48.8

It is important to distinguish between a formal contentious business agreement and the effect of the provisions of CPR Rule 48.8 and its supplemental practice direction, which preserves the freedom of the solicitor and client to make whatever agreement they desire. Rule 48.8(2)(*a*) and (*b*) provide that all costs incurred with the express or implied approval of the client shall be presumed to have been reasonably incurred and, where the amount has been expressly or impliedly approved by the client, to be reasonable in amount. This is subject to the provision of Rule 48.8(2)(*c*) that costs of an unusual nature or amount shall be presumed to have been unreasonably incurred, unless the solicitor expressly told his client that as a result he might not recover all of those costs from the other party. There is no requirement that the approval of the client shall be in writing or signed by him, and indeed the client's agreement may be implied. There is also no provision for setting aside such approval however unfair and unreasonable the resultant costs may be. It appears that the only way in which the agreement could be upset would be by the client commencing an action to have it set aside on the grounds of undue influence, or perhaps negligence by the solicitor in not advising him to obtain independent advice from another solicitor before entering the agreement. However, for the client to be bound by the presumption, his approval must be 'informed'. It must have been secured after a full and fair exposition of the relevant factors: *MacDougall v Boote Edgar Estekin* (SCCO Case No 15 of 2000). Although the presumptions under Rule 48.8 are rebuttable, while those in respect of hourly rates introduced as a result of the Courts and Legal Services Act 1990, s 98 into non-contentious business agreements and contentious business agreements are irrebuttable, the apparent advantage of this to the solicitor appears to be far outweighed by the stringent and complicated provisions relating to the formation and enforcement of non-contentious and contentious business agreements. Rule 48.8 and its supplemental practice direction are set out on pp 531–533.

(d) Differences between a contentious business agreement and CPR 48.8

1.
   (a) Under Rule 48.8 there is a presumption that hourly rates expressly or impliedly approved by the client are reasonable. The presumption is rebuttable (Costs Practice Direction 54.2).
   (b) Hourly rates in a valid CBA are binding on the client and cannot be the subject of a detailed assessment, although the *number* of hours spent and the reasonableness of those hours may be challenged. Further, a CBA cannot be enforced without the permission of the court, which will not be granted if it takes the view that *any* aspect of the CBA is unfair or unreasonable. The court may set aside the agreement and proceed as though it had never been made.
2.
   (a) Under Rule 48.8 there is a presumption that costs are unreasonably incurred if they are of an unreasonable amount or of an unusual nature and the solicitor did not inform the client that they may not be recoverable between the parties.
   (b) There is no such presumption with a CBA, although failure to give such advice might amount to negligence.
3.
   (a) Rule 48.8 does not appear to apply to an agreement to conduct litigation for a fixed fee.
   (b) A CBA is appropriate for a fixed fee agreement.

3. COUNTY COURT

The Solicitors Act 1974, s 74(3) provides: 'the amount which may be allowed on the taxation [*assessment*] of any costs or bill of costs in respect of any item relating to the proceedings in a county court shall not, except in so far as rules of court may otherwise provide, exceed the amount which could have been allowed in respect of that item as between the parties in those proceedings, having regard to the nature of the proceedings and the amount of the claim and of any counterclaim'. Under the old County Court Rules it was arguable that because there was a discretion to exceed the amounts prescribed in the Scale 1 and there was no upper limit to Scale 2 the amount at which solicitor and client costs could be awarded was not restricted by s 74(3). However, at the last minute, it was realised that the Civil Procedure Rules make no exception to the provision that solicitor and client costs may not exceed the amount recoverable between the parties with the result that they could not exceed the fixed costs on the fast track, at present limited to the trial costs but eventually to be extended to the whole of the fast track. The operation of s 74(3) would also appear to preclude a solicitor from charging the client a disproportionate amount where the party and party costs have been restricted on the grounds there were disproportionate to the issues, even though the proportionality rule does not apply as between solicitor and client! In spite of the wording of the Conditional Fee Agreements Regulations and Rules payment of a success fee could also be said to offend against s 74(3). Accordingly a new sub-rule 1A was inserted into Rule 48.8 as follows:

> 'Section 74(3) of the Solicitors Act 1974 applies unless the solicitor and client have entered into a written agreement which expressly permits payment to the solicitor of an amount of costs greater than which the client could have recovered from another party to the proceedings'.

In all county court work it is therefore prudent for the solicitor at the outset of litigation to identify the probability of a shortfall to the client as the result of fixed costs or the proportionality test, and to obtain the client's signature to an agreement that the solicitor and client charges may exceed those recoverable between the parties.

4. CONDITIONAL FEES

See Funding (Part VI) – Conditional Fee Agreements (Chapter 42).

5. QUOTATIONS AND ESTIMATES

(a) Quotations

Do you really know the difference between a quotation and an estimate in respect of solicitors' costs? A quotation is a fixed price for doing the work which cannot be exceeded in any circumstances except with the freely given consent of the client. Estimates have a chameleon quality. They have a tendency to turn into quotations when you are not looking. An unqualified estimate, for example, is for all practical purposes a fixed price quotation.

(b) Qualified estimate

A qualified estimate is still not *carte blanche*. A qualified estimate is an indication of price which is qualified by a statement that the solicitor may have to charge more if the matter involves more work than he expects. There are circumstances in which what started out in life as a qualified estimate can finish up as binding on the solicitor as a quotation. Paragraph 13.02(1)(*e*) of the Law Society's *Guide to the Professional Conduct of Solicitors 1999* provides: 'The solicitor should make it clear at the outset if an estimate, quotation or other indication of cost is not intended to be fixed'. Paragraph 13.02(6)(*c*) provides that the solicitor should 'inform the client in writing as soon as it appears that a costs estimate or agreed upper limit may or will be exceeded'. Paragraph 13.03(3) provides 'oral estimates should be confirmed in writing and clients should be informed immediately if it appears that the estimate will be, or is likely to be, exceeded. In most cases this should happen before undertaking the work that exceeds the estimate'. In other words, the final amount payable should not vary substantially from the estimate unless there has been a change in circumstances of which the client has been informed in writing.

In *Wong v Vizards (a firm)* [1997] 2 Costs LR 46, QBD, the solicitors in a letter to their client allowed for profit costs of £9,955 (*sic*) stating 'the fee proposal hopefully sets out the fullest extent of your liability to this firm for costs likely to be incurred in the future'. Although this did not amount to a binding agreement that in no circumstances would the solicitors' fees exceed their fee proposal, it was a clear and considered indication of the maximum upon which the client was likely to rely and did rely. In considering whether a reasonable amount for the work done should exceed what the fee-payer had been led to believe was a worst case assessment, regard should be had to any explanation of the divergence. It had not been suggested there was any unexpected development between the date of the solicitor's letter and the date of trial, and no satisfactory explanation had been given why the solicitors should be entitled to profit costs exceeding the amount put forward as their worst case assessment. In limiting the solicitors' costs to £9,955 the judge bore in mind two competing factors. The fee proposal was based on a trial of ten days but it took only eight days, which would justify a reduction of £1,320. On the other hand while the sum claimed by the solicitor 'should not vary substantially' from that previously estimated without warning to the client, the fee proposal was a projection or estimate rather than a warranty. In not reducing the figure of £9,955 by £1,320 the solicitor had effectively been allowed a margin of approximately 15% over the worst case estimate given. A greater divergence would be substantial and unreasonable. Similarly, in *John Anthony v Ellis & Fairbairn (a firm)* (SCCO Case No 9 of 2000), the solicitors' bill was two-and-a-half times the size of their estimate and there had been no warning to the client that the estimate would be exceeded. Even though the estimate was restricted to profit costs and limited to early settlement, which did not occur, this did not justify the solicitors in departing from it.

Accordingly, unless at the time – or preferably before – the costs have reached the estimated figure, the client is notified of this and a new basis of charging is agreed, the solicitor will be unable to recover costs in excess of the estimated amount. The fact that the solicitor had seriously underestimated the work or disbursements involved would not necessarily be a changed circumstance – indeed it could be a strong indication of negligence on the part of the solicitor in preparing the original estimate. A factor in considering whether any upward revision of an estimate is reasonable is whether the client had instructed the solicitor after shopping around and taking the lowest estimate he had been given. The qualified estimate should state the circumstances which might give rise to an increase and the client should be informed in writing when any of those circumstances arise. Paragraph 13.03(2) of the Law Society's *Guide* puts it this way: 'to give an estimate which has been pitched at an unrealistically low level solely to attract the work and subsequently to charge a higher fee for that work is improper because it misleads the client as to the true or likely cost'.

(c) Criminal offence

An estimate can, however, turn really nasty. The Consumer Protection Act 1987, ss 20 and 21, apply to the supply of services as well as to the supply of goods. These sections

(d) Solicitors should comply with paragraphs 3–6 of the code even where a client is legally aided if the client may have a financial interest in the costs because contributions are payable or the statutory charge may apply or they may become liable for the costs of another party.

(e) The code also applies to contingency fee and conditional fee arrangements with a client for the solicitor to retain commissions received from third parties.

3. Informing the client about costs

(a) Costs information must not be inaccurate or misleading.

(b) Any costs information required to be given by the code must be given clearly, in a way and at a level which is appropriate to the particular client. Any terms with which the client may be unfamiliar, for example 'disbursement', should be explained.

(c) The information required by paragraphs 4 and 5 of the code should be given to a client at the outset of, and at appropriate stages throughout, the matter. All information given orally should be confirmed in writing to the client as soon as possible.

4. Advance costs information – general

The overall costs

(a) The solicitor should give the client the best information possible about the likely overall costs, including a breakdown between fees, VAT and disbursements.

(b) The solicitor should explain clearly to the client the time likely to be spent in dealing with a matter, if time spent is a factor in the calculation of the fees.

(c) Giving 'the best information possible' includes:
   (i) agreeing a fixed fee; or
   (ii) giving a realistic estimate; or
   (iii) giving a forecast within a possible range of costs; or
   (iv) explaining to the client the reasons why it is not possible to fix, or give a realistic estimate or forecast of, the overall costs, and giving instead the best information possible about the cost of the next stage of the matter.

(d) The solicitor should, in an appropriate case, explain to a privately paying client that the client may set an upper limit on the firm's costs for which the client may be liable without further authority. Solicitors should not exceed an agreed limit without first obtaining the client's consent.

(e) The solicitor should make it clear at the outset if an estimate, quotation or other indication of cost is not intended to be fixed.

Basis of firm's charges

(f) The solicitor should also explain to the client how the firm's fees are calculated except where the overall costs are fixed or clear. If the basis of charging is an hourly charging rate, that must be made clear.

(g) The client should be told if charging rates might be increased.

Further information

(h) The solicitor should explain what reasonably foreseeable payments a client may have to make either to the solicitor or to a third party and when those payments are likely to be needed.

(i) The solicitor should explain to the client the arrangements for updating the costs information as set out in paragraph 6.

Client's ability to pay

(j) The solicitor should discuss with the client how and when any costs are to be met, and consider:
 (i) whether the client may be eligible and should apply for legal aid (including advice an assistance);
 (ii) whether the client's liability for their own costs may be covered by insurance;
 (iii) whether the client's liability for another party's costs may be covered by pre-purchased insurance and, if not, whether it would be advisable for the client's liability for another party's costs to be covered by after the event insurance (including in every case where a conditional fee or contingency fee arrangement is proposed); and
 (iv) whether the client's liability for costs (including the costs of another party) may be paid by another person eg an employer or trade union.

Cost-benefit and risk

(k) The solicitor should discuss with the client whether the likely outcome in a matter will justify the expense or risk involved including, if relevant, the risk of having to bear an opponent's costs.

5. Additional information for particular clients

Legally aided clients [now CLS funded]

(a) The solicitor should explain to a legally aided client the client's potential liability for the client's own costs and those of any other party, including:
 (i) the effect of the statutory charge and its likely amount;
 (ii) the client's obligation to pay any contribution assessed and the consequences of failing to do so;
 (iii) the fact that the client may still be ordered by the court to contribute to the opponent's costs if the case is lost even though the client's own costs are covered by legal aid; and
 (iv) the fact that even if the client wins, the opponent may not be ordered to pay or be capable of paying the full amount of the client's costs.

Privately paying clients in contentious matters (and potentially contentious matters)

(b) The solicitor should explain to the client the client's potential liability for the client's own costs and for those of any other party, including:
 (i) the fact that the client will be responsible for paying the firm's bill in full regardless of any order for costs made against an opponent;
 (ii) the probability that the client will have to pay the opponent's costs as well as the client's own costs if the case is lost;
 (iii) the fact that even if the client wins, the opponent may not be ordered to pay or be capable of paying the full amount of the client's costs; and
 (iv) the fact that if the opponent is legally aided the client may not recover costs, even if successful.

Liability for third party costs in non-contentious matters

(c) The solicitor should explain to the client any liability the client may have for the payment of the costs of a third party. When appropriate, solicitors are advised to obtain a firm figure for or agree a cap to a third party's costs.

6. Updating costs information

The solicitor should keep the client properly informed about costs as a matter progresses. In particular, the solicitor should:

(a) tell the client, unless otherwise agreed, how much the costs are at regular intervals (at least every six months) and in appropriate cases deliver interim bills at agreed intervals;

(b) explain to the client (and confirm in writing) any changed circumstances which will, or which are likely to, affect the amount of costs, the degree of risk involved, or the cost-benefit to the client of continuing with the matter;

(c) inform the client in writing as soon as it appears that a costs estimate or agreed upper limit may or will be exceeded; and

(d) consider the client's eligibility for legal aid if a material change in the client's means comes to the solicitor's attentions.

7. Client care and complaints handling

Information for clients

(a) Every solicitor in private practice must ensure that the client:
  (i) is given a clear explanation of the issues raised in a matter and is kept properly informed about its progress (including the likely timescale);
  (ii) is given the name and status of the person dealing with the matter and the name of the principal responsible for its overall supervision;
  (iii) is told whom to contact about any problem with the service provided; and
  (iv) is given details of any changes in the information required to be given by this paragraph.

Complaints handling

(b) Every principal in private practice must:
  (i) ensure the client is told the name of the person in the firm to contact about any problem with the service provided;
  (ii) have a written complaints procedure and ensure that complaints are handled in accordance with it; and
  (iii) ensure that the client is given a copy of the complaints procedure on request.

The Code requires information to be given in plain English at the outset of, and at appropriate stages throughout, the matter, with information given orally being confirmed in writing as soon as possible. At the outset the solicitor should give the client the best information possible about the likely overall costs, including a breakdown between fees, VAT and disbursements, including the basis upon which the fees are to be calculated and whether an estimate, quotation or other indication of costs is not intended to be fixed. The solicitor is required to discuss with the client how, when and by whom any costs are to be met, including consideration of Community Legal Service funding, legal expenses insurance, after-the-event insurance to cover another party's costs and whether a client's liability of costs may be payable by another person such as an employer or trade union. Costs-benefit and risk must be discussed; CLS-funded clients must be advised about the statutory charge, their liability to the CLS and liability to their opponents, whereas privately paying clients will similarly be advised as to their liability for paying their opponent's costs and that solicitor and client costs may exceed those recoverable in the event of success. Solicitors are required to tell the client, unless otherwise agreed, how much the costs are at regular intervals and not less than six months and in appropriate cases to deliver interim bills at agreed intervals. They must also explain to the client any changes of circumstances which are likely to affect (i) the amount of costs, (ii) the degree of risk involved and (iii) the costs-benefit to the client of continuing with the matter.

(c) Guide

The Law Society's *Guide to the Professional Conduct of Solicitors 1999* gave the following additional general comments relating to the giving of advance information on costs. Some refer to legal matters, others cross-refer to relevant conduct issues. They have been grouped to relate to the most relevant part of the code.

> **13.03 Advance costs information – general (paragraph 4 of the Code)**
>
> *Overall costs and basis of charges*
>
> 1. It is an implied term in law that solicitors will be paid reasonable remuneration for their services (see section 15 of the Supply of Goods and Services Act 1982). Solicitors should not, however, rely solely upon this implied term but should explain to the client, so far as possible, the work which is likely to be involved in carrying out the instructions and the time which may be taken, both of which will have direct relevance to the likely amount of fees.
> 2. Wherever possible, a solicitor should give an estimate of the likely cost of acting in a particular matter. When giving such an estimate or forecast, regard should be had to Part III of the Consumer Protection Act 1987 which deals with misleading price indications. To give an estimate which has been pitched at an unrealistically low level solely to attract the work and subsequently to charge a higher fee for that work is improper because it misleads the client as to the true or likely cost.
> 3. Oral estimates should be confirmed in writing and clients should be informed immediately it appears that the estimate will be or is likely to be exceeded. In most cases this should happen before undertaking work that exceeds the estimate. Solicitors should not wait until submitting the bill of costs. The Office for the Supervision of Solicitors deals with many complaints that have arisen simply because the solicitor does not have a system for tracking costs, and estimates are exceeded without the client's authority.
> 4. The Conditional Fee Agreement Regulations 1995 prescribe both information to be given to the client and matters to be contained in the written agreement in conditional fee cases (see 14.05, p 279 and Annex 14B, p 292). In non-contentious matters, regard must be had to the Solicitors' (Non-Contentious Business) Remuneration Order 1994 (see Annex 14D, p 296).
> 5. If the agreement is for the solicitor to be remunerated by an agreed fee, the solicitor is bound to do the work covered by the agreement for that fee, even though circumstances arise which make the work unremunerative for the solicitor. Under rule 19(5) of the Solicitors' Accounts Rules 1998, money received for or on account of an agreed fee which is paid by the client to the solicitor must not be paid into client account (see Annex 28B at p 702).
> 6. Section 57(3) of the Solicitors Act 1974 (see Annex 14A at p 284) requires a non-contentious business agreement to be in writing and signed by the

person to be bound by it. Under section 59(1) a contentious business agreement must also be in writing. (See Annex 14A at p 285.)
7. A solicitor providing property selling services must, when accepting instructions to act in the sale of a property, give the client a written statement setting out certain details of their agreement. See 26.09, p 515 of the *Guide* for further details.
8. Where clients want to set a limit on costs solicitors should warn of the consequences before accepting instructions. Any limit cannot be exceeded without the authority of the client. Further, where the limit imposed on the expenditure is insufficient the solicitor must, as soon as possible, obtain the client's instructions as to whether to continue with the matter.
9. Where a solicitor continues to act in such circumstances regardless of the limit and then presents a bill for a sum which exceeds that limit, he or she may be guilty of professional misconduct as well as having the excess disallowed on an application for a remuneration certificate and/or taxation.
10. In non-contentious matters, a solicitor may render an interim bill if the client has agreed or acquiesced. In contentious matters, the question of an interim bill in respect of costs incurred is dealt with by reference to section 65(2) of the Solicitors Act 1974.

Ability to pay

11. When discussing costs with the client, not only should the solicitor discuss the various ways of funding the case, but he or she should also explain when the costs are due. It should be clear whether payments on account will be necessary and how payment of disbursements will be dealt with.
12. Where a client may be eligible for legal aid, the availability of an emergency certificate or the 'green form' scheme should be considered. A solicitor who commences or continues work without legal aid cover runs the risk of being unable to recover pre-certificate costs.
13. The duty to advise as to legal aid applies throughout the retainer. Solicitors should ensure that any material change in a client's means, of which they become aware, is at once taken into consideration in the context of eligibility for legal aid.
14. Other methods of funding the matter should be explored with the client. The client may have insurance that will cover the matter. In respect of covering another party's costs, the solicitor should find out if the client has pre-purchased insurance, or whether it is advisable for the client to purchase after-the-event insurance. These possibilities should be explored in all cases, as well as when a conditional fee or contingency arrangement is proposed.
15. For the position where a solicitor requires a client to make a payment on account of costs see 14.01, p 277 of the *Guide*.
16. There is no objection to solicitors accepting payment for their fees by the use of a credit card facility. See 14.02 note 3, p 277 of the *Guide*.

13.04 Cost-benefit and risk (paragraph 4(k) of the Code)

1. It is in the interests of both the solicitor and the client that advice on the risks should be in writing, and that the advice is repeated at appropriate times throughout the transaction.
2. Breach of this standard will amount prima facie to inadequate professional services, giving the Office for the Supervision of Solicitors (OSS) power, inter alia, to reduce the solicitor's bill.

13.05 Responsibility for client's matter (paragraph 7(a) of the Code)

1. The code requires that the client be informed of both the name and status of the person responsible for conduct of the matter. Status refers to

qualification as well as partnership status, eg whether the person is a solicitor or a legal executive. For restriction of the term 'legal executive' to Fellows of the Institute of Legal Executives see paragraph 7(a)(ii) of the publicity code, Annex 11A at p 233.

2. If the conduct or overall supervision of the whole or part of the client's matter is transferred to another person in the firm the client should be informed and the reasons must be explained.

The importance of complying with para 13.05 was dramatically illustrated in *Pilbrow v Pearless De Rougemont & Co (a firm)* [1999] 3 All ER 355, CA, where the court upheld the client's refusal to pay his solicitor's bill on the grounds that he had asked for an appointment with a solicitor but it transpired that the person to whom he was referred by the receptionist was neither a solicitor nor a qualified legal executive. Although the work done was up to the standard of a competent solicitor the contract was one to provide legal services by a solicitor and therefore the firm did not perform that contract at all. No legal services were provided by any solicitor. The situation was not to be equated with situations where a drinker asks for a pint of one make of bitter but was mistakenly provided with a pint of another make and did not discover the difference until he had drunk the glass dry. The firm should have trained its receptionist when faced with a request to see a solicitor to do one of the following:

(i) refer the client to a solicitor;
(ii) refer the client to someone who was not a solicitor but inform the client that that person was not a solicitor; or
(iii) refer the client to someone who the receptionist knew was not a solicitor, refrain from telling the client that fact and alert the referee to the fact that the client had asked for a solicitor.

If the last course were adopted then it would be duty of the referee straight away to make clear to the client that he was not a solicitor.

The compliance with this provision in the client care letter is therefore as much for the protection of the solicitor as for the client. It is also important to note that the term 'legal executive' is restricted to Fellows of the Institute of Legal Executives. Alternatives to 'Legal Executive' are: executive; clerk; manager; secretary; paralegal and trainee solicitor.

(d) Exceptions

The exceptions to the requirement are few and far between, examples being continuous and repetitive work for the same client; the taking of instructions for a deathbed will; and emergencies. While an emergency might be a sufficient reason for not giving costs information at the outset of the retainer and before work is started, it does not excuse complete failure to give any information at any stage. Where solicitors took over the conduct of proceedings from another firm only five days before the final hearing, they inadvertently overlooked the matter of costs information. This may have been understandable, but unfortunately the retainer continued for a further 18 months, during which time the client was given no information as to costs nor were any interim bills rendered. The outcome was that the solicitors were ordered to pay compensation to the client amounting to almost one-fifth of their fees. (*Law Society Gazette*, 25 April 2002.)

7. TERMS AND CONDITIONS OF RETAINER

I suggest the lesson to be learned from this chapter is that it is as much in the interests of the solicitor as the client to agree the terms of the retainer with each client in respect of both non-contentious and contentious work. The terms can be incorporated in a terms of business letter, which may be standard, or specifically selected for a particular client from a prepared menu of provisions. My own view is that you should not aspire to achieving a contentious or non-contentious business agreement unless the work is such that both you and the client are able to agree a fixed fee in advance. In spite of the amendment allowing reference to hourly rates, the requirements of the Solicitors Act 1974, ss 57–63 (see p 10) are so forbidding and stringent that it is very difficult to produce a binding agreement, and even if that were possible the agreement would always be subject to the risk of the statutory right of challenge.

The client should be supplied with an extra copy of the letter or agreement with a request to countersign it and return it, although this is not essential to make the letter binding on the client. In litigation, another advantage from the solicitor's point of view is that the letter constitutes express authority from the client in respect of the matters contained in it and these agreed terms are therefore, pursuant to CPR Rule 48.8, presumed to be reasonable. Whatever the view of the costs officer may be as to the agreement, on a solicitor and client assessment of costs the client is bound by it.

(a) Precedent terms of business letter

The agreement must contain:

(i) All the information required by para 4 of the Law Society's Code – Advance costs information – general.

(ii) The name and status of the person responsible for the conduct of the matter on a day-to-day basis, the partner responsible for its overall supervision and whom to approach in the event of any problem with the service provided (to comply with para 7(1) of the Code).

The agreement should, or could, make provision for:

(iii) Payment on account of costs and disbursements [*'It is our normal practice to ask clients to let us have sums of money from time to time on account of the costs and disbursements which are anticipated in the following weeks or months. I shall therefore be grateful if you will now let us have an initial payment of £ ...... The acceptance by us of payments on account of costs and disbursements are not a waiver of our rights of lien in respect of unpaid fees over any of your property in our possession or recovered or preserved by us in respect of unpaid fees.'*].

(iv) The rendering of interim bills – either statute bills or bills on account [*'In accordance with our usual practice in long running cases, we shall deliver bills to you at regular intervals for the work already carried out during the conduct of the case. This enables clients to budget for costs as the matter progresses.'*].

(v) (Unless you have agreed a fixed fee) either the hourly charge-out rates of each fee earner or their hourly expense rate and the amount of their profit mark-up (but see Chapter 42) or an explanation of how it will be assessed. If you intend to render interim statute bills their effect should be explained [*'Each bill we render will be a self-contained bill being our final charge for all the work done and disbursements incurred during the period covered by the bill including all discretionary factors. On its delivery the various provisions of the Solicitors Act 1974 affecting your rights and ours will apply. We shall be happy to explain these to you at any time should you so desire.'*]. If you intend to render interim bills on account the wording of the agreement should be on these lines: [*'Each fee earner has a basic hourly expense rate which varies according to his or her experience and, to which is added a percentage uplift. This varies, according to the nature of the matter, but is generally between 25 and 100%. It is not possible for us to calculate the precise uplift in any case until the matter is completed. This is because it will depend upon a number of factors, which are prescribed by statute and which include the importance and complexity of the case, the amount involved and the difficulty or novelty of questions involved in it. It will also depend upon the nature of the work carried out at different stages of the matter. Our interim bills will therefore include a 50% uplift which may be adjusted in our final bill.'*]. (Again, see Chapter 42.)

(vi) Annual or six-monthly increases in those rates.

(vii) An explanation in contentious matters that the standard basis for costs recovered in the event of success is unlikely to cover the full solicitor and own client bill. There is an argument that it can be implied that the client has agreed to pay more to his solicitor than is recoverable as between the parties or that the client has agreed that the costs of his particular solicitor will be more than would be reasonable for any other solicitor in the area. The implication, it is said, can arise from the depth of the pile on the carpet in the waiting room and the fact that his solicitor drives a white Rolls-Royce whilst other local solicitors ride bicycles. From this a client can see that he is dealing with a firm of solicitors who are so luxurious that it is unlikely they would be able to recover all of their costs as between the parties because they are going to be considerably more expensive than any other solicitors in the district. I think that that attempted implication assumes a much more sophisticated knowledge on the part of the client than in fact many solicitors themselves possess. If your clients say 'We want the senior partner to deal with this', even though it ought to be dealt with by a Grade C or D fee earner, then you can agree the partner's rates with your client. (*'We should also explain that at the conclusion of this matter, and in the event that you are successful, it may be that you will be entitled to the payment of your costs by some other party. However it is unlikely that you will recover the full amount you have been billed by us, primarily because our full charging rates will probably not be recoverable from the other party. If you wish we will be happy to explain this aspect further.'*)

(viii) If it is known in advance that the client wishes to incur costs of an unusual nature in litigation, (for example, requiring leading counsel, an expensive expert or a shorthand writer to be instructed) a CPR Rule 48.8 warning that these costs might not be allowed on the standard basis against the other party should be included.

(ix) Interest on unpaid bills.

(x) In a matter involving exceptionally large sums of money and therefore exceptionally high liability risk, it is permissible to limit negligence liability to the maximum of your indemnity insurance – subject always to the provisions of the Unfair Contract Terms Act 1977.

(xi) In *Hunt v R M Douglas (Roofing) Ltd* [1990] 1 AC 398, HL, it was held that a litigant who had been awarded costs is entitled to interest on those costs from the date on which judgment was pronounced and not, as previously, from the date of the certificate of taxation. That interest belongs to the client even if he has made no payments on account of costs or disbursements. In order for the solicitor to be entitled to any part of the interest there must, in the words of Lord Ackner, be:

> 'An express agreement between the solicitor and his client that any interest recovered on costs and disbursements after judgment is pronounced but before the cost judge's certificate is obtained, which costs and disbursements have not in fact been paid prior to assessment, shall as to the interest on costs belong to the solicitor less the interest on disbursements held by him for and on behalf of the person or persons to whom the disbursements are ultimately paid.'

The Law Society recommends that solicitors should consider the inclusion of such a clause in their standard terms of business. 'Disbursements' will include any counsel's fees and where interest on unpaid counsel's fees is paid by a client to his solicitor this money must be passed on to counsel.

(xii) Any agreement relating to conditional fees (see Chapter 42).

(xiii) Where the costs of contentious business are to be paid by a third party, include a statement that the client is primarily liable for payment of the costs irrespective of the outcome of the proceedings in order to preclude the possibility of the indemnity principle being invoked to deprive the client of between-the-parties costs (see Chapter 17).

(b) Example letters and terms and conditions of business

The Law Society's Practice Advice Service has produced two excellent booklets, *Non-contentious Costs* (November 1999) and *Contentious Costs* (September 1999), which contain examples of client care letters and conditions of business. Each booklet contains general notes for guidance and an explanation of the letters. There are information letters for both fixed fee and hourly rate conveyancing and, if you aspire to a non-contentious business agreement, examples of these, again on the basis of a fixed fee or an hourly rate. There is an example of general terms and conditions of business for non-contentious work, while in respect of probate there are information letters for charges based on the percentage value of the estate, or hourly rates, or a mixture of both. For good measure there is a probate non-contentious business agreement based on the percentage value of the estate. The *Contentious Costs* booklet provides examples of an Hourly Rates Information Letter, Terms And Conditions Of Business with a covering letter, and an Hourly Rates Contentious Business Agreement for the ambitious (see p 23).

(c) Client care letter deficiencies

(i) Mark-up

The *Law Society Gazette* of 3 June 1998 summarised two cases before the Compliance and Supervision Committee of the Office for the Supervision of Solicitors. In the first case the client received a client care letter which made no reference to a mark-up on the firm's charges. The client did not question the standard of work or service given but he did object to the unexpected mark-up on the bill. The bill was reduced from £1,600 to £1,100 plus VAT to reflect the solicitors' failure to inform.

(ii) No information

In the second case no client care letter was sent to a client in respect of non-contentious business. The client asked the solicitors to obtain a remuneration certificate. In the absence of costs information, the certificate was issued reducing the bill from £5,400 to £4,500 plus VAT.

(iii) Hourly rates

In *Wong v Vizards (a firm)* [1997] 2 Costs LR 46, QBD the solicitors informed the client that he would be charged hourly rates of £125 for a partner and £110 for an assistant solicitor, both rates to be subject to review. That was in June 1991. In November 1993 the solicitors wrote to the client with an estimate of costs on the worst case basis showing the assistant solicitor's time at £110 per hour. However, their final bill charged rates of £140 an hour for the partner and £125 an hour for the assistant solicitor after 30 November 1993. No indication was ever given to the client of a proposed increase in the hourly rates and accordingly the solicitors were bound by their original figures.

CHAPTER 3

FORM AND CONTENT OF A BILL

1. FORM

The formalities governing the delivery of a bill are surprisingly few. The Solicitors Act 1974 is silent as to the form of a bill for non-contentious work and in respect of contentious business s 64 merely prescribes that the bill of costs may, at the option of the solicitor, be either a bill containing detailed items or a gross sum bill. Section 64(2) provides that the party chargeable may, before he is served with proceedings and within three months of the date on which the bill was delivered to them (whichever is the earlier), require the solicitor to deliver a bill containing detailed items in lieu of the original bill. This has the dramatic effect that the gross sum bill is of no effect. Accordingly, the solicitor is no longer bound by the amount of the gross sum bill and he is free to deliver a detailed bill for a higher amount if his new calculations justify this (*Polak v Marchioness of Winchester* [1956] 2 All ER 660).

What amounts to a 'requirement' of a solicitor to deliver a detailed bill for the purpose of triggering s 64(2)? Even though the client does not quote the section and is unaware of its provisions this does not prevent it being triggered by a request for details. *Carlton v Theodore Goddard & Co* [1973] 1 WLR 623, ChD held that a letter from the client saying that he wanted the costs taxed [*assessed*] was not a sufficient request – the letter did not 'contain a word about "a bill containing detailed items"'. However, in *Penningtons v Brown* (30 April 1998, unreported) the Court of Appeal upheld the judge's view that a letter from a client requesting 'a full breakdown of your firm's bill' with a view to having the gross sum bill delivered taxed [*assessed*] was a s 64(2) request. In view of this decision it would be prudent when receiving such a letter to write to the client explaining the provisions of s 64(2) and ascertaining precisely what the client wants. It would do no harm to point out that the replacement detailed bill could exceed the amount of the gross sum bill. The Court of Appeal was particularly influenced by the fact that the request was from a layman who was unlikely to appreciate the implications and consequences of his request. So, beware! Section 64(2) gives the client the additional right to an order for the detailed assessment of a gross sum bill if requested within a month of the service of proceedings. Where proceedings are commenced on a gross sum bill, s 64(2) entitles the costs officer to require such further details of the costs as are necessary for the purposes of a detailed assessment.

2. CONTENT

(a) Amount

(i) Gross not net

It is fundamental to an understanding of costs to appreciate that there are only two sources from which a solicitor can be remunerated – by their own client under contract or out of the Legal Aid or Legal Services Commission Fund under statute. All other costs arise out of the client's rights against other persons or funds, and they belong not to the solicitor but to the client. Even costs awarded out of central funds in criminal matters belong in theory to the client. However, fundamental principles are not impervious to the dictates of state funding and solicitors have an interest in costs awarded between the parties where their clients are legally aided (see Chapter 32).

The trustee looks to a trust fund for reimbursement, a successful party in litigation can expect an order for costs against the loser, the landlord may provide in the lease that his legal costs be paid by the tenant, but none of this affects the solicitor and client relationship between the trustee, the successful litigant or the landlord and their respective solicitors. The solicitor on behalf of his client seeks to recover money due to the client from the trust fund, the unsuccessful litigant or the tenant, but he does not have any personal relationship with them. The solicitor looks to his client for payment of the costs whether or not the client is reimbursed by a third party. The solicitor must therefore deliver a bill to his client for the whole of his costs and give credit for any sum that has been received. He must not treat the costs recovered as his own and merely render an account to his client for any additional payment he requires. This was dramatically illustrated as long ago as 1908 in *Cobbett v Wood* [1908] 2 KB 420, CA, when the Court of Appeal held that a bill of costs which excluded the between the parties' items and simply referred to the excess chargeable as between solicitor and own client was not a proper bill. The VAT ramifications of this principle, also dramatic, are set out in Chapter 12.

(ii) Interim bills

Where interim bills on account have been rendered pursuant to s 65(2) of the Solicitors Act 1974 (see p 5) these should be ignored for the purposes of the final bill and treated as requests for payment of money on account. The final bill should therefore be for the total amount of the solicitor's charges and disbursements with any additional mark-up (or mark-down!) on the interim bills and give credit for all payments received as a result of bills on account. If pursuant to an agreement with your client you have been rendering interim statute bills (see p 5) each bill is a self-contained account for the work done during the period which it covers.

(b) Narrative

A bill of costs must contain sufficient particulars to enable the client to judge the fairness of the charges. There are a number of decisions relating to this and surprisingly the most succinct warning of the dangers of computer printouts is *Haigh v Ousey* (1857) 7 E & B 578, which held the bill ought to be drawn so as to enable the client to judge its fairness, a solicitor to advise on it and a taxing officer to judge the propriety of the various items of which it is composed. It was held 137 years later in *Re Kingsley* (1978) 122 Sol Jo 457 that a bill merely stating 'for professional services' was void as inadequate. Although details of hours spent and letters written are not essential, a bill requires at least a sufficient summary of the work done. In my view a bill showing no more than the hours spent would be treated by the court as not being a properly delivered bill, and I also think that any client who understandably requested more details of such a bill may well not be regarded as having made a formal request justifying the delivery of a detailed itemised account for a larger amount pursuant to the Solicitors Act, s 64(3), despite *Penningtons v Brown* (p 27).

In respect of bills for contentious business it is arguable that the provisions of the Solicitors Act, s 64 for substituting a gross sum bill with a detailed bill (see p 27) made the decisions in *Haigh v Ousey* and other nineteenth century cases obsolete. In respect of non-contentious business, since the Solicitors Remuneration Order 1953, a solicitor has been entitled to such sum as may be fair and reasonable having regard to all the circumstances of the case, and the client has been entitled to apply to the Law Society to certify what this amount should be (see Chapter 5). Lord Denning in *Re: A Solicitor* [1955] 2 QB 252, CA interpreted the position as being that the solicitor could deliver:

> 'a lump sum as before, but whereas previously the client could afterwards insist on a detailed bill of charges, he now has no right to have the lump sum split up into items. He is however given a valuable new right. He can require the solicitor to put the bill before the Law Society, so that the Law Society can see whether the sum charged is fair and reasonable. If it is fair and reasonable, they will certify accordingly; or if not they will say what the proper sum should be … Such being the effect of the new Order the question is; what must a solicitors bill for non-contentious business now contain? It need not contain detailed charges as it used to do before 1920. Nor need it contain all of the details which the solicitor will have to give, if required, to the Law Society or the taxing master [*costs judge*]. But I think that it must contain a summarised statement of the work done, sufficient to tell the client what it is for which he is asked to pay. A bare account for "professional services" between certain dates, or for "work done in connection with your matrimonial affairs" would not do. The nature of the work must be stated, such as, advising on such and such a matter, instructing counsel to do so and so, drafting such and such a document and so forth.'

Surprisingly that is precisely all that the Law Society's Practice Rule 14.07 does require: 'A solicitor's bill of costs should contain sufficient information to identify the matter and period to which it relates'. A bill that did no more than comply with the Law Society's Rule exactly fits Lord Denning's description of a bill that 'will not do'!

Even in *Haigh v Ousey* (p 26) Lord Chief Justice Campbell said:

> 'I do not think that the legislature intended to throw on a solicitor the burthen (*sic*) of preparing a bill such that another solicitor on looking at it should without any further statement, see on the face of the bill all information requisite to enable him to say if the charges were reasonable … If we required in respect of every item a precise exactness of form, we should go beyond the words and meaning of the statute, and should give facilities to dishonest clients to defeat just claims upon a defence of a defect of form, in respect of which they have no real interest.'

And Erle J said:

> 'No man, unless there were interminable prolixity in the bill, could tell from the bill alone what is a fair charge for matters depending on the quantum meruit, that is for almost everything except mere steps in a cause … The bill should give reasonable information; if the client wants more, he may demand it.'

The safety net in respect of non-contentious business is the client's right to obtain a certificate as to reasonableness from the Law Society (see p 37). The safety net in respect of contentious business is the client's right to request a detailed bill (see above). I am grateful to Jeremy Morgan, of counsel, for drawing to my attention the judgment of CS Clarke QC sitting as a High Court judge in *Re a Solicitor* (10 May 1994, unreported, QB), which is a 27-page comprehensive survey of the history of the provision. The solicitor's action for the unpaid balance of their costs was met with a defence that their bill did not satisfy the law's requirements for a solicitor's bill in that it did not contain sufficient information to enable the defendant to obtain advice as to whether or not he should tax it, based on *Haigh v Ousey*. The judge in *Re: a Solicitor* held that the option given to a solicitor of submitting a gross sum bill conferred by s 64 of the Act was not available at the time of *Haigh v Ousey*, nor at that time did the clients have the rights conferred in s 64(2)–(4). He continued:

> 'In my judgment Parliament did not intend to oblige a solicitor submitting a gross sum bill for contentious business to include any more than, in the words of Lord Denning, "a summarised statement of the work done sufficient to tell the client what it is which he is asked to pay". Parliament intended to give to the solicitor the option of submitting, in contentious business, the same form of bill as was already permitted in non-contentious business. Any further obligation would render the provision wholly ineffective. Section 64 was intended to recognise that, in many cases, the client is content to accept a gross sum bill but to provide safeguards for a client who, for any reason, was not'.

He concluded:

> 'a bill which, to use Lord Denning's example, simply said "to professional services" would not, of course, be sufficient since such a document would leave it wholly unclear what the client would be paying for, if he paid it, or in respect of what the solicitor might or might not, after payment, be able to make a further claim. If such a document is a bill at all, it is certainly not a bill contemplated by the Act'.

Why should lack of information make a bill 'invalid', and not, for example, merely unenforceable? The concept of invalidity for lack of particularity is judge-made.

No doubt a bill which does not even attain the modest aspirations of Law Society Practice Rule 14.07 ought to be void on the ground that it is not really a bill at all, but should not any other deficiency merely result in the bill being unenforceable until the basic information has been supplied? The law was reviewed on 22 October 2002 by the Court of Appeal in the unreported case of *Ralph Hume Garry v Gwillim*. To establish that a bill was not in 'bona fide compliance' with the Act, a client must establish (i) it contained no sufficient narrative to identify what he was being charged for; and (ii) he did not have sufficient knowledge from documents in his possession or from information supplied to him to take advice about challenging the bill. The more the client knew, the less need for the bill to spell it out. These 'unseemly disputes' could be avoided if the bill were accompanied by a computer print-out showing the time spent, with the rate charged and some description of the work done.

A totally inadequate bill for contentious business (for example one not giving any information as to how the amount charged was calculated) cannot be saved by a request by the client for further details.

A full narrative could include details embarrassing to the client who wishes to use the bill as a VAT invoice and there are various methods of preserving this confidentiality, the most usual being to set out the narrative either on a separate sheet or on a tear-off portion at the end of the bill.

(c) Unpaid disbursements

The bill may include unpaid disbursements, but only if they are described in the bill as not yet paid; the defect is fatal to these items if they are challenged on a subsequent assessment. The only remedy would be to ask the costs judge for an adjournment, apply to the court for leave to withdraw the entire bill, re-deliver it (at the risk of being ordered to pay all the costs thrown away) and then start again (Solicitors Act 1974, s 67). However, in *Tearle & Co v Sherring* (29 October 1993, unreported, QBD), Wright J held that where a solicitor has acted in good faith but by inadvertence has omitted to describe disbursements as unpaid, the court not only had power to give him leave to withdraw his bill and deliver another one, to save costs it could in an appropriate case give leave to amend his bill by adding the words 'unpaid'. He tentatively expressed the view that a costs officer might have the same powers.

(d) Cash account

It is the duty of a solicitor when delivering a bill of costs also to deliver a cash account detailing the receipts and payments made on behalf of the client. It is important to know what disbursements should appear in the bill itself and what should be charged in the cash account. Many solicitors lose money on assessments of costs by regarding as cash account items payments which should have been included in the bill as disbursements. Disbursements have been defined as 'such payments as the solicitor in the due discharge of his duty is bound to make whether his client furnishes him with money for the purpose, with money on account, or not, as for example court fees, counsel's fees, expenses of witnesses, agents and stationers'. All of these items should appear in the bill. Other items which the solicitor is not bound by law or custom to make, such as purchase money, interest, sums paid into court, or damages, costs paid to an opponent, estate duty and land registry fees, are properly charged in the cash account (*Re Remnant* (1849) 11 Beav 603; *Re Buckwell and Berkeley* [1902] 2 Ch 596, CA; *Browne v Barber* [1913] 2 KB 553, CA).

(e) VAT

A solicitor's bill of costs must comply with the VAT regulations which apply to his services. The bill must of course contain the solicitor's VAT registration number, but there are other provisions which are so misunderstood and surprising that I have devoted the next chapter to them.

(f) Signature

Although not essential to the validity of the bill, a solicitor may not sue for his costs unless he has complied with the requirements of the Solicitors Act 1974, s 69 as to signature.

Section 69(2)(*a*) provides that the bill must be signed by the solicitor or one of his partners, either in his own name or in the name of the firm, or be accompanied by a letter which is so signed and refers to the bill. A commonly used abbreviation of the firm's name will suffice (*Bartletts de Reya v Byrne* (1983) 127 Sol Jo 69, CA). A signature impressed by means of a rubber stamp suffices (*Goodman v J Eban Ltd* [1954] 1 QB 550, CA) but the signature of an assistant solicitor or a legal executive does not. In these days of delegation it is important to ensure that this provision is complied with. Some firms instruct their accounts department not to issue or enter a bill unless it bears a partner's signature.

The practical difference between a bill which is valid but unenforceable by court proceedings because it is not signed and an invalid bill, is that the former entitles a solicitor to appropriate money paid on account in settlement of the bill or to exercise a lien until the bill is paid, while the latter is of no effect for any purpose. However, if an action on a defective bill gets before the court, the judge has the discretion in appropriate circumstances to give leave for the bill to be withdrawn and replaced without commencing fresh proceedings (*Zuliani v Veira* [1994] 1 WLR 1149, PC).

(g) Delivery

The Solicitors Act 1974, s 69(2)(*b*) also provides that the bill must be delivered to the party to be charged either personally or by being sent to him by post to, or left for him at, his place of business, dwelling house or last known place of abode.

CHAPTER 4

SOLICITOR AND CLIENT VAT

1. CHARGEABILITY

A solicitor's services to his client are subject to VAT at the standard rate unless the solicitor is not registered for VAT or the services are zero-rated.

VAT CHARGEABILITY CHART

Service Rendered by Solicitors	*Capacity of Client (See Note 1)*	*Residence of Client (See Note 2)*	*VAT Chargeability*
1. General legal services other than those below	Private or	UK	Full
		EEC (Non UK)	Full
		World (Non EEC)	Zero
	Business	UK	Full
		EEC (Non UK)	Zero
		World (Non EEC)	Zero
2. Services relating to land outside UK	Private or Business	UK	Zero
		World (Non UK)	Zero
3. Services relating to land inside UK ie: conveyancing, litigation and advice associated with land	Private or Business	UK	Full
		World (Non UK)	Full

Note 1. **Capacity of client**

It should be clearly established in every case whether a client gives instructions in a private or in a business capacity.

Note 2. **Residence of client**

Private individuals: country where they are usually resident.

Business client with premises: the country where it has any business establishment including a branch or agency. If this would give it more than one country or residence then it is to be treated as resident in the country where its establishment is located which is most directly concerned with the services rendered.

Business client without premises: for corporate clients, the country or incorporation or legal constitution; for individual clients the country of the individual's usual residence.

2. THE TAX POINT

I said in the last chapter that the effect of some of the regulations is surprising.

The basic rule is that the tax point for services is the date on which their performance is completed. VAT becomes payable on that date irrespective of when the bill is delivered.

For solicitors there is a minor exception. If a tax invoice is issued within three months of the basic tax point, the date of the invoice becomes the actual tax point. VAT is therefore payable by a solicitor when the work is completed or when his bill is delivered provided that this is within three months of the completion of the work (HM Customs and Excise Notice No 700 (Notice 700) and the Value Added Tax Act 1994, s 6(6)). This provision has the force of law and it is therefore an offence for a solicitor not to quantify his charges within three months of completing a matter for the purposes of calculating and paying VAT.

This is NOT a VAT invoice: One effect of Notice 700 is to make unlawful and ineffective the practice of a solicitor writing to a client informing him of his proposed fees but not issuing a VAT invoice until payment has been received. This erroneous philosophy was set out in the *Architect's Journal* as follows:

> 'If VAT registered it can pay to liaise with the client and give a note of what the total bill will be and not actually issue an invoice until the date the cheque arrives. This is because once an invoice for VAT is issued you are liable to pay the VAT over to HM Customs and Excise regardless of whether or not you are paid. To ensure that you keep your own cash intact, rather than having to pay it over before it reaches you from the client, you can issue your statements headed with the wording: "This is not a VAT invoice. An authenticated invoice for VAT will be sent on receipt of your cheque."'

The creation of the basic tax point cannot be circumvented by any such device.

3. DISBURSEMENTS

(a) VAT

In respect of which litigation disbursements should a client be charged VAT? The simple answer is 'none'. Unfortunately this gives rise to the much more complicated question 'what is a disbursement?'. The answer is to be found in the VAT *Guide* (HM Customs and Excise Notice 700), which sets out eight criteria. The test is whether the goods or services are supplied to the solicitor to enable him to render his service to the client, in which event they are not a disbursement and VAT is chargeable. For example, postage, telephone calls, travelling and hotel expenses are not disbursements and VAT must be charged on them. A disbursement is a payment which relates to goods or services supplied to the client, even if it is, in the first place, paid for by the solicitor. Examples are oath and court fees. A method of avoiding VAT on a payment which would not otherwise attract VAT, such as an air fare, is for the client to pay for it direct. The solicitor need not then include it in his account. An example of the importance of this was recently drawn to my attention by Simon Young of Veitch Penny. Their VAT inspector contended that all the medical reports, notes or records they had obtained in personal injury cases were obtained for their benefit and not the clients' (ie they were primarily to enable the solicitors to do their job) and as such formed part of their services to their clients, who should have been charged VAT on those items. The correspondence ended happily with HM Customs and Excise accepting that the payments satisfied the conditions of para 10.8 of Notice 700 and were true disbursements.

(b) Counsel's fees

The fees of counsel are part of the service rendered by the solicitor and should therefore be included in the solicitor's bill and attract VAT even if the barrister is not registered for VAT. However, there is a long-standing concession under which HM Customs and Excise permit solicitors to re-address counsel's fee notes to the lay client, who then makes payment direct (or is requested by the solicitor to return the fee note to him with a separate cheque payable to counsel) so that counsel's fees do not pass through the solicitor's books at all. Where this is done the fees of the unregistered barrister do not attract VAT, and the solicitor avoids incurring VAT liability on counsel's fees because he need not include them in his VAT quarterly return.

4. RECOVERY OF VAT

If the client is registered for VAT and the legal services supplied to him are for the purposes of his business he may recover the tax charged, either out of VAT received by him from his customers or by reclaiming it from HM Customs and Excise. It is therefore important for the solicitor to distinguish between a client's personal matters and his business affairs and to render separate accounts in respect of them.

5. AGREED FEES

The Solicitors' Costs Information and Client Care Code paragraph 4, requires a solicitor to give the client a breakdown between fees, VAT and disbursements in advance. If the solicitor fails to do this, the implication will be that an agreed fee included VAT (see also 'Criminal Offence' at p 14). Where a VAT inclusive fee has been agreed the solicitor must nevertheless account to HM Customs and Excise for the VAT element (for VAT at 17.5%, the magic formula is 17/74ths) and provide a VAT invoice to the client if he requests one.

6. VAT ON FIXED COSTS RECOVERED

Fixed costs recovered under CPR Rule 45, RSC Order 62 and CCR Order 38 contain no element of VAT. The solicitor may either charge the client an amount equal to the fixed costs or charge on the normal solicitor and client basis, in both cases giving credit for the sum recovered. By either method he must charge the client VAT in addition to the fixed costs. VAT is recoverable on fast track trial fixed costs under CPR Rule 46 provided the client is not registered for VAT (see section 4 above).

7. INSURANCE CLAIMS

(a) Policy holder can recover VAT

If the insurance relates to the client's business and it is VAT registered the client will be able to take a full input tax credit for the VAT on the solicitor's bill. In these circumstances the insurers will only be responsible to their policy holder for the amount of the solicitor's bill exclusive of VAT.

(b) Policy holder cannot recover VAT

Where the client is partly exempt, or the insurance does not relate to his business, or he is not VAT registered, the solicitor's bill must still be addressed to the client and include VAT. In the circumstances there is no objection to the client sending the entire bill to the insurers for payment, as previously. If, for internal accounting purposes, the insurers wish solicitors to issue invoices directly to them, this may be done but the invoice so delivered will not be a VAT invoice.

(c) The Lloyd's Underwriters, ILU and AIOA scheme

There may be cases in which the amount equivalent to the VAT payable by an insured party proves difficult or impossible to recover. The Law Society has negotiated a scheme with Lloyd's Underwriters, ILU and AIOA to cover this situation. Other insurers will usually be members of the Association of British Insurers, who have advised their members of the statement, but when dealing with these companies it is necessary for solicitors to confirm directly with them that they accept the scheme. Here is the Law Society's summary of the scheme:

LLOYD'S UNDERWRITERS, ILU AND AIOA SCHEME

1. In indemnity/liability claims, underwriters will expect to pay the solicitor's bill exclusive of the VAT equivalent when it is rendered by the solicitor. Solicitors will send the VAT invoice direct to assureds who are registered for VAT with a request for payment by them to the solicitors of the VAT equivalent. Solicitors are to use their best endeavours to obtain payment by the assured of the VAT equivalent. Underwriters will indemnify solicitors for any of the VAT equivalent remaining unpaid if, after a period of 90 days, solicitors are unable to obtain payment. In any event, solicitors will not seek to recover the VAT equivalent direct from assureds, where the amount per invoice is less than £50, and this will therefore be a cost to underwriters. If an assured pays the VAT equivalent to a solicitor after the 90-day period, the solicitor will reimburse underwriters for that amount.
2. In subrogation cases, underwriters will expect to pay the solicitor's bill inclusive of the VAT element when it is rendered by solicitors. However, solicitors are to use their best endeavours to obtain payment by the assured of the VAT equivalent. If successful, solicitors will reimburse underwriters. In any event, underwriters will not ask solicitors to pursue the payment of the VAT equivalent from assureds where the amount per invoice is less than £50. This will therefore be a cost to underwriters.
3. Nothing shall prevent an underwriter adopting a different method of invoicing for VAT purposes should any particular circumstances require such a method, save that they are not to be more onerous upon solicitors than described above.

The Law Society understands that, generally, Customs will allow solicitors to rely on underwriters' and insurers' knowledge when deciding whether their bill is entitled to zero-rating: in any case of doubt, solicitors should consult their local VAT office before treating their services as zero-rated in whole or in part. In reference to VAT invoicing generally, attention is drawn to the requirements of the relevant regulations which are now in the Value Added Tax (General) Regulations 1985 (SI 1985/886).

8. INSURANCE COMMISSIONS

The Law Society's view is that VAT is assessable on the full amount of the bill, disregarding any reduction for insurance commission set-off. Furthermore, VAT is still payable on the full amount of what the bill would have been, even if no bill at all is rendered. If this is because of offset insurance commission, the amount that the bill would have been is presumably equivalent to the whole of the commission. In the Law Society's opinion, solicitors who treat VAT in any other way in such circumstances are putting themselves at considerable risk because of the likelihood of a subsequent claim by HM Customs and Excise.

CHAPTER 5

THE CLIENT'S RIGHTS

1. FORMAL DEFECTS

If the formalities that are a prerequisite to a solicitor commencing proceedings for the recovery of his costs (see p 27) have not been complied with, his bill is nevertheless valid. Accordingly, although the solicitor cannot sue on his bill, the client can only ignore it with impunity if the solicitor has no funds of the client that he can set off against the bill and no property of the client over which he can exercise a lien.

2. REMUNERATION CERTIFICATE

(a) Right to certification

In respect of bills not exceeding £50,000 relating to non-contentious business, an 'entitled person' (a client or an entitled third party – see next paragraph) may require a solicitor to obtain a certificate from the Council of the Law Society stating what sum, in the opinion of the Council, would be a fair and reasonable charge for the business covered by the bill (whether it be the sum charged or a lesser sum). In the absence of taxation [*detailed assessment*] the sum payable in respect of such costs is the sum stated in the remuneration certificate (Solicitors' (Non-Contentious Business) Remuneration Order 1994 (SI 1994/2616), art 4).

The Order defines an 'entitled third party' as 'a residuary beneficiary absolutely and immediately (and not contingently) entitled to an inheritance, where a solicitor has charged the estate for his professional costs for acting in the administration of the estate, and either: (a) the only personal representatives are solicitors (whether or not acting in a professional capacity); or (b) the only personal representatives are solicitors acting jointly with partners or employees in a professional capacity'. The effect of this is that a residuary beneficiary of an estate where there is at least one lay executor is not an entitled third party. A residuary beneficiary of an estate in which all the personal representatives are solicitors is able to ask the solicitor billing the estate to obtain a remuneration certificate, even if the bill is from another solicitor (not a personal representative) instructed by the personal representative to do the work. A residuary beneficiary who will become entitled only upon the happening of some event – for example a person entitled subject to a life interest, or a minor entitled only on majority – is not an entitled third party (*Law Society Gazette*, 28 September 1994).

(b) Information to be given in writing to entitled person

Article 8 of the Order provides:

> When required by Art 6 or 7, a solicitor shall inform the entitled person in writing of the following matters:
> (a) where Art 4(1) applies:

(i) that the entitled person may, within one month of receiving from the solicitor the information specified in this article or (if later) of delivery of the bill or notification of the amount of the costs, require the solicitor to obtain a remuneration certificate; and

(ii) that (unless the solicitor has agreed to do so) the Council may waive the requirements of Art 11(1), if satisfied from the client's written application that exceptional circumstances exist to justify granting a waiver;

(b) that ss 70, 71 and 72 of the Solicitors Act 1974 set out the entitled person's rights in relation to taxation [*detailed assessment*];

(c) that (where the whole of the bill has not been paid, by deduction or otherwise) the solicitor may charge interest on the outstanding amount of the bill in accordance with Art 14.

(c) Loss by client of right to certification

Article 9 of the Order provides:

A client may not require a solicitor to obtain a remuneration certificate:

(a) after a bill has been delivered and paid by the client, other than by deduction;

(b) where a bill has been delivered after the expiry of one month from the date on which the client was informed in writing of the matters specified in Art 8 or from delivery of the bill if later;

(c) where a bill has been paid by deduction, three months after receiving notice of his rights. When delivering a bill the solicitor may stipulate a shorter period than three months but not less than one month (Art 7);

(d) after the solicitor and client have entered into a non-contentious business agreement in accordance with the provisions of s 57 of the Solicitors Act 1974;

(e) after a court has ordered [*a detailed assessment of the bill*].

(d) Loss by entitled third party of right to certification

Article 10 of the Order provides:

An entitled third party may not require a solicitor to obtain a remuneration certificate:

(a) after the prescribed time within the meaning of Art 7(2)(b) has elapsed without any objection being received to the amount of the costs;

(b) after the expiry of one month from the date on which the entitled third party was (in compliance with Art 7) informed in writing of the matters specified in Art 8 or from notification of the costs if later;

(c) after a court has ordered the bill to be [*a detailed assessment of the bill*].

(e) Requirement to pay a sum towards the costs

Article 11 of the Order provides:

(1) On requiring a solicitor to obtain a remuneration certificate a client must pay to the solicitor the paid disbursements and value added tax comprised in the bill together with 50% of the costs unless:

(a) the client has already paid the amount required under this article, by deduction from monies held or otherwise; or

(b) the solicitor or (if the solicitor refuses) the Council has agreed in writing to waive all or part of this requirement.

(2) The Council shall be under no obligation to provide a remuneration certificate, and the solicitor may take steps to obtain payment of his bill if the client, having been informed of his right to seek a waiver of the requirements of para (1), has not:

(a) within one month of receipt of the information specified in Art 8, either paid in accordance with para (1) or applied to the Council in writing for a waiver (which has not been refused) of the requirements of para (1); or

(b) made payment in accordance with para (1) within one month of written notification that he has been refused a waiver of those requirements by the Council.

A waiver may be granted only in exceptional circumstances, such as where an estimate has been given and apparently substantially exceeded; where the solicitor is subject to disciplinary proceedings or intervention; where the solicitor is already holding adequate security for the payment of his costs and where a client has not been given any information from the solicitors on how much he charges for his work. Being unable to pay the bill because of financial difficulty is not an exceptional circumstance. Application for a waiver must be made within one month of receiving the notice of rights to the Office for the Supervision of Solicitors (OSS) and at the same time the client must write to the solicitors informing them that he has applied for a waiver.

(f) Costs paid by deduction

Article 7 of the Order provides:

(1) If a solicitor deducts his costs from monies held for or on behalf of a client or of an estate in satisfaction of a bill and an entitled person objects in writing to the amount of the bill within the prescribed time, the solicitor must immediately inform the entitled person in writing of the matters specified in Art 8, unless he has already done so.

(2) In this article and in Art 10 'the prescribed time' means:

(a) in respect of a client, three months after delivery of the relevant bill, or a lesser time (which may not be less than one month) specified in writing to the client at the time of delivery of the bill; or

(b) in respect of an entitled third party, three months after delivery of notification to the entitled third party of the amount of the costs, or a lesser time (which may not be less than one month) specified in writing to the entitled third party at the time of such notification.

(g) The application

The solicitor must apply promptly for a remuneration certificate, the initiative lying with him. The certification process is handled by the OSS and not as previously by the Law Society. The old Chinese wall between remuneration certification and the Solicitors' Complaints Bureau was dismantled: there is now a one-door entry for both disputes and complaints.

On receipt of a request for a remuneration certificate the solicitor must obtain the application form back from the OSS and forward a copy of the completed forms to the client, requesting his comments as to why he believes the fee is too high. The forms are then returned to the OSS by the solicitors with their file of papers and the client's comments. There is no charge at this or any other stage of the remuneration certificate procedure.

When submitting an application for a remuneration certificate, the solicitor should ensure that, simply and clearly, he does justice to himself. The certifiers do not know that there is a vital letter in the middle of the file of correspondence and they certainly cannot be expected to find it by reading every document in the file. However, prolixity will not endear you to the assessor; shortly and succinctly set out the issues and relevant circumstances. Show the status of the fee earners concerned and their hourly rates if your charges are based on time.

(h) Procedure

The OSS will first ensure that the matter does not involve (i) allegations of negligence; (ii) a dispute about whether instructions were given; (iii) a question of law (iv) a dispute about disbursements or VAT; (v) the quality of advice; or (vi) whether the whole or part of the charge is payable by another person, these being matters outside the remuneration certification process.

The OSS will then endeavour to establish if there is any scope for conciliation by contacting the client for an informal discussion, if necessary seeking the solicitor's views. If the matter cannot be resolved a case worker will prepare a written report summarising the party's submissions and giving the case worker's views. A copy of the report is sent to all parties who are invited to submit comments within 14 days. After 14 days a provisional assessment, indicating the fee proposed to be certified and the reasons for it, is issued to all parties.

Parties have 28 days to lodge grounds of appeal. If no appeal is lodged the remuneration certificate will be issued based upon the provisional assessment. Either party may appeal by sending points of objection within the 28-day limit, a copy of which is sent to the other party who can make representations within 14 days. The matter is then reviewed afresh by a sub-committee of the Compliance and Supervision Committee. There is no further appeal against their decision and a remuneration certificate is issued.

(i) The assessment

On a remuneration certificate assessment the following test is applied to estimates:

1. If a figure has been given to a client, however casually, the bill will be reduced to that figure unless it is apparent that the client did not rely upon it and could not reasonably have been expected to do so.
2. If a qualified estimate has been given, then the figure may be increased if, but only if, the client was notified in writing at the time the additional work arose, of the nature of that work and its effect on costs.

According to the Law Society's publication *Non-Contentious Costs* the reasoning is to protect the reputation of the profession and to stop those solicitors who quote a low fee to get the job, with no intention of adhering to it.

(j) Solicitors Act assessment

The sum shown on the certificate is binding on the solicitor unless he subsequently applies for a Solicitors Act assessment (art 4(2)).

3. APPLICATION FOR DELIVERY OF A BILL

Section 68 of the Solicitors Act 1974 empowers the court on an application by the client to order the solicitor to deliver a bill. The jurisdiction in the High Court extends to all cases, including those in which no business has been done by the solicitor in the

High Court, while the county court has similar jurisdiction where the bill of costs relates wholly or partly to contentious business done by the solicitor in that county court. There are two usual circumstances which may give rise to such an application. The first is where the solicitor attempts to retain money paid on account without having delivered an adequate bill. The second is where the solicitor makes what the client regards as an excessive demand for an interim payment on account (see p 7).

(a) Precedent originating application to deliver bill of costs

> **CLAIM FORM N208 CPR PART 8**
>
> *Details of claim*
> the claimant seeks an order that within ... days the defendant delivers to the claimant or to his solicitor a bill of costs in all cases and matters in which he is concerned for the claimant and give credit in them for all money received by him for or on account of the claimant.

(b) Precedent order for delivery of bill of costs (CPR Schedule of Costs Precedent K)

(See overleaf.)

4. REQUEST A DETAILED BILL

In respect of contentious business, within three months of the delivery of a gross sum bill and before service of a claim for the recovery of the costs, the client may require the solicitor to deliver a bill containing detailed items (for the effect of this see p 27).

5. APPLY TO SET ASIDE A CONTENTIOUS BUSINESS AGREEMENT

Such an application may be made on the grounds that it is unfair or unreasonable, either when the solicitor applies for leave to enforce the agreement or by an application by the client (see p 11).

6. SUE FOR NEGLIGENCE

If the client alleges that he or she has suffered loss because of the solicitor's negligence, the client may sue the solicitor for damages and for a return of costs paid. A solicitor cannot charge costs for negligent work if the result of that negligence was to render the work wholly fruitless. To succeed in a claim for damages there must be proof of actual damage, but, although the court does not have the power to award exemplary damages as a mark of its disapproval of a solicitor's conduct, Peter Birts QC suggests it may be possible to claim damages for injury to feelings on the grounds that a main purpose of the solicitor's retainer was to give peace of mind and that his negligence has caused the client vexation etc (*Heywood v Wellers* [1976] 1 All ER 300). If you ever succeed with that argument, please let Peter Birts or me know!

On a solicitor and client assessment, while the costs officer can disallow items unreasonably incurred by virtue of the solicitor's negligence, a costs officer cannot disallow the entire bill because he cannot try an action for negligence.

CPR SCHEDULE OF COSTS: PRECEDENT K

Solicitor's Act: order for delivery of bill

DATED the [DATE]

IN THE HIGH COURT OF JUSTICE **[Claim No]**

[DIVISION]

[JUDGE TYPE] [JUDGE NAME]

[CLAIMANT]

BETWEEN:

Claimant

- and -

[DEFENDANT]

Defendant

UPON THE APPLICATION OF THE [PARTY]

[the parties and their representatives who attended]

AND UPON HEARING

AND UPON READING the documents on the Court File

IT IS ORDERED THAT

(1) The [PARTY] must within [NUMBER OF DAYS] deliver to the [PARTY] or to his solicitor, a bill of costs in all causes and matters in which he has been concerned for the [PARTY]

(2) The [PARTY] must give credit in that bill for all money received by him from or on account of the [PARTY]

7. WAIT UNTIL SUED

The client may wait until the solicitor institutes proceedings and then defend and counterclaim for negligence, seek a detailed assessment, or seek a quantum meruit (see *Thomas Watts & Co v Smith and Paloma SA v Turner & Co*, at p 47 below). In respect of proceedings commenced on a gross sum bill, s 64(3) of the Solicitors Act 1974 requires the court to order an assessment if the party chargeable so requests within a month of the commencement of proceedings.

(a) In the High Court

Where the solicitor sues in the High Court, if the client disputes only the amount of the bill, usually on an application for summary judgment, the order will direct that the bill be referred to a costs judge and that the solicitor be entitled to sign judgment for the costs as assessed, together with the costs of the action. The client can also obtain such an order by making an application in the action under CPR Part 23.

(b) Precedent application for a detailed assessment after action brought

APPLICATION NOTICE (FORM N244)

I [name of client] the defendant intend to apply for an order that the claimant's bills of costs and charges [*and disbursements if disputed*] delivered to the defendant for the recovery of which this action is brought be referred to a costs officer to be assessed, and that the claimant give credit for all sums of money received by him from or on account of the defendant, and that the costs officer assess the costs of the reference, and certify the amount due to or from either party in respect of the bill and of the costs of the reference (according to the statute), and that the complainant be restrained from prosecuting this action pending the reference, and that upon payment of what (if anything) is found to be due to the complainant, together with the costs of this action also to be assessed and paid, all further proceedings to be stayed.

Because I dispute that the claimant is entitled to the charges [*and disbursements*] in his bill of costs.

I rely on section 70 of the Solicitors Act 1974.

Statement of truth

(c) In the county court

If the solicitor has sued in the county court, the county court may only assess the solicitor's bill where:

(a) the bill relates wholly or in part to contentious business done in a county court;
(b) part of that work was done in the county court in which the application to tax is brought;
(c) the bill does not exceed £5,000.

(Solicitors Act 1974, s 69(3).)

Where the defendant client cannot apply for an order for a Solicitors Act assessment, there are various courses which may be adopted:

(a) Transfer the action to the High Court under the County Courts Act 1984, s 42. The court may then make a 'Smith v Edwardes Order' based on *Smith v Edwardes* (1888) 22 QBD 10, CA which provides:

> 'It is ordered that the bill of costs on which this action is brought be referred to the costs judge/district judge pursuant to the Solicitors Act 1974, s 69, and that the claimant give credit at the time of the assessment for all sums of money received by him from or on account of the defendant and that the claimant be at liberty to sign judgment for the amount of the cost judge's/district judge's certificate on the said assessment together with costs to be assessed.'

(b) Order that if the client issues an originating application in the High Court for an assessment of the costs within a fixed period the solicitor shall have leave to sign judgment for the amount to be found due on assessment or, if the client fails to institute proceedings within the requisite time, for the amount claimed.
(c) Refer to a costs judge, with his and the parties' consent, as a referee under the County Courts Act 1984, s 5(1)(*c*).
(d) Make a similar reference to a district judge for enquiry and report.
(e) Adopt the course followed by the High Court in *Lumsden v Shipcote Land Co* [1906] 2 KB 433, CA where the registrar [*district judge*] ascertained the proper amount to be paid, just as in the case of any other action for work and labour done.

These orders are, of course, subject to the client satisfying the court that he still has the right to apply for an assessment (see the Solicitors Act 1974, s 70 at p 46).

However, a frequent condition imposed by the court is that the full amount claimed by the solicitor be paid into court by the client. The solicitor should also consider applying for an interim payment (see p 8).

8. REQUEST THE SOLICITOR TO HAVE HIS COSTS ASSESSED

Frequently a client asks the solicitor to have his costs assessed. Although a solicitor may issue an application to assess their own costs, it is an invitation that should be declined unless there are some very unusual circumstances. If a solicitor issues an application to assess his own costs, unless the client attends on the assessment or the costs judge certifies there are special circumstances, there will be no order for the costs of the proceedings. In any event, the order made on the application cannot include an order for payment of the assessed costs by the client. If the client does not pay, the solicitor must institute proceedings for payment. If, therefore, a client wishes the costs to be assessed, the solicitor should advise him to make his own application. The only reason a solicitor might wish to apply for a Solicitors Act assessment would be to escape from the consequences of a remuneration certificate (see p 37). If, in spite of my advice, you do apply to assess your own costs this is the order you will get:

CPR SCHEDULE OF COSTS: PRECEDENT M

Order on Solicitor's Application for Assessment Under the Solicitor's Act 1974 Part III

Upon hearing ... upon reading ...

IT IS ORDERED THAT

(1) A detailed assessment must be made of the bill dated [ ] delivered to the defendant by the claimant.

(2) If the defendant attends the detailed assessment the court making that assessment must also assess the costs of these proceedings and certify what is due to or from either party in respect of the bill and the costs of these proceedings.

(3) Until these proceedings are concluded the claimant must not commence or continue any proceedings against the defendant in respect of the bill mentioned above.

(4) Upon payment by the defendant of any sum certified as due to the claimant in these proceedings the claimant must deliver to the defendant all the documentation in the claimant's possession or control which belong to the defendant.

9. OBTAIN AN ORDER FOR THE COSTS TO BE ASSESSED

(a) Solicitors Act 1974, s 70

The Solicitors Act 1974, s 70 provides:

(i) Where the application is made within one month of the delivery of the bill the High Court shall make an unconditional order that the bill be taxed [*assessed*] and that no action be commenced on it until the taxation [*assessment*] is completed.

(ii) After one month has expired the court may make the same order, subject to such directions and such conditions as it thinks fit.

(iii) Where 12 months have expired from the delivery of the bill or after a judgment has been obtained or where the bill has been paid within 12 months of the application, no order shall be made except in special circumstances. Such a circumstance could be where a client has paid the bill (perhaps to enable his new solicitor to obtain the papers) reserving his right to assess the bill if so advised. In *Re Norman* (1886) 16 QBD 673 the Court of Appeal held that special circumstances are not limited to overcharging so extreme as to amount to fraud or where there has been undue pressure on the client. In *Kralj v Birkbeck Montague* (18 February 1988, unreported) the Court of Appeal found special circumstances where the solicitors had dissuaded their client from having their costs taxed [*assessed*] and had charged her substantially more than was recovered between the parties, including such items as time spent with law reporters. A more recent example was in *A v BCD (a firm)* (5 June 1997, unreported, QBD), in which the court observed that the word used was 'special' and not 'exceptional'. In this case the client had exercised his right to request the solicitors to obtain a remuneration certificate but the assessment was not made until four days after the anniversary of the rendering of the bill. The court regarded this as a special circumstance even though (unfortunately) it was not exceptional. Any other course would devalue the remuneration certificate procedure and discourage the use of it. The court also discounted the practice of a client paying a bill in full while unilaterally 'reserving the right' to have the bill assessed. Although the solicitor could, by agreement in return for payment, waive the right to resist an order for taxation (assessment) out of time, the most the client could do is to pay under protest and deploy the protest as a special circumstance if possible.

(iv) The court has no power to order an assessment of an application by the party chargeable with the bill after the expiration of 12 months from the payment of the bill. It is important to remember that this provision also affects third parties liable to meet the solicitor's bill to his client, such as mortgagors and lessors. This cannot be circumvented by resort to the inherent jurisdiction of the court: *Harrison v Tew* [1990] 1 All ER 321, HL, where the House of Lords held that the Solicitors Act 1974, s 70(4), displaced the court's inherent jurisdiction to order the taxation [*assessment*] of a solicitor's bill of costs in cases where the application to tax [*assess*] had been made more than a year after the bill had been paid. The court said the claimants would have had a more attractive-looking case if it had been made to appear that, in the absence of inherent jurisdiction, a client who had been grossly overcharged would have no remedy once he had been careless or unfortunate enough to fall foul of the 12-month limit. However in some cases the solicitor would have deducted his costs from the money received on the client's behalf, in which case the client could sue under the ordinary jurisdiction described in *Re Park* (1889) 41 Ch D 326. In some other cases the client could, by making a complaint, set in motion disciplinary proceedings. While the onus of proof would lie on the complainant, the bill could be referred to the costs judge and the court could order a refund in appropriate cases.

(v) In *A v BCD* (at p 46) the court held that, whether payment in full had been made under protest or not, s 70(4) put an absolute bar on obtaining an order for taxation after the expiration of 12 months after payment. However, in *Thomas Watts & Co v Smith* (16 March 1998, unreported) the Court of Appeal held that even 12 months after payment all was not lost. Where the solicitors sued for their costs they could not simply ask the court, without any further investigation, to underwrite the amount they had chosen to claim. In such a case where solicitors are applying for payment of their bill, the situation is analogous to one in which a claimant is applying for an unquantified sum which has to be quantified by a judicial process before judgment can be awarded for the appropriate amount. This is common in damages claims. Judgment for damages to be assessed is a very common form of order under an application for summary judgment. In a quantum meruit claim for work done, the benefit of which has been obtained under a contract where the contract sum had not been agreed, there may be an order for judgment to be entered for the claimant with the quantum to be assessed. If the court is to be asked to make an order for payment by the client of the amount claimed by the solicitors, a process of judicial assessment must first take place. A costs judge should carry out the judicial assessment. It is the costs judges who have the requisite expertise for that purpose. The court should not simply leave the client liable to pay the sum the solicitors have chosen, perhaps rightly chosen, but which has not been tested, to include in their bills. The defendant should have leave to defend by making representations on quantum as to the amount claimed in the solicitor's bill. In *Watts* the court ordered that the amount that ought to be paid by the defendant client to the claimant's solicitors was to be assessed by a costs judge and judgment entered for the amount so assessed. *Paloma SA v Turner & Co* [2000] 1 WLR 37, CA was an attempt to obtain a declaration that *Watts* was wrongly decided. It backfired. The court continued the decision and held that the prohibition of a detailed assessment in s 70 did not take away the need for a solicitor suing for his fees to prove that they were reasonable if challenged, in the absence of any express agreement as to what they should be. If the hourly rate is agreed the solicitor must still prove the reasonableness of the hours spent. Although the procedure provided by the Act is convenient and advantageous for the client, perhaps for both parties, it does not take away the client's common law rights to raise the unreasonable amount of the charges as a defence if the solicitor sues on his bill. The bill was ordered to be sent for assessment (but not for detailed assessment) by a costs judge.

(vi) Where funds are transferred by a solicitor from the account of an estate into his office account in satisfaction of his bill, the account is paid for the purposes of s 70(4) when the payers know and consent to the transfer: *Gough v Chivers & Jordan (a firm)* [1996] 26 LS Gaz R 20, CA.

(b) Application

The application is under the Solicitors Act 1974, s 70 and is made by using the claims form in accordance with CPR Part 8 if it is an originating application or CPR Part 23 in existing proceedings. Part III of the Solicitors Act 1974 was not affected by the Civil Procedure Rules and it still refers to 'taxations', although CPR Rule 48.9 prescribing the procedure uses the word 'assessment' and the practice is now to refer to 'Solicitors Act Assessments'.

(c) Precedent originating application by client for Solicitors Act assessment

Details of claim

The bill of charges and disbursements delivered to the claimant by the defendants be referred to a costs judge to be assessed and that the defendant give credit for all sums of money received by him on account of the claimant, and that he refund anything that on such assessment may appear to have been overpaid.

And it is further ordered that the costs judge do assess the costs of the assessment, and certify what is due to or from either party in respect of the bill and of the costs of the assessment.

And it is further ordered that the solicitors do not prosecute or continue to prosecute any action against the claimant in respect of the said bill pending the reference.

And it is further ordered upon payment by the claimant of anything that may appear to be due to the defendants, the defendants deliver up to the claimant or as he may direction all deeds, books, papers, and writings, in the defendants' possession, custody, or power, belonging to the claimant.

Statement of truth

(d) Precedent order on client's application for detailed assessment of solicitor's bill (CPR Schedule of Costs Precedent L)

(See p 49.)

CPR SCHEDULE OF COSTS: PRECEDENT L

Order on Client's Application for Detailed Assessment of Solicitor's Bill

DATED the [DATE]

IN THE HIGH COURT OF JUSTICE **[Claim No]**

[DIVISION]

[JUDGE TYPE] [JUDGE NAME]

[CLAIMANT]

BETWEEN:

Claimant

- and -

[DEFENDANT]

Defendant

UPON THE APPLICATION OF THE [PARTY]

[the parties and their representatives who attended]

AND UPON HEARING

AND UPON READING the documents on the Court File

IT IS ORDERED THAT

(1) A detailed assessment must be made of the bill dated [ ] delivered to the claimant by the defendant.

(2) On making the detailed assessment, the court must also assess the costs of these proceedings and certify what is due to or from either party in respect of the bill and the costs of these proceedings.

(3) Until these proceedings are concluded the defendant must not commence or continue any proceedings against the claimant in respect of the bill mentioned above.

(4) Upon payment by the claimant of any sum certified as due to the defendant in these proceedings the defendant must deliver to the claimant all the documentation in the defendant's possession or control which belong to the claimant.

(e) Application in the county court

(i) Jurisdiction

Under the provisions of the Solicitors Act 1974, s 69(3) and (4), where a solicitor's bill of costs relates wholly or partly to contentious business done in a county court and the amount of the bill does not exceed £5,000, then the powers of the court relating to assessment of the solicitor's bill under the Solicitors Act 1974, ss 70 and 71 may be exercised and performed by the county court. Otherwise the assessment must be in the Supreme Court Costs office (see p 43). The fact that the solicitor has applied for a charging order under s 73 of the Solicitors Act 1974 does not disapply the jurisdictional provisions of s 69 (*Jones v Twinsectra Ltd* [2002] EWCA Civ 668, [2002] All ER (D) 87 (Apr)).

By CCR Order 49, r 18 an application under s 69(3) may be heard and determined by a district judge. The proceedings must be brought in a county court in which part of the work was done.

(ii) Limit

Unless the solicitor and client have entered into a written agreement pursuant to CPR Rule 48.8(1A) expressly permitting payment to a solicitor of an amount of costs greater than that which the client could have recovered from another party in the proceedings, the Solicitors Act 1974, s 14(3), limits the solicitor's entitlement to that amount (see p 12).

(f) Assessment procedure

CPR Rule 48.9 and its supplemental practice direction provide as follows:

CPR RULE 48.9 ASSESSMENT PROCEDURE

(1) This rule sets out the procedure to be followed where the court has made an order under Part III of the Solicitors Act 1974 for the assessment of costs payable to a solicitor by his client.
(2) The solicitor must serve a breakdown of costs within 28 days of the order for costs to be assessed.
(3) The client must serve points of dispute within 14 days after service on him of the breakdown of costs.
(4) If the solicitor wishes to serve a reply, he must do so within 14 days of service on him of the points of dispute.
(5) Either party may file a request for a hearing date—
  (a) after points of dispute have been served; but
  (b) no later than 3 months after the date of the order for the costs to be assessed.
(6) This procedure applies subject to any contrary order made by the court.

(Other rules about costs payable in special cases can be found in Schedule 1, in the following: RSC O.30 (remuneration of receivers); O.49 (costs of garnishee).)

PRACTICE DIRECTION SECTION 56 PROCEDURE ON ASSESSMENT OF SOLICITOR AND CLIENT COSTS: RULE 48.10

56.1 The paragraphs in this section apply to orders made under Part III of the Solicitors Act 1974 for the assessment of costs. In these paragraphs 'client' includes any person entitled to make an application under Part III of that Act.
56.2 The procedure for obtaining an order under Part III of the Solicitors Act 1974 is by the alternative procedure for claims under Part 8. The provisions of RSC Order 106 appear, appropriately amended, in Schedule 1 to the CPR. Precedent J of the Schedule of Costs Precedents annexed to this Practice

Direction is a model form of claim form. The application must be accompanied by the bill or bills in respect of which assessment is sought, and, if the claim concerns a conditional fee agreement, a copy of that agreement. If the original bill is not available a copy will suffice.

56.3 Model forms of order, which the court may make, are set out in Precedents K, L and M of the Schedule of Costs Precedents annexed to this Practice Direction.

56.4 Attention is drawn to the time limits within which the required steps must be taken: ie the solicitor must serve a breakdown of costs within 28 days of the order for costs to be assessed, the client must serve points of dispute within 14 days after service on him of the breakdown, and any reply must be served within 14 days of service of the points of dispute.

56.5 The breakdown of costs referred to in rule 48.10 is a document which contains the following information:

(a) details of the work done under each of the bills sent for assessment; and

(b) in applications under Section 70 of the Solicitors Act 1974, an account showing money received by the solicitor to the credit of the client and sums paid out of that money on behalf of the client but not payments out which were made in satisfaction of the bill or of any items which are claimed in the bill.

56.6 Precedent P of the Schedule of Costs Precedents annexed to this Practice Direction is a model form of breakdown of costs. A party who is required to serve a breakdown of costs must also serve—

(1) copies of the fee notes of counsel and of any expert in respect of fees claimed in the breakdown, and

(2) written evidence as to any other disbursement which is claimed in the breakdown and which exceeds £250.

56.7 The provisions relating to default costs certificates (rule 47.11) do not apply to cases to which rule 48.10 applies.

56.8 Points of dispute should, as far as practicable, be in the form complying with paragraphs 33.1–35.7.

56.9 The time for requesting a detailed assessment hearing is within 3 months after the date of the order for the costs to be assessed.

56.10 The form of request for a hearing date must be in Form N258C. The request must be accompanied by copies of—

(a) the order sending the bill or bills for assessment;

(b) the bill or bills sent for assessment;

(c) the solicitor's breakdown of costs and any invoices or accounts served with that breakdown;

(d) a copy of the points of dispute, annotated as necessary in order to show which items have been agreed and their value and to show which items remain in dispute;

(e) as many copies of the points of dispute so annotated as there are other parties to the proceedings to whom the court should give details of the assessment hearing requested;

(f) a copy of any replies served;

(g) a statement signed by the party filing the request or his legal representative giving the names and addresses for service of all parties to the proceedings.

56.11 The request must include an estimate of the length of time the detailed assessment hearing will take.

56.12 On receipt of the request for a detailed assessment hearing the court will fix a date for the hearing or if the costs judge or district judge so decides, will give directions or fix a date for a preliminary appointment.

56.13

(1) The court will give at least 14 days notice of the time and place of the detailed assessment hearing to every person named in the statement referred to in paragraph 56.10(g) above.

(2) The court will when giving notice, give all parties other than the party who requested the hearing a copy of the points of dispute annotated by the party requesting the hearing in compliance with paragraph 56.10(e) above.

(3) Attention is drawn to rule 47.14(6) and (7): apart from the solicitor whose bill it is, only those parties who have served points of dispute may be heard on the detailed assessment unless the court gives permission, and only items specified in the points of dispute may be raised unless the court gives permission.

56.14

(1) If a party wishes to vary his breakdown of costs, points of dispute or reply, an amended or supplementary document must be filed with the court and copies of it must be served on all other relevant parties.

(2) Permission is not required to vary a breakdown of costs, points of dispute or a reply but the court may disallow the variation or permit it only upon conditions, including conditions as to the payment of any costs caused or wasted by the variation.

56.15 Unless the court directs otherwise the solicitor must file with the court the papers in support of the bill not less than 7 days before the date for the detailed assessment hearing and not more than 14 days before that date.

56.16 Once the detailed assessment hearing has ended it is the responsibility of the legal representative appearing for the solicitor or, as the case may be, the solicitor in person to remove the papers filed in support of the bill.

56.17

(1) Attention is drawn to rule 47.15 (power to issue an interim certificate).

(2) If, in the course of a detailed assessment hearing of a solicitor's bill to his client, it appears to the costs judge or district judge that in any event the solicitor will be liable in connection with that bill to pay money to the client, he may issue an interim certificate specifying an amount which in his opinion is payable by the solicitor to his client. Such a certificate will include an order to pay the sum it certifies unless the court orders otherwise.

56.18

(1) Attention is drawn to rule 47.16 which requires the solicitor to file a completed bill within 14 days after the end of the detailed assessment hearing. The court may dispense with the requirement to file a completed bill.

(2) After the detailed assessment hearing is concluded the court will—

(a) complete the court copy of the bill so as to show the amount allowed;

(b) determine the result of the cash account;

(c) award the costs of the detailed assessment hearing in accordance with Section 70(8) of the Solicitors Act 1974; and

(d) issue a final costs certificate showing the amount due following the detailed assessment hearing.

56.19 A final costs certificate will include an order to pay the sum it certifies unless the court orders otherwise.

CPR SCHEDULE OF COSTS: PRECEDENT P

Solicitors Act: Breakdown of Costs

IN THE HIGH COURT OF JUSTICE — Claim Number

QUEEN'S BENCH DIVISION

SUPREME COURT COSTS OFFICE

BETWEEN

EF

Claimant

- and -

GH & Co

Defendants

BREAKDOWN OF DEFENDANT'S BILL OF COSTS DATED 26 FEBRUARY 1999
TO BE ASSESSED PURSUANT TO THE ORDER DATED 27 APRIL 1999

The claimant instructed the defendants in connection with a summons for careless or inconsiderate driving which had been served upon him. By letter dated 21 October 1998 the defendants wrote to the claimant setting out their terms of business including the hourly rates of fee earners who would act on his instructions. On 23 October 1998 the claimant dated and signed a copy of that letter and returned it to the defendants so indicating his acceptance of the terms set out.

The proceedings were of the highest importance to the claimant who feared losing his licence and who wished to defend any civil proceedings that might be taken against him as a result of the prosecution. The defendants entered into correspondence with the CPS and eventually obtained their witness statements and invited them to consent to an adjournment because of the absence overseas of an important witness for the claimant (Mr LM). Eventually the defendants successfully applied to the court for an adjournment, and also applied for and obtained a witness summons. At the trial the claimant was found guilty and was fined £300 and 4 points were endorsed on his driving licence.

Proceedings were conducted by an assistant solicitor admitted in 1990 whose time is charged at an agreed rate of £150 per hour with routine letters out and telephone calls at an agreed rate of £15 each. At the trial a trainee attended with counsel. The trainee's time is charged at an agreed rate of £75 per hour.

Cash account for client: EF

Received		**Paid**	
From client on account generally: 22 October 1998	1,500.00	Refund to client: 26 February 1999	385.00
From client on account generally: 12 February 1998	**1,000.00**	Balancing item	**2,115.00**
	2,500.00		**2,500.00**

Balance due to client EF: £2,115

CPR SCHEDULE OF COSTS: PRECEDENT P – *contd*

Item		Amount Claimed	VAT	Amount Allowed	VAT
Attendances on Court and Counsel					
5th November 1998 - application made for an adjournment for the convenience of a witness					
13th November 1998 - contested hearing of the application					
Engaged 10 minutes	25.00				
Travel and waiting 30 minutes	75.00				
(1) Total solicitor's fee for hearing		100.00	17.50		
17th November 1998 - conference with counsel					
Engaged 45 minutes	112.50				
Travel and waiting 1 hour	150.00				
(2) Total solicitor's fee for conference		262.50	45.94		
(3) Counsel's fee for conference (paid: Miss JK)		75.00	13.13		
15th February 1999 - Brief to counsel - 4 pages A4					
23rd February 1999 - attending the trial					
Trainee engaged in court 1 hour	75.00				
Engaged in conference 30 minutes	37.50				
Travel and waiting (apportioned) 45 minutes	56.25				
(4) Total trainee solicitor's fee for trial		168.75	29.53		
(5) Counsel's brief fee (paid: Miss JK)		100.00	17.50		
Claimant					
(6) 21st October 1998 - first instructions 1 hour		150.00	26.25		
(7) 16th November 1998 - finalising proof of evidence 45 minutes		112.50	19.69		
(8) Routine letters out and telephone calls - 12 (9 + 3)		180.00	31.50		
Witness (Mr LM)					
Personal attendance by trainee solicitor					
Engaged 45 minutes	56.25				
Travel and waiting 1 hour	75.00				
(9) Total trainee solicitor's fee for attendance		131.25	22.97		
(10) Routine letters out - 6		90.00	15.75		
Other persons					
(11) Routine letters out and telephone calls to the CPS - 8 (6 + 2)		120.00	21.00		
Communications with the Court					
(12) Routine letters out - 6		90.00	15.75		
Communications with counsel					
(13) Routine letters out and telephone calls - 8 (4 + 4)		120.00	21.00		
Work done on documents					
(14) Instructions to counsel - 30 minutes		75.00	13.13		
(15) Attendance note of conference 15 minutes		37.50	6.56		
(16) Brief to counsel - 30 minutes		75.00	13.13		
(17) Attendance note of trial (trainee) - 45 minutes		56.25	9.84		
Summary					
Total costs claimed in breakdown		1943.75	340.17		
(Total costs billed £1800 + £315.00 VAT)					

FORM N258C

Request for Detailed Assessment Hearing Pursuant to an Order under Part III of the Solicitors Act 1974

In the	
Claim No.	
Claimant (including ref.)	
Defendant (including ref.)	

I certify that the [party] has served a breakdown of costs in this case and the [party] has served points of dispute thereon.

I now ask the court to arrange an assessment hearing. The names, addresses and references of the parties upon whom the court should give notice of the hearing are as follows:

I enclose copies of (tick as appropriate)

- ☐ the order made under Part 111 of the Solicitors Act 1974 in this case
- ☐ Bills of Costs to be assessed
- ☐ breakdown of costs
- ☐ any fee notes of counsel and receipts or accounts for other disbursements served with the breakdown of costs
- ☐ the [party'] points of dispute plus copies to be sent to the other parties to these proceedings details of whom are given above
- ☐ points in reply (if any)

I believe the hearing will take .... (give estimate of time court should allow).

I enclose my fee of £ ....

Signed .... Date ....

(Claimant) (Defendant) (Solicitor)

(g) Costs of the assessment

The costs of the assessment are paid according to the outcome. If one-fifth of the amount of the bill is taxed off, the solicitor pays the costs, if not, the party chargeable pays (Solicitors Act 1974, s 70(9)). With this provision in mind the party chargeable may think it prudent to exercise his right when obtaining an order for assessment to limit the order to the profit costs only if there are substantial disbursements which he does not wish to challenge or, conversely, limited to counsel's or expert's fees if these are all that he wishes to challenge (s 70(6)). If non-contentious costs are reduced by more than half, the taxing officer is under an obligation to refer the matter to the Law Society by the Solicitors' (Non-Contentious Business) Remuneration Order 1994, art 5. A solicitor must not take unfair advantage of the client by overcharging for work done or to be done (paragraph 14.12, the Law Society's *Guide to the Professional Conduct of Solicitors 1999*). It is of no relevance to the question of fact in each case whether the charge is so excessive as to amount to culpable overcharging.

(h) Gross sum bills

Where the bill being assessed is a gross sum bill which has not been replaced by a detailed bill following a request by the client under the Solicitors Act 1974, s 69(3) (sec p 27) the cost officer may nevertheless for the purposes of the assessment direct the solicitor to provide a detailed breakdown of his bill showing how the gross sum is calculated or justified. It is important to appreciate that such a breakdown is for the purposes of the assessment only and that it is still the original gross sum bill delivered to the client which is being assessed and which at the end of the assessment will be either upheld or reduced. Accordingly, although the detailed breakdown may quite properly justify a figure considerably higher than the amount of the gross sum bill, it is of assistance only in considering the reasonableness of the gross sum bill and is of no relevance to the question of whether or not the gross sum bill has been reduced by one-fifth.

(i) Order made in proceedings

Many orders for solicitor and client costs to be assessed arise after the solicitors have commenced proceedings for their recovery, in either the High Court or the county court and the defence merely challenges the amount of the solicitor's bill. The procedure is set out on p 41.

10. SHODDY WORK

Schedule 1A inserted in the Solicitors Act 1974 by the Courts and Legal Services Act 1990 reads as follows:

> **SCHEDULE 1A**
> **INADEQUATE PROFESSIONAL SERVICES**
>
> **Circumstances in which Council's powers may be exercised**
>
> **1** (1) The Council may take any of the steps mentioned in paragraph 2 ('the steps') with respect to a solicitor where it appears to them that the professional services provided by him in connection with any matter in which he or his firm have been instructed by a client have, in any respect, not been of the quality which it is reasonable to expect of him as a solicitor.
> (2) The Council shall not take any of the steps unless they are satisfied that in all the circumstances of the case it is appropriate to do so.

(3) In determining in any case whether it is appropriate to take any of the steps, the Council may—

(a) have regard to the existence of any remedy which it is reasonable to expect to be available to the client in civil proceedings; and

(b) where proceedings seeking any such remedy have not been begun by him, have regard to whether it is reasonable to expect him to begin them.

Directions which may be given

2 (1) The steps are—

(a) determining that the costs to which the solicitor is entitled in respect of his services ('the costs') are to be limited to such amount as may be specified in the determination and directing him to comply, or to secure compliance, with such one or more of the permitted requirements as appear to the Council to be necessary in order for effect to be given to their determination;

(b) directing him to secure the rectification, at his expense or at that of his firm, of any such error, omission or other deficiency arising in connection with the matter in question as they may specify;

(c) directing him to pay such compensation to the client as the Council sees fit to specify in the direction;

(d) directing him to take, at his expense or at that of his firm, such other action in the interests of the client as they may specify.

(2) The 'permitted requirements' are—

(a) that the whole or part of any amount already paid by or on behalf of the client in respect of the costs be refunded;

(b) that the whole or part of the costs be remitted;

(c) that the right to recover the costs be waived, whether wholly or to any specified extent.

(3) The power of the Council to take any such steps is not confined to cases where the client may have a cause of action against the solicitor for negligence.

Compensation

3 (1) The amount specified in a direction by virtue of paragraph 2(1)(c) shall not exceed £5,000.

(2) The Lord Chancellor may by order made by statutory instrument amend sub-paragraph (1) by substituting for the sum of £1,000 such other sum as he considers appropriate.

(3) Before making any such order the Lord Chancellor shall consult the Law Society.

(4) Any statutory instrument made under this paragraph shall be subject to annulment in pursuance of a resolution of either House of Parliament.

Taxation of costs

4 (1) Where the Council have given a direction under paragraph 2(1)(a), then—

(a) for the purposes of any taxation of a bill covering the costs, the amount charged by the bill in respect of them shall be deemed to be limited to the amount specified in the determination; and

(b) where a bill covering the costs has not been taxed, the client shall, for the purposes of their recovery (by whatever means and notwithstanding any statutory provision or agreement) be deemed to be liable to pay in respect of them only the amount specified in the determination.

(2) Where a bill covering the costs has been taxed, the direction shall, so far as it relates to the costs, cease to have effect.

Failure to comply with direction

5 (1) If a solicitor fails to comply with a direction given under this Schedule, any person may make a complaint in respect of that failure to the Tribunal; but no other proceedings whatever shall be brought in respect of it.
(2) On the hearing of such a complaint the Tribunal may, if it thinks fit (and whether or not it makes any order under section 47(2)), direct that the direction be treated, for the purpose of enforcement, as if it were contained in an order made by the High Court.

Fees

6 (1) The Council may, by regulations made with the concurrence of the Lord Chancellor and the Master of the Rolls, make provision for the payment, by any client with respect to whom the Council are asked to consider whether to take any of the steps, of such fee as may be prescribed.
(2) The regulations may provide for the exemption of such classes of client as may be prescribed.
(3) Where a client pays the prescribed fee it shall be repaid to him if the Council take any of the steps in the matter with respect to which the fee was paid.
(4) In this paragraph 'prescribed' means prescribed by the regulations.

Costs

7 Where the Council take any of the steps with respect to a solicitor they may also direct him to pay to the Council—
- (a) the amount of the fee payable by the Council to the client under paragraph 6(3); and
- (b) an amount which is calculated by the Council as the cost to them of dealing with the complaint, or which in their opinion represents a reasonable contribution towards that cost.

Duty of Tribunal

8 Where the Tribunal—
- (a) is considering, or has considered, an application or complaint with respect to a solicitor; and
- (b) is of the opinion that the Council should consider whether to take any of the steps with respect to that solicitor,

it shall inform the Council.

How it works in practice is that the Council of the Law Society has delegated its disciplinary powers to the Office for the Supervision of Solicitors (OSS). Accordingly all references in the Schedule to 'the Council' may in practice be regarded as references to the OSS. When the OSS receives a complaint of shoddy work the solicitor is required to produce his file, which is considered by two report writers. If they disagree, the opinion of a third report writer is obtained. Where shoddy work is found, the solicitor's observations are invited and he can request further consideration by a review panel of practising solicitors. If it is decided that there is no evidence of shoddy work, the complainant may require the file to be referred to the Compliance and Supervision Committee. If the Compliance and Supervision Committee agree that there is no evidence of shoddy work, that is the end of the matter, subject to the right of complaint to the Legal Services Ombudsman. If an allegation of shoddy work is substantiated, the matter goes before the Adjudication Committee, which may take one or more of the following actions:

(a) Limit the costs which the solicitor may recover for the services, and require a refund of all or part of the costs.

(b) Require the solicitor to put right any error, omission or deficiency caused by the shoddy work.
(c) Direct the solicitor to pay compensation to the client of up to £1,000.
(d) Direct the solicitor to take some other action in the interests of the client.
(e) Direct the solicitor to pay to the Council of the Law Society any fee repaid to the complainant on the filing of the complaint.
(f) Direct the solicitor to pay the Council of the Law Society a sum representing the costs of dealing with the complaint, or a contribution towards those costs.

11. DISPUTING COUNSEL'S FEES

(a) Solicitors duty to challenge

Except in state-funded cases the instructing solicitor is personally liable for counsel's fees and the client is liable to the solicitor for those fees in the same way as he is to any other disbursement. The solicitor has a duty to his client to challenge any counsel's fee which he considers to be unreasonable. Paragraph 8 of the Terms of Work agreed by the Bar Council and The Law Society provides that any challenge by a solicitor to counsel's fees giving rise to an issue of competence or a dispute on quantum must be made within three months of the receipt by the solicitor of the itemised fee note.

(b) Joint tribunal

Disputes as to counsel's fees may be referred to a Joint Tribunal consisting of a member of the Council of the Law Society and a Queen's Counsel nominated respectively by the President of the Law Society and the Chairman of the Bar (see the *Guide to the Professional Conduct of Solicitors 1999*, para 20.07). The *Guide* at para 20.06 provides:

> 'Except in legal aid cases, solicitors are personally liable as a matter of professional conduct for the payment of counsel's proper fees, whether or not they have been placed in funds by the client.'

(c) Solicitors Act assessment

Section 67 of the Solicitors Act 1974 also prescribes that counsel's fees are to be paid before assessment is completed. Under the Code of Conduct of the Bar 1990, brief fees need no longer have to be agreed in advance or marked on the brief, but a prudent solicitor will agree counsel's brief and refresher fees in advance, not only with counsel but also with his client.

(d) Last-minute settlements

Last-minute settlements are another area of difficulty. Where the brief has been delivered, counsel is entitled to the full fee. However, counsel may accept no fee, or less than the agreed fee and in these circumstances the solicitor has a duty to seek to renegotiate it. If the solicitor fails to seek to renegotiate the fee he is bound to pay counsel's fee in full but will not be able to recover from his client any reduction of the fee made by the court on a Solicitors Act assessment.

CHAPTER 6

RECOVERY OF COSTS

1. PROCEEDINGS

(a) Prerequisites

(i) Final bill

It is essential that a final bill in the form and content described in Chapter 3 has been delivered. Where there has been a series of interim bills on account no proceedings may be commenced until the delivery of a final statute bill. This bill should be for the entirety of the work done and disbursements incurred throughout, either at the agreed charging rate or the direct cost with an appropriate mark-up in light of all the factors including the outcome of the matter, giving credit for payments received.

(ii) Elapse of one month

One month must have elapsed since the delivery of the bill unless the party chargeable is about to: quit England and Wales; to become bankrupt or to compound with his creditors or do any other act which tends to prevent or delay the solicitor obtaining payment. In these circumstances the solicitor can seek leave to issue proceedings within a month (Solicitors Act 1974, s 69(1)). Service of a statutory demand for payment of a solicitor's costs does not constitute the bringing of an action for the purposes of s 69(1) and may therefore be served within a month without leave. If the statutory demand is not complied with within 21 days of service the solicitor may present a bankruptcy petition, but because this is an action within the meaning of s 69 a petition may not be issued within a month without leave (*Re A Debtor (No 88 of 1991)* [1993] Ch 286, ChD).

(iii) No application or order for a detailed assessment

The client must not have either made an application to the court for a detailed assessment of the costs within one month of delivery of the bill or obtained an order for the bill to be assessed, in either of which events no action may be commenced on the bill or proceeded with until the assessment is completed: Solicitors Act 1974, ss 70(1), (2).

(iv) Solicitors' (Non-Contentious Business) Remuneration Order Notice

In respect of bills of not more than £50,000 for non-contentious business only, art 6 of the Solicitors' (Non-Contentious Business) Remuneration Order 1994 requires the solicitor before commencing proceedings to inform the client in writing of his right to obtain a certificate under art 8 of the Remuneration Order from the Law Society, stating what sum, in the opinion of the Council, would be a fair and reasonable charge for the business covered by the bill (whether it be the sum charged or a lesser sum) and of the provisions of the Solicitors Act 1974, ss 70–72 relating to the assessment of costs.

The Court of Appeal has held that merely sending a copy of the Remuneration Order and drawing attention to its provisions will not suffice. The client must be told specifically of his right to a remuneration certificate and, as 'detailed assessment' might be meaningless to him, after identifying the section of the Solicitors Act, informed of his right to have the costs checked by a costs judge. The specimen information recommended by the Law Society is set out below.

There are two surprises. First, proceedings may be commenced at any time after the notice has been given. Second, there is no provision that a request for a remuneration certificate precludes the commencement of proceedings.

Whether the notice is given with every bill or only after default in payment of a bill is a matter for decision by each individual firm.

(v) Specimen information for entitled persons under the Solicitors' (Non-Contentious Business) Remuneration Order 1994 recommended by the Law Society

REMUNERATION CERTIFICATE

1. If you are not satisfied with the amount of our fee you have the right to ask us to obtain a remuneration certificate from the Law Society.
2. The certificate will either say that our fee is fair and reasonable, or it will substitute a lower fee.
3. If you wish us to obtain a certificate you must ask us to do so within a month of receiving this notice.
4. We may charge interest on unpaid bills and we will do so at [the rate payable on judgment debts] from one month after delivery of our bill.
5.
(i) If you ask us to obtain a remuneration certificate, then unless we already hold the money to cover these, you must first pay:
    (a) half our fee shown in the bill;
    (b) all the VAT shown in the bill;
    (c) all the expenses we have incurred shown in the bill – sometimes called 'paid disbursements'.
(ii) However, you may ask the Office for the Supervision of Solicitors (at 8 Dormer Place, Royal Leamington Spa, Warwickshire, CV32 5AE) to waive this requirement so that you do not have to pay anything for the time being. You would have to show that exceptional circumstances apply in your case.
6. Your rights are set out more fully in the Solicitors' (Non-Contentious Business) Remuneration Order 1994.

ASSESSMENT

You may be entitled to have our charges reviewed by the court. (This is called 'assessment'.) The procedure is different from the remuneration certificate procedure and it is set out in the Solicitors Act 1974, ss 70, 71 and 72.

(b) High Court or county court?

The Practice Direction supplementing CPR Part 7 provides that proceedings may be started in either the High Court or a county court, except that in order to qualify for the High Court a claim must exceed £15,000. CPR 26.2 provides that, where the defendant is an individual, if a defence is filed the court will transfer the proceedings to the defendant's home court which, in High Court proceedings, means the district registry for the district in which the defendant's address for service is situated, and in the county court, the court whose jurisdiction covers the defendant's address for service.

(c) Precedent statement of case

CLAIM FORM N1 CPR PART 7

The claimant's claim is for work done and disbursements incurred as a solicitor on behalf of the defendant at the defendant's request for which [a bill] [bills] of costs [has] [have] been delivered to the defendant pursuant to the provisions of the Solicitors Act 1974.

Particulars

20 June 1999	To bill of costs number 1234
re Fagin v Yourself	£94,250
Less paid on account	£30,000
	£64,250

AND the claimant claims:

1. £64,250.
2. Interest pursuant to [Section 35A of the Supreme Court Act 1981] [Section 69 of the County Courts Act 1984] on the said sum of £50,000 to the date hereof amounting to £ being interest at the rate of [not to exceed the amount payable on judgment debts] per annum from 20 June 1999 to the date of issue hereof.
3. Continuing interest pursuant to [Section 35A of the Supreme Court Act 1981] [Section 69 of the County Courts Act 1984] on the said sum of £ at the rate of [not to exceed the rate payable on judgment debts] per annum being a daily rate of £ , from the date of issue hereof until judgment or sooner payment.

The statement that a bill or bills have been delivered 'pursuant to the provisions of the Solicitors Act 1974', refers to the prerequisites to instituting proceedings set out at the beginning of this chapter.

(d) Non-contentious and contentious business agreements

The main difference between a solicitor relying on a non-contentious and a contentious business agreement is that he must obtain the leave of the court to enforce the latter (see p 11). There is a view to which I do not subscribe that this provision precludes a solicitor who has entered into a contentious business agreement from suing for his costs without first applying for leave to enforce the agreement. The reason I disagree is that, in my view, it is only if the solicitor wishes to rely on the contentious business agreement that he needs leave to proceed. There is nothing to prevent the solicitor commencing proceedings in the usual way in the hope of obtaining judgment by default or a summary judgment. If, and only if, the matter is disputed and the solicitor wishes to rely on the contentious business agreement need he, at that stage, apply for leave to enforce it. I see no point in anticipating trouble by incurring the expense of obtaining leave to enforce an agreement until the need to rely on it arises. If the need should arise the solicitor can make an application in the proceedings for leave, similar to an application to come off the record.

(e) Interim payment

Where the client does not dispute liability but merely alleges that the charges are too high, for whatever reason, and therefore all that is in dispute is the amount of the costs, the solicitor should apply under CPR Rules 25.6 and 25.7 for an interim payment of the minimum amount he must eventually recover, even if the client were to succeed on all his objections to the bill. Disputes over quantum are often exercises in putting off the inevitable, and an order for an interim payment of a substantial amount has been known to result in the client deciding the outstanding balance was not worth incurring the expense of continuing to dispute it. The application should be supported by written evidence filed and served at least three days before the hearing. This should include an attempted quantification of all of the client's objections at their maximum and deducting these from the amount of the outstanding costs. The balance is the amount to be claimed as an interim payment.

(f) Interest

(i) Non-contentious

Article 14 of the Solicitors' (Non-Contentious Business) Remuneration Order 1994 provides:

> **14 INTEREST**
>
> (1) After the information specified in art 8 has been given to an entitled person in compliance with arts 6 or 7, a solicitor may charge interest on the unpaid amount of his costs plus any disbursements and value added tax, subject to paras (2) and (3) below.
> (2) Where an entitlement to interest arises under para (1) and subject to any agreement made between a solicitor and client, the period for which interest may be charged may run from one month after the date of delivery of a bill, unless the solicitor fails to lodge an application within one month of receipt of a request for a remuneration certificate under art 4, in which case no interest is payable in respect of the period between one month after receiving the request and the actual date on which the application is lodged.
> (3) Subject to any agreement made between a solicitor and client, the rate of interest must not exceed the rate for the time being payable on judgment debts.
> (4) Interest charged under this article shall be calculated, where applicable, by reference to the following:
>
> (a) if a solicitor is required to obtain a remuneration certificate, the total amount of the costs certified by the Council to be fair and reasonable plus paid disbursements and value added tax;
> (b) if an application is made for the bill to be assessed, the amount ascertained on assessment;
> (c) if an application is made for the bill to be assessed or a solicitor is required to obtain a remuneration certificate and for any reason the assessment or application for a remuneration certificate does not proceed, the unpaid amount of the costs shown in the bill or such lesser sum as may be agreed between the solicitor and the client, plus paid disbursements and valued added assessment.

Interest runs from one month after the delivery of the bill irrespective of when the notice is served but if the solicitor delays in applying for a remuneration certificate interest may not be charged for the period between one month after the client's request and the date on which the solicitor makes the application to the Law Society. With regard to the moneys held in the client account, the Solicitors' Accounts Rules 1991 will apply. This means that the solicitor will have to account to the client for interest earned on the moneys in the client account. This causes some difficulty with regard to the rate of interest earned because it will almost certainly be less than the judgment debt rate (currently 8%) to which the solicitor is entitled because the obligation under the Solicitors' Accounts Rules is for the solicitor to pay the sum equivalent to the interest which would have accrued had the money been kept on deposit in a separate designated account at the bank or building society where the solicitor keeps his/her general client account. This rate is likely to be very low.

Is the client entitled to interest on the amount of any reduction due back to him? It is the view of the Law Society that a bill, when delivered, represents a sum claimed by the solicitor. It is not a sum which the client is obliged to pay until he agrees it or a court decides that the sum claimed is reasonable. The solicitor has no immediate right to the sum claimed and cannot therefore avoid liability for paying interest on clients' money merely by transferring it from client account to office account or by receiving a payment which is expressed to be conditional on the outcome of the remuneration certificate application.

As we have seen, when issued, a remuneration certificate records a certified sum, which will (in the absence of a Solicitors Act assessment) be the sum payable by the client. This reinforces the view that the monies paid or transferred are client moneys until the bill is finally agreed following the issue of the remuneration certificate and have to be refunded to the client.

Where the deposit interest provisions do not apply (as in the case of money subject to a controlled trust) all interest should normally be credited to the relevant trust in accordance with the general law.

(ii) Contentious

There is no statutory or professional duty for a solicitor to inform his client of his right to have a contentious bill assessed prior to proceeding. Nor is there any right to claim interest. However, pursuant to s 35A Supreme Court Act 1981 and s 69(1) County Courts Act 1984, where proceedings are instituted the court has power to award interest from the date when payment was due.

In addition, interest runs at the prescribed rate on judgment debts including all judgments in the county court since 1 November 1998. By these means interest may be recovered on contentious costs.

(g) Effect of writing off costs

In *Slatter v Ronaldsons (a firm)* (SCCO No 2 of 2002) [2001] All ER (D) 251 (Dec) the defendant's solicitors had acted for the claimant in matrimonial proceedings for which they had outstanding costs. When the claimant became unemployed they concluded that it would be uneconomic to pursue him for the balance of their costs and accordingly 'wrote them off', obtaining the appropriate VAT refund. Subsequently the client instructed other solicitors who wrote to the defendants requesting delivery up of all relevant papers which the defendants refused to do, contending that they had a lien over the papers until their bills were discharged in full. The judge, on appeal, upheld the lien. The contractual liability to pay the balance of the bills survived their 'writing off' and there was no evidence that the claimant acted to his detriment on the basis of promissory estoppel, on the basis that the balance of the bills had been written off.

2. LIEN

(a) Acquisition of lien

(i) Retaining lien

A solicitor has, at common law, a general lien to retain any money, papers or other property belonging to his client which properly come into his possession until payment of his costs, whether or not the property was acquired in connection with the matter for which the costs were incurred. The solicitor may retain, until payment of his costs, property other than money to any value even if it greatly exceeds the amount due, but he cannot hold money in excess of the amount due. A solicitor is not entitled to sell property held under a lien or to transfer it into his ownership without an order from the court.

(ii) Property recovered

A solicitor also has at common law a particular lien on property recovered or preserved by him in litigation which extends to all costs incurred, both billed and unbilled. Unlike the general lien, a particular lien covers property not in the solicitor's possession and gives him an equitable right to have the property transferred into his possession.

(iii) Solicitors Act Charging Order

The lien on property recovered is in effect extended by the Solicitors Act 1974, s 73, which provides that any court in which a solicitor has been employed to prosecute or defend any suit, matter or proceeding may at any time:

(a) declare the solicitor entitled to a charge on any property recovered or preserved through his instrumentality for his assessed costs in relation to that suit, matter or proceedings; and
(b) make such orders for the assessment of those costs and for raising money to pay or for paying them out of the property recovered or preserved as the court thinks fit. In *Fairfold Properties Ltd v Exmouth Docks Co Ltd (No 2)* [1993] Ch 196 the claimant, in proceedings in which they were substantially successful, obtained an order that the defendant should bear their costs. Before the costs were assessed the claimant had become a dormant company with no assets other than the order for costs. The claimant's solicitors now sought a charging order under s 73 of the Solicitors Act 1974 on any costs recoverable by the claimant from the defendant and, pending such recovery, a charge on the benefit of the order. The court had jurisdiction to make such an order. Although a charging order had necessarily, by virtue of s 73(1)(*a*) of the Act, to be expressed as one for the solicitors' assessed costs, the court was not bound to order that the costs in question be assessed as between solicitor and client. It seemed impossible that the between the parties costs could exceed the same costs assessed as between solicitor and client. Nevertheless, the judge gave liberty to the solicitors to apply for an order for their costs to be assessed.

A Solicitors Act Charging Order differs from a general lien in two particular ways. First, it applies to real as well as personal property and, second, it does not apply where the claim for costs is statute-barred. The application is made under the alternative procedure prescribed by CPR Part 8 and is made pursuant to RSC Order 106 which was preserved by Schedule 1 of the CPR. Here are the precedents:

1. PRECEDENT APPLICATION FOR SOLICITOR'S CHARGING ORDER (RSC ORDER 106)

CLAIM FORM N208 CPR PART 8

Details of claim

The claimant applies for an order that he shall have a charge upon [here specify the nature and amount of the property sought to be charged] for his costs, charges and expenses of this action and that in the meantime the [property or funds, or as may be] do stand charged as stated.
The grounds of the application are [here set out the facts on which the claim is based].
Statement of truth

2. PRECEDENT CHARGING ORDER, SOLICITOR'S COSTS (RSC ORDER 106)

Upon hearing and upon reading the affidavit of , sworn the day of 20 , and It is ordered that shall have a charge upon for his costs, charges, and expenses of this action.
Dated the day of 20 .

(iv) Accounts rules

The Solicitors' Accounts Rules 1991 (Rule 29) specifically provide that nothing in those rules shall deprive a solicitor of any recourse or right, whether by way of lien, set off, counterclaim, charge or otherwise, against moneys standing to the credit of a client account.

(b) Loss of lien

A solicitor may lose his lien in the following ways:

(i) Security for costs

The Solicitors' (Non-Contentious Business) Remuneration Order 1994, art 12(3) provides that in non-contentious business a solicitor may take from his client security for the payment of any remuneration including the amount of any interest to which the solicitor may become entitled under art 14.

The Solicitors Act 1974, s 65(1) states: 'a solicitor may take security from his client for costs, to be ascertained by taxation [*assessment*] or otherwise, in respect of any contentious business to be done by him.' If a solicitor does take security from his client for costs this will preclude him from claiming a lien over subsequent money, property or documents in his possession unless that lien has been expressly reserved.

(ii) Payment into court

CPR 25.1(1)(*m*) provides that where the defendant to a claim for the recovery of personal property does not dispute the title of the party making the claim but claims to be entitled to retain the property by virtue of a lien, the court may make an order permitting the defendant to pay money into court pending the outcome of the proceedings and directing that if he does so, the property shall be given up to him.

(iii) Waiver

If at any stage the solicitor takes alternative security from a client with the intention of satisfying his claim for fees by this alternative means his lien will have been waived:

> 'Whether a lien is waived or not by taking a security depends upon the intention expressed or to be inferred from the position of the parties and all the circumstances of the case ... It appears to me that in each case the question whether the lien is waived by taking security must be decided according to the particular circumstances. I do not mean to say that taking a security necessarily imports an abandonment of the lien; but if there are circumstances in the taking of the security which are inconsistent with the continuance of the old security, it is to be inferred that the solicitor intended to abandon his lien.'

(*Re Taylor Stileman and Underwood* [1891] 1 Ch 590, CA.)
From this and other authorities it is clear that if a solicitor takes security for costs generally and that security is inconsistent with his lien and the solicitor does not in so doing reserve the lien then, on the face of it, he will be taken to have abandoned it. In *A v B* [1984] 1 All ER 265, QBD (Commercial Court) it was held that the solicitors' arrest of a vessel owned by their clients was in no way inconsistent with their lien and that no intention to waive the lien could be inferred from the fact of that arrest.

(iv) Discharge of the retainer

1. Discharge by client
If the retainer is terminated by the client other than for misconduct by the solicitor, the solicitor's lien is virtually absolute. He cannot be required to hand over or produce for inspection any papers in his possession and he is entitled to keep them until his costs have been paid (*Leo Abse & Cohen v Evan G Jones (Builders) Ltd* (1984) 128 Sol Jo 317, CA).

Nevertheless, in its commentary at para 12.14 of the *Guide to the Professional Conduct of Solicitors 1999* the Law Society comments:

> 'Where a solicitor is properly exercising a lien in respect of unpaid costs, following his or her discharge by the client during the course of proceedings, the Society recommends that the solicitor's papers should be released to the successor solicitor subject to a satisfactory undertaking as to the outstanding costs being given in lieu of the lien. There is, however, no duty on the original solicitor to accept an undertaking.'

It should be noted that the Law Society recommends that the solicitor should only give up his position of strength and security in exchange for a satisfactory undertaking as to the costs, not merely an undertaking to preserve the lien which, as we shall see in the next section, may be worthless.

2. Discharge by solicitor
(A) *Serving the interests of justice.* Where during litigation a solicitor discharges himself, the usual practice of the court is to order him to hand over the client's papers to the new solicitor against an undertaking by the new solicitor to preserve the lien of the original solicitor, even if that renders the lien worthless. However, this is not automatic and the court exercises its discretion. In approaching the matter, the overriding principle is that the order made should be that which would best serve, or at least not frustrate, the interests of justice. The principle that a litigant should not be deprived of material relevant to the

conduct of his case and so driven from the judgment seat is to be weighed against the principle that litigation should be conducted with due regard to the interests of the court's own officers, who should not be left without payment for what was justly due to them. Where the solicitors have behaved impeccably and of whose conduct there has been no criticism, whilst their clients, without any excuse, have not paid the costs and there is a default judgment against them, the balance of hardship would be far greater on the solicitors if the lien were not enforced, because they would then probably recover nothing, whereas it was open to the clients to preserve their position by paying the solicitor's costs (*A v B*, p 67).

(B) *Undertakings.* Unless there are exceptional circumstances the fact that the solicitors had reasonable cause to discharge themselves would not justify modifying the overriding principle that a solicitor discharging himself should not be allowed to exert his lien so as to interfere with the course of justice and he has therefore only a qualified lien on the papers. He is, however, entitled to the following undertakings from the new solicitors:
   (i) To hold all papers and documents delivered subject to his lien for costs.
   (ii) To afford him reasonable access to the papers and documents for the purpose of preparing his bill of costs.
   (iii) To prosecute or defend the action in an active manner.
   (iv) To redeliver the papers and documents after the conclusion of the action (*Gamlen Chemical Co (UK) Ltd v Rochem Ltd* [1980] 1 All ER 1049, CA).

(v) Rights of third parties

A solicitor cannot obtain by his lien a better title to property than that of his client. Accordingly, the solicitor of a company cannot in the exercise of his lien refuse to hand over papers to an administrative receiver seeking an order under the Insolvency Act 1986, s 236 or in defiance of a court order against the client.

(vi) State funding

As a matter of law, a solicitor's lien arises in respect of costs due for work done on the instructions of the client, for which the client has undertaken personal liability. Pre-certificate costs and disbursements (apart from those covered by legal help) will fall within this category, and this lien is protected by the Civil Legal Aid (General) Regulations 1989, reg 103. However, once a funding certificate has been issued the situation is altered, since the assisted person's solicitor has a statutory right to be paid out of the fund, and may not take any payment other than from the fund (Legal Aid Act 1988, s 31; Civil Legal Aid (General) Regulations 1989, reg 64 (see p 396)).

When a funding certificate is amended to enable a new solicitor to have the conduct of an assisted person's case the Council of the Law Society considers, therefore, that no lien arises in respect of costs and disbursements payable under a funding certificate, and that it is misleading to use the word 'lien' in relation to such costs and disbursements. The Law Society takes the view that a solicitor's costs are secured by an order for assessment or certificate and it follows that it would be inappropriate to call for a professional undertaking from the successor solicitor to pay the costs except in respect of any outstanding pre-certificate costs. A solicitor should not part with the papers on a community-funded matter until the certificate is transferred to the successor solicitor, although the papers should be made available for inspection in the meantime or copies provided. In respect of costs due from the fund it is permissible to ask for an undertaking requiring the successor solicitor to:

(a) return the papers promptly on completion to enable a bill of costs to be drawn up; or
(b) have the first solicitor's costs included in the successor solicitor's bill, collect those costs and pay them to the first solicitor.

Accordingly, where, under a community funding certificate, a change of solicitor is authorised, subject to (a) there being no lien in respect of pre-certificate costs and disbursements, and (b) an undertaking being given by the new solicitor as to the eventual assessment of costs, there is no reason why the papers should not be expeditiously transferred to the new solicitor.

(c) Documents to be handed over

What papers should be handed over by a solicitor on the termination of his retainer and lien?

Annex 12A of the Law Society's *Guide to the Professional Conduct of Solicitors 1999* gives the following guidance:

Is the client entitled to the whole file once the retainer is terminated?

Not necessarily. Most files will contain some documents which belong to you, some which belong to the client and possibly others belonging to a third party. Documents in existence before the retainer, held by you as agent for and on behalf of the client or a third party, must be dealt with in accordance with the instructions of the client or third party (subject to your lien). Documents coming into existence during the retainer fall into four broad categories (see also *Cordery on Solicitors*):

(a) *Documents prepared by you for the benefit of the client and which have been paid for by the client, either directly or indirectly, belong to the client.*

Examples: instructions and briefs; most attendance notes; drafts; copies made for the client's benefit of letters received by you; copies of letters written by you to third parties if contained in the client's case file and used for the purpose of the client's business. There would appear to be a distinction between copies of letters written to the client (which may be retained by you) and copies of letters written to third parties.

(b) *Documents prepared by you for your own benefit or protection, the preparation of which is not regarded as an item chargeable against the client, belong to you.*

Examples: copies of letters written to the client; copies made for your own benefit of letters received by you; copies of letters written by you to third parties if contained only in a filing system of all letters written in your office; tape recordings of conversations; inter-office memoranda; entries in diaries; time sheets; computerised records; office journals; books of account.

(c) *Documents sent to you by the client during the retainer, the property in which was intended at the date of despatch to pass from the client to you, belong to you.*

Examples: letters, authorities and instructions written or given to you by the client.

(d) *Documents prepared by a third party during the course of the retainer and sent to you (other than at your expense) belong to the client.*

Examples: receipts and vouchers for disbursements made by you on behalf of the client; medical and witness reports; counsel's advice and opinion; letters received by you from third parties.

(d) Client's remedy

Where there is a valid and enforceable lien, the only practical remedy for the client who wishes to obtain without delay documents on which his previous solicitor is claiming a lien is to pay his costs. Sometimes the solicitor is willing to agree to the money being paid into a joint account to await the outcome of a Solicitors Act assessment. If not, the client should obtain either the original solicitor's consent to a Solicitors Act assessment or an order from the court before making the payment, as otherwise the court might not order an assessment (see p 46). This course not only has the advantage of securing the immediate release of the papers, but it also enables the new solicitors to inspect and consider them at their leisure in order to advise whether the costs should be challenged – and, if so, on what grounds – before proceeding with the assessment.

3. STATUTORY DEMAND

Service of a statutory demand for payment of a solicitor's costs does not constitute the bringing of an action for the purposes of the Solicitors Act 1974, s 69(l) which prohibits solicitors from bringing any action to recover costs within one month of delivery of their bill without special leave of the court. The consequences to which a statutory demand leads, if not complied with, is a presumption that the debtor is unable to pay the debt in question. This, in turn, enables the creditor to present a bankruptcy petition. In general the court should exercise its discretion to set aside the statutory demand if, but only if, it would not be just for those consequences to apply in the circumstances. Arguments based on s 69 do not amount to sufficient grounds for setting aside the demand. Accordingly, a solicitor may serve a statutory demand for payment of his costs before the expiration of a month from the date of delivery of his bill of costs (*Re A Debtor (No 88 of 1991)* [1993] Ch 286, ChD). In an article in the *New Law Journal* Angharad Start, counsel for the unhappy debtor, considered that unless the courts do set aside such demands as a matter of policy, or there is a new rule of professional conduct or an amendment to s 69 of the Solicitors Act, the Insolvency Act of 1986 will have to all intents and purposes amended legislation which has been in place for over 250 years.

The Law Society recommends that solicitors should be wary of following this course of action because of the power to set aside a statutory demand on the grounds of injustice (*Re a Debtor (No 88 of 1991)* [1993] Ch 286, ChD). Another reason for caution is that the decision in *Turner & Co v O Palomo* [1999] 4 All ER 353, CA could be interpreted as precluding statutory demands based on a solicitor's bill because the amount of the bill is always open to challenge in proceedings brought to recover it even after the time limit for a detailed assessment has expired and therefore it is not a liquidated demand. In any event although a bankruptcy petition may be issued 21 days after non-compliance with a statutory demand, a petition is an 'action' within the meaning of s 69 of the Solicitors Act 1974 and cannot be issued within one month of delivery of the bill.

CHAPTER 7

THE SOLICITOR AND THIRD PARTIES

1. WRITTEN INSTRUCTIONS

Where instructions are received not from a client but from a third party purporting to represent that client, a solicitor should obtain written instructions from the client that he or she wishes him or her to act. In any case of doubt the solicitor should see the client or take other appropriate steps to confirm instructions (para 12.05, Law Society's *Guide to the Professional Conduct of Solicitors 1999*).

2. WHO IS THE CLIENT?

It is a wise solicitor who knows his own client! Is the client the trade union or its member, the driver of the car or his insurers, the employer or his insurers, the insured or the legal expenses insurers, the limited company or its director personally, a husband and wife or just one of them? The solicitor who does not ascertain clearly at the outset who may repent at leisure if it transpires he has taken instructions from the wrong person or finds his bill rejected by the person to whom he renders it.

3. WARRANTY OF AUTHORITY

A firm of solicitors instituted proceedings, including obtaining a freezing injunction, on behalf of a client whom they were unaware was an undischarged bankrupt. A bankrupt is not entitled to bring an action relating to his property, the cause of action having vested in his trustee in bankruptcy. Nevertheless, a bankrupt has the capacity and authority to retain solicitors, and solicitors acting for him without knowledge of his bankruptcy were saying no more than that they had a client and that the client had authorised the proceedings. The solicitors did not represent that the client had a good cause of action, and in commencing the proceedings warranted no more than they had authority from the client to do so. In those circumstances there had been no breach by them of their duty to the court, nor had they been negligent, and thus the court should exercise its discretion in their favour when considering an application for costs against them personally by the defendant (*Nelson v Nelson* [1997] 1 All ER 970, [1997] 1 WLR 233, CA).

4. THIRD PARTY FUNDING

Between-the-parties costs are awarded on the basis of the paying party reimbursing to the receiving party costs which he is liable to pay to his solicitors. In other words, it is on the principle of indemnifying him up to the amount of the charges he must pay his own solicitor. Where the receiving party is not liable to pay costs to his own solicitor (see Chapter 17, where, in *Gundry v Sainsbury* [1910] 1 KB 645, CA, the solicitor had agreed to act for nothing) the receiving party does not need, and is not entitled to, an indemnity. There is a danger of this argument being put forward where a client has the financial backing of a third party, such as his trade union or an insurance company. To succeed in this argument the paying party would have to show that the receiving party had no liability to his solicitor for costs – when this argument has been raised it has invariably been held that there is a dual liability or a primary liability on the client, thus entitling him to an order for between the parties costs. See, for example, *R v Miller and Glennie* [1983] 3 All ER 186. Nevertheless, where in contentious business the client is being funded by a third party, solicitors should expressly incorporate in the terms of their retainer the right to look to the client for their costs whatever the outcome of the litigation.

5. NO BILL TO THIRD PARTY

I emphasised at p 28 that all costs receivable from a third party belong to the client and not to the solicitor. The solicitor must therefore deliver a bill to his own client and give credit for any money recovered from a third party. In no circumstance may a solicitor render a bill to someone who is not his client. Misunderstandings about this arise frequently when a third party who is paying the client's costs wishes to have an invoice on which he can recover the VAT. These problems are addressed in Chapter 12.

6. LANDLORD AND TENANT

It is not improper for a landlord to request an undertaking from the tenant to pay his costs. However, a solicitor who requests an undertaking for costs should also provide a cap on the amount to be covered by the undertaking.

It has become common to include in a lease a clause providing that the landlord should be 'compensated fully' or 'indemnified' for costs and expenses incurred as a result of the tenant's breach of the lease. Similar clauses appear in most mortgage deeds. The Court of Appeal decided in *Gomba Holdings (UK) Ltd v Minories Finance Ltd (No 2)* [1993] Ch 171, CA, that mortgagees were entitled to recover costs on the indemnity basis following a review of the meaning of 'indemnity costs' clauses. The Court of Appeal in *Church Comrs for England v Ibrahim* [1997] 1 EGLR 13, CA, confirmed that the principles in *Gomba Holdings* are not confined to mortgage cases. It held that in general the landlord is not to be deprived of a contractual right to indemnity costs. Although the court always retains a discretion on costs, that discretion should be used to reflect the contractual agreement between the landlord and the tenant unless the landlord's conduct is improper or unreasonable. This decision clarifies the landlord's position on costs and should make it easier in the future either to negotiate or obtain from the court adequate compensation for the costs of litigation against defaulting tenants. However, the wording of the indemnity clause must be clear and a claim to costs should be fully pleaded in the particulars of claim.

(a) Remuneration certificates

When a solicitor is acting for a landlord, whether a lease is being granted or a licence has been applied for, the client on whose behalf the relevant costs have been incurred is the landlord. The fact that a third party is liable to pay such costs does not of itself create an entitlement to seek a remuneration certificate under the Solicitors' (Non-

Contentious Business) Remuneration Order 1994. The tenant must therefore request the landlord to seek a remuneration certificate but there is no obligation on the landlord to do so. As a matter of practice, the Law Society will accept an application for a remuneration certificate in such circumstances, but *only* if the landlord gives his consent. In appropriate cases, the Council would hope that landlords' solicitors will encourage their clients to give such consent (Statement of the Law Society Council, *Law Society Gazette*, 19 December 1984, pp 3556–3557). In either event the tenant will be required to pay half of the landlord's costs together with all of the paid disbursements and VAT comprised in the bill as a condition precedent to the application pursuant to art 11 of the Solicitors' (Non-Contentious Business) Remuneration Order 1994 (see p 38).

(b) Detailed assessment

There is judicial authority for saying that an undertaking to pay reasonable costs means costs to be assessed if not agreed (*Zaniewski v Scales* (1969) 113 Sol Jo 525). If the landlord is unwilling to give his consent to an application for a remuneration certificate, the tenant is entitled to apply to the High Court for a assessment of the bill under the Solicitors Act 1974, s 71. The client should be warned of the estimated expense of such an application and as to whether such expense might be disproportionate to the amount of the bill in dispute. Further, the client's attention should be drawn to the provisions of s 70(9) relating to payment of the costs of the assessment proceedings (Statement of the Law Society Council, *Law Society Gazette*, 19 December 1984, pp 3556–3557). A third party should be aware of the risk of losing their right to an assessment as the result of the provision in the Solicitors Act 1974, s 70(4) that no order for assessment can be made if 12 months have elapsed since the date of payment of the bill (see *Harrison v Tew*, p 46). If a mortgagee has paid his solicitor's costs in respect of possession proceedings which resulted in a suspended order, and added those costs to the mortgage debt, the mortgagor may not discover this until long after the 12-month period has expired. It would therefore be prudent for the mortgagor after any such litigation to ascertain the amount of the mortgagee's solicitor's costs so that an application for an assessment may be made within the requisite time. However, the warnings given above in respect of the assessment of a landlord's costs by the tenant apply equally here.

7. SOLICITORS ACT 1974, SECTION 71

Section 71(1) of the Solicitors Act 1974 provides:

> (1) Where a person other than the party chargeable with the bill for the purposes of section 70 has paid, or is or was liable to pay, a bill either to the solicitor or to the party chargeable with the bill, that person, or his executors, administrators or assignees may apply to the High Court for an order for the taxation [*assessment*] of the bill as if he were the party chargeable with it, and the court may make the same order (if any) as it might have made if the application had been made by the party chargeable with the bill.

The effect of this provision is 'that if a person who is not chargeable thinks fit to pay the bill it is open to him to do so, and if he does so, he should be entitled to have that bill assessed as the party chargeable therewith might himself have done' (*Re Newman* (1867) 2 Ch App 707, per Rolt LJ). Although the assessment must be conducted as between the solicitor and his own client, a third party does not, by obtaining an order to assess, increase his liability to the solicitor's client. For example, if a mortgagor has the costs of the mortgagee's solicitor assessed, items which the mortgagor would not be liable to pay as between himself and the mortgagee will be disallowed even if the solicitor is entitled to charge them against his client, the mortgagee (*Re Longbotham & Sons* [1904] 2 Ch 152, CA).

8. ENTITLED THIRD PARTIES

The Solicitors' (Non-Contentious Business) Remuneration Order 1994 gives rights to a class of beneficiaries to certain estates who may require the solicitor to obtain a remuneration certificate in respect of his costs against the estate (see p 37).

9. NO PROTECTION AGAINST CONSTRUCTIVE TRUST

In *United Mizrahi Bank Ltd v Doherty* [1998] 2 All ER 230, ChD, a provision in a freezing order permitted the defendants to use assets otherwise frozen, for reasonable legal expenses. Such a provision merely prevented the use of the assets in this way from being a breach of the order and a contempt of court. It was no advance guarantee that, if at the trial the claimant was successful in establishing a proprietary claim against the defendant, such that the money so expended turned out to have been the claimant's, the solicitors acting for the defendant could avoid a claim of constructive trust for knowing receipt being raised against them. The claimant bank was bringing an action against the first defendant for breach of his duty to the bank in which it alleged that he wrongfully obtained money from customers which had ended up in the hands of his wife and servant companies and had been used for the purchase of properties including the properties the subject matter of the application. The bank thus had a claim for breach of trust against him and in constructive trust and tracing against the other defendants. The first defendant and his solicitors had issued a notice of motion effectively seeking in advance the court's determination that the expenditure on the costs allowed by the freezing order would deprive the bank of any such claim of constructive trust. This was not a case where the court could or should say, in advance, that there would be no breach of trust by the expenditure of those moneys in legal costs.

Part II

Between the parties

CHAPTER 8

SYNOPSIS

1605–1978

Solicitors have been required to deliver detailed bills of costs since 1605. When I first encountered costs they were prescribed for the High Court in Appendix N to the Rules of the Supreme Court 1883. It contained no less than 204 items, with fixed minima and maxima. The result was a scale which, in the words of the Evershed Committee, was 'derogatory of the dignity and standing of a profession no less distinguished, learned and reputable than any of the other professions which charge on the basis of the real value of the skill and industry involved'. Nevertheless, the scale was not amended until the Supreme Court (Costs) Rules 1959 introduced Appendix 2 to RSC Ord 62, which, although it contained a mere 100 items, resulted in an even more complicated form of bill, requiring not only a skilled specialist to draw it, but someone of equal skill to check, read and assess it. The negotiations over the next 20 years comprised long periods of stagnation interspersed with short bursts of feverish activity which eventually resulted in the introduction of a new Appendix 2 on 24 April 1979. In the county court there continued to be a variety of scales depending on the amount recovered or claimed.

1979

The new High Court scale, which reduced the number of items to 12, for the first time distinguished between routine ('mechanical') work and skilled and experienced ('thinking') work which was clearly analogous to the work of non-fee earners and fee earners. The individual items in the scale related to mechanical work, while thinking work was concentrated in the instructions item. The philosophy behind it was simple and consistent with the Law Society's *The Expense of Time*, which divided the members of a solicitors' firm into the two categories of fee earner and non-fee earner and provided formulae for calculating the hourly expense of fee earners by apportioning the overheads of the firm between them. Nevertheless, the then Chief Taxing Master described the scale as a 'half-way house', while other appellations were less polite.

The new scale perpetuated some of the unfairness of the previous scale, created its own illogicalities and did not materially simplify the drawing of bills.

1986

On 28 April 1986 all the complaints about High Court costs were swept away in the culmination of the Law Society's campaign for an all-discretionary bill of costs. The fixed limits had gone. The daily rate had gone. There was a profit mark-up on all interlocutory work. In the county court there were still four scales until July 1991 and three afterwards.

However, discretion is a two-edged sword – it can be exercised both for and against – it does not automatically confer benefits. Under the old scale with fixed minimum amounts, however low the figures may have been, they were negotiated by the Law Society on behalf of all solicitors. With a discretionary scale, every solicitor must fend for himself and justify his own charges.

1999

On 26 April 1999, the Civil Procedure Rules 1998 saw the achievement of another long cherished ideal – the abolition of the difference between High Court and county court costs by the introduction of one unified regime. I accept that it was part of the equally cherished unification and simplification of all the Rules and codes of procedure in the civil courts, but unification was particularly welcome in respect of costs. All that was good in the former RSC Ord 62 and the CCR Ord 38 was incorporated in Parts 43–48 of the CPR, which also include much of the codified principle and practice that was applied in the past but were not part of the Rules. In addition, the new Rules are not a mere codification of what was already there. They introduced a new philosophy and approach to costs. In the past, the court had been concerned only to decide whether or not to award costs to one party or the other at the end of a hearing, with any costs awarded being quantified at the end of the proceedings if the parties could not agree them. Now costs permeate every aspect of civil litigation: the courts are charged with the responsibility of managing cases to ensure that the work undertaken by the parties (and therefore the costs they incur) are proportionate to the issues, while costs orders may be made as sanctions to ensure that the conduct of the parties (both before and during the proceedings) is in compliance with the new procedural code. As well as seeking to achieve proportionality and using costs orders as sanctions, the new regime also aims to make the amount of costs more predictable by requiring the parties to provide estimates of their costs at various stages of the litigation, and for costs on the fast track to be fixed, initially for the trial only, but eventually for the entire action.

Two innovations which have had an immediate dramatic impact on civil litigation are the provision for the summary assessment of costs by the judge after an interim hearing or a hearing lasting not more than one day and for those costs to be paid within 14 days (which has apparently substantially reduced the number of interim applications), and the provision in Part 36 that a *claimant* may make an offer to settle with possible favourable financial consequences if the claimant subsequently recovers more than the amount of his offer. The concepts of proportionality and of the winner of litigation no longer virtually automatically receiving all, or indeed any, of his costs, have also brought about fundamental changes in the conduct of litigation.

CHAPTER 9

VOCABULARY

COSTS PRACTICE DIRECTION RELATING TO PART 43

SECTION 1 INTRODUCTION

1.1 This Practice Direction supplements Parts 43 to 48 of the Civil Procedure Rules. It applies to all proceedings to which those Parts apply.

1.2 Paragraphs 57.1 to 57.9 of this Practice Direction deal with various transitional provisions affecting proceedings about costs.

1.3 Attention is drawn to the powers to make orders about costs conferred on the Supreme Court and any county court by Section 51 of the Supreme Court Act 1981.

1.4 In these Directions:

'counsel' means a barrister or other person with a right of audience in relation to proceedings in the High Court or in the County Courts in which he is instructed to act.

'LSC' means Legal Services Commission.

'solicitor' means a solicitor of the Supreme Court or other person with a right of audience in relation to proceedings, who is conducting the claim or defence (as the case may be) on behalf of a party to the proceedings and, where the context admits, includes a patent agent.

1.5 In respect of any document which is required by these Directions to be signed by a party or his legal representative the Practice Direction supplementing Part 22 will apply as if the document in question was a statement of truth. (The Practice Direction supplementing Part 22 makes provision for cases in which a party is a child, a patient or a company or other corporation and cases in which a document is signed on behalf of a partnership).

CPR RULE 43.2 DEFINITIONS AND APPLICATION

(1) In Parts 44 to 48, unless the context otherwise requires—
- (a) 'costs' includes fees, charges, disbursements, expenses, remuneration, reimbursement allowed to a litigant in person under rule 48.6, any additional liability incurred under a funding arrangement and any fee or reward charged by a lay representative for acting on behalf of a party in proceedings allocated to the small claims track;
- (b) 'costs judge' means a taxing master of the Supreme Court;
- (c) 'costs officer' means—
  - (i) a costs judge;
  - (ii) a district judge; and
  - (iii) an authorised court officer;
- (d) 'authorised court officer' means any officer of—
  - (i) a county court;
  - (ii) a district registry;
  - (iii) the Principal Registry of the Family Division; or
  - (iv) the Supreme Court Costs Office;

  whom the Lord Chancellor has authorised to assess costs.
- (e) 'fund' includes any estate or property held for the benefit of any person

or class of person and any fund to which a trustee or personal representative is entitled in his capacity as such;

(f) 'receiving party' means a party entitled to be paid costs;

(g) 'paying party' means a party liable to pay costs;

(h) 'assisted person' means an assisted person within the statutory provisions relating to legal aid;

(i) 'LSC funded client' means an individual who receives services funded by the Legal Services Commission as part of the Community Legal Service within the meaning of Part I of the Access to Justice Act 1999;

(j) 'fixed costs' means the amounts which are to be allowed in respect of solicitors' charges in the circumstances set out in Part 45.

(k) 'funding arrangement' means an arrangement where a person has—

  (i) entered into a conditional fee agreement or a collective conditional fee agreement which provides for a success fee within the meaning of section 58(2) of the Courts and Legal Services Act 1990;

  (ii) taken out an insurance policy to which section 29 of the Access to Justice Act 1999 (recovery of insurance premiums by way of costs) applies; or

  (iii) made an agreement with a membership organisation to meet his legal costs;

(l) 'percentage increase' means the percentage by which the amount of a legal representative's fee can be increased in accordance with a conditional fee agreement which provides for a success fee;

(m) 'insurance premium' means a sum of money paid or payable for insurance against the risk of incurring a costs liability in the proceedings, taken out after the event that is the subject matter of the claim;

(n) 'membership organisation' means a body prescribed for the purposes of section 30 of the Access to Justice Act 1999 (recovery where body undertakes to meet costs liabilities); and

(o) 'additional liability' means the percentage increase, the insurance premium, or the additional amount in respect of provision made by a membership organisation, as the case may be.

(The Conditional Fee Agreements Regulations 2000, the Collective Conditional Fee Agreements 2000 and the Access to Justice (Membership Organisations) Regulations 2000 contain further provisions about conditional fee agreements and arrangements to meet costs liabilities)

(2) The costs to which Parts 44 to 48 apply include—

(a) the following costs where those costs may be assessed by the court—

  (i) costs of proceedings before an arbitrator or umpire;

  (ii) costs of proceedings before a tribunal or other statutory body; and

  (iii) costs payable by a client to his solicitor; and

(b) costs which are payable by one party to another party under the terms of a contract, where the court makes an order for an assessment of those costs.

SECTION 2: PRACTICE DIRECTION SUPPLEMENTING CPR RULE 43.2

2.1 Where the court makes an order for costs and the receiving party has entered into a funding arrangement as defined in rule 43.2, the costs payable by the paying party include any additional liability (also defined in rule 43.2) unless the court orders otherwise.

2.2 In the following paragraphs—

'funding arrangement', 'percentage increase', 'insurance premium', 'membership organisation' and 'additional liability' have the meanings given to them by rule 43.2.

** A 'conditional fee agreement' is an agreement with a person providing advocacy or litigation services which provides for his fees and expenses, or part of them, to be payable only in specified circumstances, whether or not it provides for a success fee as mentioned in section 58(2)(b) of the Courts and Legal Services Act 1990.*

'base costs' means costs other than the amount of any additional liability.

2.3 Rule 44.3A(1) provides that the court will not assess any additional liability until the conclusion of the proceedings or the part of the proceedings to which the funding arrangement relates. (As to the time when detailed assessment may be carried out see paragraph 27.1 below).

2.4 For the purposes of the following paragraphs of this practice direction and rule 44.3A proceedings are concluded when the court has finally determined the matters in issue in the claim, whether or not there is an appeal. The making of an award of provisional damages under Part 41 will also be treated as a final determination of the matters in issue.

2.5 The court may order or the parties may agree in writing that, although the proceedings are continuing, they will nevertheless be treated as concluded.

The new rules were designed so that they and the procedures created by them are free from jargon and therefore easier to understand. This new approach resulted in old and familiar words concerning costs being replaced by new words which were and perceived to be more user-friendly. The first word to go was 'taxation' which smacked too much of the Inland Revenue for modern ears. There were various candidates to replace it; 'costs adjudication' and 'cost quantification' were two early front runners. 'Costs specification' was leading into the finishing straight, only to be overtaken by the eventual winner 'assessment'. This produced difficulties of its own because 'assessment' already had a precise and well understood meaning, but the old had to make way for the new. As a result there are now two forms of assessment: 'detailed assessment', which is the former 'taxation', and 'summary assessment' which is assessment by the judge who has conducted a hearing. Taxing Masters became 'Costs Judges' with the Chief Taxing Master as the 'Senior Costs Judge'; the Supreme Court Taxing Office became the 'Supreme Court Costs Office' and Taxing Officers are now 'Costs Officers', being Costs Judges, District Judges or authorised court officers.

The definition of 'an authorised court officer' in Rule 43.2(1)(*d*) as any officer of a county court, a District Registry, the Principal Registry of the Family Division or the Supreme Court Costs Office whom the Lord Chancellor has authorised to assess costs, is similar to a provision which caused great controversy when it was proposed to be introduced into the new RSC Ord 62 in 1986. The objection was that the assessment of costs is a judicial exercise for which Court Officers are not equipped either by legal experience or training to discharge. Eventually a compromise was reached and the practice limitations that were inserted in RSC Ord 62 r 19 are preserved in section 30 of the practice direction which can be found in Chapter 30 at pp 295–296.

In any event, with the introduction of fixed costs and summary assessments the question of assessment by authorised officers is not now of much frequency or significance.

The terms 'the paying party' and the 'receiving party' could not be in plainer English but it was proposed at one time that even they should be replaced with some gobbledygook, but this was happily abandoned. Another semantically triumph was the abolition of the archaic term 'solicitor and own client' costs and its replacement 'solicitor and client' costs, it being at last accepted that a solicitor is unlikely with any prospect of success to render a bill to someone who is not his own client! The recovery of success fees and after-the-event insurance premiums introduced more new words and concepts, including the compendium description 'additional liability' to embrace either or both of them.

CPR RULE 43.3 MEANING OF SUMMARY ASSESSMENT

'Summary assessment' means the procedure by which the court, when making an order about costs, orders payment of a sum of money instead of fixed costs or 'detailed assessment'.

SECTION 3: PRACTICE DIRECTION SUPPLEMENTING CPR RULE 43.3

3.1 Rule 43.3 defines summary assessment. When carrying out a summary assessment of costs where there is an additional liability the court may assess the base costs alone, or the base costs and the additional liability.
3.2 Form N260 is a model form of Statement of Costs to be used for summary assessments.
3.3 Further details about Statements of Costs are given in paragraph 13.6 below.

CPR RULE 43.4 MEANING OF DETAILED ASSESSMENT

'Detailed assessment' means the procedure by which the amount of costs is decided by a costs officer in accordance with Part 47.

SECTION 3: PRACTICE DIRECTION SUPPLEMENTING CPR RULE 43.4

3.4 Rule 43.4 defines detailed assessment. When carrying out a detailed assessment of costs where there is an additional liability the court will assess both the base costs and the additional liability, or, if the base costs have already been assessed, the additional liability alone.
3.5 Precedents A, B, C and D in the Schedule of Costs Precedents annexed to this Practice Direction are model forms of bills of costs to be used for detailed assessments.
3.6 Further details about bills of costs are given in the next section of these Directions and in paragraphs 28.1 to 49.1, below.
3.7 Precedents A, B, C and D in the Schedule of Costs Precedents and the next section of this Practice Direction all refer to a model form of bill of costs. The use of a model form is not compulsory, but is encouraged. A party wishing to rely upon a bill which departs from the model forms should include in the background information of the bill an explanation for that departure.
3.8 In any order of the court (whether made before or after 26 April 1999) the word 'taxation' will be taken to mean 'detailed assessment' and the words 'to be taxed' will be taken to mean 'to be decided by detailed assessment' unless in either case the context otherwise requires.

Here is an alphabetical list of some of the other changes in the litigation vocabulary.

Old	*New*
Anton Piller	Search Order
Calderbank offer	Part 36 offer
Cause	Case
Discovery	Disclosure
Ex parte	Without notice
Further and better particulars	Further information

Old	*New*
Guardian ad litem	Litigation friend
In camera	In private
Infant	Child
Interlocutory	Interim
Inter partes	With notice
Leave of the court	Permission of the court
Mareva	Freezing
Medical negligence	Clinical negligence
Minor/infant	Child
Party and party	Between the parties
Party under a disability	Patient or child
Next friend	Litigation friend
Payment into court	Part 36 payment
Plaintiff	Claimant
Pleading	Statement of case
Third party proceedings	Part 20 claim
Writ	Claim form

CHAPTER 10

COSTS ESTIMATES

Section 6 of the Costs Practice Direction makes the following provisions for costs estimates:

SECTION 6: ESTIMATES OF COSTS

6.1 This section sets out certain steps which parties and their legal representatives must take in order to keep the parties informed about their potential liability in respect of costs and in order to assist the court to decide what, if any, order to make about costs and about case management.

6.2

(1) In this section an 'estimate of costs' means—

a) an estimate of base costs (including disbursements) already incurred; and

b) an estimate of base costs (including disbursements) to be incurred, which a party intends to seek to recover from any other party under an order for costs if he is successful in the case. ('Base costs' are defined in paragraphs 2.2 of this Practice Direction.)

(2) A party who intends to recover an additional liability (defined in rule 43.2) need not reveal the amount of that liability in the estimate.

6.3 The court may at any stage in a case order any party to file an estimate of base costs and to serve copies of the estimate on all other parties. The court may direct that the estimate be prepared in such a way as to demonstrate the likely effects of giving or not giving a particular case management direction which the court is considering, for example a direction for a split trial or for the trial of a preliminary issue. The court may specify a time limit for filing and serving the estimate. However, if no time limit is specified the estimate should be filed and served within 28 days of the date of the order.

6.4

(1) When a party to a claim which is outside the financial scope of the small claims track, files an allocation questionnaire, he must also file an estimate of base costs and serve a copy of it on every other party, unless the court otherwise directs. The legal representative must in addition serve an estimate upon the party he represents.

(2) Where a party to a claim which is being dealt with on the fast track or the multi-track, or under Part 8, files a listing questionnaire ['pre-trial checklist' from 2 December 2002], *he must also file an estimate of base costs and serve a copy of it on every other party, unless the court otherwise directs. Where a party is represented, the legal representative must in addition serve an estimate on the party he represents.*

(3) This paragraph does not apply to litigants in person.

6.5 An estimate of base costs should be substantially in the form illustrated in Precedent H in the Schedule of Costs Precedents annexed to the Practice Direction.

6.6 On an assessment of the costs of a party the court may have regard to any estimate previously filed by that party, or by any other party in the same proceedings. Such an estimate may be taken into account as a factor among others, when assessing the reasonableness of any costs claimed.

Where a claim is outside the financial scope of the small claims track, a party (other than a litigant in person) filing an allocation questionnaire is required to file an estimate of costs and serve a copy of it on every other party and the client. A further estimate is required on the filing of the listing questionnaire; again the estimate must be served on every other party and the client The estimate should follow the form of Precedent H annexed to the Practice Direction, distinguishing between those costs already incurred and to be incurred. Here it is:

COSTS PRACTICE DIRECTION
PRECEDENT H

SCHEDULE OF COSTS PRECEDENTS
PRECEDENT H

IN THE HIGH COURT OF JUSTICE 2000-B-9999

QUEEN'S BENCH DIVISION

BRIGHTON DISTRICT REGISTRY

BETWEEN

AB Claimant

– and –

CD Defendant

ESTIMATE OF CLAIMANT'S COSTS DATED 12th APRIL 2001

The claimant instructed E F & Co under a conditional fee agreement dated 8th July 2000 in respect of which the following hourly rates are recoverable as base costs

Partner – £180 per hour plus VAT
Assistant Solicitor – £140 per hour plus VAT
Other fee earners – £85 per hour plus VAT

PART I: BASE

Item No.	Description of work done	V.A.T.	Disbursements	Profit Costs
	PART 1: BASE COSTS ALREADY INCURRED			
	8th July 2000 – EF & Co instructed			
	7th October 2000 Claim issued			
1	Issue fee	—	£400.00	
	21st October 2000 – Particulars of claim served			
	25th November 2000 – Time for service of defence extended by agreement to 14th January 2001			
2	Fee on allocation	£—		£80.00
	20th January 2001 – case allocated to multi-track			
	9th February 2001 – Case management conference at which costs were awarded to the claimant and the base costs were summarily assessed at £400 (paid on 24th February 2001) –			
	23rd February 2001 – Claimant's list of documents			

Item No.	Description of work done	V.A.T.	Disbursements	Profit Costs
	ATTENDANCES, COMMUNICATIONS AND WORK DONE			
	Claimant			
3	0.75 hours at £180			£135.00
4	4.4 hours at £140			£616.00
	To Summary	£—	£480.00	£751.00
	Witnesses of Fact			
5	3.8 hours at £140			£532.00
6	Paid travelling on 9th October 2000	£4.02	£22.96	
7	1.5 hours at £140			£210.00
8	Dr IJ's fee for report		£350.00	
	Defendant and his solicitor			
9	2.5 hours at £140			£350.00
	Court (communications only)			
10	0.4 hours at £140			£56.00
	Documents			
11	0.75 hours at £180 and 22.25 hours at £140			£3,250.00
	Negotiations			
12	2.75 hours at £140			£385.00
13	VAT on solicitor's base fees	£968.45		
	To Summary	£972.47	£372.96	£4,783.00
	PART 2: BASE COSTS TO BE INCURRED			
14	Fee on listing	£—	£400.00	
	Attendance at pre-trial review			
15	5 hours at £140			£700.00
16	Counsel's base fee for pre-trial review		£750.00	
	Attendance at trial			
17	20 hours at £140			£2,800.00
18	Counsel's base fee for trial including refresher		£3,000.00	
19	Fee of expert witness (Dr. IJ)		£1,000.00	
20	Expenses of witnesses of fact		£150.00	
	ATTENDANCES, COMMUNICATIONS AND WORK TO BE DONE			
	Claimant			
21	1 hour at £180			£180.00
22	8 hours at £140			£1,120.00
	Witnesses of fact			
23	5 hours at £140			£700.00
	Medical expert (Dr. IJ)			
24	1 hour at £140			£140.00
	Defendant and his solicitor			
25	2 hours at £140			£280.00
	To Summary	£—	£5,300.00	£5,920.00
	Court (communications only)			
26	1 hour at £140			£140.00
	Counsel (communications only)			
27	3 hours at £140			£420.00
	Documents			
28	1 hour at £180, 25 hours at £140 and 15 hours at £85			£4,995.00
	Negotiations			
29	5 hours at £140			£700.00

Item No.	Description of work done	V.A.T.	Disbursements	Profit Costs
	Other work			
30	5 hours at £140			£700.00
31	VAT on solicitor's base fees	£2,253.13		
	To Summary	£2,253.13	£—	£6,955.00
SUMMARY				
Part 1				
Page 1		£—	£480.00	£751.00
Page 2		£972.47	£372.96	£4,783.00
Total base costs already incurred		£972.47	£852.96	£5,534.00
Part 2				
Page 2		£—	£5,300.00	£5,920.00
Page 3		£2,253.13	£—	£6,955.00
Total base costs to be incurred		£2,253.13	£5,300.00	£12,875.00
Total of base costs		£3,225.60	£6,152.96	£18,409.00
Grand total				£27,787.56

1. ALLOCATION QUESTIONNAIRE

Although the estimate of costs does not act as a limit to the amount of costs which may be claimed, it may be taken into account and, if an estimate is substantially exceeded, this will provide ammunition for an opponent when those costs come to be assessed. When preparing the estimate for the allocation questionnaire it is not necessary to do more than enter a figure on the questionnaire but that figure must have been worked out carefully and it is advisable to be in a position to back up the estimated figure with a breakdown showing how it has been arrived at.

2. PRE-TRIAL CHECKLIST (FORMERLY 'LISTING QUESTIONNAIRE': SEE CPD S 6)

When estimating for the pre-trial checklist the estimate of costs incurred to date must be accurate and there is no reason why it should not be. With regard to the future costs it should be possible to be more accurate than at the allocation stage, since the litigation will by that time have taken on a definite pattern. Again, an estimate which is exceeded, while not limiting the amount of costs which can be claimed, may be taken into account and will provide an opponent with the opportunity to attack the figures sought.

3. ADDITIONAL LIABILITIES

Because of the desire to preserve confidentiality, additional liabilities (success fees and after-the-event insurance premiums) have been excluded from estimates. There is concern that this exclusion defeats the object of estimates and costs transparency.

4. COURT CONTROL

(a) Exceeding the estimate

There is continuing consultation with the profession as to whether costs estimates should in fact result in a limit on the recoverable costs which cannot be exceeded without a reasonable explanation.

It remains to be decided whether a party, having given an estimate, may be permitted to revise it. It seems unlikely that this will be possible in respect of the allocation questionnaire since the figures given will be the best that can be arrived at on the information available. The estimate accompanying the pre-trial checklist will provide an opportunity for revising the figures, but if there is a change of circumstance, resulting in the estimate being substantially wrong, it will probably be in the party's interests to inform the court and the opposing parties of the new figures as soon as possible.

Another question to be decided is whether a judge is entitled to exercise discretion to exceed the estimate and in what circumstances. The allocation estimate is less likely to influence the judges than the listing estimate, although both estimates should be as accurate as circumstances permit.

(b) Costs-capping

In *Griffiths v Solutia UK Ltd* [2001] EWCA Civ 736, [2001] All ER (D) 196 (Apr), the court said that although the CPR did not confer upon the court an express power to place an advance limit on the costs which would be recoverable for all or part of the litigation (equivalent to the power in the Arbitration Act 1996, s 65), case management powers surely allowed a judge to exercise the power of limiting costs, either indirectly or even directly, so that they are proportionate to the amount involved. Judges conducting cases should make full use of their powers under section 6 of the Costs Practice Direction to obtain estimates of costs and to exercise their powers in respect of costs and case management to keep costs within the bounds of the proportionate in accordance with the overriding objective.

Pioneering work on costs-capping has been done by District Judge Lethem in the Tunbridge Wells County Court. He founds his jurisdiction not only on s 6 of the CPD but also on the Supreme Court Act 1981, s 51(3) of which provides: 'The court shall have full power to determine by whom and to what extent costs are to be paid' without specifying that this shall be done at any particular stage of the proceedings. He receives further support from CPR 3.1(2)(m) which empowers the court to 'take any other step or make any other order for the purpose of managing the case and furthering the overriding objective'. There has been no appeal against his capping orders, no doubt for the very good reason that in the present costs climate an appeal would be most unlikely to succeed. DJ Lethem's philosophy is that the difficulty with the present regime is that the assessment takes place *ex post facto*. So the judge assessing the costs of the successful party is not assisting the solicitor in the budgeting exercise contemplated in *Jefferson* (see p 102) but is penalising him to the extent the judge thinks he got it wrong. Costs-capping orders are a bespoke solution tailored to each particular case. They are not a straight-jacket but a budget which is capable of revision for good reason. The procedure is to consider the costs estimates filed with the allocation questionnaire (which has not changed its name) with a view to making an order in these terms:

> 'The base costs of the parties shall not, without the permission of the court, exceed the sum of £x (save that any costs awarded in favour of a party on any interim application shall not count towards the said £x). Either party may apply without notice to increase the figure of £x and any such application shall be supported by a statement addressing the need for the increase and a revised costs estimate calculated to trial.'

The wording of the order envisages the base costs of both parties being the same, but, being bespoke and not off-the-peg, presumably adjustments can be made where appropriate.

CHAPTER 11

GENERAL RULES ABOUT COSTS (CPR PART 44)

Part 44 contains the general or core costs rules. Here it is with the supplemental practice direction:

PART 44 GENERAL RULES ABOUT COSTS

CONTENTS OF THIS PART

CPR RULE 44.1 SCOPE OF THIS PART

This Part contains general rules about costs, and entitlement to costs.
(The definitions contained in Part 43 are relevant to this Part)

CPR RULE 44.2 SOLICITOR'S DUTY TO NOTIFY CLIENT

Where—

(a) the court makes a costs order against a legally represented party; and
(b) the party is not present when the order is made,

the party's solicitor must notify his client in writing of the costs order no later than 7 days after the solicitor receives notice of the order.

SECTION 7: PRACTICE DIRECTION SUPPLEMENTING CPR RULE 44.2

7.1 For the purposes of rule 44.2 'client' includes a party for whom a solicitor is acting and any other person (for example, an insurer, a trade union or the

LSC) who has instructed the solicitor to act or who is liable to pay his fees.
7.2 Where a solicitor notifies a client of an order under that rule, he must also explain why the order came to be made.
7.3 Although rule 44.2 does not specify any sanction for breach of the rule the court may, either in the order for costs itself or in a subsequent order, require the solicitor to produce to the court evidence showing that he took reasonable steps to comply with the rule.

Rule 44.2 requires a solicitor to notify his client within seven days of a costs order being made against him if the client was not present when it was made. This is in place of the original proposal that the client should attend every interlocutory hearing to ensure he was aware of what costs were being incurred. Early drafts of this rule also included the draconian sanction that a solicitor who failed to comply with the rule should pay the costs personally, but that too did not survive. Now, no sanction is prescribed for non-compliance with this much watered-down provision, although the practice direction provides the sop that the court may order the solicitor to produce evidence that he has taken reasonable steps to comply with the rule, which sounds like a slap with a limp wrist.

CPR RULE 44.3 COURT'S DISCRETION AND CIRCUMSTANCES TO BE TAKEN INTO ACCOUNT WHEN EXERCISING ITS DISCRETION AS TO COSTS

(1) The court has discretion as to—
  (a) whether costs are payable by one party to another;
  (b) the amount of those costs; and
  (c) when they are to be paid.
(2) If the court decides to make an order about costs—
  (a) the general rule is that the unsuccessful party will be ordered to pay the costs of the successful party; but
  (b) the court may make a different order.
(3) The general rule does not apply to the following proceedings—
  (a) proceedings in the Court of Appeal on an application or appeal made in connection with proceedings in the Family Division; or
  (b) proceedings in the Court of Appeal from a judgment, direction, decision or order given or made in probate proceedings or family proceedings.
(4) In deciding what order (if any) to make about costs, the court must have regard to all the circumstances, including—
  (a) the conduct of all the parties;
  (b) whether a party has succeeded on part of his case, even if he has not been wholly successful; and
  (c) any payment into court or admissible offer to settle made by a party which is drawn to the court's attention (whether or not made in accordance with Part 36).
(Part 36 contains further provisions about how the court's discretion is to be exercised where a payment into court or an offer to settle is made under that Part)
(5) The conduct of the parties includes—
  (a) conduct before, as well as during, the proceedings, and in particular the extent to which the parties followed any relevant pre-action protocol;
  (b) whether it was reasonable for a party to raise, pursue or contest a particular allegation or issue;
  (c) the manner in which a party has pursued or defended his case or a particular allegation or issue; and

(d) whether a claimant who has succeeded in his claim, in whole or in part, exaggerated his claim.

(6) The orders which the court may make under this rule include an order that a party must pay—

(a) a proportion of another party's costs;
(b) a stated amount in respect of another party's costs;
(c) costs from or until a certain date only;
(d) costs incurred before proceedings have begun;
(e) costs relating to particular steps taken in the proceedings;
(f) costs relating only to a distinct part of the proceedings; and
(g) interest on costs from or until a certain date, including a date before judgment.

(7) Where the court would otherwise consider making an order under paragraph (6)(f), it must instead, if practicable, make an order under paragraph (6)(a) or (c).

(8) Where the court has ordered a party to pay costs, it may order an amount to be paid on account before the costs are assessed.

(9) Where a party entitled to costs is also liable to pay costs the court may assess the costs which that party is liable to pay and either—

(a) set off the amount assessed against the amount the party is entitled to be paid and direct him to pay any balance; or
(b) delay the issue of a certificate for the costs to which the party is entitled until he has paid the amount which he is liable to pay.

SECTION 8: PRACTICE DIRECTION SUPPLEMENTING CPR RULE 44.3

8.1 Attention is drawn to the factors set out in this rule which may lead the court to depart from the general rule stated in rule 44.3(2) and to make a different order about costs.

8.2 In a probate claim where a defendant has in his defence given notice that he requires the will to be proved in solemn form (see paragraph 8.3 of the Contentious Probate Practice Direction Supplementing Part 49), the court will not make an order for costs against the defendant unless it appears that there was no reasonable ground for opposing the will. The term 'probate claim' is defined in paragraph 1.2 of the Contentious Probate Practice Direction.

8.3

(1) The court may make an order about costs at any stage in a case.

(2) In particular the court may make an order about costs when it deals with any application, makes any order or holds any hearing and that order about costs may relate to the costs of that application, order or hearing.

*(3) * Rule 44.3A(1) provides that the court will not assess any additional liability until the conclusion of the proceedings or the part of the proceedings to which the funding arrangement relates. (Paragraphs 2.4 and 2.5 above explain when proceedings are concluded. As to the time when detailed assessment may be carried out see paragraph 28.1, below.)*

8.4 In deciding what order to make about costs the court is required to have regard to all the circumstances including any payment into court or admissible offer to settle made by a party which is drawn to the court's attention (whether or not it is made in accordance with Part 36). Where a claimant has made a Part 36 offer and fails to obtain a judgment which is more advantageous than that offer, that circumstance alone will not lead to a reduction in the costs awarded to the claimant under this rule.

8.5 There are certain costs orders which the court will commonly make in proceedings before trial. The following table sets out the general effect of these orders. The table is not an exhaustive list of the orders which the court may make. [This table is set out and considered in Chapter 16.]

8.6 Where, under rule 44.3(8), the court orders an amount to be paid before costs are assessed—
(1) the order will state that amount, and
(2) if no other date for payment is specified in the order rule 44.8 (Time for complying with an order for costs) will apply.

Fees of counsel

8.7
(1) This paragraph applies where the court orders the detailed assessment of the costs of a hearing at which one or more counsel appeared for a party.
(2) Where an order for costs states the opinion of the court as to whether or not the hearing was fit for the attendance of one or more counsel, a costs officer conducting a detailed assessment of costs to which that order relates will have regard to the opinion stated.
(3) The court will generally express an opinion only where:
(a) the paying party asks it to do so;
(b) more than one counsel appeared for a party or,
(c) the court wishes to record its opinion that the case was not fit for the attendance of counsel.

Fees payable to conveyancing counsel appointed by the court to assist it

8.8
(1) Where the court refers any matter to the conveyancing counsel of the court the fees payable to counsel in respect of the work done or to be done will be assessed by the court in accordance with rule 44.3.
(2) An appeal from a decision of the court in respect of the fees of such counsel will be dealt with under the general rules as to appeals set out in Part 52. If the appeal is against the decision of an authorised court officer, it will be dealt with in accordance with rules 47.20 to 47.23.

Rule 44.3 preserves the court's discretion as to costs and retains the rebuttable presumption that the loser pays the winner's costs. However, in deciding what order, if any, to make about costs the court must have regard to all the circumstances including:

(a) the conduct of the parties;
(b) whether a party has been partly, if not wholly, successful;
(c) any payment into court or any admissible offer to settle.

Consideration of the conduct of the parties is an integral part of the new philosophy of the costs of litigation. It includes:

(a) conduct *before*, as well as *during* the proceedings including compliance with any relevant pre-action protocol;
(b) whether it was *reasonable* for a party to raise, pursue or contest a particular allegation or issue;
(c) the *manner* in which a party has pursued or defended his case or a particular allegation or issue; and
(d) whether a claimant has *exaggerated* his claim in whole or in part.

(a) The philosophy

Accordingly, a party who has ignored or been cavalier about a pre-action protocol, or who has raised every possible allegation in his statement of case and failed in all but one or two minor matters or who has claimed grossly exaggerated damages may be deprived of all or part of his costs. Previously the philosophy was that if a claimant succeeded in recovering any part of a disputed claim he was entitled to his costs because it had been necessary for him to come to court to recover anything. In *Re Elgindata Ltd (No 2)* [1993] 1 All ER 232 the Court of Appeal had held that the general rule that costs should follow the event did not cease simply because the successful party raised an issue or made allegations that failed. The winner now no longer takes all. If a party only succeeds partially, they may recover only a proportionate amount of their costs. Indeed, they could in theory be ordered to pay all or some of the 'loser's' costs.

Applying the new philosophy of the CPR in *BCCI v Ali (No 4)* [1999] NLJR 1734, ChD, Lightman J said that under the CPR the straitjacket imposed by *Elgindata* had gone and that success was not now a technical term but a result in real life, the question of who had succeeded being a matter for the exercise of common sense. Before the CPR in a group action, complainants who established a breach of contract but could prove no loss would have been ordered to pay the defendant's costs. However, in this case that was only half the picture; although test case employees had lost, the judgment opened the door to possible successful claims by other employees. Accordingly, the judge held that the proper course was to make no order for costs. In *Gwembe Valley Development Co Ltd v Koshy* [2000] 11 LS Gaz R 38, ChD, Mr Justice Rimer held that even before the CPR came into force, the principle that costs should follow the event was merely the starting point from which the court could readily depart. The CPR did not alter the nature of the court's discretion so much as introducing a change of emphasis requiring the courts to be more ready to make separate orders reflecting the outcome of different issues. However, a successful party should not have to pay costs to an unsuccessful party unless the points taken by the successful party or the manner in which they were taken, or both were unreasonable. In this case, the defendant was ordered to pay 70% of the costs. In *Liverpool City Council v (1) Rosemary Chavasse Ltd (2) Walton Group plc* (19 August 1999, unreported, ChD), before the commencement of proceedings the claimant council had stuck its head in the sand and had only half-heartedly attempted negotiations; after proceedings had commenced it had left everything to the last minute and the matter could have been dealt with more quickly and cheaply if, among other things, the pressure of time had not been so great. CPR Rule 44.3 requires the court, when deciding what order to make about costs, to have regard to all the circumstances including the conduct of the parties before, as well as during, the proceedings. Applying these criteria the court awarded the successful claimant only half its costs of the proceedings with only five eighths of their costs of preparing the bundles because they had included excessive documents.

(b) The principles

In *Johnsey Estates (1990) Ltd v Secretary of State for the Environment* [2001] EWCA Civ 535, [2001] All ER (D) 135 (Apr), the court summarised the principles applicable as follows: (i) costs cannot be recovered except under an order of the court; (ii) the question of whether to make any order as to costs – and if so, what – is a matter entrusted to the discretion of the trial judge; (iii) the starting point for the exercise of discretion is that costs should follow the event; nevertheless, (iv) the judge may make different orders for costs in relation to discrete issues – and, in particular, should consider doing so where a party has been successful on one issue but unsuccessful on another issue and, in that event, may make an order for costs against a party who has been generally successful in the litigation; and (v) the judge may deprive a party of costs of an issue on which he has been successful if satisfied that the party has acted unreasonably in relation to that issue.

Spiers v English ([1907] P 122) established the principle that in contested proceedings as to the validity of a will the judge could make an alternative order to costs following the event where the testator or those interested in the residue had been the cause of the litigation, or if the circumstances led reasonably to an investigation.

In *Re Good, Carapeto v Good* [2002] 23 LS Gaz R 27 held that that principle survived CPR Rule 44.4 which prescribes that the normal order is for the unsuccessful party to pay the costs. The testator was a disabled elderly woman who left most of her £1.5 million estate to her housekeeper and her husband who had cared for her for more than 20 years. There were grounds for suspecting undue influence and the defendants were entitled to test their case. Nevertheless, the claimant had shown that the deceased knew and approved of the contents of the will and had succeeded in defending an unpleasant allegation of undue influence. In the circumstances the defendants were ordered to pay one-half of the claimant's costs.

(c) The menu

Rule 44.3(6) sets out a menu of the various orders the court may make giving a successful party less than the whole of its costs. Rule 44.3(6)(*a*) to (*f*) are in descending order of desirability for the purposes of ease of a summary judgment. Rule 43.3(7) states that (*f*) is to be avoided if it is possible to order either (*a*) or (*c*). The judge will probably start with (*a*) and try *not* to work his way down. An example of the new approach in practice was in *Grupo Torras re Sheik Fahed Mohamed Al-Sabah* (24 June 1999, unreported, QBD Comm Ct). In three cases involving allegations of conspiracy to defraud and dishonest assistance the defendants had succeeded. The judge rejected the claimant's submissions that as the defendants had only achieved a 'narrow success' they should not be awarded their costs. However, he found that the defendants had been guilty of backdating documents, deceiving the claimant's auditors and were in dereliction of their duties as directors of the claimants, so that the claimants had been justified in bringing and continuing the proceedings. Under CPR Rule 44.3(2)(*b*) the court had power to deviate from the general rule that costs follow the event and he awarded the defendants only half of their costs in one case and only one-third of their costs in the other two cases. The new thinking was also demonstrated by Park J in the Chancery Division on 10 February 1999 (before the introduction of the CPR) in the unreported case of *Frayling v Premier (3-D Designs and Christopher Hewson, third parties).* In consolidated actions involving four parties with various claims and cross-claims the judge regarded the various complaints about the behaviour of the parties as cancelling themselves out in respect of the award of costs. After weighing up all the factors he declined to make separate orders for costs, which would require two payments in opposite directions and awarded Premier, the party that had won significantly more than it had lost, three-fifths of its costs against Frayling and two-fifths of its costs against 3-D Designs. He also ordered 3-D Designs to pay one-half of Premier's costs of the third party proceedings and ordered Premier to pay Mr Hewson one-half of the aggregate costs of Mr Hewson and 3-D Designs of the third party proceedings or (if lower) the whole of Mr Hewson's own costs of the third party proceedings. There is clearly no limit to the number of permutations of costs orders where there are a number of parties and third parties.

In *Verrechia v Metropolitan Police Comr* [2002] EWCA Civ 605, [2002] 3 All ER 385 the court emphasised that the CPR require that an order which allows or disallows costs by reference to certain issues should be made only if other forms of order cannot be made which sufficiently reflect the justice of the case (CPR Rule 44.3(7)). There are good reasons for this rule. An order which allows or disallows costs on certain issues creates difficulties at the stage of the detailed assessment of costs because the costs judge would have to master the issue in detail to understand what costs were properly incurred in dealing with it, and then analyse the work done by the receiving party's legal advisers to determine whether or not it was attributable to the issue the costs of which have been disallowed. All this adds to the cost of detailed assessment and to the amount of time absorbed in dealing with costs on this basis. The costs incurred on assessment may thus be disproportionate to the benefit gained. In all the circumstances, contrary to what might be thought to be the case, a 'percentage' order under CPR Rule 44.3(6)(*a*) made by the judge who heard the application will often produce a fairer result than an 'issues-based' order under CPR Rule 44.3(6)(*f*). Moreover such an order is consistent with the overriding objective of the CPR.

These considerations will in most cases lead to the conclusion that an 'issues-based' order is not to be made. Wherever practicable, the judge should endeavour to form a view as to the percentage of costs to which the winning party should be entitled, or alternatively, whether justice would be sufficiently done by awarding costs from or until a particular date only, as suggested by CPR Rule 44.3(6)(*c*).

(d) Payment on account

Rule 44.3(8) is aimed at deterring the paying party from seeking a detailed assessment in order to delay parting with his money. Where a detailed assessment is ordered the court will usually order a substantial payment on account (see also p 283).

(e) Claim and counterclaim

Rule 44.3(9) is aimed at the situation where the claimant succeeds on the whole or on part in his claim and the defendant succeeds on the whole or on part on his counterclaim. It is infinitely preferable for there to be only one order for costs adjusted appropriately by allowing a proportion or some other partial order as to costs in favour of one party rather than making cross-orders for costs in favour of the successful claimant and the successful defendant on his counterclaim. If not, it appears that even under the new rules the lengthy, tedious and often unfair investigation of the costs attributable to the claim and those attributable to the counterclaim prescribed in the case of *Medway Oil and Storage Co Ltd v Continental Contractors Ltd* [1929] AC 88, HL will still apply. Under this approach the counterclaim will have attributed to it only the increase in the costs which it had brought about so that the result will be that the balance of the costs will almost certainly be in favour of the claimant and be unfair to the defendant. Similarly, where there is no counterclaim but the claimant only recovers 80% of his claim, implying that the defendant has been 20% successful, instead of awarding the defendant 20% of his costs the judge could consider reducing the award of costs to the claimant from 80% to perhaps 60% or 70% to compensate the defendant for that part of the claim in which he had been successful but had not been awarded any costs.

(f) No winner or loser

Shirley v Caswell [2002] Lloyd's Rep PN955, CA) was an action for damages against a barrister. The judge found that the barrister had given negligent advice on some issues, but he rejected other allegations. The judge ordered the defendant barrister to pay 60% of the claimant's costs and ordered the claimant to pay 40% of the defendant's costs on the basis that the claimant had abandoned various issues before trial after the defendant had incurred costs in preparation to those matters. The Court of Appeal held that, although the judge had been entitled to exercise his discretion in making the order for costs, the order he made exposed the claimant to the risk of being doubly penalised in respect of the costs relating to the abandoned issues because those costs would be considered on a detailed assessment in any event. The appropriate order was that the defendant should pay all of the claimant's costs and the claimant should pay 40% of the defendant's costs. The judgment referred to the decision in *AEI Rediffusion Music Ltd v Phonographic Performance Ltd (No 2) (Costs)* [1999] 1 WLR 1507, an appeal from an order for costs by the Copyright Tribunal, in which the Court of Appeal held that the Tribunal had erred in principle by seeking to find a winner and a loser and that in reality neither side had won. Accordingly, there should be no order for costs. Cross-orders for costs, either arising out of a successful claim and a successful counterclaim or, as in the present case, where the parties succeed on some points and lose on others, can give rise to serious difficulties on a detailed assessment. If, therefore, the judge is able to reach an overall decision on costs and either make no order for costs, or perhaps in the present case, have awarded the claimant, say, 50% of his costs with no award to the defendant, the assessment of costs is considerably simplified and the requirements of justice are met.

A decision with which I am not entirely happy is *Stocznia Gdanska SA v Latvian Shipping Co (No 2)* [1999] 3 All ER 822. The claimant abandoned two of the three distinct parts of its claim in tort. The claimants submitted that the court should not take into account the fact that a party had failed on an issue unless it was unreasonable for the party to have raised, pursued or contested the particular allegation or issue. This was a misapprehension. It was clear that under Rule 44.3(4)*(b)* the reasonableness of the party taking a particular point or bringing a part of the case was not necessarily relevant to the award of costs. This sub-paragraph is quite distinct from the conduct of the parties referred to in Rule 44.3(4)*(a)* and defined in Rule 44.3(5). The reasonableness of raising an issue did not necessarily have to be taken into account in applying Rule 44.3(4)*(b)*, the purpose of which was to encourage litigants to be selective as to the points they took, thus decreasing the costs of litigation. The defendant was treated as having succeeded on two parts of the claim under Rule 44.3(4)*(b)* and therefore entitled to the costs of those parts. The claimant was entitled, in all the circumstances, to 38% of the overall costs of the action. Although the logic of the award was impeccable, it did result in a detailed assessment of bills of costs from both parties, perhaps with some element of overlap, particularly as the defendants were to recover the whole of the costs in respect of two parts of the claim and the claimant to recover 38% of the overall costs of the action. Rule 44.3(9) envisages that in circumstances such as these, or where there is a successful claim and a successful counterclaim, the judge may make a broad brush order setting off the costs of one party against the other, resulting in a one-way order for costs at an appropriate percentage, or, as is happening with increasing frequency, a decision that the cross-entitlements to costs cancel each other out, resulting in the judge making no order for between-the-parties costs.

The preferred approach was exemplified in *Verrechia v Metropolitan Police Comr* [2002] EWCA Civ 605, [2002] 3 All ER 385 where the claimant sought damages of £141,500 plus aggravated and exemplary damages under the Torts (Interference with Goods) Act 1977 in respect of 65 items which the police had failed to return to him. The claimant had offered to settle for £98,000 which was followed by a payment into court by the police of the sum of £5,500 in full settlement of the whole of the claimant's claim. The judge awarded damages in the sum of £37,300 plus interest with the result that neither party succeeded to the extent of their prior offers. The judge clearly thought the action had resulted in a 'draw'. Although when the case started there were some 65 items, by the time of closing speeches, there were only 40 items in issue. The appellant won in respect of half in number of these items. There were no criticisms relevant to costs in the conduct of either party. The appellant had won one-half of his case and lost on the rest. The police as well as the appellant had come to court to win that part of the case in which they succeeded. To this extent the judge is entitled to take the view that each side was to that extent the winner. Alternatively, it was open to the judge, in the light of the wide powers conferred by the CPR, to conclude that, in any event, the appellant should only have part of his costs as he had been successful in part only of his case, and that the police should have the cost of the part of the case on which they had been successful. On either basis the judge could properly conclude that the proportion of costs which each party should receive was 50% and that the net result was nil when these two percentages were set against each other.

The Court of Appeal emphasised that the CPR require that an order which allows or disallows costs by reference to certain issues should be made only if other forms of order cannot be made which sufficiently reflect the justice of the case (CPR Rule 44.3(7)). There are good reasons for this rule. An order which allows or disallows costs on certain issues creates difficulties at the stage of the detailed assessment of costs because the costs judge would have to master the issue in detail to understand what costs were properly incurred in dealing with it, and then analyse the work done by the receiving party's legal advisers to determine whether or not it was attributable to the issue, the costs of which have been disallowed. All this adds to the cost of detailed assessment and to the amount of time absorbed in dealing with costs on this basis. The costs incurred on assessment may thus be disproportionate to the benefit gained. In all the circumstances, contrary to what might be thought to be the case, a 'percentage' order under CPR Rule 44.3(6)*(a)* made by the judge who heard the application will often produce a fairer result than an 'issues-based' order under CPR Rule 44.3(6)*(f)*. Moreover such an order is consistent with the overriding objective of the CPR. These considerations will in most cases lead to the conclusion that an 'issues-based' order is not to be made. Wherever practicable, the judge should endeavour to form a view as to the percentage of costs to which the winning party should be entitled, or alternatively, whether justice would be sufficiently done by awarding costs from or until a particular date only, as suggested by CPR Rule 44.3(6)*(c)*.

(g) Counsel

The former requirement that the costs of counsel attending an interim hearing would not be allowed unless the judge certified that counsel's attendance was reasonable has gone. It was replaced by paragraph 8.7(2) of the practice direction which envisages that the judge might express an opinion to which the costs officer should have regard. This provision led to some confusion and was resolved by paragraph 8.7(3) which sets out the only circumstances in which the court will generally express an opinion as to whether or not a hearing was fit for the attendance of counsel.

(h) Failure to mediate

In *Dunnett v Railtrack plc (in administration)* [2002] EWCA Civ 303, [2002] 2 All ER 850, on granting the claimant permission to appeal against the dismissal of his action for damages for negligence by Railtrack, the court told both parties they should attempt alternative dispute resolution, but Railtrack refused to do so, on the grounds that they were not prepared to make any further payment to the claimant and were confident that they would succeed on the appeal. Railtrack did succeed in having the appeal dismissed, but the Court of Appeal demonstrated its displeasure at their outright refusal to consider ADR by depriving them of their costs, saying 'Parties and their lawyers should ensure that they are aware that it is one of their duties fully to consider ADR, especially when the court has suggested it, and not merely to flatly turn it down. To flatly turn down ADR could place the party doing so at risk of adverse consequences in costs.

The decision was welcomed by the Centre for Effective Dispute Resolution as the decision which the mediation industry had been expecting and waiting for. Its director, Tony Allen, said: 'It makes clear that the Court of Appeal views mediation and related processes as at the heart of the overriding objective. The legal profession and its clients must take mediation seriously or face the consequences'.

(i) Failure to respond to offer

In *Kiam v MGN Ltd (No 2)* ([2002] EWCA Civ 66, [2002] 2 All ER 242) the claimant had been awarded £105,000 damages in a jury libel case against which the defendant appealed. Before the appeal was heard the claimant's solicitors wrote 'without prejudice save as to costs' offering to accept £75,000 and to return to the defendant £30,000 plus appropriate interest, an offer which the defendant simply ignored. When the appeal was dismissed the claimant sought costs on the indemnity basis under the court's general discretion under CPR Part 44. Where litigation was conducted in a way that was unreasonable, even though the conduct could not properly be regarded as lacking moral probity or deserving moral condemnation, CPR Part 44.3(4) required the court when deciding what order to make about costs, to have regard to all the circumstances, including any admissible offer to settle made by a party. The court held it would be a rare case where a refusal of a settlement offer would attract, under CPR Part 44, not merely an adverse order for costs, but an order on the indemnity rather than on the standard basis. Although conduct falling short of misconduct deserving of moral condemnation could be so unreasonable as to justify an order for indemnity costs, such conduct would need to be unreasonable to a high degree, not merely wrong or misguided in hindsight. An indemnity costs order made under Part 44, unlike one made under Part 36, did carry at least some stigma. It should not be understood that under the CPR it was now generally appropriate to condemn in indemnity costs those who declined reasonable settlement offers. In the instant case, it was quite impossible to regard the defendant's refusal of the claimant's offer as unreasonable, let alone unreasonable to so pronounced a degree as to merit an award of indemnity costs.

(j) Late amendment

In *Professional Technology Information Consultants Ltd v Jones* ([2001] EWCA Civ 2103, [2001] All ER (D) 90) the claimant succeeded in the action as a result of being given permission to make a substantial last minute amendment. The trial judge was satisfied that had the defendant known the claimant's case in its amended form from the outset she would have settled. Accordingly the judge awarded the claimant only two-thirds of her costs. The court rejected the defendant's contention that as a matter of principle she should be awarded her costs up to the date of the amendment. CPR Rule 44.3(6) empowers the court to order a party to pay a proportion of the costs and the one-third discount was an acceptable method of reflecting the amendment.

CPR RULE 44.3A COSTS ORDERS RELATING TO FUNDING ARRANGEMENTS

See Chapter 42.

CPR RULE 44.3B LIMITS ON RECOVERY UNDER FUNDING ARRANGEMENTS

See Chapter 42.

CPR RULE 44.4 BASIS OF ASSESSMENT

(1) Where the court is to assess the amount of costs (whether by summary or detailed assessment) it will assess those costs—

(a) on the standard basis; or

(b) on the indemnity basis,

but the court will not in either case allow costs which have been unreasonably incurred or are unreasonable in amount.

(Rule 48.3 sets out how the court decides the amount of costs payable under a contract)

(2) Where the amount of costs is to be assessed on the standard basis, the court will—

(a) only allow costs which are proportionate to the matters in issue; and

(b) resolve any doubt which it may have as to whether costs were reasonably incurred or reasonable and proportionate in amount in favour of the paying party.

(Factors which the court may take into account are set out in rule 44.5)

(3) Where the amount of costs is to be assessed on the indemnity basis, the court will resolve any doubt which it may have as to whether costs were reasonably incurred or were reasonable in amount in favour of the receiving party.

(4) Where—

(a) the court makes an order about costs without indicating the basis on which the costs are to be assessed; or

(b) the court makes an order for costs to be assessed on a basis other than the standard basis or the indemnity basis,

the costs will be assessed on the standard basis.

(5) [*Revoked.*]

(6) Where the amount of a solicitor's remuneration in respect of non-contentious business is regulated by any general orders made under the Solicitors Act 1974, the amount of the costs to be allowed in respect of any such business which falls to be assessed by the court will be decided in accordance with those general orders rather than this rule and rule 44.5.

1. THE TWO BASES

To fully appreciate the two bases for the assessment of costs it is necessary to go back into history before RSC Ord 62 was introduced in 1986. In those far off days judges could make any costs orders they wished. Examples were 'the defendant do indemnify the plaintiff as to costs', 'the defendant to pay all costs', and, my favourite, 'the defendant to pay the utmost costs'. No one knew what they meant but the judge felt a lot better for having made them! These orders could in theory mean that the loser had to pay whatever costs the winner claimed, however unreasonable his costs and however unreasonable his disbursements. So when RSC Ord 62 was re-drafted some prohibitory words were inserted to make the rules judge proof. Similar words are alive and well in the new Rule 44.4(4) which provides that if the court makes an order for costs to be assessed other than on the standard or indemnity basis, or makes an order which does not indicate the basis on which the costs are to be assessed the costs will be assessed on the standard basis. Both bases allow costs reasonably incurred and of a reasonable amount. Prior to the CPR the only difference between the two bases was in respect of the burden of proof of reasonableness. On the standard basis any doubt as to reasonableness is to be resolved in favour of the paying party, whilst on the indemnity basis any doubt is to be resolved in favour of the receiving party. As former Chief Taxing Master Matthews put it: 'If there is no doubt, there is no difference'. It had nothing whatsoever to do with hourly rates, profit mark up or the scope of the work. In other words, it was not the modern equivalent of 'the utmost costs'. This distinction remains.

2. PROPORTIONALITY

However, under Rule 44.4(2) there is now another important difference. On the standard basis the court will only allow costs which are not only reasonable but are also 'proportionate to the matters in issue'. 'What is proportionality?' is a conundrum the courts are still trying to solve.

(a) Rule 1.1(2)

We start with CPR Rule 1.1(2) which explains that 'proportionate' refers to (i) the amount of money involved; (ii) the importance of the case; (iii) the complexity of the issues; and (iv) the financial position of each party. The last provision arises out of the avowed aim of the CPR of equalising any disparity between the parties.

(b) Practice Direction

Section 11 of the Costs Practice Direction makes a further stab at defining 'proportionality' by saying what it *isn't*.

SECTION 11: PRACTICE DIRECTION SUPPLEMENTING CPR RULE 44.5

11.1 In applying the test of proportionality the court will have regard to rule 1.1(2)(c). The relationship between the total of the costs incurred and the financial value of the claim may not be a reliable guide. A fixed percentage cannot be applied in all cases to the value of the claim in order to ascertain whether or not the costs are proportionate.
11.2 In any proceedings there will be costs which will inevitably be incurred and which are necessary for the successful conduct of the case. Solicitors are not required to conduct litigation at rates which are uneconomic. Thus in a modest claim the proportion of costs is likely to be higher than in a large claim, and may even equal or possibly exceed the amount in dispute.
11.3 Where a trial takes place, the time taken by the court in dealing with a particular issue may not be an accurate guide to the amount of time properly spent by the legal or other representatives in preparation for the trial of that issue.
11.4 Where a party has entered into a funding arrangement the costs claimed may, subject to rule 44.3B include an additional liability.
11.5 In deciding whether the costs claimed are reasonable and (on a standard basis assessment) proportionate, the court will consider the amount of any additional liability separately from the base costs.
11.6 In deciding whether the base costs are reasonable and (if relevant) proportionate the court will consider the factors set out in rule 44.5.
11.7 Subject to paragraph 17.8(2), when the court is considering the factors to be taken into account in assessing an additional liability, it will have regard to the facts and circumstances as they reasonably appeared to the solicitor or counsel when the funding arrangement was entered into and at the time of any variation of the arrangement.
11.8
(1) In deciding whether a percentage increase is reasonable relevant factors to be taken into account may include:—
a) the risk that the circumstances in which the costs, fees or expenses would be payable might or might not occur;

b) the legal representative's liability for any disbursements;
c) what other methods of financing the costs were available to the receiving party.

(2) The court has the power, when considering whether a percentage increase is reasonable, to allow different percentages for different items of costs or for different periods during which costs were incurred.

11.9 A percentage increase will not be reduced simply on the ground that, when added to base costs which are reasonable and (where relevant) proportionate, the total appears disproportionate.

11.10 In deciding whether the cost of insurance cover is reasonable, relevant factors to be taken into account include:

(1) where the insurance cover is not purchased in support of a conditional fee agreement with a success fee, how its cost compares with the likely cost of funding the case with a conditional fee agreement with a success fee and supporting insurance cover;
(2) the level and extent of the cover provided;
(3) the availability of any pre-existing insurance cover;
(4) whether any part of the premium would be rebated in the event of early settlement;
(5) the amount of commission payable to the receiving party or his legal representatives or other agents.

11.11 Where the court is considering a provision made by a membership organisation, rule 44.3B(1) (b) provides that any such provision which exceeds the likely cost to the receiving party of the premium of an insurance policy against the risk of incurring a liability to pay the costs of other parties to the proceedings is not recoverable. In such circumstances the court will, when assessing the additional liability, have regard to the factors set out in paragraph 11.10 above, in addition to the factors set out in rule 44.5.

Paragraph 11.1 emphasises that a fixed percentage cannot be applied in all cases to the value of the claim in order to ascertain whether or not the costs are proportionate. This provision was inserted because there was gathering support for a school of thought that proportionality could be reduced to a formula that the costs should not, for example, exceed 20% or 33.3% of the claim. Paragraph 11.2 explains why this approach is erroneous. In all proceedings there will be an unavoidable base of costs and of course the lower the claim the higher the base of costs will be proportionately to the amount of the claim. Similarly, para 11.3 emphasises that the length of time taken by the court to deal with a particular issue is not necessarily relevant to the amount of time properly spent on preparing for the trial of that issue.

(c) 'Wood from the trees'

What is the difference between reasonable and proportionate?

SCCO Master O'Hare suggested a 'wood from the trees' test on the basis that proportionality cannot be applied to individual items in isolation, all of which are covered by the requirement of reasonableness, but that you must stand back and look at the matter as a whole to see if the costs are 'in all the circumstances' reasonable. Indeed, he suggests that proportionality has always been an ingredient of reasonableness and that the new rules do little more than emphasise its importance. The 'wood from the trees' test may be helpful at the end of an action, but it is difficult to stand back and apply it to interim hearings. It bears some similarities to the subsequent approach of the Court of Appeal in *Lownds* (see below).

(d) Discrete items

Writing in the *Solicitor's Journal*, 9 July 1999, Gordon Exall suggested that a glib argument that the costs are 'disproportionate' may not succeed and more profitable arguments may be on the lines that the use of an expert was inappropriate, or that the expert used was too expensive for the matters in issue or that an inordinate amount of time was spent on peripheral issues which had little effect on the overall value of the case. Although this is opposite to the 'wood from the trees' approach, it too presaged another aspect of *Lownds*.

(e) Lipton test

Then, there is what is known as the Lipton test. At first I thought it was the 'litmus' test – if the paper turns red the costs are disproportionate! But no such luck. The Lipton approach is for the judge first to calculate the reasonable sum to allow. Second, to consider arguments as to proportionality. Third, to apply any discount for disproportionality and specify to the parties both the higher reasonable figure and the proportionate figure allowed.

(f) Unprincipled ceiling

In *SCT Finance Ltd v John Bolton* ([2002] EWCA Civ 56, [2002] All ER (D) 75 (Jan)) the judge made an order for costs to be ascertained by detailed assessment on the standard basis, but limited the amount to £15,000 because the costs were disproportionate to the amount at stake and because of the paying party's limited means. The judge had already ordered that three sets of the costs of the successful party were to be ascertained by detailed assessment, so the principal effect of the judge's decision to impose a ceiling was to require the costs assessor to disallow costs which, on an overall rather than mechanical view, were disproportionate to the matters in issue and indeed to disallow them if he remained in doubt on the point. The ceiling of £15,000 imposed by the judge was unprincipled. It purported to make allowance for the perceived lack of proportionality of the amount of costs in circumstances where his orders for assessments on the standard basis had already made full allowance for any such lack of proportion. The ceiling would have effect only to the extent of requiring the costs assessor to disallow costs exceeding £15,000 which he had been satisfied were proportionate to the matters in issue. The effect of the ceiling would in that event be to excise from Mr Bolton's liability the excess element of the proportionate costs and would thus be contrary to the judge's primary reason for imposing it. Furthermore, the extent to which it was proper to have regard to Mr Bolton's perceived lack of means, was a factor which would also in any event figure in the assessor's appraisal of proportionality.

(g) Assessment at outset

Judicial guidance was given by the Lord Chief Justice when the Court of Appeal sat in Newcastle-upon-Tyne in *Jefferson v National Freight Carriers plc* [2001] EWCA Civ 2082, [2001] All ER (D) 411 (Feb). He said:

> 'Proportionality is a very important feature of the assessment of costs on the standard basis. This is particularly true in relation to the fast track and if a claimant is going to seek to recover a sum which is substantially in excess of the amount recovered, as was being sought to be recovered in this case, the legal representatives of the claimant at the hearing have to be in a position to help the judge further than was the case here. They first must bear in mind that if they are going to conduct litigation of a modest nature of the sort which was being conducted here, where the likely sum which was to be recovered, even

> on their own Part 36 offer, was a sum below £3000, they are under a heavy duty to conduct that litigation in as economical manner as possible. There is no decision which has been placed before this court indicating precisely what approach should be adopted in exercising the jurisdiction which the judge was exercising. However, we have been shown the decision of the Birmingham County Court on the 22nd June last year, when Judge Alton dealt with the issue in a manner which I regard as of considerable assistance. The judge said in particular "In modern litigation, with the emphasis on proportionality, it is necessary for the parties to make an assessment at the outset of the likely value of the claim and its importance and complexity and then to plan in advance the necessary work, the appropriate level of person to carry out the work, the overall time which it would be necessary and appropriate to spend on the various stages in bringing the action to trial and the likely overall cost. While it was not unusual for costs to exceed the amount in issue, it was, in the context of modern litigation, such as the present case, one reason for seeking to curb the amount of work done and the cost by reference to the need for proportionality." I would respectfully endorse every word of those comments of Judge Alton.'

(h) Reasonable or necessary?

Lownds v Home Office [2002] EWCA Civ 365, [2002] 1 WLR 2450 gave Lord Woolf a further opportunity to consider the application of the principle of proportionality to between-the-parties costs.

(i) Central role in CPR

He described the principle of proportionality as having a direct bearing on the policy on which the effectiveness of the Civil Procedure Rules depends. He continued:

> 'Because of the central role that proportionality should have in the resolution of civil litigation, it is essential that courts should attach the appropriate significance to the requirement of proportionality when making orders for costs and when assessing the amount of costs. What has, however, caused practitioners and the members of the judiciary who have to assess costs difficulty is how to give effect to requirements of proportionality. In particular there is uncertainty as to the relationship between the requirement of reasonableness and the requirement of proportionality. Where there is a conflict between reasonableness and proportionality does one requirement prevail over the other and, if so, which requirement is it that takes precedence? There is also the question of whether the proportionality test is to be applied globally or on an item-by-item basis, or both globally and on an item-by-item basis. These are the questions which directly arise on this appeal and explain why this judgment is so important.'

(ii) Necessary

Quoting paragraph 11.2 of the Costs Practice Direction, Lord Woolf confirmed that solicitors are not required to conduct litigation at rates which are uneconomic and that in a modest claim the proportion of costs is likely to be higher than in a large claim, and 'may even equal or possibly exceed the amount in dispute'. The court held that the words 'which are necessary' are the key to how judges in assessing costs should give effect to the requirement of proportionality. If the appropriate conduct of the proceedings makes costs necessary then the requirement of proportionality does not prevent all the costs being recovered either on an item-by-item approach or on a global approach. Where an item of costs is necessarily incurred then a reasonable amount for the item should normally be disallowed. Any item that is not necessary should be disallowed.

Although when costs are disproportionate it is necessary to determine what was necessary, the court emphasised that a sensible standard of necessity has to be adopted which takes fully into account the need to make allowances for the different judgments which those responsible for litigation can sensibly come to as to what is required. The danger of setting too high a standard with the benefit of hindsight has to be avoided. While the threshold required to meet necessity is higher than that of reasonableness, it is still a standard that a competent practitioner should be able to achieve without undue difficulty. When a practitioner incurs expenses which are reasonable but not necessary, he may be able to recover his fees and disbursements from his client, but extra expense which results from conducting litigation in a disproportionate manner cannot be recovered from the other party.

In deciding what is necessary the conduct of the other party is highly relevant. The other party, by cooperation, can reduce costs; by being uncooperative can increase costs. If he is uncooperative that may render necessary costs which would otherwise be unnecessary and that he should pay the costs for the expense which he has made necessary is perfectly acceptable. Access to justice would be impeded if lawyers felt they could not afford to do what is necessary to conduct the litigation. Giving appropriate weight to the requirements of proportionality and reasonableness will not make the conduct of litigation uneconomic if on the assessment there is allowed a reasonable sum for the work carried out which was necessary.

(iii) Two-stage approach

There has to be a global approach and an item-by-item approach. The global approach will indicate whether the total sum claimed is or appears to be disproportionate having particular regard to the considerations which CPR Rule 44.5(3) states are relevant. If the costs as a whole are not disproportionate according to that test, then all that is normally required is that each item should have been reasonably incurred and the costs for that item are reasonable. If, on the other hand, the costs as a whole appear disproportionate then the court will want to be satisfied that the work in relation to each item was necessary and, if necessary, that the costs of the item are reasonable. If, because of lack of planning or due to other causes, the global costs are disproportionately high, then the requirement that the costs should be proportionate means that no more should be payable than would have been payable if the litigation had been conducted in a proportionate manner. This in turn means that reasonable costs will only be recovered for the items which were necessary if the litigation had been conducted in a proportionate manner. The fact that the litigation had been conducted in an insufficiently rigorous manner to meet the requirement of proportionality does not mean that no costs are recoverable. It means that only those costs which would have been recoverable if the litigation had been appropriately conducted will be recovered. No greater sum can be recovered than that which would have been recoverable item-by-item if the litigation had been conducted proportionately.

(iv) Proportionality

In a case where proportionality is likely to be an issue, a preliminary judgment as to the proportionality of the costs as a whole must be made at the outset. This will ensure that the costs judge applies the correct approach to the detailed assessment. In considering that question, the costs judge will have regard to whether the appropriate level of fee earner or counsel has been deployed, whether offers to settle have been made, whether unnecessary experts have been instructed and the other matters set out in CPR Rule 44.5(3). Once a decision is reached as to proportionality of costs as a whole, the judge will be able to proceed to consider the costs, item-by-item, applying the appropriate test of reasonableness or necessity to each item.

(v) The amounts claimed and recovered

The proportionality of the costs incurred by the claimant should be determined having regard to the sum that it was reasonable for him to believe that he might recover at the time he made the claim. He should be allowed to claim the costs necessary to pursue a reasonable claim, but not allowed to recover costs increased or incurred by putting forward an exaggerated claim.

The proportionality of the costs incurred by the defendant should be determined having regard to the sum that it was reasonable for him to believe that the claimant might recover should his claim succeed. This is likely to be the amount that the claimant has claimed, for a defendant will normally be entitled to take a claim at its face value. A defendant should not be prejudiced if he assumes the claim which was made was one which was reasonable and he incurs costs in contesting the claim on this assumption.

(vi) Not inexpensive

Lord Woolf concluded by conceding that this approach will not make litigation inexpensive but it should help to ensure that costs are kept within proper bounds. Costs assessed in the way indicated will also underline the advantages to a claimant, before embarking on litigation, of making a formal offer to settle which will avoid the risks of litigation if the offer is accepted, or provide a real prospect of obtaining an indemnity order for costs if the offer is rejected.

Lord Woolf said the costs 'may even equal or possibly exceed the amount in dispute', but if the man-in-the-street were asked if he thought this was proportionate, I doubt that he would agree. However, perhaps this may now be the benchmark – a rebuttable presumption that costs which exceed the amount in dispute are disproportionate. It is ironic that in its search for clarity the Court of Appeal has disinterred the old concept of necessity which was buried by the introduction of the CPR.

CPR RULE 44.5 FACTORS TO BE TAKEN INTO ACCOUNT IN DECIDING THE AMOUNT OF COSTS

See Chapter 21.

3. THE INDEMNITY BASIS

(a) Culpability and abuse of process

The requirement that the costs must be proportionate does not apply to costs on the indemnity basis, as a result of which an order for costs on the indemnity basis has the potential to hit a paying party much harder than before. Traditionally costs on the indemnity basis have been awarded only where there has been some culpability or abuse of process such as:

(a) deceit or underhandedness;
(b) abuse of the courts procedure;
(c) not coming to court with open hands;
(d) tenuous claims;
(e) unjustified defences;
(f) voluminous and unnecessary evidence; or
(g) extraneous motives for the litigation.

Examples

Cooper v P & O Stena Line Ltd [1999] 1 Lloyd's Rep 734, QBD (Admiralty Court): In an action for personal injuries, an allegation of malingering is a serious allegation of fraud and has to be pleaded. If the defendant had undertaken a proper investigation it was unlikely they would have defended on liability at all and in terms of quantum there never had been sufficient material on which to base the allegation of fraud. The unusual circumstances of the case justified the award of costs on the indemnity basis.

Griffiths v British Coal Corpn ((1999) The Personal and Medical Injuries Law Letter, February, QBD): there were two broad generic issues, namely medical and liability. After taking into account that not all the generic medical costs had been unreasonably incurred and that only some of the liability costs would have been unreasonably incurred, the judge ordered the whole of the costs of the generic medical issues to be paid on the indemnity basis and the costs in respect of liability to be on the standard basis.

Amoco v British American Offshore Ltd (QBD Butterworths Costs Service Bulletin, January 2002): The claimant sought to avoid a contract which had become unprofitable by putting pressure on the defendant to renegotiate and, when this failed, terminating the contract. The grounds of termination were different to those subsequently put forward at the trial. The claimant lost heavily and was ordered to pay costs on the indemnity basis because it had conducted itself throughout on the basis that its commercial interests took precedence over the rights and wrongs of the matter, and had then sought to justify its stance by a constantly changing case.

(b) No culpability or abuse of process

Examples

Reid Minty (a firm) v Taylor ([2001] EWCA Civ 1723, [2002] 2 All ER 150): A party can be ordered to pay costs on the indemnity basis under CPR Rule 44.3 even though there had been no moral lack of probity or conduct deserving of moral condemnation on its part. The provision included a discretion to decide whether some or all of the costs awarded should be on the standard or indemnity basis. If costs were awarded on the indemnity basis, in many cases there would be some implicit expression of disapproval of the way in which the litigation had been conducted, but that would not necessarily be so in every case. Litigation could be conducted in a way which was unreasonable and which justified an award of costs on the indemnity basis, but which could not properly be regarded as lacking moral probity or deserving moral condemnation. It would not be right, however, that every defendant in every case could put themselves in the way of claiming indemnity costs simply by inviting the claimant at an early stage to give up and pay the defendant's costs. It might be different if the defendant offered to move some way towards the claimant's position and the result was more favourable to the defendant than that.

In the Matter of the Continental Assurance Co (in liquidation), Singer v Beckett (13 June 2001, unreported): Park J expressly disavowed his disapproval of some of the conduct of the liquidators as being the reason for his award of costs against them being on the indemnity basis. He did take into account what the consequences of the choice would be and where it would be appropriate for the benefit of any doubt to lie. There is a prima facie steer in the CPR that in the normal case costs should be awarded on the standard basis so that the benefit of any doubt should go to the paying party. However, this was not a normal, but a wholly exceptional, case where it would be wrong and unacceptable for matters to be resolved against the respondents. The liquidators had pursued all issues at full length and right to the end, with the result that the amount of costs incurred must have been enormous. It was appropriate the costs of the successful respondents should be assessed on the indemnity basis so that they, and not the liquidators, received the benefit of any doubts.

In future it will be interesting to see if a new line of awards on the indemnity basis emerges on the grounds that, although the costs were disproportionate to the matters in issue, there nevertheless were good reasons for incurring them and therefore the award should be on the indemnity basis, to avoid the risk of reduction on the ground of disproportionality on the detailed assessment.

(c) Part 36 offer

Costs on the indemnity basis may also be awarded as the result of a Part 36 offer. See Chapter 14.

(d) Indemnity costs refused

In *John v Price Waterhouse (a firm)* ([2002] 1 WLR 953) the defendants had successfully resisted the claimant's claim arising out of their conduct as auditors of the claimant companies. The defendants sought an order for costs on the indemnity basis on the grounds that as auditors they were entitled to be indemnified out of the assets of the companies against all their costs under the provisions of Table A. It was held that in their role of litigants the defendants were entitled only to an order for costs on the standard basis. There was nothing to prevent the auditors from seeking to recover the difference between standard costs and indemnity costs in separate proceedings to enforce the relevant contractual terms.

CPR RULE 44.6 FIXED COSTS

A party may recover the fixed costs specified in Part 45 in accordance with that Part.

See Chapter 25 for Part 45 with the relevant practice direction and narrative.

CPR RULE 44.7 PROCEDURE FOR ASSESSING COSTS

Where the court orders a party to pay costs to another party (other than fixed costs) it may either—

(a) make a summary assessment of the costs; or

(b) order detailed assessment of the costs by a costs officer,

unless any rule, practice direction or other enactment provides otherwise.

(The costs practice direction sets out the factors which will affect the court's decision under this rule)

SECTION 12: PRACTICE DIRECTION SUPPLEMENTING CPR RULE 44.7

12.1 Where the court does not order fixed costs (or no fixed costs are provided for) the amount of costs payable will be assessed by the court. This rule allows the court making an order about costs either

(a) to make a summary assessment of the amount of the costs, or

(b) to order the amount to be decided in accordance with Part 47 (a detailed assessment).

12.2 An order for costs will be treated as an order for the amount of costs to be decided by a detailed assessment unless the order otherwise provides.
12.3 Whenever the court awards costs to be assessed by way of detailed assessment it should consider whether to exercise the power in rule 44.3(8) (Courts Discretion as to Costs) to order the paying party to pay such sum of money as it thinks just on account of those costs.

See Chapter 29 for summary assessment and Chapter 30 for detailed assessment with the relevant practice directions and narrative.

CPR RULE 44.8 TIME FOR COMPLYING WITH AN ORDER FOR COSTS

A party must comply with an order for the payment of costs within 14 days of—

(a) the date of the judgment or order if it states the amount of those costs;
(b) if the amount of those costs (or part of them) is decided later in accordance with Part 47, the date of the certificate which states the amount; or
(c) in either case, such later date as the court may specify.

(Part 47 sets out the procedure for detailed assessment of costs)

4. REVOLUTIONARY

This rule contains the revolutionary requirement that all orders for costs, both interim and final, must be paid within 14 days of assessment. Hitherto, the rules precluded the assessment of interim costs until the conclusion of the action and therefore the order for costs had no immediate consequences. Indeed if the action were subsequently settled interim orders for costs were invariably subsumed in the overall agreement. However, now not only is it expected that interim costs will be assessed at the end of the hearing, but they are to be paid within 14 days. Clients realise that their lawyers have lost a battle and they will have to put their hands in their pockets and part with their money at an early stage of the proceedings. The provision appears to have resulted in a marked reduction in the number of interim applications, and certainly concentrates minds on costs at an early stage in the proceedings.

5. CONDITIONAL FEES

If the party who has been ordered to pay the costs of an interlocutory hearing is funded under a conditional fee agreement such an order could have serious consequences. Most indemnity insurance policies in respect of orders to pay the other party's costs, exclude orders for payment of interlocutory costs. The result will be that either the client, or his solicitors on his behalf, will have to pay the costs.

6. NON-PAYMENT

On 12 March 1999 the Vice Chancellor wrote to all judges suggesting that if there were a conditional fee agreement the judge should consider staying any order for costs until the end of the action, and consider not requiring a payment on account if he orders a detailed assessment. Why should this particular method of funding be given preferential treatment over a party who is funding the litigation himself, perhaps with a bank overdraft or by selling investments? He too will have to put his hand in his, or his funder's, pocket because his legal representative has fought and lost a battle. If it is thought unfair that the receiving party should have to wait to the end of the litigation before receiving his costs, it will not be any less unfair because his adversary has chosen one method of funding in preference to another.

The Supreme Court Costs Office *Guide to the Summary Assessment of Costs* used to advise:

> '28 Before deciding to defer payment of costs where the paying party has agreed conditional fee terms with his solicitor the court should consider:
>
> (i) whether such orders should also be made in the case of those litigants of modest means who do not agree no win no fee terms with their solicitors. Such litigants would, on the face of it, be ordered to pay the amount of any summarily assessed costs within 14 days in the normal way.
>
> (ii) Whether an order for payment of the costs forthwith might bring the action to an end and whether this would be just in all the circumstances.'

It now contents itself with:

> '33 As a general rule a paying party should be ordered to pay the amount of any summarily assessed costs within 14 days. Before making such an order the court should consider whether an order for payment of the costs might bring the action to an end and whether this would be just in all the circumstances.'

What happens if the costs are not paid within 14 days? Rule 3.1(2)(*a*) provides that the court may extend any time prescribed by the rules and therefore if a party ordered to pay interlocutory costs is unable to do so within 14 days he should apply to the judge conducting the hearing for an extension. Although the courts are concerned that an order to pay interim costs should not stifle meritorious litigation, an application for an extension must be supported by adequate evidence: *Pepin v Watts* [2000] All ER (D) 1262. It is intended that such extensions will not readily be granted. It appears that the order will be enforceable as a civil debt after the expiration of 14 days but it will not preclude the defaulting party from continuing with the proceedings. In *Stevens v School of Oriental and African Studies* (2001) Times, 2 February where an earlier action had been struck out with an order for costs, it was held to be reasonable to stay further proceedings arising out of the same facts until the costs of the first action had been paid.

CPR RULE 44.9 COSTS ON THE SMALL CLAIMS TRACK AND FAST TRACK

See Chapter 26.

CPR RULE 44.10 LIMITATION ON AMOUNT COURT MAY ALLOW WHERE A CLAIM ALLOCATED TO THE FAST TRACK SETTLES BEFORE TRIAL

See Chapter 27.

CPR RULE 44.11 COSTS FOLLOWING ALLOCATION AND RE-ALLOCATION

(1) Any costs orders made before a claim is allocated will not be affected by allocation.

(2) Where—

  (a) a claim is allocated to a track; and

(b) the court subsequently re-allocates that claim to a different track,
then unless the court orders otherwise, any special rules about costs applying—
(i) to the first track, will apply to the claim up to the date of re-allocation; and
(ii) to the second track, will apply from the date of re-allocation.
(Part 26 deals with the allocation and re-allocation of claims between tracks)

SECTION 16: PRACTICE DIRECTION SUPPLEMENTING CPR RULE 44.11

16.1 This paragraph applies where the court is about to make an order to re-allocate a claim from the small claims track to another track.
16.2 Before making the order to re-allocate the claim, the court must decide whether any party is to pay costs to any other party down to the date of the order to re-allocate in accordance with the rules about costs contained in Part 27 (The Small Claims Track).
16.3 If it decides to make such an order about costs, the court will make a summary assessment of those costs in accordance with that Part.

CPR RULE 44.12 CASES WHERE COSTS ORDERS DEEMED TO HAVE BEEN MADE

(1) Where a right to costs arises under—
(a) rule 3.7 (defendant's right to costs where claim struck out for non-payment of fees);
(b) rule 36.13 (1) (claimant's right to costs where he accepts defendant's Part 36 offer or Part 36 payment);
(c) rule 36.14 (claimant's right to costs where defendant accepts the claimant's Part 36 offer); or
(d) rule 38.6 (defendant's right to costs where claimant discontinues),
a costs order will be deemed to have been made on the standard basis.
(2) Interest payable pursuant to section 17 of the Judgments Act 1838 or section 74 of the County Courts Act 1984 on the costs deemed to have been ordered under paragraph (1) shall begin to run from the date on which the event which gave rise to the entitlement to costs occurred.

CPR RULE 44.12A COSTS-ONLY PROCEEDINGS

(1) This rule sets out a procedure which may be followed where—
(a) the parties to a dispute have reached an agreement on all issues (including which party is to pay the costs) which is made or confirmed in writing; but
(b) they have failed to agree the amount of those costs; and
(c) no proceedings have been started.
(2) Either party to the agreement may start proceedings under this rule by issuing a claim form in accordance with Part 8.
(3) The claim form must contain or be accompanied by the agreement or confirmation.
(4) In proceedings to which this rule applies the court—
(a) may
(i) make an order for costs to be determined by detailed assessment; or
(ii) dismiss the claim;
and
(b) must dismiss the claim if it is opposed.

(5) Rule 48.3 (amount of costs where costs are payable pursuant to a contract) does not apply to claims started under the procedure in this rule.
(Rule 7.2 provides that proceedings are started when the court issues a claim form at the request of the claimant).
(Rule 8.1(6) provides that a practice direction may modify the Part 8 procedure).

SECTION 17: PRACTICE DIRECTION SUPPLEMENTING CPR RULE 44.12A

17.1 A claim form under this rule should not be issued in the High Court unless the dispute to which the agreement relates was of such a value or type that had proceedings been begun they would have been commenced in the High Court.
17.2 A claim form which is to be issued in the High Court at the Royal Courts of Justice will be issued in the Supreme Court Costs Office.
17.3 Attention is drawn to rule 8.2 (in particular to paragraph (b)(ii)) and to rule 44.12A(3). The claim form must:
(1) identify the claim or dispute to which the agreement to pay costs relates;
(2) state the date and terms of the agreement on which the claimant relies;
(3) set out or have attached to it a draft of the order which the claimant seeks;
(4) state the amount of the costs claimed; and,
(5) state whether the costs are claimed on the standard or indemnity basis. If no basis is specified the costs will be treated as being claimed on the standard basis.
17.4 The evidence to be filed and served with the claim form under Rule 8.5 must include copies of the documents on which the claimant relies to prove the defendant's agreement to pay costs.
17.5 A costs judge or a district judge has jurisdiction to hear and decide any issue which may arise in a claim issued under this rule irrespective of the amount of the costs claimed or of the value of the claim to which the agreement to pay costs relates. A costs officer may make an order by consent under paragraph 17.7, or an order dismissing a claim under paragraph 17.9 below.
17.6 When the time for filing the defendant's acknowledgement of service has expired, the claimant may by letter request the court to make an order in the terms of his claim, unless the defendant has filed an acknowledgement of service stating that he intends to contest the claim or to seek a different order.
17.7 Rule 40.6 applies where an order is to be made by consent. An order may be made by consent in terms which differ from those set out in the claim form.
17.8
(1) An order for costs made under this rule will be treated as an order for the amount of costs to be decided by a detailed assessment to which Part 47 and the practice directions relating to it apply. Rule 44.4(4) (determination of basis of assessment) also applies to the order.
(2) In cases in which an additional liability is claimed, the costs judge or district judge should have regard to the time when and the extent to which the claim has been settled and to the fact that the claim has been settled without the need to commence proceedings.
17.9
(1) For the purposes of rule 44.12A(4)(b)—
(a) a claim will be treated as opposed if the defendant files an acknowledgment of service stating that he intends to contest the making of an order for costs or to seek a different remedy; and
(b) a claim will not be treated as opposed if the defendant files an acknowledgment of service stating that he disputes the amount of the claim for costs.

(2) An order dismissing the claim will be made as soon as an acknowledgment of service opposing the claim is filed. The dismissal of a claim under rule 44.12A(4) does not prevent the claimant from issuing another claim form under Part 7 or Part 8 based on the agreement or alleged agreement to which the proceedings under this rule related.

17.10

(1) Rule 8.9 (which provides that claims issued under Part 8 shall be treated as allocated to the multi-track) shall not apply to claims issued under this rule. A claim issued under this rule may be dealt with without being allocated to a track.

(2) Rule 8.1(3) and Part 24 do not apply to proceedings brought under rule 44.12A.

17.11 Nothing in this rule prevents a person from issuing a claim form under Part 7 or Part 8 to sue on an agreement made in settlement of a dispute where that agreement makes provision for costs, nor from claiming in that case an order for costs or a specified sum in respect of costs.

From 3 July, 2000 the Civil Procedure (Amendment No 3) Rules 2000 introduced this new rule which contains a useful procedure to be followed where parties to a dispute have reached an agreement on all issues, including which party is to pay the costs, but have failed to agree the amount of the costs where no proceedings have been started. In these circumstances, either party may start proceedings by issuing a claim form in accordance with Part 8. The claim form must contain or be accompanied by the agreement or confirmation. The court may either make an order for costs or dismiss the claim. It must dismiss the claim if the application is opposed.

Senior Costs Judge Peter Hurst gave guidance to the Designated Civil Judges as follows:

> 'CPR Rule 44.12A was introduced with effect from 3 July 2000 to provide a procedure enabling parties who have settled the substantive dispute between them to resolve any outstanding question relating to costs.
>
> The new procedure appears to be being misused by both claimants and defendants in breach of the overriding objective. This misuse has given rise to difficulties for District Judges. It appears that solicitors acting on behalf of claimants, having settled the amount of damages, are saying to defendants' insurers: 'Our costs are £x and if this figure is not agreed/paid within 14 days costs-only proceedings will be commenced'. In one court there has been a bulk issue of 800 applications.
>
> Defendants' representatives for their part make unreasonably low offers in respect of pre-proceedings costs and in some cases accompany the offer with a statement that the offer is made for the purpose of negotiation only and that they do not agree to the matter being resolved by use of the costs only procedure.
>
> If a claimant is forced to commence proceedings under Part 7, rather than costs only proceedings under Part 8, defendants will find themselves having to pay, not only the reasonable and proportionate costs of the claim itself, but also the costs of the Part 7 proceedings and any related assessment proceedings. If the defendant has acted unreasonably in compelling the commencement of Part 7 proceedings, consideration should be given to making an order for costs on the indemnity basis.
>
> Two distinct steps are required: firstly the Part 8 application seeking an order for costs; and secondly detailed assessment of those costs.
>
> The intention is that the proceedings should effectively be brought with the consent of both parties as a convenient means of resolving the dispute over costs. If the acknowledgement of service indicates that the application is not opposed the court may make an order for costs without a hearing. (It is recognised that at present Form N210 makes no provision for indicating that the claim is not opposed. This is being addressed).
>
> Paragraph (9) sets out the circumstances in which the court may dismiss the application without a hearing.

The procedure under Rule 44.12A is intended to be cheap and straightforward. The steps are as follows:

(1) The parties must have reached an agreement on all the issues including which party is to pay the costs.
(2) That agreement must be made or confirmed in writing.
(3) No proceedings must have been started and the parties (after a proper attempt at agreement) must have failed to agree the amount of the costs.
(4) Either party may start costs-only proceedings under Rule 44.12A.
(5) The Part 8 claim form must:
    (a) identify the claim or dispute to which the agreement to pay costs relates;
    (b) state the date and terms of the agreement on which the claimant relies:
    (c) set out a draft of the order sought;
    (d) state the amount of the costs claimed: and
    (e) state whether costs are claimed on the standard or the indemnity basis
(6) The evidence field in support of the claim must include copies of the documents on which the claimant relies to prove the defendant's agreement to pay the costs.
(7) The matter should not be listed before the District Judge until an acknowledgment of service has been filed. If the defendant agrees that the order should be made, or a consent order is filed, the court will make the order without the necessity of a hearing.
(8) If the time for filing acknowledgement of service expires, the claimant may request the court by letter to make an order in the terms of the claim. If the defendant files an acknowledgement of service out of time but before the court has made an order in the terms of the claim, paragraph (9) applies.
(9) The court may (i) make an order for costs; or, (ii) dismiss the claim. The court must dismiss the claim if it is opposed. A claim is treated as opposed if the defendant states in the acknowledgement of service that it intends to consent the proceedings or to seek a different remedy. The court will then dismiss the claim without a hearing.
(10) The court may make an order by consent in terms which differ from those set out in the claim form. The order is treated as an order or the amount of costs to be decided by detailed assessment.

In no circumstances should a District Judge or Costs Judge attempt to hear the application and then immediately embark upon a summary assessment of the costs in dispute. Arguments that the District Judge/Costs Judge should do so are incorrect, since a summary assessment is an assessment made by a Judge who has decided the substantive issue. In costs only proceedings the only issue decided by the Judge is whether or not there should be an assessment of the costs.

It is accepted that for bills of modest size detailed assessment may be unnecessarily cumbersome and consideration is being given to introducing either a disposal procedure or a short form of bill in order to overcome this problem.'

CPR RULE 44.13 SPECIAL SITUATIONS

(1) Where the court makes an order which does not mention costs—
  (a) the general rule is that no party is entitled to costs in relation to that order; but
  (b) this does not affect any entitlement of a party to recover costs out of a fund held by him as trustee or personal representative, or pursuant to any lease, mortgage or other security.

(2) The court hearing an appeal may, unless it dismisses the appeal, make orders about the costs of the proceedings giving rise to the appeal as well as the costs of the appeal.

(3) Where proceedings are transferred from one court to another, the court to which they are transferred may deal with all the costs, including the costs before the transfer.

(4) Paragraph (3) is subject to any order of the court which ordered the transfer.

Section 1 confirms that the rights of a party against a fund are not affected by the absence of an order for costs.

CPR RULE 44.14 COURT'S POWERS IN RELATION TO MISCONDUCT

See Chapter 30.

CPR RULE 44.15 PROVIDING INFORMATION ABOUT FUNDING ARRANGEMENTS

See Chapter 30.

CPR RULE 44.16 ADJOURNMENT WHERE LEGAL REPRESENTATIVE SEEKS TO CHALLENGE DISALLOWANCE OF ANY AMOUNT OF PERCENTAGE INCREASE

See Chapter 30.

CPR RULE 44.17 APPLICATION OF COSTS RULES

See Chapter 32.

CHAPTER 12

VAT BETWEEN THE PARTIES

1. THE SOLICITOR AND CLIENT BILL

In litigation the court may order one party to the action to pay costs to the other party, usually the winner, or the parties may settle the action on the basis that one party will pay the agreed or taxed costs of the other party. The winner's solicitors must nevertheless deliver to their own client a full solicitor and client bill, including VAT (see p 28).

2. WINNER NOT REGISTERED

Where the winner is not registered for VAT or the legal services are not supplied in connection with his business, he cannot recover the VAT payable on his solicitor and client costs. An amount equal to VAT at the current rate should therefore be added to the between-the-parties costs. This is not a payment of VAT but is to indemnify the winner for the VAT he will pay on the proportionate part of his solicitor and client costs. The winner's solicitors have not supplied any kind of service to the loser and there is therefore no question of the loser reclaiming or deducting VAT in respect of those costs. Because it is not a payment of VAT by the loser, he is not entitled to a VAT invoice for the between the parties costs, nor is he entitled to recoup the payment even if he is registered for VAT. Indeed, the Law Society recommends that the paying party should receive a note of the other party's costs in such terms that it cannot be mistaken for a tax invoice. This may be done, for example by clearly marking the copy of the bill sent to the paying party with the words 'this is not a tax invoice' or – if acceptable to the paying party – by issuing a summary of the bill without a VAT registration number and without the tax element identified.

3. WINNER REGISTERED

(a) Fully registered

Where the winner is registered for VAT and the legal services are supplied in the course of his business, he will be entitled to an input tax credit and therefore able to recover the VAT paid to his solicitor. In such a case the receiving party does not need indemnifying and should not claim VAT on his profit costs or disbursements, including counsel's fees, as between the parties. On an assessment of between-the-parties costs the onus is on the paying party to object to the inclusion of an indemnity for VAT.

(b) Partly exempt

Where the solicitor's client is a partly exempt registered taxable person he is not entitled to be indemnified for VAT to the extent that he can obtain credit for input tax.

4. SECTION 5: PRACTICE DIRECTION SUPPLEMENTING CPR PART 43

Section 5 of the Costs Practice Direction, 'Special Provisions Relating to VAT' (set out below) incorporates the provision of the Supreme Court Taxing Office Practice Direction of 1994. Its provisions have been agreed between HM Customs and Excise, the Lord Chancellor's Department, the Legal Aid Board (now Legal Services Commission), the Law Society and the Supreme Court Costs Office.

SECTION 5 SPECIAL PROVISIONS RELATING TO VAT

5.1 This section deals with claims for value added tax (VAT) which are made in respect of costs being dealt with by way of summary assessment or detailed assessment.

VAT Registration Number

5.2 The number allocated by HM Customs and Excise to every person registered under the Value Added Tax Act 1983 (except a Government Department) must appear in a prominent place at the head of every statement, bill of costs, fee sheet, account or voucher on which VAT is being included as part of a claim for costs.

Entitlement to VAT on costs

5.3 VAT should not be included in a claim for costs if the receiving party is able to recover the VAT as input tax. Where the receiving party is able to obtain credit from HM Customs and Excise for a proportion of the VAT as input tax, only that proportion which is not eligible for credit should be included in the claim for costs.

5.4 The receiving party has responsibility for ensuring that VAT is claimed only when the receiving party is unable to recover the VAT or a proportion thereof as input tax.

5.5 Where there is a dispute as to whether VAT is properly claimed the receiving party must provide a certificate signed by the solicitors or the auditors of the receiving party substantially in the form illustrated in Precedent F in the Schedule of Costs Precedents annexed to this Practice Direction. Where the receiving party is a litigant in person who is claiming VAT, reference should be made by him to HM Customs and Excise and wherever possible a Statement to similar effect produced at the hearing at which the costs are assessed.

5.6 Where there is a dispute as to whether any service in respect of which a charge is proposed to be made in the bill is zero rated or exempt, reference should be made to HM Customs and Excise and wherever possible the view of HM Customs and Excise obtained and made known at the hearing at which the costs are assessed. Such application should be made by the receiving party. In the case of a bill from a solicitor to his own client, such application should be made by the client.

Form of bill of costs where VAT rate changes

5.7 Where there is a change in the rate of VAT, suppliers of goods and services are entitled by ss 88(1) and 88(2) of the VAT Act 1994 in most circumstances to elect whether the new or the old rate of VAT should apply to a supply where the basic and actual tax points span a period during which there has been a change in VAT rates.

5.8 It will be assumed, unless a contrary indication is given in writing, that an election to take advantage of the provisions mentioned in paragraph 5.7 above and to charge VAT at the lower rate has been made. In any case in which an election to charge at the lower rate is not made, such a decision must be justified to the court assessing the costs.

Apportionment

5.9 All bills of costs, fees and disbursements on which VAT is included must be divided into separate parts so as to show work done before, on and after the date or dates from which any change in the rate of VAT takes effect. Where, however, a lump sum charge is made for work which spans a period during which there has been a change in VAT rates, and paragraphs 5.7 and 5.8 above do not apply, reference should be made to paragraphs 8 and 9 of Appendix F of Customs' Notice 700 (or any revised edition of that notice), a copy of which should be in the possession of every registered trader. If necessary, the lump sum should be apportioned. The totals of profit costs and disbursements in each part must be carried separately to the summary.

5.10 Should there be a change in the rate between the conclusion of a detailed assessment and the issue of the final costs certificate, any interested party may apply for the detailed assessment to be varied so as to take account of any increase or reduction in the amount of tax payable. Once the final costs certificate has been issued, no variation under this paragraph will be permitted.

Disbursements

5.11 Petty (or general) disbursements such as postage, fares etc which are normally treated as part of a solicitor's overheads and included in his profit costs should be charged with VAT even though they bear no tax when the solicitor incurs them. The cost of travel by public transport on a specific journey for a particular client where it forms part of the service rendered by a solicitor to his client and is charged in his bill of costs, attracts VAT.

5.12 Reference is made to the criteria set out in the VAT Guide (Customs and Excise Notice 700 – 1st August 1991 edition paragraph 83, or any revised edition of that Notice), as to expenses which are not subject to VAT. Charges for the cost of travel by public transport, postage, telephone calls and telegraphic transfers where these form part of the service rendered by the solicitor to his client are examples of charges which do not satisfy these criteria and are thus liable to VAT at the standard rate.

Legal Aid/LSC funding

5.13 VAT will be payable in respect of every supply made pursuant to a Legal Aid/ LSC Certificate provided only that the person making the supply is a taxable person and that the assisted person/ LSC funded client is not resident outside the European Union. Where the assisted person/ LSC funded client is registered for VAT and the legal services paid for by the LSC are in connection with that person's business, the VAT on those services will be payable by the LSC only.

5.14 Any summary of costs payable by the LSC must be drawn so as to show the total VAT on Counsel's fees as a separate item from the VAT on other disbursements and the VAT on profit costs.

Tax invoice

5.15 A bill of costs filed for detailed assessment is always retained by the Court. Accordingly if a solicitor waives his solicitor and client costs and accepts the costs certified by the court as payable by the unsuccessful party in settlement, it will be necessary for a short statement as to the amount of the certified costs and the VAT thereon to be prepared for use as the tax invoice.

Vouchers

5.16 Where receipted accounts for disbursements made by the solicitor or his client are retained as tax invoices a photostat copy of any such receipted account may be produced and will be accepted as sufficient evidence of payment when disbursements are vouched.

Certificates

5.17 In a costs certificate payable by the LSC, the VAT on solicitor's costs, Counsel's fees and disbursements will be shown separately.

Litigants acting in person

5.18 Where a litigant acts in litigation on his own behalf he is not treated for the purposes of VAT as having supplied services and therefore no VAT is chargeable in respect of work done by that litigant (even where, for example, that litigant is a solicitor or other legal representative).
5.19 Consequently in the circumstances described in the preceding paragraph, a bill of costs presented for agreement or assessment should not claim any VAT which will not be allowed on assessment.

Government departments

5.20 On an assessment between parties, where costs are being paid to a Government Department in respect of services rendered by its legal staff, VAT should not be added.

5. INSURANCE COMPANIES

Where the bill to be assessed relates to proceedings taken in the name of an insured by his insurance company, usually arising out of a road traffic accident, the fact that the insurance company is not liable for VAT is irrelevant in deciding whether or not VAT is recoverable. The question of whether or not the VAT is recoverable is answered by the lay client's VAT position and not that of the insurance company (*Law Society Gazette*, 15 January 1986, vol 83, p 90).

6. EMPLOYED SOLICITORS

Where costs have been awarded to a party, some of whose work has been done by a solicitor employee, there has been no supply of services attracting VAT and there is therefore no necessity for him to seek indemnity in respect of VAT on those legal expenses from the paying party.

7. DISPUTES

If there is a dispute about whether or not a party is liable for VAT or able to reclaim VAT and the matter cannot be resolved by agreement, the court will direct the party whose bill it is to obtain a certificate, either from HM Customs and Excise or from their accountants, as to the correct VAT position.

CHAPTER 13

SECURITY FOR COSTS

1. GENERALLY

One party to litigation may be ordered to provide security for the costs of the other party in the very limited circumstances prescribed by the Companies Act 1985, s 726(1), CPR Rules 25.12–25.15 and the Arbitration Act 1996, s 38. Only under the Arbitration Act 1996 might an individual party resident in the UK be ordered to give security.

2. AGAINST A LIMITED COMPANY

(a) Companies Act 1985, s 726(1)

> 'Where in England a limited company is plaintiff [*complainant*] in an action or other legal proceeding, the court having jurisdiction in the matter may, if it appears by credible testimony that there is reason to believe that the company will be unable to pay the defendant's costs if successful in his defence, require sufficient securities to be given for those costs, and may stay all proceedings until the security is given.'

The phrase 'other legal proceedings' refers to any matter in which the jurisdiction of the court is invoked and accordingly an application for security for costs can be made against a company which brings a petition under the Companies Act 1985, s 459 (*Re Unisoft Group Ltd* [1993] BCLC 528, Ch D). The section also empowers the court to grant security for costs against a company which has been granted leave to move by way of judicial review (*R v Westminster City Council, ex p Residents' Association of Mayfair* [1991] COD 182, QBD).

(b) Inability to pay

The fact that a company is in liquidation is, on the face of it, evidence that it is unable to pay the defendant's costs unless evidence to the contrary is given (*Northampton Coal, Iron and Waggon Co v Midland Waggon Co* (1878) 7 Ch D 500, CA). Otherwise, an application for security must be supported by an affidavit which credibly and reasonably shows the inability of the company to pay the costs if the defendant were successful. The mere issuing of a debenture charging all the company's assets is not a sufficient reason to order security. Where a company's accountant deposed to there being sufficient cash-flow to meet an order for costs despite a shortage of assets the court accepted this in the absence of expert evidence to the contrary (*Kim Barker Ltd v Aegon Insurance Co (UK) Ltd* (1989) Times, 9 October, CA).

(c) Discretion

In *Sir Lindsay Parkinson & Co Ltd v Triplan Ltd* [1973] QB 609, CA, Lord Denning identified the following circumstances which the court might take into account in exercising its discretion:

(i) Whether the claimant's claim is bona fide and not a sham.
(ii) Whether the claimant has a reasonably good prospect of success.
(iii) Whether there is an admission by the defendant on the pleadings or elsewhere that the money is due.
(iv) Whether there is a substantial payment into court or an 'open offer' of a substantial amount.
(v) Whether the application for security is being used oppressively, eg so as to stifle a genuine claim.
(vi) Whether the claimant's want of means is being brought about by any conduct by the defendants, such as delay in payment or in doing their part of the work.
(vii) Whether the application for security is made at a late stage of the proceedings.

(d) No order if oppressive

Where an order for security for costs against the claimant company might result in oppression in that the claimant company would be forced to abandon a claim which had a reasonable prospect of success, the court is entitled to refuse to make that order notwithstanding that the claimant company, if unsuccessful, will be unable to pay the defendant's costs (*Aquila Design (GRB Products) Ltd v Cornhill Insurance plc* [1988] BCLC 134, CA). It is not necessary for the company to produce evidence of its inability to pursue the proceedings if the order is made for the application to be dismissed; it is sufficient if the company shows that there is a probability that it will be unable to pursue the proceedings. Unless it is clearly demonstrable one way or the other it is not appropriate to go into the merits of the claim in such an application (*Trident International Freight Services Ltd v Manchester Ship Canal Co* [1990] BCLC 263, CA). *Europa Holdings Ltd v Circle Industries (UK) plc* [1993] BCLC 320, CA was another example. The claimants were a small company operating on a limited turnover with a net deficit in a time of great depression. It was a solvent and prudently managed company with a genuine claim for payments for work done. It would be oppressive to force the claimant to abandon its claim by ordering it to give security for costs. Yet another example was *Edmund Murray v VSP International Foundations* (1993) Current Law Week, 8 October, CA in which the Court of Appeal set aside an order for security for costs on the ground that the claimants were simply unable to meet it and would be forced to abandon their claim, which was acknowledged to be a credible one, and thus denied justice. The detriment to the claimant would be worse if the order was made than to the defendant if it were not, and the order was quashed.

On a company limited by guarantee being granted leave to move by way of judicial review the respondents applied for security for costs. The Companies Act 1985, s 726(1) empowered the court to enquire into a limited company's financial position and to stay proceedings until sufficient security for costs is provided. The application for security was granted, the court finding that in the circumstances an order for security for costs would not stifle the litigation as those behind the application would be able to find the resources if they wished the matter to proceed (*R v Westminster City Council, ex p Residents' Association of Mayfair* [1991] COD 182, QBD). See also 'Amount' on p 126.

(e) Northern Ireland company

In *Raeburn v Andrews* (1874) LR 9 QB 118, it was held that security for costs should no longer be ordered against a claimant resident in another part of the UK; there was no reason to discriminate against the claimant by treating him differently from a claimant similarly placed but resident in England. In *DSQ Property Co Ltd v Lotus*

Cars Ltd (1990) Times, 28 June, CA, the claimant company, which was incorporated and resident in Northern Ireland, was in receivership and liquidation. If the company were resident in England, security for costs could have been ordered under the Companies Act 1985, s 726 and there was no reason in principle why security for costs should not be ordered against the claimant. To order otherwise would mean that an insolvent company incorporated and resident in Northern Ireland would be in a uniquely favourable position enjoyed by no other insolvent company incorporated anywhere in the world, in or out of the UK.

(f) Co-claimant

Where the defendants obtained an order for security for costs against a claimant company which was not complied with, this did not entitle them to an order for security against an individual claimant as a condition of him being joined in the proceedings. The law offered the defendants no protection against costs which could not be paid by impoverished personal claimants (*Eurocross Sales Ltd v Cornhill Insurance plc* [1995] 4 All ER 950, CA).

(g) No assignment to avoid giving security

In *Hendry v Chartsearch Ltd* [1998] CLC 1382, CA, the claimant company was in financial difficulties and could not afford to give security for costs. Accordingly, it transferred and assigned its causes of action to its chairman and majority shareholder who commenced proceedings. The contract precluded assignment without the prior consent of the defendants, which was not to be unreasonably refused. The Companies Act 1985 gave the defendant a statutory right which protected them from being sued by an impecunious limited company without security for their costs. It could not be regarded as unreasonable for the defendant to insist upon that statutory right and refuse consent to assignment. If the individual assignee were willing to provide security on the same terms as if he were the company then the defendant could not reasonably refuse its consent on that ground. But that was not the position in this case.

3. FOREIGN CLAIMANT

RSC Order 23, Rule 1 and CCR Order 13, Rule 8 were preserved by the Schedules to the CPR but these were revoked in March 2000 and replaced by CPR Rules 25.12–25.15. Here they are:

CPR RULE 25.12 SECURITY FOR COSTS

(1) A defendant to any claim may apply under this Section of this Part for security for his costs of the proceedings.
(Part 3 provides for the court to order payment of sums into court in other circumstances. Rule 20.3 provides for this Section of this Part to apply to Part 20 claims)
(2) An application for security for costs must be supported by written evidence.
(3) Where the court makes an order for security for costs, it will—
- (a) determine the amount of security; and
- (b) direct—
  - (i) the manner in which; and
  - (ii) the time within which

  the security must be given.

CPR RULE 25.13 CONDITIONS TO BE SATISFIED

(1) The court may make an order for security for costs under rule 25.12 if—
- (a) it is satisfied, having regard to all the circumstances of the case, that it is just to make such an order; and
- (b)
  - (i) one or more of the conditions in paragraph (2) applies, or
  - (ii) an enactment permits the court to require security for costs.

(2) The conditions are—
- (a) the claimant is an individual—
  - (i) who is ordinarily resident out of the jurisdiction; and
  - (ii) is not a person against whom a claim can be enforced under the Brussels Conventions or the Lugano Convention [or the Regulation], as defined by section 1(1) of the Civil Jurisdiction and Judgments Act 1982;
- (b) the claimant is a company or other incorporated body—
  - (i) which is ordinarily resident out of the jurisdiction; and
  - (ii) is not a body against whom a claim can be enforced under the Brussels Conventions or the Lugano Convention [or the Regulation];
- (c) the claimant is a company or other body (whether incorporated inside or outside Great Britain) and there is reason to believe that it will be unable to pay the defendant's costs if ordered to do so;
- (d) the claimant has changed his address since the claim was commenced with a view to evading the consequences of the litigation;
- (e) the claimant failed to give his address in the claim form, or gave an incorrect address in that form;
- (f) the claimant is acting as a nominal claimant, other than as a representative claimant under Part 19, and there is reason to believe that he will be unable to pay the defendant's costs if ordered to do so;
- (g) the claimant has taken steps in relation to his assets that would make it difficult to enforce an order for costs against him.

(Rule 3.4 allows the court to strike out a statement of case and Part 24 for it to give summary judgment)

CPR RULE 25.14 SECURITY FOR COSTS OTHER THAN FROM THE CLAIMANT

(1) The defendant may seek an order against someone other than the claimant, and the court may make an order for security for costs against that person if—
- (a) it is satisfied, having regard to all the circumstances of the case, that it is just to make such an order; and
- (b) one or more of the conditions in paragraph (2) applies.

(2) The conditions are that the person—
- (a) has assigned the right to the claim to the claimant with a view to avoiding the possibility of a costs order being made against him; or
- (b) has contributed or agreed to contribute to the claimant's costs in return for a share of any money or property which the claimant may recover in the proceedings; and

is a person against whom a costs order may be made.

(Rule 48.2 makes provision for costs orders against non-parties)

CPR RULE 25.15 SECURITY FOR COSTS OF AN APPEAL

(1) The court may order security for costs of an appeal against—
- (a) an appellant;

(b) a respondent who also appeals,

on the same grounds as it may order security for costs against a claimant under this Part.

(2) The court may also make an order under paragraph (1) where the appellant, or the respondent who also appeals, is a limited company and there is reason to believe it will be unable to pay the costs of the other parties to the appeal should its appeal be unsuccessful.

(a) Residence abroad

CPR 25.13 provides that where the court is satisfied having regard to all the circumstances of the case, it is 'just' to do so, it may order an individual claimant or a company ordinarily resident out of the jurisdiction in a country which is not a party to the Brussels or Lugano Conventions, to give such security for the defendant's costs of the action or the proceedings. The test of whether or not a corporation is ordinarily resident outside the jurisdiction requires the court to locate its central management and control (*Re Little Olympian Each Ways Ltd* [1994] 4 All ER 561).

(b) Philosophy

The basic underlying principle is that it is, on the face of it, unjust that a foreign claimant, who by virtue of his foreign residence is more or less immune to the consequences of a costs order against him, should be allowed to proceed without making funds available within the jurisdiction against which such an order should be executed (*Corfu Navigation Co v Mobil Shipping Co Ltd* [1991] 2 Lloyd's Rep 52, CA). In *Okatcha v Voest Alpine Intertrading GmbH* [1993] BCLC 474, CA the claimants were a man and a Nigerian company wholly owned by him who were seeking commission allegedly due under an agreement. Although there was no ground for requiring the individual claimant to give security for costs, the fact that the company would not be able to meet the funds required was not a reason for refusing to order that it should give security. Nor was it right to refuse to order the company to give security on the grounds that the action would go ahead with the individual claimant anyway. The defendant should not be required to resist an action by a foreign claimant without such security as would enable them to enforce any orders for costs they obtained.

(c) Factors

(i) Residence abroad not enough

Although residence abroad is a condition precedent to the application, this alone is not sufficient to justify an order for security *(Berkeley Administration Inc v McCelland* [1990] 1 All ER 958, CA). Such an approach would be discriminatory and contrary to art 14 of the European Convention for the Protection of Human Rights. The court has now moved to a more flexible approach and the discretion should be exercised on objectively justified grounds relating to obstacles to or the burden of enforcement in the context of the particular country concerned. (*Nasser v United Bank of Kuwait* ([2001] EWCA Civ 556, [2002] 1 All ER 401).)

(ii) Poverty

The claimant's poverty alone is not a ground for ordering security but the financial viability of the claimant is a relevant factor.

(iii) Prospect of success

If it can clearly be demonstrated that the claimant has a very high probability of success, that is a matter that can properly be weighed in the balance. Similarly, if it can be shown that there is a very high probability that the defendant will succeed that also is a matter that can be weighed. The court deplores attempts to go into the merits of the case, unless it can be clearly demonstrated one way or the other that there is a high degree of probability of success or failure (*Porzelack KG v Porzelack UK* [1987] 1 All ER 1074, Ch D).

(iv) Admission

If a defendant admits so much of the claim as would be equal to the amount for which security would have been ordered, the court may refuse him security, for he can secure himself by paying the admitted amount into court (*Hogan v Hogan (No 2)* (1924) 2 Ir R 14).

(v) Summary judgment

The issuing of a summons for judgment under Part 24 does not in any way inhibit an application for security against a foreign claimant or an insolvent company, although the court will be concerned to ensure that there is a defence to the claim before granting security (*Gottlieb v Geiger* (3 July 1905, unreported, CA).

(vi) Discretion

In *Sir Lindsay Parkinson & Co Ltd v Triplan Ltd* [1973] 2 All ER 273, CA, Lord Denning identified the circumstances which the court might take into account in exercising its discretion. They are listed at pp 119–120.

(vii) Negotiations

A defendant should not be adversely affected in seeking security merely because he has attempted to reach a settlement. Evidence of negotiations conducted 'without prejudice', should not be admitted without their consent (*Simaan General Contracting Co v Pilkington Glass Ltd* [1987] 1 All ER 345, CA).

(viii) EC claimant

Data Delecta Atkiebolag v MSL Dynamics Ltd: C–43/95 [1996] All ER (EC) 961, ECJ held that a provision that security could be ordered against an individual claimant resident in the EC, even if there were cogent evidence of substantial difficulty in enforcing the judgment, was discriminatory. There is therefore now no basis upon which an order can be made against an individual claimant who resides in the EC on the grounds of his residence abroad. However, the fact that the claimant, a Dutch national residing in Florida, had assets in Holland and Switzerland did not protect him from an order for security for costs under CPR Rule 25.13(2)(*a*)(ii) as being 'a person against whom a claim [could] be enforced under the Brussels Conventions or the Lugano Convention'. The rule is aimed at the juridical characteristics of the claimant, regardless of the assets that he owned or where those assets might be situated. A claimant who was not ordinarily resident in the United Kingdom or a Convention state could not escape liability to give security for costs merely by placing an asset in a Convention state. (*De Beer v Kanaar & Co* ([2001] EWCA Civ 1318, [2002] 3 All ER 1020).)

The position in respect of insolvent limited companies is not affected by EC residence.

(ix) Convention claimant

Where the claimant resides outside the EC but in a country which is a member of either the Brussels or Lugano Conventions the ease of enforcement of the judgment for costs is a sufficient ground for denying the defendant an order for security for costs (*Thune v London Properties Ltd* [1990] 1 All ER 972, CA).

(x) English co-claimants

There is no settled rule of practice that no order will be made against a foreign claimant if there are co-claimants resident in England *(Slazengers Ltd v Seaspeed Ferries International Ltd* [1987] 3 All ER 967, CA).

(xi) Appeal

In *Antonelli v Allen* ([2001] EWCA Civ 1563) the claimant paid £100,000 to her solicitor, who had subsequently been struck off the roll of solicitors, in dubious circumstances. She retrieved £70,000 of the money but lost her claim for the balance of £30,000 from the solicitor's partner. On the claimant obtaining permission to appeal, the defendant sought an order for security for costs under the practice direction to CPR Rule 25, para 3, subparas 2(*a*) (residence outside the jurisdiction) and 2(*g*) (against a claimant who 'has taken steps in relation to his assets that would make it difficult to enforce an order for costs against him'). At the time of proceedings the claimant was living in Israel, but had now moved to New York, which made the case for security stronger, because there is no reciprocal enforcement of judgments between this country and the United States. Because the claimant had failed to respond to any questions about the fate of the £70,000 she had recovered, there was an inference that she had dealt with that sum in such a way as to put it beyond the reach of creditors. The respondent to the appeal was therefore entitled to security. The court was not prepared to assume in the absence of evidence that the costs of enforcing a judgment against the claimant in New York would not be substantial and would not, for the most part, be irrecoverable. In these circumstances the court fixed the amount of security at £10,000 with a provision that if payment was not made by a fixed date the appeal would be struck out automatically and that the appeal be stayed in the meantime.

Whether and when orders for security for costs should be made has always been a matter of practice rather than of substantive law; the court deplored a semantic dissection of judicial reasoning in an endeavour to demonstrate that there is still a rule of practice that it was only where it was certain, or virtually so, that the English claimant would become liable for all the costs if the defendant succeeded that an order for security would be made (*Corfu Navigation Co v Mobil Shipping Co Ltd* [1991] 2 Lloyd's Rep 52, CA).

4. CPR RULE 3.1

CPR Rule 3.1 provides:

(3) When the court makes an order, it may—
  (a) make it subject to conditions, including a condition to pay a sum of money into court; and
  (b) specify the consequence of failure to comply with the order or a condition.

(4) ...

(5) The court may order a party to pay a sum of money into court if that party has, without good reason, failed to comply with a rule, practice direction or a relevant pre-action protocol.

(6) When exercising its power under paragraph (5) the court must have regard to—
  (a) the amount in dispute; and
  (b) the costs which the parties have incurred or which they may incur.

In *Olatawura v Abiloye* ((2002) Times, 24 July) the Court of Appeal held that paras (4) and (5) of the Practice Direction to Rule 24 contemplated the making of orders akin to security for costs on the hearing of applications for summary judgment.

However, before ordering security for costs in any case, whether or not within Rule 25, the court should be alert and sensitive to the risk that by making such an order it might be denying the party concerned the right to access to the court.

It was right also to bear in mind that under the new rules it was not just the claimant against whom an order for security for costs could be made; it could also be made against the defendant.

If, as a condition of pursuing an unpromising defence, it was appropriate to secure the claim, why not also the claimant's costs of advancing the claim? And if that, why was it not at least as appropriate to require someone advancing an unpromising claim to secure the defendant's costs?

5. AMOUNT

The application should be supported by a skeleton bill of costs showing the amount of costs incurred to date and the estimated future costs. In considering the costs the court may well discount the sum claimed against the prospects of the settlement or the reduction of costs on assessment. However, the former 'conventional approach' that only two-thirds of the estimated costs should be awarded as security was discredited in *Procon (GB) Ltd v Provincial Building Co Ltd* [1984] 2 All ER 368, CA. An application for security for costs under the Companies Act 1985, s 726 does not have to be determined on an all-or-nothing basis. The court has power to order security in a sum less than the total potential order for costs. A balancing exercise is required (*Re Unisoft Group (No 2)* [1993] BCLC 532, Ch D). As we have seen, the court will not make an order which would prevent a claimant from proceeding with a legitimate claim. An example of this was *Innovare Displays plc v Corporate Booking Services Ltd* (1991) Times, 20 February, CA, where the Court of Appeal held that 'sufficient security' for costs does not mean complete security, but security of a sufficiency in all the circumstances of the case as to be just. Accordingly, although the defendant sought to obtain an order for security of costs in the sum of £147,655, which it estimated would be its costs, the court held that a sum of £10,000 would be appropriate! A state-funded claimant cannot be ordered to give greater security than the amount he would be likely to be ordered to pay if the defence were to succeed (*Wyld v Silver (No 2)* [1962] 2 All ER 809, CA).

6. COUNTERCLAIM

Although there can be no order for security for costs against a defendant who is exercising his right to defend himself, even though resident out of the jurisdiction, there may be such an order in respect of a counterclaim. As a general rule, where a counterclaim could properly be relied upon as a set-off and where it arose out of the same subject matter as the claim, the counter-claiming defendant ought not to be required to give security for costs of that counterclaim unless there are exceptional circumstances (*Richard Ashworth v Berkeley-Walbrood Ltd* (1989) Independent, 9 October, CA).

Security against a defendant was refused where the counterclaim raised the same issues as the claim in *BJ Crabtree (Insulation) Ltd v GPT Communications Systems Ltd* (1990) 59 BLR 43, CA. The marked discrepancy in size between the amount claimed in the action and the very much greater amount claimed by the counterclaim is relevant to an application by the claimant for security for costs in considering whether the counterclaim is a mere defence or a cross-claim in its own right which might well stand and be proceeded with even though the original claim were abandoned (*Hutchison Telephone (UK) Ltd (t/a Quadrant Communications) v Ultimate Response Ltd* [1993] BCLC 307, CA). Another example was in *L/M International Construction v Circle Partnership Ltd* [1995] CLY 4010, CA where the claimants' claim for costs and fees of about £1,000,000 was met with a counterclaim for breach of contract totalling £15,000,000. The court was of the view that the amount of the counterclaim put the defendants in the character of a claimant and they ought to be ordered to give security irrespective of the defence to the original action. The court can make such an order even in the absence of exceptional circumstances. However, in *Petromin SA v Secnav Marine Ltd* [1995] 1 Lloyd's Rep 603, QBD where both parties in a case involving a counterclaim were making substantial claims based on the same facts, the order for security for costs of the counterclaim in favour of the claimant was for the full amount of those costs and not merely for the amount by which the claimant's costs were increased in defending the counterclaim. The defendant was entitled to be secured in respect of costs no less fully than if it were merely defendant to the claim advanced in the counterclaim and not also claimant in the action. In *Flender Werft AG v Aegean Maritime Ltd* [1990] 2 Lloyd's Rep 27, QBD it was held that obtaining a freezing injunction against the claimant in an arbitration as security for a counterclaim did not preclude the defendants obtaining an order for security for costs of the counterclaim. The freezing of the funds relating to the counterclaim was not relevant to the issue of security for costs in the main action in respect of which the defendants were entitled to a separate security in the event that the claimant's claims against them failed. The defendants had offered to provide security for the costs of their counterclaim. In the circumstances it was fairer to make an order to the effect that each side should secure the other, rather than to make no order as to security at all. Neither party should be at risk in costs if successful. There is no jurisdiction to order a defendant seeking an enquiry as to damages arising out of the claimant's interlocutory injunction to provide security for the claimant's costs arising from the defendant's application (*CT Bowring & Co (Insurance) v Corsi & Partners Ltd* [1995] 1 BCLC 148, CA).

7. FUNDING BY THIRD PARTY

In *Condliffe v Hislop* [1996] 1 All ER 431, Kennedy LJ observed that if the circumstances suggested that if the litigating party were to lose, an order for costs would be difficult to enforce against a maintainer of that party, even though there was no power to order security for costs against the maintained party (who did not fall within RSC Ord 23 (now CPR Rules 25.12–25.15) or the Companies Act 1985, s 726) nevertheless a stay of the proceedings could be ordered.

In *Abraham v Thompson* [1997] 4 All ER 362, CA, the Court of Appeal disagreed. The right of a claimant to bring a properly pleaded and constituted action in good faith took precedence over the interest of a defendant who might be unable to recover costs against an impecunious claimant. It was preferable that a successful defendant should suffer the injustice of irrecoverable costs than that a claimant with a genuine claim should be prevented from pursuing it. The defendant's application for an order requiring the claimant to disclose details of any funding he was receiving from third parties to enable the defendants to make an application for an order for security for costs on the grounds that it might be difficult to enforce an order for costs against the funder was rejected.

The question of making orders for costs against the maintainer of litigation under the Supreme Court Act 1981, s 51 is considered at Chapter 35. However, under CPR Rule 25.14 an order may be sought against someone to whom a claim has been assigned with a view to avoiding an order for costs or who has contributed or agreed to contribute to the costs in exchange for an interest in the proceedings.

8. OTHER GROUNDS

CPR Rule 25.13 gives the court a discretion to order security for costs in the following circumstances:

(a) Change of address

That the claimant has changed his address during the course of the proceedings with a view to evading the consequences of litigation.

(b) No, or wrong, address

That the claimant's address is not stated in the writ or other originating process or is incorrectly stated therein, provided there shall be no such order if the claimant satisfies the court that the failure to state his address or the misstatement thereof was made innocently and without intention to deceive.

(c) Nominal claimant

That the claimant (not being a claimant who is suing in a representative capacity) is a nominal claimant who is suing for the benefit of some other person and that there is reason to believe that they will be unable to pay the costs of the defendant if ordered to do so. In *Envis v Thakkar* [1997] BPIR 189, CA the claimant was in financial difficulties when he began his action, but if he succeeded he would be able to discharge his liabilities. His creditors would benefit but so would he. Before a person could be branded a 'nominal claimant' there had to be some element of deliberate duplicity or window-dressing operating to the detriment of the defendant. In this case the claimant could not be regarded simply as a nominal claimant suing for the benefit of some other person.

(d) Dealing with assets

The claimant has taken steps that would make it difficult to enforce an order for costs against his assets.

9. ARBITRATION

The Arbitration Act 1996, s 38 (3) provides:

> 'The Tribunal may order a claimant to provide security for the costs of the arbitration. This power shall not be exercised on the ground that the claimant is:
>
> (a) An individual ordinarily resident outside the United Kingdom, or
> (b) A corporation or association incorporated or formed under the law of a country outside the United Kingdom, or whose central management and control is exercised outside the United Kingdom.'

The Arbitration Bill limited the arbitrator's discretion to the circumstances covered by the Companies Act 1985, s 726(1) and RSC Ord 23 but this limitation was omitted from the Act. This gives to the arbitrator a wide general discretion, which he must nevertheless exercise judicially – especially as the 'costs of the arbitration' include his own fees and expenses! No doubt the various factors relevant to applications for security for costs in other litigation will be taken into account by arbitrators. Also still of relevance is the decision in *K/S A/S Bani v Korea Shipbuilding and Engineering Corpn* [1987] 2 Lloyd's Rep 445, CA, in which it was held that where an international arbitration is of a type regularly conducted in London for many years and is not a one-off arbitration, security for costs should be ordered; all the more so if the litigation costs are very high.

Another practical difference between security for costs in arbitration and in other litigation is the tradition in litigation that applications for security for costs are not heard by the trial judge, because privileged and prejudicial matters, such as offers for settlement, may have to be considered on the application. Parliament must have taken the view that arbitrators are made of sterner stuff and can more readily put such matters out of their minds, because arbitrators themselves deal with applications for security.

Where a party is challenging the enforcement of a foreign arbitration award, it is right for the court to treat that party as a defendant, with the consequence that the court has jurisdiction to grant security for costs against the holder of the award (*Dardana Ltd v Yukos Oil Co* ([2002] 1 Lloyd's Rep 225)).

10. ORDER

The Court of Appeal in *Clive Brooks & Co Ltd v Baynard* (1998) Times, 30 April, CA criticised an order for security of costs which provided no time limit within which the security was to be given, and although it stayed the action in the meantime, it did not provide that the action should be dismissed if security was not given. It ruled that orders should specify a time within which security is to be given, stay all further proceedings until security is given and provide for the action or appeal to be dismissed without further order if security was not given within the time specified. A Practice Direction of 30 March 1998 prescribed the following form:

> It is ordered that the claimant by ... p.m. on .... 200 ... give security for the defendant's costs in the sum of £. ...... [by payment into court of the same] [by lodging with the defendant's solicitors] a .... (here describe the form of banker's draft etc.)] [in such manner as to the satisfaction of the Master] and that all further proceedings be stayed until security is given. In default of such security being given, the action is struck out with judgment for the defendant and his costs to be taxed if not agreed.

11. VARIATION OF ORDER

In *Gordano Building Contractors Ltd v Burgess* [1988] 1 WLR 890, CA, the claimant was ordered to give £20,000 security for the defendant's costs with 'liberty to both parties to apply'. Subsequently, the claimants obtained a letter from their bank stating that it would be willing to lend the claimants £20,000 to pay the costs if required. The claimants applied to have the order set aside but the judge held he had no jurisdiction to hear the application.

It was held on appeal that there were two questions: Can a claimant return if he can show a material change of circumstances? Can a claimant return if he produces fresh evidence as to the state of affairs extant at the date of the original order? The answer to the second question is 'No'. If a claimant wishes to have an opportunity to produce new evidence he should, no doubt at some penalty as to costs, apply for an adjournment. The answer to the first question must be that it is open to a claimant to apply to get an order for security set aside or varied in the light of changed circumstances. In the present case the judge had not considered whether there was a material change of circumstances and, if so, what as a matter of discretion he would do about it. The appeal was allowed to the extent of remitting the matter to the judge for reconsideration.

12. COURT OF APPEAL

The principles of applications for security for costs from appellants to the Court of Appeal are the same as in the court of first instance. CPR Rule 25.15, no doubt with an eye to the forthcoming Human Rights Act, removed the former fundamental difference that the impecuniosity of the appellant *was* a ground for ordering security for the costs of the appeal.

Nasser v United Bank of Kuwait [2001] EWCA Civ 556, [2002] 1 All ER 401 confirmed that the provision in CPR 25.15(1) enabling the court to make an order for security for costs of an appeal in respect of parties outside the jurisdiction of the Brussels and Lugano Conventions is not discriminatory under Schedule 1, Part 1, Article 14 of the Human Rights Act 1998, because the court retains a discretion and there is no assumption that such a party should be ordered to provide security as a matter of course. The Court of Appeal has an unfettered discretion and is unlikely to shut out a meritorious appeal by an order for security which would stifle it.

13. HOW TO GIVE SECURITY

(a) Payment into court

Payment into court may be either as the result of an order of the court or an agreement to give security, the latter being effected by completing Pay Office Form 2 and having it sealed by a High Court master or a district judge.

(b) Solicitor's undertaking

If the solicitor has sufficient faith in his client, or preferably sufficient funds in his client or other account under his control, he may give an undertaking that costs in the agreed or awarded amount will be paid, in respect of which he would of course be personally liable (*A Ltd v B Ltd* [1996] 1 WLR 665, Ch D).

(c) Bond

Another way of avoiding an unattractive investment in the court deposit account is to obtain an order or agreement that the claimant shall give security by banker's bond in a form to be agreed by the parties or settled by the court.

14. HOUSE OF LORDS

In all appeals to the House of Lords (except where the appellant has been granted state funding or the appeal is under the Child Abduction and Custody Act 1985 or is by a minister or government department) the appellant is required to pay as security

£18,000 into the House of Lords Security Fund Account. No interest is payable on money lodged as security. Security for costs can be waived if all the respondents agree. In this event the appellant's agents must, within one week of the presentation of the appeal, lodge a consent signed by all the respondents' agents agreeing to the waiver with a fee of £17.00. An appellant in a cross-appeal is not required to give security for costs (Standing Order V and Blue Book Directions).

CHAPTER 14

OFFERS TO SETTLE AND PAYMENTS INTO COURT (CPR PART 36)

What were previously known as 'payments into court' are known under the new rules as 'Part 36 Payments', whilst what were hitherto known as 'Calderbank offers' (ie offers made 'without prejudice save as to costs'), become 'Part 36 Offers'. Part 36 does not apply to proceedings being dealt with on the small claims track.

CPR PART 36 OFFERS TO SETTLE AND PAYMENTS INTO COURT

Rule 36.1	Scope of this Part
Rule 36.2	Part 36 offers and Part 36 payments—general provisions
Rule 36.3	A defendant's offer to settle a money claim requires a Part 36 payment
Rule 36.4	Defendant's offer to settle the whole of a claim which includes both a money claim and a non-money claim
Rule 36.5	Form and content of a Part 36 offer
Rule 36.6	Notice of a Part 36 payment
Rule 36.7	Offer to settle a claim for provisional damages
Rule 36.8	Time when a Part 36 offer or a Part 36 payment is made and accepted
Rule 36.9	Clarification of a Part 36 offer or a Part 36 payment notice
Rule 36.10	Court to take into account offer to settle made before commencement of proceedings
Rule 36.11	Time for acceptance of a defendant's Part 36 offer or Part 36 payment
Rule 36.12	Time for acceptance of a claimant's Part 36 offer
Rule 36.13	Costs consequences of acceptance of a defendant's Part 36 offer or Part 36 payment
Rule 36.14	Costs consequences of acceptance of a claimant's Part 36 offer
Rule 36.15	The effect of acceptance of a Part 36 offer or a Part 36 payment
Rule 36.16	Payment out of a sum in court on the acceptance of a Part 36 payment
Rule 36.17	Acceptance of a Part 36 offer or a Part 36 payment made by one or more, but not all, defendants
Rule 36.18	Other cases where a court order is required to enable acceptance of a Part 36 offer or a Part 36 payment
Rule 36.19	Restriction on disclosure of a Part 36 offer or a Part 36 payment
Rule 36.20	Costs consequences where claimant fails to do better than a Part 36 offer or a Part 36 payment
Rule 36.21	Costs and other consequences where claimant does better than he proposed in his Part 36 offer
Rule 36.22	Interest
Rule 36.23	Deduction of benefits

CPR RULE 36.1 SCOPE OF THIS PART

(1) This Part contains rules about—
- (a) offers to settle and payments into court; and
- (b) the consequences where an offer to settle or payment into court is made in accordance with this Part.

(2) Nothing in this Part prevents a party making an offer to settle in whatever way he chooses, but if that offer is not made in accordance with this Part, it will only have the consequences specified in this Part if the court so orders.
(Part 36 applies to Part 20 claims by virtue of rule 20.3)

CPR RULE 36.2 PART 36 OFFERS AND PART 36 PAYMENTS—GENERAL PROVISIONS

(1) An offer made in accordance with the requirements of this Part is called—
- (a) if made by way of a payment into court, 'a Part 36 payment';
- (b) otherwise 'a Part 36 offer'.

(Rule 36.3 sets out when an offer has to be made by way of a payment into court)
(2) The party who makes an offer is the 'offeror'.
(3) The party to whom an offer is made is the 'offeree'.
(4) A Part 36 offer or a Part 36 payment—
- (a) may be made at any time after proceedings have started; and
- (b) may be made in appeal proceedings.

(5) A Part 36 offer or a Part 36 payment shall not have the consequences set out in this Part while the claim is being dealt with on the small claims track unless the court orders otherwise.
(Part 26 deals with allocation to the small claims track)
(Rule 27.2 provides that Part 36 does not apply to small claims)

CPR RULE 36.3 A DEFENDANT'S OFFER TO SETTLE A MONEY CLAIM REQUIRES A PART 36 PAYMENT

(1) Subject to rules 36.5 (5) and 36.23, an offer by a defendant to settle a money claim will not have the consequences set out in this Part unless it is made by way of a Part 36 payment.
(2) A Part 36 payment may only be made after proceedings have started.
(Rule 36.5 (5) permits a Part 36 offer to be made by reference to an interim payment)
(Rule 36.10 makes provision for an offer to settle a money claim before the commencement of proceedings)
(Rule 36.23 makes provision for where benefit is recoverable under the Social Security (Recovery of Benefit) Act 1997)

CPR RULE 36.4 DEFENDANT'S OFFER TO SETTLE THE WHOLE OF A CLAIM WHICH INCLUDES BOTH A MONEY CLAIM AND A NON-MONEY CLAIM

(1) This rule applies where a defendant to a claim which includes both a money claim and a non-money claim wishes—
- (a) to make an offer to settle the whole claim which will have the consequences set out in this Part; and
- (b) to make an offer in respect of the money claim and a non-money offer in respect of the non-money claim.

(2) The defendant must—
- (a) make a Part 36 payment in relation to the money claim; and
- (b) make a Part 36 offer in relation to the non-money claim.

(3) The Part 36 payment notice must—

(a) identify the document which sets out the terms of the Part 36 offer; and
(b) state that if the claimant gives notice of acceptance of the Part 36 payment he will be treated as also accepting the Part 36 offer.

(Rule 36.6 makes provision for a Part 36 payment notice)

(4) If the claimant gives notice of acceptance of the Part 36 payment, he shall also be taken as giving notice of acceptance of the Part 36 offer in relation to the non-money claim.

CPR RULE 36.5 FORM AND CONTENT OF A PART 36 OFFER

(1) A Part 36 offer must be in writing.

(2) A Part 36 offer may relate to the whole claim or to part of it or to any issue that arises in it.

(3) A Part 36 offer must—
(a) state whether it relates to the whole of the claim or to part of it or to an issue that arises in it and if so to which part or issue;
(b) state whether it takes into account any counterclaim; and
(c) if it is expressed not to be inclusive of interest, give the details relating to interest set out in rule 36.22 (2).

(4) A defendant may make a Part 36 offer limited to accepting liability up to a specified proportion.

(5) A Part 36 offer may be made by reference to an interim payment.

(Part 25 contains provisions relating to interim payments)

(6) A Part 36 offer made not less than 21 days before the start of the trial must—
(a) be expressed to remain open for acceptance for 21 days from the date it is made; and
(b) provide that after 21 days the offeree may only accept it if—
(i) the parties agree the liability for costs; or
(ii) the court gives permission.

(7) A Part 36 offer made less than 21 days before the start of the trial must state that the offeree may only accept it if—
(a) the parties agree the liability for costs; or
(b) the court gives permission.

(Rule 36.8 makes provision for when a Part 36 offer is treated as being made)

(8) If a Part 36 offer is withdrawn it will not have the consequences set out in this Part.

CPR RULE 36.6 NOTICE OF A PART 36 PAYMENT

(1) A Part 36 payment may relate to the whole claim or part of it or to an issue that arises in it.

(2) A defendant who makes a Part 36 payment must file with the court a notice ('Part 36 payment notice') which—
(a) states the amount of the payment;
(b) states whether the payment relates to the whole claim or to part of it or to any issue that arises in it and if so to which part or issue;
(c) states whether it takes into account any counterclaim;
(d) if an interim payment has been made, states that the defendant has taken into account the interim payment; and
(e) if it is expressed not to be inclusive of interest, gives the details relating to interest set out in rule 36.22 (2).

(Rule 25.6 makes provision for an interim payment)

(Rule 36.4 provides for further information to be included where a defendant wishes to settle the whole of a claim which includes a money claim and a non-money claim)

(Rule 36.23 makes provision for extra information to be included in the

payment notice in a case where benefit is recoverable under the Social Security (Recovery of Benefit) Act 1997)
(3) The court will serve the Part 36 payment notice on the offeree unless the offeror informs the court, when the money is paid into court, that the offeror will serve the notice.
(4) Where the offeror serves the Part 36 payment notice he must file a certificate of service.
(Rule 6.10 specifies what must be contained in a certificate of service)
(5) A Part 36 payment may be withdrawn or reduced only with the permission of the court.

CPR RULE 36.7 OFFER TO SETTLE A CLAIM FOR PROVISIONAL DAMAGES

(1) A defendant may make a Part 36 payment in respect of a claim which includes a claim for provisional damages.
(2) Where he does so, the Part 36 payment notice must specify whether or not the defendant is offering to agree to the making of an award of provisional damages.
(3) Where the defendant is offering to agree to the making of an award of provisional damages the payment notice must also state—
- (a) that the sum paid into court is in satisfaction of the claim for damages on the assumption that the injured person will not develop the disease or suffer the type of deterioration specified in the notice;
- (b) that the offer is subject to the condition that the claimant must make any claim for further damages within a limited period; and
- (c) what that period is.

(4) Where a Part 36 payment is—
- (a) made in accordance with paragraph (3); and
- (b) accepted within the relevant period in rule 36.11,

the Part 36 payment will have the consequences set out in rule 36.13, unless the court orders otherwise.
(5) If the claimant accepts the Part 36 payment he must, within 7 days of doing so, apply to the court for an order for an award of provisional damages under rule 41.2.
(Rule 41.2 provides for an order for an award of provisional damages)
(6) The money in court may not be paid out until the court has disposed of the application made in accordance with paragraph (5).

CPR RULE 36.8 TIME WHEN A PART 36 OFFER OR A PART 36 PAYMENT IS MADE AND ACCEPTED

(1) A Part 36 offer is made when received by the offeree.
(2) A Part 36 payment is made when written notice of the payment into court is served on the offeree.
(3) An improvement to a Part 36 offer will be effective when its details are received by the offeree.
(4) An increase in a Part 36 payment will be effective when notice of the increase is served on the offeree.
(5) A Part 36 offer or Part 36 payment is accepted when notice of its acceptance is received by the offeror.

CPR RULE 36.9 CLARIFICATION OF A PART 36 OFFER OR A PART 36 PAYMENT NOTICE

(1) The offeree may, within 7 days of a Part 36 offer or payment being made, request the offeror to clarify the offer or payment notice.
(2) If the offeror does not give the clarification requested under paragraph (1)

within 7 days of receiving the request, the offeree may, unless the trial has started, apply for an order that he does so.
(3) If the court makes an order under paragraph (2), it must specify the date when the Part 36 offer or Part 36 payment is to be treated as having been made.

CPR RULE 36.10 COURT TO TAKE INTO ACCOUNT OFFER TO SETTLE MADE BEFORE COMMENCEMENT OF PROCEEDINGS

(1) If a person makes an offer to settle before proceedings are begun which complies with the provisions of this rule, the court will take that offer into account when making any order as to costs.
(2) The offer must—
  (a) be expressed to be open for at least 21 days after the date it was made;
  (b) if made by a person who would be a defendant were proceedings commenced, include an offer to pay the costs of the offeree incurred up to the date 21 days after the date it was made; and
  (c) otherwise comply with this Part.
(3) If the offeror is a defendant to a money claim—
  (a) he must make a Part 36 payment within 14 days of service of the claim form; and
  (b) the amount of the payment must be not less than the sum offered before proceedings began.
(4) An offeree may not, after proceedings have begun, accept—
  (a) an offer made under paragraph (2); or
  (b) a Part 36 payment made under paragraph (3),
without the permission of the court.
(5) An offer under this rule is made when it is received by the offeree.

CPR RULE 36.11 TIME FOR ACCEPTANCE OF A DEFENDANT'S PART 36 OFFER OR PART 36 PAYMENT

(1) A claimant may accept a Part 36 offer or a Part 36 payment made not less than 21 days before the start of the trial without needing the court's permission if he gives the defendant written notice of acceptance not later than 21 days after the offer or payment was made.
(Rule 36.13 sets out the costs consequences of accepting a defendant's offer or payment without needing the permission of the court)
(2) If—
  (a) a defendant's Part 36 offer or Part 36 payment is made less than 21 days before the start of the trial; or
  (b) the claimant does not accept it within the period specified in paragraph (1)—
    (i) if the parties agree the liability for costs, the claimant may accept the offer or payment without needing the permission of the court;
    (ii) if the parties do not agree the liability for costs the claimant may only accept the offer or payment with the permission of the court.
(3) Where the permission of the court is needed under paragraph (2) the court will, if it gives permission, make an order as to costs.

CPR RULE 36.12 TIME FOR ACCEPTANCE OF A CLAIMANT'S PART 36 OFFER

(1) A defendant may accept a Part 36 offer made not less than 21 days before the start of the trial without needing the court's permission if he gives the claimant written notice of acceptance not later than 21 days after the offer was made.

(Rule 36.14 sets out the costs consequences of accepting a claimant's offer without needing the permission of the court)

(2) If—

(a) a claimant's Part 36 offer is made less than 21 days before the start of the trial; or

(b) the defendant does not accept it within the period specified in paragraph (1)—

(i) if the parties agree the liability for costs, the defendant may accept the offer without needing the permission of the court;

(ii) if the parties do not agree the liability for costs the defendant may only accept the offer with the permission of the court.

(3) Where the permission of the court is needed under paragraph (2) the court will, if it gives permission, make an order as to costs.

CPR RULE 36.13 COSTS CONSEQUENCES OF ACCEPTANCE OF A DEFENDANT'S PART 36 OFFER OR PART 36 PAYMENT

(1) Where a Part 36 offer or a Part 36 payment is accepted without needing the permission of the court the claimant will be entitled to his costs of the proceedings up to the date of serving notice of acceptance.

(2) Where—

(a) a Part 36 offer or a Part 36 payment relates to part only of the claim; and

(b) at the time of serving notice of acceptance the claimant abandons the balance of the claim,

the claimant will be entitled to his costs of the proceedings up to the date of serving notice of acceptance, unless the court orders otherwise.

(3) The claimant's costs include any costs attributable to the defendant's counterclaim if the Part 36 offer or the Part 36 payment notice states that it takes into account the counterclaim.

(4) Costs under this rule will be payable on the standard basis if not agreed.

CPR RULE 36.14 COSTS CONSEQUENCES OF ACCEPTANCE OF A CLAIMANT'S PART 36 OFFER

Where a claimant's Part 36 offer is accepted without needing the permission of the court the claimant will be entitled to his costs of the proceedings up to the date upon which the defendant serves notice of acceptance.

CPR RULE 36.15 THE EFFECT OF ACCEPTANCE OF A PART 36 OFFER OR A PART 36 PAYMENT

(1) If a Part 36 offer or Part 36 payment relates to the whole claim and is accepted, the claim will be stayed[(GL)].

(2) In the case of acceptance of a Part 36 offer which relates to the whole claim—

(a) the stay[(GL)] will be upon the terms of the offer; and

(b) either party may apply to enforce those terms without the need for a new claim.

(3) If a Part 36 offer or a Part 36 payment which relates to part only of the claim is accepted—

(a) the claim will be stayed[(GL)] as to that part; and

(b) unless the parties have agreed costs, the liability for costs shall be decided by the court.

(4) If the approval of the court is required before a settlement can be binding, any stay[(GL)] which would otherwise arise on the acceptance of a Part 36 offer or a Part 36 payment will take effect only when that approval has been given.

(5) Any stay(GL) arising under this rule will not affect the power of the court—
(a) to enforce the terms of a Part 36 offer;
(b) to deal with any question of costs (including interest on costs) relating to the proceedings;
(c) to order payment out of court of any sum paid into court.
(6) Where—
(a) a Part 36 offer has been accepted; and
(b) a party alleges that—
(i) the other party has not honoured the terms of the offer; and
(ii) he is therefore entitled to a remedy for breach of contract,
the party may claim the remedy by applying to the court without the need to start a new claim unless the court orders otherwise.

CPR RULE 36.16 PAYMENT OUT OF A SUM IN COURT ON THE ACCEPTANCE OF A PART 36 PAYMENT

Where a Part 36 payment is accepted the claimant obtains payment out of the sum in court by making a request for payment in the practice form.

CPR RULE 36.17 ACCEPTANCE OF A PART 36 OFFER OR A PART 36 PAYMENT MADE BY ONE OR MORE, BUT NOT ALL, DEFENDANTS

(1) This rule applies where the claimant wishes to accept a Part 36 offer or a Part 36 payment made by one or more, but not all, of a number of defendants.
(2) If the defendants are sued jointly or in the alternative, the claimant may accept the offer or payment without needing the permission of the court in accordance with rule 36.11 (1) if—
(a) he discontinues his claim against those defendants who have not made the offer or payment; and
(b) those defendants give written consent to the acceptance of the offer or payment.
(3) If the claimant alleges that the defendants have a several liability(GL) to him the claimant may—
(a) accept the offer or payment in accordance with rule 36.11 (1); and
(b) continue with his claims against the other defendants if he is entitled to do so.
(4) In all other cases the claimant must apply to the court for—
(a) an order permitting a payment out to him of any sum in court; and
(b) such order as to costs as the court considers appropriate.

CPR RULE 36.18 OTHER CASES WHERE A COURT ORDER IS REQUIRED TO ENABLE ACCEPTANCE OF A PART 36 OFFER OR A PART 36 PAYMENT

(1) Where a Part 36 offer or a Part 36 payment is made in proceedings to which rule 21.10 applies—
(a) the offer or payment may be accepted only with the permission of the court; and
(b) no payment out of any sum in court shall be made without a court order.
(Rule 21.10 deals with compromise etc by or on behalf of a child or patient).
(2) Where the court gives a claimant permission to accept a Part 36 offer or payment after the trial has started—
(a) any money in court may be paid out only with a court order; and
(b) the court must, in the order, deal with the whole costs of the proceedings.
(3) Where a claimant accepts a Part 36 payment after a defence of tender

before claim(GL) has been put forward by the defendant, the money in court may be paid out only after an order of the court.
(Rule 37.3 requires a defendant who wishes to rely on a defence of tender before claim(GL) to make a payment into court)

CPR RULE 36.19 RESTRICTION ON DISCLOSURE OF A PART 36 OFFER OR A PART 36 PAYMENT

(1) A Part 36 offer will be treated as 'without prejudice(GL) except as to costs'.
(2) The fact that a Part 36 payment has been made shall not be communicated to the trial judge until all questions of liability and the amount of money to be awarded have been decided.
(3) Paragraph (2) does not apply—
  (a) where the defence of tender before claim(GL) has been raised;
  (b) where the proceedings have been stayed(GL) under rule 36.15 following acceptance of a Part 36 offer or Part 36 payment; or
  (c) where—
    (i) the issue of liability has been determined before any assessment of the money claimed; and
    (ii) the fact that there has or has not been a Part 36 payment may be relevant to the question of the costs of the issue of liability.

CPR RULE 36.20 COSTS CONSEQUENCES WHERE CLAIMANT FAILS TO DO BETTER THAN A PART 36 OFFER OR A PART 36 PAYMENT

(1) This rule applies where at trial a claimant—
  (a) fails to better a Part 36 payment; or
  (b) fails to obtain a judgment which is more advantageous than a defendant's Part 36 offer.
(2) Unless it considers it unjust to do so, the court will order the claimant to pay any costs incurred by the defendant after the latest date on which the payment or offer could have been accepted without needing the permission of the court.
(Rule 36.11 sets out the time for acceptance of a defendant's Part 36 offer or Part 36 payment)

CPR RULE 36.21 COSTS AND OTHER CONSEQUENCES WHERE CLAIMANT DOES BETTER THAN HE PROPOSED IN HIS PART 36 OFFER

(1) This rule applies where at trial—
  (a) a defendant is held liable for more; or
  (b) the judgment against a defendant is more advantageous to the claimant, than the proposals contained in a claimant's Part 36 offer.
(2) The court may order interest on the whole or part of any sum of money (excluding interest) awarded to the claimant at a rate not exceeding 10% above base rate(GL) for some or all of the period starting with the latest date on which the defendant could have accepted the offer without needing the permission of the court.
(3) The court may also order that the claimant is entitled to—
  (a) his costs on the indemnity basis from the latest date when the defendant could have accepted the offer without needing the permission of the court; and
  (b) interest on those costs at a rate not exceeding 10% above base rate(GL).
(4) Where this rule applies, the court will make the orders referred to in paragraphs (2) and (3) unless it considers it unjust to do so.
(Rule 36.12 sets out the latest date when the defendant could have accepted the offer)

(5) In considering whether it would be unjust to make the orders referred to in (2) and (3) above, the court will take into account all the circumstances of the case including—

(a) the terms of any Part 36 offer;
(b) the stage in the proceedings when any Part 36 offer or Part 36 payment was made;
(c) the information available to the parties at the time when the Part 36 offer or Part 36 payment was made; and
(d) the conduct of the parties with regard to the giving or refusing to give information for the purposes of enabling the offer or payment into court to be made or evaluated.

(6) Where the court awards interest under this rule and also awards interest on the same sum and for the same period under any other power, the total rate of interest may not exceed 10% above base rate[GL].

CPR RULE 36.22 INTEREST

(1) Unless—

(a) a claimant's Part 36 offer which offers to accept a sum of money; or
(b) a Part 36 payment notice,

indicates to the contrary, any such offer or payment will be treated as inclusive of all interest until the last date on which it could be accepted without needing the permission of the court.

(2) Where a claimant's Part 36 offer or Part 36 payment notice is expressed not to be inclusive of interest, the offer or notice must state—

(a) whether interest is offered; and
(b) if so, the amount offered, the rate or rates offered and the period or periods for which it is offered.

CPR RULE 36.23 DEDUCTION OF BENEFITS

(1) This rule applies where a payment to a claimant following acceptance of a Part 36 offer or Part 36 payment into court would be a compensation payment as defined in section 1 of the Social Security (Recovery of Benefits) Act 1997.

(2) A defendant to a money claim may make an offer to settle the claim which will have the consequences set out in this Part, without making a Part 36 payment if—

(a) at the time he makes the offer he has applied for, but not received, a certificate of recoverable benefit; and
(b) he makes a Part 36 payment not more than 7 days after he receives the certificate.

(Section 1 of the 1997 Act defines 'recoverable benefit')

(3) A Part 36 payment notice must state—

(a) the amount of gross compensation;
(b) the name and amount of any benefit by which that gross amount is reduced in accordance with section 8 and Schedule 2 to the 1997 Act; and
(c) that the sum paid in is the net amount after deduction of the amount of benefit.

(4) For the purposes of rule 36.20, a claimant fails to better a Part 36 payment if he fails to obtain judgment for more than the gross sum specified in the Part 36 payment notice.

(5) Where—

(a) a Part 36 payment has been made; and
(b) application is made for the money remaining in court to be paid out,

the court may treat the money in court as being reduced by a sum equivalent to any further recoverable benefits paid to the claimant since the date of payment into court and may direct payment out accordingly.

PRACTICE DIRECTION SUPPLEMENTING CPR PART 36

PART 36 OFFERS AND PART 36 PAYMENTS

1.1 A written offer to settle a claim[1] or part of a claim or any issue that arises in it made in accordance with the provisions of Part 36 is called:
(1) if made by way of a payment into court, a Part 36 payment[2], or
(2) if made otherwise, a Part 36 offer[3].
1.2 A Part 36 offer or Part 36 payment has the costs and other consequences set out in rules 36.13, 36.14, 36.20 and 36.21.
1.3 An offer to settle which is not made in accordance with Part 36 will only have the consequences specified in that Part if the court so orders and will be given such weight on any issue as to costs as the court thinks appropriate[4].

PARTIES AND PART 36 OFFERS

2.1 A Part 36 offer, subject to paragraph 3 below, may be made by any party.
2.2 The party making an offer is the 'offeror' and the party to whom it is made is the 'offeree'.
2.3 A Part 36 offer may consist of a proposal to settle for a specified sum or for some other remedy.
2.4 A Part 36 offer is made when received by the offeree[5].
2.5 An improvement to a Part 36 offer is effective when its details are received by the offeree[6].

PARTIES AND PART 36 PAYMENTS

3.1 An offer to settle for a specified sum made by a defendant[7] must, in order to comply with Part 36, be made by way of a Part 36 payment into court[8].
3.2 A Part 36 payment is made when the Part 36 payment notice is served on the claimant[9].
3.3 An increase to a Part 36 payment will be effective when notice of the increase is served on the claimant[10].
(For service of the Part 36 payment notice see rule 36.6(3) and (4).)
3.4 A defendant who wishes to withdraw or reduce a Part 36 payment must obtain the court's permission to do so.
3.5 Permission may be obtained by making an application in accordance with Part 23 stating the reasons giving rise to the wish to withdraw or reduce the Part 36 payment.

MAKING A PART 36 PAYMENT

4.1 To make a Part 36 payment the defendant must file the following documents:
(1) where that court is a county court or a district registry—
  (a) the Part 36 payment notice, and
  (b) the payment, usually a cheque made payable to Her Majesty's Paymaster General, with the court, and
(2) where that court is the Royal Courts of Justice—
  (a) the Part 36 payment notice with the court, and
  (b) the payment, usually a cheque made payable to the Accountant General of the Supreme Court, and
  (c) a sealed copy of the Claim Form,
  (d) the Court Funds Office form 100 with the Court Funds Office.

PART 36 OFFERS AND PART 36 PAYMENTS—GENERAL PROVISIONS

5.1 A Part 36 offer or a Part 36 payment notice must:
(1) state that it is a Part 36 offer or that the payment into court is a Part 36 payment, and
(2) be signed by the offeror or his legal representative[13].
5.2 The contents of a Part 36 offer must also comply with the requirements of rule 36.5(3), (5) and (6).
5.3 The contents of a Part 36 payment notice must comply with rule 36.6(2) and, if rule 36.23 applies, with rule 36.23(3).
5.4 A Part 36 offer or Part 36 payment will be taken to include interest unless it is expressly stated in the offer or the payment notice that interest is not included, in which case the details set out in rule 36.22(2) must be given.
5.5 Where a Part 36 offer is made by a company or other corporation, a person holding a senior position in the company or corporation may sign the offer on the offeror's behalf, but must state the position he holds.
5.6 Each of the following persons is a person holding a senior position:
(1) in respect of a registered company or corporation, a director, the treasurer, secretary, chief executive, manager or other officer of the company or corporation, and
(2) in respect of a corporation which is not a registered company, in addition to those persons set out in (1), the mayor, chairman, president, town clerk or similar officer of the corporation.

CLARIFICATION OF PART 36 OFFER OR PAYMENT

6.1 An offeree may apply to the court for an order requiring the offeror to clarify the terms of a Part 36 offer or Part 36 payment notice (a clarification order) where the offeror has failed to comply within 7 days with a request for clarification[14].
6.2 An application for a clarification order should be made in accordance with Part 23.
6.3 The application notice should state the respects in which the terms of the Part 36 offer or Part 36 payment notice, as the case may be, are said to need clarification.

ACCEPTANCE OF A PART 36 OFFER OR PAYMENT

7.1 The times for accepting a Part 36 offer or a Part 36 payment are set out in rules 36.11 and 36.12.
7.2 The general rule is that a Part 36 offer or Part 36 payment made more than 21 days before the start of the trial may be accepted within 21 days after it was made without the permission of the court. The costs consequences set out in rules 36.13 and 36.14 will then come into effect.
7.3 A Part 36 offer or Part 36 payment made less than 21 days before the start of the trial cannot be accepted without the permission of the court unless the parties agree what the costs consequences of acceptance will be.
7.4 The permission of the court may be sought:
(1) before the start of the trial, by making an application in accordance with Part 23, and
(2) after the start of the trial, by making an application to the trial judge.
7.5 If the court gives permission it will make an order dealing with costs and may order that, in the circumstances, the costs consequences set out in rules 36.13 and 36.14 will apply.
7.6 Where a Part 36 offer or Part 36 payment is accepted in accordance with rule 36.11(1) or rule 36.12(1) the notice of acceptance must be sent to the offeror and filed with the court.
7.7 The notice of acceptance:
(1) must set out—

(a) the claim number, and
(b) the title of the proceedings,
(2) must identify the Part 36 offer or Part 36 payment notice to which it relates, and
(3) must be signed by the offeree or his legal representative (see paragraphs 5.5 and 5.6 above)[15].

7.8 Where:
(1) the court's approval, or
(2) an order for payment of money out of court, or
(3) an order apportioning money in court:
(a) between the Fatal Accidents Act 1976 and the Law Reform (Miscellaneous Provisions) Act 1934, or
(b) between the persons entitled to it under the Fatal Accidents Act 1976,

is required for acceptance of a Part 36 offer or Part 36 payment, application for the approval or the order should be made in accordance with Part 23.

7.9 The court will include in any order made under paragraph 8.8 above a direction for;
(1) the payment out of the money in court, and
(2) the payment of interest.

7.10 Unless the parties have agreed otherwise:
(1) interest accruing up to the date of acceptance will be paid to the offeror,
(2) interest accruing as from the date of acceptance until payment out will be paid to the offeree.

7.11 A claimant may not accept a Part 36 payment which is part of a defendant's offer to settle the whole of a claim consisting of both a money and a non-money claim unless at the same time he accepts the offer to settle the whole of the claim. Therefore:
(1) if a claimant accepts a Part 36 payment which is part of a defendant's offer to settle the whole of the claim, or
(2) if a claimant accepts a Part 36 offer which is part of a defendant's offer to settle the whole of the claim,

the claimant will be deemed to have accepted the offer to settle the whole of the claim[16].

(See paragraph 8 below for the method of obtaining money out of court.)

PAYMENT OUT OF COURT

8.1 To obtain money out of court following acceptance of a Part 36 payment, the claimant should file a request for payment with the court[17].

8.2 The request for payment should contain the following details:
(1) where the party receiving the payment
(a) is legally represented
(i) the name, business address and reference of the legal representative, and
(ii) the name of the bank and the sort code number, the title of the account and the account number where the payment is to be transmitted, and
(2) where the party is acting in person
(a) his name and address, and
(b) his bank account details as in (ii) above.

8.3 Where the request for payment is made to the Royal Courts of Justice, the claimant should also complete Court Funds Office form 201 and file it in the Court Funds Office.

8.4 Subject to paragraph 8.5(1) and (2), if a party does not wish the payment to be transmitted into his bank account or if he does not have a bank account, he may send a written request to the Accountant-General for the payment to be made to him by cheque.

8.5 Where a party seeking payment out of court has provided the necessary information, the payment:

(1) where a party is legally represented, must be made to the legal representative,

(2) if the party is not legally represented but is, or has been, in receipt of legal aid in respect of the proceedings and a notice to that effect has been filed, should be made to the Legal Aid Board by direction of the court,

(3) where a person entitled to money in court dies without having made a will and the court is satisfied:

(a) that no grant of administration of his estate has been made, and

(b) that the assets of his estate, including the money in court, do not exceed in value the amount specified in any order in force under section 6 of the Administration of Estates (Small Payments) Act 1965,

may be ordered to be made to the person appearing to have the prior right to a grant of administration of the estate of the deceased, eg a widower, widow, child, father, mother, brother or sister of the deceased.

FOREIGN CURRENCY

9.1 Money may be paid into court in a foreign currency:

(1) where it is a Part 36 payment and the claim is in a foreign currency, or

(2) under a court order.

9.2 The court may direct that the money be placed in an interest bearing account in the currency of the claim or any other currency.

9.3 Where a Part 36 payment is made in a foreign currency and has not been accepted within 21 days, the defendant may apply for an order that the money be placed in an interest bearing account.

9.4 The application should be made in accordance with Part 23 and should state:

(1) that the payment has not been accepted in accordance with rule 36.11, and

(2) the type of currency on which interest is to accrue.

COMPENSATION RECOVERY

10.1 Where a defendant makes a Part 36 payment in respect of a claim for a sum or part of a sum:

(1) which falls under the heads of damage set out in column 1 of Schedule 2 of the Social Security (Recovery of Benefits) Act 1997 in respect of recoverable benefits received by the claimant as set out in column 2 of that Schedule, and

(2) where the defendant is liable to pay recoverable benefits to the Secretary of State,

the defendant should obtain from the Secretary of State a certificate of recoverable benefits and file the certificate with the Part 36 payment notice.

10.2 If a defendant wishes to offer to settle a claim where he has applied for but not yet received a certificate of recoverable benefits, he may, provided that he makes a Part 36 payment not more than 7 days after he has received the certificate, make a Part 36 offer which will have the costs and other consequences set out in rules 36.13 and 36.20.

10.3 The Part 36 payment notice should state in addition to the requirements set out in rule 36.6(2):

(1) the total amount represented by the Part 36 payment (the gross compensation);

(2) that the defendant has reduced this sum by £. ... ., in accordance with section 8 of and Schedule 2 to the Social Security (Recovery of Benefits) Act 1997, which was calculated as follows:

Name of benefit .... Amount ....

and ....,

(3) that the amount paid in, being the sum of £...... is the net amount after the deduction of the amount of benefit.

10.4 On acceptance of a Part 36 payment to which this paragraph relates, a claimant will receive the sum in court which will be net of the recoverable benefits.

10.5 In establishing at trial whether a claimant has bettered or obtained a judgment more advantageous than a Part 36 payment to which this paragraph relates, the court will base its decision on the gross sum specified in the Part 36 payment notice.

GENERAL

11.1 Where a party on whom a Part 36 offer, a Part 36 payment notice or a notice of acceptance is to be served is legally represented, the Part 36 offer, Part 36 payment notice and notice of acceptance must be served on the legal representative.

11.2 In a claim arising out of an accident involving a motor vehicle on a road or in a public place:

(1) where the damages claimed include a sum for hospital expenses, and

(2) the defendant or his insurer pays that sum to the hospital under section 157 of the Road Traffic Act 1988, the defendant must give notice of that payment to the court and all the other parties to the proceedings.

11.3 Money paid into court:

(1) as a Part 36 payment which is not accepted by the claimant, or

(2) under a court order,

will be placed after 21 days in a basic account[18] (subject to paragraph 11.4 below) for interest to accrue.

11.4 Where money referred to in paragraph 11.3 above is paid in respect of a child or patient it will be placed in a special investment account[19] for interest to accrue.

(A practice direction supplementing Part 21 contains information about the investment of money in court in respect of a child or patient).

(Practice directions supplementing Part 40 contain information about adjustment of the judgment sum in respect of recoverable benefits, and about structured settlements.)

(A practice direction supplementing Part 41 contains information about provisional damages awards).

1 Includes Part 20 claims.
2 See rule 36.2(1)(a).
3 See rule 36.2(1)(b).
4 See rule 36.1(2).
5 See rule 36.8(1).
6 See rule 36.8(3).
7 Includes a respondent to a claim or issue.
8 See rule 36.3(1).
9 See rule 36.8(2).
10 See rule 36.8(4).
11 Rule 36.4.
12 Practice form N242A.
13 For the definition of legal representative see rule 2.32.
14 See rule 36.9(1) and (2).
15 This should be a reference to paras 5.5 and 5.6 and not 6.5 and 6.6.
16 See rule 36.4.
17 in practice form N243.
18 See rule 26 of the Court Funds Office Rules 1987.
19 See rule 26 as above.

* These notes refer to paragraphs in an early draft which were deleted, but the numbers were not!

Payment into court

Rule 36.3(1) preserves the principle that a defendant to a money claim must make a payment into court if it is to have effective costs consequences. In the early consultation papers it was suggested that in future defendants might not have to part with their money in order to protect themselves but this was not embodied in the rules and a defendant to a money claim still has to put his money where his mouth is. If the claim is both for money and for a non-money remedy, the defendant must make a Part 36 payment in respect of the former in order to obtain full protection. It is important to note that Rule 36.1(2) provides that a party may make an offer to settle in whatever way he chooses, but if the offer is not made in accordance with Part 36 it will only have the specified costs consequences if the court so orders. It should also be remembered that under Rule 44.3(4) in deciding whether to make an order for costs the court shall have regard to any offer whether it has been made in accordance with Part 36 or not.

In *Amber v Stacey* [2001] 2 All ER 88, CA, after the commencement of proceedings, the defendant wrote offering £4000 plus costs but made no payment into court. In August 1998, the defendant paid in £2000 and this was topped up to £3000 in January 1999. At the trial in April 1999, the claimant was awarded £2300. The judge concluded the claimant had acted unreasonably in refusing the original offer of £4000 and awarded the defendant his costs from that date. The Court of Appeal held that the judge was wrong to award the defendant his full costs of the period before the payment into court of £3000. He had ignored the important difference between a Part 36 offer and a Part 36 payment. Nevertheless, because of the claimant's unreasonableness, it was appropriate to award the defendant half his costs for the period before the payment in. The court identified the following advantages of payments into court: (a) genuineness; (b) the offeror's ability to pay; (c) whether the offer is open or without prejudice and (d) the terms on which the dispute can be settled. 'They are clearly to be encouraged, and written offers, although obviously relevant, should not be treated as precise equivalents'. Commenting on the decision, Jeremy Morgan observed that despite extolling the virtues of payments into court, the decision in fact erodes the difference between an offer and a payment in. He wrote 'It is certainly not safe for a claimant's solicitor to ignore an offer in a situation where a payment could have been made, and advise his client to wait until there is a payment in'.

In *Firle Investments Ltd v Datapoint International Ltd* [2001] EWCA Civ 1106, [2001] All ER (D) 258 (Jun) the claimant had undoubtedly been at fault in being unwilling to negotiate and by persisting with hopeless issues, thereby lengthening the trial, but ultimately it had beaten the payments in and had succeeded by a substantial amount in the period up to a second payment in. The claimant recovered all of its costs up to the date of the second payment and 70% of its costs thereafter. The judge retained a discretion under CPR Rule 44.3(6)(*a*) to disapply the normal rule relating to costs and could take into account such factors as payments in, offers to settle, the conduct of the parties and whether a party had lost an issue. However, the judge should refrain from speculating on whether hypothetical offers to settle would have been accepted.

Pre-action offers

Rule 36.10(1) made the new provision that offers to settle before the commencement of proceedings have costs consequences, provided the offer is expressed to be open for at least 21 days, includes an offer to pay costs and is followed up by a payment into court within 21 days of service of the proceedings.

Rosalind Huck v Tony Robson [2002] EWCA Civ 398, [2002] 3 All ER 263 concerned a road traffic accident in which it was likely the finding on liability would be either 50/50 or 100%, the claimant made a pre-action offer to accept a 95%–5% split on liability. The defendant rejected the offer and the trial judge refused to take it into account in his award of costs on the grounds that the apportionment was 'illusory'. The Court of Appeal disagreed. Although a judge would be entitled to exercise his discretion and refuse indemnity costs where an offer was purely tactical, for example, to settle for 99.9% of the full value of the claim, that could not be said of the claimant's offer. The reduction of 5% provided the defendant with a real opportunity of settlement and did not represent the court's probable decision on liability. After applying the factors prescribed in rule 36.21 the court, by a majority, awarded the claimant her costs on the indemnity basis.

Withdrawal of offer

In *Scammell v Dicker* [2001] 1 WLR 631, CA, the claimant made an offer to settle an action under CPR Part 36, which Rule 36.5(6) provides should be 'expressed to remain open for acceptance for 21 days … '. Could the offer be withdrawn within the 21-day period? The answer was 'Yes'. There is nothing in Part 36 to the contrary. A Part 36 offer is an offer to enter into a contract with the offeree. To impose a term that the offer could not be withdrawn would lead to an addition to the contractual terms offered by the offeror. That would be possible, but should not be done by implication. If that is what Parliament had intended, the rule would have said so in clear terms. A payment into court, on the other hand, cannot be withdrawn without permission (Rule 36.6(5)).

In *Pitchmastic plc v Birse Construction Ltd* (2000) Times, 21 June, the defendants' solicitors, the day before the trial, faxed a letter marked 'without prejudice save as to costs' to the claimants' solicitors containing an offer which was rejected. During the trial, the defendants made an open offer of the same amount to which the claimants responded with a counter-offer seeking more. The defendants then withdrew their offer. After reading an unfavourable draft of the judgment, the claimants purported to accept the original offer, arguing that it was an offer under CPR Part 36 and was therefore open for acceptance for 21 days, despite its purported withdrawal. The court held that CPR Rule 36.5(8) expressly contemplates that a Part 36 offer might be withdrawn and there is no requirement that a party who has made a Part 36 offer should seek the permission of the court before withdrawing it. CPR Rule 36.1(2) also expressly contemplates that a party may make an offer to settle in whatever way he chooses and therefore the question of whether there was a compromise in pending litigation should be decided by the ordinary rules of offer and acceptance. The defendants had withdrawn the offer before the claimant had accepted it.

Discretion

In *Clark Goldring and Page Ltd v ANC Ltd* (2001) Times, 27 March, the claimants, having accepted a payment in, claimed that they were entitled to their costs as of right under CPR Rule 36.11(1) which refers to the costs consequences of timely acceptance of a Part 36 offer set out in Rule 36.13 which in turn provides that a claimant in these circumstances is entitled to his costs as of right. But CPR Rule 36.15(3) made it clear that where a payment which related only to part of a claim was accepted under Part 36, unless the parties agreed costs, liability for costs should be decided by the court. Although there appeared to be some internal conflict between Rule 36.13 and 36.15, the overall intention of the rules was unmistakably clear – that the court should have a discretion except where the payment in covered the whole of the proceedings and brought the proceedings to an end.

Claimant's offer

Another innovation was that under Rule 36.21 a *claimant* may make an offer which (if not accepted and if he recovers more than the amount of his offer at the trial) may entitle him to enhanced interest on both his claim and his costs and to costs on the indemnity basis. The first reported case of a claimant benefiting under this provision was *Little v George Little Sebire & Co* [2001] STC 1065, QBD in which the various claimants were awarded judgments totalling some £50,000 but had made a Part 36 offer indicating they would accept £30,000. The claimant sought costs on the indemnity basis with enhanced interest at a rate not exceeding 10% above base rate pursuant to Rule 36.21. The judge held that because one of the features of the overriding objective contained in CPR Rule 1.2(1) was the saving of expense, the rule should be interpreted by the court in a way that would encourage settlement. Settlement was achieved only if parties focused properly on the strengths and weaknesses of their respective cases. The powers under the rule were plainly designed to sharpen that focus. Unless the discretion conferred by the rule were exercised in a way that made a material, albeit proportionate, difference to the eventual award in the case, the rule itself would become redundant. One appropriate way in which the issue might be approached was to start with the proposition that enhanced interest of 10% above base rate (being the maximum prescribed by the rule) be awarded on the whole of the judgment, excluding interest, from the earliest date when it could be awarded and then to evaluate whether the effect of doing so would itself work an injustice or result in a disproportionate advantage to the claimants or disadvantage to the defendant. Although Rule 36.21 does not apply where there is a summary judgment (because the award is not 'at trial': *Petrotrade Inc v Texaco Ltd* [2002] 4 All ER 853, CA) the judge does have power to award costs on the indemnity basis and interest, at a rate he thinks just, under Rule 36.1 (2) and Rule 44.3(7)(*g*). Why a claimant whose case is sufficiently strong to obtain summary judgment should be in a worse position than one who goes to trial is not immediately apparent!

No stigma

In *McPhilemy v Times Newspapers Ltd (No 3)* [2001] EWCA Civ 871, [2001] EMLR 832, the court of Appeal held that there is no stigma attached to an award of indemnity costs under Part 36 and the judge had been wrong to refuse them on the grounds that they implied disapproval of the defendant's conduct.

Interest

Rule 36.22 provides that claimant's offers and defendant's payments are to be treated as inclusive of interest unless they indicate to the contrary.

Costs

Where a defendant's Part 36 payment or offer is accepted, the claimant is entitled to his costs of the proceedings up to the date of the receipt of the notice of acceptance. These include the costs of any counterclaim (Rule 36.13). However, this does not apply the other way round. If a claimant's offer is accepted, the defendant must pay his costs up to the date of service of the notice of acceptance.

In *Mitchell v James* [2002] EWCA Civ 997, [2002] All ER (D) 200 (Jul) the claimants had made a Part 36 offer, offering that each party bear its own costs. That offer was rejected and after the claimants won at trial, they asked for costs on the indemnity basis. The court held that the provisions of CPR Rule 36.14 and PD 36, paras 7.2 and 7.5 were inconsistent with a term as to costs being part of a Part 36 offer. That did not mean that a claimant could not make an offer including a term as to costs, because CPR Rule 36.1(2) states that nothing in Part 36 prevents a party from making an offer to settle in whatever way he chose. However, nothing in CPR Rule 36.1(2) permits a party to include a term as to costs in a Part 36 offer for the purpose of obtaining an order for costs on the indemnity basis.

The remainder of Part 36 has the traditional provisions as to the information which must accompany a payment into court or an offer, with strict timetables for both the making of payments and offers and their acceptance, with a variety of permutations of sticks and carrots each with consequences as to costs.

Although a party is not entitled to interrogate his opponent as to the thinking behind a Part 36 offer (other than to clarify the precise scope of the offer) the court has power to make an order for the early disclosure of admissible documents. This could enable the offeree to have additional material with which to consider the offer. The general rule that a party who failed to beat an offer paid the costs after the offer should have been accepted, should not apply when the other party has failed properly to disclose documents or information. In *R v Secretary of State for Transport, ex p Factortame (No 7)* [2001] 1 WLR 942, (2001) Butterworths Costs Service Bulletin, January, the claimants should have had an opportunity to consider expert and other evidence not previously available and therefore the government was ordered to pay their costs until the date by which it would have been reasonable for them to have had this opportunity. Similarly, in *Ford GKR Construction Ltd* [2000] 1 All ER 802, CA, although the claimant failed to beat a Part 36 payment, she still received her costs after the payment in because the defendants had waited until during the trial to obtain video evidence undermining her evidence as to the extent of her symptoms, depriving her of a real opportunity to deal with their allegations of dishonesty. Judges should consider whether or not the parties had conducted the litigation in accordance with a system designed to enable them to make informed decisions at the earliest possible stage.

Small claims track

Although Part 36 does not apply to the small claims track (Rule 27.2) there is no reason why a party to a small claim should not make an offer or a payment into court which could be taken into account when awarding costs and disbursements. This could be of particular relevance on an appeal on the small claims track, where full costs may be awarded.

Reform

The government has decided, based on the responses to its consultation paper *Payments into Court in Satisfaction of a Claim*, that the present system will be retained and will continue to be administered by the Court Service; that the system will be streamlined so that the process is the same for actions in both the High Court and the county court; that there will continue to be a facility for making payments to the county court in exceptional circumstances; and that provision is made in the rules for the Court Funds Office to receive payments via BACS in the future. The changes will take effect from 1 April 2003.

GLOSSARY

Three words in Part 36 are marked (GL), which is a reference to the glossary at the end of the Civil Procedure Rules. The glossary is expressed to be a guide to the meaning of certain legal expressions used in the rules without in any way changing their legal meaning. The words and the meanings given them are:

Rule 36.15 'Stay' A stay imposes a halt on proceedings, apart from taking any steps allowed by the rules or the terms of the stay. Proceedings can be continued if a stay is lifted.

Rule 36.19 'Without prejudice' Negotiations with a view to a settlement are usually conducted 'without prejudice' which means that the circumstances in which the content of those negotiations may be revealed to the court are very restricted.

Rule 37.3 'Defence of tender before claim' A defence that, before the claimant started proceedings, the defendant unconditionally offered to the claimant the amount due or, if no specified amount is claimed, an amount sufficient to satisfy the claim.

CHAPTER 15

FAMILY PROCEEDINGS

1. CIVIL PROCEDURE RULES

In previous editions in a chapter entitled 'Never mind the quality, feel the width', I described my nightmare about a regime of costs based on the quantity and not the quality of the work, in which the assessment of costs (because there was no reward for skill, efficiency and experience) ceased to be a judicial function and became little more than a bureaucratic arithmetical exercise. I awoke to find it was not a nightmare – it was the Matrimonial Causes (Costs) Rules 1988. When I awoke on 26 April 1999, I found that the Matrimonial Causes (Costs) Rules 1988 and the Family Proceedings (Costs) Rules 1991 which incorporated them had gone. They had been revoked by the Family Proceedings (Miscellaneous Amendments) Rules 1999 which had come into force at midnight on 25 April. It had been a close run thing. For many weeks during that spring it appeared that from 26 April, where there had previously been provision for costs in family proceedings there would just be a gaping hole, because from that date RSC Ord 62 and CCR Ord 38 would be replaced by the Civil Procedure Rules 1998 which did not apply to family proceedings. We were confident that, as in all good B movies, we should be rescued at the stroke of midnight, and of course we were, but not in the way that most of us expected. Instead of the existing costs provisions for family proceedings being preserved whilst there was a period of consultation preparatory to the introduction of a regime of costs tailor-made for family proceedings, the costs provisions of the CPR were simply superimposed onto family work, with one inspirational adaptation. Wherever the CPR used the word 'claimant' or 'defendant', this was to be treated as a reference to petitioner, applicant or respondent. Just think of the midnight oil that must have been burnt in devising that!

2. THE FAMILY PROCEEDINGS (MISCELLANEOUS AMENDMENTS) RULES 1999

This is how it was done. Parts 43 to 48 of the CPR were applied to family proceedings with these exceptions:

(a) *Rule 44.3(2)* (The general rule that costs follow the event, but see below)
(b) *Rules 44.9–44.11* (Relating to the small claims and fast tracks which of course do not apply in family proceedings)
(c) *Rule 44.12* (Costs Orders deemed to have been made, such as where notice of discontinuance is served or money in court is accepted. Again, not appropriate for family proceedings)
(d) *Part 45* (Fixed costs)
(e) *Part 46* (Fast track trial costs)

The Family Proceedings (Miscellaneous Amendment) Rules also provided that they apply to any assessment of costs taking place on or after 26 April 1999, but so that, as a general rule, no costs for work done before that date shall be disallowed if they would have been allowed on taxation before that date. Although the new rules disapplied RSC Ord 62 and CCR Ord 38 from the assessment of costs in family proceedings and replaced them with the CPR, they preserved them in respect of all other aspects of family proceedings, together with the Family Proceedings Rules 1991. For example, in family proceedings applications for a re-hearing and appeals are still governed by CCR Ord 37. So do not throw away your 1999 Green and White Books.

3. DIRECTIONS

The new costs rules were accompanied by a President's Direction of 22 April 1999. Here it is:

President's Direction 22 April 1999

[1999] 3 All ER 192, [1999] 2 FCR 1, [1999] 1 FLR 1295

It is directed that upon the coming into force on 26 April 1999 of the Civil Procedure Rules (CPR) and the Family Proceedings (Miscellaneous Amendments) Rules 1999, SI 1999/1012:

(a) [Not relevant to costs]

(b) The Practice Direction about costs supplementing CPR, Pts 43 to 48 (the costs direction) shall apply to family proceedings to which the Family Proceedings Rules 1991, SI1991/1247, apply and to proceedings in the Family Division. References in the costs direction to 'claimant' and 'defendant' are to be read as references to the equivalent terms used in family proceedings and other terms and expressions used in the costs direction shall be similarly treated. References to procedural steps and to other parts of the CPR which have not yet been applied to family proceedings are to be read as referring to equivalent or similar procedures under the rules applicable to family proceedings, as the context may permit. The previous practice in relation to 'costs reserved' will no longer be followed and such an order will have the effect specified in the costs direction. It should also be noted that the period for commencing detailed assessment proceedings will be as specified in CPR, r 47.7 (three months) in substitution for the period of six months previously applicable.

Issued with the approval and concurrence of the Lord Chancellor.

Sir Stephen Brown

It applies to family proceedings all of the practice directions supplementing CPR Parts 43 to 48, even though Parts 43 to 48 do not all apply to family proceedings; as previously noted, it substitutes the family equivalent for 'claimant' and 'defendant'; at long last the term 'costs reserved' is given the same meaning as in civil proceedings (see p 165) and there is further unification by the substitution of 'three months' for the period in which a detailed assessment must be commenced for the previous 'six months' in family proceedings.

The 1999 direction was supplemented on 24 July 2000 as follows:

Practice Direction (Family Proceedings: Application and Costs)

([1999] 1 WLR 1128 applied Practice Direction (Civil Litigation: Procedure) ([1999] 1 WLR 1124) about costs supplementing Parts 43 to 48 of the Civil procedure Rules to Family Proceedings within the Family Proceedings Rules and to proceedings in the Family Division.

A new edition of the costs direction, effective from 3 July 2000 had been published (second supplement to the Civil Procedure Rules, paragraphs 43 PD-001 to 006, pp 46–55) and all subsequent editions as and when they were published and came into effect, should extend to Family Proceedings and to proceedings and to proceedings in the Family Division in the same way as did the costs direction and to the extent applicable to such proceedings.

The further edition of the costs direction included provision applicable to proceedings following changes in the manner in which legal services were funded pursuant to the Access to Justice Act 1999. It should be noted that although the costs of the premium in respect of legal costs insurance (s 29), and all the costs of funding by a prescribed membership organisation (s 30) might be recoverable, family proceedings (within s 58A2 of the Courts and Legal services Act 1990 as inserted by s 27(1) of the 1999 Act) could not be the subject of an enforceable conditional fee agreement.

Dame Elizabeth Butler-Sloss

4. COSTS FOLLOWING THE EVENT

(a) Costs do not follow the event

As we have seen, the Family Proceedings (Miscellaneous Amendment) Rules 1999 provide that CPR Rule 44.3(2) shall not apply in family proceedings. This includes both the costs of the suit and the costs of ancillary proceedings. A between-the-parties order for costs of the suit may be inappropriate when the petition is based on two years' separation and consent or five years' separation. In a consent petition the petitioner often claims costs, or half of the costs. If the respondent agrees, there is no problem. If the respondent is not willing to pay the costs claimed he or she should refuse to consent until the claim for costs is withdrawn or agreed. In other petitions a helpful device is to include a prayer for costs 'only if the suit is defended'.

(b) The cases

Nevertheless, in *Gojkovic v Gojkovic (No 2)* [1992] 1 All ER 267, CA it was held that even in the Family Division the starting point has to be that costs on the face of it follow the event, although the presumption might be more easily displaced and in circumstances which did not apply in other Divisions of the High Court. One important example was that it was unusual to order costs in Children Act cases. Indeed, in family matters it is often difficult to identify an 'event' which costs might follow.

However, there does not have to be an identifiable event to justify an award of costs. In *Hurley v Hurley* [1998] 2 FCR 14, the Court of Appeal held that the judge had misdirected himself in refusing to order a respondent husband to pay the costs of his mother-in-law who had intervened in order to preserve her alleged beneficial interest in the matrimonial home. When the husband conceded that the home should not be sold and that the petitioner could continue to live there, it was no longer necessary for the mother-in-law to pursue her claim because her daughter was happy for her to continue living with her. The judge took the view that as the mother-in-law had not pursued her claim to adjudication, she had neither won nor lost and therefore there was no event in respect of which the court could found an order for costs against the husband. He was wrong: he should have approached the matter on the basis of whether it was reasonable in the circumstances for the intervener to intervene and, if so, whether she unnecessarily or unreasonably added to the costs of the proceedings? The judge had greatly fettered the exercise of his judicial discretion by propounding a principle for which there was no authority. I hope it will not undermine your confidence in this book when I confess that I was the judge.

Three more cases illustrate the approach of the courts. In *Re G (costs: child case)* [1999] 2 FLR 250, the Court of Appeal held that 'it was unusual to order costs in a family case, although it would be appropriate to order costs where a parent, even a litigant in person, went beyond the limit of what was reasonable to pursue the application before the court'. Even though the judge had found the father's case to be hopeless, the court held that hopelessness and reasonableness were not necessarily the same thing. Furthermore, a greater degree of generosity might be appropriate in ruling that pursuing an application had become unreasonable where the litigant was acting in person rather than where he was receiving legal advice. In *Re W (a child)* (26 August 2000, unreported), CA on the father's application to vary an order for residence with the mother, the judge confirmed the existing arrangements, extended staying contact and ordered the father to pay the costs, commenting that the proceedings had been long and protracted and that the mother had been the successful party. In allowing the father's appeal against the order for costs, the court said the judge had not criticised the father's motives or provided any other readily discernible reason for departing from the normal rule in private family law cases that each party should pay its own costs. It is essential that between-the-parties costs orders should only ever be made in exceptional cases where a party had been guilty of manipulating the litigation for their own ends rather than advancing a case which they genuinely believed to be in the best interests of the child. The third case, *Re B (costs)* [1999] 3 FCR 586, CA demonstrated that although it is rare to make costs orders in Children Act cases, the rule is not invariable. The mother had suffered from a serious manic depressive illness as a result of which the child resided with the father, who opposed the mother's application for staying contact because of his fear the mother might have a relapse which could put the child at risk. The mother produced evidence from a psychiatric consultant that the child would not be at any risk, but the father was unwilling to accept this even when a psychiatrist instructed by him agreed with the mother's psychiatrist. The Court of Appeal held the judge was right to take the view that from the date that the two psychiatrists reached agreement the father should have withdrawn his opposition to staying contact and therefore ordered him to pay the mother's costs from that date, and that the judge was also correct in assessing the costs of the father's continued and unjustified opposition at 80% of the costs of the hearing. If I now reveal that I was also the judge in that case I hope it may restore some of your confidence in me!

5. DUTY TO NEGOTIATE

Gojkovic also established that where the assets are substantial and where an order for costs, if appropriate, could be made, negotiations which might lead to a settlement were to be encouraged by the courts. For a Calderbank offer (a 'without prejudice' offer to settle) to be effective it required teeth and 'it was incumbent on the recipient of an offer to accept or reject it and, if the latter, to make (her) position clear and indicate in figures what (she) is asking for (a counter-offer). It is incumbent on both parties to negotiate if possible and at least make an attempt to settle the case'. An offer to settle should influence, but ought not to govern, the exercise of the court's wide discretion in awarding costs. There were many reasons which might affect the court in considering costs, such as culpability in the conduct of litigation, delay or excessive zeal in seeking disclosure. Where an offer to settle has been made, the starting point is that if the applicant received no more than the offer made he was at risk not only of not being awarded costs but also of paying the costs of the other party after communication of the offer and a reasonable time to consider it. Accordingly, the Court of Appeal allowed the appeal of the wife against the decision of the judge not to award her costs when she had been successful in her action against her husband and had obtained an order in excess of the offer made by him. In proceedings for financial relief the amount and incidence of costs is often an important factor to be considered when the court is dealing with the family assets. Where one or both of the parties is in receipt of state funding the operation of the statutory charge may be critical. The philosophical gulf between matrimonial and civil litigation was emphasised in *C & H Engineering v F Klucznik & Son Ltd* [1992] FSR 667, ChD where it was held that outside the Family Division the recipient of an unacceptable offer to settle is under no duty to respond to it. Unlike a spouse, a complainant is under no duty to accept anything less than that to which he believes he is entitled. However, under the CPR such an offer may be taken into account when avoiding costs and cannot be ignored with impunity. See Chapter 14.

6. 'WITHOUT PREJUDICE EXCEPT AS TO COSTS'

The Family Proceedings (Amendment No 2) Rules 1999, which came into force on 5 June 2000, amended the Family Proceedings Rules 1991 in respect of the costs of ancillary relief proceedings. They contained some surprising provisions about the costs consequences of offers to settle. Rule 2.69 is replaced and followed by new Rules 2.69A–2.69D relating to costs.

Rule 2.69 provides:

FPR RULE 2.69 OFFERS TO SETTLE

(1) Either party to the application may at any time make a written offer to the other party which is expressed to be 'without prejudice except as to costs' and which relates to any issue in the proceedings relating to the application.
(2) Where an offer is made under paragraph (1), the fact that such an offer has been made shall not be communicated to the court, except in accordance with rule 2.61E(3), until the question of costs falls to be decided.

Nothing surprising there.

FPR RULE 2.69A INTERPRETATION OF RULES 2.69B TO 2.69D

In rules 2.69B to 2.69D, 'base rate' has the same meaning as in the Civil Procedure Rules 1998.

Rule 2.69B provides:

FPR RULE 2.69B JUDGMENT OR ORDER MORE ADVANTAGEOUS THAN AN OFFER MADE BY THE OTHER PARTY

(1) This rule applies where the judgment or order in favour of the applicant or respondent is more advantageous to him than an offer made under rule 2.69(1) by the other party.
(2) The court must, unless it considers it unjust to do so, order that other party to pay any costs incurred after the date beginning 28 days after the offer was made.

There are some curious omissions. Rule 2.69B penalises a party who does not do as well as his own without prejudice offer but does not confer any corresponding benefit on that party if he does as well or better than his offer. He (or, of course, she) is on a hiding to nothing. The rule says the court *must* order him, or her, to pay the offeree's costs, unless it would be unjust to do so. ('Must' is an odd word to use when costs are by statute in the court's discretion.) The rule appears to deter the making of offers rather than to encourage them. Another omission is any provision requiring there to be a response to an offer, either by accepting it or making a counter-offer, in accordance with the principles laid down in *Gojkovic v Gojkovic (No 2)* [1992] 1 All ER 267, CA. *Gojkovic* was of course decided before 26 April 1999 and, with the CPR being a new procedural code the courts are discouraged from looking over their shoulder at cases decided under the old rules. If it was intended that these principles should still apply, then surely the rules should have so provided. Nevertheless, the judiciary appear to regard *Gojkovic* as having survived.

Rule 2.69C provides:

FPR RULE 2.69C JUDGMENT OR ORDER MORE ADVANTAGEOUS THAN OFFERS MADE BY BOTH PARTIES

(1) This rule applies where
  (a) both the applicant and the respondent have made offers under rule 2.69(1); and
  (b) the judgment or order in favour of the applicant or the respondent, as the case may be, is more advantageous to him than both of the offers referred to in paragraph (a).

(2) The court may, where it considers it just, order interest in accordance with paragraph (3) on the whole or part of any sum of money (excluding interest and periodical payments) to be awarded to the applicant or respondent, as the case may be.
(3) Interest under paragraph (2) may be at a rate not exceeding 10 per cent above base rate for some or all of the period beginning 28 days after the offer was made.
(4) The court may also order that the applicant or respondent, as the case may be, is entitled to:
  (a) his costs on the indemnity basis beginning 28 days after the offer was made; and
  (b) interest on those costs at a rate not exceeding 10 per cent above base rate.

(5) The court's powers under this rule are in addition to its powers under rule 2.69B.

Rules 2.69D and 2.69E provide:

FPR RULE 2.69D FACTORS FOR COURT'S CONSIDERATION UNDER RULES 2.69B AND 2.69C

(1) In considering whether it would be unjust, or whether it would be just, to make the orders referred to in rules 2.69B and 2.69C, the court must take into account all the circumstances of the case, including—
- (a) the terms of any offers made under rule 2.69(1);
- (b) the stage in the proceedings when any offer was made;
- (c) the information available to the parties at the time when the offer was made;
- (d) the conduct of the parties with regard to the giving or refusing to give information for the purposes of enabling the offer to be made or evaluated; and
- (e) the respective means of the parties.

(2) The power of the court to award interest under rule 2.69C(2) and (4)(b) is in addition to any other power it may have to award interest.

FPR RULE 2.69E OPEN PROPOSALS

(1) Not less than 14 days before the date fixed for the final hearing of an application for ancillary relief, the applicant must (unless the court directs otherwise) file with the court and serve on the respondent an open statement which sets out concise details, including the amounts involved, of the orders which he proposes to ask the court to make.

(2) Not more than 7 days after service of a statement under paragraph (1), the respondent must file with the court and serve on the applicant an open statement which sets out concise details, including the amounts involved, of the orders which he proposes to ask the court to make.

Rule 2.69C may make a party think carefully before responding to an offer because this could trigger an order for costs against them on the indemnity basis and for enhanced interest if the other party does better than both of the offers. Writing in the *Law Society Gazette* 27 January 2000, David Burrows suggested that the best advice to a wife now must be not to respond to any offer, unless she is a gambler or completely sure of the correctness of her response and that a solicitor who pitches a wife's response too high, risks a negligence claim where no response need have been made. Rewarding a wife for doing better than her own offer is a novel concept which makes it difficult to envisage at what level offers are expected to be pitched. Responding to this criticism, Jane Simpson, a member of the Lord Chancellor's Ancillary Relief Advisory Group, agreed there will be an element of gamble, but asked 'Is this new?'. She agreed that a wife who decides not to reply to a Calderbank offer (as they are still called in family matters) does not run the risk of paying costs on the indemnity basis with interest but she also foregoes the chance of obtaining interest on any lump sum which the court awards her if she beats both her husband's and her own offer. Mrs Simpson was also of the view that the *Gojkovic* duty to negotiate still remains. Certainly making an offer is one of the factors prescribed in rule 2.69D as being relevant to an award of costs, as indeed is CPR Rule 44.3(4). Family practitioners now have to take into account two costs regimes when advising whether or not a Calderbank offer should be made or responded to and at what level it should be pitched. The provisions appear unnecessarily to undermine and confuse the culture of negotiation and settlement which had operated so successfully in family matters from long before the introduction of the Woolf reforms in civil litigation.

Although Rule 2.69E requires the parties to make open offers, there are conflicting decisions (such as *Singer v Sharegin* [1984] FLR 114; *H v H* [1997] 2 FLR 57 and *Leadbeater v Leadbeater* [1985] FLR 789) as to whether the court should decide on the award and amount of costs before making its final decision about the family assets.

7. ESTIMATES

The importance of knowing the amount of the costs of each party was emphasised by a practice direction of 28 March 1988, requiring each party to provide an estimate of their costs incurred and expected.

Although the practice direction has not been revoked it is in effect incorporated in FPR Rule 2.61F:

FPR RULE 2.61F COSTS

(1) At every court hearing or appointment each party must produce to the court an estimate in Form H* of the costs incurred by him up to the date of that hearing or appointment.
(2) The parties' obligation under paragraph (1) is without prejudice to their obligations under paragraphs 4.1 to 4.11** of the Practice Direction relating to CPR Part 44.

* Precedent H is part of Costs Practice Direction section 6 (on p 85).
** Paragraphs 4.11 to 4.11 of the Practice Direction are now sections 12 and 13 (pp 107 and 267).

8. CURBING COSTS

(a) Guidelines

Concern over increasingly heavy legal costs was also expressed by Mrs Justice Booth in *Evans v Evans* [1990] 2 All ER 147, Fam Law when she said that the court was at times unable to make appropriate provision orders for wives and children because of the liability for costs. She issued the following general guidelines to family law practitioners in the preparation of substantial ancillary relief cases:

> 'Affidavit evidence should be confined to relevant facts and should not be prolix or diffuse. Each party should file one substantive affidavit dealing with matters to which the court should have regard under section 3 of the Matrimonial Causes Act 1973, as substituted by section 3 of the Matrimonial and Family Proceedings Act 1984, and matters which were material to the application.
>
> 1. If any further affidavit was necessary it should be confined to matters answering a serious allegation made by the other party dealing with any serious allegation made by the other party dealing with any serious issue raised or setting out any material change of circumstances.
> 2. Inquiries made under rule 2.62 of the Family Proceedings Rules should, as far as possible, be contained in one comprehensive questionnaire and should not be made piecemeal.
> 3. Wherever possible valuations of properties should be obtained from a valuer jointly instructed by both parties. Where each party instructed a valuer then reports should be exchanged and the valuers should meet in an attempt to resolve differences.

4. While it might be necessary to obtain a broad assessment of the value of a shareholding in a private company it was inappropriate to undertake an expensive and meaningless exercise to achieve a precise valuation of a private company which would not be sold (*P v P* (1989) Times, 3 February).
5. Professional witnesses should be careful to avoid a partisan approach and should maintain professional standards.
6. Care should be taken in deciding what evidence, other than professional evidence, should be adduced and emotive issues which were not material should be avoided. Where affidavit evidence was filed deponents had to be available for cross-examination on notice from the other side.
7. Duplication of documents should be avoided. Both solicitors should prepare together the bundles of documents required at the hearing and should agree what should be included and what excluded. (*This is now covered by the President's Practice Direction of 10 March 2000*).
8. A chronology of material facts should be agreed and made available to the court.
9. In a substantial case it might be desirable to have a pre-trial review to explore the possibility of settlement and to define the issues if settlement could not be reached to ensure readiness for hearing.
10. At all stages of the proceedings clients should be kept informed by solicitor and counsel of the costs incurred and they should ensure that legally aided clients understood the implications of the legal aid charge. The court required an estimate of the approximate amount of costs on each side before a lump sum award could be made.
11. The desirability of reaching a settlement should be borne in mind throughout the proceedings. While it was necessary for legal advisers to have sufficient knowledge of the financial situation of both parties before advising a client on a proposed settlement, the necessity to make further inquiries had to be balanced by a consideration of what those inquiries might be likely to achieve and the increased costs which would be incurred.'

(b) The President's Direction

On 31 January 1995 the President took matters further by issuing a case management direction. Here it is:

President's Direction 31 January 1995

[1995] 1 All ER 586, [1995] 1 WLR 332, [1995] 2 FCR 340, [1995] 1 FLR 456.

Case management

1 The importance of reducing the cost and delay of civil litigation makes it necessary for the court to assert greater control over the preparation for the conduct of hearings than has hitherto been customary. Failure by practitioners to conduct cases economically will be visited by appropriate orders for costs, including wasted costs orders.

2 The court will accordingly exercise its discretion to limit—

(a) discovery;
(b) the length of opening and closing oral submissions;
(c) the time allowed for the examination and cross-examination of witnesses;
(d) the issues on which it wishes to be addressed;
(e) reading aloud from documents and authorities.

3 Unless otherwise ordered, every witness statement or affidavit shall stand as the evidence in chief of the witness concerned. The substance of the evidence which a party intends to adduce at the hearing must be sufficiently detailed, but without prolixity; it must be confined to material matters of fact, not (except in the case of the evidence of professional witnesses) of opinion;

and if hearsay evidence is to be adduced, the source of the information must be declared or good reason given for not doing so.
4 It is a duty owed to the court both by the parties and by their legal representatives to give full and frank disclosure in ancillary relief applications and also in all matters in respect of children. The parties and their advisers must also use their best endeavours—
- (a) to confine the issues and the evidence called to what is reasonably considered to be essential for the proper presentation of their case;
- (b) to reduce or eliminate issues for expert evidence;
- (c) in advance of the hearing to agree which are the issues or the main issues.

5 Unless the nature of the hearing makes it necessary, and in the absence of specific directions, bundles should be agreed and prepared for use by the court, the parties and the witnesses, and shall be in A4 format where possible, suitably secured. The bundles for use by the court shall be lodged with the court (the Clerk of the Rules in matters in the RCJ in London) at least two clear days before the hearing. Each bundle should be paginated, indexed, wholly legible and arranged chronologically. Where documents are copied unnecessarily or bundled incompetently, the cost will be disallowed.
6 In cases estimated to last for five days or more and in which no pre-trial review has been ordered, application should be made for a pre-trial review. It should when practicable be listed at least three weeks before the hearing and be conducted by the judge or district judge before whom the case is to be heard, and should be attended by the advocates who are to represent the parties at the hearing. Whenever possible, all statements or evidence and all reports should be filed before the date of the review and in good time for them to have been considered by all parties.
7 Whenever practicable, and in any matter estimated to last five days or more, each party should, not less than two clear days before the hearing, lodge with the court, or the Clerk of the Rules in matters in the RCJ in London, and deliver to other parties, a chronology and a skeleton argument concisely summarising that party's submissions in relation to each of the issues, and citing the main authorities relied upon. It is important that skeleton arguments should be brief.
8 In advance of the hearing upon request, and otherwise in the course of their opening, parties should be prepared to furnish the court, if there is no core bundle, with a list of documents essential for a proper understanding of the case.
9 The opening speech should be succinct. At its conclusion other parties may be invited briefly to amplify their skeleton arguments. In a heavy case the court may in conjunction with final speeches require written submissions, including the findings of fact for which each party contends.
10 This Practice Direction, which follows the directions handed down by the Lord Chief Justice and the Vice-Chancellor to apply in the Queen's Bench and Chancery Divisions, shall apply to all family proceedings in the High Court and in all Care Centres, Family Hearing Centres and divorce county courts.
11 Issued with the concurrence of the Lord Chancellor.

9. CASH LIMITS?

In *Piglowska v Piglowski* [1999] 3 All ER 632, HL costs exceeding £128,000 had been expended disputing matrimonial assets of £127,400. The House of Lords commented that although the judges of the Family Division were very conscious of the problem of trying to keep the costs in an ancillary relief application proportionate to the matrimonial assets and in *Evans v Evans* had issued general guidelines, in the present case those guidelines had proved inadequate to control the costs. The costs would have been disproportionate even if the case had stopped with the District Judge, let alone having been considered by five differently-constituted tribunals by the time it had reached the Court of Appeal. It appeared that such cases were not capable of being properly brought under control until the courts or the Legal Aid Board imposed cash limits which were directly related to the value of the assets in dispute. Commenting on the case the Lord Chancellor, whilst not proposing a financial ceiling, said that the extension of the ancillary relief pilot scheme over the entire country on 5 June 2000 would address the 'twin evils of cost and delay'. This was a reference to the Family Proceedings (Amendment No 2) Rules 1999 which are considered in section 6 of this chapter.

10. SUMMARY ASSESSMENT

(a) No presumption of detailed assessment

The general rule in para 13.2 of the Practice Direction in Part 44 of the CPR did not imply a general rule requiring detailed assessment of costs in hearings lasting longer than a day. On the contrary, the exercise of the power to make a summary assessment must be considered in every case. In family cases in particular, the aggravation of detailed assessment ran counter to the satisfactory resolution of disputes. (*Q v Q (Costs: Summary assessment)* [2002] 2 FLR 668.)

(b) Discrete issues

Because so many aspects of family matters, such as the divorce, children and ancillary relief, are dealt with at the same time, often in the same attendance, telephone call or letter, it is particularly important to be able to distinguish between them for the purposes of the summary assessment of the costs of an interim application. Otherwise, there is the risk that the statement of costs may include either more or less than the work done for that particular hearing. In substantial matters you should therefore consider having separate folders or dividers within the file, or even separate files, relating to each aspect, or to a specific hearing such as an application for maintenance pending suit. Where appropriate, separate letters should be written on each aspect of the matter, with the time spent on attendances and telephone calls being similarly apportioned. By these means you will be able to satisfy the judge that you are not over-charging – and yourself that you are charging enough.

11. ENFORCEMENT

(a) Statutory demand

Rule 12.3 of the Insolvency Rules 1986 provides:

> '(1) Subject as follows, in bankruptcy … all claims by creditors are provable as debts against … the bankrupt … The following are not provable – (a) in bankruptcy, any fine imposed for an offence and any obligation arising under an order made in family proceedings or under a maintenance assessment made under the Child Support Act 1991 … '.

On this basis, Mr Levy, who was a bankrupt, applied to set aside a statutory demand served by the Legal Aid Board, now the LSC, claiming £62,732 costs incurred by his former wife in her family proceedings. Although there was jurisdiction to make a bankruptcy order on a petition based upon a non-provable debt, the jurisdiction was discretionary and would not be exercised except in special circumstances. It was puzzling that s 382(1) contemplated that a non-provable debt might be regarded as a bankruptcy debt, but it was difficult to conceive of any circumstances where that would occur (*Levy v Legal Services Commission* [2001] 1 All ER 895, CA).

(b) Judgment summons

Schedule 8 of the Administration of Justice Act 1990, which prescribes the matrimonial orders enforceable by judgment summons, does not specifically mention orders for costs, but rule 7.4 of the Family Proceedings Rules 1991 contemplates enforcement of costs orders by judgment summons by providing that on the hearing of a judgment summons the judge may make a new order for payment of the amount due where the original order is for a lump sum provision or costs.

However, in *Murbarak v Murbarak* [2001] 1 FLR 698, the Court of Appeal held that the existing judgment summons procedure under s 5 of the Debtors Act 1869 is not human rights compliant. Judgment summons proceedings for contempt are classified as criminal proceedings and the requirement that the debtor shall attend before the court to show cause why he should not be sent to prison amounts to an unacceptable reversal of the burden of proof and removes the protection against self-incrimination. It will not be safe to proceed by way of judgment summons until a new procedure has been devised.

CHAPTER 16

GETTING THE RIGHT ORDER – AND THE ORDER RIGHT

Costs are peculiarly the province of solicitors. At the end of a hearing the judge's mind is turning towards his next case. Counsel is busy endorsing and tying up the brief. Emotions are high – someone has won and someone has lost, and dealing with costs is a sordid anti-climax. Nevertheless, the fruits of victory can be soured if the proper orders are not made for costs.

It is equally important to make proper provision for costs in any terms of compromise.

1. NO AGREEMENT AS TO COSTS

It is surprising how often the parties reach agreement on all issues except the question of costs.

(a) No proceedings

Where proceedings have not been instituted and agreement cannot be reached over costs, the position is clear: there is no agreement. The matter has not been settled. Sometimes, particularly when negotiating with insurance companies, one party agrees to pay the other's costs but there is no agreement of the amount. The agreement may say 'Costs to be ascertained by detailed assessment if not agreed', but there are no proceedings in which the machinery for a detailed assessment can be set in motion. Until recently, the only possible course was to institute proceedings based upon the agreement seeking an order that the costs be assessed and paid pursuant to the agreement. This incurs the expense of instituting proceedings, which is the very thing the compromise was intended to avoid. However, the dilemma was resolved by the Civil Procedure (Amendment No 3) Rules 2000 which introduced CPR Rule 44.12A (see p 110) containing the procedure to be followed where the parties to a dispute have reached an agreement on all issues, including which party is to pay the costs, but have failed to agree the amount of the costs where no proceedings have been started. In these circumstances, either party may start proceedings by issuing a claim form in accordance with Part 8. The claim form may either make an order for costs or dismiss the claim. It must dismiss the claim if the application is opposed. Otherwise it is vital to grasp the nettle and agree the quantum of costs when compromising a dispute in respect of which proceedings have not been commenced.

(b) Proceedings

If the parties have agreed who will pay the costs but have not agreed the amount then, of course, they have reached agreement and there is no difficulty about the court ordering a detailed assessment of the costs. But what if the parties are agreed on everything but the incidence of costs: can they ask the court to resolve the issue?

In *Booker Belmont v Ashford Developments* (18 July 2000, unreported), CA the parties reached an agreement whereby the fourth party should 'pay such proportion of the claimant's costs of the action as the court shall determine and the reasonable costs of the claimant's expert … '. The judge was held to have been wrong to refuse to make an order determining the proportion of costs to be paid by the fourth party on the grounds that both as a matter of construction and jurisdiction he had no power to do so. As a matter of construction, this was a valid order for costs in a proportion to be fixed by the court. As a matter of jurisdiction, the court always had jurisdiction to decide the costs of an action. The correct approach for the judge would have been to determine the extent to which having regard to the degree of lack of success of the claimant, there should be some reduction in the amount of costs awarded.

Boxall v Waltham Forest London Borough Council [2000] All ER (D) 2445 deduced the following principles where a judicial review was resolved without a hearing:

(a) the court has power to make a costs order when the substantive proceedings have been resolved without a trial but the parties have not agreed about costs;
(b) it will ordinarily be irrelevant that the claimant is legally aided;
(c) the overriding objective is to do justice between the parties without incurring unnecessary court time and consequently additional cost;
(d) at each end of the spectrum there will be cases where it is obvious which side would have won had the substantive issues been fought to a conclusion. In between, the position will, in differing degrees, be less clear. How far the court will be prepared to look into the previously unresolved substantive issues will depend upon the circumstances of the particular case, not least the amount of costs at stake and the conduct of the parties;
(e) in the absence of a good reason to make any other order, the fall-back is to make no order as to costs;
(f) the court should take care to ensure that it does not discourage parties from settling judicial review proceedings, for example by a local authority making a concession at an early stage.

Brawley v Marczynski [2002] EWCA Civ 756, [2002] All ER (D) 110 (May) confirmed there is no tradition of there being no order as to costs where a dispute is settled, except as to costs, without judicial intervention.

2. CHILDREN AND PATIENT SETTLEMENTS

There must not only be a detailed assessment of the costs awarded to a child or a patient, but also of any adult who is a claimant – both their between the parties and solicitor and client costs. However, the Practice Direction supplementing CPR Rule 48.5 enables this to be avoided where costs are agreed between the parties and the solicitor waives any further solicitor and client costs, but only if this is specifically provided for in the order. For the full provision see 'Costs where money is payable by or to a child or patient' at p 439. The Supreme Court Costs Office takes the view that the words 'costs to be assessed if not agreed' are not a sufficient waiver to avoid a detailed assessment.

3. STATE FUNDING

The only way in which the solicitor for a funded client in litigation can avoid having a detailed assessment of his costs is if they are under £1,000 (including counsel's fees and disbursements, but not VAT) which costs may be assessed by the Area Director. Otherwise, their costs must be approved by the court. However, where the assisted person's solicitor is able to agree the costs to be paid by the other party which he and counsel are willing to accept in full satisfaction of their claim against the fund, the solicitor may avoid a detailed assessment by submitting the amount of the costs, with supporting documents, for assessment by the Area Director. It is quick, efficient and free!

In the context of legal aid costs, remember the statutory charge. It is negligent not to advise a client that all of the assisted person's costs will be deducted out of the proceeds of a consent judgment if you do not also recover costs from the other party.

4. GLOSSARY

Section 8.5 of the practice direction supplementing CPR Rule 44.3 provides a useful table of the most commonly made interim orders for costs setting out the general effect of these orders. It makes no claim to be exhaustive. Here it is:

SECTION 8: PRACTICE DIRECTION SUPPLEMENTING CPR RULE 44.3

8.5

Term	***Effect***
• *Costs* • *Costs in any event*	*The party in whose favour the order is made is entitled to the costs in respect of the part of the proceedings to which the order relates, whatever other costs orders are made in the proceedings.*
• *Costs in the case* • *Costs in the application*	*The party in whose favour the court makes an order for costs at the end of the proceedings is entitled to his costs of the part of the proceedings to which the order relates.*
• *Costs reserved*	*The decision about costs is deferred to a later occasion, but if no later order is made the costs will be costs in the case.*
• *Claimant's/defendant's costs in the case/ application*	*If the party in whose favour the costs order is made is awarded costs at the end of the proceedings, that party is entitled to his costs of the part of the proceedings to which the order relates. If any other party is awarded costs at the end of the proceedings, the party in whose favour the final costs order is made is not liable to pay the costs of any other party in respect of the part of the proceedings to which the order relates.*
• *Costs thrown away*	*Where, for example, a judgment or order is set aside, the party in whose favour the costs order is made is entitled to the costs which have been incurred as a consequence. This includes the costs of—* *a) preparing for and attending any hearing at which the judgment or order which has been set aside was made;* *b) preparing for and attending any hearing to set aside the judgment or order in question;*

Term	**Effect**
	c) preparing for and attending any hearing at which the court orders the proceedings or the part in question to be adjourned; *d) any steps taken to enforce a judgment or order which has subsequently been set aside.*
• *Costs of and caused by*	*Where, for example, the court makes this order on an application to amend a statement of case, the party in whose favour the costs order is made is entitled to the costs of preparing for and attending the application and the costs of any consequential amendment to his own statement of case.*
• *Costs here and below*	*The party in whose favour the costs order is made is entitled not only to his costs in respect of the proceedings in which the court makes the order but also to his costs of the proceedings in any lower court. In the case of an appeal from a Divisional Court the party is not entitled to any costs incurred in any court below the Divisional Court.*
• *No order as to costs* • *Each party to pay his own costs*	*Each party is to bear his own costs of the part of the proceedings to which the order relates whatever costs order the court makes at the end of the proceedings.*

The orders and definitions in the practice direction are basically the same as before the CPR, with the helpful addition of 'costs thrown away'. This has always sounded good and although everyone thought they knew what it meant, they did not always think that it meant the same thing. The detailed definition should save much confusion. In fact, there should be little prospect of orders for costs thrown away being made because, except in the most unusual circumstances, there should be a summary assessment at the end of the hearing.

5. SILENCE

Silence on the question of costs in a final judgment or order, or terms of compromise, has always been construed as meaning that each party will bear their own costs. In respect of interim hearings the glossary confirms that 'no order as to costs' continues to mean that each party bears their own costs of that application in any event. But what about silence? What if the court in fact makes no orders for costs, in other words it is silent on the subject. Prior to 26 April 1999, those costs would be included in the final order for costs and go to the receiving party. However, Rule 44.13(1) provides that if the judge says nothing about costs, no party shall in any event be entitled to the costs relating to that order. It will be the same as if the judge had actually uttered the words 'no order as to costs'. There may be a remedy under the slip rule – or just hope that on the detailed assessment no-one notices the omission!

6. APPEALS

(a) Interim

If either party appeals against an interim order, then the winner of the appeal is likely to be awarded their costs of that appeal in any event.

(b) Final

A frequent ground for applying for permission to appeal from an award of costs is the failure of the judge to give adequate reasons. This was addressed by the Court of Appeal in *English v Emery Reimbold & Strick Ltd* [2002] EWCA Civ 605, [2002] 3 All ER 385, in which it held:

(1) Where an application for permission to appeal on the ground of lack of reasons is made to the judge of first instance, he should consider whether his judgment is defective for lack of reasons, adjourning for that purpose if necessary. If he concludes that it was, then he should remedy the defect by providing additional reasons, and then refuse permission to appeal. If he concludes that his reasons were adequate, then he should refuse permission to appeal.

(2) Where an application for permission to appeal on the ground of lack of reasons is made to an appellate court, and it appears to that court that the application is well founded, it should consider adjourning the application and remitting the case to the trial judge with an invitation to provide reasons, or additional reasons. Where the appellate court is in doubt as to the adequacy of reasons, it may be appropriate to adjourn the application to an oral hearing on notice to the respondent.

(3) Where permission to appeal is granted on the ground of inadequate reasons, the appellate court should review the judgment in the light of the evidence and submissions at trial in order to determine whether it was apparent why the judge had reached the decision he did. If the reason is apparent and valid, the appeal would be dismissed. If the reasons were still not apparent the appeal court would have to consider whether to proceed to a rehearsing or direct a new trial.

(4) If the reasons for a judge's order as to costs are plain, as where costs followed the event, there was no need for the judge to give reasons for a costs order. However, the CPR sometimes require a more complex approach to costs, and judgments dealing with costs will more often need to identify the provisions of the rules which have been in play and why these have led to the order made. Where no express reason for a costs order is given the appeal court will approach the material facts on the assumption that the judge has a good reason for the order made, and where there is a perfectly rational explanation for the order the appeal court is likely to draw the inference that this is what motivated the judge in making the order. Accordingly it was only in cases where an order for costs was made with neither reasons nor any obvious explanation for the order that it is likely to be appropriate to give permission to appeal on the ground of lack of reasons.

(5) In the costs decision under consideration on this appeal, the judge had made no order as to costs without giving any reasons. However, analysis of the judgment showed that the judge thought that the action had resulted in a draw, a conclusion which was open to the judge. That appeal would therefore be dismissed.

(6) The court confirmed what was said in CPR Rule 44.3(7), namely that a trial court should ordinarily not make an order for the costs of issues, and should only make such an order if other forms of order could not be made which adequately reflected the justice of the case.

(This summary is from Butterworths Cost Service Bulletin 12, by Jeremy Morgan, to whom I am grateful.)

7. APPLICATIONS NOT ON NOTICE

If a claimant expressly or tacitly invites the defendant to be present on the hearing of a not-on-notice application, either to give evidence or to disclose his line of argument and the motion or summons is dismissed, the court can order the claimant to pay the defendant's costs, either in the case or in any event, even though the application was not on formal notice.

8. PITFALLS

(a) Costs reserved

Any interlocutory costs which have been reserved will automatically be awarded to the winner of the action unless the trial judge orders otherwise.

(b) Costs in any event

Where an action is settled, unless the terms of settlement say otherwise, any costs which have been awarded to one of the parties 'in any event' will still be recoverable. Such costs will even survive the termination of proceedings on the basis 'record withdrawn – no costs on either side'!

(c) Third parties

It is important to ensure that the final order makes provision for the costs of a third party against whom proceedings have been stayed at an earlier stage.

(d) Bullock and Sanderson Orders

These orders arise where an action founded on either contract or tort against two defendants is successful against one and unsuccessful against the other. The court has a discretion (see *Mayer v Harte* [1960] 2 All ER 840, [1960] 1 WLR 770, CA for the principles upon which such discretion is exercised) to order the unsuccessful defendant to pay the successful defendant's costs. This can be done in one of two ways:

(i) An order that the unsuccessful defendant pay directly to the successful defendant the latter's costs (known as a Sanderson Order because it was first made in *Sanderson v Blyth Theatre Co* [1903] 2 KB 533, CA).
(ii) An order that the claimant pay the successful defendant's costs, permitting the claimant to add them to the costs ordered to be paid to him by the unsuccessful defendant (a Bullock Order – *Bullock v London General Omnibus Co* [1907] 1 KB 264, CA).

Where the claimant has no means, then, subject to the court's discretion, the Sanderson Order (ie (i) above) is the fairer way of dealing with the justice of the case. Neither order is appropriate in favour of a claimant who has sued both defendants because of a doubt as to the law as opposed to the facts, or where the causes of action against each are quite distinct, nor where the respective claims are not alternative or are based upon quite distinct sets of facts.

(e) State funding

Where you are acting for two or more parties, some, but not all of whom are in receipt of state funding, ensure that the order adequately protects the claim against the fund. Otherwise the costs recoverable against the fund will be divided by the number of parties for whom you act – with a disastrous (for you) decimation of the costs payable under the funding certificate.

(f) VAT between the parties

This subject is so important and gives rise to so much misunderstanding that I devote Chapter 12 to it.

9. VARYING AND REVOKING

Prior to the introduction of the Civil Procedure Rules, once an order had been made and entered by the court neither the judge who made it nor another judge of co-ordinate jurisdiction had any jurisdiction to vary it unless the order itself contained a power permitting an application to vary. The only remedy was to appeal. However, CPR Rule 3.1(7) provides 'the power of the court under these rules to make an order includes the power to vary or revoke the order'. It will be interesting to see to what extent judges are prepared to exercise their jurisdiction under Rule 3.1(7) in respect of orders for costs. CPR Rule 40.9 provides that even a person who is not a party but who is directly affected by a judgment or order may apply to have the judgment or order set aside or varied.

10. THE SLIP RULE

Let us end on a note of comfort. Clerical mistakes in judgments, or orders or errors arising therein from any accidental slip or omission, may at any time be corrected by the court (CPR Rule 40.12). A party may apply for a correction without notice. The Practice Direction supplementing Part 40 provides as follows:

> ***PRACTICE DIRECTION SUPPLEMENTING CPR PART 40***
>
> ***CORRECTION OF ERRORS IN JUDGMENTS AND ORDERS***
>
> *4.1 Where a judgment or order contains an accidental slip or omission a party may apply for it to be corrected.*
> *4.2 The application notice (which may be an informal document such as a letter) should describe the error and set out the correction required. An application may be dealt with without a hearing:*
> *(1) where the applicant so requests,*
> *(2) with the consent of the parties, or*
> *(3) where the court does not consider that a hearing would be appropriate.*
> *4.3 The judge may deal with the application without notice if the slip or omission is obvious or may direct notice of the application to be given to the other party or parties.*
> *4.4 If the application is opposed it should, if practicable, be listed for hearing before the judge who gave the judgment or made the order.*
> *4.5 The court has an inherent power to vary its own orders to make the meaning and intention of the court clear.*

The power arises where the clearly expressed judgment of the judge has been wrongly recorded in the judgment or order. The error may be rectified on the application of either party or on the initiative of the court itself. Apart from this provision of the rules, the court has an inherent power to vary its own orders so as to carry out its own meaning and to make its meaning plain (*Thynne v Thynne* [1955] P 272, CA). The power to correct clerical mistakes extends not only to those made by an administrative officer of the court but also to those made by a party or his advisors (*Navimpriex Centrala Navala v George Moundreas & Co SA* (1983) 127 Sol Jo 392, CA). However, the slip rule cannot be invoked to rehear or amend an order for costs which correctly reflects the judge's order (*Preston Banking Co v William Allsup & Sons* [1895] 1 Ch 141, CA) or where there has been a misunderstanding as to the effect of a conventional costs order (*Mölnlycke AB v Procter & Gamble Ltd (No 6)* [1993] FSR 154). It can be used where the judge was not asked to make an order which he would have done had he been asked (*Re Earl Inchcape, Craigmyle v Inchcape* [1942] 2 All ER 157, Ch D). There is no time limit for such an application.

CHAPTER 17

THE INDEMNITY PRINCIPLE

1. NOT A FULL INDEMNITY

In England and Wales it is usual for the loser in litigation to be ordered to pay the winner's costs or, as CPR Rule 44.3(2)(*a*) puts it, 'the general rule is that the unsuccessful party will be ordered to pay the costs of the successful party'. Costs are awarded to indemnify the successful party for the costs and expenses he has incurred in the litigation. Although this is called an indemnity it is not (as we shall see in Chapter 22) a full indemnity for a variety of reasons: the winner (the receiving party) may have agreed an unreasonable charging rate with his solicitors; unreasonable work may have been done; the work may have been done by the wrong level of fee earner or counsel and unnecessary disbursements may have been incurred. All of these are matters over which the loser (the paying party) had no control and it would be wrong for the receiving party to be indemnified for them.

2. NO PROFIT

Although it is unusual for costs ordered between the parties to be as much as the receiving party's solicitor and client costs, what is certain is that costs between the parties can *never exceed* the solicitor and client costs. The receiving party is entitled only to be indemnified for his liability to his solicitor – they cannot make a profit out of the costs recovered from the other party. The first record of this principle being expounded was in *Harold v Smith* (1860) 5 H & N 381 in these terms:

> 'costs as between party and party are given by the law as an indemnity to the person entitled to them: they are not imposed as a punishment on the party who pays them, nor given as a bonus to the party who receives them. Therefore, if the extent of the indemnification can be found out, the extent to which costs ought to be allowed is also ascertained'.

3. PITFALLS

(a) Pro bono

We now come to the pitfalls. Let us start with an easy one. If the solicitor agrees to work for nothing, the client has no liability for costs to his solicitor and therefore has no need for or entitlement to an indemnity from the other party if he succeeds in the litigation.

The seminal case is *Gundry v Sainsbury* [1910] 1 KB 645 in which the Court of Appeal held that to award costs to a client whose solicitor had agreed not to charge costs would have been giving a bonus to the party receiving them. That was contrary to justice and to common sense and also to the law as laid down in *Harold v Smith.* It is understandable that a solicitor may agree to act on the basis that he will make no charge unless the action succeeds. Indeed, in practice, this is often the case when acting for an impoverished non-state funded client, but why, you might ask, would a solicitor agree to act on the basis that he would not be paid whatever the outcome of the litigation? I know of only two such reported cases. The first was *Gundry v Sainsbury* in which the client was a labourer suing for injuries caused by being bitten by a dog and who in the course of the cross-examination said: 'I could not pay costs and I had arranged with my solicitor not to pay the costs of the action'. The solicitor disagreed that those were in fact the terms of the retainer but he was precluded from giving evidence to this effect by the Attorneys and Solicitors Act 1870, s 4! As Buckley LJ said in the Court of Appeal, it was a matter of some regret that the solicitor was not allowed to go into the box and state the real facts relating to the agreement. It was for this reason that the public-spirited solicitor was deprived of the between-the-parties costs of the successful litigation. A more recent example arose in *British Waterways Board v Norman* (1993) 26 HLR 232, QBD, in which the court held that where solicitors agreed to act for a client whose financial circumstances were such that there was no prospect of the client paying the solicitors' costs unless the action succeeded, in the absence of a specific agreement to the contrary, the court concluded there must have been an understanding between the solicitor and the client that they would not look to her for any costs if she lost. This appears to be a reversal of the usual basis of a contract that either party is entitled to enforce it unless there is an express prohibition against them doing so. This case is often referred to as having been overruled by *Thai Trading v Taylor* (pp 497). But *Thai Trading* was concerned about the lawfulness of a 'no win, no fee' agreement and it was only this aspect of the judgment in *British Waterways Board v Norman* that was overruled by *Thai Trading*. The basic tenet remains that, if a solicitor expressly or impliedly agrees that he will not in any circumstances charge his client, no costs are recoverable from the other party.

Two recent cases in which the question of impecuniosity was invoked were *Leeds City Council v Carr* (1999) Times, 12 November, QBD Div.Ct, in which the local authorities sought to avoid paying costs ordered against them on the grounds that private prosecutions in respect of defective properties were funded by the solicitors on the basis that their clients would not be liable to pay any costs to them, win or lose, and that any purported agreement to the contrary was a sham. In both cases the court found there was no sufficient basis for the allegation.

A topical example of working for no fee, whatever the outcome of the litigation, is the professional pro bono groups. It has been suggested that the court should be empowered to order the loser in litigation to make a contribution to the running costs of a successful action which has been supported pro bono, but even this would be a breach of the indemnity principle.

(b) Payment by a third party

Litigation is increasingly being funded under arrangements whereby the solicitor's costs are to be paid by a third party, perhaps a trade union or an insurance company. In order to recover costs from another party it must be shown that the client had a primary, or dual, liability for his solicitor's costs, as he was able to do in *R v Miller and Glennie* [1983] 3 All ER 186. It is therefore important expressly to incorporate in the client care letter the right to look to the client for payment of the solicitor and client costs if the case is won and indeed if it is lost unless there is a valid conditional fee agreement. Otherwise, on the basis of *British Waterways Board v Norman*, it may be argued that there is an implication to the contrary and that the client has no liability to his solicitor for which he is entitled to be indemnified between the parties.

(c) Fixed fee

Where a solicitor agrees to work for a fixed fee, that is the maximum amount that can be recovered from another party.

(d) Interim bill

If during the course of litigation the solicitor delivers a bill to the client for work done to date – a stage payment – if that bill is a statute bill and not merely a request for payment on account (see p 8) then the solicitor has fixed his costs at that amount for the work done during the period covered by the bill and cannot recover a higher amount from another party for that period.

(e) Item-by-item

A dramatic development in the application of the indemnity principle was the decision of the Court of Appeal in *General of Berne Insurance Co v Jardine* [1998] 2 All ER 301, CA. Two Supreme Court Taxing Office masters (now cost judges) had reached conflicting decisions on whether the application of the indemnity principle should be on an item-by-item basis, or whether it only provides a global cap, so that the receiving party may recover on assessment uplifted hourly expense rates which are judged to be reasonable, even if they exceed the rates that the solicitors were entitled to receive from their client under a contentious business agreement, provided that the total amount allowed between the parties did not exceed the total amount the solicitors were entitled to recover from their client. There were arguments both ways and, in the words of the Court of Appeal, 'each of the parties' cases has its problems'. The court came down in favour of the item-by-item approach, even though it accepted that examples could arise where complicated and painstaking reductions could be required, commenting 'taxation [*assessment*] of costs can be a laborious procedure in any event, and can be expensive in taxing [*assessing*] fees'. No one would quarrel with that. *Nederlandse Reassurantie Groep Holding NV v Bacon & Woodrow* ([1998] 2 Costs LR 32, CA), a review of a taxation [*detailed assessment*] by Mr Justice Tucker, confirmed that the *General of Berne v Jardine* interpretation of the indemnity principle applied to all retainers, whether or not a formal contentious business agreement was in place.

The full consequences of these decisions are still emerging, for example: where interlocutory costs have been awarded against the receiving party or where parts of the receiving party's costs have been excluded; if the receiving party's solicitor was acting for a fixed fee, there cannot be an item by item comparison; if the retainer provides that the solicitor will not charge the client more than the amount of costs recovered between the parties what is the amount for which the client is entitled to be indemnified? Nil? Or perhaps the solicitor should agree not to charge the client *less* than the amount recovered between the parties! How is a retainer for a fixed expense rate with a flexible mark-up to be compared between the parties? How does the indemnity principle apply where the Legal Aid Board or the Community Legal Service has put a financial limit on the certificate? How does the amount of the success fee under a conditional fee agreement affect the application of the indemnity principle? How does the principle apply where a party is entitled to fixed costs, for example fixed trial costs on the fast track?

(f) Disclosure

A matter which has bedevilled assessments of costs for some years is how is the paying party to discover the terms of the retainer to ascertain the level of the indemnity to which the receiving party is entitled? For some time I have expressed the view that solicitors for a paying party could be negligent if they fail to obtain this information and, indeed, that the onus should be on the receiving party to satisfy the costs officer that the terms of the retainer entitle him to the indemnity for costs he is seeking. This view received support in *Bailey v IBC Vehicles Ltd* [1998] 3 All ER 570, CA, in which the court held that in future, any client care letter setting out the terms of the client's financial obligations to the solicitors should be attached to the bill of costs together with any contentious business agreement or other relevant documents. Lord Justice Henry in that case suggested that the signing of the between-the-parties bill of costs by the solicitor as an officer of the court was effectively a certificate that the receiving party's solicitors were not seeking to recover in relation to any item more than they had agreed to charge their client. There was a presumption of trust and any breach of that trust should be treated as a most serious disciplinary offence.

This approach has been exemplified in a recent case and in the Supreme Court Costs Office's *Guide to the Summary Assessment of Costs*. The case was *Hazlett v Sefton Metropolitan Borough Council* [2000] 4 All ER 887, in which it was held that for the purpose of making an order for costs between the parties, there is a presumption that the client would be personally liable for her solicitor's costs and it would not normally be necessary for the client to have to adduce evidence to that effect. However, where there was a genuine issue raised by the paying party as to whether the receiving party had properly incurred costs in the proceedings, the position would be different. If it were alleged that the receiving party was not liable to pay her solicitor's costs, whether because she had entered into an unlawful and an unenforceable conditional fee agreement with her solicitor or for any other reasons, she would be at risk if she continued to rely upon the presumption that she was liable for her solicitor's costs. If she did not then adduce evidence to prove that she had properly incurred costs in the proceedings or that the paying party could show by evidence or argument that she had not, she would be most unlikely to succeed in recovering her costs. The need for a claimant to give evidence to prove her entitlement to costs rather than relying upon the presumption in her favour would not, however, arise if the paying party simply put the claimant to proof of her entitlement to costs. Then the claimant would be justified in relying on the presumption in her favour. The SCCO *Guide* quotes the words of Lord Justice Henry in *Bailey v IBC Vehicles* and suggests that the signature of a schedule of costs (or a bill for detailed assessment) by a solicitor is, in normal circumstances, sufficient to enable the court to be satisfied that the indemnity principle has not been breached.

Dickinson v Rushmer ([2002] NLJR 58) was an appeal from a detailed assessment by a costs judge to Rimer J sitting with assessors. On the detailed assessment the paying party (the defendant) invoked the indemnity principle, asserting that the receiving party (the claimant) could not have assumed a personal responsibility to pay costs of the amount claimed in his solicitor's bills. The claimant's solicitors produced to the costs judge documents to prove the terms of the retainer and demonstrate there was no breach of the indemnity principle. The costs judge refused to allow the defendant to see the documents on the grounds they were privileged. It was held that the costs judge was wrong. It is one of the most basic principles of natural justice that each side is entitled to know what the other side's case is and to see the documentary material on which he was relying. The receiving party, without producing any documents, could ask the costs judge to direct whether he regarded the paying party as having raised a genuine issue which needed to be met by evidence, or if he accepted the signification on the bill of costs that the indemnity principle had not been offended. If the receiving party pre-empts any such decision by the costs judge by producing the documents, the paying party is entitled to see them, even though they were privileged.

In *South Coast Shipping Co Ltd v Havant Borough Council* ([2002] 3 All ER 779) the costs judge had been shown documents the paying party had not been allowed to see on the grounds that they were privileged. The appeal raised human rights issues, in particular the conflict between the right to privilege and the right to a fair trial. If the costs judge, having seen the documents in question, required the receiving party to elect between giving secondary evidence of the retainer and waiving the privilege, there was no incompatibility with the principles articulated by the Convention. That was not intended to suggest that the costs judge should put the receiving party to its election in respect of every document relied on, regardless of its degree of relevance. In the great majority of cases the paying party would be content to agree that the costs judge alone should see privileged documents. Only where it was necessary and proportionate should the receiving party be put to his election. The redaction and production of privileged documents, or the adducing of further evidence, would lead to additional delay and increase costs.

Although both *Dickinson* and *South Coast Shipping* referred to pre-CPR decisions, neither report made specific reference to *Hazlett* which confirmed the presumption that a client would be liable to pay her solicitor's costs and need only adduce evidence if a genuine issue was raised, such as the unlawfulness of the retainer or the enforceability of a CFA. What these two cases clearly establish is that right of the paying party to see documents adduced in evidence overrides their confidentiality. They are also two examples of expensive satellite litigation caused by the doomed indemnity principle.

(g) Unlawful retainer

Worst of all, if a solicitor enters into an invalid retainer with the client – a champertous agreement or a conditional fee agreement which does not comply with the regulations – it is unenforceable against the client and the client can therefore recover nothing from the other party. For disastrous examples see Chapter 42.

4. THE FUTURE OF THE INDEMNITY PRINCIPLE

In a previous edition, I wrote:

> 'It seems to me that the indemnity principle, first identified in *Harold v Smith* nearly 140 years ago, has outlived its usefulness: its application in modern times is causing horrendous and virtually insoluble problems. Why should the amount payable by the loser in litigation be influenced by the winner's liability to his own solicitor? Why should a successful litigant not be able to recover a reasonable and proportionate amount for the costs of the action irrespective of his financial arrangement with his solicitor and the method by which the litigation is being funded? At a time when reforms are aimed at achieving proportionality between costs and the subject matter of the litigation, it is ironic that the satellite litigation of drawing and assessing bills should itself be incurring costs disproportionate to the costs themselves.'

In May 1999 the Lord Chancellor produced a consultation paper entitled 'Controlling Costs and the Future of the Indemnity Principle'. The paper said it was clear that the application of the indemnity principle had become increasingly marginalised by the changes which had taken place in recent years and the question therefore arose as to whether there was any merit in its retention. The paper continued:

> 'However, whilst the principle is being observed as much in the breach, it does continue to have a central position in costs law and is inextricably linked to the general presumption that the successful party is entitled to be indemnified by

his opponent for his legal costs. It is argued that the indemnity principle operates to place some limit on the sums that can be recovered, and generally acts to keep the costs no greater than the liability of the client to his solicitor. Whilst minded to accept the thrust of the argument for the abolition of the remaining vestiges of the principle, the Lord Chancellor is concerned that its removal should not lead to an increase in legal costs being awarded by the courts over time. The indemnity principle provides a cap on the costs which can be recovered from the losing party. Without it solicitors will be technically free to claim costs without bounds, subject to assessment by the court'.

The government's conclusions following consultation on the Lord Chancellor's Department's Consultation Paper on Collective Conditional Fees are not everyone's idea of a good bedtime read, but tucked away at the end were the glad tidings that the indemnity principle is to be disapplied in respect of the assessment of costs. Respondents had commented overwhelmingly that the indemnity principle no longer served any useful purpose and should be abolished in full. The principle did not act in anyone's interest and had no impact on overall costs, given the introduction of proportionality. The government recognised the heavy burden of current work on the Civil Procedure Rules Committee would dictate the date at which any rules could be made, but recommended that the Committee considered the early introduction of any necessary rules. Here is the government's explanation of policy, giving the original paragraph numbers:

'30. The Government recognises that a constraint on an organisation or legal representative's ability to enter into a completely transparent relationship with their client concerning costs, is the threat of the opponent arguing on assessment that the indemnity principle had been breached.

31. Although there have been many changes in law which have had the effect of diluting the impact of the indemnity principle, whether in terms of Legal Aid changes, the introduction of conditional fee agreements or the growing body of case law, the indemnity principle continues to exert a major influence on the assessment of costs. By invoking the indemnity principle, paying parties have argued against any liability for costs in cases where a client has entered into an agreement where a solicitor has agreed to waive any fees if the case is unsuccessful and, if successful, seek to recover what the court allows from the paying party, without setting out the charging rate they will seek to recover. This is a particular issue where the client is indemnified for their costs by a third party. In these cases it is argued by the paying party that the client has no actual obligation to his solicitor and therefore neither do they.

32. To ensure that they do not fall victim to the indemnity principle, providers enter into agreements which set out the charging rate to be applied in the even of a successful case, even though it is clear to the providers that the charging rate will rarely apply and should they win, and not recover the full amount billed, they will not recover the excess from their clients. In third party funded cases lawyers have drawn up agreements which regard both the organisation and client as being liable to pay, thereby avoiding the indemnity principle.

33. The Government recognises that clients are not always versed in legal proceedings and misconstrue the agreements they have entered into. The client having been told that they have no liability whatever the outcome of the case does not understand why the agreement states that there is a liability. This is a particular concern in cases funded by trade unions or membership organisations. The Government believes that it is in the interests of all concerned for there to be complete clarity in the provision of these services. The operation of the indemnity principle clearly inhibits clarity. Although the introduction of CCFA regulations under s58 of the Courts and Legal Services Act 1990 (as amended) abrogates the indemnity principle for CCFAs, the Government is persuaded that there is no longer any justification for the operation of the principle when assessing costs no matter how funded.

34. Section 31 of the Access to Justice Act 1999 (when commenced) amends s 51 of the Supreme Court Act 1981 to provide that the amount recovered by way of costs may not be limited to 'what would have been payable by him (the client) to them (his lawyers) if he had not been awarded costs.'

The implementation of this section would allow rules of court to be drawn up which provide, beyond any doubt, that the receiving party can receive reasonable and proportionate costs irrespective of the terms of the agreement, in cases where an additional liability is claimed.

The method of financing litigation should be a privileged matter between the client and the solicitor. Funding may or may not be under a conditional fee agreement, which itself may be 'no win, no fee' or 'no win, lesser fee' or some other formula, it may be by a trade union or a maiden aunt and it may involve after-the-event insurance or be covered by legal expenses insurance ('before-the-event' insurance), none of which should be of concern to the court or other party.

Costs recoverable between the parties should be such sum as is reasonable and proportionate having regard to the subject matter of the litigation regardless of the terms under which those services have been provided.

The Civil Procedure Rule Committee is considering how best to implement the Lord Chancellor's policy of abrogating the indemnity principle. The proposals include:

1. Rule 40.8 should be amended to state that interest on the costs of detailed assessment should run from the date on which the liability for costs was incurred (rather than from the date of the substantive judgment).
2. Rule 47.9: amend to remove the problem caused by (iii) in cases in which directions were given extending the time to point of dispute.
3. Rule 47.9: amend to remove the problem caused by (iii) in cases in which directions were given extending the time to point of dispute.
4. Rule 48.7 (wasted costs orders): amend Rule 48.7(4) to give the court the option to make wasted costs order without specifying the amount and to direct a costs judge or district judge to decide the amount.
5. Amend the Practice Direction to indicate that the costs of ADR are capable of being 'of and incidental to' a claim, depending on the circumstances of the particular case.
6. Amend the Practice Direction to effect the introduction of collective conditional fee agreements.
7. Amend the Practice Direction to clarify the procedure under s 11(1) Access to Justice Act 1999 (costs against an LSC funded client or against the Commission).
8. Practice Direction, s 6: amend to indicate that the estimate of base costs given that an allocation need not be detailed.
9. Practice Direction, para 13.3: amend the references from '49.3 and 49.4' to '50.3 and 50.4'.
10. Practice Direction, para 13.5: amend to reflect the judgment in *Macdonald v Taree Holdings Ltd* [2001] 06 LS Gaz R 45 (failure to serve schedule of costs).
11. Practice Direction, para 17.5: amend from 'a court officer' to 'a costs officer'.
12. Practice Direction 20: clarify the practice direction to make it clear that it is limited to reductions in success fee caused by incorrect assessment risk.
13. Practice Direction, s 42: amend to disapply paras 42.2 to 42.4 in cases covered by Rule 48.10 (assessment procedure of costs payable to a solicitor by his client), and amend para 56.18 accordingly.
14. The Senior Costs Judge will welcome suggestions for any further amendments.

In his inaugural lecture as a professor, John Peysner of Nottingham Law School said that 'the long and baffling' existence of the indemnity principle, which has no place in the modern world of litigation, should be brought to a humane end by comprehensive abolition; not only was it contrary to the basis of risk management and sound business principles, it also acted as a bar to progress on introducing fixed or capped fees as a means of bringing certainty to fast track costs. David Hartley, then head of the Law Society's remuneration team added to the call for abolition, saying: 'We no longer believe that the indemnity principle serves any useful purpose. It will need to go to ensure that collective conditional fee agreements will work properly.'

The Civil Justice Council's working party on predictable costs almost unanimously agreed that the indemnity principle should be abolished, a view which has since been endorsed by Lord Philips, the Master of the Rolls, and Lord Justice May, Deputy Head of Civil Justice. Unfortunately there is not unanimity as to how this may be achieved, and, in particular, whether primary legislation is necessary. Surely what is required is the implementation of s 31 of the Access to Justice Act 1999 which amends s 51 of the Supreme Court Act 1981 (see p 177).

CHAPTER 18

INTEREST ON COSTS

1. STATUTES

The Judgments Act 1838, s 17 provides for the recovery of interest on costs in the High Court, whilst the County Court (Interest on Judgment Debts) Order 1991, made under the County Court Act 1984, s 74, provides for interest to be paid on 'relevant judgments'. A relevant judgment is one for not less than £5,000 or in respect of a 'qualifying debt' as defined by the Late Payment of Commercial Debts (Interest) Act 1998, into which we shall not delve.

2. THE INCIPITUR RULE

The dispute as to the date from which interest on costs runs from went all the way up to the House of Lords where, in *Hunt v R M Douglas Roofing (Ltd)* [1990] 1 AC 398, it was held that interest on costs ran from the date on which judgment is pronounced and not from the date of the costs officer's certificate. The former is known as the *incipitur rule* and the latter as the *allocatur rule*. Neither rule is entirely satisfactory but it was held that the balance of justice favoured the incipitur rule because the unsuccessful party had unnecessarily caused the costs to be incurred and that as neither rule covers costs incurred before the judgment the application of the allocatur rule, generally speaking, does greater injustice than the operation of the incipitur rule, even though this meant the successful party would recover interest on disbursements before they were made and costs after judgment before they were incurred. This has now been enshrined in CPR Rule 40.8(1) as follows:

> 'Where interest is payable on a judgment pursuant to section 17 of the Judgments Act 1838 or section 74 of the County Courts Act 1984, the interest shall begin to run from the date that judgment is given unless—
>
> (a) a rule in another Part or a Practice Direction makes different provision; or
> (b) the court orders otherwise.'

3. ORDERS DEEMED TO HAVE BEEN MADE

CPR Rule 44.12(2) provides that interest payable pursuant to of the Judgments Act 1838, s 17 or the County Courts Act 1984, s 74 on costs deemed to have been ordered (where a Part 36 payment or offer is accepted or where a claimant discontinues) shall begin to run from the date on which the event which gave rise to the entitlement to costs occurred.

4. ENHANCED INTEREST

CPR Rule 36.21 provides that where at trial a defendant is held liable for more, or the judgment against a defendant is more advantageous to a claimant than the proposals contained in a claimant's Part 36 offer, the court may order that the claimant is entitled to their costs on the indemnity basis and interest on those costs at a rate not exceeding 10% above base rate. For an example of this in practice, see p 146.

5. BACKDATING

Where the costs judge had made various orders for the costs of the receiving party during the course of the assessment, the interest on those costs also ran from the date of the order for costs to be assessed under the incipitur rule not from the dates of the costs officer's certificates (*Ross v Owners of the Bowbelle* [1997] 1 WLR 1159, CA). Similarly, in *Electricity Supply Nominees Ltd v Terence Farrell* [1997] 2 All ER 498, CA, where a consent order provided that the costs 'shall be taxed [*assessed*] upon the standard basis if not agreed and *such costs when taxed* [assessed] *or agreed shall be paid* by the defendants' it did not operate as a genuine postponement until after assessment of the obligation to pay the costs so as to avoid interest running from the date of the order pursuant to the rule in *Hunt v RM Douglas (Roofing) Ltd* [1990] 1 AC 398. The words in italics were probably verbiage derived from a precedent and were no more than a recitation of what in fact was to occur. Although it is open to the parties to a consent order to make a side agreement as to interest or to take account of the effect of the court's order on interest altering the wording of costs orders is unlikely to achieve the desired result. It was doubtful if even in a consent order the court could directly alter the incidence of interest on the judgment because that is governed by the Act and rules of court.

In *Nykredit Mortgage Bank plc v Edward Erdman Group Ltd (No 2)* [1998] 1 All ER 305, HL the House of Lords said that the Court of Appeal had been 'lured into error' when in *Kuwait Airways Corpn v Iraqi Airways Co (No 2)* [1994] 1 WLR 985 it held that the Rules of the Supreme Court empowered it to back date its order for costs to enable interest to run from the original judgment. Statute apart, courts have no power to award interest on costs, however desirable it might be for the court to have power to order the payment of interest on costs from a date earlier than the date on which the court gave judgment. However, although the court had no general inherent power to order the payment of interest, the result of the appeal had been that orders in the courts below should not have been made and that some of the money previously paid by the defendants to the plaintiffs as damages and costs pursuant to orders of the trial judge and the Court of Appeal had fallen to be repaid to them. This could have been an idle exercise unless the court was able to make consequential orders that achieved, as nearly as reasonably practicable, the necessary restitution which included interest on the money to be repaid. The power to do so was derived from the inherent jurisdiction of the House of Lords, which was also possessed by the Court of Appeal. To enable lesser mortals to do the same, the Civil Procedure (Modification of Enactments) Order 1998 amended the Judgments Act 1838, s 17(1) to provide that interest will run from such time as is prescribed by rules of court. The resultant rule is CPR Rule 44.3(6)(*g*) which empowers any court to award 'interest on costs from or until a certain date, including a date *before* judgment'.

6. THE RATE

Since April 1993 the rate of interest on judgment debts has been 8%, as prescribed by the Judgment Debts (Rate of Interest) Order 1993. This is despite the reduction of interest rates on funds invested in court to 7% on the special account and 5.25% on the basic account with effect from 1 August 1999. It therefore remains good investment – provided the judgment and costs are eventually paid. However, in respect of county court judgments where the judgment creditor applies to enforce payment of the judgment by execution or some other means, interest will not accrue if the enforcement process is wholly or partly successful (County Court (Interest on Judgment Debts) Order 1991, art 4). Presumably, this provision was made because, if the enforcement process is wholly successful the judgment will have been satisfied, whilst if it is only partly successful it will be too complicated to calculate the interest on the various amounts outstanding from time to time.

CHAPTER 19

COSTS OF SUCCESSFUL NON-STATE FUNDED PARTIES

1. PROCEDURE

From 1 April 2000 the Legal Aid Board was replaced by the Legal Services Commission for all civil matters commencing on or after that date and the funding of assisted persons or 'clients' (as those who receive funded services are now called), has been provided through the Community Legal Service. I deal with the present regime, including its vocabulary, in Chapter 41. Although for some years to come there will be litigation involving parties funded under the old regime, since 5 June 2001 regs 127–130 and 134–147 of the Civil Legal Aid (General) Regulations 1989 have no longer applied resulting in the amount of the liability of all state-funded parties together with applications for costs against the state, in the form of the Legal Aid Board or the Legal Services Commission, all being now decided under the Community Legal Service (Costs) Regulations 2000.

There are therefore two forms of public funding of litigation: under Legal Aid Certificates, granted before 1 April 2000 by the Legal Aid Board; and, after 1 April 2000, under Community Legal Service certificates, funded by the Legal Services Commission which replaced the Legal Aid Board. 'Public funding certificate' is a useful portmanteau description covering both forms of funding.

2. COSTS AGAINST A STATE FUNDED PARTY

(a) Liability for costs

The award of between-the-parties costs is uninfluenced by the fact that either or both of the parties is funded by the state. Awards of costs are determined by the factors prescribed in CPR Rule 44.3 (on p 90). For these purposes the funding certificate is ignored. However, a party who is in receipt of legal aid is protected by s 17 of the Legal Aid Act 1988, while an LSC-funded litigant has the protection of s 11 of the Access to Justice Act 1999.

(b) Cost protection

(i) Legal Aid funded

Where proceedings have been concluded in which an assisted person is liable or would have been liable for costs if he had not been an assisted person, no costs attributable to the period during which his certificate was in force shall be recoverable from him until the court had determined the amount of his liability in accordance with s 17 of the Legal Aid Act 1988 which provides as follows:

17 LIMIT ON COSTS AGAINST ASSISTED PARTY

(1) The liability of a legally assisted party under an order for costs made against him with respect to any proceedings shall not exceed the amount (if any) which is a reasonable one for him to pay having regard to all the circumstances, including the financial resources of all the parties and their conduct in connection with the dispute.
(2) Regulations shall make provision as to the court, tribunal or person by whom that amount is to be determined and the extent to which any determination of that amount is to be final.
(3) None of the following, namely, a legally assisted person's dwelling house, clothes, household furniture and the tools and implements of his trade shall—
- (a) be taken into account in assessing his financial resources for the purposes of this section, or
- (b) be subject to execution or any corresponding process in any part of the United Kingdom to enforce the order,

except so far as regulations may prescribe.

Where the assisted person's certificate does not relate to, or has been amended so that it no longer relates to the whole of the proceedings, the court shall nevertheless make a determination under s 17 (1) of the Act in respect of that part of the proceedings to which the certificate relates.

The amount of an assisted person's liability for costs shall be determined by the court which tried or heard the proceedings (Civil Legal Aid (General) Regulations 1989, reg 124).

Where a claimant has been granted legal aid limited to cover specific procedural steps, the certificate is spent once those steps had been accomplished. Accordingly even though the legal aid certificate had not been discharged, the assisted person is not protected from liability for costs under the Legal Aid Act 1988, s 17 in respect of any step taken outside the scope of the certificate (*Turner v Plasplugs Ltd* [1996] 2 All ER 939, CA).

(ii) Community Legal Service funded

The Community Legal Service (Cost Protection) Regulations 2000 (SI 2000/824) define 'costs protection' as the limit on costs awarded against a client set out in the Access to Justice Act 1999, s 11(1), a 'client' being defined as an individual who receives funded services.

Section 11 of the Access to Justice Act 1999 provides:

11 COSTS IN FUNDED CASES

(1) Except in prescribed circumstances, costs ordered against an individual in relation to any proceedings or part of proceedings funded for him shall not exceed the amount (if any) which is a reasonable one for him to pay having regard to all the circumstances including—
- (a) the financial resources of all the parties to the proceedings, and
- (b) their conduct in connection with the dispute to which the proceedings relate;

and for this purpose proceedings, or a part of proceedings, are funded for an individual if services relating to the proceedings or part are funded for him by the Commission as part of the Community Legal Service.
(2) In assessing for the purposes of subsection (1) the financial resources of an individual for whom services are funded by the Commission as part of the Community Legal Service, his clothes and household furniture and the tools

and implements of his trade shall not be taken into account, except so far as may be prescribed.

(3) Subject to subsections (1) and (2), regulations may make provision about costs in relation to proceedings in which services are funded by the Commission for any of the parties as part of the Community Legal Service.

(4) The regulations may, in particular, make provision—

(a) specifying the principles to be applied in determining the amount of any costs which may be awarded against a party for whom services are funded by the Commission as part of the Community Legal Service,

(b) limiting the circumstances in which, or extent to which, an order for costs may be enforced against such a party,

(c) as to the cases in which, and extent to which, such a party may be required to give security for costs and the manner in which it is to be given,

(d) requiring the payment by the Commission of the whole or part of any costs incurred by a party for whom services are not funded by the Commission as part of the Community Legal Service,

(e) specifying the principles to be applied in determining the amount of any costs which may be awarded to a party for whom services are so funded,

(f) requiring the payment to the Commission, or the person or body by which the services were provided, of the whole or part of any sum awarded by way of costs to such a party, and

(g) as to the court, tribunal or other person or body by whom the amount of any costs is to be determined and the extent to which any determination of that amount is to be final.

The Community Legal Service (Cost Protection) Regulations 2000 provide:

3 COST PROTECTION

(1) Cost protection shall not apply in relation to such parts of proceedings, or prospective proceedings, as are funded for the client by way of:

(a) Help at Court or Litigation Support;

(b) Investigative Support, except where any proceedings in respect of which the Investigative Support was given are not pursued (whether or not as funded proceedings) after the certificate for Investigative Support is discharged;

(c) subject to paragraph (2), Legal Help.

(2) Subject to paragraph (4), where the client receives Legal Help, but later receives Legal Representation or Approved Family Help in respect of the same dispute, cost protection shall apply, both in respect of:

(a) the costs incurred by the receiving party before the commencement of proceedings which, as regards the client, are funded proceedings by virtue of the client's receipt of Legal Help, and

(b) the costs incurred by the receiving party in the course of proceedings which, as regards the client, are funded proceedings by virtue of the client's receipt of Legal Representation or Approved Family Help.

(3) Subject to paragraph (4), cost protection shall apply only to costs incurred by the receiving party in relation to proceedings which, as regards the client, are funded proceedings, and:

(a) where work is done before the issue of a certificate, cost protection shall (subject to paragraphs (2) and (5)) apply only to costs incurred after the issue of the certificate;

(b) where funding is withdrawn by discharging the client's certificate, cost protection shall apply only to costs incurred before the date when funded services under the certificate ceased to be provided.

(4) Where funding is withdrawn by revoking the client's certificate, cost protection shall not apply, either in respect of work done before or after the revocation.

(5) Cost protection shall apply to work done immediately before the grant of an emergency certificate if:

(a) no application for such a certificate could be made because the Commission's office was closed; and

(b) the client's solicitor applies for an emergency certificate at the first available opportunity, and the certificate is granted.

4 ENFORCEMENT OF COSTS ORDER AGAINST CLIENT

Where, for the purpose of enforcing a costs order against a client (alone or together with any other judgment or order), a charging order under section 1 of the Charging Orders Act 1979 is made in respect of the client's interest in the main or only dwelling in which he resides:

(a) that charging order shall operate to secure the amount payable under the costs order (including, without limitation, any interest) only to the extent of the amount (if any) by which the proceeds of sale of the client's interest in the dwelling (having deducted any mortgage debts) exceed £100,000; and

(b) an order for the sale of the dwelling shall not be made in favour of the person in whose favour the charging order is made.

(iii) The costs rules

CPR RULE 44.17 APPLICATION OF COSTS RULES

This Part and Part 45 (fixed costs), Part 46 (fast track trial costs), Part 47 (procedure for detailed assessment of costs and default provisions) and Part 48 (special cases), do not apply to the assessment of costs in proceedings to the extent that—

(a) section 11 of the Access to Justice Act 1999, and provisions made under that Act, or

(b) regulations made under the Legal Aid Act 1988,

make different provision. (The costs practice direction sets out the procedure to be followed where a party was wholly or partially funded by the Legal Services Commission).

SECTION 21: PRACTICE DIRECTION SUPPLEMENTING CPR RULE 44.17

21.1 Rule 44.17(b) excludes the costs rules to the extent that regulations under the Legal Aid Act 1988 make different provision. The primary examples of such regulations are the regulations providing prescribed rates (with or without enhancement).

21.2 Rule 44.17(a) also excludes the procedure for the detailed assessment of costs in cases to which Section 11 of the Access to Justice Act 1999 applies, whether it applies in whole or in part. In these excluded cases the procedure for determination of costs is set out in Section 22 of this Practice Direction.

21.3 Section 11 of the Access to Justice Act 1999 provides special protection against liability for costs for litigants who receive funding by the LSC (Legal Services Commission) as part of the Community Legal Service. Any costs ordered to be paid by a LSC funded client must not exceed the amount which is reasonable for him to pay having regard to all the circumstances including:

a) the financial resources of all the parties to the proceedings, and
b) their conduct in connection with the dispute to which the proceedings relate.

21.4 In this Practice Direction

'cost protection' means the limit on costs awarded against a LSC funded client set out in Section 11(1) of the Access to Justice Act 1999.

'partner' has the meaning given by the Community Legal Service (Costs) Regulations 2000.

21.5 Whether or not cost protection applies depends upon the 'level of service' for which funding was provided by the LSC in accordance with the Funding Code approved under Section 9 of the Access to Justice Act 1999. The levels of service referred to are:

1) Legal Help – advice and assistance about a legal problem, not including representation or advocacy in proceedings.
2) Help at Court – advocacy at a specific hearing, where the advocate is not formally representing the client in the proceedings.
3) Family Mediation.
4) Legal Representation – representation in actual or contemplated proceedings. Legal Representation can take the form of Investigative Help (limited to investigating the merits of a potential claim) or Full Representation.
5) Approved Family Help – this can take the form of Help with Mediation (legal advice in support of the family mediation process) or General Family Help (help negotiating a settlement to a family dispute without recourse to adversarial litigation).
6) Support Funding – partial funding in expensive cases that are primarily being funded privately, under or with a view to a conditional fee agreement. Support Funding can take the form of Investigative Support (equivalent to Investigative Help) or Litigation Support (equivalent to Full Representation).

21.6 Levels of service (4) (5) and (6) are provided under a certificate (similar to a legal aid certificate). The certificate will state which level of service is covered. Where there are proceedings, a copy of the certificate will be lodged with the court.

21.7 Cost protection does not apply where:

1) The LSC funded client receives Help at Court;
2) the LSC funded client receives Litigation Support (but see further, paragraph 21.8);
3) the LSC funded client receives Investigative Support (except where the proceedings for which Investigative Support was given are not pursued after the certificate is discharged). Investigative Support will not normally cover the issue of proceedings (except for disclosure), but cost protection may be relevant if the defendant seeks an assessment of pre-action costs;
4) the LSC funded client receives Legal Help only ie where the solicitor is advising, but not representing a litigant in person. However, where the LSC funded client receives Legal Help eg to write a letter before action, but later receives Legal Representation or Approved Family Help in respect of the same dispute, cost protection does apply to all costs incurred by the receiving party in the funded proceedings or prospective proceedings.

21.8 Where cost protection does not apply, the court may award costs in the normal way. In the case of Litigation Support, costs that are not covered by the LSC funded client's insurance are usually payable by the LSC rather than the funded client, and the court should order accordingly (see Regulation 6 of the Community Legal Service (Cost Protection) Regulations 2000).

21.9 Where work is done before the issue of a certificate, cost protection does not apply to those costs, except where:

1) pre-action Legal Help is given and the LSC funded client subsequently receives Legal Representation or Approved Family Help in the same dispute; or

2) where urgent work is undertaken immediately before the grant of an emergency certificate when no emergency application could be made as the LSC's offices were closed, provided that the solicitor seeks an emergency certificate at the first available opportunity and the certificate is granted.

21.10 If a LSC funded client's certificate is revoked, costs protection does not apply to work done before or after revocation.

21.11 If a LSC funded client's certificate is discharged, costs protection only applies to costs incurred before the date on which funded services ceased to be provided under the certificate. This may be a date before the date on which the certificate is formally discharged by the LSC (Burridge v Stafford: Khan v Ali [2000] 1 WLR 927, [1999] 4 All ER 660 C.A.).

(iv) Three stages

First, the judge makes an order that the state-funded party do pay the costs of the receiving party either assessed at a specified sum (if he has summarily assessed them) or to be ascertained by detailed assessment.

That is stage one. That is the procedure for determining the full costs which a state-funded party would pay if he were not in receipt of state funding.

Stage two is the determination of the amount the state-funded party will actually have to pay under the costs protection scheme. The usual order is: 'The amount of the costs payable under section 17(1) of the Legal Aid Act or section 11 of the Access to Justice Act to be determined'. That determination will not be carried out by the trial judge, but by a costs or district judge.

However, if the trial judge is satisfied that he is in a position there and then to determine the amount payable, perhaps to be set off against an earlier award of costs in favour of the funded party, or against his damages, or even as was approved in *Williams v Walkett* [1994] CLY 3587, an order to pay the assessed costs by monthly instalments, the judge may make what is not very imaginatively called 'an order specifying the costs payable'.

There is one further action the judge may take if he is so minded when making an order for costs to be determined. Paragraph 22.6 of the Practice Direction provides he may 'make findings of fact, e.g., concerning the conduct of all the parties which are to be taken into account by the court in the subsequent determination proceedings'.

The third stage is for the receiving party to take the appropriate steps to have the costs determined within three months, although he may apply at any time within six years to vary that determination if the funded party wins the pools, the lottery or Who Wants to be a Millionaire?

(v) Interlocutory

Neither s 17 nor reg 124 prevents the court at an interlocutory stage making an order for costs in favour of the other party directing that those costs be set off against either any damages or costs to which the legally aided party had or could in future become entitled in the action. The operation of the set-off did not place the person whose chose in action was thereby reduced or extinguished under an obligation to pay. The operation of the set-off in respect of the liability of the assisted person under an order for costs did not require him to pay anything: it did not lead to any costs being recoverable against the legally aided person. Such an order would in general in equity impeach the right of the claimant to recover from the defendant the costs of the action ordered to be paid by the defendant (*Lockley v National Blood Transfusion Service* [1992] 2 All ER 589, CA).

3. COSTS AGAINST THE STATE

(a) Against the Legal Aid Board

Where one party is legally aided ('the assisted party) and the other is not ('the unassisted party) and the proceedings between them are finally decided in favour of the unassisted party, the court may, subject to the following conditions being satisfied, order the whole or, part of the costs of the unassisted party in those proceedings to be paid by the Legal Aid Board.

There can be such final decision even though it may not have been wholly in favour of the unassisted party: *Kelly v London Transport Executive* [1982] 2 All ER 842, CA.

(i) The conditions

An order under the Legal Aid Act 1988, s 18 in respect of any costs may only be made if:

(1) an order for costs would be made in the proceedings apart from this Act, as respects the costs incurred in a court of first instance, those proceedings were instituted by the assisted party and the court is satisfied that the unassisted party will suffer severe financial hardship unless the order is made; and
(2) in any case, the court is satisfied that it is just and equitable in all the circumstances of the case that provision for the costs should be made out of public funds.

In *Din v Wandsworth London Borough Council (No 2)* [1982] 1 All ER 1022, HL it was held that it is not just and equitable to make a provisional order, as a *matter of course* when an unassisted party has succeeded, that he should have his costs out of the legal aid fund, reserving to The Law Society (now the Legal Aid Board) the opportunity to make representations with regard thereto.

K v K (legal aid: costs) [1995] 2 FCR 189, CA illustrated dramatically the provision in s 18(4) that an order against the Legal Aid Board may only be made if an order for costs would have been made in the proceedings apart from the Act. The wife incurred substantial costs as a result of the husband's proceedings in respect of the children, which proceedings were finally decided in her favour. It was unusual to make an inter partes order for costs between the parties in respect of proceedings concerning the children and the wife's liability to her solicitors for costs was a factor which would be taken into account when considering ancillary relief. Although the pre-condition of s 18(4) was reasonable in the context of conventional civil litigation, where costs on the face of it followed the event, it precluded the award of costs against the Legal Aid Board cases involving children because such an order is unusual.

In *Aire Property Trust v Treeweek* [1989] 1 EGLR 61, CA, a successful respondent to an appeal which should never have been made (because there was no right of appeal without leave) and in respect of which legal aid should never have been granted was entitled to an order for his costs against the legal aid fund.

In *Adams v Riley* [1988] QB 372, QBD, in making an order against the legal aid fund under the Legal Aid Act 1974, s 13(1) the court held it should determine the proportion of the costs the successful party could pay without suffering hardship and order that he recover only the excess. It was not a question of a successful party who had got across the threshold recovering everything: he recovered only the difference between the actual costs and that sum which would have just failed to get him over the threshold.

In *O'Sullivan v Herdmans Ltd (No 2)* [1988] 1 WLR 1373, HL, the legally aided claimant with a nil contribution had successfully resisted an order for disclosure before the master and judge but failed before the Court of Appeal and the House of Lords. The House of Lords proposed ordering that the defendant's costs be paid out of the legal aid fund but it was suggested that the effect of this order would be that the amount of costs so paid would be a charge on any damages the claimant might recover. Accordingly, the House adjourned to enable representations to be made. On the restored hearing it was confirmed that the order for costs out of the legal aid fund would not give rise to a charge on any sum eventually recovered by the claimant against the defendants. The House of Lords accordingly affirmed the provisional order previously made. In the event, the argument was only over the sum of £1,000, because that is the amount for which the claimant settled her claim!

(ii) 'Financial hardship'

If his costs, if he is left to bear them himself, will so bear heavily on the unassisted person, a possible claim for hardship may be made out. The financial hardship used to have to be 'severe' but on 3 December 2001 the test of severity was removed. A limited company or body corporate is capable of suffering financial hardship so that an order may, in an appropriate case, be made in its favour. No appeal lies from a court order for payment of the costs of an unassisted party out of the fund, or a refusal to make such an order, if only a question of fact is involved. It would seem that a finding as to financial hardship or as to its absence is such a question of fact. When the unassisted party is concerned only in a representative, fiduciary or official capacity, the court is not to have regard to his personal resources, but *must* take into account the value of the property estate or fund out of which he is entitled to be indemnified and *may* have regard to the resources of the persons, including, where appropriate, the unassisted party, beneficially interested (reg 135).

The provision that it is only an unassisted person who can claim against the Legal Aid Board can cause hardship to a successful assisted person. In *Almond v Miles* (1992) Times, 4 February, ChD the claimant claimed a share of the equity in a flat in which the defendant lived. The defendant successfully resisted her claim. Both parties were in receipt of legal aid. The claimant's own flat was sacrosanct under the legal aid provision in respect of the costs awarded against her but the Legal Aid Board had a charge for their costs over the defendant's property as being property preserved by the proceedings. The court regretted that in these circumstances it could not order the defendant's costs to be paid by the Legal Aid Board and called for urgent reconsideration of the legislation. In *Re H (minors) (No 2) (Legal Aid and costs)* [1992] 2 AC 303 the House of Lords was faced with a similar situation but in that case the unsuccessful party had previously been unassisted. The fact that he was assisted at the time of the making of the order did not preclude the court from ordering payment by the Legal Aid Board of such part of the successful party's costs as had been incurred while he was unassisted.

(b) Against the Legal Services Commission

(i) The Community Legal Service (Cost Protection) Regulations 2000 (SI 2000/824)

These Regulations provide (at regs 5–7):

5 COSTS ORDER AGAINST COMMISSION

(1) The following paragraphs of this regulation apply where:

(a) funded services are provided to a client in relation to proceedings;

(b) those proceedings are finally decided in favour of a non-funded party; and

(c) cost protection applies.

(2) The court may, subject to the following paragraphs of this regulation, make an order for the payment by the Commission to the non-funded party of the whole or any part of the costs incurred by him in the proceedings (other than any costs that the client is required to pay under a section 11(1) costs order).

(3) An order under paragraph (2) may only be made if all the conditions set out in sub-paragraphs (a), (b), (c) and (d) are satisfied:

(a) a section 11(1) costs order is made against the client in the proceedings, and the amount (if any) which the client is required to pay under that costs order is less than the amount of the full costs;

(b) unless there is a good reason for the delay, the non-funded party makes a request under regulation 10(2) of the Community Legal Service (Costs) Regulations 2000 within three months of the making of the section 11(1) costs order;

(c) as regards costs incurred in a court of first instance, the proceedings were instituted by the client, the non-funded party is an individual, and the court is satisfied that the non-funded party will suffer financial hardship unless the order is made; and

(d) in any case, the court is satisfied that it is just and equitable in the circumstances that provision for the costs should be made out of public funds.

(3A) An order under paragraph (2) may be made—

(a) in relation to proceedings in the House of Lords, by the Clerk to the Parliaments;

(b) in relation to proceedings in the Court of Appeal, High Court or a county court, by a costs judge or a district judge;

(c) in relation to proceedings in a magistrates' court, by a single justice or by the justices' clerk;

(d) in relation to proceedings in the Employment Appeal Tribunal, by the Registrar of that tribunal.

(4) Where the client receives funded services in connection with part only of the proceedings, the reference in paragraph (2) to the costs incurred by the non-funded party in the relevant proceedings shall be construed as a reference to so much of those costs as is attributable to the part of the proceedings which are funded proceedings.

(5) Where a court decides any proceedings in favour of the non-funded party and an appeal lies (with or without permission) against that decision, any order made under this regulation shall not take effect:

(a) where permission to appeal is required, unless the time limit for applications for permission to appeal expires without permission being granted;

(b) where permission to appeal is granted or is not required, unless the time limit for appeal expires without an appeal being brought.

(6) Subject to paragraph (7), in determining whether the conditions in paragraph (3)(c) and (d) are satisfied, the court shall have regard to the resources of the non-funded party and of his partner.

(7) The court shall not have regard to the resources of the partner of the non-funded party if the partner has a contrary interest in the funded proceedings.

(8) Where the non-funded party is acting in a representative, fiduciary or official capacity and is entitled to be indemnified in respect of his costs from any property, estate or fund, the court shall, for the purposes of paragraph (3),

have regard to the value of the property, estate or fund and the resources of the persons, if any, including that party where appropriate, who are beneficially interested in that property, estate or fund.

6 ORDERS FOR COSTS AGAINST COMMISSION—LITIGATION SUPPORT

(1) Paragraph (2) applies where:
- (a) the client receives Litigation Support and the certificate is not revoked;
- (b) the client has effected insurance against liability in respect of costs in the proceedings, or has made other arrangements, approved by the Commission as being equivalent to such insurance;
- (c) the amount of liability insured under that insurance (or covered by those other arrangements) is subject to a maximum which has been approved by the Commission; and
- (d) a costs order has been made against the client in favour of a non-funded party and the actual amount of the client's liability in respect of costs under that costs order exceeds the maximum referred to in sub-paragraph (c).

(2) Where this paragraph applies, the amount of the excess referred to in paragraph (1)(d) shall, subject to paragraph (3), be paid by the Commission, not by the client, and the court shall order accordingly.
(3) The amount of the Commission's liability under this regulation shall not exceed the reasonable costs of the non-funded party incurred during the period in which Litigation Support was provided.

7 EFFECT OF THESE REGULATIONS

(1) No order to pay costs in favour of a non-funded party shall be made against the Commission in respect of funded proceedings except in accordance with these Regulations, and any costs to be paid under such an order shall be paid out of the Community Legal Service Fund.
(2) Nothing in these Regulations shall be construed, in relation to proceedings where one or more parties are receiving, or have received, funded services, as:
- (a) requiring a court to make a costs order where it would not otherwise have made a costs order; or
- (b) affecting the court's power to make a wasted costs order against a legal representative.

In *R v Secretary of State for the Home Department, ex p Gunn* [2001] EWCA Civ 891, [2001] 3 All ER 481, the Court of Appeal surprisingly held that the new costs regime was not compatible with the then practice of the court and an order against the LSC can only be made by a costs or district judge. Here is the relevant extract from the judgment:

> 'The Cost Protection Regulations set out the circumstances in which the Costs Judge or District Judge may make a costs order against the Commission. Regulation 5(3) makes it plain that it is for the Costs Judge or District Judge to be satisfied that it is just and equitable that provision for the costs should be made out of public funds and, in respect of proceedings at first instance, that the non-funded party will suffer severe financial hardship unless the order is made. In considering these matters the Costs Judge or District Judge is expressly required to have regard to the resources of the non-funded party and of his partner – Regulation 5(6).
>
> We have set out the new regulatory scheme in detail because we have concluded that it is not compatible with the current practices of the trial Court. The function of deciding whether or not a costs order can and should be made against the Commission is now expressly assigned to the Costs Judge or District Judge. He cannot make such an order

unless and until the prescribed formalities have been completed. It is not open to the trial Court to rule that it is just and equitable to make the order or to direct that the order is to be made before the prescribed formalities have been completed. Costs Regulation 9(6) permits the trial Court, when making a costs order, to make findings of fact relevant to the determination of the amount to be paid by the client. We consider that it must also be open to the trial Court to make any findings in relation to the conduct of the parties or facts that have emerged in the course of the proceedings that have relevance to the task to be performed by the Costs Judge or District Judge. Beyond this the trial Court should not go. It follows that, in the cases before us, this Court should not have usurped the function of the Costs Judge – in these cases the Taxing Master – in deciding that it was just and equitable to make a costs order against the Commission and to direct that such an order be made. This practice must no longer be followed, whether in the County Court, the High Court or the Court of Appeal.'

(ii) The Costs Practice Direction

Costs against the LSC

21.16 Regulation 5 of the Community Legal Service (Cost Protection) Regulations 2000 governs when costs can be awarded against the LSC. This provision only applies where cost protection applies and the costs ordered to be paid by the LSC funded client do not fully meet the costs that would have been ordered to be paid by him if cost protection did not apply.

21.17 In this Section and the following two Sections of this Practice Direction 'non-funded party' means a party to proceedings who has not received LSC funded services in relation to these proceedings under a legal aid certificate or a certificate issued under the LSC Funding Code other than a certificate which has been revoked.

21.18 The following criteria set out in Regulation 5 must be satisfied before the LSC can be ordered to pay the whole or any part of the costs incurred by a non-funded party:

(1) the proceedings are finally decided in favour of a non-funded party;

(2) the non-funded party provides written notice of intention to seek an order against the LSC within three months of the making of the section 11(1) costs order;

(3) the court is satisfied that it is just and equitable in the circumstances that provision for the costs should be made out of public funds; and

(4) where costs are incurred in a court of first instance, the following additional criteria must also be met:

(i) the proceedings were instituted by the LSC funded client; and

(ii) the non-funded party will suffer severe financial hardship unless the order is made.

(Section 11(1) costs order' is defined in paragraph 22.1, below).

21.19 In determining whether conditions (3) and (4) are satisfied, the court shall take into account the resources of the non-funded party and his partner, unless the partner has a contrary interest.

4. ASSESSMENT OF LIABILITY

(i) The Community Legal Service (Costs) Regulations 2000 (SI 2000/441)

These Regulations prescribe the procedure for assessing the amount of liability under the Access to Justice Act 1999, s 11(1). The relevant regulations are as follows:

COMMUNITY LEGAL SERVICE (COSTS) REGULATIONS 2000

PART II COSTS ORDERS AGAINST CLIENT AND AGAINST COMMISSION

5. APPLICATION OF REGULATIONS 6 TO 13

Regulations 6 to 13 apply only where cost protection applies.

6. SECURITY FOR COSTS

Where in any proceedings a client is required to give security for costs, the amount of that security shall not exceed the amount (if any) which is a reasonable one having regard to all the circumstances, including the client's financial resources and his conduct in relation to the dispute to which the proceedings relate.

7. ASSESSMENT OF RESOURCES

(1) The first £100,000 of the value of the client's interest in the main or only dwelling in which he resides shall not be taken into account in having regard to the client's resources for the purposes of section 11(1) of the Act.
(2) Where, but only to the extent that, the court considers that the circumstances are exceptional, having regard in particular to the quantity or value of the items concerned, the court may take into account the value of the client's clothes and household furniture, or the tools and implements of his trade, in having regard to the client's resources for the purposes of section 11(1) of the Act.
(3) Subject to paragraph (4), in having regard to the resources of a party for the purposes of section 11(1) of the Act, the resources of his partner shall be treated as his resources.
(4) The resources of a party's partner shall not be treated as that party's resources if the partner has a contrary interest in the dispute in respect of which the funded services are provided.
(5) Where a party is acting in a representative, fiduciary or official capacity, the court shall not take the personal resources of the party into account for the purposes of section 11(1) of the Act, but shall have regard to the value of any property or estate, or the amount of any fund out of which he is entitled to be indemnified, and may also have regard to the resources of the persons, if any, including that party where appropriate, who are beneficially interested in that property, estate or fund.

8. STATEMENTS OF RESOURCES

(1) Any person who is a party to proceedings in which another party is a client may make a statement of resources, and file it with the court.
(2) A person making and filing a statement of resources under paragraph (1) shall serve a copy of it on the client.
(3) Where a copy of a statement of resources has been served under paragraph (2) not less than seven days before the date fixed for a hearing at which the amount to be paid under a section 11(1) costs order falls, or may fall, to be decided, the client shall also make a statement of resources, and shall produce it at that hearing.

9. PROCEDURES FOR ORDERING COSTS AGAINST CLIENT AND COMMISSION

(1) Where the court is considering whether to make a section 11(1) costs

order, it shall consider whether, but for cost protection, it would have made a costs order against the client and, if so, whether it would, on making the costs order, have specified the amount to be paid under that order.
(2) If the court considers that it would have made a costs order against the client, but that it would not have specified the amount to be paid under it, the court shall, when making the section 11(1) costs order:
- (a) specify the amount (if any) that the client is to pay under that order if, but only if:
  - (i) it considers that it has sufficient information before it to decide what amount is, in that case, a reasonable amount for the client to pay, in accordance with section 11(1) of the Act; and
  - (ii) it is satisfied that, if it were to determine the full costs at that time, they would exceed the amount referred to in sub-paragraph (i);
- (b) otherwise, it shall not specify the amount the client is to pay under the costs order.

(3) If the court considers that it would have made a costs order against the client, and that it would have specified the amount to be paid under it, the court shall, when making the section 11(1) costs order:
- (a) specify the amount (if any) that the client is to pay under that order if, but only if, it considers that it has sufficient information before it to decide what amount is, in that case, a reasonable amount for the client to pay, in accordance with section 11(1) of the Act;
- (b) otherwise, it shall not specify the amount the client is to pay under the costs order.

(4) Any order made under paragraph (3) shall state the amount of the full costs.
(5) The amount (if any) to be paid by the client under an order made under paragraph (2)(b) or paragraph (3)(b), and any application for a costs order against the Commission, shall be determined in accordance with regulation 10, and at any such determination following an order made under paragraph (2)(b), the amount of the full costs shall also be assessed.
(6) Where the court makes a section 11(1) costs order that does not specify the amount which the client is to pay under it, it may also make findings of fact, as to the parties' conduct in the proceedings or otherwise, relevant to the determination of that amount, and those findings shall be taken into consideration in that determination.

10.

(1) The following paragraphs of this regulation apply where the amount to be paid under a section 11(1) costs order, or an application for a costs order against the Commission, is to be determined under this regulation, by virtue of regulation 9(5).
(2) The receiving party may, within three months after a section 11(1) costs order is made, request a hearing to determine the costs payable to him.
(3) A request under paragraph (2) shall be accompanied by:
- (a) if the section 11(1) costs order does not state the full costs, the receiving party's bill of costs, which shall comply with any requirements of relevant rules of court relating to the form and content of a bill of costs where the court is assessing a party's costs;
- (b) a statement of resources; and
- (c) if the receiving party is seeking, or, subject to the determination of the amount to be paid under the section 11(1) costs order, may seek, a costs order against the Commission, written notice to that effect.

(4) The receiving party shall file the documents referred to in paragraph (3) with the court and at the same time serve copies of them:
- (a) on the client, if a determination of costs payable under section 11(1) of the Act is sought; and

(b) on the Regional Director, if notice has been given under paragraph (3)(c).

(5) Where documents are served on the client under paragraph (4)(a), the client shall make a statement of resources.

(6) The client shall file the statement of resources made under paragraph (5) with the court, and serve copies of it on the receiving party and, if notice has been given under paragraph (3)(c), on the Regional Director, not more than 21 days after the client receives a copy of the receiving party's statement of resources.

(7) The client may, at the same time as filing and serving a statement of resources under paragraph (6), file, and serve on the same persons, a statement setting out any points of dispute in relation to the bill of costs referred to in paragraph (3)(a).

(8) If the client, without good reason, fails to file a statement of resources in accordance with paragraph (6), the court shall determine the amount which the client shall be required to pay under the section 11(1) costs order (and, if relevant, the full costs), having regard to the statement made by the receiving party, and the court need not hold an oral hearing for such determination.

(9) If the client files a statement of resources in accordance with paragraph (6), or the period for filing such notice expires, or if the costs payable by the client have already been determined, the court shall set a date for the hearing and, at least 14 days before that date, serve notice of it on:

- (a) the receiving party;
- (b) the client (unless the costs payable by the client have already been determined); and
- (c) if a costs order against the Commission is or may be sought, the Regional Director.

(10) The court's functions under this regulation may be exercised:

- (a) in relation to proceedings in the House of Lords, by the Clerk to the Parliaments;
- (b) in relation to proceedings in the Court of Appeal, High Court or a county court, a costs judge or a district judge;
- (c) in relation to proceedings in a magistrates' court, by a single justice or by the justices' clerk;
- (d) in relation to proceedings in the Employment Appeal Tribunal, by the Registrar of that Tribunal.

(11) The amount of costs to be determined under this regulation may include the costs incurred in relation to a request made under this regulation.

10A.

(1) Subject to paragraph (2), where the court makes a section 11(1) costs order but does not specify the amount which the client is to pay under it, the court may order the client to pay an amount on account of the costs which are the subject of the order.

(2) The court may order a client to make a payment on account of costs under this regulation only if it has sufficient information before it to decide the minimum amount which the client is likely to be ordered to pay on a determination under regulation 10.

(3) The amount of the payment on account of costs shall not exceed the minimum amount which the court decides that the client is likely to be ordered to pay on such a determination.

(4) Where the court orders a client to make a payment on account of costs—

- (a) it shall order the client to make the payment into court; and
- (b) the payment shall remain in court unless and until the court—
  - (i) makes a determination under regulation 10 of the amount which the client should pay to the receiving party under the section 11(1) costs order, and orders the payment on account or part of it to be

paid to the receiving party in satisfaction or part satisfaction of the client's liability under that order; or

(ii) makes an order under paragraph (5)(b) or (5)(c) of this regulation that the payment on account or part of it be repaid to the client.

(5) Where a client has made a payment on account of costs pursuant to an order under paragraph (1) of this regulation—

(a) the receiving party shall request a hearing under regulation 10 to determine the amount of costs payable to him;

(b) if the receiving party fails to request such a hearing within the time permitted by regulation 10(2), the payment on account shall be repaid to the client;

(c) if upon the hearing under regulation 10 the amount of costs which it is determined that the client should pay is less than the amount of the payment on account, the difference shall be repaid to the client.

11. APPEALS, ETC

(1) Subject to the following paragraphs of this regulation, and to regulation 12, any determination made under regulation 9 or regulation 10 shall be final.

(2) Any party with a financial interest in an assessment of the full costs may appeal against that assessment, if and to the extent that that party would, but for these Regulations, be entitled to appeal against an assessment of costs by the court in which the relevant proceedings are taking place.

(3) Where, under regulation 9(2)(a), the court has specified the amount which a client is required to pay under a section 11(1) costs order, the client may apply to the court for a determination of the full costs and if, on that determination, the amount of the full costs is less than the amount which the court previously specified under regulation 9(2)(a), the client shall instead be required to pay the amount of the full costs.

(4) The receiving party or the Commission may appeal, on a point of law, against the making of a costs order against the Commission (including the amount of costs which the Commission is required to pay under the order), or against the court's refusal to make such an order.

12. VARIATION AND LATE DETERMINATION OF AMOUNT OF COSTS

(1) The following paragraphs of this regulation apply where the court makes a section 11(1) costs order.

(2) Where the amount (if any) which the client is required to pay under the section 11(1) costs order, together with the amount which the Commission is required to pay under any costs order against the Commission, is less than the full costs, the receiving party may, on the ground set out in paragraph (4)(a), apply to the court for an order varying the amount which the client is required to pay under the section 11(1) costs order.

(3) Where the court has not specified the amount to be paid under the section 11(1) costs order, and the receiving party has not, within the time limit in regulation 10(2), applied to have that amount determined in accordance with regulation 10, the receiving party may, on any of the grounds set out in paragraph (4), apply for a determination of the amount that the client is required to pay.

(4) The grounds referred to in paragraphs (2) and (3) are the grounds that:

(a) there has been a significant change in the client's circumstances since the date of the order;

(b) material additional information as to the client's financial resources is available, and that information could not with reasonable diligence have been obtained by the receiving party in time to make an application in accordance with regulation 10; or

(c) there were other good reasons justifying the receiving party's failure to make an application within the time limit in regulation 10(2).

(5) Any application under paragraph (2) or (3) shall be made by the receiving party within six years from the date on which the section 11(1) costs order is first made.

(6) On any application under paragraph (2), the order may be varied as the court thinks fit, but the amount of costs ordered (excluding any costs ordered to be paid under paragraph (9)) shall not exceed the amount of the full costs as stated in any previous order of the court.

(7) When the amount which the client is required to pay under the section 11(1) costs order has been determined under regulation 9(2)(a), and the receiving party applies under paragraph (2) for an order varying that amount:

(a) the receiving party shall file with the application under paragraph (2) his bill of costs, which shall comply with any requirements of relevant rules of court relating to the form and content of a bill of costs where the court is assessing a party's costs; and

(b) the court shall, when determining the application, assess the full costs.

(8) Where the receiving party has received funded services in relation to the proceedings, the Commission may make an application under paragraph (2) or paragraph (3), and:

(a) when making the application the Commission shall file with the court a statement of the receiving party's costs or, if those costs have not been assessed, the receiving party's bill of costs; and

(b) paragraphs (4) to (6) shall apply to that application as if 'the Commission' were substituted for 'the receiving party' in those paragraphs.

(9) The amount of costs to be determined under this regulation may include the costs incurred in relation to an application made under this regulation.

13. RIGHTS TO APPEAR

(1) The Regional Director may appear at:

(a) any hearing in relation to which notice has been given under regulation 10(3)(c);

(b) the hearing of any appeal under regulation 11(4); or

(c) the hearing of any application under regulation 12(8).

(2) The Regional Director may, instead of appearing under paragraph (1), give evidence in the form of a written statement to the court, verified by a statement of truth.

(3) The Regional Director shall file with the court any statement under paragraph (2), and serve a copy on the receiving party, not less than seven days before the hearing to which it relates.

(ii) The Costs Practice Direction

The Costs Practice Direction provides:

Assessing a LSC funded client's resources

21.12 The first £100,000 of the value of the LSC funded client's interest in the main or only home is disregarded when assessing his or her financial resources for the purposes of Section 11 and cannot be the subject of any enforcement process by the receiving party. The receiving party cannot apply for an order to sell the LSC funded client's home, but could secure the debt against any value exceeding £100,000 by way of a charging order.

21.13 The court may only take into account the value of the LSC funded client's clothes, household furniture, tools and implements of trade to the extent that it considers that having regard to the quantity or value of the items, the circumstances are exceptional.

21.14 The LSC funded client's resources include the resources of his partner, unless the partner has a contrary interest in the dispute in respect of which funded services are provided.

Party acting in a representative, fiduciary or official capacity

21.15

(1) Where a LSC funded client is acting in a representative, fiduciary or official capacity, the court shall not take the personal resources of the party into account for the purposes of either a Section 11 order or costs against the Commission, but shall have regard to the value of any property or estate or the amount of any fund out of which the party is entitled to be indemnified, and may also have regard to the resources of any persons who are beneficially interested in the property, estate or fund.

(2) The purpose of this provision is to ensure that any liability is determined with reference to the value of the property or fund being used to pay for the litigation, and the financial position of those who may benefit from or rely on it.

Effect of appeals

21.20

(1) An order for costs can only be made against the LSC when the proceedings (including any appeal) are finally decided. Therefore, where a court of first instance decides in favour of a non-funded party and an appeal lies, any order made against the LSC shall not take effect unless:
   a) where permission to appeal is required, the time limit for permission to appeal expires, without permission being granted;
   b) where permission to appeal is granted or is not required, the time limit for appeal expires without an appeal being brought.

(2) Accordingly, if the LSC funded client appeals, any earlier order against the LSC can never take effect. If the appeal is unsuccessful, an application can be made to the appeal court for a fresh order.

SECTION 22 ORDERS FOR COSTS TO WHICH SECTION 11 OF THE ACCESS TO JUSTICE ACT 1999 APPLIES

22.1 In this Practice Direction:

'order for costs to be determined' means an order for costs to which Section 11 of the Access to Justice Act 1999 applies under which the amount of costs payable by the LSC funded client is to be determined by a costs judge or district judge under Section 23 of this Practice Direction.

'order specifying the costs payable' means an order for costs to which Section 11 of the Act applies and which specifies the amount which the LSC funded client is to pay.

'full costs' means, where an order to which Section 11 of the Act applies is made against a LSC funded client, the amount of costs which that person would, had cost protection not applied, have been ordered to pay.

'determination proceedings' means proceedings to which paragraphs 22.1 to 22.10 apply.

'Section 11(1) costs order' means an order for costs to be determined or an order specifying the costs payable other than an order specifying the costs payable which was made in determination proceedings.

'statement of resources' means

(1) a statement, verified by a statement of truth, made by a party to proceedings setting out:

(a) his income and capital and financial commitments during the previous year and, if applicable, those of his partner;
(b) his estimated future financial resources and expectations and, if applicable, those of his partner ('partner' is defined in paragraph 21.4, above);
(c) a declaration that he and, if applicable, his partner, has not deliberately foregone or deprived himself of any resources or expectations;
(d) particulars of any application for funding made by him in connection with the proceedings; and,
(e) any other facts relevant to the determination of his resources; or
(2) a statement, verified by a statement of truth, made by a client receiving funded services, setting out the information provided by the client under Regulation 6 of the Community Legal Service (Financial) Regulations 2000, and stating that there has been no significant change in the client's financial circumstances since the date on which the information was provided or, as the case may be, details of any such change.

'Regional Director' means any Regional Director appointed by the LSC and any member of his staff authorised to act on his behalf.

22.2 Regulations 8 to 13 of the Community Legal Service (Costs) Regulations 2000 set out the procedure for seeking costs against a funded client and the LSC. The effect of these Regulations is set out in this section and the next section of this Practice Direction.

22.3 As from 5 June 2000, Regulations 9 to 13 of the Community Legal Service (Costs) Regulations 2000 also apply to certificates issued under the Legal Aid Act 1988 where costs against the assisted person fall to be assessed under Regulation 124 of the Civil Legal Aid (General) Regulations 1989. In this section and the next section of this Practice Direction the expression 'LSC funded client' includes an assisted person (defined in rule 43.2).

22.4 Regulation 8 of the Community Legal Service (Costs) Regulations 2000 provides that a party intending to seek an order for costs against a LSC funded client may at any time file and serve on the LSC funded client a statement of resources. If that statement is served 7 or more days before a date fixed for a hearing at which an order for costs may be made, the LSC funded client must also make a statement of resources and produce it at the hearing.

22.5 If the court decides to make an order for costs against a LSC funded client to whom cost protection applies it may either:
(1) make an order for costs to be determined, or
(2) make an order specifying the costs payable.

22.6 If the court makes an order for costs to be determined it may also
(1) state the amount of full costs, or
(2) make findings of facts, eg concerning the conduct of all the parties which are to be taken into account by the court in the subsequent determination proceedings.

22.7 The court will not make an order specifying the costs payable unless:
(1) it considers that it has sufficient information before it to decide what amount is a reasonable amount for the LSC funded client to pay in accordance with Section 11 of the Act, and
(2) either
(a) the order also states the amount of full costs, or
(b) the court considers that it has sufficient information before it to decide what amount is a reasonable amount for the LSC funded client to pay in accordance with Section 11 of the Act and is satisfied that, if it were to determine the full costs at that time, they would exceed the amounts specified in the order.

22.8 Where an order specifying the costs payable is made and the LSC funded client does not have cost protection in respect of all of the costs awarded in that order, the order must identify the sum payable (if any) in respect of which the LSC funded client has cost protection and the sum payable (if any) in respect of which he does not have cost protection.

22.9 The court cannot make an order under Regulations 8 to 13 of the Community Legal Service (Costs) Regulations 2000 except in proceedings to which the next section of this Practice Direction applies.

SECTION 23 DETERMINATION PROCEEDINGS AND SIMILAR PROCEEDINGS UNDER THE COMMUNITY LEGAL SERVICE (COSTS) REGULATIONS 2000

23.1 This section of this Practice Direction deals with

(1) proceedings subsequent to the making of an order for costs to be determined,

(2) variations in the amount stated in an order specifying the amount of costs payable and

(3) the late determination of costs under an order for costs to be determined.

23.2 In this section of this Practice Direction 'appropriate court office' means:

(1) the district registry or county court in which the case was being dealt with when the Section 11(1) order was made, or to which it has subsequently been transferred; or

(2) in all other cases, the Supreme Court Costs Office.

23.3

(1) A receiving party seeking an order specifying costs payable by an LSC funded client and/or by the LSC may within 3 months of an order for costs to be determined, file in the appropriate court office an application in Form N244 accompanied by

- *(a) the receiving party's bill of costs (unless the full costs have already been determined);*
- *(b) the receiving party's statement of resources; and*
- *(c) if the receiving party intends to seek costs against the LSC, written notice to that effect.*

(2) If the LSC funded client's liability has already been determined and is less than the full costs, the application will be for costs against the LSC only. If the LSC funded client's liability has not yet been determined, the receiving party must indicate if costs will be sought against the LSC if the funded client's liability is determined as less than the full costs.

(The LSC funded client's certificate will contain the addresses of the LSC funded client, his solicitor, and the relevant Regional Office of the LSC.)

23.4 The receiving party must file the above documents in the appropriate court office and (where relevant) serve copies on the LSC funded client and the Regional Director. Failure to file a request within the 3 months time limit specified in Regulation 10(2) is an absolute bar to the making of a costs order against the LSC.

23.5 On being served with the application, the LSC funded client must respond by filing a statement of resources and serving a copy of it on the receiving party (and the Regional Director where relevant) within 21 days. The LSC funded client may also file and serve written points disputing the bill within the same time limit. (Under rule 3.1 the court may extend or shorten this time limit.)

23.6 If the LSC funded client fails to file a statement of resources without good reason, the court will determine his liability (and the amount of full costs if relevant) and need not hold an oral hearing for such determination.

23.7 When the LSC funded client files a statement or the 21 day period for doing so expires, the court will fix a hearing date and give the relevant parties at least 14 days notice. The court may fix a hearing without waiting for the expiry of the 21 day period if the application is made only against the LSC.

23.8 Determination proceedings will be listed for hearing before a costs judge or district judge.

23.9 Where the LSC funded client does not have cost protection in respect of all of the costs awarded, the order made by the costs judge or district judge must in addition to specifying the costs payable, identify the full costs in respect of which cost protection applies and the full costs in respect of which cost protection does not apply.

23.10 The Regional Director may appear at any hearing at which a costs order may be made against the LSC. Instead of appearing, he may file a written statement at court and serve a copy on the receiving party. The written statement should be filed and a copy served, not less than 7 days before the hearing.

Variation of an order specifying the costs payable

23.11

(1) This paragraph applies where the amount stated in an order specifying the costs payable plus the amount ordered to be paid by the LSC is less than the full costs to which cost protection applies.

(2) The receiving party may apply to the court for a variation of the amount which the LSC funded client is required to pay on the ground that there has been a significant change in the client's circumstances since the date of the order.

23.12 On an application under paragraph 23.11, where the order specifying the costs payable does not state the full costs

(1) the receiving party must file with his application the receiving party's statement of resources and bill of costs and copies of these documents should be served with the application.

(2) The LSC funded client must respond to the application by making a statement of resources which must be filed at court and served on the receiving party within 21 days thereafter. The LSC funded client may also file and serve written points disputing the bill within the same time limit.

(3) The court will, when determining the application assess the full costs identifying any part of them to which cost protection does apply and any part of them to which cost protection does not apply.

23.13 On an application under paragraph 23.11 the order specifying the costs payable may be varied as the court thinks fit. That variation must not increase:

(1) the amount of any costs ordered to be paid by the LSC, and

(2) the amount payable by the LSC funded client,

to a sum which is greater than the amount of the full costs plus the costs of the application.

23.14

(1) Where an order for costs to be determined has been made but the receiving party has not applied, within the three month time limit under paragraph 23.2, the receiving party may apply on any of the following grounds for a determination of the amount which the funded client is required to pay:

a) there has been a significant change in the funded client's circumstances since the date of the order for costs to be determined; or

b) material additional information about the funded client's financial resources is available which could not with reasonable diligence have been obtained by the receiving party at the relevant time; or

c) there were other good reasons for the failure by the receiving party to make an application within the time limit.

(2) An application for costs payable by the LSC cannot be made under this paragraph.

23.15

(1) Where the receiving party has received funded services in relation to the proceedings, the LSC may make an application under paragraphs 23.11 and 23.14 above.

(2) In respect of an application under paragraph 23.11 made by the LSC, the LSC must file and serve copies of the documents described in paragraph 23.12(1).

23.16 An application under paragraph 23.11, 23.14 and 23.15 must be commenced before the expiration of 6 years from the date on which the court made the order specifying the costs payable, or (as the case may be) the order for costs to be determined.

23.17 Applications under paragraphs 23.11, 23.14 and 23.15 should be made in the appropriate court office and should be made in Form N244 to be listed for a hearing before a costs judge or district judge.

5. WASTED COSTS ORDER AGAINST THE BOARD

In care proceedings, the judge granted continuous staying contact with the grandparents and suspended contact with the father. On appeal it was conceded that the judge's orders had been made without jurisdiction. The local authority applied for costs, indicating that it was indifferent as to whether they were awarded against the Board or against the grandparents' legal advisers under the wasted costs jurisdiction. An order against the grandparents would have no effect because they had no assets. The court laid down the following guidelines to be adopted in similar applications:

(1) Were there circumstances justifying:
   (a) an order for costs against the assisted party if that party had not been legally aided, or
   (b) a wasted costs order against that party's legal representatives?
(2) If circumstances could justify (a), such an application should be made.
(3) If it were appropriate to apply for (b), that application should be made.
(4) If the court considered it appeared to be so clear a case for making a wasted costs order against the legal representatives that it would not be just and equitable to make an order nisi against the Legal Aid Board, the court should adjourn the application against the Board and proceed to take the steps necessary to establish that a wasted costs order was necessary. If such an order were made in respect of all the relevant costs, there would ordinarily be no reason to proceed further against the Board.
(5) If the application against the Board was not adjourned:
   (a) the court should ascertain whether the requirements of s 18 of the Legal Aid Act 1988 were met, and if so make any order against the legally aided party and, if justified, an order nisi against the Board. In addition, if the court considered that there was a real possibility that a wasted costs order would be made, it should direct that that should be drawn to the Board's attention;
   (b) the lawyers representing the legally-aided litigant should regard it as their responsibility to draw to the court's attention any matters relevant in determining whether the requirements of s 18 had been met;
   (c) if the Board objected to an order, it could raise any contention it wished to pursue in respect of a wasted costs order.
(6) If an application against the Board was adjourned pending the investigation of an application for a wasted costs order and no such order was made, the application against the Board could be restored and determined.

In cases involving children, the position was complicated by the fact that the court did not attach the same significance to which party was successful, recognising that as its primary concern was the child's welfare, it was frequently inappropriate to determine questions of costs by merely asking who had won. On appeal, the approach was similar, but subject to an important qualification: that those who participate in litigation in the Court of Appeal involving the future of children had to be prepared for the appellate court to take the view that while it was reasonable for them to play an active part in proceedings at first instance, it was not so on appeal. If that was the position, they had to be prepared for an order for costs to be made against them (*Re O (a minor) (Costs: Liability of Legal Aid Board)* [1997] 1 FLR 465, CA).

CHAPTER 20

ARBITRATION

1. ARBITRATION ACT 1996

The law relating to arbitration is contained in the Arbitration Act 1996 which was greeted with universal acclaim as a model statute in both form and content when it came into force on 1 January 1997. Sections 59–65 relate to costs. Here they are:

59 COSTS OF THE ARBITRATION

(1) References in this Part to the costs of the arbitration are to—

(a) the arbitrators' fees and expenses,

(b) the fees and expenses of any arbitral institution concerned, and

(c) the legal or other costs of the parties.

(2) Any such reference includes the costs of or incidental to any proceedings to determine the amount of the recoverable costs of the arbitration (see section 63).

60 AGREEMENT TO PAY COSTS IN ANY EVENT

An agreement which has the effect that a party is to pay the whole or part of the costs of the arbitration in any event is only valid if made after the dispute in question has arisen.

61 AWARD OF COSTS

(1) The tribunal may make an award allocating the costs of the arbitration as between the parties, subject to any agreement of the parties.

(2) Unless the parties otherwise agree, the tribunal shall award costs on the general principle that costs should follow the event except where it appears to the tribunal that in the circumstances this is not appropriate in relation to the whole or part of the costs.

62 EFFECT OF AGREEMENT OR AWARD ABOUT COSTS

Unless the parties otherwise agree, any obligation under an agreement between them as to how the costs of the arbitration are to be borne, or under an award allocating the costs of the arbitration, extends only to such costs as are recoverable.

63 THE RECOVERABLE COSTS OF THE ARBITRATION

(1) The parties are free to agree what costs of the arbitration are recoverable.

(2) If or to the extent there is no such agreement, the following provisions apply.

(3) The tribunal may determine by award the recoverable costs of the arbitration on such basis as it thinks fit.

If it does so, it shall specify—

(a) the basis on which it has acted, and

(b) the items of recoverable costs and the amount referable to each.

(4) If the tribunal does not determine the recoverable costs of the arbitration, any party to the arbitral proceedings may apply to the court (upon notice to the other parties) which may—

(a) determine the recoverable costs of the arbitration on such basis as it thinks fit, or

(b) order that they shall be determined by such means and upon such terms as it may specify.

(5) Unless the tribunal or the court determines otherwise—

(a) the recoverable costs of the arbitration shall be determined on the basis that there shall be allowed a reasonable amount in respect of all costs reasonably incurred, and

(b) any doubt as to whether costs were reasonably incurred or were reasonable in amount shall be resolved in favour of the paying party.

(6) The above provisions have effect subject to section 64 (recoverable fees and expenses of arbitrators).

(7) Nothing in this section affects any right of the arbitrators, any expert, legal adviser or assessor appointed by the tribunal, or any arbitral institution, to payment of their fees and expenses.

64 RECOVERABLE FEES AND EXPENSES OF ARBITRATORS

(1) Unless otherwise agreed by the parties, the recoverable costs of the arbitration shall include in respect of the fees and expenses of the arbitrators only such reasonable fees and expenses as are appropriate in the circumstances.

(2) If there is any question as to what reasonable fees and expenses are appropriate in the circumstances, and the matter is not already before the court on an application under section 63(4), the court may on the application of any party (upon notice to the other parties)—

(a) determine the matter, or

(b) order that it be determined by such means and upon such terms as the court may specify.

(3) Subsection (1) has effect subject to any order of the court under section 24(4) or 25(3)(b) (order as to entitlement to fees or expenses in case of removal or resignation of arbitrator).

(4) Nothing in this section affects any right of the arbitrator to payment of his fees and expenses.

65 POWER TO LIMIT RECOVERABLE COSTS

(1) Unless otherwise agreed by the parties, the tribunal may direct that the recoverable costs of the arbitration, or of any part of the arbitral proceedings, shall be limited to a specified amount.

(2) Any direction may be made or varied at any stage, but this must be done sufficiently in advance of the incurring of costs to which it relates, or the taking of any steps in the proceedings which may be affected by it, for the limit to be taken into account.

2. 'NO COSTS' AGREEMENTS

Section 60 of the Act preserves the unusual prohibition in respect of arbitrations that the parties may not in the arbitration agreement provide that each party shall pay their own costs in any event, and extends the prohibition to agreements that one party shall pay the other party's costs whatever the outcome of the arbitration. The purpose is to try to create a level playing field between large contractors and small contractors.

3. AWARD OF COSTS

Section 61 of the Act empowers the arbitrator to award the whole or part of the costs of the arbitration to either party, subject to the general principle that costs follow the event except where it appears to the tribunal that in the circumstances this is not appropriate in relation to the whole or part of the costs. Matters such as conduct, proportionality and sealed offers were relevant to the award of arbitration costs long before these concepts were introduced into civil litigation by the Civil Procedure Rules 1998. Nevertheless CPR Part 49 applies the rules to arbitration and to this extent the practice has been codified in the CPR both in respect of the principles on which costs are awarded and quantified, and also in respect of offers to settle (CPR Part 36).

If a sealed offer is made in arbitration, being the arbitral equivalent of a payment into court, a respondent is normally entitled to payment of costs from the date of the offer if the award in respect of the claim and interest is less than the offer. The arbitrator is not entitled to take into account whether an award of costs would be made in favour of the claimant because that would require the claimant to assess not only the likelihood of achieving an award on his claim and interest exceeding the offer, but also, if there was a risk of an order that the claimant pay the respondent's costs, the chance of obtaining an award greater than the offer and the respondent's costs. Such a result would hinder settlement and introduce complications inconsistent with the principle that the cost should follow the event (*Everglade Maritime Inc v Schiffahrtsgesellschaft Detlef von Appen mbH* [1993] QB 780, CA.

4. QUANTIFICATION

Again in anticipation of the summary assessment introduced by the Civil Procedure Rules, arbitrators were empowered and encouraged to assess costs themselves where possible in preference to referring them to the court for assessment, subject to the right of the parties to agree what costs are recoverable. Costs were in effect on the standard basis as it was defined before 26 April 1999 unless the arbitrator ordered otherwise, but the application of the Civil Procedure Rules now incorporates the specific additional test of proportionality.

5. RECOVERABLE FEES

The definition of costs in the Arbitration Act 1996, s 59 includes the arbitrator's fees and expenses, which are defined in s 64(1) as 'such reasonable fees and expenses as are appropriate in the circumstances', while s 37(2) provides that 'expenses' may include the fees and expenses of experts, legal advisers and assessors appointed by the arbitrator, so for these to be recoverable, they too must be reasonable. Section 64(1) is subject to any order made under ss 24 and 25 of the Act on the removal or resignation of an arbitrator.

Any dispute about the reasonableness of an arbitrator's fees and expenses may be resolved by the court under s 64(2). However, this is subject to the right of the parties and the arbitrator to agree the amount of his fees and expenses at the outset, creating a contract with which the court cannot interfere (Arbitration Act 1996, s 64(4)). If the agreement relates only to hourly or daily rates, the court can investigate the reasonableness of the time spent, but not the agreed amounts.

6. COSTS LIMITATION

Again ahead of the radical philosophy of the Civil Procedure Rules, the Arbitration Act 1996, s 65 empower the arbitrator, unless the parties have agreed otherwise, to limit the costs recoverable in the arbitration either as a whole or in respect of a specified part. This enables the arbitrator either on their own initiative or, more likely, on the application of one of the parties to specify the maximum liability for costs of the arbitration. It will not of course prevent either party spending a disproportionate amount on costs, but it will put a cap on the amount they can recover from the other party. It would be helpful to support an application with a schedule of the estimate of costs, which it may not be possible to prepare until directions have been given as to the format of the arbitration.

Writing in the *New Law Journal*, 9 April 1999, Francis Miller considered the impact of a limitation of costs under s 65 on a conditional fee agreement between the claimant and their legal advisers. He suggested this could result in the actual recoverable costs from the respondent, in the event of the claimant winning, being limited to an amount which was a great deal less than the actual costs incurred by the claimant. In this event, recourse might be had to the safeguard in s 65(2) which provides:

> 'Any direction may be made or varied at any stage, but this must be done sufficiently in advance of the incurring of costs to which it relates, or the taking of any steps in the proceedings which may be affected by it, for the limit to be taken into account.'

7. THE COURT

Section 63(4) provides that if the tribunal does not determine the recoverable costs of the arbitration any party may apply to the court for a determination. Does an award of costs 'to be agreed or taxed in default of agreement' permit the arbitrator to determine the costs, or does it amount to either a reference to the court or to a failure to determine the costs, enabling the receiving party to apply to the court? In *M/S Alghanim Industries Inc v Skandia International Insurance Corpn* [2001] 2 All ER (Comm) 30 (Technology and Construction Court, *Arbitration Law Monthly*, September 2001) it was held that the phrase is not to be construed as a determination of the proceedings with a reference of taxation to the court in the event that the parties could not agree. The arbitrators had not expressly declined to tax and settle the costs, requiring the matter to go to the court. An award of costs to be agreed or taxed in default of agreement was not a refusal to tax but was neutral in its language, it left open the possibility of an application by either party to the arbitrators. This was consistent with the spirit of the Act that as far as possible matters should be resolved by arbitration rather than by application to the court.

8. CORRECTING A COSTS AWARD

Under s 57(3)(*a*) of the 1996 Act, an arbitrator has the default power to 'correct an award so as to remove any clerical mistake or error arising from an accidental slip or omission'. In *Gannet Shipping Ltd v Eastrade Commodities Inc* (Technology and Construction Court, *Arbitration Law Monthly*, May 2002) Langley J held that the arbitrator also had jurisdiction to vary the costs order at the same time. The costs error was an error 'arising from' the 'accidental slip' in the amount awarded, and accordingly it could be corrected. Furthermore, the costs award could also have been amended under the jurisdiction to intervene conferred by both s 62(2)(*a*) (failure by the tribunal to comply with the natural justice principle in s 33 of the 1996 Act and s 62(2)(*i*) (irregularity in the conduct of the proceedings or in the award which is admitted by the tribunal). The only limiting factor was the need to show substantial injustice.

9. SECURITY FOR COSTS

See Chapter 13.

Part III

Quantification

CHAPTER 21

CONTENTIOUS AND NON-CONTENTIOUS COSTS – WHAT IS THE DIFFERENCE?

1. VIVE LA DIFFERENCE?

Most approaches to costs start by distinguishing between contentious and non-contentious work, solicitors tending to identify themselves with one or the other, thereby not only relieving themselves from the responsibility of having any knowledge of the other species of costs but enabling them to say with complacent self-disparagement 'of course I don't know anything about contentious costs' (or 'non-contentious costs' as the case may be) as though they were some alien discipline. I do not in any way wish to minimise the difference between contentious and non-contentious costs – as between sexes there are differences and they are important; on the other hand, again as with the sexes, the similarities are much greater than the differences and I think that the best approach is to treat solicitors' costs as an entity, considering the differences only when they arise.

Non-contentious business is defined by the Solicitors Act 1974 as 'any business done as a solicitor which is not contentious business', and if you find that less than helpful you will also find in the Solicitors Act contentious business defined as being 'business done whether as solicitor or advocate in or for the purposes of proceedings begun before a Court or before an arbitrator appointed under the Arbitration Act 1950 other than non-contentious probate business'. The key word there is 'begun'. If you take instructions for divorce proceedings but before you present the petition the parties are reconciled that, contrary to all the appearances, is non-contentious work. Another trap for the unwary is that someone who can never have visited an Employment Tribunal has classified it (and all other tribunals except the Lands Tribunal) as non-contentious business, even though an appeal from an Employment Tribunal to the Employment Appeal Tribunal takes its rightful place as contentious business.

2. THE PRESCRIBED FACTORS

(a) Non-contentious

A solicitor's remuneration for non-contentious business is governed by the Solicitors' (Non-Contentious Business) Remuneration Order 1994, art 3 which prescribes that it:

> shall be such sum as may be fair and reasonable to both solicitor and entitled person, having regard to all the circumstances of the case and in particular to:—
> (a) the complexity of the matter or the difficulty or novelty of the questions raised;
> (b) the skill, labour, specialised knowledge and responsibility involved;
> (c) the time spent on the business;

(d) the number and importance of the documents prepared or perused, without regard to length;
(e) the place where and the circumstances in which the business or any part thereof is transacted;
(f) the amount or value of any money or property involved;
(g) whether any land involved is registered land;
(h) the importance of the matter to the client; and
(i) the approval (express or implied) of the entitled person or the express approval of the testator to:—
   (i) the solicitor undertaking all or any part of the work giving rise to the costs or
   (ii) the amount of the costs.

(b) Contentious

The quantification of contentious costs is governed by CPR Rule 44.5.

CPR RULE 44.5 FACTORS TO BE TAKEN INTO ACCOUNT IN DECIDING THE AMOUNT OF COSTS

(1) The court is to have regard to all the circumstances in deciding whether costs were—
  (a) if it is assessing costs on the standard basis—
    (i) proportionately and reasonably incurred; or
    (ii) were proportionate and reasonable in amount, or
  (b) if it is assessing costs on the indemnity basis—
    (i) unreasonably incurred; or
    (ii) unreasonable in amount.

(2) In particular the court must give effect to any orders which have already been made.

(3) The court must also have regard to—
  (a) the conduct of all the parties, including in particular—
    (i) conduct before, as well as during, the proceedings; and
    (ii) the efforts made, if any, before and during the proceedings in order to try to resolve the dispute;
  (b) the amount or value of any money or property involved;
  (c) the importance of the matter to all the parties;
  (d) the particular complexity of the matter or the difficulty or novelty of the questions raised;
  (e) the skill, effort, specialised knowledge and responsibility involved;
  (f) the time spent on the case; and
  (g) the place where and the circumstances in which work or any part of it was done.

(Rule 35.4 (4) gives the court power to limit the amount that a party may recover with regard to the fees and expenses of an expert)

3. THE BASES

Let us dispose of another difference which is more apparent than real between contentious and non-contentious costs. There are two bases for the assessment of costs, the standard basis and the indemnity basis, and on neither basis will the court allow costs which have been unreasonably incurred or are unreasonable in amount (CPR Rule 44.4(1)). They are therefore fundamentally the same. Non-contentious costs are always to be assessed on the indemnity basis (CPR Rule 48.8(2)) while CPR Rule 44.4 prescribes that contentious costs may be awarded on either basis. There are two differences between the standard and the indemnity basis: (a) the benefit of any doubt is resolved in favour of the paying party on the standard basis and in favour of the receiving party on the indemnity basis and (b) on the standard basis costs have to be proportionate to the matters in issue (CPR Rule 44.4(2); see p 99). These two exceptions apart, there is no difference between the prescribed principles governing the quantification of non-contentious and contentious business.

4. THE PAYING PARTY

An apparent difference between contentious and non-contentious costs is that in contentious work the costs are frequently ordered to be paid by somebody other than the person who ordered the work to be done. In litigation they will probably be paid by the loser, while if it is a legal aid matter, the costs may be paid out of the legal aid fund. Therefore, in litigation it is necessary much more frequently than in non-contentious business to protect the interests of a paying party who was not privy to the incurring of the costs he has to pay. But this is not a crucial difference. In non-contentious work one sees with increasing frequency provision in leases and other commercial documents for costs to be paid by someone other than the client.

5. VALUE

More imagination has been shown in applying the prescribed factors in non-contentious work than contentious. Various formulae or yardsticks have been tried – financial bands, regressive scales, the adrenalin factor, percentage service increments, time plus 25% plus half the value, time plus an overall uplift – together with a variety of ways of assessing the value of different types of non-contentious work, such as leases, options and probate. In comparison, litigation costs have become increasingly hypnotised with time – an obsession which has now led to prescribed hourly rates for summary assessments which are professed to take into account, or rather to circumscribe, all of the factors required to be taken into account by CPR Rule 44.5.

The main reason for this divergence is no doubt because in non-contentious work the value element is more readily identifiable and ascertainable than in much contentious work. What, for example, is the value element in a divorce suit or a criminal matter? Who can put a value on the liberty of the subject, whether the freedom be from a spouse or a prison? On the other hand the reverse also applies, there is often a very substantial value element identifiable in litigation while in some non-contentious work the value element may be unquantifiable or so small as to be only a minor factor in charging. What, for example, is the value of a will to the *client* as distinct from the beneficiaries?

6. CONCLUSION

There are no inherent distinctions of principle necessitating different approaches to the quantification of contentious and non-contentious costs.

CHAPTER 22

TIME

1. COSTING TIME

Time is relevant in a solicitor's practice in two distinct ways. First, it is his raw material, his stock in trade. Some years ago the young partners in an old and venerable firm were trying to persuade their elders to bring the firm into the twentieth century. One of the senior partners remonstrated with them: 'The trouble with your generation is you are trying to run the practice like a business'.

In the same way that businesses keep control over materials and stock, a solicitor should keep control over his own and his employees' time. The first relevance of time is therefore to the good running and management of a solicitor's practice. Could the time be put to better use?

The second relevance of time is to charging. Not only is time one of the prescribed factors for both contentious and non-contentious business, and in routine matters it is the most important, it also runs like a thread through the other factors. The importance and complexity of the matter, the difficulty or novelty of questions raised can all affect the amount of time spent. An hourly cost rate applied to recorded time, in the words of Donaldson J:

> 'First, informs a solicitor of the minimum figure which he must charge, if he is not to make an actual loss on the transaction. Second, it gives him an idea of the relationship between the overheads attributable to the transaction and the profit accruing to him. This latter point is plainly relevant in the broad sense that the nature of some transactions will justify much larger profits than others of a more routine type. But we must stress that it is only one of a number of cross-checks on the fairness and reasonableness of the final figure. The final figure will result from an exercise in judgment, not arithmetic, whatever arithmetical cross-checks may be employed.'

(*Property and Reversionary Investment Corpn Ltd v Secretary of State for the Environment* [1975] 2 All ER 436.)

Together with value, time is one of only two factors that are quantifiable, and if a solicitor is not able to quantify it, it is going to cast considerable doubt on his ability to quantify the other, less tangible, factors.

2. ALTERNATIVES TO COSTING TIME

(a) For management

(i) Budget

You can prepare a budget of expenses for the next year. You can divide that by 12. You now know that if in each month you do not bill at least that amount you are running at a loss. You can take it a stage further by adding to your budgeted expenses for the forthcoming year the profit you hope to make during that period and dividing that total by 12. This gives you a total target figure for bills delivered. Having calculated the figure for bills to deliver during the year, it can be apportioned among the fee earners so that the total targets of the fee earners equals your overall target. If each fee earner accepts his target as realistic, you know you should reach your overall target for the year. As a result of monthly checks you will have an early warning if any fee earner is falling behind his target. Each month you will know whether you are on, ahead of or behind your target.

(ii) Employees

There is no point in one solicitor (the principal) employing another solicitor or legal executive (the assistant), paying him a salary, supplying him free of charge with accommodation, secretarial services and all the other tools of his profession, unless that assistant either makes a profit for his principal or relieves the principal of routine work, thereby enabling the principal to undertake more profitable work. A rough formula which has stood the test of time is that a fee earner's share of the overheads is not less than one-and-a-half times his salary. An assistant with a salary of £40,000 a year will have a share of the overheads of £60,000 a year, meaning that he must bill £100,000, or two-and-a-half times his salary, to break even. If to this is added a modest profit of half his salary, this produces a target of £120,000, or three times his salary. I was interested to discover that a survey of surveyors had identified what they called a factor of 2.7–3.0; they had reached the same conclusion – that unless an assistant earns at least three times his salary, his employment must be justified by some means other than the profit he is making for the firm.

These two aspects of management control depend solely upon the calculation of expenses and projected profit. They do not require any recording or costing of time.

(b) For charging

There is a variety of ways in which solicitors' charges could be calculated, other than on the basis of time. Examples are according to value, scale, commission, salary, fixed fees, a contingency basis, and a quantum meruit.

Not only does time not enter into any of these bases, the less time a solicitor takes to do a job where time is not the basis of calculation, the bigger the profit he makes because he has more time to spend on other work.

In an article in *The Lawyer*, 12 October 1993, Anne Gallagher considered various methods of charging in the United States. She identified four basic billing methods: hourly, fixed-fee and contingency, all of which determine in advance the billing method that will be used, and 'value billing', where the lawyer retrospectively determines what the fee will be, based upon either subjective or agreed-upon criteria. Variations of billing methods included:

(i) Blended hourly rate	All services are charged at a common hourly rate whether for a senior partner, junior partner or associate.
(ii) Fixed fee plus hourly rate	Certain defined services are charged on a fixed-fee basis, while the remainder of the time expended is billed on an hourly basis.
(iii) Hourly rate plus premium	The established hourly rate is standard or lower than standard with a bonus paid if certain results are achieved.
(iv) Percentage fees	The actual amount of the fee depends on the value of the total transaction.

(v) Unit charges	For a defined segment of service, a unit charge is established, usually in combination with hourly billing.
(vi) Relative value fees	A fee is established based on the relative value of the activity. For example, time spent answering correspondence may be assigned a lower value than time spent in research or negotiation.
(vii) Availability only retainer	No services are included in this arrangement, which is established to ensure that legal counsel will be available when needed and not available to represent an adverse party. Fees are then paid as rendered.

3. THE EXPENSE OF TIME

Time recording and time costing were introduced back in the days when it was slowly dawning on the solicitors' branch of the legal profession that solicitors were no longer certain to make a profit simply by working all hours that God sent and charging as much as the matter or client would stand (subject to the time honoured exceptions that Lady So-and-So would be mortally offended if we were to send her a reminder if she did not deign to pay our bill, and of course we would not dream of charging the little old lady around the corner who had no money anyway). It was becoming increasingly clear that not all work was profitable. It was for that reason that the profession introduced time costing – to see what work was being run at a profit and at a loss. It had nothing to do with charging – indeed conveyancing was still on a fixed scale but conveyancers were exhorted to cost their time to see what profit, if any, they were making. The object, therefore, was to check whether work which was being charged on a scale or some other basis was in fact being done at a profit. As a result many Central London firms stopped doing domestic conveyancing.

For the system to work you have to know how much each job costs and to do this you have to calculate the cost to the firm of each fee earner in reasonable units of time. There was a variety of different methods of costing work but the method suggested by the Law Society in its booklet *The Expense of Time* seemed to most firms using it simple and satisfactory. In the contemporary words of *The Solicitors' Journal*, 'It recommends a simplified system suitable for near innumerate solicitors. It is a triumph that so many firms have put its provisions into practice'.

I shall not set it out here. *The Expense of Time* is now in its fifth edition and includes a simplified back-of-an-envelope approach upon which I cannot improve. Basically, it divides the firm into fee earners and non-fee earners and then divides the projected overheads of the firm, including the salaries of the non-fee earners, between the fee earners, after building in various adjustments such as notional salaries for partners, deduction of interest on the client account and applying the retail price index and the estimated rate of inflation.

It was also appreciated that if fee earners recorded non-chargeable time under various categories as well as chargeable time and the time records were fed into a computer, the partners would have an overall picture of each fee earner's day and could identify how he spent his time. This 'big brother' aspect of time recording did not commend itself to everyone, although no one could gainsay Tom Woodcock, the father of *The Expense of Time*, when he talked about the 'benefits flowing effortlessly and virtually gratuitously from computerised time recording'. His message was that the difficult part was the discipline of recording time. You could of course record time on the back of old envelopes then put them in the file. To record time on time sheets involved the fee earner in no more work, but the benefits to the firm in management control were substantial. It really is a question of what turns you on. Many partners, when they see the voluminous weekly print-outs from their computerised time recording system have a reaction similar to that of the little girl in the James Thurber story, who was set the task for her homework of reading a book about penguins and then writing an essay on the subject. Her essay started, 'This book told me more about penguins than I wanted to know'!

4. USING TIME FOR CHARGING

(a) The dangers

(i) The expense of time

We have seen that the recording and costing of time was introduced for the purpose of knowing whether work was being done at a profit or a loss and that it had the additional advantage of affording management control information for those who desired it. It was not intended as a basis of charging. What then happened was that costs judges applying the rules for the assessment of costs, those responsible for devising those rules, and indeed the profession itself, all realised that the cost of doing the work was a useful method of quantifying both contentious and non-contentious work, particularly in routine matters.

Nevertheless this was using time costing for a purpose for which it was never intended, so it was not really surprising when complaints began to ring out that the formula was too unreliable and too unsophisticated to bear the burden that had been imposed on it. As an aid to business efficiency, the costing of time was a matter of only domestic concern to each firm costing its work. If the formula they used, or their arithmetic, was wrong, it was only they who were misled into thinking they were making a bigger or smaller profit than they really were. Arithmetical sums are clearly unacceptable as a basis of charging.

Surely the answer to the problem was to be found in that worthy booklet, the Law Society's *The Expense of Time*? Alas, no! Not according to either the introduction to *The Expense of Time* or to Mr Justice Goff, when he examined it in *R v Wilkinson* [1980] 1 All ER 597:

> '*The Expense of Time* merely deals with the first but essential stage in deciding what is fair and reasonable remuneration, namely establishing the expense to the solicitor of doing his work. It does not deal with establishing what is a fair fee to charge a client …' (Introduction to first and second editions of *The Expense of Time*).

> 'This booklet is an aid to management: its use for charging purposes will be explained in detail in a separate booklet.' (Foreword to the third edition of *The Expense of Time*).

> 'It is NOT a means of calculating the charge to be made to the client.' (Introduction to the fifth (and current) edition of *The Expense of Time*).

It could also have said 'this is NOT the booklet the Law Society promised 15 years ago', which has never been written.

> 'I am unable to say that *The Expense of Time* in its present form provides a sufficiently reliable guide to be used as a basis for taxation of solicitors' costs'. (*R v Wilkinson* [1980] 1 All ER at 607, per Goff J.)

The reasons for the judge's criticisms included the number of chargeable hours (which I have seen based on figures ranging from 800 to 2,500 a year), the basing of notional salaries on the civil service salary scale, interest on clients' account, the treatment of trainee solicitors, pension provision, overtime, failure to distinguish between different types of work and the impossibility in practice for clients or costs officers to check whether a solicitor's expense of time calculations are accurate or not. The danger is that no two firms or people mean precisely the same thing when they refer to hourly expense rates. As a matter of semantics it is also difficult to see how one can describe as an 'expense rate' a calculation which includes a notional salary for partners and which covers such wide discrepancies in overheads as the thickness of the pile on the office carpets and whether the partners run white Rolls-Royces or black bicycles on the firm. Most of the criticisms in *R v Wilkinson* were met in subsequent editions of *The Expense of Time* but it is not surprising that the Law Society has still not produced its promised separate booklet to explain its use for charging purposes.

On the positive side, Mr Justice Goff did say:

> 'There is no doubt that the booklet constitutes a most praiseworthy effort to promote the calculation of the expense of time to solicitors on a scientific and uniform basis, primarily for managerial purposes, but also as a means to assist solicitors in calculating their charges and justifying them on taxation (*assessment*).'

If that were true of the second edition it is even more true of the current edition. But it is still surprising to find this complicated and sophisticated edifice of charging built upon such a nebulous foundation in shifting sand.

(ii) The painful plodder's charter

Another objection to time charging is the same as the objection to the historical quantitative methods of assessment. We now laugh at the thought of payment calculated in relation to the height of the file or the weight of papers, but payment by the metre, the kilo or the hour are all equally flawed: they all relate to quantity not quality. Payment based on time means that the longer a solicitor takes to do the work, the more he is paid. The greater his skill and expertise, the greater his expedition, the less time he will record and the less will be his reward. Where a solicitor brings to bear years of experience, or has a flash of inspiration, it happens so quickly that he does not have time to make even a mark on his time sheet. High quality work which should be encouraged is in fact severely penalised in any system of charges based solely on time. Charges based on the time spent reward the painful plodder for his slowness and inefficiency while penalising speed and efficiency in others. In contending that this basis of charging is against the client's interests an American commentator referred to the 'misaligned interests of the hourly rate'. In the words of an old catch-phrase 'Don't mind the quality, feel the width'.

(iii) Profit is not a four-letter word

The expense of time is of course concerned only with the cost of doing the work, not with profit. Profit must be calculated in some other way. It was explained in two cases:

1. Re Eastwood

In *Re Eastwood* [1973] 3 All ER 1079, Brightman J in his judgment said:

> 'During the hearing of the argument I was given certain advice by the assessors as to the manner in which a taxation proceeds at the present day. The advice given to me is this: "At the present day, on the taxation of a bill of costs of a firm of solicitors in private practice which has been engaged in litigation on behalf of a client the taxation invariably proceeds on the following basis. The firm informs the taxing master of the period of time that has been spent by any partner or employee of the firm on any 'relevant' aspect of the case: the word 'relevant' is intended to exclude time spent on a part of the case for which there is a fixed charge prescribed by statute or rule. The firm submits (a) what is the proper cost per hour of the time so spent, having regard to a reasonable estimate of the overhead expenses of the solicitors' firm including (if the time spent is that of an employee) the reasonable salary of the employee or (if the time spent is that of a partner) a notional salary. The firm will also submit at the conclusion of [the item for preparation for trial], (b) what is a proper additional sum to be allowed over and above (a) by way of further profit costs."'

2. The A and B factors

This philosophy was further expounded in *Leopold Lazarus Ltd v Secretary of State for Trade and Industry* in which the '(a)' and '(b)' were promoted to 'A' and 'B' and have ever since been known as the A factor and the B factor. *Lazarus* has never been reported in the law reports and was only briefly reported in *The Times* of 9 April 1976. As it was the first time that the expression 'direct cost' was used it may be helpful to an understanding of the concept to set out the following extract from the actual judgment of Mr Justice Kerr:

> 'In his Answer the master helpfully summarised the practice concerning the computation of Item 26 in cases such as this. Having considered the weight of the proceedings and the responsibility and skill involved, the practice is then to arrive at a total figure consisting of two elements which are referred to as A and B in the judgment of the Court of Appeal in *Eastwood*'s case.
>
> 'The computation of the A figure involves an assessment of the reasonable direct cost, that is to say the grade of person (senior solicitor, assistant solicitor, legal executive, etc) whom it was reasonable to employ at each stage; an approximation of the cost of employment of each individual by considering the number of hours for each of them to be reasonably engaged; and assessing a rate per hour sufficient to cover the salary and the appropriate share of the general overheads of each such person. The assessment of the appropriate rate per hour would be based on the taxing master's knowledge and experience of the average solicitor or executive employed by the average firm in the area concerned. The total hours of each person multiplied by an approximate cost per hour, together with an allowance for letters, telephone calls and telex messages, then produces what the Court of Appeal referred to as the A figure. The B figure is then conventionally assessed by adding a percentage to the A figure which is appropriate in all circumstances to cover matters which cannot be calculated on an hourly basis, that is to say supervision and other indirect expenses, together with what the master referred to in his Answer as "imponderables", which reflect the degree of skill, responsibility and the other factors set out in [*CPR Rule 44.5*]. As mentioned above, the increase for the B figure claimed in the present case was just under 50 per cent, which would be perfectly normal and certainly not excessive in cases of this type. This is the figure which, in the case of an independent firm of solicitors, is expected to make a contribution to the profits of the firm. The appropriateness of the total of A and B, arrived at in this way, is then considered against the background of the proceedings as a whole and rounded off to a convenient sum which appears right in all the circumstances.'

The A factor is therefore the hourly expense rate, the B factor is the profit, A and B together giving the hourly charging rate. The A factor is arrived at by ascertaining the amount and cost of the time spent, whilst the B factor is arrived at by the application of the factors prescribed in the Solicitors (Non-Contentious Business) Remuneration

Order 1994, art 3 or in CPR Rule 44.5. The greatest danger of the obsession with time is that it not only may over-reward the quantity of time spent, it may even result in the other factors being lost sight of altogether, with the result that time costing becomes time charging. That is what is in danger of happening to the costs of civil litigation.

(b) Hourly rates

(i) Ascertaining the direct cost

How is the direct cost – the A factor, the hourly rate, the expense rate or whatever you like to call it – arrived at? Back in 1979 I wrote:

> 'Ideally there should be a formula agreed between the Law Society, the Lord Chancellor's Department and the Supreme Court Taxing (*Costs*) Office for calculating expense rates; and within reason it does not matter what this formula is, provided everyone knows what it includes and what it does not'.

(Which is basically what has now been done in respect of summary assessments of costs but for charging rates, not expense rates.) In the meantime, costs officers and the profession have had to attempt to quantify the direct cost. How have they done it? I used to say that costs judges fixed the rate by pulling open the third drawer down on the right hand side of their desk and looking at a bit of paper showing the 'hourly going rate' for a particular class of work but no one knew where it had come from. A costs judge took issue with me: interestingly enough, he did not disagree that costs judges had bits of paper in the third drawer down but he said that they knew where they came from: they wrote them themselves, based on information learned from assessments. 'Sitting day in and day out, hearing other solicitors disputing or accepting them, we form a view as to market rates. We do not lay down the rates. We adjudicate on the opposing contentions of the parties.' In other words, costs judges do not fix rates, they merely reflect them.

(ii) Between the parties

The hourly expense rates arrived at by the *Leopold Lazarus* approach are known as 'the broad average direct cost'. They are arrived at by costs officers after considering the figures claimed and conceded on detailed assessments. They will, or should, vary with the level of fee earner involved. As between the parties on the standard basis, these costs, for the reasons considered on p 225, may bear little relation to the actual expense rate of the firm concerned.

The conventional method appropriate to assessing the bill of a solicitor in private practice is also appropriate for the bill of an in-house solicitor in all but special cases, where it is reasonably plain that the method will infringe the indemnity principle. Such a special case will arise where a sum can be identified, different from that used by the conventional approach, which is adequate to cover the actual cost incurred by doing the work. Such a sum may be identified by concession or presumably by the factual assessment of the assessing tribunal itself; but that possibly does not justify a detailed investigation into every case: *Cole v British Telecommunications plc* (SCCO No 14 of 2000, [2000] All ER (D) 917, CA) *and Maes Finance Ltd v WG Edwards & Partners* (2000) CLW, 21 July, QBD.

(iii) Solicitor and client

As between solicitor and client in both contentious and non-contentious costs, the costs officer starts with the retainer. If this is silent as to hourly expense rates, the costs officer must consider the actual cost to the firm of doing the work and whether that cost is reasonable in the context of the nature of the work. (If, as it should, express provision is made for hourly rates, the position is as explained in Chapter 2.)

(iv) Decisions

The position has been clarified by five decisions, four of which did not reach the law reports. They are so important that I will set out in full the extracts from the judgments that relate to the broad average direct cost.

1. STUBBS V BOARD OF GOVERNORS OF THE ROYAL NATIONAL ORTHOPAEDIC HOSPITAL [1997] COSTS LR 117, QBD

Extract from the decision of Hirst J:

> 'Stress is placed on the average cost of the average solicitor or legal executive – in the particular area concerned ... In arriving at a figure, the essence of the exercise was an appropriate apportionment of the estimated overhead expenses of the solicitors' firm having regard to the position, status, and likely rate of remuneration of the persons who were employed on the case under consideration. This is of its very nature suitable for assessment by the Taxing Master in the light of his very wide experience; it is also a matter which is properly approached by reference to averages since it is unlikely that there will be a very wide divergence between comparable firms of solicitors operating in similar fields of work in similar geographical areas.'

2. FINLEY V GLAXO LABORATORIES LTD [1997] COSTS LR 106, QBD

Although judgment was not in open court the judge, Hobhouse J, directed a tape recording of it to be made and he authorised publication of the following passages from the transcript:

> ' ... The next point – and it is the one which formed the main part of the argument before me – is the rate per hour which should be allowed. It is clear that the rate which should be allowed is the actual cost, assessed on an objective basis. In other words, it is not answered merely by reference to what has been the cost to the solicitor in question of doing the relevant work on an hourly basis. It has to be assessed on an objective basis having regard to what is reasonable. Therefore, one must consider the position of other solicitors in question. One has to consider whether it is the appropriate level of fee earner that is claimed for. In the present matter it has been accepted, and I accept, that the appropriate level of fee earner for a case of this character was a senior litigation partner; and the solicitor concerned matched that description.'

3. JOHNSON V REED CORRUGATED CASES LTD [1992] 1 ALL ER 169, QBD (COMM CT) RCJ

Extracts from the judgment of Evans J:

Figures of Individual Firms

> 'In my judgment, the registrar (*District Judge*) was in error in placing too much emphasis on the figures produced by one firm, and in basing his assessment on those figures when, as was inevitable, he could only confirm or check them as "reasonable" or average figures against his own knowledge and experience of other firms. (In *Gregory* he said "I am sure that they are well within the range of figures which would be produced by other large firms in this town". This belief must rest in part upon his knowledge of what figures those

other firms have claimed, and upon his general knowledge and experience of the economics of conducting a solicitor's practice in the area.) The registrar's assessment is neither guess work nor a precise accounting exercise (which can never be an exact science, in any event). Rather, his judicial assessment of the proper figure, based upon his general knowledge and experience, is what the Rules require. This is not to say that the figures produced by an individual firm must be disregarded. Rather the reverse, it is the registrar's responsibility to have a general awareness of the level of costs incurred by the average firm from time to time. How best he can acquire this knowledge is a separate matter about which I will say something more below. What I should emphasise here is that, as the history of the present applications shows, a detailed examination of individual accounts is likely to increase the costs and delay of taxation proceedings beyond acceptable limits. (The tail must not wag the dog. The costs of litigation are heavy enough in their own account.) The ease though not the cheapness of obtaining computer print-outs and photocopies makes the risk a substantial one, which in my view the Courts should guard against, both in the interests of litigants and of protecting their own procedures.'

The Expense of Time

'My general conclusion is that the registrar placed a wrong amount of emphasis on the figures produced in the present case, and upon the computer-aided analyses of those figures which were then made. I therefore echo the judgment in *Re Wilkinson* that, whilst *The Expense of Time* represents a policy of encouraging solicitors to estimate their actual and budgeted overhead costs in the interests of efficient financial accounting, the calculations so made should not be regarded as forming the basis (nor even the starting point) for assessing the average solicitor's average costs. The basis, and the starting point, is the Registrar's general – I emphasise the word "general" – knowledge and experience of the relevant matters.

' … There remains the question, however, of what weight, if any, the registrar should give to *Expense of Time* calculations, if they are produced in a particular case. The answer, in my judgment, is that if the figures for an individual solicitor, or firm, are produced for the purposes of the assessment in that case then they should be given very little weight … It is difficult to think of any better evidence of different solicitors' costs, as opposed to charges, than the amounts which they claim on taxation, case by case, year in, year out … Naturally enough, hourly cost is highly sensitive to variations in the "hours worked" figure. The following should be borne in mind. Allowing for a 44 week year, ie eight weeks for holidays, training, sickness and other absences, a five day week and a seven hour day i.e. 9 am until 5 pm, less one hour for lunch, the theoretical total is 1,540 hours. 1,100 hours represents a five-hour day. The "lost" two hours per day represents time which cannot be or is not charged to individual clients … It seems to me that the resulting estimate of five hours' chargeable work each day, for the average and, it must be assumed, fully occupied employee, might do less than justice to that person, for two reasons at least. The low amount of chargeable work done might suggest either a lack of diligence or of employment, with which the client or cost-paying party is not concerned. Secondly, it seems likely to me that many if not all solicitor employees in the average firm work much longer hours than this … Does it follow, then, that the information contained in such accounts must be disregarded, and that registrars should remain in ignorance of it? In my judgment, the answer to this is a vehement "no". It is part of each registrar's stock-in-trade that he has a general – again, I stress the word "general" knowledge of these matters and that if necessary he has some knowledge of the figures for local firms.'

Agreeing Going Rates

'It appears from the reasons given by registrars in other cities Newcastle and Sheffield, perhaps Birmingham also, that there have been communications between local firms, acting individually or collectively through local law societies, and registrars. I was told that similar discussions are taking place, or are proposed, between the Manchester Law Society and local registrars, all with the aim of informing registrars what the current level of overheads is and what the likely consequences of inflation are. I can see no objection to these consultations taking place and I for one would encourage them. They are the most practicable way of equipping the registrar directly with the local knowledge which he needs for the discharge of his function, and they are the only practicable way of informing him, not of the figures for one or a small number of firms, but of a range of information which enables him to form a view about the average … I suppose that a situation might arise where registrars might seem impervious to all such representations and might persist in awarding an hourly rate which was unreasonably low; in those but not in any other circumstances I can envisage that an individual party might be justified in requiring the registrar to hear evidence, not only of the party's solicitor's own costs but of other solicitors' costs for similar work also. That, however, would be an extreme case, and except in such unusual circumstances the registrar should not be required, in my view, to hear detailed accountancy evidence of solicitors' overhead costs in the course of inter party taxation … I wish to add, for the avoidance of doubt, that I do not support any idea that part of the court's functions on an inter party taxation is to discipline solicitors into charging less than they have done, or to regulate the amount of their charges to their clients. The court is not concerned with charges, only with costs, it is not concerned with any market, except indirectly, certainly not to influence any market.'

The True Starting Point

'The registrar's daily experience of the sums being claimed by local firms is an efficient way of giving him the same information, although indirectly. The reasons given in other cases, to which I have been referred, emphasise more than once the importance of this factor for individual registrars. In my judgment, that is the true starting point for assessing the hourly rate. The figure may require adjustment in the particular case. If locally a certain figure becomes the going rate for routine cases, ie ones of a particular kind with no unusual features, and that rate is unrealistically low, then local solicitors are justified, in my view, in making approaches to registrars of the kinds that already take place, these being for the purpose of providing general information and being unconnected with any particular case.'

The judge also dealt with another important aspect of the taxation of costs.

'Today's Pounds for Yesterday's Work'

'It is often argued that the hourly rate to be allowed should be that current at the date of taxation and not at the date when the work was done because payment will be made in deflated currency. This is essentially a dispute about interest. The House of Lords has held in *Hunt v R M Douglas (Roofing) Ltd* that interest runs only from the date of the judgment or order and not from the date when the work was done. Accordingly the slogan "Today's pounds for yesterday's work" is misconceived.'

4. RE A COMPANY (NO 004081 OF 1989) [1995] 2 ALL ER 155, CH D

This review by Lindsay J sitting with assessors was the first to consider the findings of a survey, involving an appraisal of the survey conducted by the City of London and the Westminster and Holborn Law Societies published in December 1992. Here is an extract dealing with hourly expense rates:

'Mr Lloyd drew our attention to *Johnson v Reed Corrugated Case Ltd* [1992] 1 All ER 169 as authority for the proposition that, at any rate on the standard basis, it was not right to look or to look only at the receiving party's solicitors' own rates but, rather (to adopt his skeleton argument) that "the proper guide is that of the average solicitor employed by the average firm in the area concerned". But how is one to find that? Mr Lloyd seeks to rely on what he calls "the going rate in the Master's corridor". But there is no evidence of the existence of anything which could be so described. Nor, were it to exist (and I am not saying it does), of what it would be. The trustees, abandoning the form of computation earlier relied on (which was based on the expense rates of the trustees' solicitors own firm uplifted by reference to the Law Society's booklet on the *Expense of Time*) now rely instead on a survey conducted by the Central London Law Societies … Those conducting the survey took the view that a response rate of not less than 40% would be needed if the results were to be capable of being fairly relied upon. In the event, the response rate was just short of 50%. Some 86 or so firms responded. The survey was published in December 1992. It is not suggested that the learned Deputy Master had the survey in mind when he held in the trustee's favour but he could, of course, have had in his mind the sort of rates of pay and overheads and so on which those who responded to the survey were experiencing and which led to the average figures I have mentioned. If, as the plaintiff's solicitors argue, the proper guide is that of the average solicitor employed by the average firm in the area concerned, then the Central London Law Societies' survey, whilst not necessarily a perfect indication of that average, is, on the evidence in this case, the closest approach we have to that average.'

5. KPMG Peat Marwick Mclintock v HLT Group Ltd [1995] 2 All ER 180, QBD

The survey conducted by the City of London and the Westminster and Holborn Law Societies received further approval from Auld J sitting with assessors. He said that if the figures in the survey continued to be disregarded, then the process of taxation (*assessment*) might set or freeze so-called reasonable levels of costs which bore no relation to the general levels of costs actually incurred. The survey was devised to assist in the assessment of broad average direct costs in the area and period in which the work in this case was done. It took no account of any perks or element of profit. It was a valuable aid and an important factor to take into account. It was a warning to taxing officers (*costs judges*) from a significant proportion of solicitors practising in the central London area that their taxing norms might be out of date.

(v) Going rates

Although *Re A Company and KPMG Peat Marwick McLintock v HLT Group Ltd* identified three categories of fee earner, and there are now four for summary assessment, there are those who advocate one hourly rate. What is this? It is the appropriate amount to be allowed between the parties for an average fee earner in an average case, such as a personal injury or road traffic accident action. It is for routine work which was done, or should have been done, by what former Chief Taxing Master Matthews described as the 12 handicap solicitor. You do not expect a solicitor to play off scratch but neither do you expect him to be a 24 handicap duffer learning at someone else's expense. Unless it is intended to embrace the philosophy of Procrustes, district judges must retain the discretion to award a higher amount if the action is sufficiently heavy to justify being dealt with by a senior partner, or a lower amount if the work has in fact been done by a legal executive or trainee solicitor. Tony Girling unkindly identifies a fourth category: the office cat, and if a fixed rate is to be allowed irrespective of the level of fee earner the office cat will certainly be the most profitable member of the firm.

Composite rates do have the advantage of certainty and simplicity, as was evident at a seminar in Guildford when Surrey solicitors were virtually unanimous in preferring a composite between-the-parties rate to a differential rate. Support for a composite rate also came from across the Irish Sea when Campbell J in *Donaldson v Eastern Health and Social Services Board* (High Court of Justice in Northern Ireland, Queen's Bench Division 19 June 1997, unreported) held that a number of different rates would lead to endless disputes about the degree of experience required to conduct various types of litigation: 'for a solicitor who is one of the large number of sole-principals the choice would be to charge at the notional hourly rate for a solicitor who ought to have done the work, possibly far below the notional rate which his experience would warrant, or to send his client to another firm with a solicitor of the appropriate grade.' Counsel appearing for the Lord Chancellor did not ask for more than one rate and the judge was satisfied that in Northern Ireland, where most solicitors are generalists rather than specialists, a composite or single hourly rate was more appropriate.

However, the death knell for composite rates, while the indemnity principle survives, was the decision in the *General of Berne Insurance Co v Jardine* (see p 173) which held that the application of the indemnity principle requires an item by item comparison between the solicitor and client costs and the between-the-parties costs. It would be difficult, and indeed undesirable, to justify a composite rate for all levels of fee earner in calculating a solicitor's charges to his client. It is probable that the four categories of fee earner adopted in summary assessments will now be used as the basis for assessing all costs and for future surveys.

(c) Will your direct cost be allowed?

Not necessarily; for the following reasons:

(i) the number of hours claimed to have been worked may not be accepted;
(ii) the number of hours worked may be excessive, disproportionate or include irrelevant work;
(iii) the work may have been done by the wrong level of fee earner;
(iv) the expense rate may be rejected;
(v) the firm's expense rate may be too high.

Let us consider each of these aspects in turn.

(i) Time spent

The costs officer must be satisfied that the amount of time claimed was actually spent. Properly kept and detailed time records are helpful in support of a bill provided they explain the nature of the work as well as recording the time involved. However, while the absence of such records could result in the disallowance or diminution of the charges claimed, the records themselves will not be accepted as conclusive evidence that the time recorded either has been spent, or if spent, is 'reasonably' or 'proportionately' chargeable. Always keep in mind the words of Payne J in *Re Kingsley* (1978) 122 Sol Jo 457:

> 'I ought to add that this case illustrates the dangers which are present if reliance is placed on a modern system of recording, without at the same time retaining the old and well tried practice of keeping attendance notes showing briefly the time taken and the purport of the work done day by day. It may be that this case will invite attention to the importance of appreciating the limits to which the computer system can be used in cases where taxation of costs must follow litigation and to the necessity of preserving as well the use of the traditional systems.'

The stage is never going to be reached of producing a computer print-out as incontrovertible evidence of the number of hours spent.

Letters received and copies of letters sent, instructions to counsel, statements of case, proofs of evidence and all other documents are tangible records and evidence of the work involved. All other work, such as attendances on the client, counsel, court and witnesses, telephone conversations, perusals, considering the facts and law, does not automatically create records of itself and a solicitor must be able to prove that he has done work of this nature. The best way is to create and keep records of it. Inferences can be drawn and oral evidence given but it is in the solicitor's interests to have available on taxation the best possible evidence of work done, and this can most easily be provided by making contemporaneous records. However, here are some words of comfort:

> 'The right to charge cannot depend upon the question whether discussions are recorded or unrecorded. It must depend, initially, upon whether they in fact took place and occupied the time claimed. If they are recorded in attendance notes this will no doubt ordinarily be accepted as sufficient evidence of those facts. If they are not so recorded it may well be that the claimant is unable to satisfy the taxing (costs) officer or master (costs judge) as to the facts. But neither the presence nor the absence of an attendance note is conclusive. It may well be for example that it is wholly impractical in some instances to keep such notes. In an exceptionally complex case, such as this which is occupying two fee earners there may be short but important discussions in respect of which it would be wholly unreasonable to expect attendance notes to be kept. In such cases an estimate of the time involved is inevitable. The question which then arises for decision is whether the estimate given is reasonable. This is a matter wholly for the taxing authorities. In general, however, all such discussions involving any substantial period of time should be recorded and an estimated addition should only be allowed for short discussions which it would be impracticable to record.'

(Parker J in *Re Frascati in Chambers* (December 1981, unreported).)

A number of points arise:

(1) We are dealing here with time which could have been recorded but for some reason was not, and not with unrecordable time, such as supervision, which is covered by general care and attention (see p 235).

(2) How the time was recorded does not, for these purposes, matter. It can be on the most sophisticated computer system or on the back of old envelopes. If the latter contains greater detail of the work which was done it is preferable to the former. The problem with most computer systems is that they do not provide a sufficient narrative. A separate file note is essential. With a mark-up for care and control on all contentious work it is not only the time but also the quality of the work that needs to be recorded. A printed form of memorandum with a panel in which to indicate the relevant CPR Rule 44.5 factors for mark-up could be invaluable.

(3) Experience shows that many solicitors have now trained themselves adequately to record the time spent on attendances but they are not so well disciplined in respect of time spent on the preparation and perusal of documents such as pleadings, instructions to counsel and, particularly in long actions, refreshing their memory from the statements of case, affidavits, attendance notes, correspondence and opinions. These are the danger areas.

(4) Time spent considering the law and procedure is usually non-chargeable – and the higher the expense rate, the more law and procedure the fee earner is expected to know. In a review of criminal costs it was held that leading and junior counsel can be assumed to be fully up-to-date with the law in the field in which they hold themselves out as practising in and they will not be paid for researching the law unless the case is unusual or infrequent (*Perry v Lord Chancellor* (1994) Times, 26 May, QBD). The same principle of course applies to civil work and to solicitors.

(5) Where there has been an omission to record time, the costs draftsman – and the costs officer – must rely on their own experience to assess from the documents in the file what time a competent solicitor would have spent on their preparation and perusal. The documents prove the work has been done but someone has to put a time and value on that work.

(6) In *Johnson v Reed Corrugated* (see p 221/223) Evans J was less enthusiastic about giving credit for unrecorded time, saying:

'In my judgement, the submission that there were unrecorded occasions when chargeable time was spent on these cases must be rejected. This leaves the Registrar's decision that in practice not all time will be fully recorded, even for those items of work in respect of which a claim is made. The claims invariably are for global figures, mostly to the nearest five minutes. No doubt there were some occasions when the periods spent were slightly more, others when it was slightly less. There is no evidence that any substantial items were not recorded at all. In my judgement, therefore, this item must be disallowed.'

(ii) Was the time reasonably, proportionately and relevantly spent?

This is an objective test between the parties. Was it reasonable to do all the work that was done and was it done within a reasonable time? If on the standard basis, was it proportionate to the matters in issue? If it was excessive or irrelevant it will be unreasonable or disallowed. In contentious costs on the standard basis any doubt as to reasonableness will be resolved in favour of the paying party. Between a solicitor and his client the same objective tests apply, together with, in respect of contentious work, the express and implied subjective assumptions prescribed by CPR Rule 48.8(2) (see p 531). Because solicitor and client costs are on the indemnity basis, any doubt will be resolved in favour of the solicitors.

(iii) The level of fee earner

This is where a detailed assessment based on a composite hourly rate is most likely to start going wrong. It is unjustifiable to seek to impose one fixed hourly rate to cover all levels of fee earner for all types of litigation – from the collection of the simplest debt to the most complicated commercial litigation – or for all kinds of non-contentious work – from the simplest conveyance to the most high-powered and onerous take over bid. If all the work has been done by a trainee solicitor, the solicitor would no doubt be delighted to be paid a fixed going expense rate of £80 an hour, or a charging rate of £120, but the client or paying party should strongly object to it. On the other hand, if the matter was properly dealt with by a senior partner it is the solicitor who would vehemently object to receiving an expense rate of only £80 an hour. It is, of course, acceptable for a costs officer to say that a particular type of work, for instance personal injury litigation or routine conveyancing, should be dealt with by, say, an assistant solicitor. However, he must exercise his discretion judicially and give the solicitor the opportunity of satisfying him that in this particular matter it was reasonable for the work to be done by someone above the level of an assistant solicitor.

(iv) Hourly rate too high

If your local law society has recently *agreed* hourly rates for different levels of fee earner you are unlikely to obtain a higher rate on a between-the-parties assessment. If there has been unusual skill, expertise, or expedition, keep your powder dry for pressing for an above-average mark-up for general care and attention, or if dealing with summary assessment charging rates, to be treated as a higher category of fee earner. If, however, there has been no communally agreed figure, or even worse, there is an unacceptable 'going rate' prescribed by your district judge, then do produce your own expense rates calculated in accordance with *The Expense of Time*. As I have said, the way ahead is for all solicitors in an area to calculate their expense rates in accordance with *The Expense of Time* and agree between them the appropriate rate for each level of fee earner which will be accepted by them on assessments, whether they are for the paying party or the receiving party. If the local costs officer will not accept these rates, appeal against his decision. Such an arrangement would not, of course, preclude the paying party from protecting his client's interests by objecting to the number of hours spent or to the level of fee earner who did the work or the mark-up for general care and conduct.

(v) Your hourly rates are too high

This is an entirely different matter and a legitimate criticism in between the parties costs. It may be that the routine going rate applied for routine cases is a fair reflection of the broad average direct cost in your area. But if you choose to be a prestigious firm with luxurious offices and expensive cars – as you are perfectly entitled to do – and your client chooses you and your firm – as he is perfectly entitled to do – it is not reasonable that the loser in litigation should have to pay your above-average expense rates because of your above-average lifestyle. Accordingly, while there is no harm in you producing your figures as part of the general process of educating and indoctrinating your district judge, do not expect him to embrace your expense rates, however accurately you may have calculated them. If, as well as being very expensive, you are also very good, the place to look for your reward is in the mark-up for general care and conduct. If, on the other hand, you are a firm with no carpets on the floor and whose partners' mode of travel is the bicycle, you will no doubt not produce your expense of time figures and be happy to be remunerated at the rate established by your more sybaritic brethren.

A disquieting exception to this rule was the decision of Buckley J in *Jones v Secretary of State for Wales* [1997] 2 All ER 507, QBD, that where a provincial firm of solicitors is more specialised than the norm for the area, a taxation of costs made in relation to its work could be calculated at a higher hourly rate than the local norm. Pitmans of Reading were in effect a London firm who had moved to Reading and were doing work that only a London firm could do. The judge was of the view that it would be odd and undesirable if the higher London rate could be recovered by a London firm, but not the somewhat lower rate claimed by Pitmans for doing a case which otherwise would probably have to be handled by a London firm. The problem with this approach is, where does it end and what happens to the constraints of averaging to ascertain local going rates if specialist firms can recover their actual expense rate without any of the levelling down that the averaging exercise inevitably achieves?

In *Truscott v Truscott and Wraith v Sheffield Forgemasters Ltd* [1998] 1 All ER 82 and *Sullivan v Co-operative Insurance Society Ltd* (1999) Times, 19 May, the Court of Appeal addressed the question of whether the liability of an unsuccessful party ordered to pay costs should be restricted to what a reasonably competent solicitor practising in the area of the court (or in the area where the successful party lived) might have been expected to charge, or whether the successful party should be entitled to recover the sums claimed by the solicitor who was in fact instructed to act on his behalf. The court held that a costs judge had to consider whether, having regard to all the relevant considerations, the successful party had acted reasonably in instructing the particular solicitors. In *Truscott* the claimant had been ill-served by local solicitors in the Brighton County Court and had instructed London solicitors who rectified the matter and obtained a wasted costs order against the original solicitors. The court held that it was reasonable for a London firm to have been instructed in these circumstances and that as their charges were reasonable by London standards they were allowed. The same principles applied in *Wraith* but in that case the only reason why the work went to London solicitors was that the claimant's trade union had adopted the practice of sending all their work to these solicitors. The action was proceeding in the Sheffield District Registry and the court was satisfied there were firms of solicitors in Sheffield or Leeds well qualified to do the work. The trade union knew, or ought to have known, what sort of legal fees it would have to expend to obtain competent services and their connection with one firm of solicitors in London was of limited relevance. *Sullivan* applied the same test over the Pennines, holding there were in Manchester, and in many other centres outside London, legal practitioners who conducted cases of substantially greater weight and complexity than the present case, every day of their working lives. Although the fact that a trade union or other organisation habitually used a particular firm of solicitors was a relevant factor it was of limited relevance in an individual case. There were no weighty factors in the context of costs justifying the trade union in employing London solicitors to conduct litigation in Manchester. Subjectively the choice may have been entirely reasonable, but between the parties the various circumstances had to be balanced objectively.

(d) Hourly rates at the crossroads

(i) Summary assessment

Under the Civil Procedure Rules, judges are encouraged to conduct a summary assessment of costs at the end of any hearing which does not last for more than one day (see p 267). To facilitate this the Supreme Court Costs Office issued its *Guide To the Summary of Assessment of Costs* to which was appended a table of suggested hourly rates for different areas of the country for three categories of fee earners which were prepared after consultation between The Supreme Court Costs Office, the Law Society and the Association of District Judges. These have now been increased to four (see p 280). The *Guide* emphasises that the figures are not intended to replace figures used by those with accurate local knowledge and are intended to provide a starting point for those faced with summary assessment who do not have that knowledge. The rates may be adjusted up or down depending on the circumstances of any particular case. They are not scale figures and costs and fees exceeding the guidelines may well be justified in appropriate cases. In other words they are not cast in stone and regular agreement of local rates is as important as ever.

In many courts there has in the past been just one composite going rate irrespective of the level of fee earner who did the work, whether it was the senior partner at one end of the scale or the office cat at the other end (see p 224). In the *Guide* the categories of fee earner range from senior partners to junior paralegals. They are:

(1) Solicitors with over eight years' post-qualification experience including at least eight years' litigation experience.
(2) Solicitors and legal executives with over four years' post-qualification experience including at least four years' litigation experience.
(3) Other solicitors and legal executives and fee earners of equivalent experience.
(4) Trainee solicitors, paralegals and other fee earners.

It is important to note that the word 'partner' appears nowhere. The categories are based upon experience, not status.

Another innovation in the table of hourly rates was that in the past solicitor's hourly rates have been allowed on the basis of an hourly expense rate (the 'A' factor) and a percentage profit mark-up (the 'B' factor). The Lord Chancellor wishes to discourage this and solicitors are urged to claim a single hourly rate which includes their profit, which should normally be the same rate at which they charge their own clients. It cannot, of course exceed it (see p 171). Accordingly, the hourly rates in the *Guide* are expressed to be inclusive of profit mark-up. This is not as revolutionary as might at first appear. It is proper commercial practice for a business to calculate the cost of doing the work in terms of time and materials and then to add on a profit. The profit element is still there whether the client or the paying party is told what it is or not. Hitherto the courts and the parties have had the advantage of knowing what it was, and what *is* revolutionary is that with guideline charging rates not distinguishing between the cost of doing the work and the profit it is not possible to know how the figures were arrived at, what represents expense and what profit, with the consequence that the CPR Rule 44.5 factors (the seven pillars of wisdom) must be applied to the total figure. Otherwise there would be no facility to enable a judge carrying out a summary assessment to reward skill, effort, specialised knowledge and responsibility or for him to acknowledge the importance, complexity, difficulty or novelty of the matter. The provisions of CPR Rule 44.5 would be negated in respect of summary assessments. Even if this approach is deemed to be acceptable as a pragmatic approach to assist trial judges in summarily assessing costs, if it were to be extended to detailed assessments, the quantification of costs would have taken a giant stride from being a judicial function to becoming a bureaucratic exercise. CPR Rule 44.5 might as well never have been written. It should also be remembered that the B factor is not solely concerned with profit, it also covers such matters as unrecordable time and supervision which would otherwise be unremunerated (see p 235). The Civil, Family and Criminal Legal Aid Regulations all embrace the concept of profit mark-up, and it would be unfortunate if, in respect of non-funded civil litigation, judges and costs officers were to be deprived of the flexibility, which the Civil Procedure Rules rightly regard as essential to the assessment of reasonable and proportionate costs, afforded by the application of the A and B factors. Solicitors are entitled to calculate and justify their charges, both to their clients and between the parties in whatever manner is fair and reasonable, and there is nothing in the Civil Procedure Rules which requires them to abandon a system which has served so well in the past. If charging is based on hourly rates, these can only be calculated on the basis of reasonable cost plus profit and whether the rate is shown as expense-plus-profit or as a charge combining both the relevant factors must still be applied in the quantification of costs. Otherwise, the simple hourly rate guide for summary assessment will turn the whole judicial function of costs assessment into mere bureaucratic number-crunching. Litigation costs should be something more sophisticated than the periodical negotiation of hourly rates.

(ii) Controlling costs

The Lord Chancellor's Department's consultation paper 'Controlling Costs' included the astonishing proposition: 'solicitors will be required to provide an inclusive charging basis, thereby abolishing the uplift for care and conduct element claimed in a bill of costs'. As I have said, the care and conduct element is the profit and one has only to substitute the word 'profit' for 'care and conduct' in the proposition to demonstrate its fallacy. Solicitors cannot be expected to work for their overheads alone: the proposal would not abolish profit (care and conduct) but merely conceal it. The premise that profit could in this way be abolished demonstrates that both the proposal and its objective are fundamentally flawed. Far from controlling costs it would in fact remove all those controls, checks and balances built into the edifice of between-the-parties costs over the years and carefully preserved in the Civil Procedure Rules. A combined rate would not in any way reduce the amount of costs, it would only make the amount (1) less transparent, (2) less flexible and (3) remove judicial discretion.

1. Less transparent

All charges must contain an element of profit. With an A and B factor the court and the paying party know how the costs claimed are calculated both as to the expense of doing the work and profit claimed. With hourly inclusive charging rates neither the court nor the paying party will know how they are calculated on either the standard or the indemnity basis. Hourly rates promulgated by the courts after consultation with the profession must be calculated on some basis – the figures cannot be plucked from the air – and if this is to be a judicial and not a fiscal exercise it must follow the normal commercial practice of ascertaining the cost of doing the work in terms of time and materials and adding to that figure a reasonable amount for profit. No other system has been suggested. Accordingly, if rates are promulgated in respect of both summary and detailed assessment inclusive of profit, then the method and figures forming the basis of their calculation must be ascertained and available.

2. Less flexible

The courts can control the amount claimed for the expense of doing the work by applying objective tests both as to what is a reasonable hourly rate in the area in which the work was done and the level of fee earner. The profit element ('care and control') enables the court to apply the discretionary factors prescribed in CPR 44.5. Without an identifiable or known element which may be varied – up or down – by applying those factors, CPR 44.5 becomes virtually meaningless and the assessment of costs becomes the rigid application of predetermined rates.

3. Remove judicial discretion

Paragraph 26 of the consultation paper suggested that if a case is complex, the added complexity will be reflected in the time taken to complete it and the hourly charging rate. This is wrong if the hourly charging rate for the level of fee earner is to be prescribed and the court has no discretion or basis for increasing it, unless it is being suggested that in future a fee earner who does work above his station in life may be rewarded by being treated as though he were a higher level of fee earner – with fine disregard for the actual cost of doing the work. Of course, if the indemnity principle were to be abandoned and replaced with the objective test of 'What is a reasonable and proportionate amount for the paying party to pay?', the test would simply be 'What level of fee earner should have done the work?' irrespective of who actually did it. Unless costs are in future to be assessed according to the philosophy of Procrustes, judicial discretion must be preserved in the concept of applying the 'A' and 'B' factors in accordance with CPR 45.5. There must therefore be transparency in how the charging rates are calculated and judicial discretion to increase or reduce them in accordance with the principles enshrined in the CPR. Whether or not the A and B factors are identified or concealed in a charging rate, they will still be there. Any commercial enterprise must base its prices and charges on costs plus profit and it is naqve to think that the legal profession could operate in some other way.

CHAPTER 23

THE OTHER FACTORS

Let us now consider the art 3 (Solicitors (Non-Contentious Business) Remuneration Order 1994) and CPR Rule 44.5 factors other than time on the basis, not of non-contentious and contentious, but of routine and non-routine.

1. NON-ROUTINE

> 'It is wrong always to start by assessing the direct and indirect expense to the solicitor, represented by the time spent on the business. This must always be taken into account, but it is not necessarily, or even usually, a basic factor to which all others are related. Thus, although the labour involved will usually be directly related to, and reflected by, the time spent, the skill and specialised knowledge involved may vary greatly for different parts of that time. Again not all time spent on a transaction necessarily lends itself to being recorded, although the fullest possible records should be kept.
>
> 'This error is compounded if, as an invariable rule, the figure representing the expense of recorded time spent on the transaction is multiplied by another figure to reflect the other factors. The present case provides an illustration of this error. The responsibility and value of the property involved were linked factors, but neither was affected by whether the recorded time spent was 30 hours or 60 hours. Yet the application of a multiplier would double the responsibility/value factor, if the recorded time spent had happened to be 60 rather than 30 hours.
>
> 'In my judgment the proper approach is to start by taking a broad look at 'all the circumstances of the case' and in particular the general nature of the business. This should be followed by a systematic consideration of the factors specified in the paragraphs of Art 2 (now Art 3) of the order.'

(*Property and Reversionary Investment Corpn Ltd v Secretary of State for the Environment* [1975] 2 All ER 436, per Donaldson J.)

> 'The magnetic attraction of time as a foundation for assessment of fair and reasonable remuneration is that in the absence of an approved scale applied to value, it is the only figure which is readily calculable. It is an attraction which must be sternly resisted in cases of this sort where one or more of the other factors is such as to dwarf it into insignificance.'

(Donaldson J, in my own firm's case of *Treasury Solicitor v Regester* [1978] 2 All ER 920.)

(a) What are the factors which may dwarf time into insignificance?

(i) Value

There is no escape from Donaldson J. In *Treasury Solicitor v Regester* he said:

> 'Turning now to value, we remind ourselves that scale fees have been abolished. Nevertheless, it is reasonable and fair to the client that the remuneration should not be

disproportionate to the value of the property involved. It is therefore useful to employ a yardstick to assess that relationship. Various yardsticks, with a regressive basis, can be suggested, and an example will be found in the Oyez Practice Notes No 20, 6th edn, at p 31. The author correctly stresses that this is only an example and each case will have to be considered on its own merits. The fact is that there is no right yardstick, although some may be wrong. For our part, we would consider that 1/2% on the first quarter of a million in a major transaction, and thereafter regressing, provides a reasonable method of assessment.'

The yardstick to which Donaldson J was giving cautious approval followed the bands suggested by Donaldson J himself in the *Property and Reversionary* case. The Council of the Law Society suggested revised bands in 1980 and took the opportunity to make further adjustments in July 1987 in their *An Approach to Non-Contentious Costs*, as follows (revised in 1994):

Band	*£ Percentage*
Up to £400,000	1/2% (0.5%)
On next £600,000 (maximum total value £1,000,000)	3/8% (0.375%)
On next £1,500,000 (maximum total value £2,500,000)	1/4% (0.25%)
On next £2,500,000 (maximum total value £5,000,000)	1/4% (0.125%)
On next £5,000,000 (maximum total value £10,000,000)	1/10% (0.1%)

What the Law Society booklet does not tell you, and what you must be desperate to know, is that Donaldson J suggested a percentage charge of 0.05% for values of over £10,000,000!

Do not however assume that this provides the profession with a yardstick, because Donaldson J continued:

> 'We must also make it clear that we disagree with the suggestion in the Oyez notes that the purpose of a scale is to arrive at remuneration for the responsibility risk element, which is then to be added to the remuneration for the other elements. This is not the case. Remuneration has to be assessed for all the circumstances taken together, and the purpose of a regressing yardstick is, as we have said, to check that the provisional figure bears a reasonable relationship to the value of the property. This is not only reasonable but also fair to both parties and in particular to the client.'

(ii) Adrenalin

In *Treasury Solicitor v Regester*, Donaldson J identified a ninth factor. He said:

> 'We then looked at the eight factors and asked ourselves, what was the factor or factors, if any, which distinguished this transaction from the general run of such transactions? The answer was clearly "the adrenalin factor". By this, we mean that the solicitor had not only to work fast but had absolutely no margin for error. The transaction had to be completed by 31 July come what might, or their client had lost not only this deal but all possibility of avoiding the effects of the development land tax. In a different case we might have found that there was plenty of time and that the transaction was very similar to one with which the solicitors had previously been concerned for the same client. This would have caused us to look in the reverse direction. Recorded time does not provide an arithmetical basis for a charge in cases such as this. Its relevance is to check whether the provisional figures for remuneration bear a reasonable relationship to the overheads attributable to the transaction. In this case, the figures which we had in mind did not seem to bear an unusual relationship to the overheads in a transaction of this type, and we therefore obtained no positive assistance from considering this factor.'

(iii) Skill, etc

It is the same where a solicitor brings to bear great skill and experience far in excess of that of the average solicitor, or where one of the other factors such as complexity, documents, place, title or importance to the client result in the amount of time spent being an irrelevance.

Although the *Property and Reversionary* and *Treasury Solicitor v Regester* cases dealt with non-contentious commercial matters, there is no reason why there should not be an identical approach in non-routine contentious matters, where the value, the adrenalin or another factor overwhelms the time involved. A gross sum bill to the client can be calculated on these principles. Should the client request a detailed bill or details be ordered on a Solicitors Act assessment the solicitor will be expected to produce a breakdown in terms of hourly rates. Even if the rates appear to be ludicrously high, the overall total can be justified on the approach of *Property and Reversionary* and *Treasury Solicitor v Regester.*

(b) The dangers

With an approach based upon factors other than time, there is always the danger that someone will come along and divide the end product by the number of hours and proclaim that the solicitors have been paid hundreds of pounds an hour. In *Treasury Solicitor v Regester*, Edward John Parris, writing in the *Estates Gazette*, by getting his figures and arithmetic wrong, calculated that my own firm had been paid £270 an hour in 1978, while in 1975 Geoffrey Bindman in the *LAG Bulletin* interpreted the *Reversionary* case as allowing £375 an hour reduced to £183, and described as 'grotesque and nonsensical' the hourly rate he calculated we had received. This sort of criticism misses the point and arises out of a fixation about time. We are dealing here with matters in which the time is irrelevant to the fee. How much an hour does a brain or heart surgeon charge? Who cares?

The most effective way of avoiding such misunderstandings is, whenever possible, to agree a fixed fee with the client in advance, and where this is not possible, to agree the basis of charging and to discuss and endeavour to agree the amount of your charges before rendering a bill.

2. ROUTINE

Here, time is the starting point. What should be added for the remaining factors? As I said in the previous chapter, no-one has suggested any way of applying the factors prescribed in CPR Rule 44.5 other than by using them to quantify the profit element to be added to a solicitor's direct costs.

(a) The B factor in contentious costs

'Why should I pay £100 an hour to my lawyers and then have to pay a 50% surcharge for them to give my matter care and attention?' 'Mark-up', 'profit element', 'service increment', 'care, skill and attention', 'personal care and conduct', the 'B factor', and simply 'profit' are some of the words for it. What it means is the factors prescribed in art 3 and CPR Rule 44.5 other than the time expended in doing the work. It includes unrecordable time, supervision and other indirect expenses.

(b) Unrecordable time

Time not capable of being recorded and not included in the A factor, was described by Walton J in *Maltby v DJ Freeman & Co* [1978] 2 All ER 913:

> 'No professional man, or senior employee of a professional man, stops thinking about the day's problems the minute he lifts his coat and umbrella from the stand and sets out on the journey home. Ideas, often very valuable ideas, occur in the train or car home, or in the bath, or even whilst watching television. Yet nothing is ever put down on a time sheet, or can be put down on a time sheet adequately to reflect this out of hours devotion of time.'

This enabled Mr Parris (whom we met at p 234), to write that solicitors were now to be paid for having baths and watching television! This was echoed by a report in the *Sun* newspaper quoting a firm of solicitors who were claiming £7,500 'thinking time' as saying 'this was a very big case which tied up one of our people for 24 hours a day. Sometimes some of our best ideas come when we are at home or in the car'.

(c) Supervision

We saw in *Frascati* (p 226) that time which should have been recorded but wasn't, should be taken into account in the A factor. What sort of time are we dealing with here? Supervision is one example.

R v Sandhu (29 November 1984, reported in the Lord Chancellor's Department's *Taxing Compendium)* identified three categories of supervision:

(i) The ordinary day-to-day supervision which is part of the overheads of the firm reflected in the basic mark-up – or indeed in the partners' non-chargeable time.
(ii) Supervision where a senior fee earner takes a direct hand in the case, in which event he should record his time and charge for it in the direct costs in the A factor.
(iii) Where a junior fee earner competently conducts the case with the assistance of regular but unquantified supervision from a senior fee earner whose time is not charged in the direct cost. This supervision is covered by the B factor.

(d) Applying the factors

(i) Add or subtract

One must either add or subtract from the direct cost the other factors. Where someone has made a meal or a mess of a case, the percentage increase for care and conduct for that work could be nothing. In other cases, it could be much higher than average. For example, where a legal executive has done work which could justifiably have been done by a senior partner he may be rewarded with a 200% mark-up for care and conduct on his hourly expense rate. Similarly, if someone has been brilliant, or had extraordinary responsibility, or has been very expeditious, this is the place to take it into account – otherwise the fee earner will be penalised by his own expedition. Twenty years ago, in *The Taxation of Contentious Costs*, I gave the true example of a solicitor friend with vast experience in personal injury matters who conducted two cases for injured workmen and, without going to counsel, negotiated substantial (in those days) settlements of £40,000 and £50,000. His recorded time was but a fraction of the time that would have been recorded had the matter been dealt with by a solicitor who was competent but who lacked my friend's expertise and who would also, quite properly, have incurred substantial counsel's fees. On the taxation of his costs my friend was quite rightly allowed a 200% profit mark-up on the time he had spent on the matter.

In neither of these examples would the paying party be penalised. The legal executive with a £60 an hour expense rate who is given a 200% mark-up receives no more than would his senior partner with a £120 an hour expense rate and a 50% mark-up. Similarly, my friend, who did all the work himself quickly and without using counsel, even with a 200% mark-up, cost the paying party no more than if the average solicitor had taken an average length of time and incurred average counsel's fees. A solicitor who is expeditious and efficient is entitled to benefit from, and not be penalised by, the lack of time he has spent on the matter. The result is reward for merit – and that is the difference between time-costing and time-charging.

Just one caveat to that. The higher the level of fee earner, the more he is expected to know. Therefore the higher the expense rate the lower the mark-up – you cannot expect to be rewarded twice.

(ii) 75%

There was consideration of mark-up in *Finley v Glaxo* (see p 221), where Hobhouse J said:

> 'The solicitor claimed 125%. The Registrar allowed 85% so as to give a composite figure of £65 per hour in conjunction with the £35 per hour rate.
>
> The solicitor was, at the material times, effectively a sole practitioner. He had another solicitor with him for part of the time but that is not material to the present case. He had a special experience and knowledge of vaccine and similar matters. He brought to the consideration of the plaintiff's case a familiarity with the subject matter and a measure of expertise appropriate to a lawyer dealing with that class of case. It must also be borne in mind that he had acted for the plaintiff previously in the tribunal matter, so that he was aware of the background through that source. He is a practitioner in Newcastle ... That takes me to the second half of the calculation, which is the question of uplift and the "B" factor. One of the matters on which the district registrar was criticised in relation to the "A" factor, in my judgment correctly, was that he got too much involved, in considering the cost assessment, with questions of profit and with the question of the uplift that he was later going to apply. The simplest way to illustrate this point is by referring to the concluding passage in his reasons, where he said:
>
> > "I cannot see, on the evidence before me, any compelling reasons why I should on this evidence increase the currently allowed hourly rate. The allowed rate is £35 per hour. This plus an 85% mark-up gives a remuneration of £65 per hour, which I consider to be both fair and reasonable having regard to the weight of the case and Mr Deas' seniority."
>
> 'The district registrar is quite right that at the end of any assessment of this kind he should stand back for a moment and consider the implications and the overall picture presented by his decision on the detail. That is what he is doing there. But it also shows that there is a relationship between the percentage that he chose to allow and the hourly rate. There are many other passages in his reasons where he allows the overall profit assessment to colour his views about the hourly rate. I consider – and counsel has not sought to argue to the contrary – that, having substantially altered the hourly rate, it is appropriate and proper for me to reconsider the uplift that has been allowed.
>
> 'The uplift factor was a subject that was referred to Kerr J in the *Leopold Lazarus* case at page 4 of the transcript. In view of the hour I will not read out what he says. He refers to Appendix 2 to Order 62 in the earlier version, which is now a slightly different version in the current Appendix. That requires the court, and indeed the taxing officer, in assessing the costs, to take into account, among other things, the complexity of the item or of the cause or matter in which it arises; the difficulty or novelty of the questions involved; the skills, specialised knowledge and responsibility required; the time and labour expended by the solicitor; the number and importance of documents; the importance of the cause or matter to the client; the amount of money involved, and so on.
>
> 'This present case did involve matters of responsibility for the solicitor, because he was taking upon himself the responsibility of assessing the evidence that was available on a

preliminary basis and advising the client. He advised against the continuation of proceedings and, far from his deserving to be marked down for that, he deserves credit for taking upon himself that responsibility and also being prepared to say, of his own judgment, that the proceedings should not continue as to do so would not be in the interests of the client and would, indeed, be a waste of time and money. It was an important case for the client. It potentially involved a very large sum of money. But the medical issues were ones which, although complicated and technical, were not outside the expertise of the solicitor; and it is because of this expertise that the matter was being dealt with by a senior partner.

'One must also bear in mind that this case was at a very early stage: it was at a stage of, essentially, perusal and advice. The solicitor was not involved in the preparation of complicated documents, nor was he involved in the conduct of any negotiations. Still less was he actually involved in the conduct of any litigation. All those factors might have put this case in a different light.

'I have to consider what is the appropriate uplift for a senior partner in the conduct of a case of this character at the stage which it had reached. The starting point for this exercise is 50%; that is the advice I received, and it is also the practice in the North East. If one is concerned with a High Court or potential High Court action, that is the appropriate starting point for the uplift. Likewise I am satisfied that 125% was far too high for a case of this kind. One of the reasons, I suspect, why 125% was even being considered by the solicitor is the too low figure that he might have feared he was going to be allowed as an hourly rate. As I have already made clear, I would not lend support to the adoption of an unduly low hourly rate and then seeking to put it right by applying a higher uplift percentage. The right approach is that which I have emphasised, namely to adopt a realistic approach to the hourly rate to reflect the actual cost of the fee earner involved, and then to apply an appropriate but not excessive uplift.

'The advice that I have had from my assessors in this matter is that no more than 75% is the maximum justifiable uplift in a case of this character, at the stage that it was at, and involving the work which it did involve at that stage. I am advised, and I have also formed the view, that 85% is too high and cannot be supported.'

(iii) 75% again

Evans J also dealt with mark-up in *Johnson v Reed Corrugated* (see p 221/223) as follows:

> 'The normal profit mark-up for the "run-of-the-mill" cases is 50%. The figure increases above 50% so as to reflect a number of possible factors – including the complexity of the case, any particular need for special attention to be paid to it, and any additional responsibilities which the solicitor may have undertaken towards the client, and others, depending upon the circumstances – but only a small percentage of accident cases results in an allowance of over 70%. To justify a figure of 100% there must be some combination of factors which mean that the case approaches the exceptional.'

He too allowed 75%.

(iv) 125%

Before you get too excited about a 125% mark up I must emphasise that this was the major test case of *Loveday v Renton (No 2)* [1992] 3 All ER 184, QBD relating to the whooping cough vaccine. The action ran between 1982 and 1988 and culminated in a 300-page judgment which took two days to read. The trial itself lasted for 65 working days. The documentation ran to some 100 lever arch files and The Wellcome Foundation had prepared a 'library' of some 50 files containing literature on the subject. The case was truly exceptional in terms of weight, complexity and responsibility. In delivering his judgment Hobhouse J emphasised that the court deplored any artificially depressed rates being compensated for by artificially inflated mark-up figures. He continued:

> 'To justify an uplift in excess of 100% it is necessary, as has recently been re-stated by Mr Justice Evans in *Johnson v Reed* to demonstrate that the case is exceptional. There has been a tendency among some firms of solicitors to put forward grossly inflated percentages by way of uplift and a failure to appreciate that to justify an uplift even as high as 100% requires the demonstration that the case is exceptional. In the present case, having regard to the features to which I have referred, I am satisfied (not without some hesitation) that the Taxing Master was wrong to alter his own original assessment on bill (A) of an uplift of 125%. I consider that 125% is at the top end of the bracket of uplift which would be proper for this case overall and I would not have interfered with a figure which lay somewhere between 125% and 100%. But I do accept the solicitors' submission before me that 100% was too low for bill (A) and I therefore shall reinstate the original allowance of 125%.'

(v) Message

Solicitors cannot expect to obtain mark-ups in excess of 75% except in the heaviest and most complex cases and probably only those which involve a contested hearing. The message to costs officers is also clear: they should not use the mark-up as an adjuster for allowing an unreasonably low hourly expense rate.

(e) Non-contentious guidance

The assessment of fair and reasonable remuneration is an art not a science. It is arrived at by a common-sense feel of the matter – not by the application of a rigid formula by a computer. The Law Society, in its publications *An Approach to Non-Contentious Costs* (1994) and *Non-Contentious Costs* (1999), gives guidance on how the quantification of costs for various categories will work. Reference should be made to those booklets, but the approach may be summarised as follows.

(i) No value element

Where there is no readily ascertainable value element, such as in simple wills, administration of trusts and all other routine non-contentious matters, the approach is the hourly cost plus a mark-up. The mark-up will rarely be less than 35%, usually 50% and, as we have seen, can be substantially higher. Each of the prescribed factors should be examined to see how they should be reflected.

(ii) Value element

1. DOMESTIC CONVEYANCING

The Law Society used to suggest either a 50% mark-up on the cost of the time or adding 1/2% of the value up to £400,000, whichever was the greater, using the regressive yardstick (on p 233) for higher values. However, the Law Society now limits its advice to taking 'a broad look at the circumstances of the transaction' and calculating 'a single charging figure incorporating the time spent and what is fair and reasonable in all the circumstances'. This is also where time costing for management comes into play – if, in order to attract conveyancing work, you are cutting your charges below what is profitable, it is as well that you should know this.

2. LEASES

To find the value take one half of the yearly rent and multiply it by the unexpired term of the lease with a maximum of 20 years. Add any premium payable by the lessee and deduct any premium payable by the lessor to or from the capitalised value or deduct any reverse premium. Then apply the following regressive scale to the value as calculated:

Value band	*£ Percentage*
Up to £400,000	1/2%
On next £600,000 (maximum total value £1 million)	3/8%
On next £1,500,000 (maximum total value £2.5 million)	1/4%
On next £2,500,000 (maximum total value £5 million)	1/8%
On next £5,000,000 (maximum total value £10 million)	1/10%

3. MORTGAGES

The Law Society suggests the following guideline charges where the solicitor is acting only for the lender:

Advance not exceeding	*Without assignment of life policy*	*With assignment of life policy*
Up to £15,000	£120	Plus flat rate £25 where there is an assignment/deposit of life policy irrespective of the number of policies or companies.
£15,001–£20,000	£121–£129	
£20,001–£25,000	£136.50	
£25,001–£30,000	£141	
£30,001–£60,000	£150	
£60,001–£100,000	£189	
Where the advance exceeds £100,000	add £188 for each £10,000 of part thereof	

In other cases the Law Society suggests the following percentages of value:

Acting for purchaser/mortgagor	1/4%
Acting for purchaser/mortgagor and mortgagee	1/4%
Acting for mortgagee alone	1/2%
Acting for mortgagor alone	1/2%

4. PROBATES AND ADMINISTRATIONS

Charge an exclusive figure of the fee earner's expense rate with a uplift of 25–33% for care and conduct plus a value element calculated as follows:

Non-solicitor executor	1%	of gross value less residence
	1/2%	of residence
Solicitor not an executor but acting for corporate executor	1/2%	gross value less residence
	1/4%	of residence
Application for probate only	1/6%	of gross value less residence
	1/4%	of residence
Solicitor executor (sole or with non corporate executor)	11/12%	of gross value less residence
	3/4%	of residence
Solicitor joint executor with corporate executor	3/4%	of gross value less residence
	3/8%	of residence

The Law Society recommends that the value of deceased's home be reduced by half the value of the deceased's interest in the property before applying the guideline percentage, ie if the property is solely owned by the deceased, the percentage will apply to half the value of the property. If the property is jointly owned, the percentage will apply to only a quarter of the value of the property.

In the ground-breaking decision of *Jemma Trust Company Ltd v Forrester and another* (SCCO 12 September 2002, unreported) Master Rogers held that a solicitor's charges for administering a large estate should no longer be based on both hourly rates and an additional element in respect of value but if he were wrong there should be a reducing scale based on *Maltby v DJ Freeman & Co* [1978] 1 WLR 431. The estate in question was worth just over £9 million for the administration of which the solicitor had elected to charge on the basis of an hourly rate for work carried out and in addition he charged 1.5% of the gross value of the estate (save for the house, which was charged at 0.5%) as a value element. This resulted in a value element of £227,000 in addition to the hourly rate charges. The master concluded that now hourly rates are calculated invariably on the basis of sophisticated time recording material, it is anachronistic and wrong to include an additional element in respect of value. He recognised that this was a bold decision for a judge to make at his judicial level but he was satisfied that in this sort of situation the solicitors should charge either an hourly rate or on the basis of value, but not both. By charging a percentage of the estate, and in addition all the hours that had been claimed, it seemed to him that the solicitors would be overpaid for what he accepted was not an easy estate to wind up. If he were to be held to be wrong he would hold that the lower percentages suggested for the parts of the estate which were worth more than the maximum figure quoted in *Maltby* should be adopted and there was logic in the figures that had been put to him as follows:

Value	*Percentage*	*Amount*
Up to £25,000	1 1/2%	£3,750.00
£25,000 to £1,000,000	1/2%	£3,750.00
£1,000,000 to £2,000,000	1/6%	£1,660.00
£2,000,000 to £5,000,000	1/12%	£2,500.00
£5,000,000 to £9,113,894.42	1/24%	£1,714.12
Total:		£13,374.12

A dramatic reduction on the traditional approach.

5. OTHER MATTERS

In all other routine non-contentious matters, where there is an ascertainable value element, consider whether the non-value factors are subsumed by value. It used to be only in exceptional circumstances that there would be a mark-up expressed as a percentage of time in addition to the value factor. However, the fall in the value of money since the value yardsticks were set means that there are now probably fewer cases where a value factor in itself is sufficient. If there is a value factor the usual mark-up on time might be less, perhaps between 25% and 33% in matters other than routine domestic conveyancing, or none at all following *Jemma Trust v Forrester*, above.

CHAPTER 24

VALUE JUDGMENT

Let Donaldson J, as he then was, have the final word on the approach to the quantification of costs:

> 'Each case will always have to be considered on its merits. Various figures will no doubt come to mind. They can be tested relative to the remuneration generally accepted or previously held to be fair and reasonable in comparable transactions, due allowance being made for all distinctions. In the end it is a value judgement based on discretion and experience. We have had to make a value judgement. Our figure may not be *the* right figure, and indeed such a figure probably does not exist, but we hope that it will be *a* right figure – one which is reasonable in all the circumstances.'

(*Property and Reversionary Investment Corpn Ltd v Secretary of State for the Environment* [1975] 2 All ER 436.)

CHAPTER 25

FIXED COSTS (CPR PART 45)

There are two kinds of fixed costs in the Civil Procedure Rules. The fixed costs dealt with by Part 45 are more or less what we were familiar with pre-26 April 1999, ie fixed costs on default and summary judgment and fixed commencement costs where payment is made in full within 14 days of service. They must be distinguished from the fixed costs on the fast track, at present limited to trials, but eventually to be extended to the whole of the fast track proceedings (see Chapter 27).

The fixed costs provisions of Part 45 apply only where the claim is for a specified sum of money and the circumstances set out in the rule apply; or the only claim is one where the court gives a fixed date for the hearing when it issues the claim and judgment is given for the delivery of goods. In either case the value of the claim must exceed £25.

Although it is not mentioned specifically in Part 45, Rule 27.14 limits the costs payable on the small claims track to the fixed costs attributable to issuing the claim (there are other circumstances in which the court may order costs on the small claims track, as to which see Chapter 26).

In addition to the fixed costs, any appropriate court fee will be allowed and the amount of costs payable is set out in the tables to the rules. Table 1 gives the fixed costs on commencement, Table 2 costs on entry of judgment and Table 3 miscellaneous fixed costs, which are largely to do with service documents.

Here is Part 45 and its supporting Practice Direction:

PART 45 FIXED COSTS

CPR RULE 45.1 SCOPE OF THIS PART

(1) This Part sets out the amounts which, unless the court orders otherwise, are to be allowed in respect of solicitors' charges in the cases to which this Part applies.

(The definitions contained in Part 43 are relevant to this Part)

(2) This Part applies where—

(a) the only claim is a claim for a specified sum of money where the value of the claim exceeds £25 and—

(i) judgment in default is obtained under rule 12.4 (1);

(ii) judgment on admission is obtained under rule 14.4 (3);

(iii) judgment on admission on part of the claim is obtained under rule 14.5 (6);

(iv) summary judgment is given under Part 24;

(v) the court has made an order to strike out[(GL)] a defence under rule 3.4 (2)(a) as disclosing no reasonable grounds for defending the claim; or

(vi) rule 45.3 applies; or

(b) the only claim is a claim where the court gave a fixed date for the hearing when it issued the claim and judgment is given for the delivery of goods and the value of the claim exceeds £25; or

(c) a judgment creditor has taken steps under Parts 70 to 73 to enforce a judgment or order.

(The practice direction supplementing rule 7.9 sets out the types of case where a court may give a fixed date for a hearing when it issues a claim)

(3) Any appropriate court fee will be allowed in addition to the costs set out in this Part.

CPR RULE 45.2 AMOUNT OF FIXED COMMENCEMENT COSTS

(1) The claim form may include a claim for fixed commencement costs.

(2) The amount of fixed commencement costs which the claim form may include shall be calculated by reference to the following Table (Table 1).

(3) Additional costs may also be claimed in the circumstances specified in Table 3.

(4) The amount claimed, or the value of the goods claimed if specified, in the claim form is to be used for determining the band in the Table that applies to the claim.

TABLE 1 FIXED COSTS ON COMMENCEMENT OF A CLAIM

Relevant Band	*Where the claim form is served by the court or by any method other than personal service by the claimant*	*Where the claim form is served personally by the claimant; and there is only one defendant*	*Where there is more than one defendant, for each additional defendant personally served at separate addresses by the claimant*
Where— the value of the claim exceeds £25 but does not exceed £500	£50	£60	£15
Where— the value of the claim exceeds £500 but does not exceed £1,000	£70	£80	£15
Where— the value of the claim exceeds £1,000 but does not exceed £5,000; or the only claim is for delivery of goods and no value is specified or stated on the claim form	£80	£90	£15
Where— the value of the claim exceeds £5,000	£100	£110	£15

CPR RULE 45.3 WHEN DEFENDANT ONLY LIABLE FOR FIXED COMMENCEMENT COSTS

(1) Where—
- (a) the only claim is for a specified sum of money; and
- (b) the defendant pays the money claimed within 14 days after service of particulars of claim on him, together with the fixed commencement costs stated in the claim form,

the defendant is not liable for any further costs unless the court orders otherwise.

(2) Where—
- (a) the claimant gives notice of acceptance of a payment into court in satisfaction of the whole claim;
- (b) the only claim is for a specified sum of money; and
- (c) the defendant made the payment into court within 14 days after service of the particulars of claim on him, together with the fixed costs stated in the claim form,

the defendant is not liable for any further costs unless the court orders otherwise.

CPR RULE 45.4 COSTS ON ENTRY OF JUDGMENT

Where—
- (a) the claimant has claimed fixed commencement costs under rule 45.2; and
- (b) judgment is entered in the circumstances specified in the table in this rule (Table 2),

the amount to be included in the judgment in respect of the claimant's solicitor's charges is the aggregate of—
- (i) the fixed commencement costs; and
- (ii) the relevant amount shown in Table 2.

TABLE 2 FIXED COSTS ON ENTRY OF JUDGMENT

	Where the amount of the judgment exceeds £25 but does not exceed £5,000	*Where the amount of the judgment exceeds £5,000*
Where judgment in default of an acknowledgment of service is entered under rule 12.4 (1) (entry of judgment by request on claim for money only)	£22	£30
Where judgment in default of a defence is entered under rule 12.4 (1) (entry of judgment by request on claim for money only)	£25	£35
Where judgment is entered under rule 14.4 (judgment on admission), or rule 14.5 (judgment on admission of part of claim) and claimant accepts the defendant's proposal as to the manner of payment	£40	£55
Where judgment is entered under rule 14.4 (judgment on admission), or rule 14.5 (judgment on admission on part of claim) and court decides the date or times of payment	£55	£70

	Where the amount of the judgment exceeds £25 but does not exceed £5,000	*Where the amount of the judgment exceeds £5,000*
Where summary judgment is given under Part 24 or the court strikes out a defence under rule 3.4 (2)(a), in either case, on application by a party	£175	£210
Where judgment is given on a claim for delivery of goods under a regulated agreement within the meaning of the Consumer Credit Act 1974 and no other entry in this table applies	£60	£85

CPR RULE 45.5 MISCELLANEOUS FIXED COSTS

The table in this rule (Table 3) shows the amount to be allowed in respect of solicitor's charges in the circumstances mentioned.

TABLE 3 MISCELLANEOUS FIXED COSTS

For service by a party of any document required to be served personally including preparing and copying a certificate of service for each individual served	£15
Where service by an alternative method is permitted by an order under rule 6.8 for each individual served	£25
Where a document is served out of the jurisdiction—	
(a) in Scotland, Northern Ireland, the Isle of Man or the Channel Islands	£65
(b) in any other place	£75

CPR RULE 45.6 FIXED ENFORCEMENT COSTS

The table in this rule (Table 4) shows the amount to be allowed in respect of solicitors' costs in the circumstances mentioned. The amounts shown in Table 3 are to be allowed in addition, if applicable.

TABLE 4 FIXED ENFORCEMENT COSTS

For an application under rule 70.5(4) that an award may be enforced as if payable under a court order, where the amount outstanding under the award:	
exceeds £25 but does not exceed £250	£30.75
exceeds £250 but does not exceed £600	£41.00
exceeds £600 but does not exceed £2,000	£69.50
exceeds £2,000	£75.50
On attendance to question a judgment debtor (or officer of a company or other corporation) who has been ordered to attend court under rule 71.2 where the questioning takes place before a court officer, including attendance by a responsible representative of the solicitor:	for each half-hour or part, £15.00 (When the questioning takes place before a judge, he may summarily assess any costs allowed.)

On the making of a final third party debt order under rule 72.8(6)(a) or an order for the payment to the judgment creditor of money in court under rule 72.10(1)(b):	
if the amount recovered is less than £150	one-half of the amount recovered
otherwise £98.50	
On the making of a final charging order under rule 73.8(2)(a):	£110.00
	The court may also allow reasonable disbursements in respect of search fees and the registration of the order.

PRACTICE DIRECTION SUPPLEMENTING CPR PART 45

SECTION 24 FIXED COSTS IN SMALL CLAIMS

24.1 Under Rule 27.14 the costs which can be awarded to a claimant in a small claims track case include the fixed costs payable under Part 45 attributable to issuing the claim.

24.2 Those fixed costs shall be the sum of

(a) the fixed commencement costs calculated in accordance with Table 1 of Rule 45.2 and;

(b) the appropriate court fee or fees paid by the claimant.

SECTION 25 FIXED COSTS ON THE ISSUE OF A DEFAULT COSTS CERTIFICATE

25.1 Unless paragraph 24.2 applies or unless the court orders otherwise, the fixed costs to be included in a default costs certificate are £80 plus a sum equal to any appropriate court fee payable on the issue of the certificate.

25.2 The fixed costs included in a certificate must not exceed the maximum sum specified for costs and court fee in the notice of commencement.

Where a default costs certificate is issued (see p 337) the receiving party is entitled to recover the amount for fixed costs specified in the Practice Direction supplementing Part 45, at present £80, and the court fee for issuing the certificate. The amount recoverable is fixed unless the court makes a different order and in any event may not exceed the maximum sum specified for costs and court fees in the notice of commencement.

The following additional fixed costs provisions have been preserved in the CPR Schedules.

RSC ORDER 62: COSTS

Appendix 3

FIXED COSTS

The scale of costs set out in this Appendix shall apply in the cases to which the Appendix refers.

PART II

COSTS ON JUDGMENT WITHOUT TRIAL FOR POSSESSION OF LAND

1.

(1) Where the claim is for the possession of land, and the claimant obtains judgment—

(a) under CPR Part 12 (default judgment); or

(c) under CPR Part 24 (summary judgment),

for possession of the land and costs, then, subject to sub-paragraph (2), there shall be allowed the costs prescribed by paragraph 2 of this Part of this Appendix.

(2) Where the claimant is also entitled under the judgment to damages to be assessed, or where the plaintiff claims any remedy of the nature specified in Order 45, rule 3(2), this Part of this Appendix shall not apply.

2. The costs to be allowed under this Part of this Appendix shall be £143.75, together with any court fee, and additional costs where appropriate set out in the Table below.

Additional costs

Amount to be allowed

(1) Where there is more than one defendant, in respect of each additional defendant served	£13.75
(2) Where service by an alternative method is ordered and effected, in respect of each defendant served	£53.25
(3) Where service out of the jurisdiction is ordered and effected, in the case of service:	
(a) in Scotland, Northern Ireland, the Isle of Man or the Channel Islands	£68.25
(b) in any other place out of the jurisdiction	£77.00
(4) In the case of default judgment under CPR Part 12 or summary judgment under CPR Part 24 the claimant makes an affidavit of service for the purpose of a judgment where the defendant failed to respond to the claim form (the allowance to include the search fee)	£20.50
(5) In the case of summary judgment under CPR Part 24 where an affidavit of service of the Part 23 application is required	£20.50
(6) In the case of summary judgment under CPR Part 24 for each adjournment of the application	£20.50

This Part shows the amount to be allowed in respect of enforcement costs.

PART III MISCELLANEOUS

2. Where a certificate in respect of money provisions contained in a judgment is registered in the High Court in the Register of United Kingdom judgments under Schedule 6 to the Civil Jurisdiction and Judgments Act 1982, there shall be allowed:	
Costs of registration	£39.00
2A. Where costs are allowed under the following paragraphs of this Part, the appropriate court fees shall be allowed in addition	
3. Where, upon the application of any person who has obtained a judgment or order against a debtor for the recovery or payment of money, a garnishee order is made under Order 49, rule 1, against a garnishee attaching debts	

due or accruing due from the debtor, the following costs shall be allowed:	
(a) to the garnishee to be deducted by him from any debt due by him as aforesaid before payment to the applicant	£23.00
(b) to the applicant, to be retained, unless the Court otherwise orders, out of the money recovered by him under the garnishee order and in priority to the amount of the debt owing to him under the judgment or order:	
(i) Basic costs	one half of the amount recovered
If the amount recovered by the applicant from the garnishee is:	
less than £150	
not less than £150	£98.50
(ii) Additional costs	
Where the garnishee fails to attend the hearing of the application and an affidavit of service is required	£18.00
4. Where a charging order is granted and made absolute there shall be allowed:	
Basic costs	£110.00
Additional costs where an affidavit of service is required	£18.00
together with such reasonable disbursements in respect of search fees and the registration of the order as the Court may allow	£18.00
5. Where leave is given under Order 45, rule 3, to enforce a judgment or order for the giving of possession of land by writ of possession, if the costs are allowed on the judgment or order there shall be allowed the following costs, which shall be added to the judgment or order:	
Basic costs	£42.50
Where notice of the proceedings has been given to more than one person, in respect of each additional person	£2.75
6. Where a writ of execution within the meaning of Order 46, rule 1, is issued against any party, there shall be allowed:	
Costs of issuing execution	£51.75

Note: Paragraphs 3 and 4 above were revoked by SI 2001/4015, r 34; date in force: 25 March 2002 (except in relation to fixed costs to be awarded in enforcement proceedings which are issued before that date): see SI 2001/4015, rr 1(c), 43(2).

CCR ORDER 38 COSTS

ORDER 38, RULE 18 FIXED COSTS

(1) Appendix B shall effect for the purpose of showing the total amount which, in the several cases to which Appendix B applies, shall be allowed to the solicitor for the claimant as fixed costs without assessment (whether by the summary or the detailed procedure), unless the court otherwise orders.
(2) In a claim to which Appendix B or CPR Part 45 does not apply no amount shall be entered on the claim form for the charges of the claimant's solicitor, but the words 'to be assessed' shall be inserted.

Appendix B

Part I Claims for the Recovery of Property

DIRECTIONS

1. The Tables in this Part of this Appendix show the amount to be entered on the claim form or application in respect of solicitors' charges—
   (a) in a claim for the recovery of property, including land, with or without a claim for a sum of money (other than a claim to which CPR Part 45 applies), for the purpose of Part II of this Appendix or of fixing the amount which the plaintiff may receive in respect of solicitors' charges without assessment whether by the detailed or summary procedure in the event of the defendant giving up possession and paying the amount claimed, if any, and costs.
2. In addition to the amount entered in accordance with the relevant Table the appropriate court fees shall be entered on the application.
3. In the Tables the expression 'claim' means—
   (a) the sum of money claimed, or
   (b) in relation to a claim for the recovery of land (with or without a claim for a sum of money), a sum exceeding £600 but not exceeding £2,000;
   (c) in relation to a claim for the recovery of property other than money or land, the value of the property claimed or in the case of goods supplied under a hire purchase agreement, the unpaid balance of the total price.
4. The Tables do not apply where the application or the claim form is to be served out of England and Wales or where service by an alternative method is ordered.

TABLES OF FIXED COSTS

Where claim exceeds £25 but does not exceed £250	
Amount of charges:	
(a) Where service is not by solicitor	£30.75
(b) Where service is by solicitor	£35.00
Where claim exceeds £250 but does not exceed £600	
Amount of charges:	
(a) Where service is not by solicitor	£41.00
(b) Where service is by solicitor	£48.50
Where claim exceeds £600 but does not exceed £2,000	
Amount of charges:	
(a) Where service is not by solicitor	£69.50
(b) Where service is by solicitor	£77.00
Where claim exceeds £2,000	
Amount of charges:	
(a) Where service is not by solicitor	£75.50
(b) Where service is by solicitor	£82.00

Part II Judgments

DIRECTIONS

Where an amount in respect of solicitors' charges has been entered on the claim form under Part I of this Appendix and judgment is given in the circumstances mentioned in paragraph (d) in column 1 of the following Table, the amount to be included in the judgment in respect of the solicitors' charges shall be the amount entered on the application or the claim form together with the amount shown in column 2 of the Table under the sum of money by reference to which the amount entered on the application or the claim form was fixed. Where judgment is given for a sum less than the amount claimed or for the delivery of goods of which the value or the balance of the total price is a sum less than the amount claimed, the foregoing paragraph shall, unless the court otherwise directs, have effect as if the amount entered on the application or the claim form had been fixed by reference to that sum.

FIXED COSTS ON JUDGMENTS

Column 1	Column 2 Sum of money A exceeding £25 but not exceeding £600	 B exceeding £600 but not exceeding £3000	 C exceeding £3000
(d) Where judgment is given in a fixed date action for: (i) delivery of goods where goods are not subject to a regulated agreement; or (ii) possession of land, where one of the grounds for possession is arrears of rent (whether or not the order for possession is suspended on terms) and the defendant has neither delivered a defence, admission or counterclaim, nor otherwise denied liability	£38.50	£57.25	£70.75

(Delivery of goods claims subject to a regulated agreement are dealt with by CPR Part 45)

MISCELLANEOUS PROCEEDINGS

The following Table shows the amount to be allowed in respect of solicitors' charges in the circumstances mentioned. The appropriate court fee shall be allowed in addition.

Amount to be allowed	
3. For filing a request for the issue of a warrant of execution for a sum exceeding £25	£2.25
4. For service of any document required to be served personally (other than an application for an attachment of earnings order or a judgment summons unless allowed under Order 27, rule 9 (1)(a), or Order 28, rule 10 (2)(a)(i)), including copy and preparation of certificate of service	£8.50
5. For service by an alternative method, including attendances, making appointments to serve claim forms, preparing and attending to swear and file affidavits and to obtain order, and the fees paid for oaths	£25.00

6. For each attendance on the hearing of an application for an attachment of earnings order of a judgment summons where costs are allowed under Order 27, rule 9, or Order 28, rule 10	£8.50
7. For the costs of the judgment creditor when allowed in garnishee proceedings or an application under Order 30, rule 12:	
(a) where the money recovered is less than £70.00	one half of the amount recovered
(b) where the money recovered is not less than £70.00	£46.50
8. For the costs of the judgment creditor when allowed on an application for a charging order	£71.00
9. For obtaining a certificate of judgment where costs allowed under Order 35, rule 5 (3)(d)	£8.00
10. Where an order for possession is made under rule 6 or rule 6A of Order 49 [Part II of CPR Part 55 (Possession claims)] without the attendance of the claimant, for preparing and filing the application, the documents attached to the application and the request for possession	£79.50
11. On examination of a witness under CCR Order 25, rule 3 where any responsible representative of the solicitor attends, for each half-hour or part thereof	£15.00

Notes:

Paragraphs 7, 8, 11 above were revoked by SI 2001/4015, r 42(c); date in force: 25 March 2002: see SI 2001/4015, r 1(c).

In paragraph 10 in column 2, the words 'Section II of CPR Part 55 (Possession claims)' in square brackets were substituted by SI 2001/256, r 29; date in force: 15 October 2001 (except in relation to claim forms issued before that date): see SI 2001/256, rr 1(d), 31.

Under the Civil Procedure Rules 2001, SI 2001/256 in Part III text in square brackets replaces text in italic with effect from 15 October 2001.

Schedules 1 and 2 to the Civil Procedure Rules set out with modification certain provisions previously contained in the Rules of the Supreme Court 1965 and the County Court Rules 1981. The schedules preserve certain fixed costs provisions not covered by Part 45, they are set out above.

TABLE OF FIXED COSTS

On 1 October 1999, the Chief Chancery Master and the Senior Queen's Bench Master approved a table of fixed costs replacing the table approved on 15 January 1997. It contained nothing new, but it is a convenient compilation of CPR Part 45 and Schedule 1 to Part 50 (RSC Order 62) and the Supreme Court Fees Order 1999 which came into operation on 26 April 1999. The table sets out the amounts which, unless the court orders otherwise, are to be allowed in respect of solicitors charges together with the court fee where appropriate. Here it is:

HIGH COURT OF JUSTICE

CHANCERY AND QUEEN'S BENCH DIVISIONS

Fixed costs

This Table replaces the one approved on 15 January which is hereby cancelled.

This Table is compiled from Part 45 and Schedule I to Part 50 (RSC Order 62) of the Civil Procedure Rules 1998 (SI 1998/3132) and The Supreme Court Fees Order 1999 (SI 1999/687) and came into operation on 26 April 1999. There is no VAT addition to this Table of Costs.

The Table sets out the amounts which, unless the court orders otherwise, are to be allowed in respect of solicitors' charges together with the court fee, where appropriate.

A. Fixed commencement costs on claim form

The following apply to all claim forms for a specified sum of money only	
Where the claim form is served by the court or by any other method other than personal service by the claimant and:	
the sum claimed exceeds £15,000 but does not exceed £50,000	£400.00
the sum claimed exceeds £50,000	£500.00
Where the claim form is served personally by the claimant and where there is more than one defendant and:	
the sum claimed exceeds £15,000 but does not exceed £50,000	£410.00
the sum claimed exceeds £50,000	£510.00
Additional costs	
Where the claim form is served personally by the claimant and where there is more than one defendant, for each additional defendant personally served at separate addresses by the claimant	£15.00*
For service by a party of any document required to be served personally including preparing and copying a certificate of service for each individual served	£15.00*
Where service by an alternative method is permitted by an order under rule 6.8 for each individual served	£25.00*
Where a document is served out of the jurisdiction:	
(a) in Scotland, Northern Ireland, the Isle of Man or in the Channel Islands	£65.00*
(b) in any other place	£75.00*

* Add application fee if appropriate

B. Fixed costs on entry of judgment

The following are to be added to the fixed commencement costs	
Where judgment in default of an acknowledgment of service is entered under rule 12.4(1) (entry of judgment by request on claim for money only)	£30.00
Where judgment in default of a defence is entered under rule 12.4(1) (entry of judgment by request on claim for money only)	£35.00
Where judgment is entered under rule 14.4 (judgment on admission of part of claim) and claimant accepts the defendant's proposal as to the manner of payment	£55.00

Where judgment is entered under rule 14.4 (judgment on admission) or rule 14.5 (judgment on admission on part of a claim) and court decides the dates or times of payment	£70.00
Where summary judgment is given under Part 24 or the court strikes out a defence under rule 3.4(2)(a), in either case, on application by a party	£260.00

C. Costs on judgment without trial for possession of land

This section does not apply where the claimant is also entitled under the judgment to damages to be assessed, or where the plaintiff claims any remedy of the nature specified in Order 88 rule 1 (mortgage claims)

Where the claim is for the possession of land, and the claimant obtains judgment under CPR Part 12 (default judgment) under CPR Part 24 (summary judgment) for possession of land and costs

£143.75 together with any court fee and additional costs (see Table below) where appropriate

Additional costs

Where there is more than one defendant, in respect of each defendant served	£13.75
Where service by an alternative method is ordered and effected, in respect of each defendant served	£53.25*
Where service out of the jurisdiction is ordered and effected, in the case of service—	
(a) in Scotland, Northern Ireland, the Isle of Man or the Channel Islands	£68.25*
(b) in any other place out of the jurisdiction	£77.00*
In the case of default judgment under CPR Part 12 or summary judgment under CPR Part 12 or summary judgment under CPR Part 24 the claimant makes and affidavit of service for the purpose of a judgment where the defendant failed to respond to the claim form (the allowance to include the search fee)	£20.50
In the case of summary judgment under CPR Part 24 where an affidavit of service of the summons is required	£20.50
In the case of summary judgment under CPR Part 24 for each adjournment of the application	£20.50

* Add application fee if appropriate

D. Enforcement costs

The following apply only where an amount in respect of solicitor's charges has been entered on the claim form under CPR Part 45 (see sections A and B above) or Schedule I (RSC O 62) (see section C above).

Scottish and Northern Ireland money judgments

Where a certificate in respect of money provisions contained in a judgment is registered in the High Court in the Register of United Kingdom judgments under Schedule 6 to the Civil Jurisdiction and Judgments Act 1982

Costs of registration	£39.00

Garnishee proceedings

Where, upon the application of any person who has obtained a judgment or order against a debtor for the recovery or payment of money, a garnishee order is made under Order 49 rule 1 against a garnishee attaching debts due accruing from the debtor, the following costs shall be allowed:

(a) to the garnishee to be deducted by him from any debt due by him as aforesaid before payment to the applicant — £23

(b) to the applicant, to be retained, unless the court otherwise orders, out of the money recovered by him under debt owing to him under the judgment or order—

(i) *Basic costs*
If the amount recovered by the applicant from the garnishee is—
less than £150 one half of the amount recovered plus £50 fee not less than £150 — £148.50

(ii) *Additional Costs*
Where the garnishee fails to attend the hearing of the application and an affidavit of service is required — £18.00

Charging order

Where a charging order is granted and made absolute there shall be allowed—

Basic costs	£160.00
Additional costs where an affidavit of service is required together with such reasonable disbursements in respect of search fees and the registration of the order as the court may allow	£18.00

Writ of possession

Where leave is given under Order 45 rule 3 to enforce a judgment or order for the possession of land by writ of possession of land by writ of possession, if the costs are allowed on the judgment or order there shall be allowed the following costs, which shall be added to the judgment or order—

Basic costs	£62.50
Where notice of the proceedings has been given to more than one person, in respect of each additional person	£2.75

Writ of execution

Where a writ of execution within the maining of Order 46 rule 1 is issued against any party, there shall be allowed—

Costs of issuing execution	£71.75

* Add application fee if appropriate

CHAPTER 26

SMALL CLAIMS TRACK

CPR Rule 26.6 provides that general claims for not more than £5,000 and claims for damages for personal injuries of not more than £1,000 shall be allocated to the small claims track. 'Damages for personal injuries' are defined as meaning damages claimed as compensation for pain, suffering and loss of amenity and does not include any other damages which are claimed.

CPR Rule 27.14 and its supplementary Practice Direction provide:

CPR RULE 27.14 COSTS ON THE SMALL CLAIMS TRACK

(1) This rule applies to any case which has been allocated to the small claims track unless paragraph (5) applies.

(Rules 44.9 and 44.11 make provision in relation to orders for costs made before a claim has been allocated to the small claims track)

(2) The court may not order a party to pay a sum to another party in respect of that other party's costs except—

- (a) the fixed costs attributable to issuing the claim which—
  - (i) are payable under Part 45; or
  - (ii) would be payable under Part 45 if that Part applied to the claim;
- (b) in proceedings which included a claim for an injunction[(GL)] or an order for specific performance a sum not exceeding the amount specified in the relevant practice direction for legal advice and assistance relating to that claim;
- (c) costs assessed by the summary procedure in relation to an appeal ...; and
- (d) such further costs as the court may assess by the summary procedure and order to be paid by a party who has behaved unreasonably.

(3) The court may also order a party to pay all or part of—

- (a) any court fees paid by another party;
- (b) expenses which a party or witness has reasonably incurred in travelling to and from a hearing or in staying away from home for the purposes of attending a hearing;
- (c) a sum not exceeding the amount specified in the relevant practice direction for any loss of earnings by a party or witness due to attending a hearing or to staying away from home for the purpose of attending a hearing; and
- (d) a sum not exceeding the amount specified in the relevant practice direction for an expert's fees.

(4) The limits on costs imposed by this rule also apply to any fee or reward for acting on behalf of a party to the proceedings charged by a person exercising a right of audience by virtue of an order under section 11 of the Courts and Legal Services Act 1990 (a lay representative).

(5) Where—

- (a) the financial value of a claim exceeds the limit for the small claims track; but
- (b) the claim has been allocated to the small claims track in accordance with rule 26.7(3),

the claim shall be treated, for the purposes of costs, as if it were proceeding on the fast track except that trial costs shall be in the discretion of the court and shall not exceed the amount set out for the value of the claim in rule 46.2 (amount of fast track trial costs).
(Rule 26.7(3) allows the parties to consent to a claim being allocated to a track where the financial value of the claim exceeds the limit for that track)

PRACTICE DIRECTION SUPPLEMENTING CPR PART 27

7.1 Attention is drawn to Rule 27.14 which contains provisions about the costs which may be ordered to be paid by one party to another.
7.2 The amount which a party may be ordered to pay under rule 27.14(2)(b) (for legal advice and assistance in claims including an injunction or specific performance) is a sum not exceeding £260.
7.3 The amounts which a party may be ordered to pay under rule 27.14(3)(c) (loss of earnings) and (d) (expert's fees) are:
(1) for the loss of earnings of each party or witness due to attending a hearing or staying away from home for the purpose of attending a hearing, a sum not exceeding £50 per day for each person, and
(2) for expert's fees, a sum not exceeding £200 for each expert.
(As to recovery of pre-allocation costs in a case in which an admission by the defendant has reduced the amount in dispute to a figure below £5,000, reference should be made to paragraph 7.4 of the Practice Direction supplementing CPR Part 26 and to paragraph 5.1(3) of the Costs Directions relating to CPR Part 44)

Rule 27.14 refers to Rules 44.9 and 44.11. Here is Rule 44.9 with its supplementary Practice Direction:

CPR RULE 44.9 COSTS ON THE SMALL CLAIMS TRACK AND FAST TRACK

(1) Part 27 (Small claims) and Part 46 (Fast track trial costs) contain special rules about—
- (a) liability for costs;
- (b) the amount of costs which the court may award; and
- (c) the procedure for assessing costs.

(2) Once a claim is allocated to a particular track, those special rules shall apply to the period before, as well as after, allocation except where the court or a practice direction provides otherwise.

SECTION 15: PRACTICE DIRECTION SUPPLEMENTING CPR RULE 44.9

15.1
(1) Before a claim is allocated to one of those tracks the court is not restricted by any of the special rules that apply to that track.
(2) Where a claim has been allocated to one of those tracks, the special rules which relate to that track will apply to work done before as well as after allocation save to the extent (if any) that an order for costs in respect of that work was made before allocation.
(3)
- *(i) This paragraph applies where a claim, issued for a sum in excess of the normal financial scope of the small claims track, is allocated to that track only because an admission of part of the claim by the defendant reduces the amount in dispute to a sum within the normal scope of that track.*

(See also paragraph 7.4 of the practice direction supplementing CPR Part 26)

(ii) On entering judgment for the admitted part before allocation of the balance of the claim the court may allow costs in respect of the proceedings down to that date.

Rule 44.11 refers to costs following allocation and reallocation. Here it is with its Practice Direction:

CPR RULE 44.11 COSTS FOLLOWING ALLOCATION AND RE-ALLOCATION

(1) Any costs orders made before a claim is allocated will not be affected by allocation.
(2) Where—
(a) a claim is allocated to a track; and
(b) the court subsequently re-allocates that claim to a different track,
then unless the court orders otherwise, any special rules about costs applying—
(i) to the first track, will apply to the claim up to the date of re-allocation; and
(ii) to the second track, will apply from the date of re-allocation.
(Part 26 deals with the allocation and re-allocation of claims between tracks)

SECTION 16: PRACTICE DIRECTION SUPPLEMENTING CPR RULE 44.11

16.1 This paragraph applies where the court is about to make an order to re-allocate a claim from the small claims track to another track.
16.2 Before making the order to re-allocate the claim, the court must decide whether any party is to pay costs to any other party down to the date of the order to re-allocate in accordance with the rules about costs contained in Part 27 (The Small Claims Track).
16.3 If it decides to make such an order about costs, the court will make a summary assessment of those costs in accordance with that Part.

1. RESTRICTIONS

These rules and sections of the Costs Practice Direction continue the restrictions on costs recoverable in small claims cases that used to be contained in County Court Rule Order 19. However, there the similarity ends. There is no automatic allocation of a case to the small claims track, and although Rule 44.9(2) provides that the limitation on costs applies both before and after the matter has been allocated to the small claims track, Rule 44.11(1) provides that if a party is able to obtain an order for costs before a claim has been allocated to a track that order will not be affected by subsequent allocation to the small claims track. Accordingly if either party makes an application for summary judgment prior to allocation, the court may make an order awarding the costs of the application to one of the parties. Where the parties consent to a case being allocated to the small claims track even though it exceeds the limit for that track, the costs restrictions do not apply and are replaced by the rules applying to the fast track contained in Part 46 (Chapter 27).

2. COSTS RECOVERABLE

The only costs recoverable are:

(a) fixed costs attributable to issuing the claim;
(b) in proceedings which include a claim for an injunction or an order for specific performance, the cost of obtaining legal advice and assistance relating to the claim not exceeding £260;
(c) loss of earnings by a party or witnesses due to attending a hearing or to staying away from home for the purpose of attending a hearing not exceeding £50 per day for each person;
(d) expert's fees not exceeding £200 each;
(e) all court fees; and
(f) costs to be summarily assessed against a party who has behaved unreasonably.

What is unreasonable conduct must depend upon each case and little help is to be gained from the authorities prior to 26 April 1999. It has been held that abandoning a defence at the last minute was unreasonable, as was the fabrication of an untruthful defence or a gross overstatement of the amount of damages claimed.

CHAPTER 27

FAST TRACK

The fast track is the normal track for any claim exceeding £5,000 and not exceeding £15,000, provided it is not likely to last for more than one day. Expert witnesses may be limited to one for each party in each field of expertise, there being not more than two such fields (CPR Rule 26.6).

1. PRE-TRIAL COSTS

The fast track was one of the great innovations of the Woolf reforms. In the past the choice was between the informality and palm-tree justice of a small claims arbitration or the full monty of the lengthy and expensive practice and procedure prescribed in both the Rules of the Supreme Court and the County Court Rules for all claims irrespective of their amount or subject matter. The idea of the fast track is to enable simple matters to be dealt with simply.

Two basic tenets of the fast track were that hearings were to last no more than one day and the costs were to be fixed so that each party knew what costs it would have to pay if it lost and what costs it might recover if it won. The one-day hearing has happened – if we ignore the 'cheating' of split trials, the eminently sensible cost-saving practice, one day being allocated for deciding liability and another day for the quantification of damages if the case gets that far. Fixed costs have not yet happened, except for fast track trials. That is unsurprising. The Access to Justice Report contained a suggested costs scale or matrix, taking into account the weight and complexity of the case and the stage it had reached, which was met with almost universal condemnation. Various pilot schemes threw out widely differing results, serving only to highlight the difficulty in obtaining the necessary data and translating it into a regime of fixed costs in respect of a practice and procedure yet to be implemented. The Lord Chancellor therefore postponed the introducing of fixed fast track pre-trial costs until the fast track had been running long enough for the amount of work involved in it to be ascertained and evaluated. Failure to implement this integral part of the Woolf Reforms would be the worst track of all – the back track! The certainty of fixed costs is at the heart of Lord Woolf's proposals and, although the costs must be fixed at the right level and regularly reviewed, giving any discretion to the court would undermine the value of the regime by introducing the uncertainty they are intended to avoid – the costs would no longer be fixed and the dispute as to whether or not the discretion should be exercised would move the litigation from its subject matter to the costs. The primary objectives of fast track fixed costs should be certainty, simplicity and proportionality to the amount in dispute. I discuss benchmark costs on p 284. It was originally envisaged that these would apply only to interim hearings in multi-track trials, but pending the introduction of fixed pre-trial costs they are to be applied to the fast track as well.

2. ESTIMATES

At present, the only guide to the parties as to their opponents' costs is the requirement of the practice direction supplementing CPR Part 43 that a party filing an allocation questionnaire shall at the same time file and serve an estimate of costs and do so again on filing a listing questionnaire. I deal with estimates in Chapter 10.

There was not perceived to be any uncertainty over fixing the costs to be allowed to an advocate preparing for and appearing at a trial. Provision is made in CPR Part 46 as follows:

CPR PART 46 FAST TRACK TRIAL COSTS

CPR RULE 46.1 SCOPE OF THIS PART

(1) This Part deals with the amount of costs which the court may award as the costs of an advocate for preparing for and appearing at the trial of a claim in the fast track (referred to in this rule as 'fast track trial costs').

(2) For the purposes of this Part—

- (a) 'advocate' means a person exercising a right of audience as a representative of, or on behalf of, a party;
- (b) 'fast track trial costs' means the costs of a party's advocate for preparing for and appearing at the trial, but does not include—
  - (i) any other disbursements; or
  - (ii) any value added tax payable on the fees of a party's advocate; and
- (c) 'trial' includes a hearing where the court decides an amount of money or the value of goods following a judgment under Part 12 (default judgment) or Part 14 (admissions) but does not include—
  - (i) the hearing of an application for summary judgment under Part 24; or
  - (ii) the court's approval of a settlement or other compromise under rule 21.10.

(Part 21 deals with claims made by or on behalf of, or against, children and patients)

SECTION 26: PRACTICE DIRECTION SUPPLEMENTING CPR RULE 46.1

26.1 Part 46 applies to the costs of an advocate for preparing for and appearing at the trial of a claim in the fast track.

26.2 It applies only where, at the date of the trial, the claim is allocated to the fast track. It does not apply in any other case, irrespective of the final value of the claim.

26.3 In particular it does not apply to:

(a) the hearing of a claim which is allocated to the small claims track with the consent of the parties given under rule 26.7(3); or

(b) a disposal hearing at which the amount to be paid under a judgment or order is decided by the court (see paragraph 12.8 of the Practice Direction which supplements Part 26 (Case Management – Preliminary Stage)).

Cases which settle before trial

26.4 Attention is drawn to rule 44.10 (limitation on amount court may award where a claim allocated to the fast track settles before trial).

CPR RULE 46.2 AMOUNT OF FAST TRACK TRIAL COSTS

(1) The following table shows the amount of fast track trial costs which the court may award (whether by summary or detailed assessment).

Value of the claim	*Amount of fast track trial costs which the court may award*
Up to £3,000	£350
More than £3,000 but not more than £10,000	£500
More than £10,000	£750

(2) The court may not award more or less than the amount shown in the table except where—
(a) it decides not to award any fast track trial costs; or
(b) rule 46.3 applies;
but the court may apportion the amount awarded between the parties to reflect their respective degrees of success on the issues at trial.

Rule 46.2(3), (4), (5) and (6) are on p 263.

CPR RULE 46.3 POWER TO AWARD MORE OR LESS THAN THE AMOUNT OF FAST TRACK TRIAL COSTS

(1) This rule sets out when a court may award—
(a) an additional amount to the amount of fast track trial costs shown in the table in rule 46.2 (1); and
(b) less than those amounts.
(2) If—
(a) in addition to the advocate, a party's legal representative attends the trial;
(b) the court considers that it was necessary for a legal representative to attend to assist the advocate; and
(c) the court awards fast track trial costs to that party,
the court may award an additional £250 in respect of the legal representative's attendance at the trial.
(Legal representative is defined in rule 2.3)
(2A) The court may in addition award a sum representing an additional liability.
(The requirements to provide information about a funding arrangement where a party wishes to recover any additional liability under a funding arrangement are set out in the costs practice direction)
('Additional liability' is defined in rule 43.2)
(3) If the court considers that it is necessary to direct a separate trial of an issue then the court may award an additional amount in respect of the separate trial but that amount is limited in accordance with paragraph (4) of this rule.
(4) The additional amount the court may award under paragraph 2A must not exceed two-thirds of the amount payable for that claim, subject to a minimum award of £350.
(5) Where the party to whom fast track trial costs are to be awarded is a litigant in person, the court will award—
(a) if the litigant in person can prove financial loss, two thirds of the amount that would otherwise be awarded; or
(b) if the litigant in person fails to prove financial loss, an amount in respect of the time spent reasonably doing the work at the rate specified in the costs practice direction.
(6) Where a defendant has made a counterclaim against the claimant, and—
(a) the claimant has succeeded on his claim; and
(b) the defendant has succeeded on his counterclaim,

the court will quantify the amount of the award of fast track trial costs to which—

(i) but for the counterclaim, the claimant would be entitled for succeeding on his claim; and

(ii) but for the claim, the defendant would be entitled for succeeding on his counterclaim,

and make one award of the difference, if any, to the party entitled to the higher award of costs.

(7) Where the court considers that the party to whom fast track trial costs are to be awarded has behaved unreasonably or improperly during the trial, it may award that party an amount less than would otherwise be payable for that claim, as it considers appropriate.

(8) Where the court considers that the party who is to pay the fast track trial costs has behaved improperly during the trial the court may award such additional amount to the other party as it considers appropriate.

The amounts prescribed are those that the court must award – or as the rule somewhat quaintly puts it 'the court may not award more or less' than those amounts – except for a £250 increase where both an advocate and a legal representative are necessary (this is the only place in the costs rules where the word 'necessary' appears) and a minimum additional payment of £350 for a split trial. When is it necessary for a legal representative to attend? Marshalling the witnesses, handling the documents, taking notes during cross-examination are traditional reasons, although these may not always be convincing in a simple road traffic accident. When the rule was first introduced the Law Society's Practice Rules required a representative from the firm of solicitors instructing counsel to attend with him on all hearings and therefore the solicitors attendance was always necessary. That professional obligation has now been removed. It was replaced by a new principle 20.04 as follows:

> 'Where counsel has been instructed, the instructing solicitor is under a duty to attend or arrange for the attendance of a responsible representative throughout the proceedings; save that attendance may be dispensed with in the magistrates' court or in certain categories of Crown court proceedings and in small claims track and fast track civil cases, where the solicitor is satisfied that it is reasonable in the particular circumstances of the case that counsel be unattended. The solicitor will be so satisfied where it is clear that the interests of the client and the interests of justice will not be prejudiced by counsel appearing alone.
>
> Attendance on counsel will normally be dispensed with in small claims track and fast track civil cases except:
>
> (a) where the case is more complex than a typical small claims or fast track case;
> (b) where the determination of costs at the conclusion of proceedings requires the presence of the solicitor;
> (c) where one of the parties in the case is a child;
> (d) where the client is unable to understand the proceedings or give adequate instructions to counsel because of inadequate knowledge of English, mental illness or other mental or physical disability;
> (e) where counsel is representing more than one party;
> (f) where the client is likely to disrupt the proceedings if counsel were to appear alone;
> (g) where there are any issues likely to arise which question the client's character or the solicitor's conduct of the case;
> (h) where there is any other exceptional circumstance which makes it desirable that counsel be attended.'

It is an anomaly that there is no similar restriction on the costs of an advocate appearing on an interim hearing on the fast track. Presumably, it was thought these would not happen on the fast track, but they do and brief fees are sometimes claimed in excess of the trial limit! Rule 46.3(6) specifically exempts from fast track trials the awarding of amounts to both the claimant and the defendant. This is done by deciding what the entitlement would be for succeeding on the claim or the counterclaim and taking one figure from the other and making an award for the difference to the party with the higher entitlement. The decision in *Medway Oil and Storage Co Ltd v Continental Contractors Ltd* [1929] AC 88, HL does not apply to fast track trial costs. Unreasonable or improper behaviour may be penalised by either awarding one party less than would otherwise have been payable to it or the other party may be awarded an additional amount. It is important to appreciate that where a fast track trial is adjourned to another day the costs limitations in respect of fast track trial costs still apply, irrespective of the length of the trial, and accordingly no additional fast track trial costs can be awarded in respect of the adjournment.

3. VALUING THE CLAIM

If costs are awarded to the claimant, the value of the claim is the total amount of the judgment, excluding interest and costs and excluding any reduction for contributory negligence. If costs are awarded to the defendant, the value of the claim is the amount specified in the claim form excluding interest and costs or, if no amount is specified, the maximum amount according to the statement of value in the claim form. For non-money claims the value is to be taken as more than £3,000 but not more than £10,000 unless the court decides otherwise. These provisions are in Rule 46.2:

CPR RULE 46.2 VALUING THE CLAIM FOR THE PURPOSES OF QUANTIFYING FAST TRACK TRIAL COSTS (*CONTINUED FROM P 261*)

(3) Where the only claim is for the payment of money—
- (a) for the purpose of quantifying fast track trial costs awarded to a claimant, the value of the claim is the total amount of the judgment excluding—
  - (i) interest and costs; and
  - (ii) any reduction made for contributory negligence;
- (b) for the purpose of the quantifying fast track trial costs awarded to a defendant, the value of the claim is—
  - (i) the amount specified in the claim form (excluding interest and costs);
  - (ii) if no amount is specified, the maximum amount which the claimant reasonably expected to recover according to the statement of value included in the claim form under rule 16.3; or
  - (iii) more than £10,000, if the claim form states that the claimant cannot reasonably say how much he expects to recover.

(4) Where the claim is only for a remedy other than the payment of money the value of the claim is deemed to be more than £3,000 but not more than £10,000, unless the court orders otherwise.

(5) Where the claim includes both a claim for the payment of money and for a remedy other than the payment of money, the value of the claim is deemed to be the higher of—
- (a) the value of the money claim decided in accordance with paragraph (3);
- (b) or the deemed value of the other remedy decided in accordance with paragraph (4),

unless the court orders otherwise.

(6) Where—

(a) a defendant has made a counterclaim against the claimant;
(b) the counterclaim has a higher value than the claim; and
(c) the claimant succeeds at trial both on his claim and the counterclaim,

for the purpose of quantifying fast track trial costs awarded to the claimant, the value of the claim is the value of the defendant's counterclaim calculated in accordance with this rule.

(Rule 20.4 sets out how a defendant may make a counterclaim)

4. MORE THAN ONE CLAIMANT OR DEFENDANT

Where the same advocate is acting for more than one party there will be only one award of costs to be apportioned between the receiving parties. However, if defendants are separately represented the court may award costs to each defendant. The rule sets out how the value of a claim is to be ascertained where the same advocate is acting for more than one claimant and each claimant has a separate claim against the defendant. Here is the rule:

CPR RULE 46.4 FAST TRACK TRIAL COSTS WHERE THERE IS MORE THAN ONE CLAIMANT OR DEFENDANT

(1) Where the same advocate is acting for more than one party—
  (a) the court may make only one award in respect of fast track trial costs payable to that advocate; and
  (b) the parties for whom the advocate is acting are jointly entitled to any fast track trial costs awarded by the court.

(2) Where—
  (a) the same advocate is acting for more than one claimant; and
  (b) each claimant has a separate claim against the defendant,

the value of the claim, for the purpose of quantifying the award in respect of fast track trial costs is to be ascertained in accordance with paragraph (3).

(3) The value of the claim in the circumstances mentioned in paragraph (2) is—
  (a) where the only claim of each claimant is for the payment of money—
    (i) if the award of fast track trial costs is in favour of the claimants, the total amount of the judgment made in favour of all the claimants jointly represented; or
    (ii) if the award is in favour of the defendant, the total amount claimed by the claimants,

  and in either case, quantified in accordance with rule 46.2 (3);
  (b) where the only claim of each claimant is for a remedy other than the payment of money, deemed to be more than £3,000 but not more than £10,000; and
  (c) where claims of the claimants include both a claim for the payment of money and for a remedy other than the payment of money, deemed to be—
    (i) more than £3,000 but not more than £10,000; or
    (ii) if greater, the value of the money claims calculated in accordance with sub paragraph (a) above.

(4) Where—
  (a) there is more than one defendant; and
  (b) any or all of the defendants are separately represented,

the court may award fast track trial costs to each party who is separately represented.

(5) Where—
  (a) there is more than one claimant; and
  (b) a single defendant,

the court may make only one award to the defendant of fast track trial costs, for which the claimants are jointly and severally liable[(GL)].

For the purpose of quantifying the fast track trial costs awarded to the single defendant under paragraph (5), the value of the claim is to be calculated in accordance with paragraph (3) of this rule.

Where a fast track case settles before the start of the trial the court will have to consider the amount of costs to be allowed in respect of the successful party's advocate for preparing for trial. The amount may not of course exceed the prescribed amount. Here is the rule:

CPR RULE 44.10 LIMITATION ON AMOUNT COURT MAY ALLOW WHERE A CLAIM ALLOCATED TO THE FAST TRACK SETTLES BEFORE TRIAL

(1) Where the court—
- (a) assesses costs in relation to a claim which—
  - (i) has been allocated to the fast track; and
  - (ii) settles before the start of the trial; and
- (b) is considering the amount of costs to be allowed in respect of a party's advocate for preparing for the trial,

it may not allow, in respect of those advocate's costs, an amount that exceeds the amount of fast track trial costs which would have been payable in relation to the claim had the trial taken place.

(2) When deciding the amount to be allowed in respect of the advocate's costs, the court shall have regard to—
- (a) when the claim was settled; and
- (b) when the court was notified that the claim had settled.

(3) In this rule, 'advocate' and 'fast track trial costs' have the meanings given to them by Part 46.

(Part 46 sets out the amount of fast track trial costs which may be awarded)

CHAPTER 28

MULTI-TRACK

The multi-track is the normal track for any claim for which the small claims track (see Chapter 26) or the fast track (see Chapter 27) is not the normal track (CPR Rule 26.6(6)). Although claims on the other two tracks will always be in a county court, claims on the multi-track may be in either the High Court or a county court. There are no specific costs rules relating only to the multi-track and therefore Parts 43, 44, 47 and 48 all apply.

CHAPTER 29

SUMMARY ASSESSMENT

Since 26 April 1999, the general rule is that at the end of any trial of a case that is being dealt with on the fast track and at the conclusion of any other hearing which has lasted not more than one day, the court will make a summary assessment of the costs unless there is good reason not to do so. What is the authority for that proposition? There is nothing in the rules. You might have thought that something so revolutionary as summary assessment by the trial judge would have been in the rules. But it is not. It is in the Practice Direction supplementing Rule 44.7.

Here are the rule and the Practice Direction:

CPR RULE 44.7 PROCEDURE FOR ASSESSING COSTS

Where the court orders a party to pay costs to another party (other than fixed costs) it may either—

(a) make a summary assessment of the costs; or

(b) order detailed assessment of the costs by a costs officer,

unless any rule, practice direction or other enactment provides otherwise.

(The costs practice direction sets out the factors which will affect the court's decision under this rule)

PRACTICE DIRECTION SECTION 13 SUMMARY ASSESSMENT: GENERAL PROVISIONS

13.1 Whenever a court makes an order about costs which does not provide for fixed costs to be paid the court should consider whether to make a summary assessment of costs.

13.2 The general rule is that the court should make a summary assessment of the costs:

(1) at the conclusion of the trial of a case which has been dealt with on the fast track, in which case the order will deal with the costs of the whole claim, and

(2) at the conclusion of any other hearing, which has lasted not more than one day, in which case the order will deal with the costs of the application or matter to which the hearing related. If this hearing disposes of the claim, the order may deal with the costs of the whole claim;

(3) in hearings in the Court of Appeal to which Paragraph 14 of the Practice Direction supplementing Part 52 (Appeals) applies;

unless there is good reason not to do so eg where the paying party shows substantial grounds for disputing the sum claimed for costs that cannot be dealt with summarily or there is insufficient time to carry out a summary assessment.

13.3 The general rule in paragraph 13.2 does not apply to a mortgagee's costs incurred in mortgage possession proceedings or other proceedings relating to a mortgage unless the mortgagee asks the court to make an order for his costs to be paid by another party. Paragraphs 50.3 and 50.4 deal in more detail with costs relating to mortgages.

13.4 Where an application has been made and the parties to the application agree an order by consent without any party attending, the parties should agree a figure for costs to be inserted in the consent order or agree that there should be no order for costs. If the parties cannot agree the costs position, attendance on the appointment will be necessary but, unless good reason can be shown for the failure to deal with costs as set out above, no costs will be allowed for that attendance.

13.5

(1) It is the duty of the parties and their legal representatives to assist the judge in making a summary assessment of costs in any case to which paragraph 13.2 above applies, in accordance with the following paragraphs.

(2) Each party who intends to claim costs must prepare a written statement of the costs he intends to claim showing separately in the form of a schedule:

(a) the number of hours to be claimed,

(b) the hourly rate to be claimed,

(c) the grade of fee earner;

(d) the amount and nature of any disbursement to be claimed, other than counsel's fee for appearing at the hearing,

(e) the amount of solicitor's costs to be claimed for attending or appearing at the hearing,

(f) the fees of counsel to be claimed in respect of the hearing, and

(g) any value added tax (VAT) to be claimed on these amounts.

*(*3) The statement of costs should follow as closely as possible Form N260 and must be signed by the party or his legal representative. Where a litigant is an assisted person or is a LSC funded client or is represented by a solicitor in the litigant's employment the statement of costs need not include the certificate appended at the end of Form N260.*

(4) The statement of costs must be filed at court and copies of it must be served on any party against whom an order for payment of those costs is intended to be sought. The statement of costs should be filed and the copies of it should be served as soon as possible and in any event not less than 24 hours before the date fixed for the hearing.

*(5) *Where the litigant is or may be entitled to claim an additional liability the statement filed and served need not reveal the amount of that liability.*

13.6 The failure by a party, without reasonable excuse, to comply with the foregoing paragraphs will be taken into account by the court in deciding what order to make about the costs of the claim, hearing or application, and about the costs of any further hearing or detailed assessment hearing that may be necessary as a result of that failure.

13.7 If the court makes a summary assessment of costs at the conclusion of proceedings the court will specify separately

(1) the base costs, and if appropriate, the additional liability allowed as solicitor's charges, counsel's fees, other disbursements and any VAT; and

(2) the amount which is awarded under Part 46 (Fast Track Trial Costs).

13.8 The court awarding costs cannot make an order for a summary assessment of costs by a costs officer. If a summary assessment of costs is appropriate but the court awarding costs is unable to do so on the day, the court must give directions as to a further hearing before the same judge.

*13.9 * The court will not make a summary assessment of the costs of a receiving party who is an assisted person or LSC funded client.*

*13.10 * A summary assessment of costs payable by an assisted person or LSC funded client is not by itself a determination of that person's liability to pay those costs (as to which see rule 44.17 and paragraphs 21.1 to 23.17 of this Practice Direction).*

13.11

(1) The court will not make a summary assessment of the costs of a

receiving party who is a child or patient within the meaning of Part 21 unless the solicitor acting for the child or patient has waived the right to further costs (see paragraph 51.1 below).

(2) The court may make a summary assessment of costs payable by a child or patient.

13.12

(1) Attention is drawn to rule 44.3A which prevents the court from making a summary assessment of an additional liability before the conclusion of the proceedings or the part of the proceedings to which the funding arrangement relates. Where this applies, the court should nonetheless make a summary assessment of the base costs of the hearing or application unless there is a good reason not to do so.

(2) Where the court makes a summary assessment of the base costs all statements of costs and costs estimates put before the judge will be retained on the court file.

13.13 The court will not give its approval to disproportionate and unreasonable costs. Accordingly:

(a) When the amount of the costs to be paid has been agreed between the parties the order for costs must state that the order is by consent.

(b) If the judge is to make an order which is not by consent, the judge will, so far as possible, ensure that the final figure is not disproportionate and/or unreasonable having regard to Part 1 of the CPR. The judge will retain this responsibility notwithstanding the absence of challenge to individual items in the make-up of the figure sought. The fact that the paying party is not disputing the amount of costs can however be taken as some indication that the amount is proportionate and reasonable. The judge will therefore intervene only if satisfied that the costs are so disproportionate that it is right to do so.

PRACTICE DIRECTION SECTION 14 SUMMARY ASSESSMENT WHERE COSTS CLAIMED INCLUDE AN ADDITIONAL LIABILITY

Orders made before the conclusion of the proceedings

14.1 The existence of a conditional fee agreement or other funding arrangement within the meaning of rule 43.2 is not by itself a sufficient reason for not carrying out a summary assessment.

14.2 Where a legal representative acting for the receiving party has entered into a conditional fee agreement the court may summarily assess all the costs (other than any additional liability).

14.3 Where costs have been summarily assessed an order for payment will not be made unless the court has been satisfied that in respect of the costs claimed, the receiving party is at the time liable to pay to his legal representative an amount equal to or greater than the costs claimed. A statement in the form of the certificate appended at the end of Form N260 may be sufficient proof of liability. The giving of information under rule 44.15 (where that rule applies) is not sufficient.

14.4 The court may direct that any costs, for which the receiving party may not in the event be liable, shall be paid into court to await the outcome of the case, or shall not be enforceable until further order, or it may postpone the receiving party's right to receive payment in some other way.

Orders made at the conclusion of the proceedings

14.5 Where there has been a trial of one or more issues separately from other issues, the court will not normally order detailed assessment of the additional liability until all issues have been tried unless the parties agree.

14.6 Rule 44.3A(2) sets out the ways in which the court may deal with the assessment of the costs where there is a funding arrangement. Where the court makes a summary assessment of the base costs:

(1) The order may state separately the base costs allowed as (a)solicitor's charges, (b) counsel's fees, (c) any other disbursements and (d) any VAT;

(2) the statements of costs upon which the judge based his summary assessment will be retained on the court file.

14.7 Where the court makes a summary assessment of an additional liability at the conclusion of proceedings, that assessment must relate to the whole of the proceedings; this will include any additional liability relating to base costs allowed by the court when making a summary assessment on a previous application or hearing.

14.8 Paragraph 13.13 applies where the parties are agreed about the total amount to be paid by way of costs, or are agreed about the amount of the base costs that will be paid. Where they disagree about the additional liability the court may summarily assess that liability or make an order for a detailed assessment.

14.9 In order to facilitate the court in making a summary assessment of any additional liability at the conclusion of the proceedings the party seeking such costs must prepare and have available for the court a bundle of documents which must include—

(1) a copy of every notice of funding arrangement (Form N251) which has been filed by him;

(2) a copy of every estimate and statement of costs filed by him;

(3) a copy of the risk assessment prepared at the time any relevant funding arrangement was entered into and on the basis of which the amount of the additional liability was fixed.

1. WHAT IS COVERED?

The general rule applies to all hearings that have lasted – the word is 'lasted', not 'listed', so the test is hindsight not foresight – not more than one day. It is not limited to fast track trials and interim hearings, 'other hearings' include multi-track trials and appeals in the Court of Appeal which do not last more than a day. Although the general rule applies to cases that last no more than one day it was held in *Q v Q* (Costs: summary assessment) [2002] 2 FLR 668, that there is no presumption against summary assessment in relation to costs where hearings last more than one day. Indeed para 13.1 of the Costs Practice Direction requires summary assessment to be considered in every case.

2. EXCEPTIONS TO THE GENERAL RULE

What is a 'good reason' for not carrying out a summary assessment? Paragraph 13.2 gives as examples of good reasons where the paying party shows substantial grounds for disputing the sum claimed for costs that cannot be dealt with summarily or there is insufficient time to carry out a summary assessment. 'Insufficient time' is not a complete bar to a summary assessment because, although para 13.8 prohibits delegation to a costs officer, it also envisages the trial judge postponing his summary assessment to another date. In *Mahmood v Penrose* [2002] EWCA Civ 457, [2002] All ER (D) 227 (Mar) the court explained the reasoning behind para 13.8 was that only the person who has actually heard the case and knows about it is in a position to make a summary assessment.

Another reason for not having a summary assessment could be legal arguments which could not properly be dealt with on a summary assessment. In *R v Cardiff City Council, ex p Brown* (11 August 1999, unreported, QBD) it was alleged that the hourly rate claimed was in breach of the indemnity principle because the work had been done by the receiving party's own legal department and the hourly cost of doing the work could not have been as much as the rate claimed between the parties. The issue required a consideration of the legal department's costings and the various relevant authorities which Harrison J concluded was not a suitable exercise for a summary assessment.

In *Neil v Stephenson* (2000) CLW, 8 December, although the claimant, acting in person, had his action struck out, he had been awarded his costs of an interim hearing. When the claim was struck out, the judge acceded to the claimant's request for a detailed assessment to give him an opportunity to demonstrate that he should be entitled to recover the value of a contract which his business had allegedly lost as a result of his attendance at the interim hearing. The fairest course was to order an expedites detailed assessment of the costs of both parties to give the litigant in person the opportunity to consider his arguments and put the case before an experienced costs judge.

Paragraph 13.3 disapplies the general rule to the mortgagee's costs of mortgage possession proceedings.

The former para 4.4(3) which provided that generally there would be no summary assessment of costs if an order has been made for costs in the case has gone. However, I contended that as both parties have gone to the trouble and expense of preparing statements of costs there would appear to be a benefit in summarily assessing the costs of each party of that hearing to await the final outcome of the proceedings. The restriction has now been removed.

Paragraph 13.4 avoids the need for a summary assessment or the attendance of the parties, provided they have either agreed the amount of the costs or agreed that there shall be no order for costs. They cannot agree to a detailed assessment.

Paragraph 13.10 provides that where one of the parties is in receipt of state funding there cannot be a summary assessment of any costs ordered to be paid to them by the other party, because the Legal Aid Act 1988 and LSC regulations require those costs to be the subject of a detailed assessment. It is the same for a child or a patient, unless their solicitor agrees not to make any further charge to his client (para 13.11). The judge may, however, assess costs ordered to be paid by a legally assisted person, a child or a patient, although you may think that in most cases that may be an academic exercise. In any event, the summary assessment of costs payable by an assisted person or LSC-funded client is not by itself determination of the assisted person's liability to pay those costs for the purposes of the Legal Aid Act 1988, s 17 or the Access to Justice Act 1999, s 11 (see Chapter 19).

The summary assessment at the end of a fast track trial will deal with the costs of the whole of the claim, remembering that the advocacy costs of the trial are fixed, and bearing in mind that there may have already been one or more summary assessments of the costs of an interim application. A summary assessment at the end of an interlocutory application will deal with the costs of the application or matter to which it related.

3. ADDITIONAL LIABILITIES

An additional liability is either a CFA success fee or an after-the-event insurance premium, and usually both. They are considered fully in Chapter 29.

On an interim hearing, the existence of an additional liability is not a reason for not carrying out a summary assessment, but the judge may only assess the base costs – he is precluded from assessing the additional liability. That is the combined effect of section 14.1 of the Costs Practice Direction and Rule 44.3A. If the judge does assess the base costs he may not make an order for them to be paid, because if the action is lost the receiving party will have no liability to his solicitor, unless he is satisfied that the receiving party is in any event liable to pay his solicitor the amount claimed. The judge may however order the costs to be paid into court pending the outcome of the proceedings, or that the order shall not be enforced without permission or fetter the receiving party in some other way.

After a final hearing, Rule 44.3A gives three options:

(1) summary assessment of all the costs;
(2) summary assessment of the base costs only. Sending the additional liability for detailed assessment; or
(3) detailed assessment of all the costs.

The revised SCCO *Guide to the Summary Assessment of Costs* gives the following advice on the summary assessment of additional liabilities.

SUMMARY ASSESSMENT WHERE COSTS CLAIMED INCLUDE AN ADDITIONAL LIABILITY

16. Rule 44.3A deals with costs orders relating to funding arrangements. An order for payment of 'costs' includes an additional liability incurred under a funding arrangement. Where the court carries out a summary assessment of base costs before the conclusion of proceedings it is helpful if the order identifies separately the amount allowed in respect of: solicitors' charges; counsel's fees; other disbursements; and any value added tax. If this is not done, the court which later makes an assessment of an additional liability, will have to apportion the base costs previously assessed.

17. Rule 44.3B sets out the limits on recovery under funding arrangements. The court will consider the amount of any additional liability separately from the base costs and when considering the factors to be taken into account under rule 44.5 in assessing an additional liability the court will have regard to the facts and circumstances as they reasonably appeared to the solicitor or counsel when the funding arrangement was entered into and at the time of any variation of the arrangement.

Orders Made before the Conclusion of Proceedings

18. Where an order for costs is made before the conclusion of the proceedings and a legal representative for the receiving party has entered into a conditional fee agreement the court may summarily assess the base costs. An order for payment of those costs will not be made unless the court is satisfied that the receiving party is at the time liable to pay to his legal representative an amount equal to or greater than the costs claimed. If the court is not so satisfied it may direct that any costs, for which the receiving party may not in the final event be liable, be paid into court to await the outcome of the case or shall not be enforceable until further order, or the court may postpone the receiving party's right to receive payment in some other way.

Orders Made at the Conclusion of Proceedings

19. Where the court makes a summary assessment of an additional liability at the conclusion of the proceedings, that assessment must relate to the whole of the proceedings; this will include any additional liability relating to base costs allowed by the court when making a summary assessment on a previous application or hearing.

FACTORS TO BE TAKEN INTO ACCOUNT IN DECIDING THE AMOUNT OF COSTS

Conditional Fee Agreements with a Success Fee

24. The factors to be taken into account when deciding whether a percentage increase is reasonable may include:
(a) the risk that the circumstance in which the costs, fees or expenses would be payable might or might not occur;
(b) the legal representative's liability for any disbursements;
(c) what other methods of financing the costs were available to the receiving party.
The court has the power to allow different percentages for different items of costs or for different periods during which costs were incurred. The court should have regard to the facts and circumstances as they reasonably appeared to the solicitor or counsel when the funding arrangement was entered into, and at the time of any variation of the agreement.
25. A percentage increase should not be reduced simply on the ground that, when added to base costs which are reasonable and (where relevant) proportionate, the total appears disproportionate.

Insurance Premiums

26. Relevant factors to be taken into account when deciding whether the cost of insurance cover is reasonable include:
(a) where the insurance cover is not purchased in support of a conditional fee agreement with a success fee, how its cost compares with the likely cost of funding the case with a conditional fee agreement with a success fee and supporting insurance cover;
(b) the level and extent of the cover provided;
(c) the availability of any pre-existing insurance cover;
(d) whether any part of the premium would be rebated in the event of early settlement;
(e) the amount of commission payable to the receiving party or his legal representatives or other agents.

Membership Organisation – Additional Amount

27. When considering a provision made by a membership organisation the court should not allow a provision which exceeds the likely cost to the receiving party of the premium of an insurance policy against the risk of incurring a liability to pay the costs of other parties to the proceedings. In those circumstances the court will have regard to the factors set out in paragraph 26 above in addition to the factors set out in rule 44.5.

4. WRITTEN STATEMENT OF COSTS

Paragraph 13.5 prescribes that any party intending to claim costs must prepare a written statement of the costs he intends to claim particularising the information specified in the practice direction, following as closely as possible Form N260 signed by the party or his legal representative. See Form N260 on pp 275–276.

The statement must be filed at court and copies served on any party against whom an order for payment is intended to be sought not less than 24 hours before the date of the hearing. The beauty of this procedure is that when the solicitor is filling in his statement of costs he does not know whether his client is going to be the receiving or the paying party, which should assist him to take a balanced view of the exercise.

Paragraph 13.6 says failure to comply will be taken into account in the decision making process and the defaulter will be at the risk of an order for costs if his failure necessitates an adjournment or a detailed assessment. Even worse, he might not get any costs at all because the practice direction makes the lodging and serving of a statement of costs a condition precedent to applying for costs.

However, in *MacDonald v Taree Holdings Ltd* [2001] 06 LS Gaz R 45, it was held that, despite the use of the word 'must', the provision is not mandatory and a deputy district judge had been wrong to refuse the successful party's application for summary assessment of his costs on the grounds that he had not served a statement of costs upon the respondent 24 hours in advance. The court has a wide discretion when deciding whether or not to award costs under Part 44 and in applications for summary judgment for costs, the failure to serve a schedule of costs was often being used for grounds for depriving a party of his costs or for curtailing a party's costs. Where, however, the only factor against awarding costs was merely a failure to serve a schedule without aggravating factors, a party should not be deprived of all his costs. The court should take the matter into account but its reaction should be proportionate. The question the court should ask itself was what, if any, prejudice there had been to the paying party and how should that prejudice be dealt with. The court should consider: first, whether it would be appropriate to have a brief adjournment for the paying party to consider the schedule and then proceed to a summary assessment of the costs. In that event, the judge should err in favour of awarding a lighter figure; secondly, whether the mater should be stood over for a detailed assessment; thirdly, whether the matter should be stood over for a summary assessment at a later data or for summary assessment to be dealt with in writing.

Where there is an adjournment for a summary assessment at a later date or an order for a detailed assessment, the receiving party will, of course, be at the risk of paying the consequential additional costs.

FORM N260

Statement of Costs (summary assessment)

In the Court	
Case Reference	

Judge/Master

Case Title

[Party]'s Statement of Costs for the hearing on *(date)* **(interim application/fast track trial)**

Description of fee earners*

(a) *(name) (grade) (hourly rate claimed)*

(b) *(name) (grade) (hourly rate claimed)*

Attendances on *(party)*				
(a) *(number)*		hours at £		£
(b) *(number)*		hours at £		£
Attendances on opponents				
(a) *(number)*		hours at £		£
(b) *(number)*		hours at £		£
Attendance on others				
(a) *(number)*		hours at £		£
(b) *(number)*		hours at £		£
Site inspections etc				
(a) *(number)*		hours at £		£
(b) *(number)*		hours at £		£
Work done on negotiations				
(a) *(number)*		hours at £		£
(b) *(number)*		hours at £		£
Other work, not covered above				
(a) *(number)*		hours at £		£
(b) *(number)*		hours at £		£
Work done on documents				
(a) *(number)*		hours at £		£
(b) *(number)*		hours at £		£
Attendance at hearing				
(a) *(number)*		hours at £		£
(b) *(number)*		hours at £		£
(a) *(number)*		hours travel and waiting at £		£
(b) *(number)*		hours travel and waiting at £		£
			Sub Total	**£**

FORM N260 – *cont*

Brought forward £

Counsel's fees *(name) (year of call)*

Fee for [advice/conference/documents] £

Fee for hearing £

Other expenses

[court fees] £

Others £

(give brief description)

Total **£**

Amount of VAT claimed

on solicitors and counsel's fees £

on other expenses £

Grand Total **£**

The costs estimated above do not exceed the costs which the *(party)* is liable to pay in respect of the work which this estimate covers.

Dated

Signed

Name of firm of solicitors [partner] for the *(party)*

* 4 grades of fee earner are suggested:

(A) Solicitors with over eight years post qualification experience including at least eight years litigation experience.

(B) Solicitors and legal executives with over four years post qualification experience including at least four years litigation experience.

(C) Other solicitors and legal executives and fee earners of equivalent experience.

(D) Trainee solicitors, para legals and other fee earners.

"Legal Executive" means a Fellow of the Institute of Legal Executives. Those who are not Fellows of the Institute are not entitled to call themselves legal executives and in principle are therefore not entitled to the same hourly rate as a legal executive.

In respect of each fee earner communications should be treated as attendances and routine communications should be claimed at one tenth of the hourly rate.

5. AGREED COSTS

The Master of the Rolls and Vice-Chancellor were anxious that the court should not be seen to be endorsing disproportionate and unreasonable costs and accordingly the practice direction was amended to provide that when the amount of the costs to be paid has been agreed, the order should make it clear that it was made by consent; where the order is not by consent the judge has a responsibility to ensure that even those items which are not challenged are reasonable and proportionate (para 13.13), although he will only intervene if the costs are clearly unreasonable or disproportionate.

6. PROPORTIONALITY

In Chapter 11, I considered the requirement of Rule 44.4 that costs shall be proportionate to the matters in issue and the various attempts to define proportionality. The SCCO *Guide to the Summary Assessment of Costs* deals with proportionality on summary assessment after a final hearing, and should now be read in the light of the decision in *Lownds* (p 103).

> **FACTORS TO BE TAKEN INTO ACCOUNT IN DECIDING THE AMOUNT OF COSTS**
>
> 20. Rule 44.5 sets out the factors to be taken into account. Those factors include: the conduct of all the parties, including in particular, conduct before as well as during the proceedings and the efforts made, if any, before and during the proceedings in order to try to resolve the dispute.
> 21. In deciding whether the costs claimed are reasonable and (on the standard basis) proportionate, the court will consider the amount of any additional liability separately from the base costs.
> 22. The Judge, before concluding a summary assessment should step back and consider the proportionality of the costs he has in mind to allow. If previous orders for summarily assessed costs have been made the Judge should, subject to paragraph 23, consider the proportionality of the total costs of the proceedings.
> 23. In arriving at a final figure the Judge should not reduce the costs of the receiving party on account of the costs awarded to that party under a previous summary assessment. To do so would impugn the decision of the earlier Judge. Where however the amount of costs previously ordered to be paid has been agreed by the parties with no judicial assessment there is nothing to prevent the court taking these figures into account when considering proportionality.

The message is that a judge cannot regard previous costs awards as mere water under the bridge but must look at the totality of the awards in considering proportionality overall.

7. THE INDEMNITY PRINCIPLE

Until the indemnity principle is disapplied, a party in whose favour an order for costs has been made may not recover more than he is liable to pay to his own solicitors (see Chapter 17). The written statement of costs (Form 1) contains the statement 'the costs estimated above do not exceed the costs which the party is liable to pay in respect of the work which this estimate covers'. The SCCO *Guide to the Summary Assessment of Costs* at paragraph 32 reads:

> 'Following the decision of Lord Justice Henry in *Bailey v IBC Vehicles Ltd* [1998] 3 All ER 570, CA it is suggested that the signature of a statement of costs (or a bill for detailed assessment) by a solicitor, is, in normal circumstances, sufficient to enable the court to be satisfied that the indemnity principle has not been breached. A solicitor is an officer of the court and as Lord Justice Henry stated: "in so signing he certifies that the contents of the bill are correct. That signature is no empty formality. The bill specifies the hourly rate supplied ... if an agreement between the receiving solicitor and his client ... restricted (say) the hourly rate payable to the client that hourly rate is the most that can be claimed or recovered on [assessment] ... the signature of the bill of costs ... is effectively the certificate of an officer of the court that the receiving party's solicitors are not seeking to recover in relation to any item more than they have agreed to charge their client ... ".'

(See *Hazlett v Sefton Metropolitan Borough Council* on p 174 for an example in practice.) Paragraph 14.3 of the practice direction confirms that the signed statement may be sufficient proof of liability.

8. PAYMENT DEFERRED

As we have seen, Rule 44.8 requires an order for costs to be paid within 14 days. If a party funded under a conditional fee agreement (CFA) has an after-the-event costs indemnity insurance policy it will usually exclude paying interim costs awarded to the other side. Who then is to pay them – the solicitor, the client or who? Conditional fee agreements are so regarded as the panacea for the funding of litigation that the problem has caused much concern in high places. On 12 March 1999 the Vice-Chancellor wrote to all judges suggesting that if there is a conditional fee agreement the judge should consider staying any order for costs until the end of the action and also consider not requiring a payment on account if he orders a detailed assessment. This gave rise to the question why a party who chose a particular method of funding should be given preferential treatment over a party who is funding the litigation himself, perhaps by mortgaging his home, or by means of a bank overdraft or by selling investments at a loss? It is in any event wrong to assume that someone who has entered into a conditional fee agreement is impecunious, much commercial litigation is now financed in this way (see Chapter 42). It also raises the question why the receiving party should have to wait until the end of the litigation before receiving interim costs just because his adversary has chosen one method of funding in preference to another. Paragraph 33 of the *SCCO's Guide to the Summary Assessment of Costs* suggests:

> 33. As a general rule a paying party should be ordered to pay the amount of any summarily assessed costs within 14 days. Before making such an order the court should consider whether an order for payment of the costs might bring the action to an end and whether this would be just in all the circumstances.

9. SOLICITORS' HOURLY RATES

As I said in Chapter 22 on Time, the Lord Chancellor wishes to discourage solicitors charging an expense rate (the A factor) with an uplift for care and conduct (the B factor) in favour of a single charge-out rate which should normally be the same rate for between-the-parties costs as between solicitor and client. Certainly the indemnity principle precludes a solicitor from recovering a higher hourly rate between the parties than he has agreed with his client, but otherwise solicitors and clients may agree anything they like as regards charging rates. The SCCO *Guide to Summary Assessment of Costs* gives guideline hourly rates for solicitors which it emphasises are broad approximations only. The figures for each locality were arrived at through a framework of local co-ordinators based on civil trial centres set up by the Vice-Chancellor, the Senior Costs Judge and the Law Society to assist in the agreeing of local rates. The co-ordinators were, and continue to be, responsible for liaising with local law societies and district judges and thereafter with the designated civil judge for each trial centre to ensure consistency across the group. In an attempt to achieve consistency across the country the agreed rates have been reported by each designated civil judge to the Senior Costs Judge. The figures are not a scale but are merely a guide for the judiciary, which may be exceeded or varied locally at any time. They are not carved in stone. They also only apply to summary assessments although they will no doubt be the starting point for some detailed assessments. I consider them more fully in Chapter 22. The grades of fee earner have been agreed between representatives of the Supreme Court Costs Office, the Association of District Judges and the Law Society and were increased in June 2001 from three to four as follows:

(1) Solicitors with over eight years' post-qualification experience including at least eight years' litigation experience.
(2) Solicitors and legal executives with over four years' post-qualification experience including at least four years' litigation experience.
(3) Other solicitors and legal executives and fee earners of equivalent experience.
(4) Trainee solicitors, paralegals and other fee earners.

Note that the word 'partner' does not appear. The grades are based upon experience, not status. 'Legal executive' means a Fellow of the Institute of Legal Executives. Although fee earners of an equivalent experience may be entitled to similar rates it must be borne in mind that Fellows of the Institute of Legal Executives generally spend two years in a solicitor's office before passing their Part 1 general examinations, a further two years before passing the Part 2 specialist examinations and then complete a further two years in practice before being able to become fellows. They have therefore acquired considerable practical and academic experience. It is semantically unfortunate that lesser beings, although they are members of the Institute of Legal Executives, may not call themselves legal executives and must be described by some other name such as, fee earner, clerk or paralegal and treated as being in the bottom grade unless the court is satisfied they have the equivalent experience. The SCCO *Guide* adds:

> Many High Court cases justify fee earners at a senior level. However the same may not be true of attendance at pre-trial hearings with counsel. The task of sitting behind counsel should be delegated to a more junior fee earner in all but the most important pre-trial hearings. As with hourly rates the costs estimate supplied by the paying party may be of assistance. What grade of fee earner did they use?
>
> In some proceedings solicitors appear as advocates more frequently than they used to. It must be borne in mind that, especially in substantial hearings, it may be more economical if the advocacy is conducted by counsel rather

than a solicitor. In all cases the court should consider whether the decision whether or not to instruct counsel has led to an increase in costs and whether that increase is justifiable.

Here are the latest rates included in the *Guide* as at June 2001 (but check locally or on the SCCO website that the rates have not been increased).

GUIDELINE HOURLY RATES (CHARGING RATES) FOR SOLICITORS (JUNE 2001)

In the table which follows the date given alongside the locality is the date when the figures were notified to the SCCO.
In those cases marked 'SCCO' no figures have been received and figures have been inserted based on comparable areas.
'Prov' indicates that the consultation for that particular area is not yet complete.

Locality	**Grade of fee earner***			
	A	B	C	D
Midland Circuit				
Birmingham Inner 1.5.01	158	158	123	80
Birmingham Outer 1.5.01	131	131	103	73
Coventry, Rugby, Nuneaton and Stratford 1.5.01	145	135	114	80
Northampton SCCO	145	135	112	80
Nottingham City 1.6.01	150	140	110	84
Nottingham & Derbyshire 1.6.01	140	135	104	78
Leicester SCCO	130	124	96	74
Lincoln 5.6.01	140	135	104	78
Stafford, Stoke, Tamworth, Shrewsbury, Telford, Ludlow, Oswestry, Kidderminster 1.5.01	130	125	100	78
Worcester, Hereford, Evesham and Redditch 1.5.01	140	130	114	80
Northern Circuit				
Liverpool 1.4.01	160	150	130	100
Birkenhead SCCO 150	150	135	125	95
Leigh 1.4.01	160	150	130	100
St Helens 14.5.01	160	150	130	100
Southport SCCO	145	130	120	90
Wigan 1.4.01	160	150	130	100
Manchester Central 4.6.01	160	130	110	80
Manchester Outer/Oldham/ Salford 4.6.01	160	130	110	80
Stockport/Altrincham/ Tameside 4.6.01	160	130	103	80
Bolton & Bury 6.6.01	155	130	108.50	85
Preston, Lancaster, Blackpool, Chorley 17.5.01	140	130	125	85
Cumbria 17.5.01	150	140	125	81
North Eastern Circuit				
Newcastle – City Centre (within a 2 mile radius of St Nicholas Cathedral) 1.6.01	160	135	115	85

Locality	Grade of fee earner*			
Newcastle (other than City Centre) 1.6.01	150	120	105	80
Teesside 25.5.01	150	120	105	80
Leeds 1.6.01	140	140	120	90
Bradford (Dewsbury, Halifax & Huddersfield) 25.5.01	140	125	110	80
Bradford (Keighley & Skipton) 25.5.01	140	125	110	80
Sheffield SCCO	140	125	105	75
Hull 18.4.01	140–150	130	120–130	80–90
Grimsby 18.4.01	140	135	100	78
Wales & Chester Circuit				
Chester & North Wales 16.5.01	130–155	110–140	110–120	70–90
Cardiff (Inner) 11.5.01	155	145	120	85
Swansea – South & West Wales, Cardiff (Outer) 11.5.01	135	125	115	80
South Eastern Circuit (London)				
City of London ** PROV	325	235	180	110
Central London PROV	250	190	155	100
Outer London *** PROV	180–210	135–180	130	95
South Eastern Circuit (Provincial)				
Oxford (Inner/Outer) 1.6.01	155	135	120	85
Lewes 1.6.01	160	140–150	130	85
Kingston/Guildford/Reigate/ Epsom 19.6.01	160	140	125	85
Luton, Milton Keynes, Aylesbury, Bedford, St Albans, Hitchin, Hertford 1.4.01	140	120	110	85
Watford 1.6.01	150	140	115	90
Chelmsford North, Cambridge 1.6.01	160	145	125	90
Cambridge City Centre 1.6.01	165	150	130	95
Norwich 21.11.00	130	105	70	
Chelmsford South 27.4.01	150	135	115	90
Croydon 26.3.01	170	150	130	90
Canterbury, Dartford, Gravesend, Maidstone & Medway SCCO	150	140	125	85
Western Circuit				
Devon, Cornwall & Exeter 27.7.01	145	125	100	80
Bristol, Bath, Weston, Cheltenham, Gloucester and Trowbridge 1.5.01	155	145	125	80
Taunton and Yeovil 1.5.01	145	125	100	80
Swindon 1.5.01	140	125	110	80
Hampshire, Dorset, Wiltshire, Isle of Wight 23.7.01	150	120	100	80

* There are four grades of fee earner:

A. Solicitors with over 8 years post qualification experience including at least 8 years litigation experience.

B. Solicitors and legal executives with over 4 years post qualification experience including at least 4 years litigation experience.

C. Other solicitors and legal executives and fee earners of equivalent experience.

D. Trainee Solicitors, para legals and fee earners of equivalent experience.

Note: 'legal executive' means a Fellow of the Institute of Legal Executives.

** Although a guideline figure is given for the top grade of fee earner in the City of

London, it is recognised that in certain complex, major commercial litigation the appropriate rate may exceed the guideline by a significant margin.

*** The wide range of rates given for the upper grades of fee earner in Outer London accommodates the fact that many sole practitioners and small partnerships practise in the area as well as very large firms. This factor must be taken into account in deciding what rate of charge to allow.

The Statement of Costs Form footnote states that routine communications should be charged at one-tenth of the fee earner's hourly rate, which is of course a six-minute unit. This should cover reading an incoming letter as well as writing the reply and routine telephone calls. Any exchange of letters or telephone call taking longer than six minutes should be timed and charged accordingly.

10. ADVOCACY FEES

(a) Solicitors

The SCCO *Guide* provides:

Solicitor Advocates

40. Remuneration of solicitor advocates is based on the normal principles for remuneration of solicitors. It is not therefore appropriate to seek a brief fee and refreshers as if the advocate were a member of the Bar. If the cost of using a solicitor advocate is more than the cost of instructing counsel, the higher cost is unlikely to be recovered. The figures properly recoverable by solicitor advocates should reflect the amount of preparation undertaken, the time spent in court and the weight and gravity of the case.

41. Where the solicitor advocate is also the solicitor who does the preparation work, the solicitor is entitled to charge normal solicitors' rates for that preparation, but once the solicitor advocate starts preparation for the hearing itself the fees recoverable should not exceed those which would be recoverable in respect of counsel.

42. It is clearly wrong for the fees of a solicitor acting as a junior counsel to exceed the fee appropriate for the leading counsel.

(b) Counsel

The SCCO *Guide* quotes from the judgment of Mr Justice Pennycuick in *Simpsons Motor Sales (London) Ltd v Hendon Corpn* [1965] 1 WLR 112:

> 'a proper measure for counsel's fees is to estimate what fee a hypothetical counsel, capable of conducting the case effectively, but unable or unwilling to insist on the higher fees sometimes demanded by counsel of pre-eminent reputation, would be content to take on the brief: but there is no precise standard of measurement and the judge must, using his or her knowledge and experience, determine the proper figure'.

The *Guide* now provides the following table of figures based upon Supreme Court Costs Office statistics dealing with run-of-the-mill proceedings in the Queen's Bench and Chancery Division and in the Administrative Court. The table gives figures for cases lasting up to an hour and up to half a day, in respect of counsel up to five years call, up to ten years call and over ten years call. It is emphasised that these figures are not recommended rates but it is hoped that they may provide a helpful starting point for judges when assessing counsel's fees. The appropriate fee in any particular case may be more or less than the figures appearing in the table, depending upon the circumstances.

The table does not include any figures in respect of leading counsel's fees since such cases would self evidently be exceptional. Similarly, no figures are included for the Commercial Court or the Technology & Construction Court.

TABLE OF COUNSEL'S FEES

Queen's Bench	**1 hour hearing**	**1/2 day hearing**
Junior up to 5 years call	£220	£385
Junior 5–10 years call	£330	£655
Junior 10+ years call	£500	£1000
Chancery Division	**1 hour hearing**	**1/2 day hearing**
Junior up to 5 years call	£250	£475
Junior 5–10 years call	£425	£800
Junior 10+ years call	£650	£1200
Administrative Court	**1 hour hearing**	**1/2 day hearing**
Junior up to 5 years call	£325	£500
Junior 5–10 years call	£600	£1000
Junior 10+ years call	£850	£1500

If the paying parties were represented by counsel, the fee paid to their counsel is an important factor but not a conclusive one on the question of fees payable to the receiving party's counsel.

In deciding upon the appropriate fee for counsel, the question is not simply one of counsel's experience and seniority but also of the level of counsel which the particular case merits.

Counsel's fees should not be allowed in cases in which it was not reasonable to have instructed counsel, but it must be borne in mind that, especially in substantial hearings, it may be more economical if the advocacy is conducted by counsel rather than a solicitor. In all cases, the court should consider whether the decision whether or not to instruct counsel has led to an increase in costs and whether that increase is justifiable.

It has not yet been possible to publish more specific guideline figures because of the lack of sufficient data. These figures are averages based upon SCCO statistics and figures supplied by the Bar.

11. PAYMENT ON ACCOUNT

CPR Rule 44.3(8) (on p 91) contains the important provision that if the trial judge does order a detailed assessment he may order a payment on account. The attraction of a detailed assessment to a paying party is the delay before he has to part with his money. An order for an interim payment removes that attraction. Statements of costs will be available to help the judge order a realistic amount. A robust example of this was in *Mars UK Ltd v Teknowledge Ltd (No 2)* [1999] 2 Costs LR 44, ChD. It is a judgment of Mr Justice Jacob, who with Mr Justice Laddie pioneered summary assessment of costs for some years before their introduction in the Civil Procedure Rules. He confirmed that in general an interim order for costs on account should be made. However, in exercising its discretion the court had to take into account all the circumstances, one of which might be an unsuccessful party's wish to appeal; other considerations were the relative financial position of each party and the court's overriding objective to deal with cases justly. Jacob J ordered the defendants to make an interim payment of £80,000 but he allowed the money to be paid in instalments of £30,000 within the first month and five monthly sums of £10,000 each thereafter so as not to preclude the defendants from being able to afford an appeal against his decision. In estimating the amount at which the costs might eventually be assessed the court took into account the claimant's pre-action heavy-handedness and misconduct during the proceedings as a result of which the judge thought it unlikely that on a detailed assessment the claimant would recover more than 40% of their solicitor and client costs.

12. CONDUCTING THE ASSESSMENT

Solicitors and counsel should be aware that the summary assessment of costs at the end of the hearing will be dealt with by the advocate who conducted the hearing. If counsel has been briefed, counsel will have to either justify his client's statement of costs if he succeeds or to attack the other side's statement if he loses. When I spoke to young barristers on behalf of the Bar Council I told them they must become costs experts. Solicitors might forgive them for losing a case, but they will never forgive them for making a mess of the costs! I advise solicitors that counsel must be fully briefed on how to justify their own statement of costs or attack that of the other side depending on the outcome. It is, for example, helpful to have available a detailed breakdown of how the figures in the statement of costs were arrived at. The absence of the solicitor's file can also cause difficulty if a query arises as to the number, length or content of documents.

13. DUPLICATION

On the summary assessment of costs of an interim hearing, the bill will inevitably include a claim for work which often has a dual purpose, being both costs of the application and costs in the main action. If a judge disallows an element of the claim he should give his reasons for doing so. He should distinguish between disallowing costs because the work was not done or was unreasonable or disproportionate and between disallowances of costs of the main action: *Sterling Publications v Burroughs* [2001] 2 Costs LR 155, QB.

14. BENCHMARK COSTS

The name is new, the concept is not. For example, prior to 26 April 1999, many courts had a going rate for possession summonses which was the amount awarded by judges and accepted, usually without demur, by practitioners. In his Final Report, Lord Woolf said:

> 'there are, however, some multi-track proceedings in which further steps could be taken to assist the parties and the courts. These are proceedings which have a limited and fairly constant procedure. Here the court with the assistance of user groups and the information available to them (the SCCO), should over time be able to produce figures indicating a standard of guideline costs or a range of costs for a class of proceedings. An obvious candidate for this approach will be cases which did not substantially turn on issues of fact … judicial review is … a possible example. The steps taken in the majority of cases are standard'.

Although Lord Woolf there referred to multi-track, the same approach can be applied to the fast track pending the introduction of fixed costs, which are themselves a form of benchmark costs. The object of benchmark costs is to set a figure, or perhaps a bracket of figures, for the amount of costs normally awarded for particular kinds of cases or applications. This is the amount the receiving party may accept without further investigation or assessment, or which the receiving party may seek to have increased by summary or detailed assessment if he can justify it, or which the paying party could seek to have reduced. Some of the advantages of benchmark costs are the avoidance of the necessity of preparing a written statement of costs, the avoidance of summary assessments and getting away from a system of payment by reward based on the length of time spent rather than the skill and expertise with which the work was done. Provided that benchmark costs are a guide and are not simply fixed costs in Woolf's clothing, are of realistic amounts and revised regularly, then they are to be welcomed. They are a halfway-house between summary assessment and fixed costs. The introduction of pre-trial fixed costs on the fast track, on which the Woolf reforms were based, was postponed until there was sufficient fast track experience to enable them to be formulated. Benchmark costs may apply to a particular type of hearing, such as a routine interim application, or to a particular type of action, such as possession proceedings or a road traffic accident action. In exceptional circumstances, either party may apply for the benchmark costs to be increased or reduced, but by and large they will be accepted, avoiding the need for a summary assessment. Benchmark costs also emphasise that the assessment of between-the-parties costs involves applying the objective test of what is reasonable and proportionate, irrespective of what work the solicitors in fact did. The SCCO has prepared a preliminary paper on benchmark costs indicating various Queen's Bench Division and insolvency applications and proceedings which might be susceptible of benchmarking. The Family Division is also undertaking consultation. It is not of course necessary to await guidance from on high for any court, after consultation, to promulgate its own benchmark costs in respect of particular types of hearings or applications.

(a) Report

In his Report on Benchmark Costs to the Master of the Rolls, the Senior Costs Judge set out the following conclusions:

(a) Benchmarks should be limited to those proceedings having a limited and fairly constant procedure.
(b) An award of benchmark costs should be a form of summary assessment. The court should retain its discretion as to what (if any) costs to allow and whether to award benchmark costs.
(c) It is important that the benchmark figures should be at the correct level to avoid constant applicants to escape from the benchmark figure.
(d) There should be adequate consultation prior to implementation.
(e) Setting accurate benchmarks requires a substantial system of data collection.
(f) There should be differential benchmark figures for different levels of fee earner.
(g) The benchmark figures should be fixed by reference to the type of hearing rather than the length of hearing.
(h) Benchmark costs should be available in cases where an order for costs in the case is made. Similarly, there is nothing to stop the court ordering benchmark costs against a LSC-funded client.
(i) Benchmark costs should not be used as a means of driving down remuneration.
(j) Benchmark costs are intended to supplement summary assessment rather than impede or restrict it.

(b) List of proceedings

Accompanying the draft Report is a Proposed List of 20 proceedings, which have been identified as suitable for benchmarking. They are:

NON-FAMILY PROCEEDINGS

Benchmark	**Court of Appeal Civil Division**
1	Appeals on quantum
2	Simple applications for security for costs
3	Applications by solicitors to come off the record
	High Court Judge/Circuit Judge
4	Simple appeals from Masters/District Judges
	Masters/District Judges
5	Applications for an extension of time
6	Applications by solicitors to some off the record
7	Simple applications for security for costs
8	Simple applications without notice
	Bankruptcy Registrars/District Judges
9	Applications for substituted service of bankruptcy petitions
10	Bankruptcy hearings adjourned to another appointment
11	Dismissal of bankruptcy petition with costs payable by the debtor
	Costs Judges and District Judges
12	Applications to set aside default costs certificates
13	Part 8 applications under Part III of the Solicitors Act 1974
14	Detailed assessment proceedings between parties

FAMILY PROCEEDINGS

Benchmark	**Circuit Judge/District Judge**
15	Contact cases listed for up to one hour
16	Applications to commit for breach of orders
17	Applications for maintenance pending suit
18	Applications by solicitors to come off the record
19	Applications for extension of time
	Cost Judges and District Judges
20	Detailed assessment proceedings between parties

(c) The bands

The original proposal was for placing different localities into five bands including London. Having considered the guideline rates, bearing in mind the apparent inconsistencies between localities of similar type, the proposal now is that there should be four bands covering the whole country except London, with a further three bands for the City of London, Central London and Outer London. It is suggested that it would be preferable to publish a limited number of bands specifying rates for each grade of fee earner in each band and proposing which locality belongs where. The Designated Civil Judges could then be asked whether these proposals were acceptable, and if not, what adjustment was necessary. This exercise might make it easier for each Designated Civil Judge to approve rates having regard to the rates proposed by other Designated Judges for comparable locations in other areas.

(d) The prospects

There has been so much slippage of time and opposition both in principle and detail that the prospect of benchmarks has receded. The impetus is now with fixed or predictable costs which I consider at the end of this chapter.

15. NO TARIFF

Pending the introduction of benchmark costs, the court must be careful not to use summary assessment as a 'vehicle for the introduction of a scale of judicial tariffs for different categories of case'. In *1-800 Flowers Inc v Phonenames Ltd* [2001] EWCA Civ 721, [2001] 2 Costs LR 286, the Court of Appeal said it was of the essence of a summary assessment of costs that the court should focus on the detailed break-down of costs actually incurred by the party in question as shown in its statement of costs; and that is should carry out the assessment by reference to the items appearing in that statement. In so doing the court might find it helpful to draw to a greater or lesser extent on its own experience of summary assessment of costs in what it considered to be comparable cases. Equally, having dealt with the costs by reference to the detailed items in the statement of costs which was before it, the court might find it helpful to look at the total sum at which it had arrived in order to see whether that sum fell within the bounds of what it considered reasonable and proportionate. If the court considered the total sum to be unreasonable or disproportionate, it might wish to look again at the various detailed items in order to see what further reductions should be made. Such an approach was wholly unobjectionable. However, the judge in this case did not appear to have focused at all on the detailed items in the opponent's statement of costs. Rather, having concluded that the total of the detailed items was unreasonably high he then proceeded to apply his own tariff, which appeared to have been derived primarily from a case in which the opponent had not been involved and about which it and its advisers knew nothing. However general the approach which the court chose to adopt when assessing costs summarily, and however broad the brush which the court chose to use, the assessment must be directed to and focused upon the detailed breakdown of costs contained in the receiving party's statement of a costs.

16. COURT OF APPEAL

The SCCO *Guide* describes the regime as follows:

GUIDE TO THE SUMMARY ASSESSMENT OF COSTS IN THE COURT OF APPEAL

48. The Practice Direction supplementing CPR Part 52 identifies five types of hearing at which costs are likely to be assessed by way of summary assessment and states that parties attending any of those hearings should be prepared to deal with the summary assessment. The Costs Practice Direction (Section 13 paragraph 13.5) places a duty on the parties and their legal representatives to file and serve a statement of any costs they intend to claim in respect of such hearings.

49. In this Guide the term 'counsel' includes a solicitor-advocate who is instructed by another solicitor.

(1) Contested Directions Hearings (2) Applications for Permission to Appeal at which the Respondent is Present and (4) Appeals from Case Management Decisions

50. The guidance given below in relation to contested directions hearings, applications for permission to appeal at which the respondent is present and appeals from case management decisions relates to hearings which, although important, are not difficult or complex and are not of general public

importance and are listed either for a hearing not exceeding one hour or for a hearing not exceeding one half day.
51. If these hearings are attended by solicitor and counsel the number of hours which it is reasonable to presume that the solicitor will undertake (in respect of preparation, attendance, travel in Central London and waiting) is 4 hours for a one hour appointment and 7.5 hours for a half day appointment. It is reasonable to presume that counsel who has between 5 and 10 years' experience merits a fee of approximately £500 (exclusive of VAT) for a one hour appointment and merits a fee of approximately £800 (exclusive of VAT) for a half day appointment.
52. If these hearings were attended by a solicitor without counsel it is reasonable to presume that the total number of hours the solicitor will spend (in respect of preparation, attendance, travel in Central London and waiting) is 5 hours for a one hour appointment and 10 hours for a half day appointment.
53. If these hearings are attended by a litigant in person it is reasonable to presume that the total number of hours the litigant in person will spend (in respect of preparation, attendance and waiting) is 9 hours for a one hour appointment and 14 hours for a half day appointment. In each case a further allowance should be made for time and expense in travelling to the appointment.

(3) Dismissal List Hearings at which the Respondent is Present

54. The guidance given below in relation to dismissal list hearings in the Court of Appeal at which the respondent is present, relates to cases which are listed for less than one hour and are of significantly less weight than the contested directions hearings, applications for permission to appeal and appeals from case management decisions described above.
55. If the hearing is attended by solicitor and counsel (for the appellant or the respondent), it is reasonable to presume that the total number of hours to allow the solicitor (in respect of preparation, attendance, travel in Central London and waiting) is 2 hours, and it is reasonable to presume that counsel who has between 5 and 10 years' experience merits a fee of approximately £350 (exclusive of VAT).
56. If an appeal is dismissed and costs are awarded to the respondent, it will probably be appropriate to allow further costs in respect of work previously done in responding to the appeal. Consideration should be given to whether it is in fact appropriate to carry out a summary assessment, depending on the amount of work done by the respondent.
57. Subject to paragraph 56 if the hearing is attended by a solicitor without counsel it is reasonable to presume that the total number of hours to allow the solicitor (in respect of preparation, attendance, travel in Central London and waiting) is 3 hours.
58. Subject to paragraph 56, if the hearing is attended by a litigant in person it is reasonable to presume that the total number of hours to allow the litigant in person (in respect of preparation, attendance and waiting) is 6 hours with a further allowance for time and expense in travelling to the appointment.

(5) Appeals Listed for One Day or Less

59. Appeals listed for one day or less vary enormously as to weight, complexity and importance. Thus, it is not at present possible to give guidance as to the number of hours reasonably spent by solicitors (in respect of preparation, attendances, travel and waiting) in such appeals. However, after research and consultation, it may be possible in future to give such guidance in relation to particular types of general and specialist appeals. Pending such research and consultation, the only guidance which can be given is as follows.

(1) It may not be appropriate to carry out a summary assessment if a case lasts more than half a day or involves leading counsel since in those circumstances the case is likely to be complex and weighty. It will often be unwise for the court summarily to assess costs in a matter which is not simple and straightforward, unless the difference between the parties is comparatively small, or unless the correct allowance appears clear.

(2) The reasonable fees of counsel are likely to exceed the reasonable fees of the solicitor.

(3) The fact that the same counsel appeared in the lower court does not greatly reduce the reasonable fee unless, for example, the lower court dealt with a great many more issues than are raised on the appeal. It is reasonable for counsel to spend as much time preparing issues for the Court of Appeal hearing as he spent preparing those issues for the lower court hearing.

(4) If the case merits leading counsel it may merit also the instruction of a junior to assist him. The junior's fees should be allowed at one half of the leader's fees unless:
   (a) the junior is a senior junior and the case merited both a leader and a senior junior.
   (b) The junior took a responsibility which was equal to or larger than that taken by the leader.
   (c) The junior undertook work not covered by the brief.

(5) In many cases the largest element in the solicitors' reasonable fees for work in the Court of Appeal concerns instructing counsel and preparing the appeal bundles. Time spent by the solicitor in the development of legal submissions will only be allowed where it does not duplicate work done by counsel and is claimed at a rate the same or lower than the rate counsel would have claimed.

(6) Although the solicitor may have spent many hours with the client, the client should have been warned that little of this time is recoverable against a losing party. Reasonable time spent receiving instructions and reporting events should not greatly exceed the time spent on attending the opponents.

(7) Given that the case will be presented by a barrister or a solicitor advocate there is usually no reason for any other solicitor to spend many hours perusing papers. A large claim for such perusal probably indicates that a new fee earner was reading in. Reading in fees are not normally recoverable from an opponent.

(8) Although it is usually reasonable to have a senior fee earner sitting with counsel in the Court of Appeal, it is not usually reasonable to have two fee earners. The second fee earner may be there for training purposes only.

(9) In most appeals it will be appropriate to make an allowance for copy documents. The allowance for copying which is included in the solicitor's hourly rates will have already been used up or exceeded in the lower court. An hourly rate charge is appropriate for selecting and collating documents and dictating the indices. If the paperwork is voluminous much of this should be delegated to a trainee. Note that:
   (a) For the copying itself, a fair allowance is 10p per page, i.e. £100 per 1,000 sheets. This includes an allowance for checking the accuracy of the copying.
   (b) Time spent standing at the photocopier and time spent taking the papers to a local photocopy shop is not recoverable. Such work is not fee earner work; it is secretarial.

(10) It must be borne in mind that skeleton arguments will have been lodged at an early stage, and, in respect of floating appeals, the case may have come into and out of the list. In those circumstances it may be necessary to change counsel which would inevitably increase the costs. New

counsel may decide to submit a different skeleton argument. Where this has occurred, detailed assessment is to be preferred.

Solicitors Charges

60. Although many appointments in the Court of Appeal merit the attendance of a senior fee earner familiar with the case, the most minor appointments may not. For example, on an application in the dismissal list in a case tried in Newcastle, if counsel who was briefed for the trial attends it may be unreasonable for a solicitor familiar with the case to travel from Newcastle to attend also. In order to arrive at a notional figure to represent the instruction of and costs of an agent, it may be appropriate to disallow most of the travel time and travelling expenses claimed by the solicitor.

61. The Court of Appeal has stated that it is the duty of litigators (particularly unions and insurers) to keep down the cost of litigation. This means that if they instruct London solicitors who charge London rates for a case which has no obvious connection with London and which does not require expertise only to be found there, they will, even if successful, recover less than the solicitors have charged (see *Wraith v Sheffield Forgemasters Ltd* [1998] 1 WLR 132 CA).

62. In relation to the first four types of hearing appropriate for summary assessment in the Court of Appeal, some guidance is given above suggesting the number of hours which may be reasonable for the solicitor to spend. That guidance should be used as a starting point only. The court should also have regard to the number of hours actually claimed.

Counsel's Fees in the Court of Appeal

63. Counsel's fees depend upon the seniority of counsel which it was reasonable to instruct and the market price for the item of work in question. It is not appropriate to specify an hourly rate for counsel and to remunerate them at a multiple of that rate according to the number of hours reasonably spent. Such an approach would reward the indolent and penalise the expeditious.

64. In previous paragraphs (paragraphs 51 and 55), figures were suggested for brief fees for counsel who has between 5 and 10 years' experience. For less experienced counsel it may be appropriate to reduce these figures; for more experienced counsel it may be appropriate to increase these figures. The guideline figures are a starting point only and the Court has the discretion to allow fees appropriate to the particular circumstances of the appeal.

Costs Awarded to Litigants in Person

65. The starting point for most litigants in person is £9.25 per hour reasonably spent. The number of hours reasonably spent by a litigant in person will almost invariably exceed the number of hours which would have been reasonably spent by a solicitor.

66. It is open to a litigant in person to prove a financial loss greater than the starting point amount. That loss may be in respect of a period greater than the time reasonably spent by the litigant. For example, attendance at a one hour hearing may necessitate the litigant taking two days unpaid leave from his employment.

67. In all cases there is an absolute cap on the amount recoverable by a litigant in person, namely the reasonable costs of disbursements plus two thirds of the amount which would have been allowed if the litigant in person had been legally represented (rule 48.6(2)).

Conditional Fee Agreements with Success Fees

68. Although not common for appellants to enter into such agreements, it is common for respondents (the successful party at first instance) whose claim or defence was conducted under a conditional fee agreement: such agreements usually also cover appeals brought by the opponent.
69. Attention is drawn to paragraph 3 of this Guide dealing with summary assessment of an additional liability at the conclusion of proceedings.
70. Paragraphs 24 and 25 set out the factors to be taken into account when deciding whether a percentage increase is reasonable.

17. APPEALS AGAINST SUMMARY ASSESSMENT

See Chapter 29.

18. THE END OF SUMMARY ASSESSMENTS?

(a) ALCD

The Council of the Association of Law Costs Draftsmen recommends that the summary assessment procedures should be withdrawn, subject to the right of any party at the conclusion of an interim application to seek summary assessment of the costs relating to that application and the right of the court in straightforward cases to summarily assess costs. Their proposal is based on the 'enormous' variations arising from some summary assessments: assessments appearing to have been carried out arbitrarily; the procedure increasing rather than reducing costs; preparation of statements of costs resulting in unnecessary work for solicitors; solicitors being ill-able to afford to release papers for the preparation of a statement of costs at a time when they are preparing for a hearing; there being often insufficient time for a summary assessment to be carried out satisfactorily and there being a variety of exceptions to the requirement for summary assessment. The proposal is in conjunction with the Association's proposal for revised procedures for detailed assessment, based on two pilot schemes, one for lower-value claims where the profit costs do not exceed £10,000 and there is no disputed fact, and the second applying to assessments where the profit costs exceed £10,000. It is claimed that the proposed procedures would be fairer and more workable than the present summary assessment, judicial time would be reduced and the courts freed for more essential business at the end of a trial. The receiving party would be able to produce a claim for costs that is better explained than the existing model form used for summary assessment, while the paying party would be provided with more detail of the claim and better able to identify what costs claimed or items of costs claimed may reasonably be challenged. The court would be afforded cogent written reasons summarising the disputes to assist it in its requirement that the parties be proactive before any assessment in trying to resolve disputes and limiting the issues to be determined by the court. In particular, dispute resolution and mediation should be considered in appropriate cases.

(b) Litigation funding

Here are my views as expressed in an article in the Law Society's publication, *Litigation Funding*:

It is a truth universally acknowledged that the costs provisions are the least successful part of the Civil Procedure Rules, and that the least successful part of the costs provisions is summary assessment. That is because summary assessment has imposed on the judiciary a function that Lord Woolf never intended it to perform. The linchpin of Lord Woolf's proposals was a fast track with fixed costs. We have the fast track, but not the fixed costs, except for the trial itself. As a result, at the end of an exhausting fast track hearing there is often the pantomime of two barristers addressing a former barrister (the trial judge), who has had a one-hour JSB crash course on costs, on matters of which none of them has any practical experience, in circumstances where even the most experienced costs judge or costs draftsman would flounder. There is a one-page statement (why do people persist in calling it a 'schedule'?) of costs containing no information other than the time spent on various activities and the amount claimed. It has usually been prepared by someone who is not present in court, and relates to a file of papers which is also conspicuous by its absence. The judge has to choose between two sets of figures apparently plucked from the air, or arrive at his own by the same route. Because the whole exercise is based on hourly rates, without any enhancement for care, skill and attention as previously, we now have a painful plodder's charter with the rewards going to the slowest, least able and most imaginative. Is it any wonder that instead of costs being controlled and certain, as was envisaged for the fast track, costs for both interim and final hearings have spiralled out of all recognition? Instead of certainty we have a lottery. The answer is simple and not as Draconian as may at first sight appear: abolish summary assessments. There are no summary assessments on the small claims track because only exceptionally are between-the-parties costs awarded. It is unusual for costs to be summarily assessed after a multi-track trial, which usually lasts for more than one day, and are sent for detailed assessment. There is no summary assessment of the costs of a fast track trial, which are fixed. There is no summary assessment of additional liabilities after an interim hearing and after a final hearing the judge has the option of sending additional liabilities, together with the basic costs, for detailed assessment. Accordingly, there is no necessity for a summary assessment where the receiving party is funded under a CFA with recoverable additional liabilities. This leaves pre-trial costs on the fast track and the costs of interim hearings. Even here there are many exceptions to the requirement for a summary assessment, these include: orders for 'costs in the case'; where there is insufficient time; where there are arguments about the law, the calculations or the retainer; mortgagee's costs; where the receiving party is state funded, a child or a patient and, of course, where the costs are agreed. As for the remainder, fixed or predictable pre-trial costs for all fast track actions should be introduced as a matter of urgency, with provision for an additional prescribed amount for the costs of any interim application necessitated by the unreasonable conduct of one of the parties. All multi-track trial costs should go for detailed assessment, with benchmark costs for interim hearings. The introduction of fixed pre-trial costs on the fast track was delayed to enable the government to monitor fast track proceedings and collect and collate data. It is unfortunate that this was not done. There are many forms and models of fixed or predictable costs and these are under active consideration by the Civil Justice Council in the following circumstances.

When it became increasingly clear that problems in relation to costs were impeding the access to justice, spawning what the Master of the Rolls described as a cottage industry of costs, the Civil Justice Council held a Costs Forum in November 2001 which included representatives of the litigation and insurance industries. As well as supporting the abolition of the indemnity principle the Forum recommended the Council should initiate further work to try to make costs more certain, controlled and transparent, particularly on the fast track, using the description 'predictable' rather than 'fixed'.

As a result, a Civil Justice Council's Predictable Costs Working Party was set up which held its first meeting in June 2002, when everyone concerned with litigation costs was either present or represented. It is know as the 'Big Tent'. I do not know the derivation of the name Big Tent – 'Marquee' might sound less like a circus, or taking a cue from Afghanistan, *Loya Jirga*, which I am informed means a meeting of tribal chieftains.

The meeting underwent a surprising sea-change when it transpired that the majority of those attending were not much concerned about pre-trial costs or even the recoverability of CFA success fees and ATE premiums, but about pre-issue costs, which constitute 95% of between-the-parties costs.

One idea which found some favour was based on the old Family Division practice of the petitioner being able to opt for either the prescribed fixed costs of a petition, or for the costs to be taxed. Most opted for the immediacy of fixed costs until they were overtaken by inflation because the fixed costs were not adequately updated. This idea led to considerable discussion in the Big Tent about schemes for 'opting in' and 'opting out'.

There was also talk about a system of basic costs with add-ons for factors such as the subject matter of the litigation, whether or not liability was admitted, the amount involved and, in respect of post-issue costs, the stage the proceedings had reached. I had the feeling that if we had talked for long enough we might have come up with the concept of hourly rates with a mark-up to reflect the variables (to be known as the 'A' and 'B' factors) or a list of the amounts to be awarded taking into account all of these matters, which could be called a 'scale' of costs. We should then have re-invented the wheel!

It is hoped that another Costs Forum in December 2002 will result in recommendations being put to the Lord Chancellor and the Rules Committee.

CHAPTER 30

DETAILED ASSESSMENT

CPR Rule 44.7 (see p 107) provides that the amount of any costs ordered to be paid by one party to another shall be ascertained either by summary assessment by the judge at the end of a hearing (Chapter 29) or by a costs officer by a detailed assessment. The provisions for detailed assessment are contained in CPR Part 47.

CPR PART 47

SECTION I GENERAL RULES ABOUT DETAILED ASSESSMENT

CPR RULE 47.1 TIME WHEN DETAILED ASSESSMENT MAY BE CARRIED OUT

The general rule is that the costs of any proceedings or any part of the proceedings are not to be assessed by the detailed procedure until the conclusion of the proceedings but the court may order them to be assessed immediately.

(The costs practice direction gives further guidance about when proceedings are concluded for the purpose of this rule)

SECTION 28: PRACTICE DIRECTION SUPPLEMENTING CPR RULE 47.1

28.1

(1) For the purposes of rule 47.1, proceedings are concluded when the court has finally determined the matters in issue in the claim, whether or not there is an appeal.

(2) For the purposes of this rule, the making of an award of provisional damages under Part 41 will be treated as a final determination of the matters in issue.

(3) The court may order or the parties may agree in writing that, although the proceedings are continuing, they will nevertheless be treated as concluded.

(4)

(a) A party who is served with a notice of commencement (see paragraph 32.3 below) may apply to a costs judge or a district judge to determine whether the party who served it is entitled to commence detailed assessment proceedings.

(b) On hearing such an application the orders which the court may make include: an order allowing the detailed assessment proceedings to continue, or an order setting aside the notice of commencement.

(5) A costs judge or a district judge may make an order allowing detailed assessment proceedings to be commenced where there is no realistic prospect of the claim continuing.

The purpose of this rule in the past was to ensure that all costs were assessed by the same person at the same time, but its usefulness and importance were eroded by the introduction of summary assessments at the end of interim hearings which have lasted not more than one day. The rule does, however, exclude detailed assessments of interim orders for costs in any event, unless the judge making the order has been persuaded to order an immediate detailed assessment. Paragraph 28.1(5) contains the useful provision that where there has been an order for a detailed assessment of interim costs, presumably against the claimant, and there is no prospect of the claim continuing, a costs judge or district judge may authorise the commencement of detailed assessment proceedings.

CPR RULE 47.2 NO STAY OF DETAILED ASSESSMENT WHERE THERE IS AN APPEAL

Detailed assessment is not stayed pending an appeal unless the court so orders.

SECTION 29: PRACTICE DIRECTION SUPPLEMENTING CPR RULE 47.2

29.1

(1) Rule 47.2 provides that detailed assessment is not stayed pending an appeal unless the court so orders.

(2) An application to stay the detailed assessment of costs pending an appeal may be made to the court whose order is being appealed or to the court who will hear the appeal.

How refreshing to find a rule which means what it says and says what it means. Previously there was a widespread misapprehension that an appeal acted as a stay in respect of orders for costs.

CPR RULE 47.3 POWERS OF AN AUTHORISED COURT OFFICER

(1) An authorised court officer has all the powers of the court when making a detailed assessment, except—

- (a) power to make a wasted costs order as defined in rule 48.7;
- (b) power to make an order under—
  - (i) rule 44.14 (powers in relation to misconduct)
  - (ii) rule 47.8 (sanction for delay in commencing detailed assessment proceedings);
  - (iii) paragraph (2) (objection to detailed assessment by authorised court officer); and
- (c) power to make a detailed assessment of costs payable to a solicitor by his client, unless the costs are being assessed under rule 48.5 (costs where money is payable to a child or patient).

(2) Where a party objects to the detailed assessment of costs being made by an authorised court officer, the court may order it to be made by a costs judge or a district judge.

(The costs practice direction sets out the relevant procedure)

SECTION 30: PRACTICE DIRECTION SUPPLEMENTING CPR RULE 47.3

30.1

(1) The court officers authorised by the Lord Chancellor to assess costs in the Supreme Court Costs Office and the Principal Registry of the Family Division are authorised to deal with claims for costs not exceeding £30,000 (excluding VAT) in the case of senior executive officers, or their equivalent and £75,000 (excluding VAT) in the case of principal officers.

(2) In calculating whether or not a bill of costs is within the authorised amounts, the figure to be taken into account is the total claim for costs including any additional liability.

(3) Where the receiving party, paying party and any other party to the detailed assessment proceedings who has served points of dispute are agreed that the assessment should not be made by an authorised court officer, the receiving party should so inform the court when requesting a hearing date. The court will then list the hearing before a costs judge or a district judge.

(4) In any other case a party who objects to the assessment being made by an authorised court officer must make an application to the costs judge or district judge under Part 23 (General Rules about Applications for Court Orders) setting out the reasons for the objection and if sufficient reason is shown the court will direct that the bill be assessed by a costs judge or district judge.

An authorised court officer is defined in CPR Rule 43.2(1)(*d*) as any officer of (i) a county court; (ii) a district registry; (iii) the Principal Registry of the Family Division; or (iv) the Supreme Court Costs Office whom the Lord Chancellor has authorised to assess costs. When Lord Hailsham, as Lord Chancellor, sought to introduce a similar provision in the 1986 Rules, there was rioting in the streets and the solicitor and barrister members of the Supreme Court Rules Committee refused to sign the new Order 62. The objection was that the assessment of costs is a judicial function not an administrative act and that officers of district registries and county courts are not lawyers, most have never worked in a solicitor's office and are equipped neither by training nor experience to exercise judicial discretion. A twelfth-hour compromise resulted in RSC Rule 19.4(*b*) providing that authorisation was limited to principal or senior executives of (i) the Supreme Court [*Costs*] Office, or a principal or a senior executive of (ii) a district registry who had previously served in either of such capacities for at least two years in the Supreme Court [*Costs*] Office or in one of the Birmingham, Bristol, Cardiff, Leeds, Liverpool or Manchester District Registries. The CPR contain no such provision but following the Lord Chancellor's assurance that he would follow the previous criteria, para 30.1 of the practice provides that the only authorised court officers are to be found in the SCCO and in the Principal Registry of the Family Division with financial limits on their jurisdiction. A further safeguard is that the parties may agree that the detailed assessment should not be dealt with by an authorised costs officer; if one party only objects he may make an application under Part 23 to a costs judge or district judge and, because a party is entitled to have a dispute resolved by a qualified judge, it is difficult to envisage any ground on which the application could be refused. Authorised court officers do not have the penal powers of a costs judge or district judge and this could be a reason for one of the parties objecting to them – or preferring them!

CPR RULE 47.4 VENUE FOR DETAILED ASSESSMENT PROCEEDINGS

(1) All applications and requests in detailed assessment proceedings must be made to or filed at the appropriate office.
(The costs practice direction sets out the meaning of 'appropriate office' in any particular case)
(2) The court may direct that the appropriate office is to be the Supreme Court Costs Office.
(3) A county court may direct that another county court is to be the appropriate office.

(4) A direction under paragraph (3) may be made without proceedings being transferred to that court.
(Rule 30.2 makes provision for any county court to transfer the proceedings to another county court for detailed assessment of costs)

SECTION 31: PRACTICE DIRECTION SUPPLEMENTING CPR RULE 47.4

31.1 For the purposes of rule 47.4(1) the 'appropriate office' means
(1) the district registry or county court in which the case was being dealt with when the judgment or order was made or the event occurred which gave rise to the right to assessment, or to which it has subsequently been transferred; or
(2) in all other cases, including Court of Appeal cases, the Supreme Court Costs Office.
31.2
(1) A direction under rule 47.4(2) or (3) specifying a particular court, registry or office as the appropriate office may be given on application or on the court's own initiative.
(2) Before making such a direction on its own initiative the court will give the parties the opportunity to make representations.
(3) Unless the Supreme Court Costs Office is the appropriate office for the purposes of Rule 47.4(1) an order directing that an assessment is to take place at the Supreme Court Costs Office will be made only if it is appropriate to do so having regard to the size of the bill of costs, the difficulty of the issues involved, the likely length of the hearing, the cost to the parties and any other relevant matter.

Detailed assessments will generally take place at the court in which the case was proceeding, subject to the ability of the court to direct the detailed assessment to take place at another county court or district registry, presumably for the convenience of the parties or if one court has a serious backlog of work. In the latter event the transfer would no doubt only be with the prior agreement of the receiving court. However, the Senior Costs Judge, Peter Hurst, has announced that the SCCO is able to accept bills at all levels. Bills below £75,000 will usually be given a hearing date four to six weeks ahead, above that figure, the hearing date is likely to three to four months ahead. The SCCO is able to deal with all bills from the Court of Appeal, High Court, Principal Registry of the Family Division, Divorce County Courts and other county courts.

Transfer to the SCCO can be achieved by a simple direction to this effect.

A case which is of high value, complex, or which is going to take a considerable time to assess is clearly suitable for transfer. The same may be true of a low-value bill containing a novel or complex point of principle.

The parties must, of course, be given the opportunity to make representations as to whether or not the case should be transferred. The first and most obvious criterion is the cost of requiring the parties to attend the SCCO in London as against the actual amount in dispute in the bill. In general in London it is no more expensive for the parties to attend the SCCO than it is to attend a county court. In non-London cases the time and cost of attending the SCCO may be a significant factor. Where the cost of transporting the papers and the travel and hotel expenses of those involved in what will inevitably be a lengthy hearing become disproportionate, it may be possible to arrange for a costs judge to sit outside the SCCO in order to deal with the matter. I have the impression that some of the costs judges would welcome an away day.

SECTION II COSTS PAYABLE BY ONE PARTY TO ANOTHER – COMMENCEMENT OF DETAILED ASSESSMENT PROCEEDINGS

CPR RULE 47.5 APPLICATION OF THIS SECTION

This section of Part 47 applies where a costs officer is to make a detailed assessment of costs which are payable by one party to another.

CPR RULE 47.6 COMMENCEMENT OF DETAILED ASSESSMENT PROCEEDINGS

(1) Detailed assessment proceedings are commenced by the receiving party serving on the paying party—
  (a) notice of commencement in the relevant practice form; and
  (b) a copy of the bill of costs.
(Rule 47.7 sets out the period for commencing detailed assessment proceedings)
(2) The receiving party must also serve a copy of the notice of commencement and the bill on any other relevant persons specified in the costs practice direction.
(3) A person on whom a copy of the notice of commencement is served under paragraph (2) is a party to the detailed assessment proceedings (in addition to the paying party and the receiving party).

(The costs practice direction deals with:
other documents which the party must file when he requests detailed assessment; the court's powers where it considers that a hearing may be necessary; the form of a bill; the length of notice which will be given if a hearing date is fixed)

SECTION 32: PRACTICE DIRECTION SUPPLEMENTING CPR RULE 47.6

*32.1 * Precedents A, B, C and D in the Schedule of Costs Precedents annexed to this Practice Direction are model forms of bills of costs for detailed assessment. Further information about bills of costs is set out in Section 4.*
32.2 A detailed assessment may be in respect of:
(1) base costs, where a claim for additional liability has not been made or has been agreed;
(2) a claim for additional liability only, base costs having been summarily assessed or agreed;
or
(3) both base costs and additional liability.
32.3 If the detailed assessment is in respect of costs without any additional liability, the receiving party must serve on the paying party and all the other relevant persons the following documents:
(a) a notice of commencement;
(b) a copy of the bill of costs;
(c) copies of the fee notes of counsel and of any expert in respect of fees claimed in the bill;
(d) written evidence as to any other disbursement which is claimed and which exceeds £250;
(e) a statement giving the name and address for service of any person upon whom the receiving party intends to serve the notice of commencement.
32.4 If the detailed assessment is in respect of an additional liability only, the receiving party must serve on the paying party and all other relevant persons the following documents:
(a) a notice of commencement;
(b) a copy of the bill of costs;
(c) the relevant details of the additional liability;

(d) a statement giving the name and address of any person upon whom the receiving party intends to serve the notice of commencement.

32.5 The relevant details of an additional liability are as follows:

(1) In the case of a conditional fee agreement with a success fee:

(a) a statement showing the amount of costs which have been summarily assessed or agreed, and the percentage increase which has been claimed in respect of those costs;

(b) a statement of the reasons for the percentage increase given in accordance with Regulation 3(1)(a) of the Conditional Fee Agreements Regulations or Regulation 5(1)(c) of the Collective Conditional Fee Agreements Regulations 2000.

(2) If the additional liability is an insurance premium: a copy of the insurance certificate showing whether the policy covers the receiving party's own costs; his opponents costs; or his own costs and his opponent's costs; and the maximum extent of that cover, and the amount of the premium paid or payable.

(3) If the receiving party claims an additional amount under Section 30 of the Access of Justice Act 1999: a statement setting out the basis upon which the receiving party's liability for the additional amount is calculated.

32.6 Attention is drawn to the fact that the additional amount recoverable pursuant to section 30 of the Access to Justice Act 1999 in respect of a membership organisation must not exceed the likely cost of the premium of an insurance policy against the risk of incurring a liability to pay the costs of other parties to the proceedings as provided by the Access to Justice (Membership Organisation) Regulations 2000 Regulation 4.

32.7 If a detailed assessment is in respect of both base costs and an additional liability, the receiving party must serve on the paying party and all other relevant persons the documents listed in paragraph 32.3 and the documents giving relevant details of an additional liability listed in paragraph 32.5.

32.8

(1) The Notice of Commencement should be in Form N252.

(2) Before it is served, it must be completed to show as separate items;

(a) the total amount of the costs claimed in the bill;

(b) the extra sum which will be payable by way of fixed costs and court fees if a default costs certificate is obtained.

32.9

(1) This paragraph applies where the notice of commencement is to be served outside England and Wales.

(2) The date to be inserted in the notice of commencement for the paying party to send points of dispute is a date (not less than 21 days from the date of service of the notice) which must be calculated by reference to Part 6 Section III as if the notice were a claim form and as if the date to be inserted was the date for the filing of a defence.

32.10

(1) For the purposes of rule 47.6(2) a 'relevant person' means:

(a) any person who has taken part in the proceedings which gave rise to the assessment and who is directly liable under an order for costs made against him;

(b) any person who has given to the receiving party notice in writing that he has a financial interest in the outcome of the assessment and wishes to be a party accordingly;

(c) any other person whom the court orders to be treated as such.

(2) Where a party is unsure whether a person is or is not a relevant person, that party may apply to the appropriate office for directions.

(3) The court will generally not make an order that the person in respect of whom the application is made will be treated as a relevant person, unless within a specified time he applies to the court to be joined as a party to

the assessment proceedings in accordance with Part 19 (Parties and Group Litigation).

32.11

(1) This paragraph applies in cases in which the bill of costs is capable of being copied onto a computer disk.

(2) If, before the detailed assessment hearing, a paying party requests a disk copy of a bill to which this paragraph applies, the receiving party must supply him with a copy free of charge not more than 7 days after the date on which he received the request.

The commencement of detailed assessment proceedings by serving documents on the paying party rather than filing them at court was entirely new. Notice of commencement must be served on Form N252 (p 301).

Rule 47.5(2) requires service to be on the 'paying party and on any other relevant persons' who are defined in para 32.10 of the practice direction. Where there is any doubt as to who is a relevant person, para 32.10 (2) provides for there to be an application to the court for directions, which should be made in accordance with CPR Part 23. The importance of service where the paying parties are jointly and severally liable was emphasised in *Mainwaring v Goldtech Investments Ltd (No 2)* [1999] 1 WLR 745 where the receiving party delayed for about six years in serving a bill of costs on one of two paying parties. The first paying party's assessment had been completed and a certificate issued. When the second party successfully applied to set aside the certificate and had the costs against them disallowed in their entirety because of the delay the first paying party succeeded in having the costs award against her also set aside in its entirety, because there could not be two certificates in different amounts arising from a single costs order imposing joint and several liability. There was only one bill and there could therefore be only one penalty.

Paragraph 32.3 provides that the notice of commencement must be accompanied by: a copy of the bill of costs; copies of the fee notes of counsel and of any expert in respect of fees claimed in the bill; written evidence as to any other disbursement which is claimed which exceeds £250; a statement giving the name and address for service of any person on whom the receiving party intends to serve the notice of commencement. Writing in the *New Law Journal*, Costs Judge John O'Hare pointed out that although failing to serve copies of the fee notes of counsel and of any expert did not nullify the notice of commencement they do make irregular both the notice and any default costs certificate obtained in respect of it. A receiving party who obtains a default costs certificate while ignoring a request for relevant fee notes, or who obtains a default costs certificate earlier than he should have done, may expect his certificate to be set aside with costs payable by him, such costs to be set off against any costs payable under the bill for assessment.

FORM AND CONTENTS OF BILLS OF COSTS

The Schedule of Costs precedents annexed to the Costs Practice Direction provides four model forms of bills of costs for detailed assessment. Before we look at the models it is necessary to revert to the Practice Direction supplementing Part 43 which prescribes the form and contents of bills of costs.

FORM N252

Notice of Commencement of Assessment of Bill of Costs

In the	
Claim No.	
Claimant (include Ref.)	
Defendant (include Ref.)	

To the claimant(defendant)

Following an .... *(insert name of document eg. order, judgement)* dated ....

(copy attached) 1 have prepared my Bill of Costs for assessment. The Bill totals *£ .... If you choose to dispute this bill and your objections are not upheld at the assessment hearing, the full amount payable (including the assessment fee) will be £ .... together with interest *(see note below)* I shall also seek the costs of the assessment hearing

Your points of dispute must include

- details of the items in the bill of costs which are disputed
- concise details of the nature and grounds of the dispute for each item and, if you seek a reduction in those items, suggest, where practicable, a reduced figure

You must serve your points of dispute by .... *(insert date 21 days from the date of service of this notice)* on me at: - (give full name and address for service including any DX number or reference)

You must also serve copies of your points of dispute on all other parties to the assessment identified below. (you do not need to serve your points of dispute on the court)

I certify that I have also served the following (persons)(person) with a copy of this certificate and my Bill of Costs: - (give details of persons served)

If I have not received your points of dispute by the above date, I will ask the court to issue a default costs certificate for the full amount of my bill (see above*) plus fixed costs and court fee in the total amount of

£.......................................

Signed.. **Date** ....
(Claimant)(Defendant)('s Solicitor)

Note: Interest may be added to all High Court judgments and certain county court judgments under the Judgments Act 1838, the County Courts Act 1984 and the Late Payment of Commercial Debts (Interest) Act 1998.

The court office at

is open between 10 am and 4 pm Monday to Friday. When corresponding with the court, please address forms or letters to the Court Manager and quote the claim number.

1

SECTION 4: PRACTICE DIRECTION SUPPLEMENTING CPR PART 43

4.1 A bill of costs may consist of such of the following sections as may be appropriate:—
(1) title page;
(2) background information;
(3) items of costs claimed under the headings specified in paragraph 4.6;
(4) summary showing the total costs claimed on each page of the bill;
(5) schedules of time spent on non-routine attendances; and
(6) the certificates referred to in paragraph 4.15.

4.2 Where it is necessary or convenient to do so, a bill of costs may be divided into two or more parts, each part containing sections (2), (3) and (4) above. A division into parts will be necessary or convenient in the following circumstances:—
(1) Where the receiving party acted in person during the course of the proceedings (whether or not he also had a legal representative at that time) the bill should be divided into different parts so as to distinguish between;
  (a) the costs claimed for work done by the legal representative; and
  (b) the costs claimed for work done by the receiving party in person.
(2) Where the receiving party was represented by different solicitors during the course of the proceedings, the bill should be divided into different parts so as to distinguish between the costs payable in respect of each solicitor.
(3) Where the receiving party obtained legal aid or LSC funding in respect of all or part of the proceedings the bill should be divided into separate parts so as to distinguish between;
  (a) costs claimed before legal aid or LSC funding was granted;
  (b) costs claimed after legal aid or LSC funding was granted; and
  (c) any costs claimed after legal aid or LSC funding ceased.
(4) Where value added tax (VAT) is claimed and there was a change in the rate of VAT during the course of the proceedings, the bill should be divided into separate parts so as to distinguish between;
  (a) costs claimed at the old rate of VAT; and
  (b) costs claimed at the new rate of VAT.
(5) Where the bill covers costs payable under an order or orders under which there are different paying parties the bill should be divided into parts so as to deal separately with the costs payable by each paying party.
*(*6) Where the bill covers costs payable under an order or orders, in respect of which the receiving party wishes to claim interest from different dates, the bill should be divided to enable such interest to be calculated.*

4.3 Where a party claims costs against another party and also claims costs against the LSC only for work done in the same period, the costs claimed against the LSC only can be claimed either in a separate part of the bill or in additional columns in the same part of the bill. Precedents C and D in the Schedule of Costs Precedents annexed to this Practice Direction show how bills should be drafted when costs are claimed against the LSC only.

4.4 The title page of the bill of costs must set out:—
(1) the full title of the proceedings;
(2) the name of the party whose bill it is and a description of the document showing the right to assessment (as to which see paragraph 40.4, below);
(3) if VAT is included as part of the claim for costs, the VAT number of the legal representative or other person in respect of whom VAT is claimed;
(4) details of all legal aid certificates, LSC certificates and relevant amendment certificates in respect of which claims for costs are included in the bill.

4.5 The background information included in the bill of costs should set out:—

(1) a brief description of the proceedings up to the date of the notice of commencement;

(2) A statement of the status of the solicitor or solicitor's employee in respect of whom costs are claimed and (if those costs are calculated on the basis of hourly rates) the hourly rates claimed for each such person.

It should be noted that 'legal executive' means a Fellow of the Institute of Legal Executives.

Other clerks, who are fee earners of equivalent experience, may be entitled to similar rates. It should be borne in mind that Fellows of the Institute of Legal Executives will have spent approximately 6 years in practice, and taken both general and specialist examinations. The Fellows have therefore acquired considerable practical and academic experience.

Clerks without the equivalent experience of legal executives will normally be treated as being the equivalent of trainee solicitors and para-legals.

(3) a brief explanation of any agreement or arrangement between the receiving party and his solicitors, which affects the costs claimed in the bill.

4.6 The bill of costs may consist of items under such of the following heads as may be appropriate:—

(1) attendances on the court and counsel up to the date of the notice of commencement;

(2) attendances on and communications with the receiving party;

(3) attendances on and communications with witnesses including any expert witness;

(4) attendances to inspect any property or place for the purposes of the proceedings;

(5) attendances on and communications with other persons, including offices of public records;

(6) communications with the court and with counsel;

(7) work done on documents: preparing and considering documentation, including documentation relating to pre-action protocols where appropriate, work done in connection with arithmetical calculations of compensation and/or interest and time spent collating documents;

(8) work done in connection with negotiations with a view to settlement if not already covered in the heads listed above;

(9) attendances on and communications with London and other agents and work done by them;

(10) other work done which was of or incidental to the proceedings and which is not already covered in the heads listed above.

4.7 In respect of each of the heads of costs:—

(1) 'communications' means letters out and telephone calls;

(2) communications, which are not routine communications, must be set out in chronological order;

(3) routine communications should be set out as a single item at the end of each head;

4.8 Routine communications are letters out, e mails out and telephone calls which because of their simplicity should not be regarded as letters or e mails of substance or telephone calls which properly amount to an attendance.

4.9 Each item claimed in the bill of costs must be consecutively numbered.

4.10 In each part of the bill of costs which claims items under head (1) (attendances on court and counsel) a note should be made of:

(1) all relevant events, including events which do not constitute chargeable items;

(2) any orders for costs which the court made (whether or not a claim is made in respect of those costs in this bill of costs).

4.11 The numbered items of costs may be set out on paper divided into columns. Precedents A, B, C and D in the Schedule of Costs Precedents annexed to this Practice Direction illustrate various model forms of bills of costs.

4.12 In respect of heads (2) to (10) in paragraph 4.6 above, if the number of attendances and communications other than routine communications is twenty or more, the claim for the costs of those items in that section of the bill of costs should be for the total only and should refer to a schedule in which the full record of dates and details is set out. If the bill of costs contains more than one schedule each schedule should be numbered consecutively.

4.13 The bill of costs must not contain any claims in respect of costs or court fees which relate solely to the detailed assessment proceedings other than costs claimed for preparing and checking the bill.

4.14 The summary must show the total profit costs and disbursements claimed separately from the total VAT claimed. Where the bill of costs is divided into parts the summary must also give totals for each part. If each page of the bill gives a page total the summary must also set out the page totals for each page.

4.15 The bill of costs must contain such of the certificates, the texts of which are set out in Precedent F of the Schedule of Costs Precedents annexed to this Practice Direction, as are appropriate.

4.16 The following provisions relate to work done by solicitors:

(1) Routine letters out and routine telephone calls will in general be allowed on a unit basis of 6 minutes each, the charge being calculated by reference to the appropriate hourly rate. The unit charge for letters out will include perusing and considering the relevant letters in and no separate charge should be made for in-coming letters.

(2) E-mails received by solicitors will not normally be allowed. The court may, in its discretion, allow an actual time charge for preparation of e-mails sent by solicitors, which properly amount to attendances provided that the time taken has been recorded. The court may also, in its discretion, allow a sum in respect of routine e-mails sent to the client or others on a unit basis of 6 minutes each, the charge being calculated by reference to the appropriate hourly rate.

(3) Local travelling expenses incurred by solicitors will not be allowed. The definition of 'local' is a matter for the discretion of the court. While no absolute rule can be laid down, as a matter of guidance, 'local' will, in general, be taken to mean within a radius of 10 miles from the court dealing with the case at the relevant time. Where travelling and waiting time is claimed, this should be allowed at the rate agreed with the client unless this is more than the hourly rate on the assessment.

(4) The cost of postage, couriers, out-going telephone calls, fax and telex messages will in general not be allowed but the court may exceptionally in its discretion allow such expenses in unusual circumstances or where the cost is unusually heavy.

(5) The cost of making copies of documents will not in general be allowed but the court may exceptionally in its discretion make an allowance for copying in unusual circumstances or where the documents copied are unusually numerous in relation to the nature of the case. Where this discretion is invoked the number of copies made, their purpose and the costs claimed for them must be set out in the bill.

(6) Agency charges as between a principal solicitor and his agent will be dealt with on the principle that such charges, where appropriate, form part of the principal solicitor's charges. Where these charges relate to head (1) in paragraph 4.6 (attendances at court and on counsel) they should be included in their chronological order in that head. In other cases they should be included in head (9) (attendances on London and other agents).

4.17

(1) Where a claim is made for a percentage increase in addition to an hourly rate or base fee, the amount of the increase must be shown separately, either in the appropriate arithmetic column or in the narrative column. (For an example see Precedent A or Precedent B.)

(2) Where a claim is made against the LSC only and includes enhancement and where a claim is made in family proceedings and includes a claim for uplift or general care and conduct, the amount of enhancement uplift and general care and conduct must be shown, in respect of each item upon which it is claimed, as a separate amount either in the appropriate arithmetic column or in the narrative column. (For an example, see Precedent C.)

'Enhancement' means the increase in prescribed rates which may be allowed by a costs officer in accordance with the Legal Aid in Civil Proceedings (Remuneration) Regulations 1994 or the Legal Aid in Family Proceedings Regulations 1991.

Costs of preparing the bill

4.18 A claim may be made for the reasonable costs of preparing and checking the bill of costs.

This practice direction helpfully incorporates all of those aspects of practice directions and decisions under the old costs regime which apply equally to the new. It is a mine of practice and procedure.

(a) Six-minute unit

Paragraph 4.16 is a particularly useful guide on various matters which have caused problems in the past. It is important to understand that the six-minute unit (one-tenth of the fee earner's hourly rate) referred to in para 4.16 applies not only to letters but also routine telephone calls. If an exchange of letters or a telephone call which replaces a personal attendance and materially progresses the matter exceeds six minutes, the time should be recorded and charged (*Bwanaoga v Bwanaoga* [1979] 2 All ER 105, in which I, for the first and last time, represented the Lord Chancellor).

(b) Travelling and waiting

I deal with the use of expense rates and mark-up as opposed to charge-out rates in Chapter 22. It is, however, worth noting that a windfall to solicitors arising out of the use of charge-out rates, both on summary and detailed assessments is in respect of travelling and waiting times. Under the old regime the solicitor recovered his expense rate but no profit mark-up. Now, if the retainer does not differentiate between the rates chargeable for preparation and for travelling and waiting, there will be no difference in the amount recoverable from the other party if it is reasonable and proportionate. If the agreement with the client provides for a reduced rate for travelling and waiting, then under the indemnity principle only the reduced rate is recoverable from the paying party. However, old habits die hard – one costs officer reduces the rate by half if travelling by train on the basis that the fee earner can do other work on the train. Assuming of course that he can get a seat and it is a mobile phone-free compartment.

(c) Counsel's fees

Although the practice direction is silent, there has been judicial guidance.

(i) Justifying counsel's fees
Armitage v Nurse (assessment of costs) (2000) CLW 11 August, Ch D

On an appeal against the reduction of counsel's fees on a detailed assessment it is doubtful whether the appellant may be entitled to rely on material which had not been put before the costs judge. Where substantial counsel's fees are being assessed on a detailed assessment under a funding certificate evidence should be provided that the fees were appropriate. Counsel should prepare a short note commenting on their fees which could be submitted to the court together with the relevant fee notes.

(ii) Brief fees and skeleton arguments
Hornsby v Clark Kenneth Leventhal (a firm) [2000] 4 All ER 567, QBD

Following an unsuccessful appeal to the Court of Appeal, leading counsel claimed a fee of £30,000 for settling the skeleton argument and a further fee of £30,000 on the brief, but was allowed on assessment only £6000 on each. Junior counsel claimed £6650 for drafting the skeleton argument and a brief fee of £20,000. He was allowed £3000 on each.

The correct approach for assessing fees for skeleton arguments and briefs in the Court of Appeal is in three stages. In the first stage, the fee for the skeleton argument should be assessed, usually by reference to the amount of time which counsel had reasonably and proportionately devoted to reading the documents, researching the law and drafting the skeleton argument. The second stage is assessing the brief fee, bearing in mind there is an overlap between the work covered by the skeleton argument fee and the work covered by the brief fee. Where the skeleton argument was drafted shortly before the hearing, then the overlap is greater than it would have been if the skeleton argument had been drafted far in advance of the hearing. This exercise involves considering both the amount of time properly spent and the various factors in CPR Rule 44.5. The guidance given in *Loveday v Renton (No 2)* [1992] 3 All ER 184 at 195 is still effective. The third stage, having arrived at an appropriate skeleton argument fee and brief fee, is a cross-check. The two figures should be aggregated to see whether the total appears too large or too small for the overall conduct of the case in the Court of Appeal. In the present case, counsel had spent some 150 hours in relation to the skeleton argument. That was the equivalent of 20 days or four working weeks. It was not reasonable or proportionate. Half that time would have been reasonable and accordingly the appropriate fee was £15,000. In reaching his figure of £6000, the costs judge had erred by placing considerable reliance on the fees charged by leading junior counsel for the other appellants. First, counsel for the other appellants would have been able to adopt and rely upon many of the submissions made on behalf of the first and second appellants. Second, as a matter of principle, the fees charged by other counsel in a case is only one of the relevant factors and it should not have been given disproportionate weight. Having regard to the time spent by junior counsel and all the circumstances of the case, his proper fee was £5000. Turning to the brief fee, leading counsel had spent 103 hours preparing for the hearing, excluding time relating to the skeleton argument. His proper brief fee was £25,000. Junior counsel had taken an active role and in all the circumstances his fee should have been 60% of leading counsel's brief fee, namely £15,000. The cross-check gave leading counsel £40,000 of fees and junior counsel £20,000. Those figures were reasonable and proportionate remuneration.

Although this appeal related to an appeal to the Court of Appeal, the approach would appear to be appropriate in all cases where counsel charges a separate fee for preparing a skeleton argument.

(iii) Junior counsel's brief fee
Matthews v Dorkin and Motor Insurers' Bureau (SCCO No 16 of 2000, 26 October 2000) Garland J Sitting with Assessors)

In a routine road traffic accident claim leading counsel claimed a brief fee of £10,000, which had not been negotiated, and junior counsel claimed £5000, being 50% of that claimed by his leader. On a between-the-parties detailed assessment the leader's brief fee was allowed at £8000 and accordingly junior counsel's brief fee was reduced to £4000. Junior counsel appealed, arguing that he should still be allowed £5000 even though his leader had not appealed. He criticised the costs judge for not taking into account the allowances made in, what he said was, a similar case, and for making comparison of his fees for the claimant with those of the defendant's counsel.

On appeal it was held that the proper approach was to look at the time spent and the work actually carried out. Because these were not negotiated fees, and junior counsel's fee had been submitted at 50% of his leader's fee it was impossible to criticise the costs judge's approach, and therefore no increase would be granted on the brief fee allowed to junior counsel.

Under the Code of Conduct of the Bar 1990, brief fees no longer have to be agreed in advance or marked on the brief, but it is surprising in this case that they do not appear to have been agreed even before the detailed assessment. If the client has not negotiated and agreed his liability to counsel, how is he to know the amount for which he is seeking to be indemnified by the paying party? Or is the agreement, express or implied, that counsel will be paid whatever is allowed between party and party? That would appear to leave it open to the paying party to argue that nothing should be awarded in respect of counsel's fee with the result that the receiving party would owe nothing to counsel, and thereby be fully indemnified! Although the judge held that the proper approach was to look at the time spent and the work actually carried out, the Bar Council has been concerned to ensure that it is not seen to be advocating remuneration for barristers upon the basis of an hourly rate. It supports the practice of barristers being paid for each item of work which involves taking into account all the relevant factors as well as the time spent. This is a principle which solicitors, with increasing lack of success, have been fighting to preserve for many years and this decision is an indication that barristers are now joining solicitors on the slippery slope to payment based on time spent and hourly rates alone. This and other aspects of counsel's remuneration are now covered comprehensively in Division J of *Butterworths Costs Service*, edited by Peter Birts QC. See also the table of counsel's fees in the SCCO *Guide to the Summary Assessment of Costs* on p 283.

(iv) Settlement
Martin v Holland & Barratt Ltd (SCCO No 11 of 2001, 19 October)

This was an appeal to Holland J (presumably no relation) sitting with assessors. A personal injury trial had been fixed for 28 October. On 14 October counsel advised in conference following a further payment into court. The brief was delivered on 15 October and agreement was reached on 16 October. Counsel's brief fee was £3,500 plus VAT. On the detailed assessment the district judge accepted that counsel was fully prepared for the hearing. She allowed £2,350 plus VAT to cover both the conference and the brief. On appeal the judge and assessors agreed that a brief fee of £3,500 would have been reasonable if the case had proceeded. However, given the proximity of the conference on 14 October and delivery of the brief on 15 October, with settlement on 16 October the brief fee allowed by the district judge was too high. It exceeded the generous ambit within which reasonable disagreement was possible. A reasonable discounted brief fee, to include the conference and to reflect the early settlement, was £1,500 plus VAT.

(d) Costs draftsmen's costs

Solicitors cannot charge for the cost of preparing a bill to their own client any more than can any supplier of goods or services. However, in civil litigation, before a successful party can recover costs from a paying party, the rules require him to prepare a detailed statement or bill of costs. Paragraph 4.18 of the practice direction belatedly recognised that the preparation and checking of a statement or bill of costs is as much a part of the costs of conducting litigation as any other work done in the course of proceedings. It is fee-earning work and the person who does it is therefore a fee earner. It is generally accepted that there are three categories of fee earner and the inescapable logic is that a costs draftsman must fall into one of these and be paid the appropriate hourly rate for the time he has spent. Whether the costs draftsman is an employee of the receiving party's solicitors or independent is of no relevance, as was demonstrated in *Smith Graham v Lord Chancellor's Department* [1999] NLJR 1443, QBD where a solicitor was permitted to charge for preparation work done by an enquiry agent as though the work had been done by a member of the firm. The same principle has also applied for many years where one solicitor uses another as his agent (see section (f) Outsourcing, below). Whether the solicitor pays an independent costs draftsman an hourly rate or a percentage of the bill as drawn or assessed is also irrelevant – provided the client has agreed to pay for the preparation of the bill at no lower rate than is claimed from the paying party in order to comply with the indemnity principle. All the problems and anomalies which arise from treating law costs draftsmen as some alien race outside the recognised categories of fee earners disappear if they are classified as fee earners. The costs must of course be reasonable and not, for example, include putting a file into the order in which it should have been kept, and, on the standard basis, the costs of preparing the bill must be proportionate to the matters in issue.

Having established that costs draftsmen are fee earners, it is then necessary to decide into which category they fall. A conference of the Designated Civil Judges published a paper 'Guidance in Relation to the Fees of Costs Draftsmen' which, after making some derogatory and inaccurate remarks about the nature of a costs draftsman's work (do remember that I am the honorary president of the Association of Law Costs Draftsmen), concluded that in the vast majority of cases, the appropriate rate would be that of a Grade 3 (now Grade D) fee earner based in the locality in which the receiving party's solicitor works. They were clearly unaware of the exacting standards and experience necessary to qualify as an Associate or Fellow of the Association. Grade D is only the equivalent of a trainee solicitor and although this might be acceptable for routine bills, the preparation of substantial bills and advocacy on detailed assessments is at least the equivalent of the work done by Grade C or B fee earners. This was raised at a meeting of the Costs Practitioners' Group at the Supreme Court Costs Office whose view was that while Grade D fee earners might be able to draw straightforward bills of under £10,000, all other bills ought to be drafted by a Grade C fee earner, since costs are a technical matter, and matters such as the operation of the indemnity principle need more experience than a Grade D fee earner is likely to possess. In bills which are not entirely straightforward, a Grade C costs draftsman is often used for the advocacy before the costs officer and it was arguable that the bill should be prepared by the costs draftsman who was going to argue it. (I would add, that in heavy bills involving amounts considerably in excess of the fast track jurisdiction of £15,000, in which Grade A or B fee earners are regularly engaged, the use of a Grade A or B costs draftsman, for example a Fellow of the ALCD, would be reasonable and proportionate.) The SCCO Costs Practitioners' Group also commented that the lower the grade of fee earner who prepared the bill, the longer the time that would have to be spent by a partner checking it, to enable him to comply with the stringent requirement that he should approve and sign it.

(e) Outsourcing

(i) Litigation support

An increasing number of solicitors, rather than incur the overheads and liabilities of employing fee earners, use outside agencies, to do work for them. In a bill of between-the-parties costs should the charges of an outside agency be treated as a disbursement or are the solicitors entitled to treat the work done by their agents as though it had been done by their own fee earner and charge on this basis?

An understandable initial reaction might be – why should a solicitor make a profit out of someone else's work? The answer is that solicitors, as with most commercial enterprises, professional or otherwise, do it all the time. They make a profit out of those they employ. Otherwise, what would be the point or purpose of having employees? Most firms of solicitors employ qualified or unqualified fee earners for whose work they make an hourly charge to their clients, usually calculated on the cost of the fee earner to the firm, including his share of the overheads, together with an appropriate profit margin. It is a practice which has long been recommended and supported by the Law Society in its publication *The Expense of Time*. An historic example of a solicitor charging as though he had done work actually done by someone else is where a firm of solicitors pay counsel for his advice out of their own pockets, but charge the client as though they themselves had given the advice. Another long-standing practice is enshrined in para 4.16(6) of the Costs Practice Direction which provides:

> 'Agency charges as between a principal solicitor and his agent will be dealt with on the principle that such charges, where appropriate, form part of the principal solicitors' charges'.

The various threads of this philosophy were drawn together in the judgment of Mrs Justice Hale in *Smith Graham (a firm) v Lord Chancellor's Department* (QBD [1999] NLJR 1443), when she held that a retired police officer, who was not an employee of the firm of solicitors who instructed him to carry out investigative work, was not excluded from the definition of 'fee earner'. She rejected the contention of the defendant that the police officer as an independent contractor should be treated as a disbursement and not a fee earner. That case concerned the assessment of costs under a legal aid certificate in criminal proceedings, but the principle and philosophy are of equal application to privately-funded civil work.

(ii) Medical agencies

In routine personal injury cases, where a medical report is required, it has become a common practice to instruct a medical agency to arrange a medical examination of the claimant; undertake the collation and obtaining of relevant medical reports; arrange the appointment with the medical expert and the claimant; deal with any cancellations or rearrangements and deliver the resultant medical report to the solicitors. Because of the specialisation, experience, expertise and contacts of the medical agency they are able to do this administrative work at least as efficiently, expeditiously and economically as most firms of solicitors using their own fee earners. There can be no objection in principle to the fees of the medical agency being recoverable between the parties, provided it is demonstrated that their charges do not exceed the reasonable and proportionate costs of the work if it had been done by the solicitors. Where the invoice, or 'fee note', from the medical agency shows the medical consultant's fees and their own charges separately, it is possible for the costs officer to assess them both. A practice of some concern is where a medical agency charges a composite fee, without differentiating between the amount of the medical consultant's fee and their own charges. The medical fees and the agency's charges should be shown separately, with the latter being sufficiently particularised to enable the costs officer to be satisfied they do not exceed the reasonable and proportionate cost of a solicitor's fee earner doing the work.

This section is based on a judgment delivered by me in *Stringer v Copley* in the Kingston-upon-Thames County Court on 17 May 2002.

(f) Work done by employees

Admiral Management Services Ltd v Para-Protect Europe Ltd [2002] NLJR 518 ChD: The reasonable costs of the claimant's expert employees in investigating, formulating and presenting claims against the defendants (after the claimant had formed the suspicion of wrongdoing by the defendants) which, if done by someone who was not an employee, would have been recoverable between the parties, could qualify for a costs order. In *In re Nossen's Letter Patent* [1969] 1 WLR 638, it was held that the costs of expert employees investigating a claim of wrongful use of intellectual property was an exception to the general rule that the work of a party's employees in investigating, formulating and prosecuting a claim by legal proceedings did not qualify for an order for the payment of costs of and incidental to those proceedings. There is no reason why a different principle in regard to the recoverability of costs should apply to intellectual property as against other claims.

(g) Narrative

Paragraph 4.5 twice uses the word 'brief' in regard to the background information to be included in a bill of costs. It may be worth recalling the wording of the pre-CPR practice direction: 'the bill should commence with a brief narrative indicating the issues and the relevant circumstances. This narrative should be short and succinct; the assessment of allowances which depend partly on arithmetical computation and partly on judgments of value is not assisted by prolixity'.

Let us now look at the four precedent model bills:

(i) Precedent A is the suggested form of bill for a case conducted under a CFA where both the solicitor's base costs and the success fee are to be assessed. It also includes counsel's success fee under a CFA.

(ii) Precedent B deals with the same case, but assumes that base costs have been summarily assessed. The bill therefore suggests the format for claiming success fees only. Both Precedents A and B are similar in layout to the old 'three-column' bill except that the 'taxed off' column has disappeared.

(iii) Precedent C illustrates the situation in which the receiving party is publicly-funded and also benefits from an order for costs between parties. It is similar in layout to the old 'six-column' bill.

(iv) Precedent D is the original model bill suggested in the first costs practice direction published in April 1999. In the words of Harry Birks:

> 'It provoked great controversy in the costs drafting profession, most draftsmen expressing strong opposition to the change, along the lines of "if it ain't broke, don't fix it". An enlightened minority looked beyond the immediate effects of change and saw benefits for lay clients in the easier-to-follow format and for themselves in the potential to apply computer technology to bills of costs, both in the drafting process and after detailed assessment. They were out-voted.'

COSTS PRACTICE DIRECTION: PRECEDENT A

SCHEDULE OF COSTS PRECEDENTS
PRECEDENT A

IN THE HIGH COURT OF JUSTICE 2000 – B – 9999

QUEEN'S BENCH DIVISION

BRIGHTON DISTRICT REGISTRY

BETWEEN

AB Claimant

– and –

CD Defendant

CLAIMANT'S BILL OF COSTS TO BE ASSESSED PURSUANT TO THE ORDER DATED 26th JULY 2000

V.A.T. No. 33 4404 90

In these proceedings the claimant sought compensation for personal injuries and other losses suffered in a road accident which occurred on Friday 1st January 1999 near the junction between Bolingbroke Lane and Regency Road, Brighton, East Sussex. The claimant had been travelling as a front seat passenger in a car driven by the defendant. The claimant suffered severe injuries when, because of the defendant's negligence, the car left the road and collided with a brick wall.

The defendant was later convicted of various offences arising out of the accident including careless driving and driving under the influence of drink or drugs.

In the civil action the defendant alleged that immediately before the car journey began the claimant had known that the defendant was under the influence of alcohol and therefore consented to the risk of injury or was contributorily negligent as to it. It was also alleged that, immediately before the accident occurred, the claimant wrongfully took control of the steering wheel so causing the accident to occur.

The claimant first instructed solicitors, E F & Co, in this matter in July 2000. The claim form was issued in October 2000 and in February 2001 the proceedings were listed for a two day trial commencing 25th July 2001. At the trial the defendant was found liable but the compensation was reduced by 25% to take account of contributory negligence by the claimant. The claimant was awarded a total of £78,256.83 plus £1,207.16 interest plus costs.

The claimant instructed E F & Co under a conditional fee agreement dated 8th July 2000 which specifies the following base fees and success fees.

Partner – £180 per hour plus VAT
Assistant Solicitor – £140 per hour plus VAT
Other fee earners – £85 per hour plus VAT
Success fees exclusive of disbursement funding costs: 40%
Success fee in respect of disbursement funding costs: 7.5% (not claimed in this bill)

Except where the contrary is stated the proceedings were conducted on behalf of the claimant by an assistant solicitor, admitted November 1999.

E F & Co instructed Counsel (Miss GH, called 1992) under a conditional fee agreement dated 5th June 2001 which specifies a success fee of 75% and base fees, payable in various circumstances, of which the following are relevant

Fees for interim hearing whose estimated duration is up to 2 hours: £600
Brief for trial whose estimated duration is 2 days: £2,000
Fee for second and subsequent days: £650 per day

Item No.	Description of work done	V.A.T.	Disbursements	Profit Costs
	8th July 2000 – EF & Co instructed 22nd July 2000 – AEI with Eastbird Legal Protection Ltd			
1	Premium for policy	£—	£120.00	
	7th October 2000 – Claim issued			
2	Issue fee	£—	£400.00	
	21st October 2000 – Particulars of claim served 25th November 2000 – Time for service of defence extended by agreement to 14th January 2001			
3	Fee on allocation	£—	£80.00	
	20th January 2001 – case allocated to multi-track 9th February 2001 – Case management conference at which costs were awarded to the claimant and the base costs were summarily assessed at £400 (paid on 24th February 2001) 23rd February 2001 – Claimant's list of documents 12th April 2001 – Payment into court of £25,126.33 13th April 2001 – Filing listing questionnaire			
4	Fee on listing	£—	£400.00	
	28th June 2001 – Pre trial review: costs in case			
	Engaged 1.5 hours	£210.00		
	Travel and waiting 2.00 hours	£280.00		
5	Total solicitor's base fee for attending			£490.00
6	Counsel's base fee for pre trial review (Miss GH)		£600.00	
	25th July 2001 – Attending first day of trial: adjourned part heard			
	Engaged in Court 5.00 hours	£700.00		
	Engaged in conference 0.75 hours	£105.00		
	Travel and waiting 1.5 hours	£210.00		
7	Total solicitor's base fee for attending		£1,015.00	

Item No.	Description of work done	V.A.T.	Disbursements	Profit Costs
8	Counsel's base fee for trial (Miss GH)	£2,000.00		
9	Fee of expert witness (Dr. IJ)	£ —	£850.00	
10	Expenses of witnesses of fact	£ —	£84.00	
	26th July 2001 – Attending second day of trial when judgment was given for the claimant in the sum of £78,256.53 plus £1207.16 interest plus costs			
	Engaged in Court 3.00 hours	£420.00		
	Engaged in conference 1.5 hours	£210.00		
	Travel and waiting 1.5 hours	£210.00		
11	Total solicitor's base fee for attending			£840.00
12	Counsel's base fee for second day (Miss GH)	£650.00		
To Summary		£ —	£5,184.00	£2,345.00
	Claimant			
13	8th July 2000 – First instructions:			
	0.75 hours by Partner: base fee			£135.00
	Other timed attendances in person and by telephone – see Schedule 1			
14	Total base fee for Schedule 1 – 7.5 hours			£1,050.00
15	Routine letters out and telephone calls – 29 (17 + 12) total base fee			£406.00
	Witnesses of Fact			
	Timed attendances in person, by letter out and by telephone – see Schedule 2			
16	Total base fee for Schedule 2 – 5.2 hours			£728.00
17	Routine letters out, e mails and telephone calls – 8 (4 + 2 + 2) total base fee			£112.00
18	Paid travelling on 9th October 2000	£4.02	£22.96	
	Medical expert (Dr. IJ)			
19	11th September 2000 – long letter out 0.33 hours: base fee			£46.20
20	30th January 2001 – long letter out			
	0.25 hours base fee			£35.00

Item No.	Description of work done	V.A.T.	Disbursements	Profit Costs
21	23rd May 2001 – telephone call 0.2 hours base fee			£28.00
22	Routine letters out and telephone calls – 10 (6 + 4) total base fee			£140.00
23	Dr. IJ's fee for report	£ —	£350.00	
	Defendant and his solicitor			
24	8th July 2000 – timed letter sent 0.5 hours: base fee			£70.00
25	19th February 2001 – telephone call 0.25 hours: base fee			£35.00
26	Routine letters out and telephone calls – 24 (18 + 6) total base fee Communications with the court			£336.00
27	Routine letters out and telephone calls – 9 (8 + 1) total base fee			£126.00
	Communications with Counsel			
28	Routine letters out, e mails and telephone calls – 19 (4 + 7 + 8) total base fee			£266.00
	Work done on documents			
	Timed attendances – see Schedule 3			
29	Total base fees for Schedule 3 – 0.75 hours at £180, 44.5 hours at £140, 12 hours at £85			£7,385.00
	Work done on negotiations			
	23rd March 2001 – meeting at offices of Solicitors for the Defendant			
	Engaged – 1.5 hours	£210.00		
	Travel and waiting – 1.25 hours	£175.00		
30	Total base fee for meeting			£385.00
	Other work done			
	Preparing and checking bill			
	Engaged: Solicitor – 1 hour	£140.00		
	Engaged: Costs Draftsman – 4 hours	£340.00		
31	Total base fee on other work don		£480.00	
	To Summary	£4.02	£372.96	£11,763.20
32	Success fee on solicitor's base fee on interim orders which were summarily assessed (40% of £400) plus VAT at 17.5%	£28.00		£160.00
33	VAT on solicitor's other base fees (17.5% of £14,108.20)	£2,468.94		

Item No.	Description of work done	V.A.T.	Disbursements	Profit Costs
34	Success fee on solicitor's other base fees (40% of £14,108.20) plus VAT at 17.5%	£987.58		£5,643.28
35	VAT on Counsel's base fees (17.5% of £3,250)	£568.75		
36	Success fee on Counsel's base fee (75% of £3,250) plus VAT at 17.5%	£426.57	£2,437.50	
	To Summary	£4,479.84	£2,437.50	£5,803.28
SUMMARY		£ —	£5,184.00	£2,345.00
Page 3		£4.02	£372.96	£11,763.20
Page 4		£4,479.84	£2,437.50	£5,803.28
Page 5				
Totals		£4,483.86	£7,994.46	£19,911.48
Grand total				£32,389.80

COSTS PRACTICE DIRECTION: PRECEDENT B

SCHEDULE OF COSTS PRECEDENTS
PRECEDENT B

IN THE HIGH COURT OF JUSTICE 2000 – B – 9999

QUEEN'S BENCH DIVISION

BRIGHTON DISTRICT REGISTRY

BETWEEN

AB Claimant

– and –

CD Defendant

CLAIMANT'S BILL OF COSTS TO BE ASSESSED PURSUANT TO THE ORDER DATED 26th JULY 2000

V.A.T. No. 33 4404 90

In these proceedings the claimant sought compensation for personal injuries and other losses suffered in a road accident which occurred on Friday 1st January 1999 near the junction between Bolingbroke Lane and Regency Road, Brighton, East Sussex. The claimant had been travelling as a front seat passenger in a car driven by the defendant. The claimant suffered severe injuries when, because of the defendant's negligence, the car left the road and collided with a brick wall.

The defendant was later convicted of various offences arising out of the accident including careless driving and driving under the influence of drink or drugs.

In the civil action the defendant alleged that immediately before the car journey began the claimant had known that the defendant was under the influence of alcohol and therefore consented to the risk of injury or was contributorily negligent as to it. It was also alleged that, immediately before the accident occurred, the claimant wrongfully took control of the steering wheel so causing the accident to occur.

The claimant first instructed solicitors, E F & Co, in this matter in July 2000. The claim form was issued in October 1999 and in February 2000 the proceedings were listed for a two day trial commencing 25th July 2001. At the trial the defendant was found liable but the compensation was reduced by 25% to take account of contributory negligence by the claimant. The claimant was awarded a total of £78,256.83 plus £1,207.16 interest plus costs, and the base costs were summarily assessed

The claimant instructed E F & Co under a conditional fee agreement dated 8th July 2000 which specifies the following base fees and success fees.

Partner – £180 per hour plus VAT
Assistant Solicitor – £140 per hour plus VAT
Other fee earners – £85 per hour plus VAT
Success fees exclusive of disbursement funding costs: 40%
Success fee in respect of disbursement funding costs: 7.5% (not claimed in this bill)
Except where the contrary is stated the proceedings were conducted on behalf of the claimant by an assistant solicitor, admitted November 1999.
E F & Co instructed Counsel (Miss GH, called 1992) under a conditional fee agreement dated 5th June 2001 which specifies a success fee of 75% and base fees, payable in various circumstances, of which the following are relevant.
Fees for interim hearing whose estimated duration is up to 2 hours: £600
Brief for trial whose estimated duration is 2 days: £2,000
Fee for second and subsequent days: £650 per day

Item No.	Description of work done	V.A.T.	Disbursements	Profit Costs
	8th July 2000 – EF & Co instructed 22nd July 2000 – AEI with Eastbird Legal Protection Ltd			
1	Premium for policy	£—	£120.00	
	9th February 2001 – Case management conference at which costs were awarded to the Claimant and the base costs were summarily assessed at £400			
2	Success fee on costs of case management conference (40% of £400) plus VAT	£28.00		£160.00
	28th June 2001 – Pre trial review: costs in the case (base costs included base costs at trial)			
	25th July 2001 – First day of trial			
	26th July 2001 – Second day of trial at which judgment was given for the claimant as follows: Compensation: £78,256.83 Interest thereon: £1,207.16 Base costs to trial Solicitor's fees: £12,500.00 plus £2187.50 VAT thereon Counsel's fees: £3,200.00 plus £560.00 VAT thereon			

Item No.	Description of work done	V.A.T.	Disbursements	Profit Costs
	Other disbursements: £2,300.00 plus £4.02 VAT thereon			
3	Success fee on solicitor's base costs awarded at trial (40% of £12,500) plus VAT	£875.00		£5,000.00
4	Success fee on Counsel's base costs awarded at trial (75% of £3,200) plus VAT	£420.00	£2,400.00	
	Other work done			
	Preparing and checking bill	£ 35.00		
	Engaged: Solicitor – 0.25 hours			
	Engaged: Costs draftsman – 1.75 hours	£148.75		
5	Total base fee for other work done plus VAT	£32.16		£183.75
6	Success fee for other work done (40% of £183.75) plus VAT	£12.87		£73.50
	Totals:	£1,368.03	£2,520.00	£5,417.25
	Profit Costs		£5,417.25	
	Disbursements		£2,520.00	
	VAT		£1,368.03	
	Grand total:		£9,305.28	

COSTS PRACTICE DIRECTION: PRECEDENT C

SCHEDULE OF COSTS PRECEDENTS
PRECEDENT C

IN THE HIGH COURT OF JUSTICE 1999 – B – 9999

QUEEN'S BENCH DIVISION

BRIGHTON DISTRICT REGISTRY

BETWEEN

AB Claimant

– and –

CD Defendant

CLAIMANT'S BILL OF COSTS TO BE ASSESSED PURSUANT TO THE ORDER DATED 26th JULY 2000 AND IN ACCORDANCE WITH REGULATION 107A OF THE CIVIL LEGAL AID (GENERAL) REGULATIONS 1989

Legal Aid Certificate No. 01. 01. 99. 32552X issued on 9th September 1999.
V.A.T. No. 33 4404 90

In these proceedings the claimant sought compensation for personal injuries and other losses suffered in a road accident which occurred on Friday 1st January 1999 near the junction between Bolingbroke Lane and Regency Road, Brighton, East Sussex. The claimant had been travelling as a front seat passenger in a car driven by the defendant. The claimant suffered severe injuries when, because of the defendant's negligence, the car left the road and collided with a brick wall.

The defendant was later convicted of various offences arising out of the accident including careless driving and driving under the influence of drink or drugs.

In the civil action the defendant alleged that immediately before the car journey began the claimant had known that the defendant was under the influence of alcohol and therefore consented to the risk of injury or was contributorily negligent as to it. It was also alleged that, immediately before the accident occurred, the claimant wrongfully took control of the steering wheel so causing the accident to occur.

The claimant first instructed solicitors, E F & Co, in this matter in July 1999. The claim form was issued in October 1999 and in February 2000 the proceedings were listed for a two day trial commencing 25th July 2000. At the trial the defendant was found liable but the compensation was reduced by 25% to take account of contributory negligence by the claimant. The claimant was awarded a total of £78,256.83 plus £1,207.16 interest plus costs.

The proceedings were conducted on behalf of the claimant by an assistant solicitor, admitted November 1998. The bill is divided into two parts.

Part 1 Costs payable by the defendant to the date of grant of legal aid

This covers the period from 8th July 1999 to 8th September 1999. In this part the solicitor's time is charged at £140 per hour (including travel and waiting time) and letters out and telephone calls at £14.00 each.

Part 2 Costs payable by the defendant and L.S.C. from the date of grant of legal aid

This part covers the period from 9th September 1999 to the present time, the client having the benefit of a legal aid certificate covering these proceedings. In this part, solicitor's time in respect of costs payable by the defendant has been charged as in Part 1 plus costs draftsman's and trainee's time charged at £85 per hour. Solicitor's time in respect of costs payable by the LSC only are charged at the prescribed hourly rates plus enhancement of 50%.

Preparation: £74
Attending counsel in conference or at court: £36.40
Travelling and waiting: £32.70
Routine letters out: £7.40
Routine telephone calls: £4.10

Item No	Description of work done Part 1: COSTS FROM DATE OF GRANT OF LEGAL AID	Payable by L.S.C. only V.A.T.	Disbursements	Profit Costs	Payable by Defendant V.A.T.	Disbursements	Profit Costs
	Claimant						
1	8th July 1999 – First Instructions – 0.75 hours:						£105.00
2	Routine Letters out – 3						£42.00
	Witnesses of Fact						
3	Routine Letters out – 2						£28.00

Description of work done		Payable by L.S.C. only			Payable by Defendant		
Item No	**Part 1: COSTS FROM DATE OF GRANT OF LEGAL AID**	**V.A.T.**	**Disbursements**	**Profit Costs**	**V.A.T.**	**Disbursements**	**Profit Costs**
	The Defendant						
4	8th July 1999 – Timed letter sent – 0.5 hours						£70.00
5	VAT on total profit costs (17.5% of £245)				£42.88		
	To Summary				£42.88	£—	£245.00
	Part 2: COSTS FROM DATE OF GRANT OF LEGAL AID						
	7th October 1999 – Claim issued						
6	Issue fee—					£400.00	
	21st October 1999 – Particulars of claim served						
	25th November 1999 – Time for service of defence extended by agreement to 14th January 2000						
	17th January 2000 – Filing allocation questionnaire						
7	Fee on allocation—					£80.00	
	20th January 2000 – Case allocated to multi-track						
	9th February 2000 – Case management conference						
	Engaged 0.75 hours	£105.00					
	Travel and waiting 2.00 hours	£280.00					
8	Total solicitor's fee for attending						£385.00
	23rd February 2000 – Claimant's list of documents						
	12th April 2000 – **Payment into court** of £25,126.33						
	13th April 2000 – Filing listing questionnaire						
9	Fee on listing						£400.00
	Engaged 0.75 hours	£105.00					
	Travel and waiting 2.00 hours	£280.00					
10	Total solicitor's fee for attending						£490.00
11	Counsel's brief fee for attending pre-trial review (Miss GH)					£105.00	£600.00
	To Summary	£—	£—	£—	£105.00	£1,480.00	£875.00
	25th July 2000 – Attending first day of trial: Adjourned part heard						
	Engaged in court 5.00 hours	£700.00					
	Engaged in conference 0.75 hours	£105.00					
	Travelling and waiting 1.5 hours	£210.00					
12	Total solicitor's fee for attending						£1,015.00
13	Counsel's brief fee for trial (Miss GH)				£350.00	£2,000.00	

Description of work done		Payable by L.S.C. only			Payable by Defendant		
Item No	Part 1: COSTS FROM DATE OF GRANT OF LEGAL AID	V.A.T.	Disbursements	Profit Costs	V.A.T.	Disbursements	Profit Costs
14	Fee of expert — witness (Dr IJ)					£850.00	
15	Expenses of witnesses of fact				—	£84.00	
	26th July 2000 Attending second day of trial when judgment was given for the claimant in the sum of £78,256.83 plus £1,207.16 interest plus costs						
	Engaged in court 3.00 hours	£420.00					
	Engaged in conference 1.5 hours	£210.00					
	Travel and waiting 1.5 hours	£210.00					
16	Total solicitor's fee for attending						£840.00
17	Counsel's fee for second day (Miss GH)				£113.75	£650.00	
	Claimant – (1) Payable by Defendant Timed attendances in person and by **telephone – see** Schedule 1						
18	Total fees for Schedule 1 – 7.50 hours						£1,050.00
19	Routine letters out and telephone calls – 26 (14 + 12)						£364.00
	Claimant – (2) Payable by LSC only 11th September 1999 – telephone call						
	Engaged 0.25 hours	£18.50					
	Enhancement 50%	£9.25					
20	Total solicitor's fee			£27.75			
	10th April 2000 – telephone call						
	Engaged 0.1 hours	£4.10					
	Enhancement 50%	£2.05					
21	Total solicitor's fee	£6.15					
	Timed attendances in person, by letter out and by telephone – see Schedule 2 **Witnesses of fact**						
22	Total fees for Schedule 2 – 5.2 hours						£728.00
23	Routine letters out (including e mails) and telephone calls – **6 (4 + 2)**						£84.00
24	Paid travelling on 9th October 1999				£4.02	£22.96	
	To Summary	£—	£—	£33.90	£467.77	£3,606.96	£4,081.00
	Medical expert (Dr IJ)						
25	11th September 1999 – long letter out 0.33 hours						£46.20
26	30th January 2000 – long letter out 0.25 hours						£35.00

Description of work done		Payable by L.S.C. only			Payable by Defendant		
Item No	**Part 1: COSTS FROM DATE OF GRANT OF LEGAL AID**	**V.A.T.**	**Disbursements**	**Profit Costs**	**V.A.T.**	**Disbursements**	**Profit Costs**
27	23rd May 2000 – telephone call 0.2 hrs					£28.00	
28	Routine letters out and telephone calls – 10 (6 + 4)						£140.00
29	Dr IJ's fee for report				£—	£350.00	
	Solicitors for the defendant						
30	19th February 2000 – telephone call 0.25 hours						£35.00
31	Routine letters out and telephone calls – 24 (18 + 6)						£336.00
	Communications with the court						
32	Routine letters out and telephone calls – 9 (8 + 1)						£126.00
	Communications with Counsel						
33	Routine letters out (including e mails) and telephone calls – 19 (11 + 8)						£266.00
	Legal Aid Board and LSC – Payable by LSC only						
	2nd August 2000 – Report on case						
	Engaged 0.5 hours	£37.00					
	Enhancement 50%	£18.50					
34	Total solicitor's fee			£55.50			
	Routine letters out and telephone calls						
	Letters out – 2	£14.80					
	Telephone calls – 4	£16.40					
35	Total solicitor's fee	£31.20					
	Work done on documents						
	Timed attendances – see Schedule 3						
36	Total fees for Schedule 3 – 45.25 hours at £140 + 12 hours at £85						£7,355.00
	Work done on negotiations						
	23rd March 2000 – meeting at offices of solicitors for the Defendant						
	Engaged – 1.5 hours	£210.00					
	Travel and waiting – 1.25 hours	£175.00					
37	Total solicitor's fee for meeting						£385.00
	Other work done – (1)						
	Payable by Defendant						
	Preparing and checking bill						
	Engaged: Solicitor – 1 hour	£140.00					
	Engaged: Costs Draftsman 4 hours	£340.00					
38	**Total on other work done (1)**						£480.00
	To Summary	£—	£—	£86.70	£—	£350.00	£9,232.20

Description of work done		Payable by L.S.C. only			Payable by Defendant		
Item No	**Part 1: COSTS FROM DATE OF GRANT OF LEGAL AID**	**V.A.T.**	**Disbursements**	**Profit Costs**	**V.A.T.**	**Disbursements**	**Profit Costs**
	Other work done – (2) Payable by LSC only Preparing and checking bill Engaged: Solicitor – no claim Engaged: Costs Draftsman – 1 hour	£74.00					
39	Total on other work done (2)			£74.00			
40	VAT on total profit costs payable by Defendant (17.5% of £14,176.20)				£2,480.84		
41	VAT on total profit costs payable by LSC only (17.5% of £205.60)	£35.98					
	To Summary	£35.98	£—	£74.00	£2,480.84	£—	£—
	SUMMARY						
	Part 1 – Pre Legal Aid Page 3	£—	£—	£—	£42.88	£—	£245.00
	Part 2 – Costs since grant of legal aid						
	Page 3	£—	£—	£—	£105.00	£1,480.00	£875.00
	Page 4	£—	£—	£33.90	£467.77	£3,606.96	£4,081.00
	Page 5	£—	£—	£86.70	£—	£350.00	£9,232.20
	Page 6	£35.98	£—	£74.00	£2,480.84	£—	£—
	Totals	£35.98	£—	£194.60	£3,096.49	£5,436.96	£14,433.20
	Grand totals						
	Costs payable by Defendant					£22,966.65	
	Costs payable by LSC only					£230.58	
	Grand total:						£23,197.23

COSTS PRACTICE DIRECTION: PRECEDENT D

SCHEDULE OF COSTS PRECEDENTS PRECEDENT D

IN THE HIGH COURT OF JUSTICE 1999 – B – 9999

QUEEN'S BENCH DIVISION

BRIGHTON DISTRICT REGISTRY

BETWEEN

AB Claimant

– and –

CD Defendant

CLAIMANT'S BILL OF COSTS TO BE ASSESSED PURSUANT TO THE ORDER DATED 26th JULY 2000 AND IN ACCORDANCE WITH REGULATION 107A OF THE CIVIL LEGAL AID (GENERAL) REGULATIONS 1989

Legal Aid Certificate No. 01. 01. 99. 32552X issued on 9th September 1999. V.A.T. No. 33 4404 90

In these proceedings the claimant sought compensation for personal injuries and other losses suffered in a road accident which occurred on Friday 1st

January 1999 near the junction between Bolingbroke Lane and Regency Road, Brighton, East Sussex. The claimant had been travelling as a front seat passenger in a car driven by the defendant. The claimant suffered severe injuries when, because of the defendant's negligence, the car left the road and collided with a brick wall.

The defendant was later convicted of various offences arising out of the accident including careless driving and driving under the influence of drink or drugs.

In the civil action the defendant alleged that immediately before the car journey began the claimant had known that the defendant was under the influence of alcohol and therefore consented to the risk of injury or was contributorily negligent as to it. It was also alleged that, immediately before the accident occurred, the claimant wrongfully took control of the steering wheel so causing the accident to occur.

The claimant first instructed solicitors, E F & Co, in this matter in July 1999. The claim form was issued in October 1999 and in February 2000 the proceedings were listed for a two day trial commencing 25th July 2000. At the trial the defendant was found liable but the compensation was reduced by 25% to take account of contributory negligence by the claimant. The claimant was awarded a total of £78,256.83 plus £1,207.16 interest plus costs.

The proceedings were conducted on behalf of the claimant by an assistant solicitor, admitted November 1998. The bill is divided into three parts.

Part 1 Costs payable by the defendant to the date of grant of legal aid: This covers the period from 8th July 1999 to 8th September 1999. In this part the solicitor's time is charged at £140 per hour (including travel and waiting time) and letters out and telephone calls at £14.00 each.

Part 2 Costs payable by the defendant from the date of grant of legal aid: This part covers the period from 9th September 1999 to the present time, the client having the benefit of a legal aid certificate covering these proceedings. In this part, solicitor's time in respect of costs payable by the defendant has been charged as in Part 1 plus costs draftsman's and trainee's time charged at £85 per hour.

Part 3 Costs payable by the LSC only: This part covers the same period as Part 2. In this part solicitor's time in respect of costs payable by the LSC only are charged at the prescribed hourly rates plus enhancement of 50%.

Preparation: £74
Attending counsel in conference or at court: £36.40
Travelling and waiting: £32.70
Routine letters out: £7.40
Routine telephone calls: £4.10

Item No.	**Item**	**Amount claimed**	**VAT**	**Amount allowed**	**VAT**
	Part 1: COSTS PAYABLE BY THE DEFENDANT Claimant				
1	8th July 1999 – First Instructions – 0.75 hours	£105.00	£18.38		
2	Routine Letters out – 3 Witnesses of Fact	£42.00	£7.35		
3	Routine Letters out – 2 The Defendant	£28.00	£4.90		
4	8th July 1999 – Timed letter sent – 0.5 hours	£70.00	£12.25		

Item No.	Item	Amount claimed	VAT	Amount allowed	VAT
	To Summary	£245.00	£42.88		
	Part 2: COSTS PAYABLE BY THE DEFENDANT				
	7th October 1999 – Claim issued				
5	Issue fee	£400.00	£—		
	21st October 1999 – Particulars of claim served				
	25th November 1999 – Time for service of defence extended by agreement to 14th January 2000				
	17th January 2000 – Filing allocation questionnaire				
6	Fee on allocation	£80.00	£—		
	20th January 2000 – Case allocated to multi-track				
	9th February 2000 – Case management conference				
	Engaged 0.75 hours	£105.00			
	Travel and waiting 2.00 hours	£280.00			
7	Total solicitor's fee for attending	£385.00	£67.38		
	23rd February 2000 – Claimant's list of documents				
	12th April 2000 – Payment into court of £25,126.33				
	13th April 2000 – Filing listing questionnaire				
8	Fee on listing	£400.00			
	28th June 2000 – Pre-trial review				
	Engaged 1.5 hours	£210.00			
	Travel and waiting 2.00 hours	£280.00			
9	Total solicitor's fee for attending	£490.00	£85.75		
10	Counsel's brief fee for attending pre-trial review (Miss GH)	£600.00	£105.00		
	25th July 2000 – Attending first day of trial: adjourned part heard				
	Engaged in court	£700.00			

Item No.	Item	Amount claimed	VAT	Amount allowed	VAT
	5.00 hours				
	Engaged in conference 0.75 hours	£105.00			
	Travel and waiting 1.5 hours	£210.00			
11	Total solicitor's fee for attending	£1,015.00	£177.63		
12	Counsel's brief fee for trial (Miss GH)	£2,000.00	£350.00		
13	Fee of expert witness (Dr IJ)	£850.00			
14	Expenses of witnesses of fact	£84.00			
	26th July 2000 – Attending second day of trial when judgment 'was given for the claimant in the sum of 78,256.83 plus' '£1,207.16 interest plus costs'				
	Engaged in court 3.00 hours	£420.00			
	Engaged in conference 1.5 hours	£210.00			
	Travel and waiting 1.5 hours	£210.00			
15	Total solicitor's fee for attending	£840.00	£147.00		
16	Counsel's fee for second day (Miss GH)	£650.00	£113.75		
	Claimant Timed attendances in person and by telephone – see Schedule 1				
17	Total fees for Schedule 1 – 7.50 hours		£1,050.00	£183.75	
18	Routine letters out and telephone calls – 26 (14 + 12)	£364.00	£63.70		
	Witnesses of fact Timed attendances in person, by letter out and by telephone – see Schedule 2				
19	Total fees for Schedule 2 – 5.2 hours	£728.00	£127.40		
20	Routine letters out (including e mails) and telephone calls – 6 (4 + 2)	£84.00	£14.70		
21	Paid travelling on 9th October 1999	£22.96	£4.02		
	Medical expert (Dr IJ)				

Item No.	Item	Amount claimed	VAT	Amount allowed	VAT
22	11th September 1999 – long letter out 0.33 hours	£46.20	£8.09		
23	30th January 2000 – long letter out 0.25 hours	£35.00	£6.13		
24	23rd May 2000 – telephone call 0.2 hours	£28.00	£4.90		
25	Routine letters out and telephone calls – 10 (6 + 4)	£140.00	£24.50		
26	Dr IJ's fee for report	£350.00	£ —		
	Solicitors for the defendant				
27	19th February 2000 – telephone call 0.25 hours	£35.00	£6.13		
28	Routine letters out and telephone calls – 24 (18 + 6)	£336.00	£58.80		
	Communications with the court				
29	Routine letters out and telephone calls – 9 (8 + 1)	£126.00	£22.05		
	Communications with Counsel				
30	Routine letters out (including e mails) and telephone calls – 19 (11 + 8)	£266.00	£46.55		
	Work done on documents				
	Timed attendances – see Schedule 3				
31	Total fees for Schedule 3 – 45.25 hours at £140 + 12 hours at £85	£7,355.00	£1,287.13		
	Work done on negotiations				
	23rd March 2000 – meeting at offices of solicitors for the Defendant				
	Engaged – 1.5 hours	£210.00			
	Travel and waiting – 1.25 hours	£175.00			
32	Total solicitor's fee for meeting	£385.00	£67.38		
33	Other work done				
	Preparing and checking bill				
	Engaged: Solicitor – 1 hour	£140.00			

Item No.	Item	Amount claimed	VAT	Amount allowed	VAT
	Engaged: Costs Draftsman 4 hours	£340.00			
	Total on other work done	£480.00	£84.00		
	To Summary	£19,625.16	£3,055.70		
	Part 3: COSTS PAYABLE BY LSC ONLY				
	Claimant				
	11th September 1999 – telephone call				
	Engaged 0.25 hours	£18.50			
	Enhancement 50%	£9.25			
34	Total solicitor's fee	£27.75	£4.86		
	10th April 2000 – telephone call				
	Engaged 0.1 hours	£4.10			
	Enhancement 50%	£2.05			
35	Total solicitor's fee	£6.15	£1.08		
	Legal Aid Board and LSC				
	2nd August 2000 – Report on case				
	Engaged 0.5 hours	£37.00			
	Enhancement 50%	£18.50			
36	Total solicitor's fee	£55.50	£9.71		
	Routine letters out and telephone calls				
	Letters out – 2	£14.80			
	Telephone calls – 4	£16.40			
37	Total solicitor's fee	£31.20	£5.46		
	Other work done				
	Preparing and checking bill				
	Engaged: Solicitor – no claim				
	Engaged: Costs Draftsman – 1 hour	£74.00			
38	Total on other work done	£74.00	£12.95		
	To Summary	£194.60	£34.06		
	SUMMARY				
	Costs payable by the Defendant				
	Part 1	£245.00	£42.88		
	Part 2	£19,625.16	£3,055.70		
	Total costs payable by the Defendant	£19,870.16	£3,098.58		

Item No.	Item	Amount claimed	VAT	Amount allowed	VAT
	Costs payable by LSC only				
	Part 3	£194.60	£34.06		
	Grand Totals				
	Costs payable by the Defendant	£19,870.16	£3,098.58		
	Costs payable by LSC only	£194.60	£34.06		
	Grand total	£20,064.76	£3,132.63		

As I have indicated, the original model bill caused more difficulty than almost any other aspect of the CPR costs rules and practice direction. Not only was there understandable criticism of various aspects of the bill but there was also confusion arising out of the wording of the practice direction supplementing Part 43 as to whether use of the 'model' form of bill was compulsory and, if not, why the previous form of bill could not continue to be used. Some district judges insisted on no deviation from the model form, whilst others were more relaxed. This led to the Vice-Chancellor in September 1999 writing to all designated civil judges:

> 'a number of district judges have interpreted [para 3.5] of the practice direction as imposing a mandatory obligation upon the parties to use the new form of bill. This was never the intention. The model form of bill is an attempt to improve upon the form previously used. It had, however, never been tried before and there are clearly some situations in which it would not be appropriate'.

This was followed up by an amendment of para 3.7 to make it clear that the use of the model form of bill is not compulsory. Although para 3.5 of the practice direction still says that the model bills of costs are 'to be used for detailed assessments', para 3.7 makes it clear that they are not mandatory.

The way in which a bill must be drawn is not prescribed except that para 4.1 of the practice direction requires there to be a title page, background information, the items of costs claimed, a summary showing the total costs claimed on each page with schedules of time spent and the relevant certificates as in Precedent F, which you will find at the end of this section. Paragraph 4.12 provides that if the number of attendances and communications other than routine communications is 20 or more the claim for costs of those items in that section of the bill of costs should be for the total only and should refer to a schedule in which the full record of dates and details is set out. This number was increased by amendment from the original figure of five.

In practice, costs draftsmen have produced a variety of formats, based upon the precedents and incorporating their own particular preferences. One inevitable result of the changes is that modern technology has largely taken over from the former practice of typing an original 'red line' bill on pre-printed stationery, most bills now being generated by word processors. When combined with the use of spreadsheets, the process of 'casting' a bill has become at once simpler and less prone to errors. Whatever precedent or hybrid bill is used, accuracy and clarity are obviously paramount. With the increasing variety of situations to be covered, including partial costs orders, summary assessment of interim costs, conditional fees and the new enhancement provisions in family proceedings, to name but a few, bills of costs are often not the easiest of documents to follow, particularly for the lay client. Clear and careful presentation of the bill in a manner which assists the parties and the costs officer is a factor to be taken into account in deciding the reasonable costs of preparing the bill.

For the reasons given in the chapter on the indemnity principle (Chapter 17) the certificate of the receiving party's solicitors that the indemnity principle has not been breached is important. It is also important for the court to ensure that there is no double recovery of costs as a result of costs of interim hearings which have already been summarily assessed. Accordingly, the rules prescribe certificates in respect of these and other matters which must be signed as appropriate. They are in Precedent F:

COSTS PRACTICE DIRECTION: PRECEDENT F

SCHEDULE OF COSTS PRECEDENTS
PRECEDENT F

Certificates for inclusion in bill of costs

- Appropriate certificates under headings (1) and (2) are required in all cases. The appropriate certificate under (3) is required in all cases in which the receiving party is an assisted person or a LSC funded client. Certificates (4), (5) and (6) are optional. Certificate (6) may be included in the bill, or, if the dispute as to VAT recoverability arises after service of the bill, may be filed and served as a supplementary document amending the bill under paragraph 39.10 of this Practice Direction.
- All certificates must be signed by the receiving party or by his solicitor. Where the bill claims costs in respect of work done by more than one firm of solicitors, certificate (1), appropriately completed, should be signed on behalf of each firm.

(1) Certificate as to accuracy

I certify that this bill is both accurate and complete [and]
☐ (where the receiving party was funded by legal aid/LSC) [in respect of Part(s) ... of the bill] all the work claimed was done pursuant to a certificate issued by the Legal Aid Board/Legal Services Commission granted to [the assisted person] [the LSC funded client].
☐ (where costs are claimed for work done by an employed solicitor) [in respect of Part(s) ... of the bill] the case was conducted by a solicitor who is an employee of the receiving party.
☐ (other cases where costs are claimed for work done by a solicitor) [in respect of Part(s) ... of the bill] the costs claimed herein do not exceed the costs which the receiving party is required to pay me/my firm.

(2) Certificate as to interest and payments

I certify that:
☐ No rulings have been made in this case which affects my/the receiving party's entitlement (if any) to interest on costs.
or
☐ The only rulings made in this case as to interest are as follows:
[give brief details as to the date of each ruling, the name of the Judge who made it and the text of the ruling]
and
☐ No payments have been made by any paying party on account of costs included in this bill of costs.
or
☐ The following payments have been made on account of costs included in this bill of costs:
[give brief details of the amounts, the dates of payment and the name of the person by or on whose behalf they were paid]

(3) Certificate as to interest of assisted person/LSC funded client pursuant to regulation 119 of the Civil Legal Aid (General) Regulations 1989

I certify that the assisted person/LSC funded client has no financial interest in the detailed assessment.
or
I certify that a copy of this bill has been sent to the assisted person/LSC funded client pursuant to Regulation 119 of the Civil Legal Aid General Regulations 1989 with an explanation of his/her interest in the detailed assessment and the steps which can be taken to safeguard that interest in the assessment. He/she has/has not requested that the costs officer be informed of his/her interest and has/has not requested that notice of the detailed assessment hearing be sent to him/her.

(4) Consent to the signing of the certificate within 21 days of detailed assessment pursuant to regulations 112 and 121 of the Civil Legal Aid (General) Regulations 1989

I certify that notice of the fees reduced or disallowed on detailed assessment has been given in writing to counsel on [date].
or
I certify that: there having been no reduction or disallowance of counsel's fees it is not necessary to give notice to counsel.
I/we consent to the final costs certificate being issued immediately.

(5) Certificate in respect of disbursements not exceeding £500

I hereby certify that all disbursements listed in this bill which individually do not exceed £500 (other than those relating to counsel's fees) have been duly discharged.

(6) Certificate as to recovery of VAT

With reference to the pending assessment of the [claimant's/defendant's] costs and disbursements herein which are payable by the [claimant/defendant] we the undersigned [solicitors to] [auditors of] the [claimant/defendant] hereby certify that the [claimant/defendant] on the basis of its last completed VAT return [would/would not be entitled to recover would/be entitled to recover only percent of the] Value Added Tax on such costs and disbursements, as input tax pursuant to Section 14 of the Value Added Tax Act 1983.

CPR RULE 47.7 PERIOD FOR COMMENCING DETAILED ASSESSMENT PROCEEDINGS

The following table shows the period for commencing detailed assessment proceedings.

SOURCE OF RIGHT TO DETAILED ASSESSMENT	TIME BY WHICH DETAILED ASSESSMENT PROCEEDINGS MUST BE COMMENCED
Judgment, direction, order, award or other determination	3 months after the date of the judgment etc. Where detailed assessment is stayed pending an appeal, 3 months after the date of the order lifting the stay.
Discontinuance under Part 38	3 months after the date of service of notice of discontinuance under rule 38.3; or 3 months after the date of the dismissal of application to set the notice of discontinuance aside under rule 38.4.
Acceptance of an offer to settle or payment into court under Part 36	3 months after the date when the right to costs arose.

SECTION 33: PRACTICE DIRECTION SUPPLEMENTING CPR RULE 47.7

33.1 The parties may agree under rule 2.11 (Time limits may be varied by parties) to extend or shorten the time specified by rule 47.7 for commencing the detailed assessment proceedings.
33.2 A party may apply to the appropriate office for an order under rule 3.1(2)(a) to extend or shorten that time.
33.3 Attention is drawn to rule 47.6(1). The detailed assessment proceedings are commenced by service of the documents referred to.
33.4 Permission to commence assessment proceedings out of time is not required.

Family practitioners should note that now the civil procedure rules apply to family proceedings the time by which detailed assessment proceedings must be commenced has been reduced from six months to three months.

CPR RULE 47.8 SANCTION FOR DELAY IN COMMENCING DETAILED ASSESSMENT PROCEEDINGS

(1) Where the receiving party fails to commence detailed assessment proceedings within the period specified—
(a) in rule 47.7; or
(b) by any direction of the court,
the paying party may apply for an order requiring the receiving party to commence detailed assessment proceedings within such time as the court may specify.
(2) On an application under paragraph (1), the court may direct that, unless the receiving party commences detailed assessment proceedings within the time specified by the court, all or part of the costs to which the receiving party would otherwise be entitled will be disallowed.
(3) If—
(a) the paying party has not made an application in accordance with paragraph (1); and
(b) the receiving party commences the proceedings later than the period specified in 47.7,
the court may disallow all or part of the interest otherwise payable to the receiving party under—
(i) section 17 of the Judgments Act 1838; or
(ii) section 74 of the County Courts Act 1984,
but must not impose any other sanction except in accordance with rule 44.14 (powers in relation to misconduct).
(4) Where the costs to be assessed in a detailed assessment are payable out of the Community Legal Service Fund, this rule applies as if the receiving party were the solicitor to whom the costs are payable and the paying party were the Legal Services Commission.

SECTION 34: PRACTICE DIRECTION SUPPLEMENTING CPR RULE 47.8

34.1
(1) An application for an order under rule 47.8 must be made in writing and be issued in the appropriate office.
(2) The application notice must be served at least 7 days before the hearing.

In other words, the period for commencing detailed assessment proceedings is three months after the event giving rise to the right of assessment.

In the past if a receiving party did not get on with the assessment proceedings the paying party was able to do so. Now, if the receiving party does not commence detailed assessment proceedings within the time prescribed by the rules or any direction of the court, the paying party's remedy is to make an application under Part 23 for an order that unless the receiving party commences proceedings within a specified period all or part of the costs will be disallowed. Where the paying party has not obtained such an order there is nothing to prevent the receiving party from commencing the assessment proceedings at any time, the only sanction being the court's power to disallow interest under Rule 47.8(3)(*b*). Some costs officers require justification of the delay in writing when considering whether or not to disallow interest. Rule 44.14(2)(*a*) and (*b*) also empowers the court to disallow all or part of the costs.

In the Matter of Homes Assured Corpn plc, Official Receiver v Dobson, Sampson v Wilson (28 November 2001, unreported) were appeals from detailed assessments to Mr Justice Park sitting with assessors. In the first case, under the Civil Legal Aid (General) Regulations 1989 the assisted party's solicitors' bill should have been lodged for assessment within three months, but it was lodged four years out-of-time. In the absence of any adequate explanation for the delay, the deputy costs judge, after assessing the profit costs at £29,500, disallowed them in their entirety, under reg 109 and CPR Rule 44.14. On appeal it was held on the authorities relating to delay that the court was not confronted with the stark choice between a reprimand but no sanction, on the one hand, and a total striking-out on the other. The court can graduate the penalty between these two extremes. There is the built-in sanction in delay in lodging a public funding bill that no interest is payable on the outstanding costs and it is only the solicitors who are prejudiced by the delay. The delay is positively beneficial to the Legal Services Commission who suffer no discernible prejudice, while the delay in no way impeded the normal and efficient assessment of the bill. The delay was such that the deputy costs judge had been right to impose a sanction, but it should have been a reduction of 30%, not 100%.

In the second case, the costs judge also disallowed the profit costs in their entirety, but did not assess them. The bill when first lodged for assessment was only five months out-of-time, but by the time the solicitors had corrected various errors of omission and got the fee right, it was 17 months overdue. After some further months had elapsed the SCCO informed the solicitors that the costs judge had in mind disallowing the whole of their costs, to which the solicitors responded that as the matter was still ongoing they were withdrawing their legal aid bill from assessment at that stage. There then followed months of communications in which the solicitors demonstrated, contrary to the suspicions of the costs judge, not malice but muddle. The costs judge gave as his reason for disallowing the whole of the profit costs claimed by the solicitors, of some £58,000, 'the way that they have dealt with the whole of this matter' and in particular referred to 'the long delay in lodgement' and 'because you withdrew the bills of costs lodged'. The costs judge had misinterpreted reg 109(1) in considering it authorised him to disallow costs because he disapproved of the firm's conduct of the assessment. Whether an item of costs in a bill was wasted or not must depend on circumstances as they existed when the item was incurred. That was not a good reason for disallowing any profit costs in this matter. The delay could not justify a disallowance of all the profit costs by way of penalty, which was disproportionate to such an extent that it went beyond the acceptable limits for the exercise of the costs judge's discretion.

The purpose of Rule 47.8(4) is to enable the Legal Services Commission to put pressure on a solicitor who has delayed commencing detailed assessment proceedings. Solicitors who have received payment on account, particularly, as sometimes happens, if it exceeds the ultimate amount of the bill, have no incentive to commence detailed assessment proceedings, which causes difficulty for counsel who remain unpaid but cannot themselves commence detailed assessment proceedings.

CPR RULE 47.9 POINTS OF DISPUTE AND CONSEQUENCE OF NOT SERVING

(1) The paying party and any other party to the detailed assessment proceedings may dispute any item in the bill of costs by serving points of dispute on—

(a) the receiving party; and
(b) every other party to the detailed assessment proceedings.

(2) The period for serving points of dispute is 21 days after the date of service of the notice of commencement.

(3) If a party serves points of dispute after the period set out in paragraph (2) he may not be heard further in the detailed assessment proceedings, unless the court gives permission.

(The costs practice direction sets out requirements about the form of points of dispute)

(4) The receiving party may file a request for a default costs certificate if—

(a) the period set out in rule 47.9 (2) for serving points of dispute has expired; and
(b) he has not been served with any points of dispute.

(5) If any party (including the paying party) serves points of dispute before the issue of a default costs certificate the court may not issue the default costs certificate.

(Section IV of this Part sets out the procedure to be followed after points of dispute have been filed)

SECTION 35: PRACTICE DIRECTION SUPPLEMENTING CPR RULE 47.9

35.1 The parties may agree under rule 2.11 (Time limits may be varied by parties) to extend or shorten the time specified by rule 47.9 for service of points of dispute. A party may apply to the appropriate office for an order under rule 3.1(2)(a) to extend or shorten that time.

35.2 Points of dispute should be short and to the point and should follow as closely as possible Precedent G of the Schedule of Costs Precedents annexed to this Practice Direction.

35.3 Points of dispute must—

(1) identify each item in the bill of costs which is disputed,
(2) in each case, state concisely the nature and grounds of dispute,
(3) where practicable suggest a figure to be allowed for each item in respect of which a reduction is sought, and
(4) be signed by the party serving them or his solicitor.

35.4

(1) The normal period for serving points of dispute is 21 days after the date of service of the notice of commencement.
(2) Where a notice of commencement is served on a party outside England and Wales the period within which that party should serve points of dispute is to be calculated by reference to Part 6 Section III as if the notice of commencement was a claim form and as if the period for serving points of dispute were the period for filing a defence.

35.5 A party who serves points of dispute on the receiving party must at the same time serve a copy on every other party to the detailed assessment proceedings, whose name and address for service appears on the statement served by the receiving party in accordance with paragraph 32.3 or 32.4 above.

35.6

(1) This paragraph applies in cases in which Points of Dispute are capable of being copied onto a computer disk.

(2) If, within 14 days of the receipt of the Points of Dispute, the receiving party requests a disk copy of them, the paying party must supply him with a copy free of charge not more than 7 days after the date on which he received the request.

35.7

(1) Where the receiving party claims an additional liability, a party who serves points of dispute on the receiving party may include a request for information about other methods of financing costs which were available to the receiving party.

(2) Part 18 (further information) and the Practice Direction supplementing that part apply to such a request.

Paragraph 35.1 is a reminder that under CPR Rule 2.11 the parties may agree to extend (or shorten) the 21-day time limit for service of points of dispute. If there is no agreement the paying party may also apply under CPR Rule 3.1(2)(*a*) for an extension of the time for service of points of dispute, the application being made in accordance with Part 23. The receiving party may also apply to shorten the time although it is not easy to imagine the circumstances in which such an application would succeed, or, in many courts, when the application would even be heard before the 21-day time limit had expired. This provision is the nub of the new detailed assessment regime. If points of dispute are not served, the receiving party may request a default costs certificate for the full amount of the bill without any other judicial intervention. If points of dispute are served the judicial intervention will be limited to the points identified. It is, in effect, the voluntary pilot scheme run for several years in the Supreme Court Costs Office and which is now embodied in the rules. If points of dispute are not served within the time limit and no extension has been agreed between the parties or ordered by the court, all is not lost. Service of points of dispute out of time will prevent the issue of a default costs certificate necessitating a hearing at which the points in dispute must be taken into account, whether or not the costs officer is prepared to hear argument on behalf of the paying party. Setting aside a default certificate is covered by CPR Rule 47.12 (p 338). Points of dispute should be in Precedent G of the Schedule of Costs forms to the Costs Practice Direction. Here it is:

COSTS PRACTICE DIRECTION: PRECEDENT G

SCHEDULE OF COSTS PRECEDENTS
PRECEDENT G

IN THE HIGH COURT OF JUSTICE 2000 – B – 9999

QUEEN'S BENCH DIVISION

BRIGHTON DISTRICT REGISTRY

BETWEEN

AB Claimant

– and –

CD Defendant

POINTS OF DISPUTE SERVED BY THE DEFENDANT

Item	Dispute	Claimant's Comments
General point	Base rates claimed for the assistant solicitor and other fee earners are excessive. Reduce to £100 and £70 respectively plus VAT. Each item in which these rates are claimed should be recalculated at the reduced rates.	
(1)	The premium claimed is excessive. Reduce to £95.	
(14)	The claim for timed attendances on claimant (Schedule 1) is excessive. Reduce to 4 hours ie. £400 at reduced rates.	
(29)	The total claim for work done on documents by the assistant solicitor is excessive. A reasonable allowance in respect of documents concerning court and counsel is 8 hours, for documents concerning witnesses and the expert witness, 6.5 hours, for work done on arithmetic, 2.25 hours and for other documents, 5.5 hours. Reduce to 22.25 hours ie. £2,225 at reduced rates (£3,380 in total).	
(31)	The time claimed is excessive. Reduce solicitor's time to 0.5 hours ie. to £50 at reduced rates and reduce the costs draftsman's time to three hours ie. £210 (£260 in total).	
(32)	The success fee claimed is excessive. Reduce to 25% ie. £100 plus VAT of £17.50.	
(33)	The total base fees when recalculated on the basis of the above points amounts to £7,788, upon which VAT is £1,362.90.	
(34)	The success fee claimed is excessive. Reduce to 25% of £7,788 ie. £1,947.50 plus VAT of £340.73.	
(36)	The success fee claimed is excessive. Reduce to 50% ie. £1,625 plus VAT of £284.38.	

Served on .... [date] by .... [name] [solicitors for] the Defendant.

CPR RULE 47.10 PROCEDURE WHERE COSTS ARE AGREED

(1) If the paying party and the receiving party agree the amount of costs, either party may apply for a costs certificate (either interim or final) in the amount agreed.
(Rule 47.15 and Rule 47.16 contain further provisions about interim and final costs certificates respectively)
(2) An application for a certificate under paragraph (1) must be made to the court which would be the venue for detailed assessment proceedings under rule 47.4.

SECTION 36: PRACTICE DIRECTION SUPPLEMENTING CPR RULE 47.10

36.1 Where the parties have agreed terms as to the issue of a costs certificate (either interim or final) they should apply under rule 40.6 (Consent judgments and orders) for an order that a certificate be issued in terms set out in the application. Such an application may be dealt with by a court officer, who may issue the certificate.
36.2 Where in the course of proceedings the receiving party claims that the paying party has agreed to pay costs but that he will neither pay those costs nor join in a consent application under paragraph 36.1, the receiving party may apply under Part 23 (General Rules about Applications for Court Orders) for a certificate either interim or final to be issued.
36.3 An application under paragraph 36.2 must be supported by evidence and will be heard by a costs judge or a district judge. The respondent to the application must file and serve any evidence he relies on at least two days before the hearing date.
36.4 Nothing in rule 47.10 prevents parties who seek a judgment or order by consent from including in the draft a term that a party shall pay to another party a specified sum in respect of costs.
36.5
(1) The receiving party may discontinue the detailed assessment proceedings in accordance with Part 38 (Discontinuance).
(2) Where the receiving party discontinues the detailed assessment proceedings before a detailed assessment hearing has been requested, the paying party may apply to the appropriate office for an order about the costs of the detailed assessment proceedings.
(3) Where a detailed assessment hearing has been requested the receiving party may not discontinue unless the court gives permission.
(4) A bill of costs may be withdrawn by consent whether or not a detailed assessment hearing has been requested.

If the costs are agreed there will be no need to trouble the court if they are to be paid without delay. If the costs are agreed before the final judgment or order the agreed amount may be included in the judgment or order (para 36.4). If a certificate is to be obtained, the agreement may relate to part only of the costs, in which event it will be an interim certificate, or to the whole of the costs, when it will be a final certificate.

An application may be made either before or after the court has become involved in the detailed assessment proceedings. If the agreement is after the commencement of detailed assessment proceedings the application will be to the 'appropriate office' as specified in Rule 47.4, otherwise it will be to the court where the judgment or order was made. Paragraph 37.4 makes provision for discontinuance of detailed assessment proceedings and for withdrawal of a bill of costs by consent.

SECTION III COSTS PAYABLE BY ONE PARTY TO ANOTHER – DEFAULT PROVISIONS

CPR RULE 47.11 DEFAULT COSTS CERTIFICATE

(1) Where the receiving party is permitted by rule 47.9 to obtain a default costs certificate, he does so by filing a request in the relevant practice form. (The costs practice direction deals with the procedure by which the receiving party may obtain a default costs certificate)
(2) A default costs certificate will include an order to pay the costs to which it relates.
(3) Where a receiving party obtains a costs certificate, the costs payable to him for the commencement of detailed assessment proceedings shall be the sum set out in the costs practice direction.

SECTION 37: PRACTICE DIRECTION SUPPLEMENTING CPR RULE 47.11

37.1
(1) A request for the issue of a default costs certificate must be made in Form N254 and must be signed by the receiving party or his solicitor.
(2) The request must be accompanied by a copy of the document giving the right to detailed assessment. (Section 40.4 of the Costs Practice Direction identifies the appropriate documents).
37.2 The request must be filed at the appropriate office.
37.3 A default costs certificate will be in Form N255.
37.4 Attention is drawn to Rules 40.3 (Drawing up and Filing of Judgments and Orders) and 40.4 (Service of Judgments and Orders) which apply to the preparation and service of a default costs certificate. The receiving party will be treated as having permission to draw up a default costs certificate by virtue of this Practice Direction.
37.5 The issue of a default costs certificate does not prohibit, govern or affect any detailed assessment of the same costs which are payable out of the Community Legal Service Fund.
37.6 An application for an order staying enforcement of a default costs certificate may be made either—
(1) to a costs judge or district judge of the court office which issued the certificate; or
(2) to the court (if different) which has general jurisdiction to enforce the certificate.
37.7 Proceedings for enforcement of default costs certificates may not be issued in the Supreme Court Costs Office.
*37.8 * The fixed costs payable in respect of solicitor's charges on the issue of the default costs certificate are £80.*

The ability to obtain a default costs certificate is a continuation of the philosophy of not involving the court until it is clear that there is a dispute for the court to resolve. Again the rules impose tight time limits. We have seen that points of dispute must be served within 21 days of service of the notice of commencement, and that because a default costs certificate includes an order to pay, the provisions of Rule 44.8 mean that it must be paid within 14 days. To further expedite these matters para 3.3 of the practice direction allows the receiving party to draw up the default costs certificate. See Forms N254 and N255 on pp 339 and 340.

Form N255(HC) is the same form for the High Court, without the reference to the Register of County Court Judgments. Because the time limits are so strict, it is expected that there will be many applications either to stay enforcement under para 37.6 of the practice direction or to extend the time for payment under CPR Rule 44.8. Paragraph 37.7 points out that although the Supreme Court Costs Office can grant a stay of enforcement, enforcement proceedings themselves may not be issued in the Supreme Court Costs Office.

CPR RULE 47.12 SETTING ASIDE DEFAULT COSTS CERTIFICATE

(1) The court must set aside a default costs certificate if the receiving party was not entitled to it.
(2) In any other case, the court may set aside or vary a default costs certificate if it appears to the court that there is some good reason why the detailed assessment proceedings should continue.
(3) Where—
- (a) the receiving party has purported to serve the notice of commencement on the paying party;
- (b) a default costs certificate has been issued; and
- (c) the receiving party subsequently discovers that the notice of commencement did not reach the paying party at least 21 days before the default costs certificate was issued,

the receiving party must—
- (i) file a request for the default costs certificate to be set aside; or
- (ii) apply to the court for directions.

(4) Where paragraph (3) applies, the receiving party may take no further step in
- (a) the detailed assessment proceedings; or
- (b) the enforcement of the default costs certificate,

until the certificate has been set aside or the court has given directions.
(The costs practice direction contains further details about the procedure for setting aside a default costs certificate and the matters which the court must take into account)

SECTION 38: PRACTICE DIRECTION SUPPLEMENTING CPR RULE 47.12

38.1
(1) A court officer may set aside a default costs certificate at the request of the receiving party under rule 47.12(3).
(2) A costs judge or a district judge will make any other order or give any directions under this rule.
38.2
(1) An application for an order under rule 47.12(2) to set aside or vary a default costs certificate must be supported by evidence.
(2) In deciding whether to set aside or vary a certificate under rule 47.12(2) the matters to which the court must have regard include whether the party seeking the order made the application promptly.
(3) As a general rule a default costs certificate will be set aside under rule 47.12(2) only if the applicant shows a good reason for the court to do so and if he files with his application a copy of the bill and a copy of the default costs certificate, and a draft of the points of dispute he proposes to serve if his application is granted.
38.3
(1) Attention is drawn to rule 3.1(3) (which enables the court when making an order to make it subject to conditions) and to rule 44.3(8) (which enables the court to order a party whom it has ordered to pay costs to pay an amount on account before the costs are assessed).
(2) A costs judge or a district judge may exercise the power of the court to make an order under rule 44.3(8) although he did not make the order about costs which led to the issue of the default costs certificate.
38.4 If a default costs certificate is set aside the court will give directions for the management of the detailed assessment proceedings.

FORM N254

Request for a Default Costs Certificate

In the	
Claim No.	
Claimant (include Ref.)	
Defendant (include Ref.)	

I certify that the attached Notice of Commencement was served on the paying party ---
(and give details of any other party served with the notice)

on -- *(insert date)*

I also certify that I have not received any points of dispute and that the time for receiving them has now elapsed.

I now request the court to issue a certificate for the amount of the bill of costs plus such fixed costs and court fees as are appropriate in this case.

Signed ____________________________________ Date ---------------------------

(Claimant (Defendant)('s Solicitor)

The court office at

is open between 10 am and 4 pm Monday to Friday. When corresponding with the court, please address forms or letters to the Court Manager and quote the claim number.

FORM N255

Default Costs Certificate

In the	
County Court	
Claim No.	
Claimant (including Ref.)	
Defendant (including Ref.)	
Date	

To [Claimant] [Defendant] ['s Solicitor]

As you have not raised any points of dispute on the [defendant's][claimant's] bill of costs, the costs of the claim have been allowed and the total sum of £ is now payable.

You must pay this amount to the [defendant] [claimant] [within 14 days from the date of this order] [on or before [ ]]

The date from which any entitlement to interest under this certificate commences is [ ]

Take Notice

To the defendant (claimant)

If you do not pay in accordance with this order your goods may be removed and sold or other enforcement proceedings may be taken against you. If your circumstances change and you cannot pay, ask at the court office about what you can do

Further interest may be added if judgment has been given for £5,000 or more or is in respect of a debt which attracts contractual or statutory interest for late payment.

If you do not pay as ordered, this judgment may be registered on the Register of County Court Judgments. This may make it difficult for you to get credit. **If you then pay in full within one month** you can ask the court to cancel the entry on the Register. You will need to give proof of payment. You can (for a fee) also obtain a Certificate of Cancellation from the court. If you pay the debt in full after one month you can ask the court to mark the entry on the Register as satisfied and (for a fee) obtain a Certificate of Satisfaction to prove that the debt has been paid.

Address for Payment

How to Pay

- **PAYMENT(S) MUST BE MADE to the person named at the address for payment quoting their reference and the court case number.**
- **DO NOT bring or send payments to the court. THEY WILL NOT BE ACCEPTED.**
- You should allow at least 4 days for your payment to reach the claimant (defendant) or his representative.
- Make sure that you keep records and can account for all payments made. Proof may be required if there is any disagreement. It is not safe to send cash unless you use registered post.
- A leaflet giving further advice about payment can be obtained from the court.
- If you need more information you should contact the claimant (defendant) or his representative.

The court office at

is open between 10 am and 4 pm Monday to Friday. Address all communications to the Court Manager quoting the claim number

If, for whatever reason, the receiving party was not entitled to a default costs certificate, perhaps because the paying party did not have 21 days' notice, or had served points of dispute within this time, the court must set aside the certificate: it has no discretion. Rule 47.12(3) contains the unusual provision making it obligatory on a *receiving* party who discovers that the notice of commencement did not reach the paying party at least 21 days before the default costs certificate was issued to either file a request for the certificate to be set aside or to apply to the court for directions. Where a valid default costs certificate has been obtained it is for the paying party to establish that there is some good reason why the assessment proceedings should continue. The application is to be made in accordance with CPR Part 23, supported by evidence and will be unlikely to succeed unless it is accompanied by a draft of the points of dispute. It should be made promptly. If the court does set aside the certificate it can impose conditions, including ordering the paying party to make a payment on account.

SECTION IV COSTS PAYABLE BY ONE PARTY TO ANOTHER – PROCEDURE WHERE POINTS OF DISPUTE ARE SERVED

CPR RULE 47.13 OPTIONAL REPLY

(1) Where any party to the detailed assessment proceedings serves points of dispute, the receiving party may serve a reply on the other parties to the assessment proceedings.
(2) He may do so within 21 days after service on him of the points of dispute to which his reply relates.
(The costs practice direction sets out the meaning of reply)

SECTION 39: PRACTICE DIRECTION SUPPLEMENTING CPR RULE 47.13

39.1

(1) Where the receiving party wishes to serve a reply, he must also serve a copy on every other party to the detailed assessment proceedings. The time for doing so is within 21 days after service of the points of dispute.

(2) A reply means:
  - *(i) a separate document prepared by the receiving party; or*
  - *(ii) his written comments added to the points of dispute.*

(3) A reply must be signed by the party serving it or his solicitor.

Although a reply is not obligatory, it is probably tactically advisable except in the simplest of cases. It could also be relevant when the court considers its order in respect of the costs of the detailed assessment proceedings.

CPR RULE 47.14 DETAILED ASSESSMENT HEARING

(1) Where points of dispute are served in accordance with this Part, the receiving party must file a request for a detailed assessment hearing.
(2) He must file the request within 3 months of the expiry of the period for commencing detailed assessment proceedings as specified—
  (a) in rule 47.7; or
  (b) by any direction of the court.
(3) Where the receiving party fails to file a request in accordance with paragraph (2), the paying party may apply for an order requiring the receiving party to file the request within such time as the court may specify.
(4) On an application under paragraph (3), the court may direct that, unless the receiving party requests a detailed assessment hearing within the time

specified by the court, all or part of the costs to which the receiving party would otherwise be entitled will be disallowed.

(5) If—

(a) the paying party has not made an application in accordance with paragraph (3); and

(b) the receiving party files a request for a detailed assessment hearing later than the period specified in paragraph (2),

the court may disallow all or part of the interest otherwise payable to the receiving party under—

(i) section 17 of the Judgments Act 1838; or

(ii) section 74 of the County Courts Act 1984,

but must not impose any other sanction except in accordance with rule 44.14 (powers in relation to misconduct).

(6) No party other than—

(a) the receiving party;

(b) the paying party; and

(c) any party who has served points of dispute under rule 47.9,

may be heard at the detailed assessment hearing unless the court gives permission.

(7) Only items specified in the points of dispute may be raised at the hearing, unless the court gives permission.

(The costs practice direction specifies other documents which must be filed with the request for hearing and the length of notice which the court will give when it fixes a hearing date)

SECTION 40: PRACTICE DIRECTION SUPPLEMENTING CPR RULE 47.14

40.1 The time for requesting a detailed assessment hearing is within 3 months of the expiry of the period for commencing detailed assessment proceedings.

40.2 The request for a detailed assessment hearing must be in Form N258. The request must be accompanied by:

(a) a copy of the notice of commencement of detailed assessment proceedings;

(b) a copy of the bill of costs,

(c) the document giving the right to detailed assessment (see paragraph 40.4 below);

(d) a copy of the points of dispute, annotated as necessary in order to show which items have been agreed and their value and to show which items remain in dispute and their value;

(e) as many copies of the points of dispute so annotated as there are persons who have served points of dispute;

(f) a copy of any replies served;

(g) a copy of all orders made by the court relating to the costs which are to be assessed;

(h) copies of the fee notes and other written evidence as served on the paying party in accordance with paragraph 32.3 above;

(i) where there is a dispute as to the receiving party's liability to pay costs to the solicitors who acted for the receiving party, any agreement, letter or other written information provided by the solicitor to his client explaining how the solicitor's charges are to be calculated;

(j) a statement signed by the receiving party or his solicitor giving the name, address for service, reference and telephone number and fax number, if any, of–

(i) the receiving party;

(ii) the paying party;

(iii) any other person who has served points of dispute or who has given notice to the receiving party under paragraph 31.10(1)(b) above;

and giving an estimate of the length of time the detailed assessment hearing will take;

(k) where the application for a detailed assessment hearing is made by a party other than the receiving party, such of the documents set out in this paragraph as are in the possession of that party;

(l) where the court is to assess the costs of an assisted person or LSC funded client—

(i) the legal aid certificate, LSC certificate and relevant amendment certificates, any authorities and any certificates of discharge or revocation;

(ii) a certificate, in Precedent F(3) of the Schedule of Costs Precedents;

(iii) if the assisted person has a financial interest in the detailed assessment hearing and wishes to attend, the postal address of that person to which the court will send notice of any hearing;

(iv) if the rates payable out of the LSC fund are prescribed rates, a schedule to the bill of costs setting out all the items in the bill which are claimed against other parties calculated at the legal aid prescribed rates with or without any claim for enhancement: (further information as to this schedule is set out in Section 48 of this Practice Direction);

(v) a copy of any default costs certificate in respect of costs claimed in the bill of costs.

40.3

(1) This paragraph applies to any document described in paragraph 40.2(i) above which the receiving party has filed in the appropriate office. The document must be the latest relevant version and in any event have been filed not more than 2 years before filing the request for a detailed assessment hearing.

(2) In respect of any documents to which this paragraph applies, the receiving party may, instead of filing a copy of it, specify in the request for a detailed assessment hearing the case number under which a copy of the document was previously filed.

40.4 'The document giving the right to detailed assessment' means such one or more of the following documents as are appropriate to the detailed assessment proceedings:

(a) a copy of the judgment or order of the court giving the right to detailed assessment;

(b) a copy of the notice served under rule 3.7 (sanctions for non-payment of certain fees) where a claim is struck out under that rule;

(c) a copy of the notice of acceptance where an offer to settle is accepted under Part 36 (Offers to settle and payments into court);

(d) a copy of the notice of discontinuance in a case which is discontinued under Part 38 (Discontinuance);

(e) a copy of the award made on an arbitration under any Act or pursuant to an agreement, where no court has made an order for the enforcement of the award;

(f) a copy of the order, award or determination of a statutorily constituted tribunal or body;

(g) in a case under the Sheriffs Act 1887, the sheriff's bill of fees and charges, unless a court order giving the right to detailed assessment has been made;

(h) a notice of revocation or discharge under Regulation 82 of the Civil Legal Aid (General) Regulations 1989;

(j) in the county courts certain Acts and Regulations provide for costs incurred in proceedings under those Acts and Regulations to be assessed in the county court if so ordered on application. Where such an application is made, a copy of the order.

40.5 On receipt of the request for a detailed assessment hearing the court will fix a date for the hearing, or, if the costs officer so decides, will give directions or fix a date for a preliminary appointment.

40.6

(1) The court will give at least 14 days notice of the time and place of the detailed assessment hearing to every person named in the statement referred to in paragraph 40.2(j) above.

(2) The court will when giving notice, give each person who has served points of dispute a copy of the points of dispute annotated by the receiving party in compliance with paragraph 40.2(d) above.

(3) Attention is drawn to rule 47.14(6)&(7): apart from the receiving party, only those who have served points of dispute may be heard on the detailed assessment unless the court gives permission, and only items specified in the points of dispute may be raised unless the court gives permission.

40.7

(1) If the receiving party does not file a request for a detailed assessment hearing within the prescribed time, the paying party may apply to the court to fix a time within which the receiving party must do so. The sanction, for failure to commence detailed assessment proceedings within the time specified by the court, is that all or part of the costs may be disallowed (see rule 47.8(2)).

(2) Where the receiving party commences detailed assessment proceedings after the time specified in the rules but before the paying party has made an application to the court to specify a time, the only sanction which the court may impose is to disallow all or part of the interest which would otherwise be payable for the period of delay, unless the court exercises its powers under rule 44.14 (court's powers in relation to misconduct).

40.8 If either party wishes to make an application in the detailed assessment proceedings the provisions of Part 23 (General Rules about Applications for Court Orders) apply.

40.9

(1) This paragraph deals with the procedure to be adopted where a date has been given by the court for a detailed assessment hearing and
   (a) the detailed assessment proceedings are settled; or
   (b) a party to the detailed assessment proceedings wishes to apply to vary the date which the court has fixed; or
   (c) the parties to the detailed assessment proceedings agree about changes they wish to make to any direction given for the management of the detailed assessment proceedings.

(2) If detailed assessment proceedings are settled, the receiving party must give notice of that fact to the court immediately, preferably by fax.

(3) A party who wishes to apply to vary a direction must do so in accordance with Part 23 (General Rules about Applications for Court Orders).

(4) If the parties agree about changes they wish to make to any direction given for the management of the detailed assessment proceedings—
   (a) they must apply to the court for an order by consent; and
   (b) they must file a draft of the directions sought and an agreed statement of the reasons why the variation is sought; and
   (c) the court may make an order in the agreed terms or in other terms without a hearing, but it may direct that a hearing is to be listed.

40.10

(1) If a party wishes to vary his bill of costs, points of dispute or a reply, an amended or supplementary document must be filed with the court and copies of it must be served on all other relevant parties.

(2) Permission is not required to vary a bill of costs, points of dispute or a reply but the court may disallow the variation or permit it only upon

conditions, including conditions as to the payment of any costs caused or wasted by the variation.

40.11 Unless the court directs otherwise the receiving party must file with the court the papers in support of the bill not less than 7 days before the date for the detailed assessment hearing and not more than 14 days before that date.

40.12 The following provisions apply in respect of the papers to be filed in support of the bill;

(a) If the claim is for costs only without any additional liability the papers to be filed, and the order in which they are to be arranged are as follows:
  (i) instructions and briefs to counsel arranged in chronological order together with all advices, opinions and drafts received and response to such instructions;
  (ii) reports and opinions of medical and other experts;
  (iii) any other relevant papers;
  (iv) a full set of any relevant pleadings to the extent that they have not already been filed in court.
  (v) correspondence, files and attendance notes;

(b) where the claim is in respect of an additional liability only, such of the papers listed at (a) above, as are relevant to the issues raised by the claim for additional liability;

(c) where the claim is for both base costs and an additional liability, the papers listed at (a) above, together with any papers relevant to the issues raised by the claim for additional liability.

40.13 The provisions set out in Section 20 of this Practice Direction apply where the court disallows any amount of a legal representative's percentage increase, and the legal representative applies for an order that the disallowed amount should continue to be payable by the client in accordance with Rule 44.16.

40.14 The court may direct the receiving party to produce any document which in the opinion of the court is necessary to enable it to reach its decision. These documents will in the first instance be produced to the court, but the court may ask the receiving party to elect whether to disclose the particular document to the paying party in order to rely on the contents of the document, or whether to decline disclosure and instead rely on other evidence.

40.15 Costs assessed at a detailed assessment at the conclusion of proceedings may include an assessment of any additional liability in respect of the costs of a previous application or hearing.

40.16 Once the detailed assessment hearing has ended it is the responsibility of the legal representative appearing for the receiving party or, as the case may be, the receiving party in person to remove the papers filed in support of the bill.

The notice of commencement will have been served, followed by points of dispute, but the request for a detailed assessment will be the first occasion in which the court has been involved. The request must be filed within three months of the expiry of the period for commencing detailed assessment proceedings, which in effect means the receiving party has six months from the date of the award of costs in which to request a detailed assessment hearing. If the receiving party fails to file a request the paying party may apply for an order with default provisions requiring the receiving party to request a hearing. See the request form on p 346.

The request for a detailed assessment hearing helpfully lists the documents which should accompany it, which include the solicitor's client care letter or retainer where the receiving party alleges the indemnity principle is of relevance. Paragraph 40.12 of the practice direction specifies the supporting papers which should be filed.

FORM N258

Request for detailed assessment hearing (general form)

In the	
Claim No.	
Claimant (include Ref.)	
Defendant (include Ref.)	

I certify that the attached Notice of Commencement was served on the paying party ....

(and give details of any other party served with the notice)

on .... *(insert date)*

I now ask the court to arrange an assessment hearing.

I enclose copies of *(tick as appropriate)*

- ☐ the document giving the right to detailed assessment;
- ☐ a copy of the Notice of Commencement;
- ☐ the bill of costs;
- ☐ the paying party's point of dispute, annotated as necessary in order to show (1) which items have been agreed and their value and (2) which items remain in dispute and their value;
- ☐ points in reply (if any);
- ☐ a statement giving the names, addresses for service and references of all persons to whom the court should give notice of the hearing;
- ☐ the relevant details of any additional liability claimed;
- ☐ a copy of all the orders made by the court relating to the costs of the proceedings which are to be assessed;
- ☐ any fee notes of counsel and receipts or accounts for other disbursements relating to items in dispute;
- ☐ [where solicitors' costs are disputed] the client care letter delivered to the receiving party or the solicitor's retainer.

I believe the hearing will take .... *(give estimate of time court should allow)*.

I enclose my fee of £ ....

Signed .... **Date** ....

(Claimant) (Defendant) ('s solicitor)

The court office at

is open between 10 am and 4 pm Monday to Friday. When corresponding with the court, please address forms or letters to the Court Manager and quote the claim number.

SECTION V INTERIM COSTS CERTIFICATE AND FINAL COSTS CERTIFICATE

CPR RULE 47.15 POWER TO ISSUE AN INTERIM CERTIFICATE

(1) The court may at any time after the receiving party has filed a request for a detailed assessment hearing—
- (a) issue an interim costs certificate for such sum as it considers appropriate;
- (b) amend or cancel an interim certificate.

(2) An interim certificate will include an order to pay the costs to which it relates, unless the court orders otherwise.
(3) The court may order the costs certified in an interim certificate to be paid into court.

SECTION 41: PRACTICE DIRECTION SUPPLEMENTING CPR RULE 47.15

41.1
- *(1) A party wishing to apply for an interim certificate may do so by making an application in accordance with Part 23 (General Rules about Applications for Court Orders).*
- *(2) Attention is drawn to the fact that the court's power to issue an interim certificate arises only after the receiving party has filed a request for a detailed assessment hearing.*

In addition to the court's power to order costs on account in CPR Rule 44.3(8), this rule gives the court a complete discretion to award an interim certificate even though there has been no assessment or agreement on quantum. The points of dispute should enable the court to calculate the minimum amount the receiving party will eventually be awarded, but no doubt busy district judges would appreciate it if the calculations and the resulting minimum amount accompanied the application. The court may order that the amount in an interim certificate shall be paid either to the receiving party or into court.

CPR RULE 47.16 FINAL COSTS CERTIFICATE

(1) In this rule a completed bill means a bill calculated to show the amount due following the detailed assessment of the costs.
(2) The period for filing the completed bill is 14 days after the end of the detailed assessment hearing.
(3) When a completed bill is filed the court will issue a final costs certificate and serve it on the parties to the detailed assessment proceedings.
(4) Paragraph (3) is subject to any order made by the court that a certificate is not to be issued until other costs have been paid.
(5) A final costs certificate will include an order to pay the costs to which it relates, unless the court orders otherwise.
(The costs practice direction deals with the form of a final costs certificate)

SECTION 42: PRACTICE DIRECTION SUPPLEMENTING CPR RULE 47.16

42.1 At the detailed assessment hearing the court will indicate any disallowance or reduction in the sums claimed in the bill of costs by making an appropriate note on the bill.
42.2 The receiving party must, in order to complete the bill after the detailed assessment hearing make clear the correct figures agreed or allowed in respect of each item and must re-calculate the summary of the bill appropriately.

42.3 The completed bill of costs must be filed with the court no later than 14 days after the detailed assessment hearing.

42.4 At the same time as filing the completed bill of costs, the party whose bill it is must also produce receipted fee notes and receipted accounts in respect of all disbursements except those covered by a certificate in Precedent F(5) in the Schedule of Costs Precedents annexed to this Practice Direction.

42.5 No final costs certificate will be issued until all relevant court fees payable on the assessment of costs have been paid.

42.6 If the receiving party fails to file a completed bill in accordance with rule 47.16 the paying party may make an application under Part 23 (General Rules about Applications for Court Orders) seeking an appropriate order under rule 3.1 (The court's general powers of management).

42.7 A final costs certificate will show:

(a) the amount of any costs which have been agreed between the parties or which have been allowed on detailed assessment;

(b) where applicable the amount agreed or allowed in respect of VAT on the costs agreed or allowed.

This provision is subject to any contrary provision made by the statutory provisions relating to costs payable out of the Community Legal Service Fund.

42.8 A final costs certificate will include disbursements in respect of the fees of counsel only if receipted fee notes or accounts in respect of those disbursements have been produced to the court and only to the extent indicated by those receipts.

42.9 Where the certificate relates to costs payable between parties a separate certificate will be issued for each party entitled to costs.

42.10 Form N257 is a model form of interim costs certificate and Form N256 is a model form of final costs certificate.

42.11 An application for an order staying enforcement of an interim costs certificate or final costs certificate may be made either:

(1) to a costs judge or district judge of the court office which issued the certificate; or

(2) to the court (if different) which has general jurisdiction to enforce the certificate.

42.12 Proceedings for enforcement of interim costs certificates or final costs certificates may not be issued in the Supreme Court Costs Office.

FORM N257

Interim costs certificate

In the	
Claim No.	
Claimant (including ref.)	
Defendant (including ref.)	
Date	

To [Claimant] [Defendant] ['s Solicitor]

Upon application by the [claimant] [defendant] for [a detailed assessment hearing] [the issue of an interim Costs certificate by agreement].

[Master] [District Judge][ ]has ordered that you must pay £ to the [claimant] [defendant] [within 14 days from the date of this order] [on or before [ ] [[into court to await the issue of a final costs certificate].

Take Notice

To the defendant (claimant)

If you do not pay in accordance with this order your goods may be removed and sold or other enforcement proceedings may be taken against you. If your circumstances change and you cannot pay, ask at the court office about what you can do

Address for Payment

How to Pay

- **PAYMENT(S) MUST BE MADE to the person named at the address for payment quoting their reference and the court case number.**
- **DO NOT bring or send payments to the court. THEY WILL NOT BE ACCEPTED.**
- You should allow at least 4 days for your payment to reach the claimant (defendant) or his representative.
- Make sure that you keep records and can account for all payments made. Proof may be required if there is any disagreement. It is not safe to send cash unless you use registered post.
- A leaflet giving further advice about payment can be obtained from the court.
- If you need more information you should contact the claimant (defendant) or his representative.

The court office at

is open between 10 am and 4 pm Monday to Friday. Address all communications to the Court Manager quoting the claim number

FORM N256

Final Costs Certificate

In the	
County Court	
Claim No.	
Claimant (including ref.)	
Defendant (including ref.)	
Date	

To [Claimant] [Defendant] ['s Solicitor]

Upon the [claimant] [defendant] filing a completed bill of costs in this claim

District Judge [ ] has assessed the total costs as £ [including £ for the costs of the detailed assessment]

[And £ already having been paid under the interim costs certificate issued on [ ]]

You must pay [the balance of] £ to the [claimant] [defendant] [within 14 days from the date of this order] [on or before [ ]]

The date from which any entitlement to interest under this certificate commences is [ ]

Take Notice

To the defendant (claimant)

If you do not pay in accordance with this order your goods may be removed and sold or other enforcement proceedings may be taken against you. If your circumstances change and you cannot pay, ask at the court office about what you can do

Further interest may be added if judgment has been given for £5,000 or more or is in respect of a debt which attracts contractual or statutory interest for late payment.

This judgment has been registered on the Register of County Court Judgments. This may make it difficult for you to get credit. **If you pay in full within one month** you can ask the court to cancel the entry on the Register. You will need to give proof of payment. You can (for a fee) also obtain a Certificate of Cancellation from the court. If you pay the debt in full after one month you can ask the court to mark the entry on the Register as satisfied and (for a fee) obtain a Certificate of Satisfaction to prove that the debt has been paid.

Address for Payment

How to Pay

- **PAYMENT(S) MUST BE MADE to the person named at the address for payment quoting their reference and the court case number.**
- **DO NOT bring or send payments to the court. THEY WILL NOT BE ACCEPTED.**
- You should allow at least 4 days for your payment to reach the claimant (defendant) or his representative.
- Make sure that you keep records and can account for all payments made. Proof may be required if there is any disagreement. It is not safe to send cash unless you use registered post.
- A leaflet giving further advice about payment can be obtained from the court.
- If you need more information you should contact the claimant (defendant) or his representative.

he court office at

s open between 10 am and 4 pm Monday to Friday. Address all communications to the Court Manager quoting the claim number

At the conclusion of the detailed assessment proceedings the receiving party must complete the bill by calculating the amounts due, filing the completed bill together with fee notes and receipted accounts for disbursements exceeding £500 and all outstanding court fees. A tip from Harry Birks:

> 'If there has not been time at the end of the detailed assessment hearing to agree the final total of the bill, it is a good idea for the solicitors for the parties (or their costs draftsmen) to communicate to agree the figures before the completed bill is filed. This can avoid the necessity for a further application to the court if the paying party disputes the figure on the final costs certificate.'

The final costs certificate will include an order to pay the costs, which, as ever, under Rule 44.8 must be complied with within 14 days unless an extension is obtained.

SECTION VI DETAILED ASSESSMENT PROCEDURE FOR COSTS OF A LSC FUNDED CLIENT OR AN ASSISTED PERSON WHERE COSTS ARE PAYABLE OUT OF THE COMMUNITY LEGAL SERVICE FUND

CPR RULE 47.17 DETAILED ASSESSMENT PROCEDURE FOR COSTS OF A LSC FUNDED CLIENT OR AN ASSISTED PERSON WHERE COSTS ARE PAYABLE OUT OF THE COMMUNITY LEGAL SERVICE FUND

See Chapter 32.

CPR RULE 47.17A DETAILED ASSESSMENT PROCEDURE WHERE COSTS ARE PAYABLE OUT OF A FUND OTHER THAN THE COMMUNITY LEGAL SERVICE FUND

See Chapter 37.

SECTION VII COSTS OF DETAILED ASSESSMENT PROCEEDINGS

CPR RULE 47.18 LIABILITY FOR COSTS OF DETAILED ASSESSMENT PROCEEDINGS

(1) The receiving party is entitled to his costs of the detailed assessment proceedings, except where—
- (a) the provisions of any Act, any of these Rules or any relevant practice direction provide otherwise; or
- (b) the court makes some other order in relation to all or part of the costs of the detailed assessment proceedings.

(2) In deciding whether to make some other order, the court must have regard to all the circumstances, including—
- (a) the conduct of all the parties;
- (b) the amount, if any, by which the bill of costs has been reduced; and
- (c) whether it was reasonable for a party to claim the costs of a particular item or to dispute that item.

SECTION 45: PRACTICE DIRECTION SUPPLEMENTING CPR RULE 47.18

45.1 As a general rule the court will assess the receiving party's costs of the detailed assessment proceedings and add them to the bill of costs.
45.2 If the costs of the detailed assessment proceedings are awarded to the paying party, the court will either assess those costs by summary assessment or make an order for them to be decided by detailed assessment.

45.3 No party should file or serve a statement of costs of the detailed assessment proceedings unless the court orders him to do so.
45.4 Attention is drawn to the fact that in deciding what order to make about the costs of detailed assessment proceedings the court must have regard to the conduct of all parties, the amount by which the bill of costs has been reduced and whether it was reasonable for a party to claim the costs of a particular item or to dispute that item.
45.5
(1) In respect of interest on the costs of detailed assessment proceedings, the interest shall begin to run from the date of the default, interim or final costs certificate as the case may be.
(2) This provision applies only to the costs of the detailed assessment proceedings themselves. The costs of the substantive proceedings are governed by rule 40.8(1).

The costs of the detailed assessment proceedings will generally be awarded to the receiving party unless at some previous hearing the court has ordered otherwise or the costs officer disallows all or part of the costs on the grounds of misconduct in relation to the detailed assessment proceedings. Such misconduct could be the inclusion of an unjustifiable item or amount in the bill. The amount of the costs of the detailed assessment proceedings will almost certainly be dealt with by way of summary assessment, although the costs officer could for good reason order a detailed assessment. The receiving party would be well advised to be prepared for a summary assessment even though the provisions of para 13.5 of the Costs Practice Direction (on p 268) for a statement of costs do not apply to the receiving party, because he is already entitled to the costs of the assessment under the order for the costs being assessed. Supplying the costs officer with your figures in writing is all part of the art of advocacy.

CPR RULE 47.19 OFFERS TO SETTLE WITHOUT PREJUDICE SAVE AS TO COSTS OF THE DETAILED ASSESSMENT PROCEEDINGS

(1) Where—
- (a) a party (whether the paying party or the receiving party) makes a written offer to settle the costs of the proceedings which gave rise to the assessment proceedings; and
- (b) the offer is expressed to be without prejudice(GL) save as to the costs of the detailed assessment proceedings,

the court will take the offer into account in deciding who should pay the costs of those proceedings.
(2) The fact of the offer must not be communicated to the costs officer until the question of costs of the detailed assessment proceedings falls to be decided.
(The costs practice direction provides that rule 47.19 does not apply where the receiving party is a LSC funded client or an assisted person, unless the court orders otherwise)

SECTION 46: PRACTICE DIRECTION SUPPLEMENTING CPR RULE 47.19

46.1 Rule 47.19 allows the court to take into account offers to settle, without prejudice save as to the costs of detailed assessment proceedings, when deciding who is liable for the costs of those proceedings. The rule does not specify a time within which such an offer should be made. An offer made by the paying party should usually be made within 14 days after service of the notice of commencement on that party. If the offer is made by the receiving party, it should normally be made within 14 days after the service of points of

dispute by the paying party. Offers made after these periods are likely to be given less weight by the court in deciding what order as to costs to make unless there is good reason for the offer not being made until the later time.
46.2 Where an offer to settle is made it should specify whether or not it is intended to be inclusive of the cost of preparation of the bill, interest and value added tax (VAT). The offer may include or exclude some or all of these items but the position must be made clear on the face of the offer so that the offeree is clear about the terms of the offer when it is being considered. Unless the offer states otherwise, the offer will be treated as being inclusive of all these items.
46.3 Where an offer to settle is accepted, an application may be made for a certificate in agreed terms, or the bill of costs may be withdrawn, in accordance with rule 47.10 (Procedure where costs are agreed).
46.4 Where the receiving party is an assisted person or an LSC funded client, an offer to settle without prejudice save as to the costs of the detailed assessment proceedings will not have the consequences specified under rule 47.19 unless the court so orders.

The provision for the court to take into account offers by *either* party was a significant change. It means that receiving parties cannot afford to sit back, ignore offers they expect to beat and go along to the assessment hearing in the expectation that they will recover their full costs of the detailed assessment proceedings. Costs officers are now more likely to penalise the receiving party even when they beat the paying party's offer, if they have made little or no attempt to compromise – unless the offer is derisory and the bill demonstrably reasonable. In any event every paying party should make a Rule 47.19 offer, even where the receiving party is publicly-funded, and comply with the statement of costs provision to support his claim for costs of the assessment if the receiving party does not beat his offer.

SECTION 57 TRANSITIONAL ARRANGEMENTS

57.1 In this section 'the previous rules' means the Rules of the Supreme Court 1965 ('RSC') or County Court Rules 1981 ('CCR'), as appropriate.

GENERAL SCHEME OF TRANSITIONAL ARRANGEMENTS CONCERNING COSTS PROCEEDINGS

57.2

(1) Paragraph 18 of the Practice Direction which supplements Part 51 (Transitional Arrangements) provides that the CPR govern any assessments of costs which take place on or after 26th April 1999 and states a presumption to be applied in respect of costs for work undertaken before 26th April 1999.

(2) The following paragraphs provide five further transitional arrangements:

  (a) to provide an additional presumption to be applied when assessing costs which were awarded by an order made in a county court before 26th April 1999 which allowed costs 'on Scale 1' to be determined in accordance with CCR Appendix A, or 'on the lower scale' to be determined in accordance with CCR Appendix C;
  (b) to preserve the effect of CCR Appendix B Part III, paragraph 2;
  (c) to clarify the approach to be taken where a bill of costs was provisionally taxed before 26th April 1999 and the receiving party is unwilling to accept the result of the provisional taxation;

(d) to preserve the right to carry in objections or apply for a reconsideration in all taxation proceedings commenced before 26th April 1999;
(e) to deal with funding arrangements made before 3 July 2000.

SCALE 1 OR LOWER SCALE COSTS

57.3 Where an order was made in county court proceedings before 26th April 1999 under which the costs were allowed on Scale 1 or the lower scale, the general presumption is that no costs will be allowed under that order which would not have been allowed in a taxation before 26th April 1999.

FIXED COSTS ON THE LOWER SCALE

57.4 The amount to be allowed as fixed costs for making or opposing an application for a rehearing to set aside a judgment given before 26th April 1999 where the costs are on lower scale is £11.25.

BILLS PROVISIONALLY TAXED BEFORE 26TH APRIL 1999

57.5 In respect of bills of costs provisionally taxed before 26th April 1999:
(1) The previous rules apply on the question who can request a hearing and the time limits for doing so; and
(2) The CPR govern any subsequent hearing in that case.

BILLS TAXED BEFORE 26TH APRIL 1999

57.6 Where a bill of costs was taxed before 26th April 1999, the previous rules govern the steps which can be taken to challenge that taxation.

OTHER TAXATION PROCEEDINGS

57.7
(1) This paragraph applies to taxation proceedings which were commenced before 26th April 1999, were assigned for taxation to a Taxing Master or District Judge, and which were still pending on 26th April 1999.
(2) Any assessment of costs that takes place in cases to which this paragraph applies which is conducted on or after 26th April 1999, will be conducted in accordance with the CPR.
(3) In addition to the possibility of appeal under rules 47.20 to 47.23 and Part 52 any party to a detailed assessment who is dissatisfied with any decision on a detailed assessment made by a costs judge or district judge may apply to that costs judge or district judge for a review of the decision. The review shall, for procedural purposes, be treated as if it were an appeal from an authorised court officer.
(4) The right of review provided by paragraph (3) above, will not apply in cases in which, at least 28 days before the date of the assessment hearing, all parties were served with notice that the rights of appeal in respect of that hearing would be governed by Part 47 Section VIII (Appeals from Authorised Court Officers in Detailed Assessment Proceedings) and Part 52 (Appeals).
(5) An order for the service of notice under sub-paragraph (4) above may be made on the application of any party to the detailed assessment proceedings or may be made by the court of its own initiative.

TRANSITIONAL PROVISIONS CONCERNING THE ACCESS TO JUSTICE ACT 1999 SECTIONS 28 TO 31

57.8

(1) Sections 28 to 31 of the Access to Justice Act 1999, the Conditional Fee Agreements Regulations 2000, the Access to Justice (Membership Organisations) Regulations 2000, and the Access to Justice Act 1999 (Transitional Provisions) Order 2000 came into force on 1 April 2000. The Civil Procedure (Amendment No 3) Rules come into force on 3 July 2000.

(2) The Access to Justice Act 1999 (Transitional Provisions) Order 2000 provides that no conditional fee agreement or other arrangement about costs entered into before 1 April 2000 can be a funding arrangement, as defined in rule 43.2. The order also has the effect that where an conditional fee agreement or other funding arrangement has been entered into before 1 April 2000 and a second or subsequent funding arrangement of the same type is entered into on or after 1 April 2000, the second or subsequent funding arrangement does not give rise to a liability which is recoverable from a paying party.

(3) The Collective Conditional Fee Agreements Regulations 2000 came into force on 30 November 2000. The Regulations apply to agreements entered into on or after that date. Agreements entered into before that date are treated as if the Regulations had not come into force.

57.9

(1) Rule 39 of the Civil Procedure (Amendment No 3) Rules 2000 applies where between 1 April and 2 July 2000 (including both dates)—

a funding arrangement is entered into, and

proceedings are started in respect of a claim which is the subject of that agreement.

(2) Attention is drawn to the need to act promptly so as to comply with the requirements of the Rules and the Practice Directions by 31 July 2000 (ie within the 28 days from 3 July 2000 permitted by Rule 39) if that compliance is to be treated as compliance with the relevant provision. Attention is drawn in particular to Rule 44.15 (Providing Information about Funding Arrangements) and Section 19 of this Practice Direction.

(3) Nothing in the legislation referred to above makes provision for a party who has entered into a funding arrangement to recover from another party any amount of an additional liability which relates to anything done or any costs incurred before the arrangement was entered into.

SECTION VIII APPEALS FROM AUTHORISED COURT OFFICERS IN DETAILED ASSESSMENT PROCEEDINGS

CPR RULE 47.20 RIGHT TO APPEAL

See Chapter 31.

CPR RULE 47.21 COURT TO HEAR APPEAL

See Chapter 31.

CPR RULE 47.22 APPEAL PROCEDURE

See Chapter 31.

CPR RULE 47.23 POWERS OF THE COURT ON APPEAL

See Chapter 31.

CHAPTER 31

APPEALS AGAINST ASSESSMENTS

1. NO SPECIAL PROCEDURE

In the bad old days before the introduction of the Civil Procedure Rules, an appeal against a decision made on the taxation of costs, as detailed assessment was then called, was to the very person whose decision was being appealed against. The reasoning behind this apparently bizarre process was that by the dissatisfied party taking in objections, as they were known, the original adjudicator was given a further opportunity to consider the decision away from the hurly-burly of the taxation. It was also an opportunity for him to give his considered reasons to be available if the matter proceeded to an appeal. The CPR removed this second bite of the cherry but CPR Rule 47.21 still required the dissatisfied party to obtain written reasons from the costs officer who had conducted a detailed assessment. Appeals from summary assessments were in accordance with the general rules relating to appeals. The remaining special provisions in respect of detailed assessments were removed by a new CPR Part 52 and now all costs appeals (except from authorised court officers, which are covered below) are dealt with in the same way as all other appeals.

2. REASONS

I agree with Jeremy Morgan's comments that a difficulty now inherent in appeals against detailed assessments under CPR Part 52 is that in order to succeed the appellant has to show that the costs judge was wrong either in law or in the exercise of his discretion, but the former procedure for obtaining written reasons has gone and, often, the reasons uttered by the costs judge in the course of the assessment are incomplete. He suggested that either the costs judge must give, and the parties note, sufficient reasons for every decision made in the course of a detailed assessment or the procedure for obtaining written reasons has to be re-introduced.

In the rough and tumble of an assessment of costs, decisions are made on a number of disputed matters without the court delivering a reasoned judgment on each decision. It is now necessary for the court to enunciate its reasons and for the court and parties to keep a record of them for the purposes of any appeal. The way forward is indicated in *English v Emery Reimbold & Strick* on p 167. If the costs officer does not give adequate reasons and feels unable to provide them voluntarily, include lack of reasons in the application for permission to appeal. This should trigger the sequence of events as described in *English v Emery*.

The problem was encountered in *Griffiths v Solutia UK Ltd*, [2001] EWCA Civ 736, [2001] All ER (D) 196 (Apr), the relevant part of the judgment of the Court of Appeal being:

> 'The question before us is whether the deputy judge was entitled to conclude that the decision of the costs judge was wrong. The test which the deputy judge had to apply, in determining whether or not the costs judge's decision was wrong, was explained by this court in *Tanfern v Cameron-McDonald* [2000] 1 WLR 1311, paragraph 32, where Brooke LJ says as follows:

"The first ground for interference speaks for itself. The epithet 'wrong' is to be applied to the substance of the decision made by the lower court. If the appeal is against the exercise of a discretion by the lower court, the decision of the House of Lords in *G v G (minors: custody appeal)* [1985] 1 WLR 647 warrants attention. In that case Lord Fraser of Tullybelton said, at page 652:

> 'Certainly it would not be useful to inquire whether different shades of meaning are intended to be conveyed by words such as "blatant error" used by the President in the present case, and words such as "clearly wrong", "plainly wrong" or "simply wrong" used by other judges in other cases. All these various expressions were used in order to emphasise the point that the appellate court should only interfere when they consider that the judge of first instance has not merely preferred an imperfect solution, which is different from an alternative imperfect solution which the Court of Appeal might or would have adopted, but has exceeded the generous ambit within which a reasonable disagreement is possible.'

The task that faces us is to apply that same test. Essentially the test requires the appellate court to consider whether or not, in a case involving the exercise of discretion, the judge has approached the matter applying the correct principles, has taken into account all relevant considerations and has not taken into account irrelevant considerations, and has reached a decision which is one which can properly be described as a decision which is within the ambit of reasonable decisions open to the judge on the facts of the case."'

3. ROUTE

Appeals from detailed or summary assessments of a district judge are to a circuit judge. Appeals from detailed and summary assessments of a costs judge and against summary assessments by a circuit judge are to a High Court judge. Appeals from summary assessments by a High Court judge are to the Court of Appeal. In an earlier edition, I said this would be an event for which they could sell tickets – but it has happened. See *1-800 Flowers Inc v Phonenames Ltd* on p 287, but they didn't charge for admission!

4. PERMISSION

Appeals against assessments are no longer as of right, but require permission either from the tribunal being appealed against or from the appellate court. An appeal does not act as a stay and it is likely that a court granting a stay will make it dependent upon at least the minimum amount conceded being paid forthwith.

The Court of Appeal has no jurisdiction to entertain an appeal against the refusal of a judge to grant permission to appeal against a decision of a costs judge. Nor has it any jurisdiction to review the judge's decision: *Riniker v University College London* [2001] 1 WLR 13, CA.

5. REVIEW, NOT RE-HEARING

Another substantial change is that appeals against assessment decisions will no longer be a full re-hearing (unless the appellate court so orders) but will be limited to a review of the decision under appeal. In *Johnsey Estates (1990) v Secretary of State for the Environment, Transport and the Regions* [2001] EWCA Civ 535, [2001] All ER (D) 135 (Apr) the Court of Appeal held that an appellate court should not interfere with the judge's exercise of discretion merely because it takes the view that it would have exercised that discretion differently. This requires an appellate court to exercise a degree of self-restraint. It must recognise the advantage which the trial judge enjoys as a result of his 'feel' for the case which he has tried. Indeed, it is not for an appellate court even to consider whether it would have exercised the discretion differently unless it has first reached the conclusion that the judge's exercise of his discretion is flawed. That is to say, that he has erred in principle, taken into account matters which should have been left out of account, left out of account matters which should have been taken into account or reached a conclusion which is so plainly wrong that it can be described as perverse.

6. ASSESSORS

The costs rules used to provide for the appointment of assessors to sit with the judge on a review of taxation, usually a costs officer and a practising solicitor (or a barrister if counsel's fees were in dispute). Although there is now no such specific provision, judges hearing costs appeals may think it helpful to continue the practice by exercising their powers under the Supreme Court Act 1981, s 70 or the County Courts Act 1984, s 63. The costs of the assessors will not, as in the past, be borne by the court, but by the parties. The traditional rate of pay is that of a deputy costs judge or district judge.

Assessors are appointed by the court under the Supreme Court Act 1981, s 70 in the High Court and the County Courts Act 1984, s 63 in the county court. The former procedure of appointing two assessors, one being a district judge and the other a solicitor nominated by the Law Society or a local law society has gone. CPR 35.15 introduced the new provision that an assessor's remuneration shall be determined by the court and shall form part of the costs of the proceedings. The court may order any party to deposit in the court office a specified sum in respect of assessor's fees and, where it does so, the assessor will not be appointed until the sum has been deposited; the SCCO has no knowledge of any such order having been made. CPR Practice Direction 35 provides that not less than 21 days before making any appointment, the court must notify each party. Any objection must be filed with the court within seven days.

7. TIME FOR APPEALING

In *Kasir v DSRM* noted at [2001] 12 LS Gaz R 39, at the end of a four-day detailed assessment in May 2000, it was left to the costs draftsmen to agree the calculations arising out of the costs judge's findings and submit to him the result. Unfortunately, they were unable to reach agreement which necessitated a further hearing in August which was followed by further correspondence lasting until a final figure was agreed in October. The claimant lodged an appellant's notice within 14 days from the date of the final agreement of the costs figure, which was some six months after the decisions on the items under appeal. The judge held that under CPR Rule 52.4, time runs from the decision of the lower court that the appellant wishes to appeal. The appeal was therefore out of time. It was pointed out to the judge that in long and detailed assessments spread over a period of time, a dissatisfied party might have to lodge several appellant's notices and further might not know until the end of the assessment whether the global result was such that he wanted to appeal. The judge suggested either the parties could agree, and the costs judge order, at the beginning of a long assessment that time for appeals should not start running until the last day or such an application could be made in the course of the assessment when a party received a decision that he was likely to want an appeal.

8. APPEALS FROM AUTHORISED COURT OFFICERS IN DETAILED ASSESSMENT PROCEEDINGS

CPR RULE 47.20 RIGHT TO APPEAL

(1) Any party to detailed assessment proceedings may appeal against a decision of an authorised court officer in those proceedings.
(2) For the purposes of this Section, a LSC funded client or an assisted person is not a party to detailed assessment proceedings.
(Part 52 sets out general rules about appeals)

SECTION 47: PRACTICE DIRECTION SUPPLEMENTING CPR RULE 47.20

47.1 This Section and the next Section of this Practice Direction relate only to appeals from authorised court officers in detailed assessment proceedings. All other appeals arising out of detailed assessment proceedings (and arising out of summary assessments) are dealt with in accordance with Part 52 and the Practice Direction which supplements that Part. The destination of appeals is dealt with in accordance with the Access to Justice Act 1999 (Destination of Appeals) Order 2000.
47.2 In respect of appeals from authorised court officers, there is no requirement to obtain permission, or to seek written reasons.

CPR RULE 47.21 COURT TO HEAR APPEAL

An appeal against a decision of an authorised court officer is to a costs judge or a district judge of the High Court.

CPR RULE 47.22 APPEAL PROCEDURE

(1) The appellant must file an appeal notice within 14 days after the date of the decision he wishes to appeal against.
(2) On receipt of the appeal notice, the court will—
- (a) serve a copy of the notice on the parties to the detailed assessment proceedings; and
- (b) give notice of the appeal hearing to those parties.

SECTION 48: PRACTICE DIRECTION SUPPLEMENTING CPR RULE 47.22

48.1 The appellant must file a notice which should be in Form N161 (an appellant's notice).
48.2 The appeal will be heard by a costs judge or a district judge of the High Court, and is a re-hearing.
48.3 The appellant's notice should, if possible, be accompanied by a suitable record of the judgment appealed against. Where reasons given for the decision have been officially recorded by the court an approved transcript of that record should accompany the notice. Photocopies will not be accepted for this purpose. Where there is no official record the following documents will be acceptable:
(1) The officer's comments written on the bill.
(2) Advocates' notes of the reasons agreed by the respondent if possible and approved by the authorised court officer.
When the appellant was unrepresented before the authorised court officer, it is the duty of any advocate for the respondent to make his own note of the reasons promptly available, free of charge to the appellant where there is no

official record or if the court so directs. Where the appellant was represented before the authorised court officer, it is the duty of his/her own former advocate to make his/her notes available. The appellant should submit the note of the reasons to the costs judge or district judge hearing the appeal.
48.4 The appellant may not be able to obtain a suitable record of the authorised court officer's decision within the time in which the appellant's notice must be filed. In such cases, the appellant's notice must still be completed to the best of the appellant's ability. It may however be amended subsequently with the permission of the costs judge or district judge hearing the appeal.

CPR RULE 47.23 POWERS OF THE COURT ON APPEAL

On an appeal from an authorised court officer the court will—

(a) rehear the proceedings which gave rise to the decision appealed against; and

(b) make any order and give such directions as it considers appropriate.

9. COSTS

Appeals against summary assessment are in accordance with the general rules relating to appeals prescribed in CPR Part 52. Where an appeal is allowed and the appellate court makes an order for costs of the appeal and of the proceedings in the court below, the appellate court may, if it is appropriate, summarily assess the costs of the appeal but that court will probably not be in a position to deal with the costs in the court below, nor should the matter be remitted to the judge in the court below for summary assessment to be carried out. The whole purpose of summary assessment is that it should be carried out on the day of the hearing or very shortly after. The prospect of asking the judge at first instance to carry out an assessment months or perhaps years later is not sensible. In those circumstances the only option is to order detailed assessment of all the costs which the appellate court does not deal with.

CHAPTER 32

STATE-FUNDED COSTS

The current regime of state funding with its special vocabulary and concepts is the subject of Chapter 41. Anyone unfamiliar with the Community Legal Service may find it helpful to look at Chapter 41 before this chapter, which is concerned with the quantification of state-funded costs.

Article 4 of the Community Legal Service (Funding) Order 2000 preserved reg 107 of the Civil Legal Aid (General) Regulations 1989 so that it applies to cases funded under a Community Legal Service Funding Certificate as well as to those cases still funded under a Legal Aid Certificate. Article 6 made similar provision in respect of family proceedings, so we are able to consider both types of state funding in this chapter.

1. LEGAL AID LEGAL ADVICE AND ASSISTANCE AND CLS LEGAL HELP

(a) Scope

This was known to its friends as the Green Form Scheme. They now call it Legal Help. It covers advice and help with any legal problems by way of giving general advice, writing letters, negotiating, getting counsel's opinion and preparing a written case to go before a tribunal. It extends to all assistance short of actual representation. To qualify for advice under Legal Help the matter must be one of English law and must not be in respect of conveyancing services (except rental purchase agreements or conditional sale agreements for the sale of land and any conveyancing necessary to give effect to an order of the court or the terms of the matrimonial agreement) or to wills (except where a client is aged 70 or over, or is mentally or physically disabled; where a parent or guardian wants to provide for a child in care, or where a one-parent family wishes to appoint a guardian for a minor living with the client). It does not cover the taking of any step in the institution or conduct of proceedings, except to a limited degree in undefended divorce suits, and it is not therefore available for obtaining a grant of representation to an estate, because a grant is an order of court for which application must be made to the court.

(b) Eligibility

See Chapter 41.

(c) Fees

The initial fee limit is three hours work at the current rates of remuneration for a petition for divorce or judicial separation and two hours work for all other cases including disbursements, which include counsel's fees but not VAT.

Since 1 April 1996 there have been separate rates applicable to work done inside London and work done outside London, and separate rates for franchisees and non-franchisees.

(d) Disbursements

The Legal Aid Board published this list of disbursements which will normally be treated as recoverable and those which are unlikely to find favour.

Recoverable	*Irrecoverable*
Accident report fees	Ad valorem stamp duties
Birth and other Certificates	Capital duty
Conciliation referral fees to approved services [see also below]	Client's travelling and accommodation expenses
Counsel's fees	Discharge of debts owed by the client, eg rent or mortgage arrears
Enquiry agent's and interpreter's fees	Mortgagee's or lessor's solicitor's costs and disbursements
Expert's fees including for medical reports	Passport fees
Newspaper advertisements	Fees payable on voluntary petitions in bankruptcy
Fees recoverable on oaths	Court fees (unless for a search/photocopies/bailiff service)
Photographers' accounts	Probate fees
Search fees	
Stamp Duties of a nominal amount	
Travelling expenses of a solicitor, including a solicitor in the capacity of McKenzie friend	

Where a solicitor refers a client to a recognised conciliation service (outside the mediation pilot scheme, to which separate provisions apply), a fixed amount can be allowed. This is currently £33.13 (£33.00 for non-franchisees), which is broken down to £23.35 for the report (ie the disbursement for the service's fee) and £9.78 (£9.65 for non-franchisees) for the solicitor's costs. An extension to the costs limit may or may not be needed to undertake this work, depending on the work already reasonably undertaken when the referral is to be made.

(e) Extension

Where the limit is likely to be exceeded it is important to make an application for an extension in good time. A solicitor may not start to charge a Legal Help client privately until a request for an extension has been turned down. Since under no circumstances can proceedings be covered by the scheme, it is also important to submit an application for legal aid as soon as possible where proceedings are envisaged. Various retainers have been devised in recent years to enable solicitors acting for clients under the Green Form scheme to recover from defendants costs not covered by the Scheme but incurred prior to the granting of a legal aid certificate. Only if the client was personally liable to the solicitor for such costs would he be entitled to recover them under an order for costs against an unsuccessful defendant. The matter is of such importance and prevalence that in *Joyce v Kammac (1988) Ltd* [1996] 1 All ER 923, QBD the Senior Costs Judge travelled to Mold where he sat with Morland J and a solicitor assessor on an appeal by the plaintiff against the disallowance of his pre-legal aid certificate costs. The judge identified the following principles from the common law and statutory provisions, which no doubt apply to Legal Help.

1. Once a person became a client under the Green Form scheme in relation to a claim receiving advice and assistance the solicitor had a mandatory obligation to comply with the relevant regulations.
2. Breach of the solicitor's statutory obligations to apply for extensions for increases in the statutory limit to the green form scheme or any device, including any purported agreement with the client, having the purpose of evading the statutory restrictions was unlawful. Once the Green Form scheme with extensions was exhausted, a client, if he chose, might enter into an agreement with a solicitor on a private retainer basis.
3. It followed that the plaintiff's solicitor's 'general authority' was unlawful. In particular the following sentence flouted the statutory regime and was illegal:

> 'I understand that I am personally responsible for all the above described costs but notwithstanding instruct my solicitor to commence proceedings … irrespective of any green form advice or application for legal aid … and I further instruct my solicitor not to increase the possibility of my personal costs liability by making application for extension of the financial limit of the Green Form'.

4. In practice, it was conceded, no client had ever been asked to pay his solicitor's costs under the purported obligation in the 'general authority'. There was no doubt that from the outset no client was ever expected to pay. It was a sham to enable the solicitor to recover costs incurred with the Green Form scheme from the defendant if he was unsuccessful. It was a device to surmount what would otherwise be a contingency agreement. It purported to create a potential primary liability upon the client for his solicitor's costs thus enabling the costs to be recoverable from the unsuccessful defendant on the indemnity principle.
5. It was submitted that on the ground of public policy a client should he allowed to be subject to a private retainer during the currency of the statutory Green Form retainer and while a legal aid certificate application was being processed which normally took about three months. Otherwise investigation into a claim and the taking of witness statements would be delayed to the prejudice of the client. However, in most cases sufficient preliminary investigations could be undertaken under the Green Form scheme especially if extended. If there were problems of great urgency there was in practice no difficulty in obtaining emergency legal aid certificates to cover urgent work.

A client could not at the same time be subject to both a statutory retainer and a private retainer in relation to the same matter. In effect that was what the plaintiff's solicitor's 'general authority' sought to achieve.

2. LEGAL AID ASSISTANCE BY WAY OF REPRESENTATION (ABWOR) AND CLS HELP AT COURT

(a) Scope

In the county court, the Family Proceedings Court, and Mental Health Review Tribunals, ABWOR may be granted under Regulations 7 and 8 of the Legal Advice and Assistance (Scope) Regulations 1989 only where these conditions are met:

(a) the party to be granted representation is not already receiving representation (legal aid) and has not been refused it;
(b) the party has not been refused representation (legal aid) in connection with the proceedings;
(c) the court is satisfied that the hearing should take place on the same day;
(d) the court is satisfied that the party would not otherwise be represented;
(e) the court requests a solicitor who is in the precincts of the court for purposes other than the provision of ABWOR or approves a proposal from such a solicitor that he should provide the party in question with ABWOR.

This prevents a solicitor from providing ABWOR if he has come to the court for that specific purpose.

(b) Eligibility

See Chapter 41.

(c) Fees

The fees are as for the Legal Help scheme with the exception of Mental Health Review Tribunals in which the prescribed rates are higher, again with differentials between London and outside London. The distinction between franchisees and non-franchisees was abolished for work done on or after 2 April 2001. The previous rates can be found on page 344 of *Cook on Costs 2001/02*. The fees for work done on or after 2 April 2001 are below:

(i) Legal Help and Help at Court – Table 1

Immigration, Mental Health, Actions against the Police etc, Public Law, Education and Community Care

	Outside London £	London £
Preparation	52.55	57.35
Travelling and Waiting	29.45	30.30
Routine letters written and routine telephone calls	4.10	4.40

(ii) Legal Help and Help at Court – Table 2

Family, Housing and Employment

	Outside London £	London £
Preparation	50.05	53.10
Travelling and waiting	28.05	28.05
Routine letters written and routine telephone calls	3.95	4.10

(iii) Legal Help and Help at Court – Table 3

All categories of work not falling within Tables 1 or 2 above or work carried out under contract tolerances

	Outside London £	London £
Preparation	47.80	50.70
Travelling and waiting	26.80	26.80
Routine letters written and routine telephone calls	3.75	3.90

3. PRESCRIBED FAMILY PROCEEDINGS

On any assessment, review or taxation of the costs of an assisted person where the costs are, or may be, paid out of the Fund they shall be determined on the standard basis subject to:

(a) the Legal Aid in Civil Proceedings (Remuneration) Regulations 1994 in proceedings to which those regulations apply;
(b) the Legal Aid in Family Proceedings (Remuneration) Regulations 1991 in proceedings to which those regulations apply (reg 107A).

(a) Definition

The definition in reg 2 of the Legal Aid in Family Proceedings (Remuneration) Regulations 1991 is tortuous. In effect it means all family proceedings except Wardship, Inheritance (Provision for Family and Dependants) Act 1975 and Domestic Violence and Matrimonial Proceedings Act 1976 proceedings, these being covered with the provisions for civil legal aid on p 399.

(b) Rates and items

Schedule 2 of the Matrimonial Causes (Costs) Rules 1988 relating to legal aid costs was replaced by the Legal Aid in Family Proceedings (Remuneration) Regulations 1991 as follows, incorporating the amendments of 2 April 2001 for franchisees (note that the distinction between franchisees and non-franchisees remains):

LEGAL AID IN FAMILY PROCEEDINGS (REMUNERATION) REGULATIONS 1991
(SI 1991/2038)

Schedule 1

Care Proceedings

[Non-franchisees]

Column 1	Column 2 *High Court*	Column 3 *County Court or Magistrate's Court*
ITEM **PART I** **PREPARATION**		
1 Writing routine letters.	£4.25 per item	£3.65 per item
2 Receiving routine letters.	£2.10 per item	£1.85 per item
3 Routine telephone calls.	£4.25 per item	£3.65 per item
4 All other preparation work including any work which was reasonably done arising out of or incidental to the proceedings, interviews with client, witnesses, and other parties; obtaining evidence; preparation and consideration of, and dealing with, documents, negotiations and notices; dealing with letters written and received and telephone calls which are not routine.	£65.50 per hour	£58.00 per hour
	(£69.75 per hour for a fee-earner whose office is situated within legal aid area 1)	£61.25 per hour
5 Travelling and waiting time in connection with the above matters.	£32.00 per hour	£29.25 per hour
PART II **CONFERENCES WITH COUNSEL**		
6 Attending counsel in conference.	£37.00 per hour	£32.50 per hour
7 Travelling and waiting.	£32.00 per hour	£29.25 per hour
PART III **ATTENDANCES**		
8 Attending with counsel at the trial or hearing of any cause or the hearing of any summons or other application at court, or other appointment.	£37.00 per hour	£32.50 per hour
9 Attending without counsel at the trial or hearing of any cause or the hearing of any summons or other application at court, or other appointment.	£64.00 per hour	£64.00 per hour
10 Travelling and waiting.	£32.00 per hour	£29.25 per hour

Column 1		Column 2 *High Court*	Column 3 *County Court or Magistrate's Court*
PART IV **FEES FOR JUNIOR COUNSEL**			
11 With a brief on an unopposed application for an injunction, or procedural issue.			
	Standard	£88.25	£76.25
	Maximum	£146.25	£127.00
12 With a brief on the trial of a cause or matter or on the hearing of an application where the hearing lasts for			
(a) one hour	Standard	£133.50	£114.25
	Maximum	£268.00	£228.50
(b) a half day	Standard	£184.75	£159.25
	Maximum	£304.50	£268.00
(c) a full day	Standard	£368.50	£317.75
	Maximum	£584.75	£508.50
(d) more than a full day.		Discretionary	Discretionary
13 For each day or part of a day on which the trial of a cause or matter, or the hearing of an ancillary application, or a children appointment, is continued after the first day.		Discretionary	Discretionary
14 Conference (including time reasonably spent in preparation and conference, but not otherwise remunerated).		Standard £20.25 per 1/2 hour	Standard £17.75 per 1/2 hour
15 (a) Complex items of written work (such as advices on evidence, opinions and affidavits of a substantial nature, requests for particulars or answers).		Standard £96.25 per item	Standard £82.75 per item
(b) All other written work.		Standard £57.00 per item	Standard £50.25 per item
16 Except where the court is within 40 kilometres of Charing Cross or where there is no local Bar in the court town, or within 40 kilometres thereof, for travelling time.		Standard £18.50 per hour + expenses	Standard £15.85 per hour + expenses
PART V **DETAILED ASSESSMENT AND APPEAL IN RELATION TO DETAILED ASSESSMENT (HIGH COURT AND COUNTY COURT ONLY)**			
17 Preparing the bill (where allowable) and completing the detailed assessment (excluding preparing for and attending the detailed assessment).		£32.00–£89.25	£32.00–£51.00
18 Preparing for and attending the detailed assessment (including travelling and waiting).		Discretionary	Discretionary
19 Appeal to costs judge, district judge or judge (including preparation).		Discretionary	Discretionary

SCHEDULE 1A

Care Proceedings

[Franchisees]

Column 1	Column 2 *High Court*	Column 3 *County Court or Magistrate's Court*
ITEM **PART I** **PREPARATION**		
1 Writing routine letters	£4.70 per item	£4.10 per item
2 Receiving routine letters	£2.35 per item	£2.05 per item
3 Routine telephone calls	£4.70 per item	£4.10 per item
4 All other preparation work including any work which was reasonably done arising out of or incidental to the proceedings, interviews with client, witnesses, and other parties; obtaining evidence; preparation and consideration of, and dealing with, documents, negotiations and notices; dealing with letters written and received and telephone calls which are not routine	£73.15 per hour (£77.85 per hour for a fee-earner whose office is situated in the Legal Services Commission's London Region)	£64.90 per hour (£68.20 per hour for a fee-earner whose office is situated in the Legal Services Commission's London Region)
5 Travelling and waiting	£35.75 per hour	£32.45 per hour
PART II **CONFERENCES WITH COUNSEL**		
6 Attending with counsel in conference	£41.25 per hour	£36.30 per hour
7 Travelling and waiting	£35.75 per hour	£32.45 per hour
PART III **ATTENDANCES**		
8 Attending with counsel at the trial or hearing of any cause or the hearing of any summons or other application at court, or other appointment	£41.25 per hour	£36.30 per hour
9 Attending without counsel at the trial or hearing of any cause or the hearing of any summons or other application at court, or other appointment	£73.15 per hour (£77.85 per hour for a fee-earner whose office is situated in the Legal Services Commission's London Region)	£71.50 per hour
10 Travelling and waiting	£35.75 per hour	£32.45 per hour

Column 1	Column 2 *High Court*	Column 3 *County Court or Magistrate's Court*
PART V **DETAILED ASSESSMENT AND APPEAL IN RELATION TO DETAILED ASSESSMENT (HIGH COURT AND COUNTY COURT ONLY)**		
17 Preparing the bill (where allowable) and completing the detailed assessment (excluding preparing for and attending the hearing of the detailed assessment)	£35.75–£99.85	£35.75–£56.95
18 Preparing for and attending the hearing of the detailed assessment (including travelling and waiting)	Discretionary	Discretionary
19 Appeal to costs judge, district judge or judge (including preparation)	Discretionary	Discretionary

SCHEDULE 2

Prescribed Family Proceedings

[Non-franchisees]

(a) High Court and county court proceedings

Column 1	Column 2 *High Court*	Column 3 *County Court or Magistrate's Court*
ITEM **PART I** **PREPARATION**		
1 Writing routine letters.	£4.25 per item	£3.65 per item
2 Receiving routine letters.	£2.10 per item	£1.85 per item
3 Routine telephone calls.	£4.25 per item	£3.65 per item
4 All other preparation work including any work which was reasonably done arising out of or incidental to the proceedings, interviews with client, witnesses, and other parties; obtaining evidence; preparation and consideration of, and dealing with, documents, negotiations and notices; dealing with letters written and received and telephone calls which are not routine.	Where the proceedings were conducted in the divorce registry or in another court on the South Eastern Circuit at the time when the relevant work was done:	
	£46.75 per hour All other circuits: £43.75 per hour	£41.00 per hour £38.75 per hour
5 In addition to items 1–4 above, to cover the general care and conduct of the proceedings.	+50%	+50%
6 Travelling and waiting time in connection with the above matters.	£32.00 per hour	£29.25 per hour

Column 1		Column 2 *High Court*	Column 3 *County Court or Magistrate's Court*
PART II **CONFERENCES WITH COUNSEL**			
7 Attending counsel in conference.		£37.00 per hour	£32.50 per hour
8 Travelling and waiting.		£32.00 per hour	£29.25 per hour
PART III **ATTENDANCES**			
9 Attending with counsel at the trial or hearing of any cause or the hearing of any summons or other application at court, or other appointment.		£37.00 per hour	£32.50 per hour
10 Attending without counsel at the trial or hearing of any cause or the hearing of any summons or other application at court, or other appointment.		£55.75 per hour	£55.25 per hour
11 Travelling and waiting.		£32.00 per hour	£29.25 per hour
PART IV **FEES FOR JUNIOR COUNSEL**			
12 With a brief on an unopposed application for an injunction, or procedural issue.			
	Standard	£88.25	£76.25
	Maximum	£146.25	£127.00
13 With a brief on the trial of a cause or matter or on the hearing of an ancillary application or on a children appointment where the hearing lasts for			
(a) one hour	Standard	£133.50	£114.25
	Maximum	£268.00	£228.50
(b) a half day	Standard	£184.75	£159.25
	Maximum	£304.50	£268.00
(c) a full day	Standard	£368.50	£317.75
	Maximum	£584.75	£508.50
(d) more than a full day		Discretionary	Discretionary
14 For each day or part of a day on which the trial of a cause or matter, or the hearing of an ancillary application, or a children appointment, is continued after the first day.		Discretionary	Discretionary
15 Conference (including time reasonably spent in preparation and conference, but not otherwise remunerated).		Standard £20.25 per 1/2 hour	Standard £17.75 per 1/2 hour
16 (a) Complex items of written work (such as advices on evidence, opinions and affidavits of a substantial nature, requests for particulars or answers).		Standard £96.25 per item	Standard £82.75 per item
(b) All other written work.		Standard £57.00 per item	Standard £50.25 per item

Column 1	Column 2 *High Court*	Column 3 *County Court or Magistrate's Court*
17 Except where the court is within 40 kilometres of Charing Cross or where there is no local Bar in the court town, or within 40 kilometres thereof, for travelling time.	Standard £18.50 per hour + expenses	Standard £15.85 per hour + expenses
PART V DETAILED ASSESSMENT AND APPEAL IN RELATION TO DETAILED ASSESSMENT		
18 Preparing the bill (where allowable) and completing the taxation [detailed assessment] (excluding preparing for and attending the taxation [detailed assessment]).	£32.50–£89.25	£32.00–£51.00
19 Preparing for and attending the taxation [detailed assessment] (including travelling and waiting).	Discretionary	Discretionary
20 Review by district judge or judge [Appeal to costs judge, district judge or judge] (including preparation).	Discretionary	Discretionary

(b) Magistrates' court proceedings

Class of work	*Rate*
Preparation	£44.00 per hour—(£46.75 per hour for a fee-earner whose office is situated within legal aid area 1)
Advocacy	£55.25 per hour
Attendance at court where counsel assigned	£30.00 per hour
Travelling and waiting	£24.60 per hour
Routine letters written and routine telephone	£3.40 per item—(£3.55 per item for a fee-earner whose office is situated within legal aid area 1)

SCHEDULE 2A

Prescribed Family Proceedings

[Franchisees]

(a) High Court and county court proceedings

Column 1	Column 2 *High Court*	Column 3 *County Court or Magistrate's Court*
ITEM **PART I PREPARATION**		
1 Writing routine letters	£7.05 per item	£6.15 per item
2 Receiving routine letters	£3.50 per item	£3.10 per item

Column 1	Column 2 *High Court*	Column 3 *County Court or Magistrate's Court*
3 Routine telephone calls	£7.05 per item	£6.15 per item
4 All other preparation work including any work which was reasonably done arising out of or incidental to the proceedings, interviews with client, witnesses, and other parties; obtaining evidence; preparation and consideration of, and dealing with, documents, negotiations and notices; dealing with letters written and received and telephone calls which are not routine	Where proceedings were conducted in the divorce registry or in another court on the South Eastern Circuit at the time when the relevant work was done: £78.40 per hour All other circuits: £73.05 per hour	Where proceedings were conducted in the divorce registry or in another court on the South Eastern Circuit at the time when the relevant work was done: £68.50 per hour All other circuits: £64.80 per hour
6 Travelling and waiting time in connection with the above matters	£35.75 per hour	£32.45 per hour
PART II CONFERENCES WITH COUNSEL		
7 Attending counsel in conference	£41.25 per hour	£36.30 per hour
8 Travelling and waiting	£35.75 per hour	£32.45 per hour
PART III ATTENDANCES		
9 Attending with counsel at the trial or hearing of any cause or hearing of any summons or other application at court, or other appointment	£41.25 per hour	£36.30 per hour
10 Attending without counsel at the trial or hearings of any cause or the hearing of any summons or other application at court, or other appointment	Where proceedings were conducted in the divorce registry or in another court on the South Eastern Circuit at the time when the relevant work was done: £78.40 per hour All other circuits: £73.05 per hour	Where proceedings were conducted in the divorce registry or in another court on the South Eastern Circuit at the time when the relevant work was done: £68.50 per hour All other circuits: £68.80 per hour
11 Travelling and waiting	£35.75 per hour	£32.45 per hour

Column 1	Column 2 *High Court*	Column 3 *County Court or Magistrate's Court*
PART V **DETAILED ASSESSMENT AND APPEAL IN RELATION TO DETAILED ASSESSMENT**		
18 Preparing the bill (where allowable) and completing the detailed assessment (excluding preparing for and attending the hearing of the detailed assessment)	£35.70–£99.85	£35.70–£56.95
19 Preparing for and attending the hearing of the detailed assessment (including travelling and waiting)	Discretionary	Discretionary
20 Appeal to costs judge, district judge or judge (including preparation)	Discretionary	Discretionary

(b) Magistrates' court proceedings

Class of work	*Rate*
Preparation	£48.95 per hour—(£52.25 per hour for a fee-earner whose office is situated in the Legal Services Commission's London Region)
Advocacy	£61.90 per hour
Attendance at court where counsel assigned	£33.30 per hour
Travelling and waiting	£27.50 per hour
Routine letters written and telephone calls	£3.80 per item—(£4.00 per item for a fee-earner whose office is situated in the Legal Services Commission's London Region)

(c) Graduated Fee Scheme for barristers

On 1 May 2001, the Lord Chancellor introduced a new payment scheme for barrister advocates who undertake publicly-funded family work. Family work is divided into four categories: domestic violence injunctions; public law children; private law children and all other family work. While family certificated work may contain a number of proceedings, and therefore a mix of categories, counsel will be asked to choose one category when applying for payment. The scheme does not apply to appeals to the Divisional Court, Court of Appeal or House of Lords or cases where the final trial or hearing exceeds ten days, which continue to operate under the previous payment arrangements.

Under the scheme, counsel is able to claim a base fee for defined pieces of work ('a function fee') for the following functions:

F:1 pre-issue work;
F:2 injunctive, declaratory or enforcement work;
F:3 interim or review hearings;
F:4 the main conference
F:5 final trial or hearing.

The base fees for each function include all related advice, any conferences, drafting or other work performed as well as advocacy (where relevant). F1 and F4 will only be paid once during the case. There may be more than one F2 and F3 payments. F5 will only be paid once per proceeding and the scheme builds in provision for split hearings.

(i) Additional payments

In certain circumstances, additional payments may be added onto the basic fee to graduate it. While there are a number of potential additional payments, only those that directly concern judges are discussed here. There are as follows:

(1) Special Issue Payment (SIP)
(2) Court Bundle Payment (CBP)
(3) Settlement Supplement Payment (SS)
(4) Special Preparation Fees

SPECIAL ISSUE PAYMENTS (SIP)

The circumstances of a case may require extra work or an additional payment may need to be made to reflect its complexity. Such payments are known as Special issue Payments (SIP) and are paid as a percentage of the base fee or hearing unit fee. Deciding whether to 'certify' a special issue payment in respect of the hearing is a judicial function and must be certified by the judge on the prescribed form at the end of each relevant hearing.

COURT BUNDLE PAYMENTS (CBP)

Payments are made relative to the size of the court bundle to reflect variation in preparation. The judge's certificate must be obtained for bundles in excess of 700 pages.

SETTLEMENT SUPPLEMENT PAYMENT (SSP)

To encourage early settlement, supplemental payments are made if the case settles while counsel is instructed and if the settlement falls within the criteria set. These are not the concern of the judge but if a case listed for two days or more settles on the first day, counsel will be entitled to a settlement supplement payment. This is a percentage of the hearing unit fee and in the case of ancillary relief proceedings, an additional payment (£171.88 in respect of Queen's Counsel and £68.75 for junior counsel) is made where the settlement takes place prior to the FDR appointment if it leads to resolution of the proceedings.

SPECIAL PREPARATION FEES

Further payments are made to reflect additional and exceptional preparation and are within the discretion of the judge.

IPS

Additional payments may also include incidental sums that counsel may have incurred, eg, the listening to, or watching of, audio or visual tapes, discs or cassettes; travel, hotel expenses or travel time.

(ii) Current rates

Here are the current rates:

CATEGORY 1 – FAMILY INJUNCTIONS (A)

Base Rates for Queen's Counsel

Function	Base Fee	Hearing Unit	Settlement
F1	150		
F2		287.50	100%
F3			
F4	125		
F5 Primary		800	10%
F5 Secondary		550	

Base Rates for Junior Counsel

Function	Base Fee	Hearing Unit	Settlement
F1	60		
F2		115	100%
F3			
F4	50		
F5 Primary		320	10%
F5 Secondary		220	

	Category 1 – Queen's Counsel	Category 1 – Junior Counsel
	SIPs %	**SIPs %**
LIP (litigant in person)	5%	5%
2+ parties	5%	5%
Multi-clients	5%	5%
Experts	10%	10%
Foreign	0%	0%
Assets	0%	0%
Conduct	0%	0%

CATEGORY 2 – PUBLIC LAW CHILDREN (B)

Base Rates for Queen's Counsel

Function	Base Fee	Hearing Unit	Settlement
F1	175		
F2		212.50	100%
F3		412.50	100%
F4	150		
F5 Primary		1075	20%
F5 Secondary		575	

Base Rates for Junior Counsel

Function	Base Fee	Hearing Unit	Settlement
F1	70		
F2		85	100%
F3		165	100%
F4	60		
F5 Primary		430	20%
F5 Secondary		230	

	Category 1 – Queen's Counsel	Category 1 – Junior Counsel
	SIPs %	SIPs %
LIP (litigant in person)	40%	40%
2+ parties	40%	40%
Multi-clients	5%	5%
Experts	20%	20%
Foreign	30%	30%
Assets	0%	0%
Conduct	50%	50%

CATEGORY 3 – PRIVATE LAW CHILDREN (C)

Base Rates for Queen's Counsel

Function	Base Fee	Hearing Unit	Settlement
F1	150		
F2		187.50	100%
F3		300	100%
F4	125		
F5 Primary		812.50	10%
F5 Secondary		550	

Base Rates for Junior Counsel

Function	Base Fee	Hearing Unit	Settlement
F1	60		
F2		75	100%
F3		120	100%
F4	50		
F5 Primary		325	10%
F5 Secondary		220	

	Category 1 – Queen's Counsel	Category 1 – Junior Counsel
	SIPs %	SIPs %
LIP (litigant in person)	30%	30%
2+ parties	30%	30%
Multi-clients	5%	5%
Experts	50%	50%
Foreign	30%	30%
Assets	0%	0%
Conduct	50%	50%

CATEGORY 4 – ANCILLARY RELIEF AND ALL OTHER FAMILY WORK (D)

Base Rates for Queen's Counsel

Function	Base Fee	Hearing Unit	Settlement
F1	150		171.88*
F2		162.50	50%
F3		300**	50%
F4	125		
F5 Primary		812.50	10%
F5 Secondary		550	

Base Rates for Junior Counsel

Function	Base Fee	Hearing Unit	Settlement
F1	60		68.75*
F2		65	50%
F3		120	50%
F4	50		
F5 Primary		325	10%
F5 Secondary		220	

* Settlement in ancillary relief only
** FDR hearing receive an additional sum of £150.00 (QC) and £60.00 (JC)

	Category 1 – Queen's Counsel	Category 1 – Junior Counsel
	SIPs %	**SIPs %**
LIP (litigant in person)	10%	10%
2+ parties	10%	10%
Multi-clients	5%	5%
Experts	10%	10%
Foreign	25%	25%
Assets	50%	50%
Conduct	50%	50%

ADDITIONAL PAYMENTS

Special preparation fee	1. exceptional cases	All paid at the hourly rate of QC £100.50 JC £40.20	
	2. adjourned care case – same hourly rate 3. court bundle C		
High Court uplift	33% increase on total graduated fee		
Financial Dispute Resolution hearings	Additional sum paid	QC £150.00 JC £60.00	
Ancillary relief settlement in F1	Settlement fee paid at	QC £171.88 JC £68.75	
Court Bundle 1 payments	176–350 pages		
	Functions	QC	JC
	F1	40	16
	F2	47	19
	F3	82	33
	F4	33	13
	F5P	221	88
	F5S	135	54
Court Bundle 2 payments	351–700 pages		
	Functions	QC	JC
	F1	79	32
	F2	94	37.50
	F3	165	66
	F4	67	27
	F5P	442	177
	F5S	271	108

(d) South Eastern Circuit

Schedule 2 provides a higher rate for the South Eastern Circuit than for the rest of the country. As this includes King's Lynn and Ramsgate as well as Central London, there should be some thriving matrimonial practices on the Norfolk Broads and the Isle of Thanet, while firms in the great metropolises outside the South Eastern Circuit may wonder whether some other form of regional differentiation might be more appropriate.

(e) Routine letters

The Civil Procedure Rules adopt the six-minute unit for writing routine letters, to include perusing routine incoming letters. Schedule 2 permits a charge for both, which results in higher remuneration that if the six-minute unit had been adopted.

(f) Travel: time spent and costs incurred

In determining the amount to be allowed in respect of travel:

(1) On the face of it, the amount to be allowed is the cost of the time expended on and the expenses incurred in making the journey by public transport, provided that public transport is available and is reasonably convenient, having regard to the relevant circumstances in each case, and

(2) Allowances made should include the time spent and expense incurred in getting from the starting point to the railhead or coach station and also the time spent and expense in getting from the terminus to the destination (Ref: *CRIMLA 33* (Amended) – 30.7.92 and 30.1.95).

(g) Photocopying

The making of copies of documents is part of the solicitor's normal overhead expense, and thus would not normally be remunerated separately. However, an allowance may be made for copying in unusual circumstances or where the documents copied are unusually numerous in relation to the nature of the case. The cost should be claimed as a disbursement. If copies have been made out of the office the actual cost should be claimed. If made in the office, a charge equivalent to the commercial cost should be claimed. A charge based on the time expended by a member of the solicitor's staff will not be allowed (Ref: *CRIMLA 1* (Amended) – 18.12 89 and 30.1.95).

(h) Attending counsel

Although letters, telephone calls and all the preparation work carry a 50% mark-up, there is no mark-up for attending counsel either in conference or at court. See the explanation in respect of civil costs at p 386.

(i) Enhancement

(i) Entitlement

Regulation 3(4)(*c*) empowers a costs officer to allow a larger amount than specified in column 2 or column 3 of Parts I, II, III and V of Schs 1 and 2(a) where it appears to him reasonable to do so having regard to:

(i) the exceptional competence with which the work was done, or
(ii) the exceptional expedition with which the work was done, or
(iii) any other exceptional circumstances of the case including, in the case of care proceedings, the fact that the solicitor was a member of the Law Society's Children Act Panel.

Regulation 3(5) gives a similar discretion in respect of counsel's fees.

(ii) Quantification

Regulation 3(7) prescribes that the costs officer shall exercise his discretion to allow a larger amount in accordance with para l(2) of Pt l of Sch l to the Rules which are our old friends, the seven pillars of wisdom. Here they are again:

(a) the complexity of the item or of the cause or matter in which it arises and the difficulty or novelty of the questions involved;
(b) the skill, specialised knowledge and responsibility required of, and the time and labour expended by, the solicitor or counsel;
(c) the number and importance of the documents (however brief) prepared or perused;
(d) the place and circumstances in which the business involved is transacted;
(e) the importance of the cause or matter to the client;
(f) where money or property is involved, its amount or value;
(g) any other fees and allowances payable to the solicitor or counsel in respect of other items in the same cause or matter, but only where work done in relation to those items has reduced the work which would otherwise have been necessary in relation to the item in question.

(iii) Two stages

It is a two-stage process. First, the entitlement to enhancement is decided by considering the threshold circumstances prescribed in reg 3(4)(*c*) and, if the threshold is crossed, it is followed by quantification of the enhancement by applying the discretionary factors prescribed in reg 3(7).

(iv) Family and civil

There are important differences between the provisions for enhancement in respect of legal aid costs in prescribed family proceedings and in other proceedings. I deal with them fully under the heading of Civil and Non-Prescribed Family Proceedings at p 384 and shall here consider only the judicial decisions relating to enhancement in prescribed family proceedings.

(v) Membership of the Law Society's Children Act and Solicitors Family Law Association Panels

Membership of these panels is itself an exceptional circumstance under reg 3(4)(*c*)(iii) of the Legal Aid in Family Proceedings (Remuneration) Regulations 1991 which gives a discretion to the assessing officer to allow a larger amount than that specified where it appears to him to be reasonable to do so in any particular part of the hill of costs in question. (Ref: *CLA 8* (Amended) – 23 September 1996.)

The enhancement provisions within the Legal Aid in Family Proceedings (Remuneration) Regulations 1991 (LAFP(R)R) have been amended so that cases where enhancement is currently available now attract a guaranteed minimum enhancement of 15% where the work is done by a fee earner who is on the accredited specialist panel of the Solicitors Family Law Association (SFLA) or the Law Society's Children Act Panel but higher amounts may still be obtained if justified. The enhancement is available to all work done in a family case by a member of the accredited specialist panel of the SFLA. For a member of the Law Society's Children Act Panel, the enhancement is available for all work done under a certificate that includes proceedings relating to children (as defined below). This will mean that if a certificate covers both children proceedings and ancillary relief, all the work done by the specialist fee earner under the certificate will attract the minimum enhancement. This is not so if the certificate only covers ancillary relief. Proceedings relating to children are defined as 'proceedings within which the welfare of children is determined, without limitation, proceedings under the Children Act 1989 or under the inherent jurisdiction of the High Court in relation to children'. There was dismay when the enhancement provisions were not extended to the Law Society's Family Panel (LSFP) but the Lord Chancellor has now agreed to the creation of two tiers in the Family Panel, the second tier qualifying for enhancement. It is now in place (see SI 2001/830, reg 4 which amended the LAFP(R)R 1991).

The minimum guaranteed enhancement is not available for supervision nor to work done by other fee earners. While such work is not subject to the guaranteed minimum enhancement, it may attract enhancement on assessment in the normal way if the criteria in reg 3(4)(*c*) are satisfied. When preparing a bill for detailed assessment, the narrative should clearly state the fee earner for whom the enhancement is claimed and the basis of the enhancement under the amended regulations.

As a general rule, where a solicitor appeared as an advocate, this is not an exceptional circumstance. Where, however, a Children Panel solicitor appeared as an advocate in care proceedings, this will be an exceptional circumstance. Whether this justifies of itself allowance of a 'larger amount' is a question for the exercise of discretion, in consideration of all the circumstances of the case. An uplift in hourly rate for panel membership in cases properly lasting more than two days would normally be justified. (Ref: *CLA 9* (Amended) – 23 September 1996.)

When considering a claim for enhanced rates on the basis of reg 3(4)(*c*)(iii) of the Legal Aid in Family Proceedings (Remuneration) Regulations 1991 consideration should, when deciding if there are 'any other exceptional circumstances' of the case, be given to whether any of the following exist:

1. FACTORS WHICH MIGHT RAISE AN EXCEPTIONAL CIRCUMSTANCE:

(i) innate difficulties of communication with the client, eg mental health problems, deaf, speech-impaired, or autistic clients, or clients requiring an interpreter (although attention should first be given as to whether this has been covered by longer than normal hours of attendance being claimed);
(ii) a conflict of detailed expert evidence (as opposed to merely contested expert evidence, and/or a proliferation of expert witnesses);
(iii) a hearing in excess of two days without counsel;
(iv) conflict between the guardian ad litem and the child, where the child instructs his own solicitor.

2. FACTORS WHICH MIGHT BUT NOT NECESSARILY WOULD RAISE EXCEPTIONAL CIRCUMSTANCES:

(i) detailed contested allegation of sexual or serious abuse;
(ii) a large number of parties with competing applications;
(iii) involvement of children with different needs.

The transfer of the case to a care centre or from a care centre to the High Court is indicative of complexity and weight only and are not conclusive of exceptional circumstances.

Where exceptional circumstances are said to arise there must be a factor, or combination of factors, in the particular case which is exceptional or are unusual in care proceedings.

The factors set out above are a non-exhaustive list. They relate to the circumstances of the case itself and not to claims for enhanced rates based on reg 3(4)(*c*)(i) and (ii) of the Legal Aid in Family Proceedings (Remuneration) Regulations 1991 which have regard to the manner in which the work was done.

Where exceptional circumstances are sought to be established and solicitors seek remuneration on the basis of the exercise of the assessing officer's discretion pursuant to reg 3(4)(*c*) the solicitor must precisely identify the exceptional circumstances and those specific items of work in respect of which enhancement is sought (see *Re Children Act 1989 Taxation of Costs* [1994] 2 FLR 934).

(vi) The authorities

Eastham J in *Freeman v Freeman* (21 February 1992, unreported, *Butterworths Costs Service* para N[201]) Fam in respect of Prescribed Family Proceedings:

> 'Where a court is satisfied or a taxing officer is satisfied that there are exceptional circumstances in the case, then he the taxing officer is completely freed from the fixed amount specified in the Second Schedule and it is his duty thereafter to assess what in all the circumstances is a fair and reasonable fee both in relation to the hourly rate and also in relation to the mark-up.'

The LAB Appeal Committee in *CRIMLA 36* (26 September 1994) held that:

> 'The proper test of "exceptional" within "exceptional circumstances of the case" in paragraph 3 (b) of Part 1 Schedule 1 Legal Aid in Criminal and Care Proceedings (Costs) Regulations 1989 is the ordinary and actual meaning of the word "exceptional" ie "unusual or out of the ordinary".'

Cazalet J in *London Borough of A v M and S F* [1995] 1 FCR 688, Fam in respect of care proceedings:

> '(a) "Exceptional Circumstances"
> We do not feel that a legal definition can be given to the words "Exceptional Circumstances" or is necessary. The courts are well used to dealing with these words and taxing officers are well able to recognise exceptional circumstances. ... We emphasise that there is no basis for limiting a taxing officer's discretion by attempting to compile an exhaustive list of "exceptional circumstances". These will change as the law, procedure, society and its problems change. What is exceptional today may not be exceptional tomorrow ... We emphasise that in each case where "exceptional circumstances" are said to arise there must be a factor or combination of factors in the particular case being taxed which is/are exceptional/unusual in care proceedings. The category of circumstances which might qualify as "exceptional" must have an effect in a qualitative or quantitative sense on the work required of the lawyer seeking an exercise of the discretion. In care cases the following factors may give rise to "exceptional circumstances":
>
> 1. Where a case is transferred upwards, this is not conclusive of exceptional circumstances but is no more than an indicator of complexity and weight.
> 2. Innate difficulties of communication with the client, eg through mental health problems, deafness, speech impairment, the client being autistic or requiring an interpreter, may constitute exceptional circumstances, although consideration may first be given to whether the matter has not in fact been covered by longer than normal hours of attendance being claimed.
> 3. A conflict of detailed expert evidence as opposed merely to contested expert

evidence and/or a proliferation of expert witnesses is more likely to constitute an exceptional circumstance.

4. Detailed contested allegations of sexual or other serious abuse may, but will not necessarily, constitute exceptional circumstances.
5. Hearings in excess of two days undertaken by solicitors without reliance upon counsel may well raise exceptional circumstances.
6. A large number of parties with competing applications may, but will not necessarily, constitute an exceptional circumstance.
7. A conflict between the guardian ad litem and the child.
8. The involvement of children with different needs may, but will not necessarily, constitute an exceptional circumstance.

(b) How much?

The "larger amount" that we are required to assess is, in my view, linked and referable to the specified sums under the Regulations themselves … The empowering words "may allow a larger amount" are specific and can only be referring to a sum which is assessed by reference to the prescribed rates … The district judge's knowledge and experience of work carried out at the prescribed rate will provide him with a suitable yardstick by which to assess the larger amount of costs to be allowed when exceptional circumstances arise. That this yardstick should be one of the factors brought into account in the exercise of discretion is, in my view, further supported by the words of Regulation 3(4)(c) and Regulation 7 which do not seek (whether by inclusion or exclusion) to limit the exercise of discretion, save that it can only be based on circumstances which are relevant. That is not to say that the taxing officer will not carry out the broad average direct costs and care and conduct uplift approach. His experience of rates in his locality should enable him to do this quite readily and he will no doubt have in mind the product of that calculation … However I take the view that a district judge when standing back and formulating his overall assessment must keep in mind as a controlling yardstick for the larger amount the fact that numbers of solicitors are carrying out work, not within the exceptional circumstance range, at the prescribed rates.'

In respect of advocacy the court increased the prescribed rate of £63 an hour to £75 an hour representing an uplift to reflect membership of the Law Society's Children Act Panel of about 20% in respect of attendances where there were no other exceptional circumstances. In respect of advocacy, at the substantive hearing the court took the view that there were exceptional circumstances justifying an increase in the advocacy figure to £95 an hour, being approximately 50% more than the prescribed hourly rate in order to reflect both membership of the Children Panel and the other exceptional circumstances. Where a case might be considered as most exceptional, a district judge would be likely to arrive at a higher figure whilst an exceptional element lower down the scale could result in a figure of less than £95 an hour. The judge said 'We do not prescribe £95 per hour as a figure set in stone, but it may be a useful benchmark for practitioners and taxing officers'. In respect of attendances on a volatile, aggressive and difficult witness the prescribed rate was increased by 20% to £72 an hour in respect of panel membership with a further increase to £84 to reflect the difficulties. On the same basis, attendances on the client were increased to £90 an hour which was also allowed for consideration of documents and preparation for trial to reflect panel membership.

(vii) Confusion

In saying that £95 was intended to reflect membership of the panel and other exceptional circumstances and that in a case that might be most exceptional a district judge would be likely to arrive at a higher figure, the judge appears to have confused two concepts. The first concept is the threshold criteria prescribed in reg 3(4)(*c*). If a case is exceptional, the costs officer is empowered to exercise his discretion; if not,

not. It does not matter for this purpose by how much the threshold is exceeded, the case either gets over it or it does not. If the case does get over the threshold of exceptional circumstances then the entirely different set of criteria prescribed by reg 3(7) applies as to how the discretion is to be exercised – the seven pillars of wisdom. When assessing the 'larger amount' to be allowed it is to these factors that the court's attention should be directed – the question of whether the case or the work was exceptional is no longer relevant. A case involving exceptional circumstances cannot become unexceptional each and every time a fee earner does an item of routine work.

(viii) Between-the-parties costs

See p 394.

(j) Costs of preparing the bill

The 'costs of preparing the bill' in item 17 of the Legal Aid in Family Proceedings (Remuneration) Regulations 1991 covers all the costs of drawing up a bill which is fit to be presented to the paying party: that is not only the costs of the costs draftsman but also the costs of the solicitor in checking and signing the bill. This is to be distinguished from the costs of preparing for and attending the taxation hearing which are covered by item 18. It is an essential part of preparing the bill, rather than a part of the court's process if scrutinising that bill. However, when there is a provisional assessment, the solicitor then has to look through the bill as provisionally assessed and decide whether to accept it or proceed to an assessment hearing. That work must be part of 'preparing for and attending the taxation', under item 18 of the regulations. In practice, it should be possible for the solicitor to make a fair estimate of how long this will take and add a provisional figure in respect of it. It is likely to take longer in those cases where the result of the provisional assessment is such that the solicitor is likely to want to proceed to an assessment hearing, in which case the matter can be argued there: *A Local Authority v Mother and Child (family proceedings: Legal Aid assessment* [2000] All ER (D) 2389.

4. CIVIL AND NON-PRESCRIBED FAMILY PROCEEDINGS

(a) The regulations

The Civil Legal Aid (General) (Amendment) Regulations 1994, the Legal Aid in Civil Proceedings (Remuneration) Regulations 1994 and the Legal Aid in Family Proceedings (Remuneration) (Amendment) Regulations 1994 came into force on 25 February 1994. They were followed by a practice direction. The Schedules to the Remuneration Regulations were amended from 1 April 1996:

Schedule 1

[NON-FRANCHISEES]

Column 1	Column 2 *High Court*	Column 3 *County Court or Magistrates' Court*
WORK		
1 Routine letters out.	£7.40 per item	£6.50 per item
2 Routine telephone calls.	£4.10 per item	£3.60 per item
3 All other preparation work including any work which was reasonably done arising out of or incidental to the proceedings, interviews with client, witnesses, and other parties; obtaining evidence; preparation and consideration of, and dealing with, documents, negotiations and notices; dealing with letters written and received and telephone calls which are not routine.	£74.00 per hour	£65.00 per hour
	(£78.50 per hour where solicitor's office situated within legal aid area 1)	£69.00 per hour
4 Attending counsel in conference or at the trial or hearing of any summons or application at court, or other appointment.	£36.40 per hour	£32.00 per hour
5 Attending without counsel at the trial or hearing of any cause or the hearing of any summons or other application at court, or other appointment.	£74.00 per hour	£65.00 per hour
6 Travelling and waiting in connection with the above matters.	£32.70 per hour	£28.75 per hour

Schedule 2

[FRANCHISEES]

Column 1	Column 2 *High Court*	Column 3 *County Court or Magistrates' Court*
WORK		
1 Routine letters out.	£7.50 per item	£6.60 per item
2 Routine telephone calls.	£4.15 per item	£3.65 per item
3 All other preparation work including any work which was reasonably done arising out of or incidental to the proceedings, interviews with client, witnesses, and other parties; obtaining evidence; preparation and consideration of, and dealing with, documents, negotiations and notices; dealing with letters written and received and telephone calls which are not routine.		£66.00 per hour
	(£79.50 per hour where solicitor's office situated within legal aid area 1)	£70.00 per hour

Column 1	Column 2 *High Court*	Column 3 *County Court or Magistrates' Court*
4 Attending counsel in conference or at the trial or hearing of any summons or application at court, or other appointment.	£37.00 per hour	£32.50 per hour
5 Attending without counsel at the trial or hearing of any cause or the hearing of any summons or other application at court, or other appointment.	£75.00 per hour	£66.00 per hour
6 Travelling and waiting in connection with the above matters.	£33.25 per hour	£29.20 per hour

(b) The figures

(i) One rate

Let us face the bad news first. The same rate is prescribed for the entire country (with an increase in respect of Legal Aid Area 1) and it is a single rate irrespective of the level of fee earner. Also it is not, as was originally intended, limited to the county court: the prescribed fees and hourly rates apply to both High Court and county court proceedings.

(ii) £74 an hour

And then the even worse news. The rate has not been increased since 1 April 1996. A prescribed rate of £74 an hour including profit mark-up. As many county courts on summary assessment now allow rates of £150 and more, how can this be? I shall tell you. The Lord Chancellor abandoned his original intention that the rates should be costs neutral, ie set at figures which would maintain the current level of remuneration. It was decided to pitch the rates at a level which would attract a sufficient number of firms of solicitors who were prepared to undertake legal aid work. A 1991 survey showed that the average expense rate allowed on taxations was £48.86. To this was added a 3% uprating for inflation. And then 50% profit mark-up? No. Having read the various authorities those advising the Lord Chancellor observed that in a 50% mark-up is an element of unrecorded time but, they argued, solicitors are now so sophisticated at time recording such a provision is no longer necessary and would result in double remuneration. Therefore a 30% mark-up was added, resulting in the final figure of £65 an hour in the county court and £74 an hour in the High Court when the rates were introduced in February 1994 and they have been static ever since.

(iii) Routine letters out

The fixed fee is based on the six minute unit, being one-tenth of the prescribed hourly rate to include reading an incoming letter and replying to it. If perusing an incoming letter and writing an outgoing letter takes more than six minutes the time should be recorded and charged under preparation at the hourly rate. For routine telephone calls the six minute unit has not been applied. Indeed little over three minutes for a routine telephone call is allowed. Again, the remedy is that all telephone calls lasting more than three minutes should be timed and charged at the hourly rate.

(iv) Attending counsel

£36.40 per hour in the High Court and £32 per hour in the county court. Incredible? It is only three-quarters of the Lord Chancellor's Department's own survey figure for the expense rate alone without mark-up. The argument is that at a conference it is counsel who takes the lead and does the work. The solicitor merely leads the client to counsel's chambers and sits throughout the conference struck dumb in awe and admiration at counsel's wit, wisdom and erudition, or perhaps just at the thought of how much more the solicitor could be earning if he were back at the office. In any event, it does not make sense to require solicitors to be present at every conference and pay them less than their minimum expense rate. The only mitigation is to ensure you charge at your full rate for all time spent in preparation for the attendance – or don't have conferences!

(v) Enhancement

1. REGULATION 5

Now for the good news. Regulation 5 of the Legal Aid in Civil Proceedings (Remuneration) Regulations 1994 provides:

5. ENHANCEMENT

(1) Upon a determination the relevant authority may allow fees at more than the prescribed rate subject to the provisions of this regulation where it appears to the relevant authority, taking into account all the relevant circumstances, that

(a) the work was done with exceptional competence, skill or expertise;
(b) the work was done with exceptional dispatch; or
(c) the case involved exceptional circumstances or complexity.

(2) Where the relevant authority considers that any item or class of work should be allowed at more than the prescribed rate, it shall apply to that item or class of work a percentage enhancement in accordance with the following provisions of this regulation.

(3) In determining the percentage by which fees should be enhanced above the prescribed rate the relevant authority shall have regard to:—

(a) the degree of responsibility accepted by the solicitor;
(b) the care, speed and economy with which the case was prepared;
(c) the novelty, weight and complexity of the case.

(4) Except in proceedings to which paragraph (5) applies, the percentage above the prescribed rate by which fees for work may be enhanced shall not exceed 100 per cent.

(5) In proceedings in the High Court, the relevant authority may allow an enhancement exceeding 100 per cent where it considers that, in comparison with work in other High Court proceedings which would merit 100 per cent enhancement, the item or class of work relates to exceptionally complex matters which have been handled with exceptional competence or dispatch.

(6) In proceedings to which paragraph (5) applies, the percentage above the prescribed rate by which fees for work may be enhanced may exceed 100 per cent but shall not exceed 200 per cent.

(7) The relevant authority may have regard to the generality of proceedings to which these Regulations apply in determining what is exceptional within the meaning of this regulation.

2. REGULATION 6

Before you get too excited let me remind you of reg 6. It is not one-way traffic:

6. REDUCTION OF COSTS

(1) Upon a determination the relevant authority may allow costs in respect of any item or class of work at less than the prescribed rate where it appears reasonable to do so having regard to the competence or dispatch with which the item or class of work was done.
(2) Paragraph (1) is without prejudice to regulation 109 of the General Regulations.

Regulation 109 of the Civil Legal Aid (General) Regulations 1989 provides for any wasted costs to be disallowed or reduced on any taxation of an assisted person's costs and for disallowance or reduction of costs for delay in proceeding with the taxation.

3. JUDICIAL DISCRETION

Enhancement is all that stands between the assessment of costs remaining a judicial process and not becoming a bureaucratic arithmetical exercise. It is all that prevents the paying party (the state) being the arbiter of the fees it is willing to pay. It is all that preserves any semblance of judicial discretion in costs officers under the principle of payment of a reasonable amount for work reasonably done. Costs officers are empowered to double remuneration in the county court and treble it in the High Court. It is a vital escape clause which must be considered in respect of every bill. Will the profession appreciate it and take advantage of it? The answer on past performance is a resounding 'No'. The prescribed family proceedings enhancement provisions were obtained by the Law Society in 1991 after hard bargaining and yet district judge after district judge has told me that no-one has ever applied to him for enhancement of their matrimonial costs! It appears that many practitioners prefer to whinge about their unhappy lot rather than to use their minds and energies in taking advantage of remedies that are available to them.

4. ENTITLEMENT

THE THRESHOLD CIRCUMSTANCES

Look carefully at the circumstances in reg 5(1) and compare them with the similar provisions in the Legal Aid in Family Proceedings (Remuneration) Regulations 1991, reg 3(4)(*c*) on p 379.

The civil enhancement provisions are considerably wider. They are exceptional:

(i) competence;
(ii) skill;
(iii) expertise;
(iv) dispatch;
(v) circumstances;
(vi) complexity.

In the Law Society's negotiations over their wording, every comma and conjunction was debated and they represent major concessions secured by the Law Society. There are six separate prescribed circumstances any one of which gives entitlement to enhancement. (See also 'Confusion' on p 382.) In every case consider which of them apply and seek enhancement where appropriate.

GENERALITY

Regulation 5(7) is pregnant with meaning and importance. 'The generality of proceedings' precludes the practitioner being met with the argument 'this is a run-of-the-mill medical negligence case and therefore you are not entitled to enhancement'. All medical negligence cases should come within some or all of the prescribed circumstances if they are compared with routine litigation and all should qualify for enhancement. The principle was exemplified in the criminal costs decision of *R v Legal Aid Board, ex p RM Broudie & Co* (1994) 138 Sol Jo LB 94, Div Ct in which it was held that in deciding whether a murder case was exceptional one compared it with the ordinary run of criminal cases generally and not with other murder cases. Broudie was in fact armed robbery.

Cazalet J in the *London Borough of A v M and SF* (see p 381) said 'The early cases of child sexual abuse may well have been viewed as exceptional. However such cases are now regularly before the courts'. I suggest that such an observation would not have been relevant if reg 5(7) applied to care cases. All sexual abuse cases are exceptional compared with the generality of care proceedings.

5. QUANTIFICATION

CALCULATING THE PERCENTAGE

Having got over the threshold of entitlement to enhancement the second stage is the entirely separate one of assessing how much it should be. Regulation 5(3) prescribes the factors. Although for some unknown reason, unlike the equivalent provision for prescribed family proceedings, these regulations do not specifically set out the seven pillars of wisdom, but the factors are virtually the same. How, therefore, are they to be applied to quantification? Regulation 5 requires that a percentage enhancement shall be applied to the prescribed hourly rates which shall not exceed 100% in the county court or 200% in the High Court. The question therefore becomes how is the percentage enhancement to be arrived at? Before the arrival of prescribed hourly rates it has been well established since *Eastwood and Lazarus* (see p 218) that the prescribed factors are to be applied by ascertaining the direct cost of doing the work, the A factor, and adding to it the B factor for profit mark-up expressed as a percentage. As I have shown, even the prescribed hourly rates were calculated in this way. Is the percentage increase to be assessed in some way other than that established by authority and statute? Unless an arbitrary figure is to be plucked from the air and applied to the prescribed hourly rate, which itself consists of both the direct cost and profit mark-up, the only way to evaluate enhanced costs is to ascertain the direct cost and profit uplift and then convert it into a percentage of the prescribed hourly rate or fixed item. That appears to have been done in *London Borough of A v M and SF* by Cazalet J and the assessors. They arrived at figures of £75 and £95 an hour and then expressed them to be about 20% and 50% respectively above the prescribed hourly rate.

THE AUTHORITIES

There is considerable authority for this approach. The principle was enunciated in *R v Backhouse*, a criminal appeal to the SCTO (now SCCO) Master in March 1986 applying regulations comparable to the Civil and Non-Prescribed Family Proceedings Regulations 1994. The Master accepted that solicitors were entitled to enhancement because the case had been handled with exceptional competence and dispatch and also because of the exceptional circumstances of the case. The master quoted the decision in *R v Hussain*, 3 January 1984, Case No 820498/9 in which the Master concluded that:

'The taxing (*costs*) officer should proceed in accordance with the general principle that where any scale of costs is avoided by reason of the exercise of a discretion to do so, the allowance to be made should be fixed without reference to the scale item because the scale has ceased to be relevant. He should accordingly make this assessment in accordance with the directions contained in reg 3(5) ... save that he will ignore the limitation placed on his discretion by reg 5(3) which would otherwise require him to allow fees in accordance with Schedule 1. To carry out that task he must assess a rate which reflects first the direct cost of the work at the time when it was done bearing in mind the status of the relevant fee earner, and secondly, the burden of the relevant circumstances. The exercise is unavoidably arbitrary and can be no more than a value judgment based on experience.'

In *Backhouse* the costs judge in his judgment said:

'I have considered the decision in *R v Hussain* and I notice that before expressing his view the learned master indicated that it was necessary to assess a rate which reflects first the direct cost of the work at the time when it was done bearing in mind the status of the relevant fee earner and, secondly, to assess the burden of the relevant circumstances, that is those circumstances set out in reg 3(5) which are listed as including the nature, importance, complexity or difficulty of the work and the time involved. It seems to me that what the master was saying was that A plus B calculation should be made in order to reach an enhanced rate. That seems to me to be the only possible logical approach once the rates prescribed by the regulations cease to apply, but I would go further and say the proper approach is to arrive at an A figure for the broad average direct cost of the work and add to that a percentage uplift (the B figure) to take into account all the relevant circumstances of the case as required by reg 3(5).'

As we have seen, Evans J applied the Legal Aid in Family Proceedings (Remuneration) Regulations 1991 in *Freeman* (p 381) as follows:

'Where a court is satisfied or a taxing officer is satisfied that there are exceptional circumstances in the case, then he the taxing officer is completely freed from the fixed amount specified in the Second Schedule and it is his duty thereafter to assess what in all the circumstances is a fair and reasonable fee both in relation to the hourly rate and also in relation to the mark-up.'

This approach was confirmed by the Legal Aid Board in *CRIMLA 13* (Amended) 17 May 1994 and 26 September 1994 relating to enhanced rates in criminal and care cases in respect of which the prescribed factors are now identical to those in the 1994 Regulations. On the appeal it was held:

'Where the criteria for paying enhanced rates in criminal proceedings under the Legal Aid in Criminal and Care Proceedings (Costs) Regulations 1989 are met, such claims will be assessed on the basis of the broad average direct cost of the work (the A figure) to which is added a percentage uplift (the B figure) to take into account all the relevant circumstances of the case. The A figure will represent the broad average direct cost of undertaking the work. Factors to be taken into account in identifying this figure may include the rate likely to be allowed in an enhanced rates case by the appropriate Crown Court for the relevant level of fee earner at the time to which the cost claim relates and evidence of the results of surveys of local solicitors' expense rates. As to the B figure, 35% should be considered as a starting point in respect of preparation. Solicitor advocacy would normally be expected to carry an uplift of 40–60% and attendances with counsel 20%. In the majority of cases where enhancement is claimed and allowed it will, nonetheless, be usual to pay travel and waiting without enhancement at the prescribed legal aid rate. Each case must be considered on its own particular merits having regard to all the relevant circumstances of the case. A claim for travel and waiting at the A figure may be allowed in exceptional cases. Even then travel and waiting would not be expected to attract an uplift on the A figure. When enhanced rates apply to routine letters written and to telephone calls made or received and they are not timed, the method of assessment

> is to allow them at one tenth of the hourly rate plus , in appropriate cases, an uplift for preparation.'

In *London Borough of A v M and SF* Cazalet J was construing the words 'may allow a larger amount' in the 1991 Regulations. The equivalent words in the 1994 Regulations are, 'may allow fees at more than the prescribed rate'. There may or may not be a significant difference between these two phrases but there is a significant difference between the two sets of regulations in that in the 1994 Regulations there is a cap or cut-off point of 100% in the county court and 200% in the High Court above the prescribed rate whilst there is no such ceiling under the 1991 Regulations. Nevertheless Cazalet J said:

> 'The district judge's knowledge and experience of work carried out at the prescribed rate will provide him with a suitable yardstick by which to assess the larger amount of costs to be allowed when exceptional circumstances arise. That this yardstick should be one of the factors brought into account in the exercise of discretion is, in my view, further supported by the words of reg 3(4)(c) and reg 7 which do not seek (whether by inclusion or exclusion) to limit the exercise of discretion, save that it can only be based on circumstances which are relevant. That is not to say that the taxing officer will not carry out the broad average direct costs and care and conduct uplift approach. His experience of rates in his locality should enable him to do this quite readily and he will no doubt have in mind the product of that calculation. Indeed such a calculation may well produce the highest limit of the bracket which commences at the level of the prescribed rate. The taxing officer must then however exercise the discretion in the manner so clearly stated by Evans J in *Johnson v Reed Corrugated Cases Ltd* (above cited). It seems to me in exercising that discretion that the district judge's general knowledge and experience as well as his particular knowledge of the numerous taxations carried out by him and/or others upon the basis of the prescribed rates is one of the beacons that will guide him in the exercise of his discretion in assessing the larger amount to be paid for exceptional work. As I have said I do not consider that the decision of Eastham J in *Freeman* (above cited) sought to indicate otherwise. However if I am wrong about this then whilst this decision must be of considerable persuasive authority I respectfully take the view that a district judge when standing back and formulating his overall assessment must keep in mind as a controlling yardstick for a larger amount the fact that numbers of solicitors are carrying out work, not within the exceptional circumstance range, at the prescribed rates.'

THREE APPROACHES

1. *Direct costs plus mark-up.* How are the direct costs and mark-up to be ascertained? In exactly the same way as in all other cases. Is it too much to suggest that enhanced state-funded expense rates should not be less than those for run-of-the mill cases as in non-state-funded litigation? To these is to be applied a mark-up where appropriate, remembering that the total cannot exceed 100% of the prescribed rate in the county court or 200% in the High Court. For example, at the present prescribed rates of £65 and £74 the enhanced hourly rate could not exceed £86 an hour plus 50% mark-up (£129 in the county court) or £98 an hour plus 50% (£147) at 100% and £196 an hour plus 50% at 200% in the High Court. This traditional approach overcomes the perceived objection that as prescribed hourly rates include an element of mark-up, a straight percentage enhancement results in a mark-up upon a mark-up, even though the figure calculated must be converted into a percentage increase of the prescribed rate to comply with the regulations.
2. *A formula.* The other difficulty in rejecting the A factor and the B factor is that any percentage increase is necessarily arbitrary. An ingenious attempt to apply some rationale and logic into a straight percentage mark-up is shown by the following formula. Before the introduction of prescribed rates the usual mark-

up for profit was between 50% and 75% of the expense rate. This gave a spread of five bands each of 5%. The prescribed enhancement percentage in the county court is between 0% and 100% which consists of five bands of 20%. Accordingly if a 60% mark-up would have been allowed on the old basis this was the equivalent of two bands at 5%. The equivalent enhancement percentage would therefore be two bands at 20%, totalling 40%. Therefore 60% under the old regime would be 40% under the new.

3. *Seat-of-the-pants.* If the costs officer declines to adopt the A factor and B factor calculation and uses a seat-of-the-pants approach to award a straight, say, 10% enhancement, what should you do? One course is to express your eternal gratitude and go on your poverty-stricken way. Or you could argue for a higher percentage from the seat of your own pants. On this basis I suggest that the maxima are taken as the guide. It is prescribed that there may be 100% enhancement in some county court and 200% in some High Court cases. The starting point therefore is to ask what sort of work will attract the maximum enhancement and where does a particular case stand in relation to such a case. Unless 100% and 200% are allowed in a reasonable number of cases there is a danger of taxing officers confining themselves to the lower end of the percentage scale and never getting halfway up it. Prima facie, where all seven pillars of wisdom are present, this should indicate an entitlement to the maximum percentage enhancement. The final course when faced with a 10% seat-of-the-pants enhancement is to appeal on the grounds that the costs officer has applied the wrong part of his or her anatomy to the assessment.

6. Claiming enhancement in the bill

How should (i) entitlement to enhancement (the reg 5(1) threshold factors) and (ii) quantification of enhancement (the reg 5(3) quantification factors) be claimed? As I have said, the two were so confused in *London Borough of A v M and SF* that I do not think that judgment is a useful starting point, although I shall revert to it later.

Claiming entitlement

There can be no doubt that it is possible to claim entitlement to enhancement for an entire case. Regulation 5(1)(*c*) prescribes as a relevant circumstance that 'the *case* involved exceptional circumstances or complexity' (reg 5(3)), although dealing with the quantification of enhancement, refers to the care, speed and economy with which the case was prepared and the novelty, weight and complexity of the *case* and reg 5(7) permits regard to be had 'the generality of proceedings' and all the other threshold factors could well apply to an entire case. On the other hand, a routine case, like war, may have many months of boredom interspersed with periods of sheer panic. Interlocutory injunctions are an example. In such a case it would be appropriate to claim entitlement to enhancement for only those items which justified it. In either event I suggest that entitlement to enhancement should be claimed at the head of the bill identifying one or more of the six threshold circumstances which justify it.

Claiming enhancement

If the A factor plus the B factor approach is used, we are on familiar ground with no problems. The A factor is the direct cost measured by the appropriate inter partes hourly expense rate plus a B factor percentage mark-up arrived at by applying the prescribed circumstances, remembering always that the total cannot exceed the legal aid cut-off point of 100% or 200% of the prescribed hourly rate or fixed item. Having done the necessary calculation to arrive at the total rate claimed this must then be converted into a percentage of the prescribed rate (as in *London Borough of A v M and SF*) and shown at the head of the bill if it is claimed for the entire bill, or after each item or class of work for which it is sought, referring to the reg 5(3) quantification factors relied on to justify the figures claimed. If the approach adopted is a seat-of-the-pants percentage increase of the prescribed hourly rates, the same approach should be adopted and justified as best you can, perhaps using one of the methods in the last section.

1. *The entire bill?* Although, as I have said above, reg 5(3) envisages enhancement based on factors relating to the entire case, can there be a broad brush approach of applying the same enhancement to the entire bill? The answer on basic principles must be 'no' except in those matters which are so heavy that it is apparent that even the maximum permitted percentage increase of every item would still not result in adequate remuneration. I have in mind cases such as *Loveday v Renton (No 2)* (p 237). In the vast majority of cases the profit mark-up for interlocutory work is less than for preparation and there is no mark-up for travelling and waiting time. Although the hourly expense rate remains the same throughout, the profit mark-up does not. The costs judge in the criminal costs appeal of *R v Shah* (Case No T 932101) [1994] Crim LR 125 encapsulated the position:

   > 'Once the claim for enhanced rates based upon the exceptional circumstances of the case is allowed, all the work becomes an integral part of the case. Mark-up is a different matter and that will not apply to some aspects of the enhanced rate like waiting but they are still entitled to an enhanced fee for the work. I often suspect there is a confusion between mark-up and the claim for enhanced rates.'

   His reference to confusion is in line with the views I expressed on p 383.
2. *Routine letters*. Some costs officers cavil at 'absurdities such as enhancement claimed for, inter alia, letters to the Legal Services Commission or the court or preparing the Report on Case'. While sympathising with this view, the profession and costs officers must avoid a situation where every letter and telephone conversation is analysed to decide whether or not it qualifies for enhancement, and if so by how much. In *CRIMLA 13* (p 390) it was held, 'where enhanced rates apply, they apply to all letters written and telephone calls made or received'. In *R v McIlkenny and Hunter* (unreported) another criminal costs appeal, the costs judge held, 'in a matter of this nature, the letters and telephone calls were as much part of the preparation of the case as attendances on the client, or in conference. The solicitors are entitled to the same enhancement thereon as on other rates'. In any event, where the costs officer has freed himself from the prescribed rates by accepting entitlement to enhancement, would 30% above the prescribed rates in fact be an 'absurdity' compared with normal expense rates and mark-up?
3. *Travelling and waiting*. In *R v Shah* [1994] Crim LR 125, CA the costs judge thought the expense rate should be enhanced but with no mark-up, and it is difficult to see why if enhancement is appropriate that travelling and waiting should be done at an actual loss. However, in *R v Backhouse* (p 389) in regard to the claim for an enhanced rate for travelling and waiting time the costs judge said that in normal circumstances it was difficult to see how travelling and waiting time could attract an enhanced rate, but in that case it was accepted the circumstances were wholly exceptional and a modest increase in the standard rate was allowed. The Board took exactly the same view in *CRIMLA 13* (p 390), while in *R v McIlkenny and Hunter* the master found no justification for payment of any enhancement on travelling.
4. *London Borough of A v M and SF*. It must be remembered that this was a care

case concerned with the 1991 Regulations in which the judge either disagreed with or distinguished the judgment in Freeman which was also dealing with those regulations in respect of prescribed family proceedings, *London Borough of A* is therefore not an authority for not following *Freeman* and it is certainly not an authority on the interpretation of the Civil and Non-Prescribed Family Proceedings Regulations 1994. In any event, this is what happened.

In his judgment the district judge had said that solicitors and costs draftsmen were finding it very difficult to identify and isolate those circumstances of the case which were likely to qualify as exceptional. He referred to a succession of bills of costs which contained no specific particulars and made vague general assertions followed by a request that the taxing officer allow throughout the bill a charging rate well in excess of the prescribed rate or a mark-up or both with no attempt to distinguish those items of work which were exceptional from those which were not. The district judge pointed out that this made it almost impossible for the costs officer on the one hand to ensure that the solicitor is remunerated reasonably for those items of work which were genuinely exceptional and on the other hand to protect the legal aid fund.

Here is how Cazalet J dealt with the problem. He said:

> 'Where such an exceptional circumstance is said to arise it is insufficient for the solicitor simply to claim in a narrative of the bill that "This was a complex and extremely arduous case with voluminous paperwork and difficult issues", or that "This was a difficult and complex case in which instructions on the many complex and lengthy reports and statements were not always easy to obtain" or some other generalised phrase followed by a request that the taxing officer allow throughout the bill a charging rate in excess of the prescribed rate or mark-up or both. Taxing officers cannot be expected to sort the wheat from the chaff and unless bills of costs are drafted in a way which identifies and particularises those specific items of work in respect of which the taxing officer's discretion is sought, the taxing officer will have difficulty in identifying specific "exceptional circumstances" and will therefore be bound by the specified rates in Schedule 1 to the 1991 Regulations. Where "exceptional circumstances" are sought to be established and solicitors seek remuneration on the basis of the exercise of the taxing officer's discretion pursuant to Regulation 3(4)(c) then the exceptional circumstances must be specifically identified. The existence of an exceptional circumstance is unlikely normally to lead to an enhanced discretionary rate throughout the bill. Rather the taxing officer will apply a "larger amount" to such parts of the bill as may be appropriate. For example, if a solicitor needs the assistance of an interpreter in order to take instructions then this may justify a "larger amount" in respect of attendances upon the client and/or conferences and/or correspondence to and from the client and telephone calls. It would be unlikely to attract a "larger amount" in respect of dealing with witnesses and other parties, preparation and consideration of and dealing with documents, negotiations and notices, instruction of counsel, and any other matter where the inability to communicate direct with a client has not affected the particular class of work which that solicitor is conducting.
>
> There will be many attendances and applications which will not be exceptional and which will attract the specified rate. Where an hourly rate is sought in excess of the specified amount this should be stated and an explanation of how it is calculated provided. The bill should also identify and justify the specific areas of activity where it is claimed that the larger amount should apply. This will add to the burden of solicitors and costs draftsmen in preparing bills and of taxing officers in determining them but, as has already been pointed out, if the taxing officer is to protect the Legal Aid Fund on the one hand and ensure on the other that the solicitor is properly remunerated for those items of work which are genuinely exceptional this procedure must, in our view, be adopted'.

(vi) A curate's egg

Can it have been intended at a time of concern about the cost and complexity of litigation to introduce a regime that so complicated the drawing assessment and completion of bills of costs that it created a nightmare for the profession, costs draftsmen and costs officers alike, adding substantially to the time and cost of evaluating work which already had a small profit margin? To superimpose a chameleon quality to different parts of a case is as implausible as the curate's egg and would involve all concerned in an exercise akin to the mediaeval counting of the number of angels on a pin-head. If that is how the regulations are to be interpreted the result will be, to quote the Evershed Committee on Appendix N to the 1883 Rules, 'derogatory to the dignity and standing of a profession no less distinguished, learned and reputable than any of the other professions which charge on the basis of the real value of the skill and industry involved'.

WHO DECIDES?

Regulation 5(1) provides 'Upon a determination the relevant authority may allow fees at more than the prescribed rate'. That means the costs officer. It does not mean and cannot mean the trial judge. It may of course be of some persuasive value on the assessment that the trial judge expressed such an opinion, but the mischief is that where such a direction has not been sought or has been refused, some district judges refuse to exercise their discretion on the grounds that the application should have been made to the judge at the hearing. As we shall see in the next section, it is insufficient for a solicitor simply to seek enhancement for the whole case: but he must identify the specific areas of work in respect of which enhancement is sought. A general certificate of enhancement from the trial judge does not satisfy that requirement. If authority is required for this proposition it is to be found in the judgment of Cazalet J in *London Borough of A v M and SF* where he said:

> 'The fact that the judge certified there should be a special allowance is not, in my view, of relevance to a taxation under Schedule 1 to the 1991 Regulation. If the taxing officer is to step outside the prescribed rates he must be satisfied that he is entitled to exercise his discretion under Regulation 3(4). This regulation is not concerned with "special allowances" as such, and accordingly such a phrase is irrelevant to any taxation carried out in care proceedings.'

Only the costs officer is empowered to exercise first the discretion to enhance and then to quantify the enhancement. And perhaps requests for a 'special allowance for solicitor' have finally been laid to rest.

(vii) Between-the-parties costs

THE CHINESE WALL

More good news. For many years I complained that low legal aid rates had an inhibiting effect on true expense rates in non-state-funded work. The legal aid tail was wagging the litigation dog. I argued that it should be acknowledged that the lawyers were subsidising state funding by being paid rates that were artificially low, and that there should in effect be a Chinese wall between legal aid rates and the rates recoverable between the parties. General regulation 107B(1), introduced by the Civil Legal Aid (General) (Amendment) Regulations 1994, enables the solicitors for a successful assisted party to recover costs at the full going rate from a party against whom a between-the-parties costs order is made. The solicitors are entitled to keep the difference between the prescribed rate legal aid costs and the between-the-parties costs. I have got my Chinese wall. The legal aid tail need no longer wag the litigation dog.

Or, to put it another way, a legal aid certificate was the first form of conditional fee basis for the solicitor with a safety net. If the client wins, the solicitor recovers full costs from the other party. If the client loses, the solicitor is at least paid at the prescribed rate out of the fund. To enable this to be done reg 107B(3) purported to disapply the indemnity costs rule (see *Gundry v Sainsbury*, Chapter 17) to between-the-parties costs in state-funded cases and also disapplies reg 64 which restricts payment to a solicitor otherwise than from the legal aid fund. I say 'purported' because doubt has been expressed as to whether the substantive law can be disapplied by a mere regulation. I am surprised that it has never been challenged by an insurance company. This provision also breached for the first time the principle that costs recovered belong either to the client or to the state fund. These costs belong to the solicitor. This provision also gives rise to a potential conflict of interest between the solicitor and the client, it being in the solicitor's financial interests to secure an agreement or order for between-the-parties costs at the full rate, whereas the client may be prepared to accept an offer which included costs but did not differentiate between the claim and costs, or did not include costs, particularly if the statutory charge did not bite on the compromise.

5. DETAILED ASSESSMENT

From 26 April 1999, the procedure for the assessment of all state-funded costs has been governed by CPR Rule 47.17 which, since 3 July 2000 has been supplemented by Sections 43 and 49 of the Costs Practice Direction.

CPR RULE 47.17 DETAILED ASSESSMENT PROCEDURE FOR COSTS OF A LSC FUNDED CLIENT OR AN ASSISTED PERSON WHERE COSTS ARE PAYABLE OUT OF THE COMMUNITY LEGAL SERVICE FUND

(1) Where the court is to assess costs of a LSC funded client or an assisted person which are payable out of the Community Legal Service Fund, that person's solicitor may commence detailed assessment proceedings by filing a request in the relevant practice form.

(2) A request under paragraph (1) must be filed within 3 months after the date when the right to detailed assessment arose.

(3) The solicitor must also serve a copy of the request for detailed assessment on the LSC funded client or the assisted person, if notice of that person's interest has been given to the court in accordance with legal aid regulations.

(4) Where the solicitor has certified that the LSC funded client or the assisted person wishes to attend an assessment hearing, the court will, on receipt of the request for assessment, fix a date for the assessment hearing.

(5) Where paragraph (3) does not apply, the court will, on receipt of the request for assessment provisionally assess the costs without the attendance of the solicitor, unless it considers that a hearing is necessary.

(6) After the court has provisionally assessed the bill, it will return the bill to the solicitor.

(7) The court will fix a date for an assessment hearing if the solicitor informs the court, within 14 days after he receives the provisionally assessed bill, that he wants the court to hold such a hearing.

SECTION 43: PRACTICE DIRECTION SUPPLEMENTING CPR RULE 47.17

43.1 The provisions of this section apply where the court is to assess costs which are payable only out of the community legal service fund. Paragraphs 39.1 to 40.14 and 49.1 to 49.8 apply in cases involving costs payable by another person as well as costs payable only out of the community legal service fund.

43.2 The time for requesting a detailed assessment under rule 47.17 is within 3 months after the date when the right to detailed assessment arose.

43.3 The request for a detailed assessment of costs must be in Form N258A. The request must be accompanied by:

(a) a copy of the bill of costs;

(b) the document giving the right to detailed assessment (for further information as to this document, see paragraph 40.4 above);

(c) a copy of all orders made by the court relating to the costs which are to be assessed;

(d) copies of any fee notes of counsel and any expert in respect of fees claimed in the bill;

(e) written evidence as to any other disbursement which is claimed and which exceeds £250;

(f) the legal aid certificates, LSC certificates, any relevant amendment certificates, any authorities and any certificates of discharge or revocation;

(g) in the Supreme Court Costs Office the relevant papers in support of the bill as described in paragraph 40.12 above; in cases proceeding in District Registries and county courts this provision does not apply and the papers should only be lodged if requested by the costs officer;

(h) a statement signed by the solicitor giving his name, address for service, reference, telephone number, fax number and, if the assisted person has a financial interest in the detailed assessment and wishes to attend, giving the postal address of that person, to which the court will send notice of any hearing.

43.4 Rule 47.17 provides that the court will hold a detailed assessment hearing if the assisted person has a financial interest in the detailed assessment and wishes to attend. The court may also hold a detailed assessment hearing in any other case, instead of provisionally assessing a bill of costs, where it considers that a hearing is necessary. Before deciding whether a hearing is necessary under this rule, the court may require the solicitor whose bill it is, to provide further information relating to the bill.

43.5 Where the court has provisionally assessed a bill of costs it will send to the solicitor a notice, in Form N253 annexed to this practice direction, of the amount of costs which the court proposes to allow together with the bill itself. The legal representative should, if the provisional assessment is to be accepted, then complete the bill.

43.6 The court will fix a date for a detailed assessment hearing if the solicitor informs the court within 14 days after he receives the notice of the amount allowed on the provisional assessment that he wants the court to hold such a hearing.

43.7 The court will give at least 14 days notice of the time and place of the detailed assessment hearing to the solicitor and, if the assisted person has a financial interest in the detailed assessment and wishes to attend, to the assisted person.

43.8 If the solicitor whose bill it is, or any other party wishes to make an application in the detailed assessment proceedings, the provisions of Part 23 (General Rules about Applications for Court Orders) applies.

43.9 It is the responsibility of the legal representative to complete the bill by entering in the bill the correct figures allowed in respect of each item, recalculating the summary of the bill appropriately and completing the Community Legal Service assessment certificate (Form EX80A).

SECTION 49: COSTS PAYABLE BY THE LSC AT PRESCRIBED RATES

49.1 This section applies to a bill of costs of an assisted person or LSC funded client which is payable by another person where the costs which can be claimed against the LSC are restricted to prescribed rates (with or without enhancement).

49.2 Where this section applies, the solicitor of the assisted person or LSC funded client must file a legal aid/ LSC schedule in accordance with Paragraph 39.2(I) above. The schedule should follow as closely as possible Precedent E of the Schedule of Costs Precedents annexed to this Practice Direction.

49.3 The schedule must set out by reference to the item numbers in the bill of costs, all the costs claimed as payable by another person, but the arithmetic in the schedule should claim those items at prescribed rates only (with or without any claim for enhancement).

49.4 Where there has been a change in the prescribed rates during the period covered by the bill of costs, the schedule (as opposed to the bill) should be divided into separate parts, so as to deal separately with each change of rate. The schedule must also be divided so as to correspond with any divisions in the bill of costs.

49.5 If the bill of costs contains additional columns setting out costs claimed against the LSC only, the schedule may be set out in a separate document or, alternatively, may be included in the additional columns of the bill.

49.6 The detailed assessment of the legal aid/ LSC schedule will take place immediately after the detailed assessment of the bill of costs.

49.7 Attention is drawn to the possibility that, on occasions, the court may decide to conduct the detailed assessment of the legal aid/ LSC schedule separately from any detailed assessment of the bill of costs. This will occur, for example, where a default costs certificate is obtained as between the parties but that certificate is not set aside at the time of the detailed assessment pursuant to the Legal Aid Act 1988 or regulations thereunder.

49.8 Where costs have been assessed at prescribed rates it is the responsibility of the legal representative to enter the correct figures allowed in respect of each item and to recalculate the summary of the legal aid/ LSC schedule.

FORM N258A

Request for detailed assessment (Legal aid/ Legal Services Commission only)

In the	
Claim No.	
Claimant (include Ref.)	
Defendant (include Ref.)	

I now ask the court to provisionally assess the bill (arrange an assessment hearing as the assisted person/LSC funded client wishes to be heard)

I enclose copies of *(tick as appropriate)*

- ☐ The document giving the right to detailed assessment;
- ☐ the bill of costs;
- ☐ a statement giving the names, addresses for service and references of all persons to whom the court should give notice of the hearing;
- ☐ a copy of all the orders made by the court relating to the costs of the proceedings which are to be assessed;
- ☐ any fee notes of counsel and receipts or accounts for other disbursements relating to items claimed;
- ☐ all civil legal aid certificates and LSC certificates and amendments to them; notice of discharge or revocation and specific legal aid authorities;
- ☐ the relevant papers in support of the bill (Supreme Court Costs Office/ PRFD assessments only)

*I certify that the assisted person/LSC funded client wishes to attend the assessment hearing and I believe the hearing will take . . . . *(give estimate of time court should allow).*

I enclose my fee of £ . . . .

**(delete if not applicable)*

Signed .... **Date** ....

(Claimant) (Defendant) ('s solicitor)

The court office at

is open between 10 am and 4 pm Monday to Friday. When corresponding with the court, please address forms or letters to the Court Manager and quote the claim number.

FORM N253

Notice of Amount Allowed on Provisional Assessment
(Legal Aid only)

In the	
Claim No.	
Claimant (including ref.)	
Defendant (including ref.)	
Date	

To [Claimant] [Defendant] ['s Solicitor]

Take notice that the [claimant's] [defendant's] bill of costs in this action has been provisionally assessed and is returned with this notice

If you wish to be heard on the assessment, you must, within 14 days of the receipt of this notice inform the court in writing and return the bill of costs to the court. A date for assessment will then be fixed.

If you (and counsel, if any) accept the provisional assessment as final, please return the bill together with the balance of the assessment fee.

The court office at

is open between 10 am and 4 pm Monday to Friday. Address all communications to the Court Manager quoting the claim number

FORM EX80A

Legal aid assessment certificate

Claimant/Petitioner

[ ]

Defendant/Respondent

[ ]

In the	
Claim/Case No.	
Legal Aid Certificate No.	
Solicitors Ref.	

The costs in this matter have been assessed as set out in boxes A, B and C below and are claimed from the Legal Aid Fund.

SEAL

The costs are those of the ☐ Claimant ☐ Petitioner ☐ Defendant ☐ Respondent ☐ Other

They were assessed in the ☐ High Court ☐ County Court

Total pre-certificate costs, which are not being claimed, were £
(including disbursements, profit costs and VAT)

Dated____________________ Signed____________________________________
(Solicitor)

A. Costs payable by another party as allowed or as in legal aid schedule if appropriate
(Do not include any pre-certificate costs, or the costs of assessment).

Profit costs	
VAT	
Counsel's Fees	
VAT	
Disbursements	
VAT (where appropriate)	
Total	**£**

B. Legal aid only costs
(Do not include the costs of assessment)

Profit costs	
VAT	
Counsel's Fees	
VAT	
Disbursements	
VAT (where appropriate)	
Total	**£**

C. Costs of Assessment
(Allowed in respect of A and B above)

For Part A	
VAT	
Court fee (where appropriate)	
For Part B	
VAT	
Court fee (where appropriate)	
Total	**£**

D. Total Claimed
(Add totals A, B and C)

Total part A	
Total part B	
Total part C	
Total	**£**

Sealed by the court on ____________________

COSTS PRACTICE DIRECTION: PRECEDENT E

SCHEDULE OF COSTS PRECEDENTS

PRECEDENT E

Legal Aid/LSC Schedule of Costs **1999 – B – 9999**

IN THE HIGH COURT OF JUSTICE

QUEEN'S BENCH DIVISION

BRIGHTON DISTRICT REGISTRY

BETWEEN	**AB**	**Claimant**
	– and –	
	CD	**Defendant**

CLAIMANT'S BILL OF COSTS: LEGAL AID/LSC SCHEDULE

Item No.	Description of work done	V.A.T.	Disbursements	Profit Costs
6	Issue fee		£—	£400.00
7	Allocation fee		£—	£80.00
8	Solicitor's fee for hearing			
	Engaged 0.75 hours	£55.50		
	Enhancement thereon at 50%	£27.75		
	Travel and waiting 2.00 hours	£65.40		
	Total solicitor's fee for attending			£148.65
9	Fee on listing		£—	£400.00
10	Solicitor's fee for hearing			
	Engaged 1.5 hours	£111.00		
	Enhancement thereon at 50%	£55.50		
	Travel and waiting 2.00 hours	£65.40		
	Total solicitor's fee for attending			£231.90
11	Counsel's fee		£105.00	£600.00
12	Solicitor's fee for trial			
	Engaged in court 5.00 hours	£182.00		
	Engaged in conference 0.75 hours	£27.30		
	Enhancement thereon at 50%	£104.65		
	Travel and waiting 1.50 hours	£49.05		
	Total solicitor's fee for attending			£363.00
13	Counsel's brief fee for trial		£350.00	£2,000.00
14	Expert's fee for trial		£—	£850.00
15	Witnesses' expenses		£—	£84.00
	To summary	£455.00	£4,414.00	£743.55
16	Solicitor's fee for trial (second day)			
	Engaged in court 3.00 hours	£109.20		
	Engaged in conference 1.50 hours	£54.60		
	Enhancement thereon at 50%	£81.90		
	Travel and waiting 1.50 hours	£49.05		
	Total solicitor's fee for attending			£294.75
17	Counsel's fee for second day of trial		£113.75	650.00
18	Timed attendances on Claimant (1)			
	7.5 hours	£555.00		
	Enhancement thereon at 50%	£277.50		£832.50
19	Routine communications with Claimant (1)			
	Letters out – 14	£103.60		
	Telephone calls – 12	£49.20		£152.80

Item No.	Description of work done	V.A.T.	Disbursements	Profit Costs
22	Timed attendances on and communications with witnesses of fact			
	5.2 hours	£384.80		
	Enhancement thereon at 50%	£192.40		£577.20
23	Routine communications with witnesses of fact			
	Letters out – 4	£29.60		
	Telephone calls – 2	£8.20		£37.80
24	Paid travelling		£4.02	£22.96
25	Timed attendance on medical expert			
	0.33 hours	£24.42		
	Enhancement thereon at 50%	£12.21		£36.63
26	Timed communications with medical expert			
	0.25 hours	£18.50		
	Enhancement thereon at 50%	£9.25		£27.75
27	Timed communications with medical expert			
	0.2 hours	£14.80		
	Enhancement thereon at 50%	£7.40		£22.20
28	Routine communications with medical expert			
	Letters out – 6	£44.40		
	Telephone calls – 4	£16.40		£60.80
29	Expert's fee for report		£ —	£350.00
30	Timed communications with solicitors for Defendant			
	0.25 hours	£18.50		
	Enhancement thereon at 50%	£9.25		£27.75
31	Routine communications with solicitors for Defendant			
	Letters out – 18	£133.20		
	Telephone calls – 6	£24.60		£157.80
32	Routine communications with the court			
	Letters out – 8	£59.20		
	Telephone calls – 1	£4.10		£63.30
	To summary	£117.77	£1,022.96	£2,291.28
33	Routine communications with Counsel			
	Letters out – 11	£81.40		
	Telephone calls – 8	£32.80		£114.20
36	Work done on documents			
	57.25 hours	£4,236.50		
	Enhancement thereon at 50%	£2,118.25		£6,354.75
37	Work done on negotiations			
	Engaged – 1.5 hours	£111.00		
	Enhancement thereon at 50%	£55.50		
	Travel and waiting – 1.25 hours	£40.88		£207.38
38	Other work done (1)			
	Preparing and checking bill			£370.00

Item No.	Description of work done	V.A.T.	Disbursements	Profit Costs
40	VAT on total profit costs set out above (17.5% of £10,216.86)		£1,787.95	
	To summary	£1,78795	£ —	£7,046.33
	SUMMARY			
	Page 1	£455.00	£4,414.00	£743.55
	Page 2	£117.77	£1,022.96	£2,291.28
	Page 3	£1,787.95	£—	£7,046.33
	Totals:	£2,360.72	£5,436.96	£10,081.16
	Grand total:			£17,878.84

CPR RULE 44.17 APPLICATION OF COSTS RULES

This Part and Part 45 (fixed costs), Part 46 (fast track trial costs), Part 47 (procedure for detailed assessment of costs and default provisions) and Part 48 (special cases), do not apply to the assessment of costs in proceedings to the extent that—

(a) section 11 of the Access to Justice Act 1999, and provisions made under that Act, or

(b) regulations made under the Legal Aid Act 1988,

make different provision. (The costs practice direction sets out the procedure to be followed where a party was wholly or partially funded by the Legal Services Commission).

Part IV

Sanctions and penalties

CHAPTER 33

WASTED COSTS

1. WASTED COSTS ORDERS

(a) The Law

From 1 October 1991, s 4 of the Courts and Legal Service Act 1990 inserted a new s 51 in the Supreme Court Act 1981 relating to both the High Court and the county courts introducing the concept of 'wasted costs', as follows:

> 6. In any proceedings mentioned in sub-section (1) [in the Court of Appeal, High Court and county court], the court may disallow or, (as the case may be) order the legal or other representative concerned to meet the whole of any wasted costs or such part of them as may be determined in accordance with Rules of Court.
> 7. In sub-section (6) 'wasted costs' means any costs incurred by a party: (a) as a result of any improper, unreasonable or negligent act or omission on the part of any legal or other representative or any employee of such a representative; or (b) which in the light of any such act or omission occurring after they were incurred, the costs considers it unreasonable to expect that party to pay.

CPR RULE 48.7 PERSONAL LIABILITY OF LEGAL REPRESENTATIVE FOR COSTS—WASTED COSTS ORDERS

(1) This rule applies where the court is considering whether to make an order under section 51 (6) of the Supreme Court Act 1981 (court's power to disallow or (as the case may be) order a legal representative to meet, 'wasted costs').
(2) The court must give the legal representative a reasonable opportunity to attend a hearing to give reasons why it should not make such an order.
(4) When the court makes a wasted costs order, it must specify the amount to be disallowed or paid.
(5) The court may direct that notice must be given to the legal representative's client, in such manner as the court may direct—
 (a) of any proceedings under this rule; or
 (b) of any order made under it against his legal representative.
(6) Before making a wasted costs order, the court may direct a costs judge or a district judge to inquire into the matter and report to the court.
(7) The court may refer the question of wasted costs to a costs judge or a district judge, instead of making a wasted costs order.

Although *Re Wiseman Lee (Solicitors) (wasted costs order) (No 5 of 2000)* ((2001) Times, 5 April) was a criminal case the principle applies equally to civil matters. The court made a wasted costs order against the defendant solicitors in their absence with permission to make representations against the order by a given date. When no representations were received, the order was drawn up. The solicitors' appeal was allowed on the grounds that a legal representative must be allowed to make representations before a wasted costs order is made against him under CPR Rule 48.7(2).

SECTION 53: PRACTICE DIRECTION SUPPLEMENTING CPR RULE 48.7

53.1 Rule 48.7 deals with wasted costs orders against legal representatives. Such orders can be made at any stage in the proceedings up to and including the proceedings relating to the detailed assessment of costs. In general, applications for wasted costs are best left until after the end of the trial.

53.2 The court may make a wasted costs order against a legal representative on its own initiative.

53.3 A party may apply for a wasted costs order—

(1) by filing an application notice in accordance with Part 23; or

(2) by making an application orally in the course of any hearing.

53.4 It is appropriate for the court to make a wasted costs order against a legal representative, only if—

(1) the legal representative has acted improperly, unreasonably or negligently;

(2) his conduct has caused a party to incur unnecessary costs, and

(3) it is just in all the circumstances to order him to compensate that party for the whole or part of those costs.

53.5 The court will give directions about the procedure that will be followed in each case in order to ensure that the issues are dealt with in a way which is fair and as simple and summary as the circumstances permit.

53.6 As a general rule the court will consider whether to make a wasted costs order in two stages—

(1) in the first stage, the court must be satisfied—

(a) that it has before it evidence or other material which, if unanswered, would be likely to lead to a wasted costs order being made; and

(b) the wasted costs proceedings are justified notwithstanding the likely costs involved;

(2) at the second stage (even if the court is satisfied under paragraph (1)) the court will consider, after giving the legal representative an opportunity to give reasons why the court should not make a wasted costs order, whether it is appropriate to make a wasted costs order in accordance with paragraph 53.4 above.

53.7 On an application for a wasted costs order under Part 23 the court may proceed to the second stage described in paragraph 53.6 without first adjourning the hearing if it is satisfied that the legal representative has already had a reasonable opportunity to give reasons why the court should not make a wasted costs order. In other cases the court will adjourn the hearing before proceeding to the second stage.

53.8 On an application for a wasted costs order under Part 23 the application notice and any evidence in support must identify—

(1) what the legal representative is alleged to have done or failed to do; and

(2) the costs that he may be ordered to pay or which are sought against him.

53.9 A wasted costs order is an order—

(1) that the legal representative pay a specified sum in respect of costs to a party; or

(2) for costs relating to a specified sum or items of work to be disallowed.
53.10 Attention is drawn to rule 44.3A(1) and (2) which respectively prevent the court from assessing any additional liability until the conclusion of the proceedings (or the part of the proceedings) to which the funding arrangement relates, and set out the orders the court may make at the conclusion of the proceedings.

(b) Cases

Although neither s 51 nor Rule 48.7 specifically said so, the power of the court to disallow costs not only enables the court to order a legal representative to pay costs, it may also order him to indemnify his own client against a costs order against him, or to indemnify another party in respect of costs ordered against them, or order that the legal representative's costs against his own client be disallowed. If such a provision is not included in a wasted costs order against a legal representative, there would appear to be nothing to prevent him from charging his client for the work he had done in the proceedings giving rise to the wasted costs order.

In *Medcalf v Mandell* [2002] UKHL 27, [2002] 3 All ER 721 the House of Lords rejected the argument that s 51 conferred no right on a party to seek a wasted costs order against any legal representative other than his own. It did, however, hold that in these circumstances if the party for whom the legal representative was acting refused to waive legal privilege thereby preventing the practitioner from telling the whole story the court should not make a wasted costs order unless it is (a) satisfied there is nothing the practitioner could say, if unconstrained, to resist the order and (b) it is in all the circumstances fair to make the order. However, it was held in *Brown v Bennett (No 3)* ((2002) Times, 4 January) on a wasted costs application that it was permissible for the respondent barristers to be asked whether they saw or knew of non-privileged documents, provided that the purpose of the question was not to discover what was in the barristers' brief or instructions, even though answering the question might reveal the contents of the instructions or brief. That distinction might appear to be a very narrow and technical one. However, it was self-evident that it would be quite impermissible for the barristers to answer the question if the purpose of putting the question was to find out if a particular document was in his instructions, even if the document was open. But, it was by no means self-evident that if the purpose of asking the question was solely to discover whether the document was seen by or known to counsel that the question should not be answered. The question was permissible even if it happened to reveal that open documents, as opposed to privileged documents, were included in counsels' brief or instructions, provided that no prejudice was thereby caused to the client.

Applications under the wasted costs provisions started as a trickle which turned into a stream, consisting mainly of applications for orders against the legal representatives of unsuccessful state-funded claimants. It was becoming a new area of satellite litigation which the Court of Appeal was anxious to deter. Accordingly, they addressed all aspects of wasted costs applications in *Ridehalgh v Horsefield* [1994] 3 All ER 848, CA, where, in appeals backed by the Bar Council, The Law Society and the Solicitors Indemnity Fund, the Court of Appeal set aside wasted costs orders against two solicitors and a barrister and in the lead case declined to make an order in a case referred to them by a different division of the Court of Appeal. In delivering the judgment of the court, the Master of the Rolls said that while judges must not reject the weapon which Parliament intended to be used for the protection of those injured by the unjustifiable conduct of the other side's lawyers, they must be astute to control what threatened to become a new and costly form of satellite litigation.

Lord Bingham re-iterated this view in *Medcalf v Mandell*, approving the approach of the Privy Council in a New Zealand case that wasted costs orders should be confined to questions which are apt for summary disposal by the court, such as failures to appear; conduct which leads to an otherwise avoidable step in the proceedings; the prolongation of a hearing by gross repetition or extreme slowness in the presentation of evidence or argument. Such matters can be dealt with summarily on agreed facts or after a brief enquiry. Any hearing to investigate the conduct of a complex action is itself likely to be expensive and time-consuming. Compensating litigating parties who have been put to unnecessary expense is only one of the public interests to be considered.

In future, anyone considering applying for a wasted costs order should think twice.

The practice direction supplementing Rule 48.7 helpfully embodies the major findings of the Court of Appeal in *Ridehalgh*. Because wasted costs orders are made under the statute and Rule 48.7 and its supplementary practice direction govern merely the practice and procedure, not the principles, this is an area in which decisions made prior to 26 April 1999 are still of relevance and assistance.

(c) Three-stage test

In *Wasted Costs Order (No 1 of 1991)* (1992) Independent 23 April, the Court of Appeal identified a three-stage test to be applied. It is incorporated in paragraph 53.4 of the practice direction.

(d) *Ridehalgh v Horsefield*

(i) Improper, unreasonable or negligent conduct

(1) 'Improper' covers, but is not confined to, conduct which would ordinarily be held to justify disbarment, striking off, suspension from practice or other serious professional penalty. It also covers conduct which according to the consensus of professional, including judicial, opinion could be fairly stigmatised as being improper whether it violated the letter of a professional code or not.

(2) 'Unreasonable' includes conduct which is vexatious, designed to harass the other side rather than advance the resolution of the case and it made no difference that the conduct was the product of excessive zeal and not improper motive. Legal representatives could not lend assistance to proceedings which were an abuse of process and they were not entitled to use litigious procedures for purposes for which they were not intended, as by issuing or pursuing proceedings for purposes unconnected with success in the litigation or pursuing a case known to be dishonest nor was he entitled to evade rules intended to safeguard the interests of justice as by knowingly failing to make full disclosure on an ex parte application or knowingly conniving at incomplete disclosure of documents. However, conduct is not unreasonable simply because it leads to an unsuccessful result or because other more cautious legal representatives would have acted differently. The acid test is whether the conduct permitted of a reasonable explanation. It is not unreasonable to be optimistic.

(3) 'Negligent' does not mean conduct which is actionable as a breach of the legal representative's duty to his own client. There is of course no duty of care to the other party. Negligence should be understood in an untechnical way to denote failure to act with the competence reasonably expected of ordinary members of the profession. However the court firmly discountenanced any suggestion that

an applicant for a wasted costs order needed to prove under the negligence head anything less than he would have had to prove in an action for negligence. It adopted the test in *Saif Ali v Sydney Mitchell & Co* [1980] AC 198, HL 'advice, acts or omissions in the course of their professional work which no member of the profession who is reasonably well-informed and competent would have given or done or omitted to do'; an error 'such as no reasonably well-informed and competent member of that profession could have made'.

(ii) Causation

The causal link must be established by the applicant and failure to do so will result in no award being made.

(iii) Two-stage discretion

Jurisdiction to make the order depended upon the exercise of the court's discretion at two stages. First, on the initial application that the lawyer be given an opportunity to show cause. That was not something to be done automatically. The discretion was to be exercised judicially, but judges might not infrequently decide that further proceedings were not likely to be justified. Second, even if the court was satisfied that legal representatives had acted improperly, unreasonably or negligently so as to waste costs, the court was not bound to make an order, but would have to give sustainable reasons for the exercise of its discretion in that way. The Court of Appeal emphasised that judges should approach their task with caution and where possible consider the applicability of other sanctions of a disciplinary nature.

(iv) Threats

The threat of a wasted costs order should not be used as a means of intimidation. However, if one side considered that the conduct of the other was improper, unreasonable or negligent and likely to cause a waste of costs it was not objectionable to alert the other side to that view. There appears to be a fine line between 'threatening' and 'alerting'.

(v) Legal Aid

It is incumbent on courts to bear prominently in mind the peculiar vulnerability of legal representatives acting for assisted persons. It would subvert the benevolent purposes of state funding legislation if such representatives were subject to any unusual personal risk and their advice and conduct was not to be tempered by the knowledge that their client was not their paymaster and so not, in all probability, liable for the costs of the other side. This was clearly a reference to what the Master of the Rolls called a new and costly form of satellite litigation arising out of attempts by successful litigants to obtain costs against counsel and solicitors for unsuccessful state-funded litigants on the grounds that the Legal Aid Board (now replaced by the LSC) should have been advised either of the outset or after discovery that the action had no realistic prospect of success.

(vi) Advocacy

Although the legislation intended to encroach upon the traditional immunity of the advocate by subjecting him to the wasted costs jurisdiction, full allowance must be made for the fact that an advocate in court often has to make decisions quickly and under pressure. Mistakes would inevitably be made, things done which the outcome showed to have been unwise. Advocacy is more an art than a science, it could not be conducted according to formulae. It was only when, with all allowances made, an advocate's conduct of court proceedings was quite plainly unjustifiable that it could be appropriate to make a wasted costs order against him. One of the appeals was *Antonelli v Wade Gery Farr* [1994] Ch 205, CA in which the Court of Appeal had set aside an order that counsel should pay the costs of one day of a trial on the grounds that her acceptance of an unseen brief at very short notice was unreasonable and amounted to improper conduct as it was improbable that she had time to grasp properly the issues involved in the matter. She had been unclear about the issues involved, her submissions had been rambling, had contained many embarrassing pauses and she had failed to prepare written submissions when requested by the judge. The judge had failed to take into account para 209 of the Bar Code, known as the 'cab-rank' rule, which in the opinion of the Court of Appeal precluded the barrister from refusing the brief. She did not then know how inadequate her instructions would be, but even if she had known, she would not have been entitled to refuse. Even when the inadequacy of her instructions became only too plain, para 506 of the Bar Code precluded her from returning the brief or withdrawing from the case in such a way or in such circumstances that the client may be unable to find other legal assistance in time to prevent prejudice being suffered by the client. There is no reason to think anyone else would have been better placed to conduct the case than she.

The question of an advocate's immunity from suit was re-visited by the House of Lords in *Arthur JS Hall & Co (a firm) v Simons and two other actions* [2000] 3 All ER 673 when it was decided that advocates no longer enjoy immunity from suit in respect of their conduct of civil and criminal proceedings.

(vii) Reliance on counsel

A solicitor did not abdicate his professional responsibility when he sought the advice of counsel. He had to apply his mind to the advice received. But the more specialist the nature of the advice the more reasonable it was likely to be for him to accept it.

(viii) The application

The court agreed with the decision in *Filmlab Systems International Ltd v Pennington* [1994] 4 All ER 673, Ch D that save in exceptional circumstances an application for a wasted costs order should only be made after the trial of the action. In the ordinary way applications were best left until after the end of the trial but it was impossible to lay down rules of universal application. In *Melchior v Vettivel* ([2001] All ER (D) 351 (May)) the court made a wasted costs order after the conclusion of the trial and the sealing of the costs order.

(ix) Initiation

The court should be slow to initiate an enquiry because:

(i) The court does not serve a pleading informing the lawyer of the precise charges to be answered.
(ii) The court will be both the prosecutor and the adjudicator.
(iii) Difficult and embarrassing issues on costs could arise if an order were not made. The costs of the enquiry would have to be borne by someone and it would not be the court.

Judges should not make lawyers 'show cause' where the issue went to the merits. That should be left to the parties. An example of a case where the court did intervene was *Abbassi v Secretary of State for the Home Department*, [1992] Imm AR 349, CA where counsel and solicitors applied for judicial review of the decision of an immigration officer to refuse leave to their client, Mr Abbassi, to enter the United Kingdom. Ordinarily, the correct course open to a person who disputed facts relied upon by the Home Office for refusing leave to enter was to appeal to a tribunal and not to apply for leave for judicial review. Although counsel and solicitors owed a duty to their clients, they also owed a duty to the courts. Not only had there been no possible prospect of the appeal succeeding, but it had been irresponsible to seek to advance arguments once it was clear that the court was not prepared to accept the evidence upon which the arguments were based.

The court adjourned to give counsel and the solicitors an opportunity to be heard and on hearing that the solicitors did not wish to take advantage of that opportunity the court ordered the costs thrown away by the appeal, of £500, should be borne equally by the counsel and solicitors, as agreed between them.

(x) Procedure

The application should be heard by the trial judge (*In re P (a barrister) (wasted costs order)* (2001) Times, 31 July, CA). The court should determine the procedure to be followed to meet the requirements of the individual case. The overriding requirements were that any procedure had to be fair and as simple and summary as fairness permitted. Elaborate pleadings should in general be avoided. No formal process of discovery or interrogatories would be appropriate. The court could not imagine any circumstances in which the applicant should be permitted to interrogate the respondent lawyer. On the other hand, the respondent must be entitled to present a full defence and must be informed of the conduct complained of, the amount claimed and the alleged causal link between the two. Hearings should be measured in hours, not days or weeks.

(xi) Burden of proof

Although RSC Ord 62, r 11(4) (now CPR Rule 48.7(2)) provided no order should be made without giving the legal representative opportunity to show cause why an order should not be made, that should not be understood to mean the burden was on the legal representative to exculpate himself.

(e) Sheltering behind counsel

To what extent can a solicitor avoid personal liability by reliance on counsel? In addition to *Ridehalgh v Horsefield* (see above) a number of answers have been given, some more encouraging to solicitors than others. The low watermark was *Davy-Chiesman v Davy-Chiesman* [1984] 1 All ER 321, where counsel had advised in writing that the husband should not seek a lump sum payment from his wife payable directly to him as otherwise it would be taken immediately by his trustee in bankruptcy. At a subsequent conference, counsel advised that the husband should seek a lump sum payable to him direct and abandon all his other claims. It must have been glaringly apparent to any reasonable solicitor that the form of relief for which alone counsel was going to ask fell foul of the fundamental requirement that because of the bankruptcy any capital sum should not go direct to the husband. The duty the solicitor owed to inform the legal aid fund of any change of circumstances was not just to pass on any views expressed by counsel but to consider for himself the effect of any change of circumstances. The solicitor was at that stage guilty of 'a serious dereliction of duty' or 'serious misconduct' and it was not sufficient to absolve the solicitor that he acted in accordance with the advice of counsel. The solicitor was in many circumstances protected from personal liability if he had acted on the advice of experienced counsel properly instructed. The protection to the solicitor was not automatically total. The solicitor was highly-trained and expected to be experienced in his particular fields of law and he did not abdicate all responsibility whatever by instructing counsel. In this particular case, the solicitor had allowed his own skill and ability to be entirely subordinated to the dominant and forceful personality of counsel. Obviously, the Legal Aid Committee was not to be bombarded with notifications of every minute fluctuation in the estimate of the percentage prospects of success but only when it appeared, or should appear to a reasonable solicitor, that the assisted person no longer had any reasonable chance of success. The Law Society's application that the solicitor should pay both the husband's and wife's costs personally was allowed.

The culprit was counsel and yet it was the solicitors who were ordered to pay the costs of both parties. Counsel was not even named in the law report!

In *R v Oxfordshire County Council, ex p Wallace* [1987] NLJ Rep 542, QBD, the applicant commenced judicial review proceedings against the local education authority and the local health authority. On the first day of the hearing he was given leave to discontinue the proceedings against the health authority who at the end of the hearing applied for an order for their costs to be paid personally by the applicant's solicitors.

Counsel for the health authority argued that counsel's advice that the health authority should be joined as a party was based quite clearly on his stating the statutory position inaccurately and his advice that the decision of the health authority had been perverse was, or ought to have been, realised to be patently wrong by anyone with experience in this field, as had the applicant's solicitors. He relied on the decision in *Davy-Chiesman v Davy-Chiesman* that because the solicitors should have realised that there was not an arguable case for judicial review against the health authority they should be personally liable for costs in spite of the advice of counsel.

For the solicitors it was argued that they had obtained counsel's specific advice on the point as follows:

> 'I take the view that no reasonable health authority properly directing itself as to the law could possibly reach this decision (to provide no more speech therapy for the infant applicant than it was then providing) and that therefore there are good grounds for joining the health authority on an application for judicial review. This is the same sort of case as where a plaintiff is faced with two defendants, one blaming the other, and it is quite proper to join both defendants and let the unsuccessful defendant pay the costs.'

In addition it was contended for the solicitors that the single judge had granted leave to move against both authorities after hearing argument.

It was held that the case could be distinguished on its facts on *Davy-Chiesman*. In that case, counsel propounded a claim which he had earlier advised was bound to fail, as the solicitors in the case knew, and it was not the one for which, on his advice, the client had been granted legal aid. In *R v Oxfordshire County Council*, counsel had been specifically asked to advise against whom the proceedings should begin and the form they should take. A mere mistake or error of judgment is insufficient to attract liability of a solicitor for the costs of the other parties, for which purpose it was necessary to establish gross or serious negligence.

The case against the applicant's solicitors was not as strong as the authorities required it to be before any order for costs could be made against them. Accordingly an order for costs on behalf of the health authority against the solicitors was refused.

In striking out a copyright action in *Swedac Ltd v Magnet and Southerns plc* [1990] FSR 89, QBD, the trial judge criticised counsel and his solicitors. He refused to order the plaintiff's solicitors to pay the costs personally. It was held on appeal that although the solicitors could not automatically shelter behind counsel, in this particular case they had been justified in relying upon his advice.

However, in *Locke v Camberwell Health Authority* [1991] 2 Med LR 249, CA, it was held at first instance that the failure of a solicitor to ensure that pertinent information was before counsel advising on the merits in a negligence action constituted a gross dereliction of the solicitor's duty as an officer of the court and made him liable for the defendant's costs, thereafter thrown away. In advising on the merits, counsel did not have photocopies of the hospital notes, which it was his duty to request and the solicitor's duty to supply, as a result his advice was short and inadequate. However when it was established on appeal that the defendants had not in fact disclosed the relevant hospital notes, counsel and the solicitors were exonerated and the order set aside. As a general rule, a solicitor is entitled to rely upon the advice of counsel properly instructed but they must not do so blindly and must exercise their own independent judgment.

The pendulum swung back again in *Tolstoy-Miloslavsky v Lord Aldington* [1996] 2 All ER 556) (after the decision in *Ridehalgh*), where the Court of Appeal upheld an order that Count Tolstoy should pay 60% of Lord Aldington's costs of an action brought by Count Tolstoy to set aside on the grounds of fraud the monumental libel damages awarded against him, said that 'although the solicitors relied on fully experienced and very experienced, respected leading counsel who put his name to a statement of claim … counsel having extensive knowledge of the background of the case … this does not absolve the solicitors exercising their independent judgment nor allow them to close their eyes to the blindingly obvious … '. The document the solicitors were expected to overrule had been signed by both leading and junior counsel. Ouch!

(f) Against barrister for advice

In *Brown v Bennett (No 2)* ([2002] 2 All ER 273) it was submitted that a wasted costs order could only be made against a barrister by virtue of his conduct when actually exercising a right of audience, in other words, when actually conducting a case in court. The basis for this argument was that a wasted costs order could only be made as a result of inappropriate conduct on the part of any 'legal or other representative' which s 51(13) limited to 'any person exercising a right of audience or right to conduct litigation'. As a barrister, unlike a solicitor, did not 'conduct litigation' he could only be liable when he was exercising a right of audience. Rejecting this argument the court held that although it was true that the concept of conducting litigation would in many circumstances be understood to involve the traditional litigation activities of a solicitor, 'a right to conduct litigation' was not defined in the Act and it was quite permissible to give that expression a meaning which was less technical and more vernacular. There was no reason why it should not extend to such activities such as drafting or settling of documents and advising on prospects or procedure.

(g) Causation

Also in *Brown v Bennet* the defendants contended that the court must be satisfied that there was a real prospect that the applicants would not have incurred all the costs that they did incur if the lawyers had not acted and advised as they did and if the court were not so satisfied any uncertainty would have to be taken into account when assessing the level of costs or order against the lawyers. The court held that although there was a powerful argument in logic for awarding only a proportion of the total costs on the 'loss of chance' basis, that was not the appropriate approach to take. The court should ask itself whether, on the balance of probabilities, the applicant would have incurred the costs that he claimed from the lawyers if they had not acted or advised as they did.

(h) Orders made

Examples we have considered were the decisions in *Davy-Chiesman* (p 413), *Tolstoy v Aldington* (p 415) and *Abbassi v Secretary of State for the Home Department* (p 413).

Re a Company (006798 of 1995) [1996] 2 All ER 417, ChD

A solicitor swore an affidavit in support of a winding-up petition, asserting on oath a belief that a company was insolvent on the ground that a debt was owing and that the company was unable to pay its debts as they fell due. There were in fact no grounds upon which a competent solicitor could have reached that view on the material available to him and he was ordered to pay the costs of the company personally.

General Mediterranean Holidays v Patel (27 January 2000, unreported, QBD)

The defendants denied an allegation of fraud until shortly before the trial when they admitted it. The action was compromised on terms that there be no order for costs, but the claimants obtained a wasted costs order against the defendants' solicitor on the grounds that the solicitor knew the defendants had admitted the existence of the fraud in other proceedings.

(i) Orders refused

Trill v Sacher (No 2) [1992] 40 LS Gaz R 32, CA

Where a statement of claim was struck out for want of prosecution the defendants sought wasted costs orders against the solicitors for the legally-aided claimant. The solicitors' explanation for the delay related to the difficulties experienced in complicated cases such as the present, where the plaintiffs had only a limited legal aid certificate. The solicitors' hands were tied in dealing with the Legal Aid authorities. The slow action by the authorities and by counsel in preparing written opinions had contributed to the delay. An order that they be personally liable for wasted costs was set aside.

Re a Solicitor (wasted costs order) [1993] 2 FLR 959, CA

In this case a solicitor who was having difficulty resolving the position regarding his client's Legal Aid Certificate had not sought an adjournment until the day before the fixed hearing date, causing expense to the other side and to their witnesses. His failure to warn the court or his opponents in sufficient time was an error of judgment. However, the material now available showed that the Law Society accepted that the solicitor had found himself in an extremely difficult position. It would not be right to go further than to say the solicitor had been guilty of an error of judgment: he had not acted in dereliction of his duty. A wasted costs order against him personally was not warranted.

Wall v Lefever [1998] 1 FCR 605, CA

The wasted costs provisions of s 51 involve the tension between two important public interests. First, that lawyers should not be deterred from pursuing their client's interests by fear of incurring a personal liability to their clients' opponents, and second, that litigants should not be financially prejudiced by the unjustifiable conduct of litigation by their or their opponents' lawyers. Care should be exercised before launching an appeal against the refusal of a wasted costs order by a judge at first instance who had heard the evidence. If the judge concluded that the conduct complained of had not fallen within that proscribed by s 51 an appeal was only justified if some point of principle indicated that the judges approach had been wholly wrong. That was not the present case.

Re a Barrister (wasted costs order No 4 of 1993) (1995) Times, 21 April, CA

It is important for a judge considering making a wasted costs order, which is a draconian order, to remember that he is removed from the daily demands of practice and to make allowance for difficulties with time estimates. The appellant had accepted a brief for a two-day trial listed at Derby Crown Court immediately prior to another trial in which he was to appear at Nottingham Crown Court. The first trial was late starting and progressed more slowly than anticipated. In granting an adjournment of the second trial the judge ordered the barrister to pay the consequential wasted costs. In quashing the order, the court said that although the barrister had been over-optimistic in failing to anticipate delays in the first trial, his conduct could not be described as unreasonable.

Turner Page Music v Torres Design Associates Ltd (1998) Times, 3 August, CA

The ability of the court to make a wasted costs order can have advantages, but it will be of no advantage if it is going to result in complex proceedings which involve detailed investigation of fact. If the situation involves detailed investigation of facts and indeed allegations of dishonesty then it may well be that the wasted costs procedure is largely inappropriate to cover the situation, except in what would be an exceptional case. If the situation involved breach of a solicitor's professional duty to a client that too might make it unsuited to a summary procedure. The claimant's application for a wasted costs order against the defendant's solicitors was dismissed.

Byrne v Sefton Health Authority [2001] EWCA Civ 1904, [2002] 1 WLR 775

The solicitors had acted for the claimant in connection with his allegations of clinical negligence by the defendant, but ceased to act for the claimant before he instructed other solicitors, who commenced proceedings. When the action was dismissed as out-of-time the defendant applied for a wasted costs order against the solicitors on the grounds that its costs had been incurred as a result of the solicitors' failure to bring proceedings within the limitation period. Section 51(6) of the Supreme Court Act 1981 empowers costs to be awarded against 'a legal or other representative', while s 51(13) defines a legal or other representative as a person who has issued proceedings, exercised rights of audience or performed ancillary functions in relation to the conduct of litigation. The defendant's case against the solicitors rested on the very fact that they had failed to do any of these things. Furthermore there was no causative link between the solicitors' conduct and the costs incurred by the defendant. The defendant's costs had not been incurred by the defendant's failure to act, but by the claimant's current solicitors' decision to bring an action outside the limitation period.

B v Pendlebury [2002] NLJR 1072

On an application for wasted costs in a case in which there has been no adjudication of the primary facts, the court should be reluctant to enquire into a state of affairs in which it has no solid foundation from which the process of analysis essential to the wasted costs procedure can proceed. The process and procedure envisaged in the

Practice Direction is not readily to be equated with what was involved on a trial of issues. The phrases 'simple and summary as the circumstances will permit' and 'after giving the legal representative an opportunity to give reasons' did not lend themselves as appropriate to a disputed trial involving consideration and resolution of complex and disputed evidence. It is axiomatic that a solicitor is bound by the instructions of his client. He is not obliged to act as a filter between the instructions provided by the client and the opposing party. Quite simply, a solicitor owes no duty to the opposing party although he does, of course, owe such a duty to the court: *Orchard v Southeastern Electricity Board* [1987] 1 All ER 95, CA.

(j) Appeals

An appeal against a wasted costs order does not relate only, or indeed primarily, to costs: it relates to the conduct of the solicitor, and accordingly does not fall within the ambit of s 18(1)(*f*) of the Supreme Court Act 1981 which prohibits appeals against orders for costs only, unless the judge has mis-exercised his discretion (*Wilkinson v Kenny* [1993] 3 All ER 9, [1993] 1 WLR 963, CA).

(k) Non-parties

There is jurisdiction to make an order for wasted costs even though the applicant was not a party to the proceedings within s 51(6) and (7) of the Act (*Lubrizol v Tyndallwoods Solicitors* (1998) Lawyer, 21 April, QBD, where the applicants were directly interested in the subject matter of an application for judicial review). However, there is no power in the court to make a wasted costs order in favour of, or (by parity of reasoning) against, a person who elected to oppose an ex parte application for leave to apply for judicial review. Such a person is not a party for present purposes. The modern practice of the court in regularly hearing and sometimes inviting the participation of such persons could not make it otherwise; only legislation or a rule change could make it so (*R v Camden London Borough Council, ex p Martin* [1997] 1 All ER 307, QBD). The test for determining whether the court should exercise its power under the Supreme Court Act 1981, s 51(1) and (3) to order a non-party firm of solicitors to pay the costs of an action is whether it would be just to do so. While ordering a non-party to pay the costs would not normally be merited in the ordinary case where a party was prosecuting or defending a claim for its own advantage through the medium of solicitors acting as such, in cases where one or both of those characteristics was missing, the issue would be one for the judge's discretion (*Globe Equities Ltd v Kotrie* (1999) Independent, 15 March, CA).

2. WRONG COURT

(a) Reduction of costs

The second penalty introduced by the new s 51 of the Supreme Court Act 1981 may be imposed by 'the person responsible for determining the amount which is to be awarded' and arises where, in the opinion of the court, a case brought in the High Court should have been brought in the county court. The costs officer may reduce the costs by an amount not exceeding 25%, this being a figure which may be varied by order of the Lord Chancellor.

(b) Striking out

Section 40 of the County Courts Act 1984 as amended by s 2(1) of the Courts and Legal Services Act 1990 provides:

> '(1) where the High Court is satisfied that any proceedings before it are required by any provision of the kind mentioned at sub-section (8) ... to be in a county court it shall – (a) order the transfer of the proceedings to a county court; or (b) if the court is satisfied that the person bringing the proceedings knew, or ought to have known, of that requirement, order that they be struck out.'

In *Restick v Crickmore* [1994] 2 All ER 112, CA the judge had followed a decision of Turner J in *Groome v Nonnan Motors (Wallisdown) Ltd* (30 June 1992, unreported) in holding there was no discretion and they had no alternative but to strike out. This was because the word 'shall' in s 40(1) had been treated as being mandatory and governing paragraph (*b*) giving the court no option but to strike out when the relevant conditions were satisfied. That construction ignored the word 'or'. The use of the word 'shall', positioned where it was, did not require the court to adopt one course rather than the other, simply because the necessary precondition for exercising choice (*b*) was satisfied. The court was required to make a choice between two alternatives, but it could only strike out if the additional condition was satisfied, namely that the person bringing the proceedings knew or ought to have known, of the requirement to bring the case in the county court. Otherwise the choice or discretion was unfettered. That construction accorded with the policy of the courts that provided proceedings were started within the time permitted by the statute of limitations, were not frivolous, vexatious, or an abuse of the court and disclosed a cause of action, they would not as a rule be struck out because of a mistake in procedure on the part of the plaintiff or his advisers. The discretion to strike out might, for example, be exercised where there was a deliberate attempt to harass a defendant by running up unnecessary costs or in defiance of a warning of the defendants as to the proper venue or where a party persistently started actions in the wrong court.

Writing in the *Law Society Gazette* of 13 April 1994, Diana Bretherick identified some of the circumstances in which the court would exercise its discretion to strike out as being the persistent commencement of actions wrongly in the High Court, attempts to harass a defendant or where the claim is obviously below the threshold value. She observed that one of the temptations to commence in the High Court is that a generally endorsed writ may be issued and served without the need for a detailed statement of claim in cases where prognosis, and hence quantum, is uncertain. It is a temptation to be avoided unless the solicitor is prepared to swear an affidavit with calculations showing the claim appeared to be worth £50,000 or more in a personal injury claim and £25,000 or more in other claims.

CHAPTER 34

MISCONDUCT

CPR RULE 44.14 COURT'S POWERS IN RELATION TO MISCONDUCT

(1) The court may make an order under this rule where—
 (a) a party or his legal representative, in connection with a summary or detailed assessment, fails to comply with a rule, practice direction or court order; or
 (b) it appears to the court that the conduct of a party or his legal representative, before or during the proceedings which gave rise to the assessment proceedings, was unreasonable or improper.

(2) Where paragraph (1) applies, the court may—
 (a) disallow all or part of the costs which are being assessed; or
 (b) order the party at fault or his legal representative to pay costs which he has caused any other party to incur.

(3) Where—
 (a) the court makes an order under paragraph (2) against a legally represented party; and
 (b) the party is not present when the order is made,

the party's solicitor must notify his client in writing of the order no later than 7 days after the solicitor receives notice of the order.

SECTION 18: PRACTICE DIRECTION SUPPLEMENTING CPR RULE 44.14

18.1 Before making an order under rule 44.14 the court must give the party or legal representative in question a reasonable opportunity to attend a hearing to give reasons why it should not make such an order.

18.2 Conduct before or during the proceedings which gave rise to the assessment which is unreasonable or improper includes steps which are calculated to prevent or inhibit the court from furthering the overriding objective.

18.3 Although rule 44.14(3) does not specify any sanction for breach of the obligation imposed by the rule the court may, either in the order under paragraph (2) or in a subsequent order, require the solicitor to produce to the court evidence that he took reasonable steps to comply with the obligation.

There has been a misunderstanding about the purpose of this rule. The misunderstanding is that this rule had been envisaged as providing a simple summary procedure to deal with misconduct without involving the sledgehammer procedure of a wasted costs inquiry under the Supreme Court Act 1981, s 51. It was even proposed originally that an order could be made in the absence of the defaulting party, but it was appreciated that natural justice required the absent party to be heard on such an application and this was remedied in the practice direction. However, the misunderstanding has been to think that this provision applies to the court's powers generally in relation to misconduct, while in fact it relates solely to either during the course of a detailed assessment or in respect of misconduct before or during the main proceedings which only comes to light during the assessment. The heading should therefore be 'Court's Powers on Assessment in Relation to Misconduct'. Its primary object is to invest costs officers with disciplinary powers.

The misconduct may be either that of the legal representative of a party or of the party personally. If the allegation is in respect of the legal representative, all the factors relating to a wasted costs order under the Courts and Legal Services Act 1990, s 51 (see Chapter 33) will apply.

The investigation into misconduct can be initiated by the judge or costs officer or at the request of one of the parties.

An apparent omission from Rule 44.14 is that, unlike under the Supreme Court Act 1981, s 51, it contains no provision to prevent the solicitor from rendering a charge to his client in respect of any between-the-parties costs which are being disallowed. The remedy may be to invite the solicitor to undertake not to render a charge to his client as the alternative to the court initiating an investigation under s 51. In any event, Rule 44.14(3) requires the solicitor to notify his client in writing of any order based upon his misconduct no later than seven days after the solicitor receives notice of the order if the party is not present when the order is made.

Although one approaches pre-26 April 1999 decisions with caution, two decisions cast some light on the meaning of the words 'unreasonable or improper'. In *Sinclair-Jones v Kay* [1989] 1 WLR 114, the Court of Appeal held that the test was that a solicitor was liable to pay personally the costs of other parties to the proceedings where such costs had been incurred improperly or unreasonably or where they had been wasted by his failure to conduct the proceedings with reasonable competence and expedition. *Mainwaring v Goldtech Investments Ltd* (1991) Times, 19 February, CA, identified the following guidelines for making an order under the predecessor to Rule 44.14:

(i) The criteria to be applied are those in *Sinclair-Jones*.
(ii) Any order is purely compensatory.
(iii) The court must be satisfied that the amount of costs claimed was caused by the impropriety.
(iv) A high standard of proof is required because the order affects the solicitor's reputation.

PART V

PARTICULAR PEOPLE

CHAPTER 35

NON-PARTIES

CPR RULE 48.1 PRE-COMMENCEMENT DISCLOSURE AND ORDERS FOR DISCLOSURE AGAINST A PERSON WHO IS NOT A PARTY

(1) This paragraph applies where a person applies—

(a) for an order under—

(i) section 33 of the Supreme Court Act 1981; or

(ii) section 52 of the County Courts Act 1984,

(which give the court powers exercisable before commencement of proceedings); or

(b) for an order under—

(i) section 34 of the Supreme Court Act 1981; or

(ii) section 53 of the County Courts Act 1984,

(which give the court power to make an order against a non-party for disclosure of documents, inspection of property etc).

(2) The general rule is that the court will award the person against whom the order is sought his costs—

(a) of the application; and

(b) of complying with any order made on the application.

(3) The court may however make a different order, having regard to all the circumstances, including—

(a) the extent to which it was reasonable for the person against whom the order was sought to oppose the application; and

(b) whether the parties to the application have complied with any relevant pre-action protocol.

This is one of the few costs rules that does not have a supplementary practice direction.

This rule gives a party against whom an order for pre-commencement or non-party disclosure is made the general right to his costs but emphasises that the court may make some other order. Rule 48.1(3)(*a*) suggests that the court may well make different orders relating to the costs if an application is unsuccessfully opposed. Similarly, the person required to comply with a pre-action disclosure order will not only be awarded the costs of the application but the costs of complying with the order although, again, unreasonable behaviour, perhaps failure to comply with a pre-action protocol, may result in the court making a different order.

In *Totalise plc v Motley Fool Ltd* ([2001] EWCA Civ 1897, [2002] 1 WLR 1233, CA) Interactive Investor Ltd (Interactive) ran a website providing financial information to individual investors, on which subscribers could post information and opinions likely to be of interest to other investors. An investor under the name of 'Zeddust' posted defamatory statements questioning the competency and integrity of the claimants. When the claimants complained, Interactive removed the offending messages and suspended the account of Zeddust. However, they declined to reveal the identity of Zeddust on the grounds that, in the absence of a court order, they were precluded from disclosing personal details about any account to a third party under the provisions of the Data Protection Act 1998 and under the terms of the contract with their investors. The judge, in making the order sought by the claimants, ordered Interactive Investor to pay the costs of the application. Interactive's appeal against the order was allowed. 'Norwich Pharmacal' applications (see *Norwich Pharmacal v Customs and Excise Comrs*, ([1974] AC 133)) are not ordinary adversarial proceedings but are akin to proceedings for pre-action disclosure where costs are governed by CPR Rule 48.3. In general the costs incurred should be recovered from the wrongdoer rather than from an innocent party. Although there may be exceptions requiring a different order, these did not include cases where:

- the party required to make the disclosure had a genuine doubt that the person seeking the disclosure was entitled to it;
- the party was under an appropriate obligation not to reveal the information or where the legal position was not clear, or the party had a reasonable doubt as to the obligations; or
- the party could be subject to proceedings if disclosure was voluntary; or
- the party would or might suffer damage by voluntarily giving the disclosure; or
- the disclosure would or might infringe a legitimate interest of another.

If a party refusing disclosure had supported or was implicated in a crime or tort or sought to obstruct justice being done, the court would require that party to bear its costs and, if appropriate, pay the other party's costs.

In *Habib Bank Ltd v Customs and Excise Comrs* (28 January 1999, unreported, QBD), HM Customs and Excise had given an undertaking to indemnify third parties against expenses incurred in complying with a freezing order. The bank claimed that one provision contained within the order had been poorly drafted and caused some confusion. It had felt obliged to seek the advice of outside solicitors and the court held that as the applicant was unfamiliar with orders of the kind in question it was, therefore, reasonable for independent solicitors to be instructed for the purpose of interpretation and that the claimant should pay their costs of so doing.

CPR RULE 48.2 COSTS ORDERS IN FAVOUR OF OR AGAINST NON-PARTIES

(1) Where the court is considering whether to exercise its power under section 51 of the Supreme Court Act 1981 (costs are in the discretion of the court) to make a costs order in favour of or against a person who is not a party to proceedings—

- (a) that person must be added as a party to the proceedings for the purposes of costs only; and
- (b) he must be given a reasonable opportunity to attend a hearing at which the court will consider the matter further.

(2) This rule does not apply—

- (a) where the court is considering whether to—
  - (i) make an order against the Legal Services Commission;
  - (ii) make a wasted costs order (as defined in 48.7);
- (b) in proceedings to which rule 48.1 applies (pre-commencement disclosure and orders for disclosure against a person who is not a party).

Another rule without a practice direction.

The approach of the court to making orders for costs against non-parties was set out in *Symphony Group plc v Hodgson* [1994] QB 179, CA and exemplified in subsequent cases.

1. THE GENERAL APPROACH

In *Symphony Group plc v Hodgson* the claimant obtained injunctive relief against the defendant who had left his employment to join Halvanto, a competitor, in breach of restrictive covenants in his contract of employment. The claimant did not add Halvanto as a defendant or initiate proceedings against it or tell Halvanto that it might seek to make it liable for costs. Halvanto's managing director gave evidence for the defendant. The defendant was protected by a legal aid certificate and the complainant successfully applied for an order that Halvanto should pay the claimant's costs of the action. In allowing Halvanto's appeal the court said that since *Aiden Shipping Co Ltd v Interbulk* [1986] 2 All ER 409, HL the courts had entertained claims for costs against non-parties where a person had some management of or financed the action, where the person had caused the action, where the person was a party to a closely-related action which had been heard at the same time but not consolidated, and in group litigation. The court identified the following material considerations to be taken into account:

(a) An order for the payment of costs by a non-party would always be exceptional. The judge should treat any application for such an order with considerable caution.
(b) It would be even more exceptional for such an order to be made where the applicant had a cause of action against the non-party and could have joined him. Joinder as a party gave the person concerned all the protection conferred by the rules, eg the framing of issues, discovery and the knowledge of what the issues were before giving evidence. (Rule 48.2(*a*) now requires that he must be added as a party.)
(c) Even if the applicant could provide a good reason for not joining the non-party against whom he had a valid cause of action, he should warn the non-party that he might apply for costs against him.
(d) An application should normally be determined by the trial judge.
(e) The fact that the trial judge might have expressed views on the conduct of the non-party neither constituted bias nor the appearance of bias.
(f) The procedure for the determination of costs is a summary procedure, not necessarily subject to all the rules that would apply in an action. Thus, subject to any statutory exceptions, judicial findings were inadmissible as evidence of the facts on which they were based in proceedings between one of the parties to the original proceedings and a stranger. Yet, in the summary procedure, for a solicitor to pay the costs of an action to which he was not a party, the judge's findings of fact might be admissible. That departure from basic principles could only be justified if the connection of the non-party with the original proceedings was so close that he would not suffer any injustice by allowing the exception to the general rule.
(g) The normal rule was that witnesses in either civil or criminal proceedings enjoyed immunity from any form of civil action in respect of evidence given during the proceedings. In so far as the evidence of a witness in proceedings might lead to an application for costs against him or his company, it introduced an exception to a valuable general principle.
(h) The fact that an employee or even a director or managing director of a company gave evidence in an action did not normally mean that the company was taking part in that action.
(i) The judge should be alert to the possibility that an application for costs against a non-party was motivated by resentment or an inability to obtain an effective order for costs against a state-funded litigant.

In *Wiggins v Richard Read (Transport) Ltd* (1999) Times, 14 January, CA, David Wiggins, who was disabled, was suing by his brother and next friend. After a trial of a preliminary issue, the judge determined that the claimant did not have a cause of action, struck out the proceedings and ordered his parents to pay the costs of the defendant. In allowing their appeal, the court said that Note 62/2/7 in the White Book had misled the judge into thinking that the closeness of a third party to litigation on its own allowed a costs order to be made against the third party. The categories of case where an order could be made and the guiding principles were set out by Lord Justice Balcombe in *Symphony Group plc v Hodgson* (p 426) which was cited in the Note. Lord Justice Balcombe had identified nine guidelines but the Note in relation to the sixth guideline did not include all the words of Lord Justice Balcombe. Because of the omission of some of those words, the sixth principle was elided and misshapen. It could never be enough simply to show a close relationship or than an action was inspired by a parent for his disabled son in order for a costs order to be made against a parent. There must be something more. The judge did not ask whether it had been shown that the parent had consciously brought the action for his own benefit and not for his son's or whether he had consciously encouraged a hopeless action.

2. INSURERS

Insurers who took over the defence of an action and conducted it for their own benefit could properly be said to have been the real defendants and were ordered to pay the costs although they were not a party to the action (*Pendennis Shipyard Ltd v Margrathea (Pendennis) Ltd (in liquidation)* [1998] 1 Lloyd's Rep 315, QBD. However, legal expenses insurers were not liable to pay more than the limit of their cover merely on the grounds that they had funded the litigation under a commercial agreement (*Murphy v Young & Co Brewery plc* [1997] 1 All ER 518, CA).

In *TGA Chapman Ltd v Christopher and Sun Alliance* [1998] 2 All ER 873, the Court of Appeal held that the defendant's negligence insurers were liable for the full amount of a judgment of £1,100,000 plus costs even though their liability under the insurance policy was limited to £1,000,000 inclusive of opponents costs. The insurers were in a different position from those in *Murphy* because, as in *Pendennis*, above, the litigation was funded, controlled and directed by the insurance company motivated entirely by its own interest.

3. DIRECTORS

In *Taylor v Pace Developments Ltd* [1991] BCC 406, the Court of Appeal held that the controlling director of a one-man company should not be personally liable for the costs of defending an action even though he knew the company would not be able to meet the plaintiffs costs should the company prove unsuccessful. That would be far too great an inroad on the principle of limited liability, although the director might be made liable if the company's defence was not bona fide, as, for example, where the company had been advised that there was no defence.

Gardiner v FX Music Ltd [2000] All ER (D) 144 confirmed that an order for costs against a non-party is always an exceptional order. In the case of a sole or guiding director of an insolvent company, such an order is not normally made unless it can be shown that the director caused the company to bring or defend proceedings improperly.

In *H Leverton Ltd v Crawford Offshore (Exploration) Services Ltd (in liquidation)* (1996) Times, 22 November, QBD, an application succeeded where a Mr Crawford was found to be the defendant company for all practical purposes. He had acted in bad faith by concocting false claims supported by forged documents, destroyed and suppressed documents, given false evidence, and had substantially financed the proceedings. These were exceptional circumstances making it appropriate to order costs against him.

In *Re Land and Property Trust & Co plc (No 2)* [1993] BCC 462, CA provided a good illustration of the dangers inherent in treating an application for costs against a third party in the same manner as one against a party to the proceedings. On refusing a petition by a company for an administration order, the judge had ordered the costs incurred by a creditor to be paid by the directors personally. Although he had jurisdiction to make such an order for costs, he had refused the directors' application for an adjournment to enable them to have a proper opportunity of putting in evidence and his failure to do so caused him to err in principle. On the fresh evidence that was available before the Court of Appeal the order for costs ought not to have been made.

In *Robertson Research International Ltd v ABG Exploration BV* (1999) Times, 3 November, Patents Court, QBD, after directions for trial had been given in a robustly-defended action, the defendant company gave notice that it was ceasing to trade, its solicitors came off the record and it consented to judgment for the entire sum claimed. By then it was an empty shell. The claimants joined as parties a director and the financial controller of the defendant company alleging that they had known there was no defence and seeking an order for costs against them. The defendants argued that in view of the strictures of the Court of Appeal in *Turner Page Music* (p 417) in wasted costs matters that such applications will not be heard unless they can be dealt with summarily, the present applications should be dismissed. The master accepted these submissions, but on appeal, Laddie J held that unlike the wasted costs jurisdiction, applications against non-parties were solely compensatory and it was irrelevant whether there was any impropriety on the part of those responsible. Although such orders would always be exceptional, it was not necessary that the applications had to be capable of being dealt with summarily. The matter could be dealt with appropriately by, for example, limiting it to principle issues, limiting or disposing with cross examination and limiting the length of the hearing.

In *Secretary of State for Trade and Industry v Backhouse* [2001] 09 LS Gaz R 38, CA, two companies were ordered to be wound up, the judge having found that no proper books of account had been kept, that the businesses of the companies were intertwined with the defendant personally, who treated the companies' moneys as his own and that a savings scheme marketed through the companies lacked intrinsic merit. After judgment, the Secretary of State warned the defendant for the first time that he intended to apply for a costs order against him personally. The judge ordered the defendant to pay the costs personally because he had defended to protect his own reputation and position without seriously considering the interests of the companies or their creditors. The crucial question was whether the relevant director held a bona fide belief that the company had an arguable defence and that it was in the companies' interests to advance that defence. If he did so believe, to make a non-party pay the costs would constitute an unlawful inroad into the principle of limited liability. However, on the facts, the defendant had not considered the companies' interests but only his own; there was ample evidence to justify the costs order despite the absence of an early warning concerning costs.

4. LIQUIDATORS

Although the court has jurisdiction to order a liquidator as a non-party to proceedings brought by an insolvent company to pay costs personally, it will only exercise that jurisdiction in exceptional circumstances where there has been impropriety on the part of the liquidator, particularly in view of the fact that the normal remedy of obtaining an order for security for costs is available to the defendant. The caution necessary in all cases when attempt is made to render a non-party liable for costs would be the greater in the case of a liquidator having regard to public policy considerations (*Metalloy Supplies Ltd (in liquidation) v MA (UK) Ltd* [1997] 1 All ER 418).

5. TRIBUNALS

The court has power to order costs against a tribunal whose decision was overturned on appeal, but only if the tribunal made itself a party by appearing on the appeal or taking steps to defend the determination (*Providence Capitol Trustees Ltd v Ayres* [1996] 4 All ER 760, ChD. Where in a successful appeal against a decision of the Pensions Ombudsman the ombudsman had appeared at the appeal and made representations in support of his determination, the costs recoverable from him were not limited to the amount by which they had been increased by his appearance but could, in principle, extend to the whole of the successful party's costs in making the appeal. The decisions in *Elliott v Pensions Ombudsman* ([1998] OPLR 21) and *University of Nottingham v Eyett (No 2)* ([1999] 1 WLR 594) that the ombudsman could be ordered to pay the costs of a successful appeal only to the extent that those costs were increased by his participation was wrong and would not be followed (*Moore's (Wallisdown) Ltd v Pensions Ombudsman* [2002] 1 All ER 737).

6. FUNDERS

In *Shah v Karanjia* [1993] 4 All ER 792 an application against a non-party failed both because he had been given no adequate warning of the application and because of lack of evidence that he had funded the proceedings.

In *Locabail (UK) Ltd v Bayfield Properties Ltd (No 3)* (2000) Times, 29 February, ChD, the first husband of one of the defendants had given evidence on her behalf at the trial when he had been found to be an unsatisfactory witness, prone to exaggeration. He admitted to funding his former wife's action and recommending a solicitor to her. The complainants sought costs against him and he was joined in the action solely in relation to the claim for costs. It was not appropriate to punish the former husband by awarding costs solely on the basis of his funding the litigation of another and behaving unsatisfactorily as a witness. However he was ordered to pay the claimants' costs on the following bases:

(a) he had funded proceedings knowing that his former wife would be unable to satisfy a costs order if unsuccessful;
(b) his intense identification with his former wife's position in his own evidence;
(c) his indifference to the legal and factual issues in the case; and
(d) the court's rejection of the factual basis of his former wife's case.

Hamilton v Al Fayed (No 2) [2002] EWCA Civ 665, [2002] 3 All ER 641 distinguished between 'pure' funders who made donations in support of a litigant as an act of charity and 'professional' funders, such as insurers, who were almost always contractually bound to fund the litigation. An order for costs would rarely be made against a charitable, philanthropic, altruistic or merely sympathetic donor who, on the information before him, had reasonable grounds for believing that the litigant had reasonable grounds for asserting his right or a defence to the claim, and who wished to ensure that a genuine dispute was not lost by default or inadequately contested. If pure funders were regularly exposed to liability under s 51, such funds would dry up and access to justice would thereby on occasions be lost. They should not, however, ordinarily be held liable. So long as the law continued to allow impoverished parties to litigate without having to provide security for their opponents' costs, those sympathetic to their plight should not be discouraged from assisting them to secure representation.

7. INTERVENORS

In the course of proceedings concerning children, the court gave directions for an assessment by a family centre. The father made a statement in intemperate terms attacking the personal and professional integrity of the social worker responsible for the family centre's report. The centre was granted leave to intervene in the proceedings in order to defend these allegations. The centre was formally joined in the proceedings for the purpose of a costs application in accordance with CPR Rule 48.2. The father's attack on the centre had gone far beyond the limits of toleration. The centre's intervention had been warranted and an order for their costs was made against the father: *Re A (family proceedings: expert witnesses)* [2001] 1 FLR 723, Fam D.

CHAPTER 36

COSTS PAYABLE UNDER A CONTRACT

Rule 48.3 and its supplementary practice direction deal with the amount of costs where costs are payable pursuant to a contract.

CPR RULE 48.3 AMOUNT OF COSTS WHERE COSTS ARE PAYABLE PURSUANT TO A CONTRACT

(1) Where the court assesses (whether by the summary or detailed procedure) costs which are payable by the paying party to the receiving party under the terms of a contract, the costs payable under those terms are, unless the contract expressly provides otherwise, to be presumed to be costs which—

(a) have been reasonably incurred; and

(b) are reasonable in amount,

and the court will assess them accordingly.

(The costs practice direction sets out circumstances where the court may order otherwise)

(2) This rule does not apply where the contract is between a solicitor and his client.

SECTION 50: PRACTICE DIRECTION SUPPLEMENTING CPR RULE 48.3

50.1 Where the court is assessing costs payable under a contract, it may make an order that all or part of the costs payable under the contract shall be disallowed if it is satisfied by the paying party that costs have been unreasonably incurred or are unreasonable in amount.

50.2 Rule 48.3 only applies if the court is assessing costs payable under a contract. It does not—

(1) require the court to make an assessment of such costs; or

(2) require a mortgagee to apply for an order for those costs that he has a contractual right to recover out of the mortgage funds.

50.3 The following principles apply to costs relating to a mortgage—

(1) An order for the payment of costs of proceedings by one party to another is always a discretionary order: section 51 of the Supreme Court Act 1981.

(2) Where there is a contractual right to the costs the discretion should ordinarily be exercised so as to reflect that contractual right.

(3) The power of the court to disallow a mortgagee's costs sought to be added to the mortgage security is a power that does not derive from section 51, but from the power of the courts of equity to fix the terms on which redemption will be allowed.

(4) A decision by a court to refuse costs in whole or in part to a mortgagee litigant may be—

(a) a decision in the exercise of the section 51 discretion;

(b) a decision in the exercise of the power to fix the terms on which redemption will be allowed;

(c) a decision as to the extent of a mortgagee's contractual right to add his costs to the security;

or

(d) a combination of two or more of these things.

The statements of case in the proceedings or the submissions made to the court may indicate which of the decisions has been made.

(5) A mortgagee is not to be deprived of a contractual or equitable right to add costs to the security merely by reason of an order for payment of costs made without reference to the mortgagee's contractual or equitable rights, and without any adjudication as to whether or not the mortgagee should be deprived of those costs.

50.4

(1) Where the contract entitles a mortgagee to—

(a) add the costs of litigation relating to the mortgage to the sum secured by it;

(b) require a mortgagor to pay those costs, or

(c) both,

the mortgagor may make an application for the court to direct that an account of the mortgagee's costs be taken.

(Rule 25.1(1)(n) provides that the court may direct that a party file an account)

(2) The mortgagor may then dispute an amount in the mortgagee's account on the basis that it has been unreasonably incurred or is unreasonable in amount.

(3) Where a mortgagor disputes an amount, the court may make an order that the disputed costs are assessed under rule 48.3

Many contracts, particularly mortgages, contain provisions to the effect that one or other party will be liable for the costs incurred pursuant to the contract. Under the terms of a mortgage deed, the mortgagee is usually entitled to add to his security his usual and proper costs of proceedings between himself and the mortgagor or any surety. He does not require an order from the court to do so. However, the court has an equitable jurisdiction to disallow all or part of a mortgagee's costs as being unreasonably incurred or of an unreasonable amount, in fixing the terms of redemption. In addition to his costs of proceedings between himself and the mortgagor, a mortgagee may recover the reasonable and proper costs of proceedings between himself and a third party where what is impugned is the title to the estate. But where a third party impugns the title to a mortgage or the enforcement or exercise of some right or power accruing to the mortgagee under it, the mortgagee's costs of the proceedings, even though reasonable and proper, are not recoverable from the mortgagor (*Parker-Tweedale v Dunbar Bank plc (No 2)* [1991] Ch 26).

There is a presumption that costs payable under a mortgage or any other contract are reasonably and properly incurred and such costs are to be paid on the indemnity basis (*Gomba Holdings (UK) Ltd v Minories Finance Ltd (No 2)* [1993] Ch 171, CA). Rule 48.3 is a summary of the law as I have explained it. There was, however, uncertainty arising out of the original practice direction which was para 50.1 only. This was interpreted by some as meaning that the court now had to assess the costs payable under a contract and that mortgagees had to obtain an order before they could add their costs to the mortgage debt. Accordingly the practice direction was expanded into its present comprehensive statement of the law and practice. But even that was not enough. Paragraph 13.2 of the practice direction supplementing Rule 44.7 provides that the general rule is that the court *should* make a summary assessment of the costs at the end of fast track trial or any hearing that has lasted not more than a day. That necessitated inserting a new para 13.3 as follows:

'The general rule in paragraph 1 does not apply to a mortgagee's costs incurred in mortgage possession proceedings or other proceedings relating to a mortgage unless the mortgagee asks the court to make an order for his costs to be paid by another party. Paragraphs 49.3 and 49.4 deal in more detail with costs relating to mortgages'.

The additional para 50.4 contains the useful provision for a mortgagor to apply for a direction that an account of the mortgagee's costs be taken and for any disputed costs to be assessed under Rule 48.3.

CHAPTER 37

TRUSTEES AND PERSONAL REPRESENTATIVES

CPR RULE 48.4 LIMITATIONS ON COURT'S POWER TO AWARD COSTS IN FAVOUR OF TRUSTEE OR PERSONAL REPRESENTATIVE

(1) This rule applies where—
- (a) a person is or has been a party to any proceedings in the capacity of trustee or personal representative; and
- (b) rule 48.3 does not apply.

(2) The general rule is that he is entitled to be paid the costs of those proceedings, insofar as they are not recovered from or paid by any other person, out of the relevant trust fund or estate.

(3) Where he is entitled to be paid any of those costs out of the fund or estate, those costs will be assessed on the indemnity basis.

There is no supplemental practice direction to this rule.

1. ENTITLEMENT TO COSTS OUT OF THE TRUST OR ESTATE

Trustees and personal representatives have a duty to protect the trust fund or the estate and are entitled to their costs on the indemnity basis of any proceedings undertaken in their capacity of trustee or personal representative out of the trust fund or estate, less, of course, any costs recovered from or paid by another party or source. Such costs are presumed to have been of a reasonable amount and properly incurred, unless they were incurred contrary to the duty of the trustees or personal representatives or the trustee or personal representative has acted for a benefit other than that of the fund or estate.

2. PRE-EMPTIVE ORDERS

If trustees or personal representatives are concerned that it might be suggested that they have acted unreasonably or in their own interests they may apply to the court before commencing or defending proceedings for an order that, win or lose, they will be entitled to their costs out of the property in dispute, before the facts have been fully investigated and before the law has been fully argued. Because, however, such an order could involve the expenditure of a substantial part of the funds or estate, there is a strong public interest in the Attorney-General being represented on the application (*Re Beddoe* [1893] 1 Ch 547). It is known as a 'Beddoe application'.

3. PROSPECTIVE COSTS ORDERS

Practice Statement 1 May 2001

(Trust Proceedings: Prospective Costs Orders) Chancery Division

(1) The practice statement is about the costs of applications by trustees, or beneficiaries, or other person concerned, in relation to the administration of a trust including questions of construction, questions relating to the exercise of powers conferred by the trust, or questions as to the validity of the trust.

(2) Where trustees have the power to agree to pay the costs of some other party to such an application, and exercise properly such a power, CPR Rule 48.3 applies. In such a case, an order is not required and the trustees are entitled to recover out of the trust fund any costs which they pay pursuant to the agreement made in the exercise of such power.

(3) Where the trustees do not have, or decide not to exercise, a power to make such an agreement, the trustees or the party concerned may apply to the court at any stage of the proceedings for an order that the costs of any party to the application referred to in paragraph 1 above (including the costs of the trustees) shall be paid out of the fund (a 'prospective costs order').

(4) The court, on an application for a prospective costs order, may (a) in the case of the trustees' costs, authorise the trustees to raise and meet such costs out of the fund; (b) in the case of the costs of any other party, authorise or direct the trustees to pay such costs (or any part of them, or the costs incurred up to a particular time) out of the trust fund to be assessed, if not agreed by the trustees, on the indemnity basis or, if the court directs, on the standard basis, and to make payments from time to time on account of such costs. A model form of order is set out at the end of this practice statement.

(5) The court will always consider whether it is possible to deal with the application for a prospective costs order on paper without a hearing and in an ordinary case would expect to be able to do so. The trustees must consider whether a hearing is needed for any reason. If they consider that it is they should say so and explain why in their evidence. If any party to the application referred to in paragraph 1 above (or any other person interested in the trust fund) considers that a hearing is necessary (for instance because he wishes to oppose the making of a prospective costs order) this should be stated, and the reasons explained, in his evidence, if any, or otherwise in a letter to the court.

(6) If the court would be minded to refuse the application on a consideration of the papers alone, the parties will be notified and given the opportunity, within a stated time to ask for a hearing.

(7) The evidence in support of an application for a prospective costs order should be given by witness statement. The trustees and the applicant (if different) must ensure full disclosure of the relevant matters to show that the case is one which falls within the category of case where a prospective costs order can properly be made.

(8) The model form of order is designed for use in the more straightforward cases, where a question needs to be determined which has arisen in the administration of the trust, whether the claimants are the trustees or a beneficiary. The form may be adapted for use in less straightforward cases, in particular where the proceedings are hostile, but special factors may also have to be reflected in the terms of the order in such a case.

Sir Andrew Morritt
Vice Chancellor

4. COSTS AGAINST TRUSTEES

A trustee or personal representative who has acted outside his duty or has acted in his own interests or otherwise unreasonably not only will be unable to recover his costs out of the fund or estate, but he may be ordered to pay the costs of another party personally. Similarly, although trustees and personal representatives will generally be justified in making an application to obtain the opinion of the court on a matter of construction or difficulty, if they appeal against the court's decision unsuccessfully, they may expect to be ordered to pay the costs of the appeal *personally (Re Earl of Radnor's Will Trusts* (1890) 45 ChD 402). Only in exceptional circumstances, say, for example, where large interests are at stake or where the interests of unborn persons are affected, will the costs be ordered to be paid out of the estate.

CPR RULE 47.17A DETAILED ASSESSMENT PROCEDURE WHERE COSTS ARE PAYABLE OUT OF A FUND OTHER THAN THE COMMUNITY LEGAL SERVICE FUND

(1) Where the court is to assess costs which are payable out of a fund other than the Community Legal Service Fund, the receiving party may commence detailed assessment proceedings by filing a request in the relevant practice form.
(2) A request under paragraph (1) must be filed within 3 months after the date when the right to detailed assessment arose.
(3) The court may direct that the party seeking assessment serve a copy of the request on any person who has a financial interest in the outcome of the assessment.
(4) The court will, on receipt of the request for assessment, provisionally assess the costs without the attendance of the receiving party, unless it considers that a hearing is necessary.
(5) After the court has provisionally assessed the bill, it will return the bill to the receiving party.
(6) The court will fix a date for an assessment hearing if the party informs the court, within 14 days after he receives the provisionally assessed bill, that he wants the court to hold such a hearing.

SECTION 44: PRACTICE DIRECTION SUPPLEMENTING CPR RULE 47.17A

44.1 Rule 47.17A provides that the court will make a provisional assessment of a bill of costs payable out of a fund (other than the Community Legal Service Fund) unless it considers that a hearing is necessary. It also enables the court to direct under rule 47.17A(3) that the receiving party must serve a copy of the request for assessment and copies of the documents which accompany it, on any person who has a financial interest in the outcome of the assessment.

44.2

(a) A person has a financial interest in the outcome of the assessment if the assessment will or may affect the amount of money or property to which he is or may become entitled out of the fund.

(b) Where an interest in the fund is itself held by a trustee for the benefit of some other person, that trustee will be treated as the person having such a financial interest.

(c) 'Trustee' includes a personal representative, receiver or any other person acting in a fiduciary capacity.

44.3 The request for a detailed assessment of costs out of the fund should be in Form N258B, be accompanied by the documents set out at paragraph 42.3(a) to (e) and (g) above and the following—

(a) a statement signed by the receiving party giving his name, address for service, reference, telephone number, fax number and,

(b) a statement of the postal address of any person who has a financial interest in the outcome of the assessment, to which the court may send notice of any hearing; and

(c) in respect of each person stated to have such an interest if such person is a child or patient, a statement to that effect.

44.4 The court will decide, having regard to the amount of the bill, the size of the fund and the number of persons who have a financial interest, which of those persons should be served. The court may dispense with service on all or some of them.

44.5 Where the court makes an order dispensing with service on all such persons it may proceed at once to make a provisional assessment, or, if it decides that a hearing is necessary, give appropriate directions. Before deciding whether a hearing is necessary under this rule, the court may require the receiving party to provide further information relating to the bill.

44.6

(1) Where the court has provisionally assessed a bill of costs, it will send to the receiving party, a notice in Form N253 of the amount of costs which the court proposes to allow together with the bill itself. If the receiving party is legally represented the legal representative should, if the provisional assessment is to be accepted, then complete the bill.

(2) The court will fix a date for a detailed assessment hearing, if the receiving party informs the court within 14 days after he receives the notice in Form N253 of the amount allowed on the provisional assessment, that he wants the court to hold such a hearing.

44.7 Where the court makes an order that a person who has a financial interest is to be served with a copy of the request for assessment, it may give directions about service and about the hearing.

44.8 The court will give at least 14 days notice of the time and place of the detailed assessment hearing to the receiving party and, to any person who has a financial interest in the outcome of the assessment and has been served with a copy of the request for assessment.

44.9 If the receiving party, or any other party or any person who has a financial interest in the outcome of assessment, wishes to make an application in the detailed assessment proceedings, the provisions of Part 23 (General Rules about Applications for Court Orders) applies.

44.10 If the receiving party is legally represented the legal representative must in order to complete the bill after the assessment make clear the correct figures allowed in respect of each item and must recalculate the summary of the bill if appropriate.

CHAPTER 38

CHILDREN AND PATIENTS

1. GLOSSARY

The useful umbrella description of a 'party under a disability' was perceived to be politically incorrect and has gone. The word 'minor', itself a recent replacement for 'infant', has now given way to the word 'child'– despite the irrefutable fact that we are all someone's child. CPR Rule 21.1(2) defines 'child' as a person under 18 and defines 'patient' as a person who by reason of mental disorder within the meaning of the Mental Health Act 1983 is incapable of managing and administering his own affairs. The terms 'next friend' and 'guardian ad litem' were replaced by 'litigation friend' in civil litigation. Guardians ad litem are alive and well in Children Act 1989 proceedings.

2. LITIGATION FRIEND

A patient must have a litigation friend to conduct proceedings on his behalf (CPR Rule 21.2(1)) and a child must have one unless the court permits the child to conduct his own proceedings (CPR Rule 21.2(3)). Where the child or patient is a claimant, the litigation friend must give an undertaking to pay any costs which the child or patient may be ordered to pay in relation to the proceedings, subject to any right he may have to be repaid from the assets of the child or patient whether the litigation friend has become one without a court order (CPR Rule 2.3(1)(*e*)) or has been appointed under a court order (CPR Rule 3.4(4)). The litigation friend's liability for costs continues until the child or patient serves notice that the litigation friend's appointment has ceased (giving his address for service and stating whether or not he intends to carry on the proceedings) or the litigation friend serves notice on the parties that his appointment to act has ceased (CPR Rule 21.9(6)).

CPR RULE 48.5 COSTS WHERE MONEY IS PAYABLE BY OR TO A CHILD OR PATIENT

(1) This rule applies to any proceedings where a party is a child or patient and—

- (a) money is ordered or agreed to be paid to, or for the benefit of, that party; or
- (b) money is ordered to be paid by him or on his behalf.

('Child' and 'patient' are defined in rule 2.3)

(2) The general rule is that—

- (a) the court must order a detailed assessment of the costs payable by any party who is a child or patient to his solicitor; and
- (b) on an assessment under paragraph (a), the court must also assess any costs payable to that party in the proceedings, unless the court has issued a default costs certificate in relation to those costs under rule 47.11.

(3) The court need not order detailed assessment of costs in the circumstances set out in the costs practice direction.

(4) Where—

(a) a claimant is a child or patient; and

(b) a detailed assessment has taken place under paragraph (2)(a),

the only amount payable by the child or patient to his solicitor is the amount which the court certifies as payable.

(This rule applies to a counterclaim by or on behalf of child or patient by virtue of rule 20.3)

SECTION 51: PRACTICE DIRECTION SUPPLEMENTING CPR RULE 48.5

51.1 The circumstances in which the court need not order the assessment of costs under rule 48.5(3) are as follows:

(a) where there is no need to do so to protect the interests of the child or patient or his estate;

(b) where another party has agreed to pay a specified sum in respect of the costs of the child or patient and the solicitor acting for the child or patient has waived the right to claim further costs;

(c) where the court has decided the costs payable to the child or patient by way of summary assessment and the solicitor acting for the child or patient has waived the right to claim further costs;

(d) where an insurer or other person is liable to discharge the costs which the child or patient would otherwise be liable to pay to his solicitor and the court is satisfied that the insurer or other person is financially able to discharge those costs.

Rule 48.5 is designed to protect the interests of a child or patient and to prevent exploitation by unscrupulous legal representatives or litigation friends. Generally, detailed assessment is required of any costs payable by a child or patient to his solicitor and when such an assessment takes place the court must also assess any costs payable to that party in the proceedings, unless a default costs certificate has been issued.

The court is given the discretion to dispense with a detailed assessment where it is not needed to protect the interests of the child or patient:

(a) where another party has agreed to pay a specified sum in respect of the costs and the solicitor has waived the right to claim any further costs from the child or patient;

(b) where the court has decided the amount of costs payable by way of summary assessment; and

(c) where an insurer or other person is liable to discharge the costs which the child or patient would otherwise be liable to pay and the court is satisfied that the person liable is financially able to discharge the costs.

CHAPTER 39

LITIGANTS IN PERSON

1. THE STATUTE

The Litigants in Person Costs and Expenses Act 1975 provides that where any costs of a litigant in person (known affectionately as LIPs or 'lippies') are ordered to be paid by any other party to proceedings there may be allowed (subject to any rule of the court) on assessment or determination of the costs, sums in respect of any work done and any expenses and losses incurred by the litigant in or in connection with the proceedings. The provisions of the Act apply to all civil proceedings in the House of Lords, The Supreme Court, the Lands Tribunal and county courts in which any order is made that the costs of a LIP are to be paid by any other party to those proceedings or in any other way. Prior to the coming into force of the Act in April 1976, LIPs (other than those who were practising solicitors) whose costs were ordered to be paid were entitled to recover from the paying party no more than such out-of-pocket expenses as had been properly incurred. The Act enabled LIPs to recover the same category of costs as would have been allowed if the work had been done by a solicitor on the litigant's behalf, limited in amount to such sum as was required to compensate the litigant for the time he had reasonably spent on preparing and conducting his case, subject to any rules of court.

2. RULE AND PRACTICE DIRECTION

CPR RULE 48.6 LITIGANTS IN PERSON

(1) This rule applies where the court orders (whether by summary assessment or detailed assessment) that the costs of a litigant in person are to be paid by any other person.
(2) The costs allowed under this rule must not exceed, except in the case of a disbursement, two-thirds of the amount which would have been allowed if the litigant in person had been represented by a legal representative.
(3) The litigant in person shall be allowed—
- (a) costs for the same categories of—
  - (i) work; and
  - (ii) disbursements,

  which would have been allowed if the work had been done or the disbursements had been made by a legal representative on the litigant in person's behalf;
- (b) the payments reasonably made by him for legal services relating to the conduct of the proceedings; and
- (c) the costs of obtaining expert assistance in assessing the costs claim.

(The costs practice direction deals with who may be an expert for the purpose of paragraph (2)(c))
(4) The amount of costs to be allowed to the litigant in person for any item of work claimed shall be—

(a) where the litigant can prove financial loss, the amount that he can prove he has lost for time reasonably spent on doing the work; or

(b) where the litigant cannot prove financial loss, an amount for the time reasonably spent on doing the work at the rate set out in the practice direction.

(5) A litigant who is allowed costs for attending at court to conduct his case is not entitled to a witness allowance in respect of such attendance in addition to those costs.

(6) For the purposes of this rule, a litigant in person includes—

(a) a company or other corporation which is acting without a legal representative; and

(b) a barrister, solicitor, solicitor's employee or other authorised litigator (as defined in the Courts and Legal Services Act 1990) who is acting for himself.

SECTION 52: PRACTICE DIRECTION SUPPLEMENTING CPR RULE 48.6

52.1 In order to qualify as an expert for the purpose of rule 48.6(3)(c) (expert assistance in connection with assessing the claim for costs), the person in question must be a

(1) barrister,

(2) solicitor,

(3) Fellow of the Institute of Legal Executives,

(4) Fellow of the Association of Law Costs Draftsmen,

(5) law costs draftsman who is a member of the Academy of Experts,

(6) law costs draftsman who is a member of the Expert Witness Institute.

52.2 Where a litigant in person wishes to prove that he has suffered financial loss he should produce to the court any written evidence he relies on to support that claim, and serve a copy of that evidence on any party against whom he seeks costs at least 24 hours before the hearing at which the question may be decided.

52.3 Where a litigant in person commences detailed assessment proceedings under rule 47.6 he should serve copies of that written evidence with the notice of commencement.

52.4 The amount, which may be allowed to a litigant in person under rule 46.3(5)(b) and rule 48.6(4), is £9.25 per hour.

52.5 Attention is drawn to rule 48.6(6)(b). A solicitor who, instead of acting for himself, is represented in the proceedings by his firm or by himself in his firm name, is not, for the purpose of the Civil Procedure Rules, a litigant in person.

The rules have always limited the costs recoverable by a litigant in person to two-thirds of the amount which would have been allowed to a legal representative. The reasoning behind this figure is that a solicitor's charges have usually included a 50% profit mark-up on his expense rate, but as an LIP may not make a profit out of the costs of litigation, the 50% is deducted, leaving two-thirds.

3. FINANCIAL LOSS

(a) Two categories

In previous editions I said this rule was less than satisfactory. It has now been amended with effect from 2 December 2002. Because work done before 2 December 2002 will be governed by the previous Rule 48.6(3) and (4), here they are:

(3) Costs allowed to the litigant in person shall be—
  (a) such costs which would have been allowed if the work had been done or the disbursements made by a legal representative on the litigant in person's behalf;
  (b) the payments reasonably made by him for legal services relating to the conduct of the proceedings; and
  (c) the costs of obtaining expert assistance in connection with assessing the claim for costs.

(The costs practice direction deals with who may be an expert for the purpose of paragraph (2)(c))

(4) Subject to paragraph (2), the amount of costs to be allowed to the litigant in person for any item of work to which the costs relate shall, if he fails to prove financial loss, be an amount in respect of the time spent reasonably doing the work at the rate specified in the costs practice direction.

The anomaly that an LIP who could prove *any* financial loss, however small, was over the threshold and entitled to recover up to two-thirds of what a solicitor would have charged for *all* the work that he had done, whether or not it all caused a financial loss. Under the amended Rule 48.6(4)(*a*) the amount an LIP can claim cannot exceed his financial loss. That is the first category. An LIP who cannot prove financial loss continues, under the new Rule 48.6(4)(*b*), to recover for the amount of time reasonably spent at the prescribed rate, at the time of writing £9.25 an hour. That is the second category. But are the categories mutually exclusive? When the costs of an LIP in category 1 reach the limit of his financial loss, may he switch to category 2? Or may the wording of sub-rule (4)(*a*) be interpreted as confining the LIP to category 1? I hope not, but if not, may an LIP jump from one category to the other for each item of work, depending on whether or not it resulted in financial loss, resulting in LIPs calculating which category would be most favourable to them at any particular stage?

(b) Legal costs

Although a litigant may have acted in person without a solicitor on the record, he is nevertheless entitled to recover payments reasonably made for legal services relating to the conduct of the proceedings and the costs of obtaining expert assistance in connection with assessing the claim for costs, including representation on a detailed assessment. The categories of expert are identified in paragraph 5.1 of the practice direction.

(c) Fast track trial costs

The effect of the test of financial loss can become bizarre when applied to the fixed costs of fast track trials. Rule 46.3, which has not been amended, provides:

(5) Where the party to whom fast track trial costs are to be awarded is a litigant in person, the court will award—
  (a) if the litigant in person can prove financial loss, two-thirds of the amount that would otherwise be awarded; or
  (b) if the litigant in person fails to prove financial loss, an amount in respect of the time spent reasonably doing the work at the rate specified in the costs practice direction.

This provision throws up a ludicrous anomaly. Rule 48.6(3) still provides that the costs allowed to a LIP shall be such costs as would have been allowed if the work had been done by a legal representative. Rule 46.2 provides that the court may not award less than the prescribed amounts and therefore any LIP who can show that he has suffered any financial loss, however small, must be awarded two-thirds of the prescribed amount. Surprisingly, it has not been possible to devise a means of circumventing this anomalous windfall to a LIP; the provision is clearly in breach of the indemnity principle, but, by their nature, no fixed costs take into account the receiving party's liability to his own solicitor.

(d) Re-appraisal

Despite the amendment of Rule 48.6(3) and (4) there is still a need for a full re-appraisal of the philosophy, practice and procedure relating to costs awarded to LIPs, which is now underway.

4. CASES

In *Law Society v Persaud* (1990) Times, 10 May, QBD, the defendant, who lived in South Africa, successfully contested proceedings brought by the Law Society and obtained an order for costs against them. On the assessment of his costs two items were disallowed: the cost of travelling from South Africa to England to defend the action in person of £1,391.25 and the cost of travelling between Birmingham and London of £74.

The claimants did not suggest that the defendant had been extravagant or acted in bad faith but that the disbursements did not come within the terms of Ord 62, r18(1) (now Rule 48.6(3)) because no solicitor would have been allowed to charge as a disbursement the cost of travel from South Africa to England because the solicitor would already be in England and similarly the cost of travelling from Birmingham to London would not be incurred because the solicitor would already be in London.

The defendant justified his disbursements on the grounds that they were less than would have been the cost of instructing solicitors and counsel. The costs officer had assessed the costs of solicitors at £2,457 and allowed the defendant £1,643, being two-thirds of this, resulting in a saving to the claimants of £821 of the amount if the defendant had instructed solicitors. To this, the defendant argued, must be added the estimated cost of instructing counsel. The Law Society and the costs officer took the view that this was wrong, following the decision in *Hart v Aga Khan Foundation (UK)* [1984] 2 All ER 439, CA, where the Court of Appeal had said that one should not allow the cost of counsel who were not in fact employed. To apply that decision in this matter was too literal an approach; it did not preclude the costs officer from allowing reasonable disbursements which had in fact been incurred. The costs sought to be recovered by the defendant did not exceed what would have been the actual cost and disbursements allowable to a London solicitor, including counsel's fees. There was still an overall saving to the other side as a result of the relevant party having chosen to represent himself, and therefore, both sets of disallowed disbursements were restored.

The *New Law Journal* of 1 July 1994, p 890 reported that a litigant in person who after a three-and-a-half-day hearing was granted leave to proceed under the Mental Health Act against seven defendants with the costs of the application awarded against those defendants, was allowed on taxation her costs in excess of £59,000 for obtaining legal assistance in the preparation and presentation of a case from solicitors who were not on the record.

In *R v Common Professional Examination Board, ex p Mealing-McCleod* (2000) SCCO No 7 (2000) Times, 2 May, CA it was held:

(a) CPR Rule 48.6(4) suggests that more time should be allowed to a litigant in person than to a solicitor doing the same task.
(b) When a litigant in person is restricted to the litigant in person charging rate of £9.25 per hour, it is likely that the costs of the other side, if legally represented are likely to be very much higher. The proportionality mentioned in CPR Rule 48.5 is that the costs incurred by a party must be proportionate to the amount of the claim and the litigation generally. It does not mean that the costs of a legally represented party must be reduced below a reasonable level of remuneration because the other side is a litigant in person restricted to payment over £9.25 per hour.

However, in *Greville v Sprake* [2001] EWCA Civ 234, the Court of Appeal, without referring to *Mealing-McCleod*, held that a litigant in person is limited to the time which would reasonably have been spent by a solicitor on the preparation of his or her case based on Rule 48.6(3)(*a*). This appears to be another demonstration of the urgent need for a complete overhaul of LIPs' costs.

5. WHO IS A LITIGANT IN PERSON?

After much debate and various amendments the rule and the practice direction now provide that a litigant in person includes a company or other corporation which is acting without a legal representative, a barrister, solicitor, solicitor's employee or other authorised litigator who is acting for himself. However, a solicitor who instead of acting for himself is represented in the proceedings by his firm, or by himself in his firm's name, is not, for the purposes of the Civil Procedure Rules, a litigant in person. If he were this would preclude a solicitor acting on his own behalf, for example suing for unpaid costs, from recovering his normal charges. When this was appreciated, it was too late to change the rule so it was circumvented by para 52.5 of the practice direction by providing that a solicitor, who, instead of acting for himself, is represented in the proceedings by his firm or by himself in his firm name (presumably even if he is a sole practitioner) is not, a litigant in person.

6. OFFICIAL RECEIVER IS A LITIGANT IN PERSON

In *Re Minotaur Data Systems Ltd* [1998] 4 All ER 500, ChD the judge had with some regret come to the conclusion that the Official Solicitor acting as an applicant in proceedings under the Company Director Disqualification Act 1986, s 6 without the aid of a Solicitor was not a litigant in person and therefore not entitled to an allowance in respect of costs. The judge therefore would have been pleased to have been reversed by the Court of Appeal on 18 March 1999, which held that the Official Solicitor could not be said to be acting for the Crown as a litigant in person but that he was himself a litigant in person for the purposes of recovering his costs.

7. ASSESSMENT

The provision that a LIP may only recover two-thirds of what a notional solicitor would have charged limits the amount the LIP may claim for any particular item. The correct approach therefore for the assessment of a LIP claiming at the specified rate is to ascertain what the total of that item is. Then compare that with two-thirds of the notional solicitors rate and allow the lower of the two items. This means that the bill of costs drawn by the LIP must be gone through in some detail, item by item (*Morris v Wiltshire and Woodspring District Council* (16 January 1998, unreported, QBD).

In *R (on the application of Wulfsohn) v Legal Services Commission* [2002] EWCA Civ 250, [2002] All ER (D) 120 (Feb) a successful litigant in person produced a rough costs schedule purporting to show that he had been engaged for over 1,200 hours on research and he also gave oral evidence, which the court had no reason to disbelieve, that he had spent well in excess of 1,200 hours. In these circumstances the right course is to start with the cap imposed by CPR Rule 48.6(2) which provides that the costs of a litigant in person shall not exceed two-thirds of the amount which would have been allowed if the litigant in person had been represented by a legal representative. The litigant in person also produced a letter to him from a firm of solicitors saying: 'On the limited information that we have been provided by yourself and the Citizens Advice Bureau in the Royal Courts of Justice and having seen at a very preliminary stage the documentation with regards the matter we would estimate that the legal costs would be in the region of £15,000 to £20,000 plus VAT'. Doing the best it could on the information in front of it the court 'being extremely rough-and-ready' about it took the figure of £15,000 which resulted in a cap of £10,000. In addition to that the court allowed photocopying, postage and travelling totalling £460, resulting in a total award of costs of £10,460, instead of the £120 awarded by the trial judge.

CHAPTER 40

GROUP (MULTI-PARTY) LITIGATION

CPR RULE 48.6A COSTS WHERE THE COURT HAS MADE A GROUP LITIGATION ORDER

This rule applies where the court has made a Group Litigation Order ('GLO').
(2) In this rule—
  (a) 'individual costs' means costs incurred in relation to an individual claim on the group register;
  (b) 'common costs' means—
    (i) costs incurred in relation to the GLO issues;
    (ii) individual costs incurred in a claim while it is proceeding as a test claim, and
    (iii) costs incurred by the lead solicitor in administering the group litigation; and
  (c) 'group litigant' means a claimant or defendant, as the case may be, whose claim is entered on the group register.
(3) Unless the court orders otherwise, any order for common costs against group litigants imposes on each group litigant several liability([GL]) for an equal proportion of those common costs.
(4) The general rule is that where a group litigant is the paying party, he will, in addition to any costs he is liable to pay to the receiving party, be liable for—
  (a) the individual costs of his claim; and
  (b) an equal proportion, together with all the other group litigants, of the common costs.
(5) Where the court makes an order about costs in relation to any application or hearing which involved—
  (a) one or more GLO issues; and
  (b) issues relevant only to individual claims,
the court will direct the proportion of the costs that is to relate to common costs and the proportion that is to relate to individual costs.
(6) Where common costs have been incurred before a claim is entered on the group register, the court may order the group litigant to be liable for a proportion of those costs.
Where a claim is removed from the group register, the court may make an order for costs in that claim which includes a proportion of the common costs incurred up to the date on which the claim is removed from the group register.
(Part 19 sets out rules about group litigation).
[([GL]) Several liability: A person who is severally liable with others may remain liable for the whole claim even where judgment has been obtained against the others.]

This rule was introduced on 3 July 2000 in an attempt to codify the guidance in the authorities on some of the costs issues arising in group litigation. Some of the problems where a few claims are selected out of a large number as test cases are concerned with how the costs of those cases are to be apportioned among all of the claimants in a variety of circumstances, such as when a between-the-parties costs award in their favour is obtained which is less than the solicitor and client costs, or where there is an adverse costs order. A frequent complication is where some, but not all of the claimants are state-funded. In *BCCI v Ali* (13 April 2000, unreported, ChD) of some 300 claimants, five were chosen as test cases. They were not awarded any between-the-parties costs, although not ordered to pay any (see p 93) but the non-test case claimants argued that the solicitor and client costs should be paid solely by the test case claimants, on the grounds that they had lost because of their own dishonesty. Surprisingly, no costs sharing order or agreement had been made. The court found that when the test cases were chosen it was the common expectation of all the claimants that the test case costs would be shared equally, and it so ordered. In *Ochwat v Watson Burton (a firm)* [1999] All ER (D) 1407, the test case claimants won on the general issues of duty of care and breach of that duty, but failed on causation. The judge awarded the defendants 75% of their costs of which he ordered the test case claimants to pay 75% and the remaining claimants 25%. On appeal it was held that this was unfair to the test case claimants and that the costs awarded to the defendants should be paid by all the claimants.

Rule 48.6A provides that, unless the court orders otherwise, orders against group litigants impose several liability for an equal proportion of common costs and that a group litigant will be responsible for his own individual solicitor and client costs and an equal share of the common costs. The court may make provision for the costs contribution of a party who joins the group late, or leaves it early.

In *Sayers v Smith Kline Beecham plc* [2001] EWCA Civ 2017, [2001] All ER (D) 365 (Dec) appeals arose in relation to the details of costs-sharing in three separate multi-party actions. However likely it might be that, if common issues were directed at trial, the costs of those issues would be ordered to follow the determination of those issues rather than await the individual fate of each claimant's action, it would be wrong to say that that should always be the presumptive position. Parties who settle their cases did not usually need any presumptive order as to the incidence of costs since costs would be part of the discussion leading to a settlement in any event. Discontinuers, however, gave rise to a more difficult problem. The order usually made in these circumstances was too blunt an instrument and was unnecessarily favourable to defendants, at a stage of the proceedings when it was as yet unknown whether the claimants as a whole were to be successful in the common issues which were to be tried. The orders in the present case should be amended to read:

> 'If in any quarter a claimant discontinued his claim against any one or more of the defendants or it is dismissed by an order of the court whereby the claimant is ordered to pay such defendant's costs, then he will be liable for his individual costs incurred by such defendants up to the last day of that quarter; liability for common costs and disbursement to be determined following the trial of common issues, with permission to apply if such trial does take place.'

This form of order should in future be used in multi-party actions.

Michael Goldberg of Davies Arnold Cooper regarded the judgment as an opportunity lost to reinforce a restraint on claimants. In the *New Law Journal* of 22 March 2002 he wrote:

> 'Claimants ought to be able to leave a group action knowing their liability for costs, pay them, and then put the litigation behind them. Instead, claimants wishing to forget their unsuccessful foray into group litigation may have their claims re-examined. Quite how the court will be able to embark on such re-examination remains unanswered.
>
> Group actions function as a cost-effective and administratively convenient way of ensuring that large numbers of claimants are able to have claims litigated with minimal delay. Whilst the judgment might be perceived by some as good news for the lawyers

acting on both sides in group actions, who can now anticipate a drawn-out enquiry on costs at the end of each trial, one cannot help wondering whether justice is truly being served.

Ultimately, it is the litigants themselves who are being short changed.'

PART VI

FUNDING

CHAPTER 41

THE COMMUNITY LEGAL SERVICE

In 1945 the new Labour Government gave the legal and medical professions the alternatives of either being nationalised, or of voluntarily coming up with proposals for providing their services free to those who could not afford to pay for them. The medical profession came up with nothing, and they got the National Health Service. The legal profession avoided the creation of a National Legal Service by proposing the Legal Aid Scheme, funded by a 15% reduction in lawyers' fees to those clients who qualified for legal aid, subject to contributions. Prior to that a key concept in the running of a solicitors' practice had been 'cross-subsidisation' – whereby the more profitable work (mainly probate and conveyancing) subsidised the less profitable or unprofitable work (such as crime and litigation), with work being done *pro bono* for deserving clients who could not afford to pay anything. It was contemplated that the new legal aid scheme would embrace this philosophy and that all firms of solicitors would offer legal aid as a method of funding to those who qualified for it. The National Health Service may or may not be in a mess, but the Legal Aid Scheme, as originally envisaged, is dead. It went wrong at both ends of the spectrum. It was not obligatory for firms of solicitors to undertake legal aid work, and not all of them did. Over the years, the number of firms not accepting legal aid work, and, indeed, not now being allowed to accept it because they have neither a public funding contract or franchise, has increased from a trickle to a flood. At the other end of the spectrum are firms of solicitors seeking to make a living out of publicly funded work, much of which had previously been done at a loss or *pro bono*. The result is that instead of legal aid being provided by the legal profession as a whole – which was the consideration for not being nationalised – we have the present polarisation, with legal aid being provided by a diminishing number of specialist firms and the majority of the profession being unwilling, and now unable, to undertake publicly funded work.

A survey by the Law Society's *Gazette*, supported by the Legal Aid Practitioners Group, among 150 firms of solicitors throughout the country, found that:

- 57% had given up legal aid contracts or were considering doing so.
- 21% had dropped more than one area of work or were considering doing so in the future.
- 15% of firms had stopped, or were stopping, doing all publicly funded family work, as were 14% in respect of crime and 11% in respect of housing.
- 85% of firms had no intention of taking on new areas of publicly funded work.
- 54% said they had given up the work because it was unprofitable.
- 23% could not meet the supervisory requirements governing the amount of work they needed to do to get a contract.
- 20% blamed bureaucracy.

The Legal Aid Practitioners Group in a consultation paper refers to an 'unimaginable crisis' ahead unless the problems in recruiting and maintaining senior staff, trainees and support staff are rapidly addressed. The report went on:

> 'Where there is no private work to subsidise the legal aid sector, it is difficult to make a reasonable living. Where there is, those partners doing private work increasingly resent having their income so significantly reduced by the comparative lack of income from the legal aid parts of the firm.'

No concept of cross-subsidisation or *pro bono* there. It may be the object of the Legal Services Commission to achieve efficiency and economy by having fewer and larger specialist firms providing state-funded litigation services, but we have come a long way from the vision of 1945, and perhaps a step closer to a National Legal Service.

On 1 April 2000, the Legal Aid Board was replaced by the Legal Services Commission (LSC). The LSC runs two schemes, the civil scheme working with those legal service providers (solicitors and not-for-profit agencies) who are members of the Community Legal Service (CLS) and the criminal scheme, the Criminal Defence Service. Both schemes deliver services primarily through contracts with legal service providers who have satisfied the LSC's prescribed standards, which entitles them to display the CLS civil logo.

Since February 1999, only legal service providers with a contract with the LSC have been able to take on publicly-funded clinical negligence cases, and since 1 January 2000 only contracted organisations have been able to give initial help in any civil matter or provide any level of LSC-funded service in family and immigration cases. Since 1 April 2000, most personal injury cases (except clinical negligence) have been excluded from public funding. On 1 April 2001, the civil contracting scheme was extended to cover all levels of service for all types of case, which can now only be supplied under a LSC contract.

1. A NEW VOCABULARY

There are some different words for old concepts and new words for new concepts:

- **Legal Services Commission** *(formerly the Legal Aid Board)*
- **Community Legal Service Fund** *(formerly the Legal Aid Fund)*
- **Funding Code Certificate** *(formerly a Legal Aid Certificate)*
- **funded client** *(formerly an assisted person)*
- **costs protection** *(the limit on costs awarded against a client set out in the Access to Justice Act 1999, s 11(1))*
- **funding code** *(the code approved under the Access to Justice Act 1999, s 9)*
- **funded services** *(services which are provided directly for a client and funded for that client by the LSC through the CLS under the Access to Justice Act 1999, ss 4–11)*
- **funded partner** *(except in the expression 'partner in a business' means a person with whom the person concerns lives as a couple, and includes a person with whom the person concerned is not currently living, but from whom he or she is not living separate and apart)*
- **personal injury proceedings** *(proceedings for damages in respect of death or any disease or impairment of the client's physical or mental condition, excluding proceedings for clinical negligence)*
- **solicitor** *(solicitor or other person who is an authorised litigator within the meaning of the Courts and Legal Services Act 1990, s 119 (1))*
- **supplier** *(the solicitor, mediator or agency being requested to provide or providing funded services to the client)*

2. SERVICES INCLUDED

Section 4 of the Access to Justice Act 1999 describes the services to be provided by the CLS as:

(a) The provision of general information about the law and legal system and the availability of legal services.
(b) The provision of help by the giving of advice as to how the law applies in particular circumstances.
(c) The provision of help in preventing, settling or otherwise resolving, disputes about legal rights and duties.
(d) The provision of help in enforcing decisions by which such disputes are resolved.
(e) The provision of help in relation to legal proceedings not relating to disputes.

3. SERVICES EXCLUDED

Schedule 2 to the Access to Justice Act provides that the following services may not be funded as part of the CLS:

(a) Allegations of negligently caused injury, death or damage to property, apart from allegations relating to clinical negligence.
(b) Conveyancing.
(c) Boundary disputes.
(d) The making of wills.
(e) Matters of trust law.
(f) Defamation or malicious falsehood.
(g) Matters of company or partnership law.
(h) Other matters arising out of the carrying on of a business.
(i) Advocacy in any proceedings except in the House of Lords, the Judicial committee of the Privy Counsel in the exercise of its jurisdiction under the Government of Wales Act 1998, The Scotland Act 1998 or the Northern Ireland Act 1998, the Court of Appeal, the High Court, any county court, the Employment Appeal Tribunal or any Mental Health Review Tribunal.

4. THE LEVELS OF SERVICE

The LSC funds various levels of service under the CLS in various categories. Here they are:

(a) Help

Help comes in the form of Legal Help and Help at Court.

Legal Help provides initial advice and assistance and is the equivalent of the Legal Advice and Assistance formerly provided under the Green Form Scheme.

Help at Court replaces the former Assistance by Way of Representation, known as ABWOR, authorising legal representation for the purposes of a particular hearing, but not in the proceedings generally.

These two levels of service provide help from a legal service provider up to an amount of £500 (with a higher figure for immigration asylum cases). Once the cost limit is reached the solicitor or adviser can only carry out further work at this level with the authority of the LSC Regional Office. Legal Help cannot be applied for retrospectively.

(b) Legal Representation

There are two forms of Legal Representation which are equivalent to the former Civil Legal Aid.

(i) Investigative Help

This is similar to a former Legal Aid Certificate limited to making enquiries, obtaining counsel's opinion and issuing, but not serving, proceedings. It is intended for fast track and multi-track claims where substantial investigative work is necessary to assess the strength of a proposed claim. It is only available where the prospects of success are not clear and the investigation is likely to be expensive. Its purpose is to enable the prospect of success to be assessed for the purposes of a conditional fee agreement or for full CLS funding.

(ii) Full Representation

This is the equivalent of a former full Legal Aid Certificate and is the main form of legal representation. Although the LSC may impose limitations and conditions on the extent of funding, in principle, full representation can cover all work needed to take legal proceedings to trial and beyond.

(c) Support Funding

This is a new concept of mixed funding, which previously was not allowed, with part of the costs being financed by the state and the balance privately with the assistance of a conditional fee agreement. When support funding is granted, the LSC does not take over general responsibility for funding the costs of the proceedings. The case will continue on a private basis with the solicitor being paid limited payments by the LSC during the case towards the overall legal costs. It again comes in two forms:

(i) Investigative Support

This provides limited funding for the investigation of the strength of a proposed claim with a view to proceeding under a conditional fee agreement. It covers only work done in investigating the strength of the claim and does not cover other investigative work, for example the amount of the claim. As soon as sufficient investigative work has been carried out to estimate prospects of success and to decide whether to proceed under a conditional fee agreement, this must be reported to the LSC and no further work will be funded. It is only available where the reasonable costs of investigation are exceptionally high, ie disbursements, such as experts' reports, are likely to exceed £1,000 or the solicitor's fees to investigate the case are likely to exceed £3,000. Other merits criteria apply to this level of funding, including a requirement that the likely damages exceed £5,000.

(ii) Litigation Support

This is any type of Support Funding other than Investigative Support. It is intended to provide partial funding support for high-cost litigation already proceeding under a conditional fee agreement. It is only available where the reasonable costs of the litigation are exceptionally high, ie disbursements such as experts' reports, are likely to exceed £5,000 or the solicitor's costs and the barrister's fees together are likely to exceed £15,000 calculated at the rate of £70 an hour. The other merits criteria apply to this level of funding.

(d) Family

In addition to Legal Help and Legal Representation there are additional services in respect of family matters.

(i) Approved Family Help

Approved Family Help provides help in family cases short of Full Representation in contested proceedings. It includes the services covered by Legal Help, but also includes issuing proceedings and representation where necessary to obtain disclosure of information from another party, or to obtain a consent order following an agreement of matters in dispute. It is also available in two forms:

1. Help with mediation

This is only available to those who are actually participating in Family Mediation or have successfully reached an agreement or settlement as a result of Family Mediation, and are in need of legal advice or assistance. It may be provided only by solicitors with a contract with the LSC in family law. The charges for the work may not exceed £150 where mediation relates to children issues only; £250 for financial issues only; and £350 where mediation covers both. These limits can be extended where necessary by the LSC regional office. The result of all work properly carried out under this level of service is exempt from the statutory charge (see p 484).

2. General family help

General Family Help covers negotiations in a family dispute where no mediation is in progress, although it will not usually be granted unless the suitability of the case for mediation has been considered by a mediator. It also includes representation in proceedings where this is necessary to obtain disclosure of information (for example, about their finances) from another party. It is only available from solicitors with a family law contract. The solicitor or adviser's charges are limited to an initial £1,500, which can be extended where necessary on application to a LSC regional office. The statutory charge will apply to any money or property recovered or preserved under this level of service (see p 483).

(ii) Family Mediation

Family Mediation provides funding for mediation of a family dispute for couples who qualify financially. The dispute may relate to children, money and property. It is important to remember that a mediator does not make decisions for the parties but helps them to reach their own decisions in a neutral environment. It is an alternative to reaching agreements or obtaining court orders, although it does not replace legal or other advice. Those eligible for mediation can obtain legal advice and assistance from a solicitor to support them during mediation either through Legal Help or Help with Mediation.

5. FINANCIAL ELIGIBILITY

I am grateful to the Community Legal Service for their permission to reproduce their *Guide to assessing financial eligibility for all levels of service*.

Guide to assessing financial eligibility for all levels of service

Section 7

Summary of Eligibility Limits

Level of Service	Income Limit	Capital Limit
Legal Help, Help at Court, and Legal Representation before Immigration Adjudicators and the Immigration Appeal Tribunal	Gross income not to exceed £2,250** per month. Disposable income not to exceed £611 per month. Passported if in receipt of income support or income-based jobseeker's allowance.	£3,000 No passporting, capital must be assessed in all cases.
Family Mediation, Help with Mediation, General Family Help, Support Funding and *Other Legal Representation	Gross income not to exceed £2,250** per month. Disposable income not to exceed £695 per month. Passported if in receipt of income support or income-based jobseeker's allowance.	£8,000 Passported if in receipt of income support or income-based jobseeker's allowance.

* may be subject to contribution from income and/or capital (see ... step 10 below)
** a higher gross income limit applies if you have more than 4 dependant children (see table below)

No of children in family	Gross monthly income not to exceed
0–4	£2250
5	£2395
6	£2540
7	£2685
8 or more	Add £145 to above figure for each additional child

The following guide shows how your solicitor or adviser will work out whether you are likely to qualify financially for funding. This guide does not apply to Legal Representation before the mental health appeal tribunal (see Section 5.5).

Remember that for some Legal Representation this is only a rough guide and it is for the LSC to assess eligibility (see Section 5.3). Note that also the assessment officer may take into account the assets of others where they have transferred resources to the client, maintained the client in the proceedings or have made resources available to the client.

Step 1: Identify whether the client has a partner whose means should be included in the assessment

Step 2: Identify clients in receipt of income support or income-based jobseeker's allowance

Clients in receipt (either directly or indirectly) of income support or income-based jobseeker's allowance are eligible on income for all levels of service but clients applying for Legal Help, Help at Court or Legal Representation before Immigration Adjudicators and the Immigration Appeal Tribunal must still have their capital assessed (see step 7). If the client is not in receipt of income support, or income-based jobseeker's allowance, move on to step 3. Other types of benefit, such as Working Families Tax Credit and Disabled Persons Tax Credit, do not give automatic entitlement.

Step 3: Work out monthly gross income

Add together the client's monthly gross income (i.e. before tax) and that of his/her partner if appropriate.
Income includes:
- earnings or profits from business;
- maintenance payments;
- pensions;
- welfare benefits (please see below);
- income from savings and investments;
- dividends from shares;
- monies received from friends and relatives;
- student grants and loans.

Income excludes:
the full amount of any of the following welfare benefits: attendance allowance, council tax benefit, housing benefit, social fund payments, disability living allowance, constant attendance allowance, invalid care allowance, severe disablement allowance, exceptionally severe disablement allowance, any war pensions, independent living fund payments, fostering allowance (to the extent it exceeds the relevant dependant's allowance), back to work bonus under section 26 of the Job Seeker's Act 1995, payments made under the Earnings Top-up Scheme and payments under the Community Care Direct Payment Scheme.

Gross monthly income £

If over £2,250** the client will not get funding.

Step 4: Work out deductible allowances and expenses

Deduct the following from monthly income:
- Income tax, National Insurance contributions;
- maintenance payments made;
- £45 for client and/or partner in receipt of salary or wage;
- child care expenses incurred because of employment;
- housing costs:
  - rent or mortgage repayments (less any housing benefit), although the amount allowed if the client has no dependants is limited to £545;
  - endowment policy premiums (if paid in connection with a mortgage);
  - actual costs of accommodation if the client is neither a tenant nor owner-occupier.
- fixed amounts for each dependent relative (adult or child) living with the client.

The monthly amounts of allowances for dependants are:

Partner		£133.40
Dependants	Aged 15 or under	£145.57
	Aged 16 or over	£149.04

Note that no other deductions may be made by the Assessment Officer.

Step 5: Work out monthly disposable income

Monthly gross income (see step 3)
£________________________________ minus
deductions (see step 4) £________________________________
to give
Monthly disposable income £________________________________

Step 6: Does the monthly disposable income qualify the client for funding?

For Legal Help, Help at Court, Legal Representation before Immigration Adjudicators and the Immigration Appeal Tribunal you will not get funding if your disposable income exceeds £611 per month.

For all other levels of service you will not get funding if your disposable income exceeds £695 per month.

If your disposable income is below these limits then you qualify for funding but you may have to pay a contribution from income (see step 10 below).

Step 7: Work out capital

Add together all the capital of the client (and partner if appropriate).
Capital includes:

- all land and buildings other than the client's home, including interest in timeshares, and the market value of the client's home in excess of £100,000, after allowing for any outstanding mortgage but only up to £100,000. A maximum of £100,000 is allowed in respect of all mortgages on all the client's properties;
- money in the bank, building society, Post Office, premium bonds, National Savings certificates etc.;
- investments, stocks and shares;
- money that can be borrowed against the surrender value of insurance policies;
- money value of valuable items, for example, boat, caravan, antiques, jewellery (but not wedding or engagement rings or usually the client's car);
- money owing to the client;
- money due from an estate or Trust Fund;
- money that can be borrowed against business assets.

Do not include:

- loans or grants from the Social Fund;
- back to work bonus under section 26 of the Job Seeker's Act 1995;
- home contents, for example (unless exceptionally valuable) furniture and household effects;
- personal clothing;
- personal tools and equipment of trade;
- payments under the Community Care Direct Payment scheme;
- savings, valuable items or property the ownership of which is the specific subject of the court case; for example, a holiday cottage would normally count but not if it was under attack as part of a disputed divorce settlement.

Total disposable Capital
£________________________________

Step 8: Does the disposable capital qualify the client for funding?

For Legal Help, Help at Court, and Legal Representation before Immigration Adjudicators and the Immigration Appeal Tribunal you will not get funding if your disposable capital exceeds £3,000.

For all other levels of service you will not get funding if your disposable capital exceeds £8,000 unless the Commission considers the probable costs would exceed the contribution payable (see step 9).

If your disposable capital is below these limits then you may qualify for funding but you must have your income assessed (see steps 3–5 above). You may also have to pay a contribution from capital (see step 9 below).

Step 9: Work out the size of the client's likely capital contribution

If your disposable capital is £3,000 or below you will pay no capital contribution for any level of service.

There are no contributions from capital for Legal Help, Help at Court, Legal Representation before Immigration Adjudicators and the Immigration Appeal Tribunal, Family Mediation, and Help with Mediation.

For other levels of service if your disposable capital exceeds £3,000 you will have to pay a capital contribution as follows:

Total disposable Capital (see step 7)
£______________________________

Deduct £3,000 to give
Capital contribution £________________

Pensioners on low incomes are allowed capital disregards for some forms of Legal Representation (see section 5.11).

Step 10: Work out amount of contribution from income

If your disposable income is £263 per month or less you will pay no income contribution for any level of service.

There are no contributions from income for Legal Help, Help at Court, Legal Representation before Immigration Adjudicators and the Immigration Appeal Tribunal, Family Mediation, and Help with Mediation.

For other levels of service if your disposable income exceeds £263 per month you will have to pay a monthly contribution from income. Such contributions will be assessed in accordance with the following bands depending on the level of the assessed income:

Band	Monthly disposable income	Monthly contribution
A	£264 to £386	1/4 of income in excess of £259
B	£387 to £513	£31.75 + 1/3 of income in excess of £386
C	£514 to £695	£74.08 + 1/2 of income in excess of £513

So if disposable income is £299 per month, the contribution will be in band A, the excess income is £40 and therefore the monthly contribution will be £10 per month.

If the disposable income was £401 per month, the contribution would be in band B, the excess income would be £15 (£401 – £386), and the monthly contribution would therefore be £36.75 i.e. £31.75 + £5.

If the disposable income was £533 per month, the contribution would be in band C, the excess income would be £20 (£533 – £513), and the monthly contribution would therefore be £84.08 i.e. £74.08 + £10.

Step 11: Work out the total initial contribution

Add together:

Monthly Contribution (see step 10)	£______
and Capital Contribution (see step 9)	£______
to give	
Total Initial Contribution	£______

6. ELIGIBILITY ON MERITS

(a) Costs-benefit

The CLS General Funding Code prescribes a costs-benefit matrix for deciding whether a case merits the grant of funding. Where the prospects of success are very good (80% or more) the anticipated damages must exceed the costs. Where the prospects of success are classified as good (60–80%) the estimated damages must exceed the costs by a ratio of two to one. Moderate prospects of success (50–60%) require that the estimated damages must exceed the costs by a ration of four to one. Poor prospects of success (less than 50%) will not qualify for funding in the absence of specified circumstances.

(b) The merits criteria

The Legal Aid Handbook was replaced by the Legal Services Commission Manual with effect from 1 April 2000. The manual now fills four large ring binders, the whole of the contents of which I could not even summarise in a work of this nature. One of the aspects on which I have concentrated is eligibility for state funding, which is based on the three criteria of financial eligibility (see p 458), prospects of success and cost-benefit. The latter two criteria are covered comprehensively in Part I of the Legal Services Commission's Funding Code, which apart from the introductory sections, I am reproducing in full below.

7. THE FUNDING CODE: PART 1 – CRITERIA

Section 1 – Levels of Service

1.1. Levels of Service Available

The Commission will fund only the following levels of service as part of the Community Legal Service, subject to the provisions of the Act, orders regulations and directions made under the Act, these criteria and the Funding Code Procedures:

1. Legal Help.
2. Help at Court.
3. Approved Family Help – this can be either General Family Help or Help with Mediation.
4. Legal Representation – this can be either Investigative Help or Full Representation.
5. Support Funding – this can be either Investigative Support or Litigation Support.
6. Family Mediation.

7. Such other services as are authorised by specific orders or directions from the Lord Chancellor.

1.2 Representation

Legal Representation and Support Funding will be funded only in relation to proceedings for which advocacy may be funded in accordance with paragraph 2 of Schedule 2 to the Act. Help at Court will be funded only in proceedings before the High Court, any county court and those magistrates' court proceedings specified at paragraph 2(3) of the Schedule.

1.3 Disbursements

Contracts or guidance may specify what items may or may not be charged as disbursements under each level of service.

Section 2 – Definitions

2.1 Levels of Service

Note: Nothing in these definitions limits the power of the Commission to place conditions or limitations on any grant.

'Legal Help' is a level of service the grant of which authorises services falling within Section 4(2) of the Access to Justice Act 1999 other than:

(i) The provision of general information about the law and legal system and the availability of legal services (except where such provision is incidental to the provision of help in a specific case).

(ii) Issuing or conducting court proceedings.

(iii) Advocacy or instructing an advocate in proceedings.

(iv) The provision of mediation or arbitration (but this does not prevent legal help being given in relation to mediation or arbitration or covering payment of a mediator's or arbitrator's fees as a disbursement).

'Help at Court' is a level of service the grant of which authorises help and advocacy for a client in relation to a particular hearing, without formally acting as legal representative in the proceedings.

'Legal Representation' is a level of service the grant of which authorises legal representation for a party to proceedings or for a person who is contemplating taking proceedings. This includes the following:

(i) Litigation services.

(ii) Advocacy services.

(iii) All such help as is usually given by a person providing representation in proceedings, including steps preliminary or incidental to proceedings.

(iv) All such help as is usually given by such a person in arriving at or giving effect to a compromise to avoid or bring to an end any proceedings.

Legal representation does not include the provision of mediation or arbitration (but this does not prevent help being given in relation to mediation or arbitration, or the payment of a mediator's or arbitrator's fees as a disbursement).

'Investigative Help' means Legal Representation which is limited to investigation of the strength of a proposed claim. Investigative Help includes the issue and the conduct of proceedings only so far as necessary to obtain disclosure of relevant information or to protect the client's position in relation to any urgent hearing or time limit for the issue of proceedings.

'Full Representation' means a grant of Legal Representation other than Investigative Help.

'Support Funding' is a level of service the grant of which authorises the same services as Legal Representation, but which is limited to partial funding of proceedings which are otherwise being pursued privately, under or with a view to a conditional fee agreement.

'Investigative Support' means Support Funding which is limited to investigation of the strength of a proposed claim with a view to a conditional fee agreement.

'Litigation Support' means a grant of Support Funding other than Investigative Support. It covers partial funding of high cost litigation proceeding under a conditional fee agreement.

'Approved Family Help' is a level of service the grant of which authorises help in relation to a family dispute including assistance in resolving that dispute through negotiation or otherwise. This includes the services covered by Legal Help as well as issuing proceedings and representation in proceedings where necessary to obtain disclosure of information from another party, or to obtain a consent order following settlement of part or all of the dispute and related conveyancing work.

'Help with Mediation' means Approved Family Help limited to advice to a client in support of family mediation, help in drawing up any agreement reached in mediation and where appropriate help in confirming such an agreement in a court order and related conveyancing work.

'General Family Help' means a grant of Approved Family Help other than Help with Mediation.

'Family Mediation' is a level of service the grant of which authorises mediation of a family dispute, including assessing whether mediation appears suitable to the dispute and the parties and all the circumstances.

2.2 Case Categories

'Clinical Negligence Proceedings' means proceedings which include:
- (i) a claim for damages in respect of an alleged breach of duty of care or trespass to the person committed in the course of the provision of clinical or medical services (including dental or nursing services); or
- (ii) a claim for damages in respect of alleged professional negligence in the conduct of such a claim.

'Family Dispute' means a legal dispute arising out of a family relationship, including disputes concerning the welfare of children or which may give rise to Family Proceedings.

'Family Proceedings' means proceedings which arise out of family relationships, including proceedings in which the welfare of children is determined (other than judicial review proceedings). Family Proceedings also include all proceedings under any one or more of the following:
- (a) the Matrimonial Causes Act 1973;
- (b) the Inheritance (Provision for Family and Dependants) Act 1975;
- (c) the Adoption Act 1976;
- (d) the Domestic Proceedings and Magistrates' Courts Act 1978;
- (e) Part III of the Matrimonial and Family Proceedings Act 1984;
- (f) Parts I, II and IV of the Children Act 1989;
- (g) Part IV of the Family Law Act 1996; and
- (h) the inherent jurisdiction of the High Court in relation to children.

'Special Children Act Proceedings' means proceedings under the Children Act 1989 (other than appeal proceedings) where Legal Representation is applied for on behalf of:
- (i) a child in respect of whom an application is made for an order under:
  - (a) Section 31 (a care or supervision order);
  - (b) Section 43 (a child assessment order);
  - (c) Section 44 (an emergency protection order); and
  - (d) Section 45 (extension or discharge of an emergency protection order);
- (ii) any parent of such a child or person with parental responsibility for the child within the meaning of the 1989 Act;
- (iii) a child who is brought before a Court under Section 25 (use of

accommodation for restricting liberty) who is not, but wishes to be, legally represented before the Court.

'Other public law children cases' means public law proceedings concerning the welfare of children other than Special Children Act Proceedings or related proceedings (see Section 11.8) but including:

(i) Appeals (whether interim or final) from orders made in Special Children Act Proceedings;

(ii) Other proceedings under Part IV or V of the 1989 Act;

(iii) Adoption proceedings, including freeing for adoption;

(iv) Proceedings under the inherent jurisdiction of the High Court in relation to children.

2.3 Merits, Costs and Damages

'Prospects of Success' means the likelihood of the client obtaining a successful outcome in the proceedings, assuming the case were determined at trial or other final hearing. Guidance may give examples of what may constitute a successful outcome for different types of proceeding.

Different categories of Prospects of Success have the following meanings:

'Very Good' means 80% or more;

'Good' means 60%–80%;

'Moderate' means 50%–60%;

'Borderline' means that Prospects of Success are not Poor, but because there are difficult disputes of fact, law or expert evidence, it is not possible to say that Prospects of Success are better than 50%;

'Poor' means clearly less than 50% so that the claim is likely to fail;

'Unclear' means that the case cannot be put into any of the above categories because further investigation is needed;

'Likely Costs' means an estimate of the likely total gross costs to be incurred on behalf of the client to disposal of the proceedings. This includes counsel's fees, disbursements and any enhancement or uplift on costs. Where appropriate, costs should be calculated by reference to standard or prescribed remuneration rates set by the Lord Chancellor or the Commission. Likely Costs and all cost thresholds specified in the Code are exclusive of VAT;

'Likely Damages' means a realistic estimate of the size of any money award the client would receive if substantially successful at trial or final hearing, after allowing for any likely reduction through contributory negligence or otherwise. Likely Damages should be discounted (by anything up to 100%) if there is doubt as to whether the opponent will be able to pay the money award.

2.4 Other Definitions

'the Act' means the Access to Justice Act 1999 and terms defined in the Act have the same meaning in the Code.

'Central Budget' means the budget set by the Lord Chancellor for the funding of very expensive cases in accordance with Code Procedures.

'Contract' means a contract with the Commission under which services are provided which are funded as part of the Community Legal Service.

'Excluded Services' means services which are excluded under Schedule 2 of the Act and are not covered by any direction or authorisation under section 6(8) of the Act.

'Guidance' means guidance published by the Lord Chancellor or the Commission for the purpose of making decisions under the Code.

'Hague Convention' means the convention defined in section 1(1) of the Child Abduction and Custody Act 1985.

'European Convention' means the convention defined in section 12(1) of that Act.

'Hague Convention Countries' has the same meaning as in the Reciprocal Enforcement of Maintenance Orders (Hague Convention Countries) Order 1979.
'Maintenance Orders (Reciprocal Enforcement) Act 1972' means the Act as applied with such exceptions, adaptations and modifications as are specified in the 1979 Order.
'Immigration Adjudicator' and **'Immigration Appeal Tribunal'** mean the adjudicators and Tribunal referred to in Part IV of the Immigration and Asylum Act 1999.
'Multi-Party Action' or **'MPA'** means any action or actions in which a number of clients have causes of action which involve common issues of fact or law arising out of the same cause or event.
'the 1989 Act' means the Children Act 1989.
'Overwhelming importance to the client' means a case which has exceptional importance to the client, beyond the monetary value (if any) of the claim, because the case concerns the life, liberty or physical safety of the client or his or her family, or a roof over their heads.
'Prescribed' means either set out in Regulations or specified by the Commission.
'Proceedings' means legal proceedings before any court, tribunal, arbitrator or panel in England and Wales, but mediation and any form of dispute resolution which cannot make a determination which is binding on the client do not count as proceedings.
'Public Authority' has the meaning given in section 6 of the Human Rights Act 1998.
'Regulations' means orders or regulations under the Access to Justice Act 1999.
'Special Cases Unit' means a unit established by the Commission under the Code Procedures whose functions include administering the central budget and issuing contracts in very expensive cases.
'Wider Public Interest' means the potential of the proceedings to produce real benefits for individuals other than the client (other than benefits to the public at large which normally flow from proceedings of the type in question).

Section 3 – Case Categories

3.1 The General Funding Code

Applications for funding will be considered under the General Funding Code except to the extent that different criteria are specified for specific categories of case or proceeding. Definitions and criteria for specific categories are given in sections 6–13 of these Criteria.

3.2 Disputed Categories

Where any issue arises as to which category a case falls into, the Commission will apply the criteria which appear to it to be most relevant to the substance of the application.

3.3 Mixed Claims

Where it appears to the Commission that an application for Legal Representation or Support Funding relates to proceedings covering more than one category, the Commission may apply the criteria which appear to it most appropriate to the proceedings as a whole. If proceedings have not been started, the Commission may consider each aspect of the case under the criteria relevant to it and may apply appropriate restrictions on any grant.

3.4 Excluded Proceedings

The Commission will refuse an application for Legal Representation if, in the view of the Commission, effective representation cannot be provided in the proceedings without the provision of excluded services.

3.5 Guidance

Guidance may give examples of descriptions of proceedings in particular case categories.

3.6 Foreign Orders and Judgments

Cases within the scope of section 11.14 shall be subject only to the criteria in that section (whether or not the proceedings in question are Family Proceedings).

Section 4 – Standard Criteria

4.1 Scope of this section

The criteria in this section apply to all applications under the Code.

4.2 English Law

An application will be refused if it relates to law other than that of England and Wales, save where this is permitted by or under section 19 of the Act.

4.3 Excluded Services

An application for the provision of excluded services will be refused.

4.4 Directions on Scope

Where an application relies upon a direction or authorisation under section 6(8) of the Act the application will be refused if any conditions specified in the direction or authorisation are not satisfied.

4.5 Identity of Client

An application will be refused unless it is for the benefit of a client who is an individual and who satisfies such other conditions as are specified in the Code Procedures.

4.6 Identity of Supplier

An application will be refused unless the proposed supplier of services is of a description specified in the Code Procedures.

4.7 Contract Scope

Where an application is for services which under the Code Procedures can be provided only under contract, the application will be refused unless the supplier has a contract and is permitted to provide those services under the terms of the contract.

4.8 Procedures

An application may be refused or rejected if any Code Procedures have not been complied with.

4.9 Financial Eligibility

An application will be refused unless the client is assessed as financially eligible under regulations, except where:
(i) under Regulations services are available without reference to means; or
(ii) Regulations or Code Procedures authorise services to be provided before completion of the financial assessment.

4.10 Conduct

An application may be refused if it appears unreasonable to grant funding in the light of the conduct of the client in connection with this or any other application or in connection with any proceedings.

Section 5 – The General Funding Code

5.1 Application of General Funding Code

This section applies, in addition to the criteria in section 4, to any application for funding, save to the extent that different criteria are applied for specific categories of case or proceedings in sections 6 to 13.

5.2 Criteria for Legal Help

5.2.1 SUFFICIENT BENEFIT TEST

Help may only be provided where there is sufficient benefit to the client having regard to the circumstances of the matter, including the personal circumstances of the client, to justify work or further work being carried out.

5.2.2 FUNDING AS PART OF CLS

Help may only be provided if it is reasonable for the matter to be funded out of the Community Legal Service Fund, having regard to any other potential sources of funding.

5.3 Criteria for Help at Court

5.3.1 CRITERIA FOR LEGAL HELP

The criteria for Legal Help apply to an application for Help at Court, in addition to the following two criteria.

5.3.2 THE NEED FOR REPRESENTATION

Help at Court may only be provided if the nature of the proceedings and the circumstances of the hearing and the client are such that advocacy is appropriate and will be of real benefit to the client.

5.3.3 LEGAL REPRESENTATION

Help at Court may not be provided if the contested nature of the proceedings or the nature of the hearing is such that, if any help is to be provided, it is more appropriate that it should be given through Legal Representation.

5.4 Standard Criteria for Legal Representation and Support Funding

5.4.1 Scope of this Section

The following criteria apply to all applications for Legal Representation or Support Funding, in addition to the criteria relevant to the specific level of service applied for.

5.4.2 Alternative Funding

An application may be refused if alternative funding is available to the client (through insurance or otherwise) or if there are other persons or bodies, including those who might benefit from the proceedings, who can reasonably be expected to bring or fund the case. For the purpose of this criterion only, alternative funding does not include funding by means of a conditional fee agreement.

5.4.3 Alternatives to Litigation

An application may be refused if there are complaint systems, ombudsman schemes or forms of alternative dispute resolution which should be tried before litigation is pursued.

5.4.4 Other Levels of Service

An application may be refused if it appears premature or if it appears more appropriate for the client to be assisted by some other level of service under the Code, such as Legal Help or Help at Court.

5.4.5 The Need for Representation

An application may be refused if it appears unreasonable to fund representation, for example in the light of the existence of other proceedings or the interests of other parties in the proceedings to which the application relates.

5.4.6 Small Claims

An application will be refused if the case has been or is likely to be allocated to the small claims track.

5.5 Emergency Representation

5.5.1 Urgency

Legal Representation may only be granted as a matter of urgency where it appears in the interests of justice to do so.

5.5.2 Limited Information

Where only limited information is available to determine whether the criteria for Legal Representation are satisfied, emergency representation may be granted only if it appears likely on the information available that those criteria would be satisfied.

5.6 Criteria for Investigative Help

5.6.1 Potential for a Conditional Fee Agreement

Investigative Help may be refused if the nature of the case and circumstances of the client are such that investigative work should be carried out privately with a view to a conditional fee agreement or that funding should take the form only of Investigative Support.

5.6.2 The Need for Investigation

Investigative Help may only be granted where the prospects of success of the claim are uncertain and substantial investigative work is required before those prospects can be determined. Guidance may indicate what constitutes substantial investigative work for this purpose.

5.6.3 Damages

If the client's claim is primarily a claim for damages and has no significant wider public interest, Investigative Help will be refused unless the damages are likely to exceed £5,000.

5.6.4 Prospects after Investigation

Investigative Help may only be granted if there are reasonable grounds for believing that when the investigative work has been carried out the claim will be strong enough, in terms of prospects of success and cost benefit, to satisfy the relevant criteria for Full Representation.

5.7 Criteria for Full Representation

5.7.1 Conditional Fee Agreements

If the nature of the case is suitable for a CFA, and the client is likely to be able to avail himself or herself of a CFA, Full Representation will be refused.

5.7.2 Prospects of Success

Full Representation will be refused if:
(i) Prospects of success are unclear;
(ii) Prospects of success are borderline and the case does not appear to have a significant wider public interest or to be of overwhelming importance to the client; or
(iii) Prospects of success are poor.

5.7.3 Cost Benefit – Quantifiable Claims

If the claim is primarily a claim for damages by the client and does not have a significant wider public interest, Full Representation will be refused unless the following cost benefit criteria are satisfied:
(i) If prospects of success are very good (80% or more), likely damages must exceed likely costs;
(ii) If prospects of success are good (60%–80%), likely damages must exceed likely costs by a ratio of 2:1;
(iii) If prospects of success are moderate (50%–60%), likely damages must exceed likely costs by a ratio of 4:1.

5.7.4 Cost Benefit – Unquantifiable Claims

If the claim is not primarily a claim for damages (including any application by a defendant or a case which has overwhelming importance to the client), but does not have a significant wider public interest, Full Representation will be refused unless the likely benefits to be gained from the proceedings justify the likely costs, such that a reasonable private paying client would be prepared to litigate, having regard to the prospects of success and all other circumstances.

5.7.5 Cost Benefit – Public Interest Cases

If the claim has a significant wider public interest, Full Representation may be refused unless the likely benefits of the proceedings to the applicant and others justify the likely costs, having regard to the prospects of success and all other circumstances.

5.8 Criteria for Investigative Support

5.8.1 High Investigative Costs

Investigative Support may only be granted where the prospects of success are uncertain and the reasonable costs of investigating the claim to determine prospects of success are such that:

(i) disbursements (including counsel's fees) are, or are likely to exceed, £1,000; or
(ii) Investigative costs at prescribed rates other than disbursements have reached or are likely to exceed £3,000.

5.8.2 Damages

Investigative Support will be refused unless the damages are likely to exceed £5,000.

5.8.3 Prospects after Investigation

Investigative Support may only be granted if there are reasonable grounds for believing that when the investigative work has been carried out the claim will be strong enough, in terms of prospects of success and cost benefit, to proceed privately, together with Litigation Support if appropriate.

5.9 Litigation Support

5.9.1 Form of Conditional Fee Agreement

Litigation Support will be refused unless the form of the conditional fee agreement is satisfactory and complies with any relevant conditions set out in Code Procedures.

5.9.2 Insurance

Litigation Support will be refused unless the conditional fee agreement will be supported by satisfactory insurance cover or equivalent arrangements in accordance with Code Procedures.

5.9.3 High Overall Costs

Litigation Support will be refused unless the reasonable costs of the litigation, including the costs of the investigative stage but excluding any sums already funded by the Commission or other bodies, are such that:

(i) disbursements are or are likely to exceed £5,000; or
(ii) the costs of the case at prescribed rates, excluding disbursements, have reached or are likely to exceed £15,000,

but the Commission may vary the above threshold if satisfied that the case has a significant wider public interest.

5.9.4 Prospects of Success

Litigation Support will be refused if the prospects of success are unclear, borderline or poor.

5.9.5 Cost Benefit

Save where the case has a significant wider public interest, Litigation Support will be refused unless the following cost benefit criteria are satisfied:

(i) If prospects of success are very good (80% or more), likely damages must exceed likely costs;
(ii) If prospects of success are good (60%–80%), likely damages must exceed likely costs by a ratio of 2:1;
(iii) If prospects of success are moderate (50%–60%), likely damages must exceed likely costs by a ratio of 4:1.

5.9.6 Cost Benefit – Public Interest Cases

If the claim has a significant wider public interest, Litigation Support may be refused unless the likely benefits of the proceedings to the applicant and others justify the likely costs, having regard to the prospects of success and all other circumstances.

5.10 Criteria for Other Services

5.10.1 Orders and Directions

Levels of service other than those provided for in the General Funding Code or elsewhere in these criteria may be funded only if a specific order or direction from the Lord Chancellor so provides, and then only in accordance with the terms of the order or direction.

5.10.2 Reasonableness

An application for such services may be refused if it appears unreasonable in all the circumstances to grant it.

Section 6 – Very Expensive Cases

6.1 Scope

This section applies to applications or certificates for Legal Representation or Support Funding which have been referred to the Special Cases Unit in accordance with Code Procedures.

6.2 Relevant Criteria

All Criteria relevant to the level of service and category of case in question shall apply, as modified in this section, in addition to the Criteria set out in this section.

6.3 The Costed Case Plan

Funding may be refused if the proposals put forward for progressing the litigation including proposals as to cost do not appear to the Commission to be satisfactory.

6.4 Affordability

Subject to 6.5 below, funding will be refused or deferred unless it appears reasonable for funding to be granted in the light of the resources available in the Central Budget and likely future demands on those resources.

6.5 Top Priority Cases

The Affordability criterion in 6.4 shall not apply to:
(i) Special Children Act Proceedings;
(ii) judicial review proceedings under section 7 of the Criteria in which funding is to continue by virtue of criterion 7.5.2;

(iii) other proceedings in which the life or liberty of the client is at risk.

6.6 Clinical Negligence

Where a clinical negligence case (as defined in section 9) is referred under this section for the cost benefit ratio specified at criterion 9.3.2(iii) (minimum cost benefit ratio where prospects of success are moderate) there shall be substituted a ratio of 4:1.

Section 7 – Judicial Review

7.1 Scope

This section applies to applications for Legal Representation in relation to court proceedings concerning public law challenges to the acts, omissions or decisions of public bodies, including in particular challenges by way of judicial review or habeas corpus and proceedings under Part VII of the Housing Act 1996.

7.2 Criteria for Investigative Help

7.2.1 General Funding Code Criteria

Criteria 5.6.1 (potential for a conditional fee agreement) and 5.6.3 (minimum damages level) do not apply to applications for Investigative Help under this section.

7.2.2 Is Judicial Review Available?

An application may be refused if the act or decision complained of in the proposed proceedings does not appear to be susceptible to challenge.

7.2.3 Administrative Procedures

Investigative Help may be refused if there are administrative appeals or other procedures which should be pursued before proceedings are considered.

7.3 Criteria for Full Representation

If, at the time the application for funding is made, the court has not granted permission to bring the proceedings or if according to rules of court such permission is not required, the criteria in section 7.4 apply. If at the time the application is made the court has granted permission, the criteria in 7.5 apply.

7.4 Pre-Permission Criteria

7.4.1 General Funding Code

The following criteria replace those in section 5.7 of the General Funding Code.

7.4.2 Is Judicial Review available?

An application may be refused if the act or decision complained of in the proposed proceedings does not appear to be susceptible to challenge.

7.4.3 Administrative Procedures

Full Representation may be refused if there are administrative appeals or other procedures which should be pursued before proceedings are considered.

7.4.4 NOTIFICATION TO RESPONDENT

Full Representation will be refused unless the proposed respondent has been given a reasonable opportunity to respond to the challenge or deal with the applicant's complaint, save where this is impracticable in the circumstances.

7.4.5 PROSPECTS OF SUCCESS

Full Representation will be refused if the prospects of successfully obtaining the substantive order sought in the proceedings are:
(i) unclear;
(ii) borderline and the case does not appear to have significant wider public interest, to be of overwhelming importance to the client or to raise significant human rights issues; or
(iii) poor.

7.4.6 COST BENEFIT

Full Representation may be refused unless the likely benefits of the proceedings justify the likely costs, having regard to the prospects of success and all other circumstances.

7.5 Post-Permission Criteria

7.5.1 GENERAL FUNDING CODE

The following criteria replace those in section 5.7 of the General Funding Code.

7.5.2 THE PRESUMPTION OF FUNDING

If the case has a significant wider public interest, is of overwhelming importance to the client or raises significant human rights issues, then, provided the standard criteria in Section 4 are satisfied, funding shall be granted save where, in light of information which was not before the court at the permission stage or has subsequently come to light, it appears unreasonable for Legal Representation to be granted.

7.5.3 REFUSAL ON THE MERITS

Where the case does not appear to have a significant wider public interest, to be of overwhelming importance to the client or to raise significant human rights issues, Legal Representation will be refused if:
(i) prospects of success are borderline or poor; or
(ii) the likely benefits of the proceedings do not appear to justify the likely costs having regard to the prospects of success and all the circumstances.

Section 8 – Claims Against Public Authorities

8.1 Scope

This section applies to applications for Legal Representation in relation to proceedings or proposed proceedings against public authorities concerning serious wrong-doing, abuse of position or power or significant breach of human rights, other than cases falling within the scope of section 7 (Judicial Review) or section 10 (Housing).

8.2 Criteria for Investigative Help

Criteria 5.6.1 (potential for a conditional fee agreement) and 5.6.3 (minimum damages level) do not apply to applications for Investigative Help under this section.

8.3 Criteria for Full Representation

8.3.1 General Funding Code

The following criteria replace the criteria in section 5.7 of the General Funding Code in applications to which this section applies.

8.3.2 Prospects of Success

Full Representation will be refused if:
(i) Prospects of success are unclear;
(ii) Prospects of success are borderline and the case does not appear to have a significant wider public interest, to be of overwhelming importance to the client or to raise significant human rights issues;
(iii) Prospects of success are poor.

8.3.3 Cost Benefit

Legal Representation may be refused unless the likely benefits of the proceedings justify the likely costs, having regard to the prospects of success and all other circumstances.

Section 9 – Clinical Negligence

9.1 Scope

This section applies to applications for Legal Representation in Clinical Negligence Proceedings.

9.2 Criteria for Investigative Help

9.2.1 Potential for a Conditional Fee Agreement

Criterion 5.6.1 does not apply to applications under this section, unless the application relates to a multi-party action.

9.2.2 The Complaints Scheme

If the likely value of the claim does not exceed £10,000, Investigative Help may be refused if pursuing the NHS complaints procedure is more appropriate for the client than litigation.

9.3 Criteria for Full Representation

9.3.1 Conditional Fee Agreements

Criterion 5.7.1 (refusal on grounds that the case is of a type suitable for a CFA) does not apply to applications under this section, unless the application relates to a multi-party action.

9.3.2 Cost Benefit – Quantifiable Claims

In applications to which this section applies, the cost benefit criteria set out in criterion 5.7.3 in the General Funding Code shall be replaced with the following:

(i) If prospects of success are very good (80% or more), likely damages must exceed likely costs;
(ii) If prospects of success are good (60%–80%), likely damages must exceed likely costs by a ratio of at least 1.5:1;
(iii) If prospects of success are moderate (50%–60%), likely damages must exceed likely costs by a ratio of at least 2:1.

Section 10 – Housing

10.1 Scope

This section applies to applications for legal representation for a client in proceedings which concern possession of the client's home, the client's legal status in the home, or the obligations of a landlord or other person to keep the client's home in good repair and allow quiet enjoyment of the property.

However, this section does not apply to cases within the scope of section 7 (Judicial Review).

10.2 Criteria for Investigative Help

10.2.1 POTENTIAL FOR A CONDITIONAL FEE AGREEMENT

Criterion 5.6.1 does not apply to applications under this section.

10.2.2 DAMAGES

In applications under this section the figure for minimum damages in criterion 5.6.3 shall be £1,000.

10.3 Criteria for Full Representation – Possession Cases

10.3.1 GENERAL FUNDING CODE

The following criteria replace those in section 5.7 of the General Funding Code for proceedings which concern possession of the client's home.

10.3.2 PROSPECTS OF SUCCESS

Full Representation will be refused if the client has no substantive legal defence to the proceedings or the prospects of successfully avoiding an order for possession (or, if the client is bringing proceedings, the prospects of obtaining such an order) are poor.

10.3.3 COST BENEFIT

Full representation may be refused unless the likely benefits of the proceedings to the client justify the likely costs, having regard to the prospects of success and all other circumstances.

10.4 Criteria for Full Representation – Other Housing Cases

10.4.1 GENERAL FUNDING CODE

The following criteria replace the criteria in section 5.7 of the General Funding Code in applications within the scope of this section other than possession cases.

10.4.2 NOTIFICATION TO LANDLORD

Where the client is applying for Full Representation to bring proceedings the application may be refused unless the landlord or other person responsible for dealing with the matters complained of has been notified of the client's complaint and given a reasonable opportunity to respond and put matters right, save where this is impracticable in the circumstances.

10.4.3 PROSPECTS OF SUCCESS

Full Representation will be refused if:
(i) Prospects of success are unclear;
(ii) Prospects of success are borderline and the case does not appear to have a significant wider public interest or to be of overwhelming importance to the client;
(iii) Prospects of success are poor.

10.4.4 COST BENEFIT

Full Representation may be refused unless the likely benefits of the proceedings to the client justify the likely costs, having regard to the prospects of success and all other circumstances.

Section 11 – Family

11.1 Scope

This section applies to applications for Approved Family Help, Family Mediation or Legal Representation in Family Proceedings.

11.2 Criteria for Help with Mediation

11.2.1 NEED FOR HELP WITH MEDIATION

Help with Mediation may only be granted if the client is participating in family mediation or has reached an agreement or settlement in family mediation and is in need of the services covered by Help with Mediation.

11.2.2 LEGAL HELP

Help with Mediation may be refused if it is more appropriate for the client to be assisted by way of Legal Help.

11.2.3 SUFFICIENT BENEFIT TEST

Help with Mediation may only be provided where there is sufficient benefit to the client, having regard to the circumstances of the matter, including the personal circumstances of the client, to justify work or further work being carried out.

11.3 Criteria for General Family Help

11.3.1 REFERRAL TO FAMILY MEDIATION

General Family Help will be refused if, in accordance with Code Procedures, the case must first be referred to a mediator for a determination as to whether mediation is suitable to the dispute and the parties and all the circumstances.

11.3.2 SUITABILITY FOR MEDIATION

General Family Help may be refused if mediation, supported if necessary by Help with Mediation, is more appropriate to the case than General Family Help.

11.3.3 Legal Help

General Family Help may be refused if it is more appropriate for the client to be assisted by way of Legal Help.

11.3.4 Sufficient Benefit Test

General Family Help may only be provided where there is sufficient benefit to the client, having regard to the circumstances of the matter, including the personal circumstances of the client, to justify work or further work being carried out.

11.4 Criteria for Family Mediation

11.4.1 The Intake Assessment

An assessment of whether mediation is suitable to the dispute and the parties and all the circumstances ('an intake assessment') may only be provided if the standard criteria in Section 4 are satisfied.

11.4.2 Substantive Mediation

Mediation beyond the intake assessment may be provided only where the mediator is satisfied that mediation is suitable to the dispute and the parties and all the circumstances.

11.5 Investigative Help

Investigative Help is not available in Family Proceedings. Legal Representation in Family Proceedings shall take the form only of Full Representation.

11.6 Criteria for Full Representation

The criteria at Section 5.7 of the General Funding Code (criteria for Full Representation) and criterion 5.4.6 (small claims) do not apply to applications for Legal Representation in Family Proceedings.

11.7 Criteria for Special Children Act Proceedings

Legal Representation shall be granted in Special Children Act Proceedings (as defined in Section 2) provided the relevant criteria in Section 4 are satisfied. The standard criteria in Section 5.4 of the General Funding Code shall not apply.

11.8 Related Proceedings

Where Legal Representation has been granted to a person in Special Children Act Proceedings, Legal Representation may also be granted for that person in related proceedings which are being heard together with the Special Children Act Proceedings or in which an order is being sought as an alternative to an order in the Special Children Act Proceedings.

11.9 Criteria for other Public Law Children Cases

11.9.1 Standard Criteria

The standard criteria for Legal Representation in Section 5.4 of the General Funding Code do not apply in other public law children cases, save for the following criteria:

(i) 5.4.2 (refusal on the ground of the availability of alternative sources of funding);
(ii) 5.4.5 (refusal on the ground that representation is not necessary).

11.9.2 Prospects of Success

Where Legal Representation is sought on behalf of a client who is making or supporting an application or appeal, Legal Representation will be refused if the prospects of the application or appeal being successful are poor.

11.9.3 Reasonableness

An application for Legal Representation may be refused if it appears unreasonable for funding to be granted, having regard to the importance of the case to the client and all other circumstances.

11.10 Domestic Violence Cases

11.10.1 Scope

These criteria apply to proceedings seeking an injunction, committal order or other orders for the protection of a person from harm (other than public law children proceedings).

11.10.2 Prospects of Success

Legal Representation will be refused if the prospects of obtaining the order sought in the proceedings are poor.

11.10.3 Cost Benefit

Legal Representation will be refused unless the likely benefits to be gained from the proceedings for the client justify the likely costs, having regard to the prospects of obtaining the order sought and all other circumstances.

11.11 Private Law Children Cases

11.11.1 Scope

These criteria apply to proceedings concerning residence, contact and other private law issues concerning children (other than issues of financial provision).

11.11.2 Referral to Family Mediation

Legal Representation will be refused, if in accordance with Code Procedures, the case must first be referred to a mediator for a determination as to whether mediation is suitable to the dispute and the parties and all the circumstances before Legal Representation can be provided.

11.11.3 Suitability for Mediation

Legal Representation may be refused if mediation, supported if necessary by Help with Mediation, is more appropriate to the case than Legal Representation.

11.11.4 Attempts at Settlement

Legal Representation may be refused unless reasonable attempts have been made to resolve the dispute without recourse to proceedings, through negotiation or otherwise.

11.11.5 Prospects of Success

Legal Representation will refused if prospects of success are poor.

11.11.6 Cost Benefit

Legal Representation will be refused unless the likely benefits to be gained from the proceedings for the client justify the likely costs, such that a reasonable private paying client would be prepared to take or defend the proceedings in all the circumstances.

11.12 Financial Provision and Other Proceedings

11.12.1 Scope

These criteria apply to ancillary relief and other family proceedings concerning financial provision, and to all other family proceedings which are not covered by criteria elsewhere in this section.

11.12.2 Referral to Family Mediation

Legal Representation will be refused if, in accordance with Code Procedures, the case must first be referred to a mediator for a determination as to whether mediation is suitable to the dispute and the parties and all the circumstances before Legal Representation can be provided.

11.12.3 Suitability for Mediation

Legal Representation may be refused if mediation, supported if necessary by Help with Mediation, is more appropriate to the case than Legal Representation.

11.12.4 Attempts at Settlement

Legal Representation may be refused unless reasonable attempts have been made to resolve the dispute without recourse to proceedings, through negotiation or otherwise.

11.12.5 Prospects of Success

Legal Representation will be refused if prospects of success are:
(i) borderline or unclear, save where the case has overwhelming importance to the client or a significant wider public interest;
(ii) poor.

11.12.6 Cost Benefit

Legal Representation will be refused unless the likely benefits to be gained from the proceedings for the client justify the likely costs, such that a reasonable private paying client would be prepared to take or defend the proceedings in all the circumstances.

11.13 Child Abduction Cases

Subject only to Section 4, Legal Representation shall be granted to a person whose application under the Hague Convention or the European Convention has been submitted to the central authority in England and Wales pursuant to Section 3(2) or Section 14(2) of the Child Abduction and Custody Act 1985 and on whose behalf a legal representative has been instructed in England and Wales in connection with the application.

11.14 Registration of foreign orders and judgments

11.14.1 SCOPE

This section applies to a person who:
(i) appeals to a Magistrates' Court against the registration of or the refusal to register a maintenance order made in a Hague Convention country pursuant to the Maintenance Orders (Reciprocal Enforcement) Act 1972; or
(ii) applies for the registration of a judgment under Section 4 of the Civil Jurisdiction and Judgments Act 1982,
and who satisfies the criterion set out below.

11.14.2 LEGAL AID ABROAD

Legal representation under this provision shall be granted if the standard criteria in Section 4 are satisfied and if the client benefited from complete or partial legal aid, other public funding or exemption from costs or expenses in the country in which the maintenance order was made or the judgment was given.

Section 12 – Mental Health

12.1 Scope

This section applies to applications for Legal Representation in proceedings before a Mental Health Review Tribunal under the Mental Health Act 1983 on behalf of a person whose case or whose application to the Tribunal is or is to be the subject of the proceedings.

12.2 Investigative Help

Investigative Help is not available in applications under this section. Applications for Legal Representation under this section shall take the form of Full Representation.

12.3 General Funding Code

The criteria in Sections 5.4 and 5.7 of the General Funding Code shall not apply to applications under this section (but this should not be taken as restricting the scope of the reasonableness criterion below).

12.4 Reasonableness

An application may be refused if it is unreasonable in the particular circumstances of the case for Legal Representation to be granted.

Section 13 – Immigration

13.1 Scope

This section applies to applications for Legal Representation for a client whose case is before an Immigration Adjudicator or the Immigration Appeal Tribunal, and any further appeals from that tribunal to the Court of Appeal or House of Lords.

13.2 Investigative Help

Investigative Help is not available in applications under this section. Applications for Legal Representation under this section shall take the form of Full Representation.

13.3 General Funding Code

The standard criteria for Legal Representation in Section 5.4 of the General Funding Code apply to applications under this section, save for criterion 5.4.6 (small claims). The criteria for Full Representation under Section 5.7 of the General Funding Code do not apply to applications under this section.

13.4 Prospects of Success

Legal Representation will be refused if the prospects of achieving a successful outcome for the client are:
(i) unclear or borderline, save where the case has a significant wider public interest, is of overwhelming importance to the client or raises significant human rights issues; or
(ii) poor.

13.5 Cost Benefit

Save where the case has a significant wider public interest, Legal Representation will be refused unless the likely benefits to be gained from the proceedings justify the likely costs, such that a reasonable private paying client would be prepared to take the proceedings, having regard to the prospects of success and all other

Section 14 – Withdrawal of Funding

14.1 Scope

This section applies where funding has already been granted under the Code Criteria. Funding may be withdrawn in accordance with the following criteria and the Code Procedures. Code Procedures may in particular specify the grounds for withdrawal of emergency representation.

14.2 Criteria No Longer Satisfied

Funding may be withdrawn where the criteria under which funding was originally granted are no longer satisfied.

14.3 Reasonableness

Funding may be withdrawn where it is unreasonable for funding to continue in all the circumstances of the case, taking into account the interests of the client, any wider public interest and the interest of the Community Legal Service Fund.

14.4 Investigations

Investigative Help or Investigative Support will cease where it appears that sufficient work has been carried out to enable prospects of success to be determined. Investigative Support will also cease when a conditional fee arrangement is entered into.

14.5 Other Grounds

Without prejudice to any of the above criteria, funding may be withdrawn:
(i) where the client has died;
(ii) where the client has had a bankruptcy order made against him or her;
(iii) on financial grounds, in accordance with Code Procedures and Regulations;

(iv) with the consent of the client;
(v) where all work authorised by the Commission has been completed;
(vi) where, in accordance with Code Procedures, it is unreasonable for funding to continue in the light of the conduct of the client.

8. THE STATUTORY CHARGE

Regulations 43–53 of the Community Legal Service (Financial) Regulations 2000 provide that where any money or property is recovered for a client in a relevant dispute or proceedings, the amount of the statutory charge shall be the aggregate of the sums referred to in s 10(7)(*a*) and (*b*) of the Access to Justice Act 1999. These are sums expended by the LSC in funding the services and other sums payable by the individual by virtue of regulations which shall constitute a first charge on any property recovered or preserved by an individual (whether for himself or any other person) in any proceedings or in any compromise or settlement of any dispute in connection with which the services were provided. The charge does not cover sums expended by the LSC in funding (a) Legal Help; (b) Help at Court; (c) Family Mediation or (d) Help with Mediation, except (a), (c) and (d) do not apply where the funded services were given in relation to family, clinical negligence or personal injury proceedings or a dispute which may give rise to such proceedings.

(a) The law

(i) Cases under the Legal Aid Act 1988

Where a client had advice and assistance under Part II of the Legal Aid Act 1988, the relevant law is in s 11 of that Act and regulations 31–33 and Sch 4 of the Legal Advice and Assistance (Scope) Regulations 1989. Where a certificate was granted for representation under the Legal Aid Act 1988, the relevant law is in s 16 of that Act and Part XI of the Civil Legal Aid (General) Regulations 1989.

(ii) Cases under the Access to Justice Act 1999

Where the Commission funds a service for a client as part of the Community Legal Service, unless regulations provide otherwise, the unrecovered cost of funding the service gives rise to a first charge on any property recovered or preserved by the client in any proceedings, or in any compromise or settlement of any dispute, in connection with which the services were funded – see the Access to Justice Act 1999, s 10(7).

(b) Extent

The charge consists of:

(a) the amount of money the Commission has spent on funding services at all levels in connection with the proceedings or dispute; (note: when a contract does not distinguish the costs of the client's individual case and other cases, the cost is what the Commission specifies in writing);
(b) less any costs recovered by the client in the proceedings or dispute;
(c) less any payment by the client by way of contribution or otherwise; see s 10(7) of the Access to Justice Act 1999. (*LSC Manual.*)

(c) Amount

For the purposes of calculating the amount of the charge, the cost of funding services does not include the costs of assessment proceedings under the CPR, or taxation proceedings in the House of Lords. The costs of drawing up a bill are not part of the costs of assessment proceedings. Those costs will therefore form part of the deficiency to the fund: reg 40(4) of the Community Legal Service (Financial) Regulations 2000.

When a client had a certificate under the 1988 Act, the Commission treated the value of the charge as the value of the property recovered or preserved, or the net deficiency, whichever was less. Regulation 99(6) of the Civil Legal Aid (General) Regulations 1989 supported this approach. But s 10(7) of the 1999 Act and reg 43 of the Community Legal Service (Financial) Regulations 2000 do not permit the Commission to value the charge in this way. The charge is always the cost of the funded services, less costs and contributions actually received, even if the property to which it attaches is worth less on recovery or preservation.

If the client pays off the charge at the end of the case, the changed approach to valuation is unlikely to make any difference. The Commission cannot seek more than the value of the charged property in satisfaction of the deficiency to the Fund. But if we agree to defer enforcing the charge by securing it on the client's home, and the home increases in value before the client pays off the charge, we may enforce the charge up to its full amount, depending on how much the property is worth at the time.

In determining the value of the property at the time the charge is enforced, the £2,500 or £3,000 exemption in most family proceedings will take effect to the extent that it has not already been used up on any other asset or assets. (*LSC Manual.*)

(d) Exemptions

Regulation 44 (1) provides that the charge shall not apply to any of the following:

(a) any periodical payment of maintenance;

(b) other than in circumstances which are exceptional having regard in particular to the quantity or the value of the items concerned, the client's clothes or household furniture or the tools or implements of his trade;

(c) any sum or sums ordered to be paid under Section 5 of the Inheritance (Provision for Family and Dependants) Act 1975 or Part IV of the Family Law Act 1996;

(d) the first £2,500 (£3,000 if the application is made after 1 December 2001) of any money or the value of any property recovered by virtue of an order made or deemed to have been made under any enactments specified in paragraph (2), or an agreement which has the same effect as such an order;

(e) one-half of any redundancy payment within the meaning of Part XI of the Employment Rights Act 1996 recovered by the client;

(f) any payment of money made in accordance with an order made by the Employment Appeal Tribunal (excluding an order for costs);

(g) where the statutory charge is in favour of the supplier, the client's main or only dwelling, or

(h) any sum, payment or benefit which, by virtue of any provision of or made under an Act of Parliament, cannot be assigned or charged (which generally covers state benefits and pensions).

(e) Waiver

The LCS may grant a supplier authority, either in respect of individual cases or generally, to waive either all or part of the statutory charge where its enforcement would cause grave hardship or distress to the client or would be unreasonably difficult because of the nature of the property.

The LCS may, if it considers it equitable to do so, waive some or all of the amount of the statutory charge in respect of proceedings which it considers have a significant wider public interest and the Commission considers it cost-effective to fund those services for a specified claimant or claimants, but not for other claimants or potential claimants who might benefit from the litigation. 'Wider public interest' is defined as meaning that the potential of the proceedings to produce real benefits for individuals others than the client (other than any general benefits which normally flow from proceedings of the type in question) (Regulation 47).

(f) Enforcement

The LCS may enforce the statutory charge in any manner which would be available to a chargee in respect of the charge given between parties (Regulation 51).

(g) Deferment

The Commission may postpone the enforcement of the statutory charge where (but only where):

(a) by order of the Court or agreement it relates to property to be used as a home by the client or his dependants, or, where the relevant proceedings were family proceedings, to money to pay for such a home;
(b) the LCS is satisfied that the property in question will provide such security for the statutory charge as it considers appropriate;
(c) as soon as it is possible to do so, the LCS registers a charge under the Land Registration Act 1925 to secure the amount in Regulation 43 or, as appropriate, takes equivalent steps to protect its interests in the property.

Where the client wishes to purchase a property in substitution for the property over which a charge is registered under paragraph (c) the Commission may release the charge if the conditions in paragraph (b) and (c) are satisfied. Where the enforcement of the statutory charge is postponed interest shall accrue to the Commission from the date on which the charge is first registered at the rate of 8% calculated on the lesser of the amount of the statutory charge outstanding from time to time or where the value of the client's interest in the property at the time it was recovered was less than the amount of the statutory charge, such lower sum as the LCS considers equitable in the circumstances. All conveyances and acts done to defeat or operate to defeat any charge shall, except in the case of a bona fide purchaser for value without notice, be void as against the LSC, without prejudice to the provisions of the Land Registration Act 1925 and the Land Charges Act 1972 (Regulations 52 and 53).

9. PROPERTY AND COSTS RECOVERED FOR A FUNDED CLIENT

There are strict rules to ensure that a funded client meets all his obligations to the CLS Fund before he receives the benefit of the litigation. The provisions are contained in Part III of the Community Legal Service (Costs) Regulations 2000 as follows:

COMMUNITY LEGAL SERVICE (COSTS) REGULATIONS 2000

(SI 2000/441)

PART III PROPERTY AND COSTS RECOVERED FOR A FUNDED CLIENT

14 APPLICATION OF THIS PART

(1) In this Part:

'the awarded sum' means the amount of costs to be paid in accordance with a client's costs order or a client's costs agreement;

'client's costs order' and 'client's costs agreement' mean, respectively, an order and an agreement that another party to proceedings or prospective proceedings pay all or part of the costs of a client;

'Fund' means the Community Legal Service Fund established under section 5 of the Act;

'the funded sum' means the amount of remuneration payable by the Commission to a supplier for the relevant work under a contract or any other arrangements that determine that supplier's remuneration, including those that apply by virtue of article 4 of the Community Legal Service (Funding) Order 2000; and, where funding is provided by the Commission under a contract which does not differentiate between the remuneration for the client's case and remuneration for other cases, means such part of the remuneration payable under the contract as may be specified in writing by the Commission as being the funded sum;

'relevant work' means the funded services provided in relation to the dispute or proceedings to which the client's costs order or client's costs agreement relates;

'remuneration' includes fees and disbursements and value added tax on fees and disbursements;

'statutory charge' means the charge created by section 10(7) of the Act.

15 AMOUNT OF COSTS UNDER CLIENT'S COSTS ORDER OR CLIENT'S COSTS AGREEMENT

(1) Subject to the following paragraphs of this regulation, the amount of the costs to be paid under a client's costs order or client's costs agreement shall, subject to regulation 16, be determined on the same basis as it would be if the costs were to be paid to a person who had not received funded services.

(2) Subject to paragraph (3), the amount of the awarded sum shall not be limited to the amount of the funded sum by any rule of law which limits the costs recoverable by a party to proceedings to the amount he is liable to pay to his legal representatives.

(3) Paragraph (2) applies only to the extent that the Commission has authorised the supplier under section 22(2)(b) of the Act to take payment for the relevant work other than that funded by the Commission.

16 COSTS OF SERVING NOTICES AND OTHER DOCUMENTS

The amount of costs to be paid under a client's costs order or client's costs agreement may include costs incurred in filing with the court, or serving on any other party to proceedings, notices or any other documents in accordance with these Regulations, the Financial Regulations or the Funding Code.

17 APPLICATION OF REGULATIONS 18 TO 24

(1) Regulations 18 to 24 apply only where funded services have been provided under a certificate.
(2) If the client is no longer being represented by a solicitor, all money to which regulation 18(1) applies shall be paid (or repaid) to the Commission, and all references in regulations 18(1) and 19 to the client's solicitor shall be construed as references to the Commission.

18 MONEY RECOVERED TO BE PAID TO SOLICITOR

(1) Subject to the following paragraphs of this regulation, and to regulation 17(2), all money payable to or recovered by a client in connection with a dispute by way of damages, costs or otherwise, whether or not proceedings were begun, and whether under an order of the court or an agreement or otherwise, shall be paid to the client's solicitor, and only the client's solicitor shall be capable of giving a good discharge for that money.
(2) Paragraph (1) shall not apply to:
- (a) any periodical payment of maintenance; or
- (b) any money recovered or preserved by a client in any proceedings which:
  - (i) has been paid into, or remains in, court, and is invested for the client's benefit; and
  - (ii) under regulation 50 of the Financial Regulations, is not subject to the statutory charge.

(3) Where the client's solicitor has reason to believe that an attempt may be made to circumvent the provisions of paragraph (1), he shall inform the Commission immediately.

19 NOTICE TO THIRD PARTIES

(1) Where money is payable under regulation 18, and that money is payable by a trustee in bankruptcy, a trustee or assignee of a deed of arrangement, a liquidator of a company in liquidation, a trustee of a pension fund or any other third party ('the third party') the client's solicitor shall send to the third party notice that funded services have been funded for the client by the Commission.
(2) Notice under paragraph (1) shall operate as a request by the client that money payable under regulation 18 be paid to his solicitor, and shall be a sufficient authority for that purpose.

20 SOLICITOR TO PAY MONEY RECOVERED TO COMMISSION

(1) The client's solicitor shall forthwith:
- (a) inform the Regional Director of any money or other property recovered or preserved, and send him a copy of the order or agreement by virtue of which the property was recovered or preserved;
- (b) subject to the following paragraphs of this regulation, pay to the Commission all money or other property received by him under regulation 18.

(2) Paragraph (1)(b) shall not apply to any money or other property to which the statutory charge does not apply, by virtue of the Financial Regulations.
(3) Where he considers it essential to protect the client's interests or welfare, the Regional Director shall pay, or direct the client's solicitor to pay, to the client any money received by way of any interim payment made in accordance with an order made under CPR rule 25.6, or in accordance with an agreement having the same effect as such an order.

(4) The Regional Director may direct the client's solicitor to:

(a) pay to the Commission under paragraph (1)(b) only such sums as, in the Regional Director's opinion, should be retained by the Commission in order to safeguard its interests; and

(b) pay any other money to the client.

(5) Where the solicitor pays money to the Commission in accordance with this regulation, he shall identify what sums relate respectively to:

(a) costs;

(b) damages;

(c) interest on costs; and

(d) interest on damages.

21 POSTPONEMENT OF STATUTORY CHARGE

(1) In this regulation:

'conveyancer' means a solicitor or any other person who lawfully provides conveyancing services;

'family proceedings' means proceedings which arise out of family relationships, including proceedings in which the welfare of children is determined. Family proceedings also include all proceedings under any one or more of the following:

(a) the Matrimonial Causes Act 1973;

(b) the Inheritance (Provision for Family and Dependants) Act 1975;

(c) the Adoption Act 1976;

(d) the Domestic Proceedings and Magistrates' Courts Act 1978;

(e) Part III of the Matrimonial and Family Proceedings Act 1984;

(f) Parts I, II and IV of the Children Act 1989;

(g) Part IV of the Family Law Act 1996; and

(h) the inherent jurisdiction of the High Court in relation to children;

'purchase money' means money recovered or preserved by the client in family proceedings which, by virtue of an order of the court or an agreement, is to be used to purchase a home to be used by the client or the client's dependants, and 'the purchased property' means the property purchased or to be purchased with that money.

(2) The following paragraphs of this regulation apply, and (subject to paragraph (6)) regulation 20(1)(b) does not apply, where the Commission decides to postpone enforcement of the statutory charge under regulation 52 of the Financial Regulations.

(3) The solicitor may release the purchase money to the seller or the seller's representative on completion of the purchase of the purchased property; and shall as soon as practicable provide the Commission with sufficient information to enable it to protect its interest in accordance with regulation 52(1)(c) of the Financial Regulations.

(4) The client's solicitor may release the purchase money to a conveyancer acting for the client in the purchase of the purchased property, if he is satisfied that adequate steps have been, or will be, taken to protect the interests of the Commission.

(5) The steps referred to in paragraph (4) shall include, but are not limited to, the securing of an undertaking from the conveyancer referred to in that paragraph to:

(a) provide the information referred to in paragraph (3); and

(b) repay the purchase money under paragraph (6).

(6) Where the purchase of the purchased property has not been completed within 12 months after the date of the Commission's decision referred to in paragraph (2), or such longer period as the Commission considers reasonable, regulation 20(1)(b) shall apply and the purchase money shall accordingly be repaid to the Commission.

22 RETENTION AND PAYMENT OUT OF MONEY BY THE COMMISSION

(1) The Commission shall deal with the money paid to it under this Part in accordance with this regulation.
(2) The Commission shall retain:
 (a) an amount equal to the costs incurred in taking steps under regulation 23;
 (b) an amount equal to that part of the funded sum already paid to the supplier in respect of the relevant work; and
 (c) where costs are paid to the Commission together with interest, an amount equal to that interest, less the amount of any interest payable to the supplier under paragraph (3)(b)(ii).
(3) The Commission shall pay to the supplier:
 (a) any outstanding amount of the funded sum payable to him in respect of the relevant work;
 (b) where costs are ordered or agreed to be paid to the client, and those costs are received by the Commission, and those costs (less any amount retained under paragraph (2)(a) or payable under paragraph (5)) exceed the funded sum:
  (i) an amount equal to the amount of the excess; and
  (ii) where those costs are paid to the Commission together with interest, an amount equal to the interest attributable to the excess referred to in sub-paragraph (i).
(4) Paragraph (5) applies where a solicitor has acted on behalf of the client in proceedings before that client receives funded services in respect of the same proceedings, or has a lien on any documents necessary to proceedings to which a client is a party, and has handed them over subject to the lien, but applies only so far as is consistent with the express terms of any contract between the Commission and the solicitor.
(5) Where the solicitor referred to in paragraph (4) gives the Commission written notice that this paragraph applies, the Commission shall pay to that solicitor the costs to which that solicitor would have been entitled if those costs had been assessed on an indemnity basis.
(6) Where the amount of costs payable under paragraph (5) have not been assessed by the court, they may instead be assessed by the Commission.
(7) Where the amount received by the Commission, less any amount retained under paragraph (2)(a), is insufficient to meet the funded sum and any sum payable under paragraph (5), the Commission shall apportion the amount received proportionately between the two.
(8) The Commission shall pay all the money paid to it under this Part, which is not paid or retained under paragraphs (2) to (5), to the client.

23 ENFORCEMENT OF ORDERS ETC IN FAVOUR OF CLIENT

(1) Where, in relation to any dispute to which a client is a party, whether or not proceedings are begun:
 (a) an order or agreement is made providing for the recovery or preservation of property by the client (whether for himself or any other person); or
 (b) there is a client's costs order or client's costs agreement

the Commission may take any steps, including proceedings in its own name, as may be necessary to enforce or give effect to that order or agreement.
(2) A client may, with the consent of the Regional Director, take proceedings to give effect to an order or agreement under which he is entitled to recover or preserve money or other property.
(3) Subject to paragraph (4), the client's solicitor may take proceedings for the recovery of costs where a client's costs order or a client's costs agreement has been made.

(4) Where the client's costs order or client's costs agreement relates wholly or partly to costs incurred in carrying out work which is remunerated, or to be remunerated, in the funded sum, but those costs have not been reimbursed by payment from any other party in favour of the client, the solicitor shall require the consent of the Regional Director before taking proceedings to which paragraph (3) refers.
(5) Where the Commission takes proceedings, it may authorise any person to make a statement, file a proof or take any other step in the proceedings in its name.
(6) The costs incurred by the Commission in taking any step to enforce an order or agreement where paragraph (1) applies shall be a first charge on any property or sum so recovered.

24 INTEREST ON DAMAGES

(1) Where the Commission receives damages paid in favour of a client it shall, subject to the following paragraphs, pay to the client a sum representing gross interest earned while the damages are being held by the Commission.
(2) Without prejudice to its other powers to invest money, the Commission shall maintain and may deposit damages to which this regulation refers in one general account at a deposit taker.
(3) The rate of interest payable to the client under this regulation shall be 0.5% per annum less than the rate payable on damages deposited in the general account.
(4) The Commission shall not be required to pay interest where the damages received do not exceed £500 or where the period during which they are held by the Commission is less than 28 days.
(5) Interest shall be payable for the period beginning on the third business day after the date on which damages are received by the Commission to and including the date on which the Commission determines the amount to be paid under regulation 22(8).
(6) In this regulation:

'business day' means a day other than a Saturday, a Sunday, Christmas Day, Good Friday or a bank holiday under the Banking and Financial Dealings Act 1971;

'deposit taker' means the Bank of England, or the branch, situated in England or Wales, of either—

(a) a person with permission under Part 4 of the Financial Services and Markets Act 2000 to accept deposits, or
(b) an EEA firm of the kind mentioned in paragraph 5(b) of Schedule 3 to that Act, which has permission under paragraph 15 of that Schedule (as a result of qualifying for authorisation under paragraph 12(1) of that Schedule) to accept deposits;

'general account' means an interest bearing account opened in the name of the Commission, the title of which does not identify any client.

(7) The definition of 'deposit taker' in paragraph (6) must be read with—

(a) section 22 of the Financial Services and Markets Act 2000;
(b) any relevant order under that section; and
(c) Schedule 22 to that Act.

10. OBTAINING PAYMENT

The Legal Services Commission has provided the following helpful charts and guidance. I am again grateful for their permission to reproduce them.

REGULATION	TIME LIMIT APPLICABLE
Retainer determined before proceedings begun – costs must be assessed by LSC (reg 105(2)).	Within three months of determination of the solicitor's retainer
Proceedings begun, costs not more than £500 – costs must be assessed by LSC (reg 105(2A)); or	All other cases If the certificates revoked or discharged within three months of the termination of the retainer. Otherwise within the period CPR 47.7 would have specified.
Proceedings begun and costs not more than £1000 – costs may be assessed by LSC (reg 105(3)(c)); or	
Special circumstances (reg 105(3)(2)); or	
Following direction/order for detailed assessment, recovery costs are incurred (reg 105(3)(d)).	

SOURCE OF RIGHT TO DETAILED ASSESSMENT	TIME BY WHICH DETAILED ASSESSMENT PROCEEDINGS MUST BE COMMENCED
Judgment, direction, order, award or other determination.	Three months after the date of the judgment etc, but where detailed assessment is stayed pending an appeal, three months after the date of the order lifting the stay.

REGULATION	TIME LIMIT APPLICABLE
Discontinuance under Part 38.	Three months after the date of service of notice of discontinuance under Rule 38.3 or three months after the date of the dismissal of any application to set the notice of discontinuance aside under Rule 38.4.
Acceptance of an offer to settle or a payment into court under Part 36.	Three months after the date when the rights to the cost arose.

Guidance

4. There are now strict limits for the submission of civil bills. The legal provisions are set out in reg 105 (as amended) of the Civil Legal Aid (General) Regulations 1989.
5. Although claims may be submitted out of time, a fair balance has to be achieved between the interests of the Community Legal Service in securing prompt submission of bills and those of the profession in not being deprived, merely due to late submission, of costs for work properly carried out.
6. It will, however, generally be reasonable to expect solicitors to be aware of, and to comply with the time limits, particularly as time limits already apply to the submission of bills for detailed assessment and in relation to other types of costs claims. Firms will wish to obtain payment as soon as possible and should have access to appropriate support systems to monitor their cashflow.

7. The three month time limit for the submission of claims may be extended for 'good reason'. A common example may be where linked or related actions are awaiting final disposal or where the court has delayed in sending the final order. What constitutes 'good reason' is a question of fact in every case, although regard can be had to the particular firm's history of late claims, particularly where the 'good reason' put forward relates to the firm's own conduct.
8. To avoid difficulties on assessment, the solicitor should apply to the regional office for an extension to the time limit before it expires. However, the regional office may still extend the time limit, on receipt of a costs claim after the three month period, provided the solicitor can show 'good reason'. Where 'good reason' has been shown, the solicitor's costs should not be reduced only because of late submission.
9. Where the solicitor is unable to show 'good reason', the regional office must then go on to consider whether there are any 'exceptional circumstances' which would justify extending the time in the particular case. Each case will be judged on its own merits, although regard can be had to the particular firm's history of late claims.
10. Where the regional office decides that there were 'exceptional circumstances' it must then go on to consider whether to impose a penalty for late submission. Deductions will be imposed to a maximum of:

- 5 per cent for bills submitted up to three months out of time;
- 10 per cent for bills submitted up to six months out of time;
- 15 per cent for bills submitted up to nine months out of time.

11. Generally it should be possible for late claims to be submitted within twelve months of the conclusion of the matter (ie, up to nine months out of time) but there may be truly exceptional circumstances where the claim is submitted so late that higher deductions may be warranted.
12. Where a solicitor has failed to show either 'good reason' or 'exceptional circumstances', his claim for costs will be disallowed in full. He may then appeal to the Costs Committee.
13. Deductions are calculated on the total of the solicitor's profit costs. The deductions will be made from the solicitor unless counsel has been responsible for the delay. Counsel's fees are preserved provided he/she has not caused or contributed to the delay.
14. Where costs are disallowed in full, the solicitor is still bound to discharge both counsel's and (any) experts' fees. It is the Commission's view that payment in these circumstances would not breach reg 64 of the Civil Legal Aid (General) Regulations 1989.
15. Many queries over apparent non-payment of claims which are raised with the regional offices may arise from cases where payment has in fact been made, but solicitors have not posted the payment. It is reasonable to expect solicitors to monitor the receipt of payments on a regular basis and therefore to be in a position to raise such queries promptly after having posted payments and checked remittance advices. Except in a small minority of cases, civil bills are paid by the Commission within a maximum of four to six weeks of receipt of the claim for costs. The solicitor should therefore only make an enquiry of the regional office if payment is not received within two months of the submission of the claim.
16. Before raising a query with the relevant regional office, the solicitor should specifically check for payment and, if an enquiry of the regional office is appropriate, should confirm that all the remittance advices since the submission of the original claim have been checked for the appropriate payment and a copy of the claim previously submitted together with any proof of receipt should be forwarded to the regional office. The process of the solicitor checking for payment and the inclusion of a copy of the claim (and any supporting documents available) will reduce unnecessary queries and assist the regional offices in dealing with such queries as are received. Where

the solicitor cannot provide proof of receipt of the claim by the regional office, the matter may be treated as a late claim (see above).

Detailed assessment

See Chapter 30.

Chapter 42

CONDITIONAL FEES

PART 1 THE COMMON LAW

1. CONTINGENCY FEES

(a) A change of attitude

Since the Statute of Westminster in 1275 it had been inculcated into each generation of English lawyers as a tenet of professional ethics that contingency fees were not merely unlawful but, in the words of the judges, 'inherently immoral', 'deeply corrupting' and 'definitely sinister'. They were the scarlet women of the law. They might make suitable consorts for brash American lawyers, but no respectable clean-living English barrister or solicitor should associate with, let alone embrace, them. Yet, acting on a recommendation by the Civil Justice Review in 1989 a Scottish Presbyterian Lord Chancellor published a Green Paper on contingency fees inviting English lawyers seriously to consider getting into bed and cohabiting with this method of funding litigation. What had happened? Was it that contingency fees were not as bad as they had been painted over the centuries? Had it been a case of mistaken identity? Could they even now be redeemed and reformed? Had our moral values changed? Or was it simply that to keep the purse strings tight the Treasury was able to view with equanimity the prospect of the legal profession living on immoral earnings. The change was as sudden as it was dramatic, two converts being the Law Society and the government. In 1979, the government had accepted the view of the Royal Commission on Legal Services that in a contingency fee system 'the lawyer is exposed to strong temptation to settle the claim before incurring the heavy expense of preparing for trial, and of trial itself, although it may not be in his client's interest to do so. Alternatively, the client, having nothing to lose, may insist that a hopeless or irresponsible claim be pursued to litigation in the hope some profit will result'. ('Having nothing to lose' overlooked the possibility of between-the-parties costs being awarded against the client.)

In July 1987, a Law Society working party (in its report 'Improving Access to Civil Justice') agreed with the views of the Royal Commission and added 'we would go further and say that conflict of interest between solicitor and client is inherent in contingency fee arrangements' and 'it would be impossible to overcome the ethical and consumer protection problems'.

However, by 1989 the government in its Green Paper believed 'that it is appropriate to consider the introduction in England and Wales of speculative actions on the Scottish model' (para 5.3), while the Law Society's working party in its second report advised the Council of the Law Society 'to seek an opportunity to remove the statutory bars on contingency fees … and that if they are removed the Council should immediately permit "speculative" funding of all types of case'.

(b) For and against

The arguments propounded in favour of contingency fees included: greater access to justice; avoiding the client funding litigation during its currency; protection against costs on failure; an incentive to lawyers; assurance to clients of their lawyer's motivation and extra work for lawyers with higher rewards for success. The arguments against were that contingency fee agreements would conflict with a lawyer's duty to the court; be a temptation for unprofessional conduct; lead to unmeritorious 'blackmailing' actions; removed lawyer's objective independence from their clients; afford clients no protection against between-the-parties costs, expert fees and other disbursements; result in lawyers sharing in their client's awards and being paid by results leading to conflicts of interest between the lawyer and the client.

(c) The White Paper

In July 1989 in its White Paper 'Legal Services: a Framework for the Future' the government reported:

> 'The Green Paper stimulated lively debate on the acceptability in principle of any contingency fee arrangement, and on the differences between those jurisdictions where it is permitted in some form or other and the legal and commercial arrangements in England and Wales. There was a clear consensus that it would not be right in principle, and would be likely to have a number of undesirable side-effects, for a lawyer to be permitted to undertake a case in return for some percentage of whatever damages might be received. That form of contingency fee was also thought likely to create an unacceptable degree of conflict of interest between the lawyer and his client, which could result in his being unable to give the client or the court advice of the required degree of impartiality. There was, however, little objection to the proposal that arrangements following the model of the Scottish speculative action (payment of normal fees only if successful) should be allowed in England and Wales, and some support for the proposition that the client and his lawyers should be able to agree an uplift to those costs when acting on this basis. There was, moreover, a very clear consensus that the general rule that costs follow the event should not be changed. (para 14.2)
>
> The Government accordingly proposes to remove the existing prohibitions to enable clients to agree with any or all of their lawyers payment of a conditional fee on the speculative basis already permitted in Scotland. This relaxation will not, however, extend to criminal and family (matrimonial, care and wardship) proceedings which the Government believes are inappropriate for conditional funding. (para 14.3)
>
> The Government also accepts that it would be reasonable for a lawyer who represents a client on this basis to balance the risk of losing the case and ending up with no costs by charging at a higher rate than would have been appropriate but for the conditional factor.' (para 14.4)

(d) Still unlawful

The outcome of the debate was a triumph for semantics. Contingency fees were still an abhorrence, but conditional fees were given cautious approval. It was a distinction without a difference. A contingency agreement provides that the successful lawyer will receive a share of the proceeds, while under a conditional fee agreement before April 2000 the lawyer received a higher fee than normal – payable, of course, out of the proceeds. The end result was the same under both a contingency fee agreement and a conditional fee agreement – the client got less and the lawyer got more. Conditional fees were thus described as 'contingency fees by the back door'.

Nevertheless, semantics apart, contingency fee agreements, whereby the lawyers receive a direct share of the proceeds of the litigation were and, for the time being, continue to be unlawful. The change brought about in April 2000 was the potential recovery of the success fee (and insurance premium) from the losing opponent, thereby to a great extent protecting the damages retained by the client and removing the similarity with contingency fees. All of this applies to lawyers but not to members of other professions who may provide services in support of litigation on a contingency fee basis, that is, in return for a direct share of the proceeds, without being champertous. This is the decision of the Court of Appeal in *Factortame v Secretary of State for Transport* [2002] EWCA Civ 932 [2002] 4 All ER 97 which concluded that such an agreement was not contrary to the common law nor governed by the Courts and Legal Services Act 1990. That leaves of course regulation by professional bodies. The court expressly disapproved of any such arrangement with expert witnesses.

2. CATEGORIES OF CONDITIONAL FEES

All conditional fee agreements allow a lawyer to act for a client on the basis he will not charge his client, or not charge as much, if an agreed result is not achieved. Most agreements allow the solicitor to charge a success fee if the agreed result is achieved. Any fee agreement whereby the solicitor is to be paid different sums in different circumstances will amount to a conditional fee agreement under s 58 of the Courts and Legal Services Act 1990 as substituted by s 27 of the Access to Justice Act 1999. There are at least four varieties of fee arrangements which are within this statutory provision. It must be emphasised that in each of these, the full statutory regime must be followed because each is a CFA.

(a) Conditional fee with success fee

These have also been called 'enhanced fee agreements' or 'conditional uplift fee agreements' (CUFAs). If the case is won, the lawyer is not only entitled to charge his normal fee, he may also charge a success fee calculated as a percentage of his normal charges, to recompense him for the risk he has run of not being paid and of having to fund the litigation. The Lord Chancellor's Department's consultation paper of March 1998 said 'Conditional fees ensure that the risks of litigation are shared between the lawyer and the client: clients do not pay their lawyer's fees unless they win; and lawyers when they win receive a level of fees that recognises the risk they have taken'.

(b) Conditional fee agreements with no success fee

These have also been variously known as contingent fee agreements; no-win, no-fee agreements; *Thai Trading* agreements and conditional normal fee agreements (CNFAs). In previous editions of this book, after considering the law of champerty and maintenance I wrote:

> 'As Lord Denning said, many forms of maintenance are considered justifiable today and not contrary to public policy. Examples are funding by trade unions, negligence insurers, legal expenses insurers, motoring organisations, employers, trade protection associations and the Legal Aid Fund. … I very much doubt that it is now against public policy for a solicitor to agree with a client that he will not charge a fee unless a particular result is achieved … All that prevents a litigator or advocate from entering into an agreement not to receive payment unless a specified result is achieved are the practice rules of the Bar and the Law Society'.

In *Thai Trading Co v Taylor* [1998] 3 All ER 65, the Court of Appeal quoted those words and agreed with me. Delivering judgment, Lord Justice Millet summarised the position as follows:

> 'In my judgment, there is nothing unlawful in a solicitor acting for a party to litigation to agree to forego all or part of his fee if he loses, provided that he does not seek to recover more than his ordinary profit costs and disbursements if he wins'.

The judgment dealt with my comments about the practice rules by saying that the fact that a professional rule prohibited a particular practice did not itself make the practice contrary to law, especially as those rules were based on an outdated perception of public policy.

However, a QBD Divisional Court subsequently held in *Hughes v Kingston-upon-Hull City Council* [1999] QB 1193, following *Swain v Law Society* [1982] 2 All ER 827 (which was not drawn to the attention of the court in *Thai Trading*), that the Solicitors' Practice Rules had the force of statute just as much as if they had been set out in a schedule to the Solicitors Act 1974. Law Society Practice Rule 8 defines a contingency fee as 'any sum (whether fixed, or calculated either as a percentage of the proceeds or otherwise howsoever) payable only in the event of success in the prosecution or defence of any action, suit or other contentious proceeding'. Therefore the practice rules prohibited solicitors from entering into no-win, no-fee agreements which did not comply with the Conditional Fee Agreements Regulations 1995 (which were replaced on 1 April 2000). As a result of the decision in *Hughes*, Practice Rule 8(1) was amended with effect from 8 January 1999 to read 'a solicitor who is retained or employed to prosecute or defend any action, suit or other contentious proceeding shall not enter into any agreement to receive a contingency fee in respect of that proceeding, save one permitted under statute or by the common law'.

This was on the assumption that the common law did not regard it as against public policy for solicitors to assist impecunious litigants in their search for justice by not charging a fee unless the action were successful, but, on the contrary, it encouraged them to do so. Everyone breathed a sigh of relief, and many such agreements, with the encouragement of the Law Society, were entered into (indeed both the Senior Costs Judge and I wrote articles saying that we thought no-win, no-fee agreements would eventually replace the statutory scheme of conditional fee agreements with a success fee), until the decision of a differently constituted Court of Appeal. In *Awwad v Geraghty & Co (a firm)* [2000] 1 All ER 608, CA, the court held that there was no difference in principle between conditional fee agreements with a success fee and those without a success fee, because they were both based on payment by results and were therefore giving the lawyer a financial interest in the outcome of the litigation, which was against the common law and public policy and therefore unlawful unless sanctioned by statute. The court held that the same objection applied to an agreement to charge a reduced fee if the case was lost and a normal fee if it was won. Leave was given to appeal to the House of Lords, but no one was prepared to fund the appeal, partly because the position would be rectified by a new s 58 of the Courts and Legal Services Act 1990 to be introduced by the Access to Justice Act 1999 on 1 April 2000. However, the legislation would not be retrospective and the profession was left to wrestle with the problem of the enforceability of no-win, no-fee agreements entered into both before January 1999, at a time when the practice rule prohibited them, and after that date up to 1 April 2000, during which period *Geraghty* proclaimed them to be illegal (the case is always referred to as '*Geraghty*' even though Miss Geraghty was the respondent to a Solicitors Act originating application). On the face of it, the solicitor could not enforce such an agreement against his client and, because of the indemnity principle, the costs were also irrecoverable between the parties. The Law Society's advice, after obtaining the opinion of counsel, was based on the fact that in *Geraghty* the agreement was entered into in as long ago as 1993, long before the practice rule was amended, and that the approval of the subsequent change in the practice rule by the Master of the Rolls implied that by 1999 the common law permitted conditional fee agreements. In other words, *Thai Trading* (and *Cook on Costs*!) can be regarded as a general reflection of public policy and the common law. It would certainly be surprising if the court in *Geraghty* had decided that a principle which Parliament had enshrined in a statute (the Access to Justice Act 1999) which was awaiting implementation was contrary to public policy. I thought Parliament was public policy! Nonetheless, the fee arrangement made in *Geraghty* would not have complied with the statute had it been in force and it cannot be advised that the same arrangement made in the same way in 1998 or 1999 would be enforceable. It seems the decision in *Geraghty* was that Parliament had created a statutory being under close control and no more. The case also decided that an arrangement which breaches the Practice Rules is unlawful, in respect of Rule 8 this leads to a circular argument along the lines of the chicken and the egg. Nonetheless, it seems that the common law has not evolved in the way described in *Thai Trading* and that the only lawful conditional fee agreement is one which fully complies with the statute – a view which forms the basis of the decision of Master Wright in *Woods v Chaleff* [2002] NLJR 1276 that a defective CFA cannot be enforced at common law.

(c) Discounted conditional fee agreements

On this basis, the lawyer receives payment whatever the result, but at a discounted rate if a specific result is not achieved. Tony Girling suggests two options. An example of the first is an agreement that provides for charges of £150 an hour if the case is won and an order for costs is secured, but only £100 an hour if the prescribed result is not achieved. His other option is an attractive variation on the lines of '£150 an hour if the case is won with a success fee of (*for example*) 50%; if the case is lost, this fee arrangement be discounted to £100 an hour'. This formula gives the solicitor and the client the best of both worlds. Justifying the various figures in such arrangements will need care. In particular account must be taken of the fact that by no means all of the solicitor's fees are being risked so that the success fee needs to reflect the real level of risk.

(d) Speccing agreements

This is where a solicitor speculates by acting for an impecunious client who has no prospect of paying the solicitor's fees unless the proceedings are successful. The solicitor in effect agrees to act for such costs as are recovered from the opponent. English law seems to have considerable difficulty in dealing with this everyday reality. In these circumstances it was held in *British Waterways Board v Norman* (1993) 26 HLR 232, QBD that in the absence of a specific agreement to the contrary, the presumption is that there must have been an understanding between the solicitors and the client that they would not look to her if she lost and accordingly the arrangement infringed the indemnity principle and was unlawful as a contingency fee (see p 172 and Section (b) above). More recently the Divisional Court has held in two cases that agreements with clients who have no prospect of meeting a liability under them were nevertheless valid agreements – *R v Liverpool Magistrates' Court* [2001] 2 All ER 705 and *R (on the application of Hazlett) v South Sefton Magistrates' Court* [2001] EWHC Admin 791, [2001] All ER (D) 18 (Oct). In the latter case the judgment of Millett LJ in *Thai Trading* was relied upon:

> 'It is not uncommon for solicitors to take on a case for an impecunious client with a meritorious case, knowing that there is no realistic prospect of recovering their costs from

> the client if the case is lost, without thereby waiving their legal right to their fees in that event. As every debt collector knows, what is legally recoverable and what is recoverable in practice are no the same.'

It is therefore essential to the validity of such agreements that the solicitor and the client enter into a cast iron agreement that the client is liable for the solicitor's costs whatever the outcome of the proceedings, even though the solicitor realises that if nothing is recovered he will not be paid unless his client wins the lottery or the football pools. The judge in the *South Sefton* case dealt with the allegation of sham on the basis that a sham requires both parties to intend to deceive. So, I shall not use the word 'sham', but simply enquire what the client would answer if asked, 'Are you going to have to pay?' It is another example of the tortuous reasoning the moribund indemnity principle (Chapter 17) leads to when the courts wish to apply common sense.

PART 2 THE STATUTES

1. COURTS AND LEGAL SERVICES ACT 1990

Statutory provision for conditional fee agreements with or without a success fee was first made by the Courts and Legal Services Act 1990, s 58. It authorised the Lord Chancellor to permit conditional fee agreements in respect of all categories of work except criminal and family proceedings by Order after consultation with the designated judges, the General Council of the Bar, the Law Society and such other authorised bodies he thought appropriate. All of this took time, and it was not until 5 July 1995 that the Conditional Fee Agreements Order 1995 and accompanying Regulations came into force. At first they were restricted to a few specified proceedings, but on 30 July 1998 the Conditional Fee Agreements Order 1998 extended the categories to all work except those prohibited by the Act.

2. ACCESS TO JUSTICE ACT 1999

On 1 April 2000 s 27 of the Access to Justice Act 1999 substituted a new s 58 of the Courts and Legal Services Act 1990 and introduced a new s 58A:

27 CONDITIONAL FEE AGREEMENTS

(1) For section 58 of the Courts and Legal Services Act 1990 substitute—

'58 Conditional fee agreements

(1) A conditional fee agreement which satisfies all of the conditions applicable to it by virtue of this section shall not be unenforceable by reason only of its being a conditional fee agreement; but (subject to subsection (5)) any other conditional fee agreement shall be unenforceable.

(2) For the purposes of this section and section 58A—

(a) a conditional fee agreement is an agreement with a person providing advocacy or litigation services which provides for his fees and expenses, or any part of them, to be payable only in specified circumstances; and

(b) a conditional fee agreement provides for a success fee if it provides for the amount of any fees to which it applies to be increased, in specified circumstances, above the amount which would be payable if it were not payable only in specified circumstances.

(3) The following conditions are applicable to every conditional fee agreement—
   (a) it must be in writing;
   (b) it must not relate to proceedings which cannot be the subject of an enforceable conditional fee agreement; and
   (c) it must comply with such requirements (if any) as may be prescribed by the Lord Chancellor.

(4) The following further conditions are applicable to a conditional fee agreement which provides for a success fee—
   (a) it must relate to proceedings of a description specified by order made by the Lord Chancellor;
   (b) it must state the percentage by which the amount of the fees which would be payable if it were not a conditional fee agreement is to be increased; and
   (c) that percentage must not exceed the percentage specified in relation to the description of proceedings to which the agreement relates by order made by the Lord Chancellor.

(5) If a conditional fee agreement is an agreement to which section 57 of the Solicitors Act 1974 (non-contentious business agreements between solicitor and client) applies, subsection (1) shall not make it unenforceable.

58A Conditional fee agreements: supplementary

(1) The proceedings which cannot be the subject of an enforceable conditional fee agreement are—
   (a) criminal proceedings, apart from proceedings under section 82 of the Environmental Protection Act 1990; and
   (b) family proceedings.

(2) In subsection (1) "family proceedings" means proceedings under any one or more of the following—
   (a) the Matrimonial Causes Act 1973;
   (b) the Adoption Act 1976;
   (c) the Domestic Proceedings and Magistrates' Courts Act 1978;
   (d) Part III of the Matrimonial and Family Proceedings Act 1984;
   (e) Parts I, II and IV of the Children Act 1989;
   (f) Part IV of the Family Law Act 1996; and
   (g) the inherent jurisdiction of the High Court in relation to children.

(3) The requirements which the Lord Chancellor may prescribe under section 58(3)(c)—
   (a) include requirements for the person providing advocacy or litigation services to have provided prescribed information before the agreement is made; and
   (b) may be different for different descriptions of conditional fee agreements (and, in particular, may be different for those which provide for a success fee and those which do not).

(4) In section 58 and this section (and in the definitions of "advocacy services" and "litigation services" as they apply for their purposes) "proceedings" includes any sort of proceedings for resolving disputes (and not just proceedings in a court), whether commenced or contemplated.

(5) Before making an order under section 58(4), the Lord Chancellor shall consult—
   (a) the designated judges;
   (b) the General Council of the Bar;
   (c) the Law Society; and
   (d) such other bodies as he considers appropriate.

(6) A costs order made in any proceedings may, subject in the case of

court proceedings to rules of court, include provision requiring the payment of any fees payable under a conditional fee agreement which provides for a success fee.

(7) Rules of court may make provision with respect to the assessment of any costs which include fees payable under a conditional fee agreement (including one which provides for a success fee).'

Section 28 of the 1999 Act will create a new s 58B but has yet to be brought into force:

28 LITIGATION FUNDING AGREEMENTS

In the Courts and Legal Services Act 1990, after section 58A (inserted by section 27 above) insert—

'58B Litigation funding agreements

(1) A litigation funding agreement which satisfies all of the conditions applicable to it by virtue of this section shall not be unenforceable by reason only of its being a litigation funding agreement.

(2) For the purposes of this section a litigation funding agreement is an agreement under which—

(a) a person ("the funder") agrees to fund (in whole or in part) the provision of advocacy or litigation services (by someone other than the funder) to another person ("the litigant"); and

(b) the litigant agrees to pay a sum to the funder in specified circumstances.

(3) The following conditions are applicable to a litigation funding agreement—

(a) the funder must be a person, or person of a description, prescribed by the Lord Chancellor;

(b) the agreement must be in writing;

(c) the agreement must not relate to proceedings which by virtue of section 58A(1) and (2) cannot be the subject of an enforceable conditional fee agreement or to proceedings of any such description as may be prescribed by the Lord Chancellor;

(d) the agreement must comply with such requirements (if any) as may be so prescribed;

(e) the sum to be paid by the litigant must consist of any costs payable to him in respect of the proceedings to which the agreement relates together with an amount calculated by reference to the funder's anticipated expenditure in funding the provision of the services; and

(f) that amount must not exceed such percentage of that anticipated expenditure as may be prescribed by the Lord Chancellor in relation to proceedings of the description to which the agreement relates.

(4) Regulations under subsection (3)(a) may require a person to be approved by the Lord Chancellor or by a prescribed person.

(5) The requirements which the Lord Chancellor may prescribe under subsection (3)(d)—

(a) include requirements for the funder to have provided prescribed information to the litigant before the agreement is made; and

(b) may be different for different descriptions of litigation funding agreements.

(6) In this section (and in the definitions of "advocacy services" and "litigation services" as they apply for its purposes) "proceedings" includes any sort of proceedings for resolving disputes (and not just

proceedings in a court), whether commenced or contemplated.

(7) Before making regulations under this section, the Lord Chancellor shall consult—
  (a) the designated judges;
  (b) the General Council of the Bar;
  (c) the Law Society; and
  (d) such other bodies as he considers appropriate.

(8) A costs order made in any proceedings may, subject in the case of court proceedings to rules of court, include provision requiring the payment of any amount payable under a litigation funding agreement.

(9) Rules of court may make provision with respect to the assessment of any costs which include fees payable under a litigation funding agreement.'

3. BASE COSTS

(a) Section 58

The new s 58 refers to a fee which is 'above the amount which would be payable if it were not payable only is specified circumstances', while its predecessor defined a success fee as 'an amount above the amount which would be payable if it were not a conditional fee agreement'. For ten years, I have been trying to discover what the 'amount that would be payable' is. In 1990 I asked the Chief Taxing Master, as he then was, the Lord Chancellor's Department and the Law Society what they thought it was. The Chief Taxing Master said that he was as perplexed as I. The Lord Chancellor's Department replied: 'The uplift will fall upon the fees which the solicitor would charge his client under the normal remuneration procedure. As you point out in your letter, the solicitor and client can agree any amount as the fee'. Precisely. No two firms of solicitors have exactly the same rates and system of charging; some firms have different rates for different classes of work and different charges for different clients, depending on such factors as the level of fee earner, the difficulty, complexity, importance, expertise and urgency involved. A solicitor may charge all red-headed clients 100% more than other clients, if they agree his charges. Similarly a solicitor could charge 100% more for personal injury work than for other types of litigation, if he and the client so agree. Solicitors do not even have to quote hourly rates – they may agree to litigate for a fixed fee. The Law Society replied to my question in this way:

> 'You mention the difficulty caused by the fact that solicitors are free to agree whatever hourly rate they wish with their clients; are free to charge different clients different rates and are not obliged to publish their rates (and indeed rarely do so). We drew attention to these difficulties during the passage of the Courts and Legal Services Act, but we did not think it wise to press the point very strongly since one solution (which would have been undesirable from our point of view) would have been to provide that the uplift should operate on the [*between-the-parties*] costs. The answer to your question is that the uplift does indeed relate to the amount that would indeed have been charged in the individual case on the ordinary basis. If the client believes that the solicitor has falsely stated the hourly rate which would otherwise be charged, he or she can challenge the rate on [*assessment*]. If the basic rate seemed unusually high, the [*assessing*] authorities might no doubt expect the solicitor to demonstrate that there were other clients, instructing the solicitor on the ordinary basis, who were charged roughly the same as the rate the solicitor was seeking to uphold as the basic rate for the conditional fee client. For example, a solicitor whose conditional fee agreement was based on £200 an hour plus 100% uplift might well be struggling to justify his fee if clients acting on the ordinary basis were charged £80 an hour'.

The advent of the recoverable success fee has somewhat lessened the importance of the regime since, in effect, the success fee will be applied to the between-the parties-costs that have been allowed. It is inconceivable that on an assessment the paying party would be ordered to pay a success fee on base costs he has not been ordered to pay, even though the CFA applies the success fee to the whole of the base costs payable by the client.

I think that it would now be very difficult to show that any reasonable contingent no-win, no-fee agreement was champertous. There is, in principle, no need for a success fee. There is no reason why solicitors should not charge ordinary rates which recognise that a proportion of the cases they handle on a conditional fee basis fail. Different types of litigation may give rise to different levels of 'ordinary' charging rates. Thus in personal injury actions the level of success is normally higher than in clinical negligence cases. Conditional fee agreements at an appropriately high charging rate would appear to be particularly suitable where a client has a strong case but cannot afford to litigate and does not qualify for state funding, and also in high profile public interest cases (for individual or group clients) and, indeed, in all litigation where the risk of losing can be compensated for by a reasonable adjustment in the charging rate. In other words, it should now only be necessary to enter into a conditional fee agreement where the circumstances justify and require the imposition of a substantial and identifiable success fee. However, because success fees may now be recovered between the parties, this has ensured their survival, because a modest hourly charging rate with a success fee is more likely to be recovered in full than a high hourly charging rate without a success fee and in any event s 58 as now worded precludes the simpler route.

Section 58 embodied in the statute the common law position as identified in *Thai Trading* until the decision in *Geraghty* , that it is not unlawful for lawyers to agree to work for less than their normal fees in the event that they are unsuccessful, provided they do not seek to recover more than their normal fees if they succeed. However, the price of legitimacy is that they too must comply with regulations prescribed by the Lord Chancellor. Section 58 defines a conditional fee agreement as an agreement which provides for the fees, or any part of them, to be payable only in specified circumstances. Because 'any part of them' covers the four categories identified in Part 1 of this chapter and *Geraghty* declared any agreement not sanctioned by statute to be unlawful, this creates a problem for conditional fee agreements in family proceedings, where they are, of course, not permitted. In the past they were merely unenforceable which meant the solicitor was entitled to keep any money paid to him for costs, but as the agreement is now unlawful, the solicitor must return to the client any money paid under the agreement. Since 1 April 2000 (or earlier if *Geraghty* was right) any agreement satisfying the definition in s 58(2) must comply with the statute. In family litigation it is not possible at all to satisfy the statute because family proceedings are not within the statutory scheme. Thus a speccing agreement will be unenforceable by virtue of s 58.

(b) Section 58A

The new s 58A presaged regulations which distinguish between agreements which do, and those which do not, provide for enhanced fees, making provisions similar to those already existing in respect of agreements which include a success fee. It also included the revolutionary, but long-awaited, provision that success fees payable to the receiving party's lawyer under a conditional fee agreement should be recoverable from the paying party.

(c) Section 58B

Section 58B will create the litigation funder. There has been no indication that this provision is to be brought into force in the foreseeable future. A litigation funder must be a person or body prescribed by the Lord Chancellor who will pay the lawyers in the usual way and, in successful cases, be able to recover those costs plus a success fee from the other side. Success fees recovered will be paid into the fund and used towards payment of lawyers' fees in unsuccessful actions. This is to facilitate the introduction of funding on lines similar to the Bar's preferred option of a Contingency Legal Aid Fund, which I discuss on p 543.

(d) Other costs provisions in the 1999 Act

As well as amending the Courts and Legal Services Act 1990, the Access to Justice Act 1999 contained the following provisions as to costs:

29 RECOVERY OF INSURANCE PREMIUMS BY WAY OF COSTS

Where in any proceedings a costs order is made in favour of any party who has taken out an insurance policy against the risk of incurring a liability in those proceedings, the costs payable to him may, subject in the case of court proceedings to rules of court, include costs in respect of the premium of the policy.

30 RECOVERY WHERE BODY UNDERTAKES TO MEET COSTS LIABILITIES

(1) This section applies where a body of a prescribed description undertakes to meet (in accordance with arrangements satisfying prescribed conditions) liabilities which members of the body or other persons who are parties to proceedings may incur to pay the costs of other parties to the proceedings.
(2) If in any of the proceedings a costs order is made in favour of any of the members or other persons, the costs payable to him may, subject to subsection (3) and (in the case of court proceedings) to rules of court, include an additional amount in respect of any provision made by or on behalf of the body in connection with the proceedings against the risk of having to meet such liabilities.
(3) But the additional amount shall not exceed a sum determined in a prescribed manner; and there may, in particular, be prescribed as a manner of determination one which takes into account the likely cost to the member or other person of the premium of an insurance policy against the risk of incurring a liability to pay the costs of other parties to the proceedings.
(4) In this section 'prescribed' means prescribed by regulations made by the Lord Chancellor by statutory instrument; and a statutory instrument containing such regulations shall be subject to annulment in pursuance of a resolution of either House of Parliament.
(5) Regulations under subsection (1) may, in particular, prescribe as a description of body one which is for the time being approved by the Lord Chancellor or by a prescribed person.

31 RULES AS TO COSTS

In section 51 of the Supreme Court Act 1981 (costs), in subsection (2) (rules regulating matters relating to costs), insert at the end 'or for securing that the amount awarded to a party in respect of the costs to be paid by him to such representatives is not limited to what would have been payable by him to them if he had not been awarded costs.'

(e) Section 29

Section 29 made provision for rules to allow the court to order the party ordered to pay the costs in litigation to pay the premium on any after-the-event insurance policy taken out by the receiving party in respect of costs, whether or not the receiving party has entered into a conditional fee agreement.

(i) The vital difference

The vital difference between the system of funding litigation in the USA and in this country is not that the former is on a contingency basis and the latter is on a conditional basis. That, as I have said, I regard as a distinction of semantics and not substance. No, the real difference is between-the-parties costs. In the USA the client has a free ride if he loses. He has no liability to his own lawyer and no liability to the other party. In the UK (it applies to Scotland as well) there is a double whammy – the unsuccessful litigant is liable for his own lawyer's costs and the costs of the other side. A conditional fee agreement protects a losing client against his own lawyer's costs but not against those of the other side. 'The good news is that you are only going bankrupt for the other party's costs, not for your own costs as well' has a hollow ring to it.

(ii) Accident Line Protect

The Law Society resolved the dilemma and made conditional fee agreements possible by a brilliant stroke. They negotiated 'after-the-event insurance' (known by the irreverent as 'the morning after pill') with Accident Line Protect whereby after a conditional fee agreement had been entered into the client could for a mere £85 insure himself against an order for between the parties costs up to £100,000. He was also insured against his own disbursements. Such a low premium was achieved by limiting the availability of the policy to clients whose solicitors were members of the Accident Line Scheme and who entered into conditional fee agreements similar to the Law Society's model. As Frances McCarthy, the president of the Association of Personal Injury Lawyers, said at a costs seminar 'anyone embarking on litigation financed under a conditional fee agreement without insurance for the other party's costs would be mad'. In terms of attractiveness to clients this has been a great success. It was an experiment that seemed to have worked.

(iii) The future

Before we get carried away, let us pause for breath. Conditional fee agreements have worked, at least in personal injury cases, because of after-the-event insurance. After-the-event insurance has worked because the premium was so low and the cover so high. That was because of two very special reasons. First, the insurance was limited to non-medical negligence personal injury actions in which the prospects of success are at least 90%. Second, Accident Line Protect insurance was available only to specialist solicitors on the Law Society's panel. Even so, after two years the premiums had to be dramatically increased. In November 1997 premiums for personal injury policies went up by almost double to £161.20 and in respect of road traffic accidents to £95.68. In 2000 the whole scheme was re-launched with new underwriters, a much reduced panel of solicitors and further increased premiums. That was in respect of work in which the chances of success are high and the work involved is reasonably clear from the outset. But how are the chances of success to be evaluated in a medical negligence claim and who is to finance the gathering of the evidence and reports upon which that evaluation is to be based? Flat rate premiums appear to be out of the question. The state is now only prepared to finance litigation where there is more than a 50% chance of winning. Are commercial insurance companies going to accept any longer odds, and if so, at what price the premiums? If it does not make sense to have non-profit-making state funding is it likely to make any more sense to profit-making insurance companies? And what amount of cover will be on offer? £100,000 will cover the cost of virtually any road traffic accident case, but what about medical negligence cases with heavy experts' fees, and defamation actions? When he was Chairman of the Bar, Robert Owen QC, referred to a medical negligence case in which he was involved in which the client had to pay a premium of £15,000 to obtain £100,000 of cover. Who will insure the 60/40 case, let alone the 50/50 case, even if a firm of solicitors and a barrister can be found to act on a conditional fee agreement basis? Will there now be a substantial class of litigants whom no one will back – not the state, not the lawyers and not the insurers because they are not racing certainties? These are some of the questions to which answers must be found before conditional fee agreements become a realistic way of financing all forms of litigation. See 'Gatekeepers to Justice' on p 542.

(iv) The insurers

There has been no shortage of companies offering after-the-event insurance (known as ATE or AEI), although the nature of the cover and the terms vary considerably. Here is a recent list taken from the Law Society's excellent publication Litigation Funding. Some movement into and out of this market means that by the time you read this, the list will be neither up-to-date nor comprehensive.

Accident Claim Protect (01772 272 064)
Accident Line Protect (0500 192939). Insured through Abbey Legal Protection (020 7702 3636)
Albion Legal (0113 223 7350)
Amicus Legal Ltd (01206 871287)
Capital Assistance (was Eastgate) (08705 234 567)
Claims Advance (01204 393 133)
Collegiate Underwriting (020 7459 3450)
Composite Legal Expenses (02920 222 033)
Conditional Fee Insurance Services underwritten by CAS (0870 241 1345)
8oe (DAS) (0117 934 0087)
Fastrack Indemnity (01539 732 211)
First Assist Group Ltd (020 8652 1313)
First Legal Indemnity (020 7623 3653)
Glenshield Ltd (01963 33580)
IMS (020 8408 7600)
Lawclub Legal Protection (0870 243 4340)
Law Assist (020 8771 7772), run by Greystoke Legal Services
Litco (08707 322 233)
Litigation Protection Ltd (01903 883811)
Motor Accident Solicitors Society (MASS) (0117 929 2560)
M Young Legal Associates (0161 247 8633)
NFL (020 8661 1111)
Oracle Legal Services (0171 685 5480)
QLP (020 7626 0191)
Royal & Sun Alliance (020 8652 1437)
Saturn Professional Risks (01494 774431)

Solicitors Services (01689 885 050)
Temple Legal protection (01483 577 877)
Vision Underwriting (0117 917 5080)
Wren Insurance Services (01242 222767)

(f) Section 30

Section 30 enables a prescribed body which has undertaken to meet the costs liabilities of a party to recover an additional sum for having provided the facility. The Access to Justice (Membership Organisations) Regulations 2000 which came into force on 1 April 2000 defined the bodies which are prescribed for the purpose of section 30 as able to recover a sum as part of legal costs from unsuccessful opponents to reflect the provision of legal help for members and their families. CPR Rule 44.3B (1)(*b*) on p 524 provides that any provision for an additional liability by a membership organisation which exceeds the likely cost of an after-the-event insurance premium shall not be recoverable between the parties.

The Lord Chancellor has approved as prescribed bodies all trade unions listed by the Certification Office for Trade Unions and Employers Organisations and:

RAC Motoring Services
Defence Police Federation
Engineering Employer's Federation
Police Federation of England and Wales
The Automobile Association

The Lord Chancellor's Department published guidance in April 2000 relating to applications for approval as a prescribed body.

(g) Section 31

In order to avoid the operation of the indemnity principle, s 31 is to amend s 51 of the Supreme Court Act 1981 to allow rules to be made providing that the amount of costs ordered to be paid by the paying party need not be limited to the amount which the receiving party would have been liable to pay to his own lawyers if he had not been awarded costs. The amendment of the indemnity principle would certainly simplify collective CFA's and pave the way for more transparent arrangements for guaranteeing that damages will be retained by the client. But s 31 has still not been brought into force and even were it to be, we would have to wait for new rules and then the debate will begin as to whether the new rules apply retrospectively to cover agreements entered into before they were written.

PART 3 THE ORDER

CONDITIONAL FEE AGREEMENTS ORDER 2000

1 CITATION, COMMENCEMENT AND INTERPRETATION

(1) This Order may be cited as the Conditional Fee Agreements Order 2000 and shall come into force on 1st April 2000.
(2) In this Order 'the Act' means the Courts and Legal Services Act 1990.

2 REVOCATION OF 1998 ORDER

The Conditional Fee Agreements Order 1998 is revoked.

3 AGREEMENTS PROVIDING FOR SUCCESS FEES

All proceedings which, under section 58 of the Act, can be the subject of an enforceable conditional fee agreement, except proceedings under section 82 of the Environmental Protection Act 1990, are proceedings specified for the purposes of section 58(4)(a) of the Act.

4 AMOUNT OF SUCCESS FEES

In relation to all proceedings specified in article 3, the percentage specified for the purposes of section 58(4)(c) of the Act shall be 100%.

1. ALL AGREEMENTS

For the purposes of s 58(4)(*a*) of the Courts and Legal Services Act 1990 provision for a success fee may be made in all enforceable conditional fee agreements except in proceedings under the Environmental Protection Act 1990, s 82.

2. THE MAXIMUM UPLIFT

The percentage increase of costs in a success fee permitted under the amended section 58(4)(*c*) of the Courts and Legal Services Act 1990 remains at 100%, despite at one time it being contemplated that there should be no limit for proceedings in the Commercial, Technology and Construction and Admiralty Courts. In such cases the prospect of reflecting in a success fee both the risk of losing and the cost of the substantial delay in payment within the 100% maximum would seem to be a hopeless task. It remains to be seen what view emerges from the judges dealing with this category of work.

The term 'maximum uplift' sounds like an advertisement for a ladies' undergarment, but it was the phrase used in the draft of the original order when conditional fee agreements were being introduced. The final version became the 'maximum permitted percentage' by which the solicitor's fees might be increased. The original figure proposed was 10% but the Law Society pointed out that on this basis solicitors would have to win ten out of eleven cases to break even. Lord Donaldson called it 'silly'. The uplift was then increased to 20% resulting in breaking even if only one out of six cases was lost (a success rate of 83.6%). Still no big deal. Then the Lord Chancellor increased the mark-up to 100%, in spite of the advice of his own advisory committee.

3. PROFIT INCREASED BY MORE THAN 100%

In the House of Lords debate, Baroness Hamwee, a practising solicitor, pointed out that a 100% increase in a solicitor's charges amounted to considerably more than a doubling of the profit, because hourly rates include overheads. A charge-out hourly rate which is calculated on the basis of the direct cost of doing the work plus a 50% profit mark-up comprises two-thirds cost and one third profit. Accordingly a success fee of 100% on the total base costs is in fact a 300% increase of the profit element, whilst even a modest 10% success fee results in a 30% increase in the profit.

PART 4 THE REGULATIONS

The Access to Justice Act was followed, eventually, by the Conditional Fee Agreements Regulations 2000 which also came into force on 1 April 2000, replacing the Conditional Fee Agreements Regulations 1995. Here they are:

CONDITIONAL FEE AGREEMENTS REGULATIONS 2000

1 CITATION, COMMENCEMENT AND INTERPRETATION

(1) These Regulations may be cited as the Conditional Fee Agreements Regulations 2000.
(2) These Regulations come into force on 1st April 2000.
(3) In these Regulations—
'client' includes, except where the context otherwise requires, a person who—
- (a) has instructed the legal representative to provide the advocacy or litigation services to which the conditional fee agreement relates, or
- (b) is liable to pay the legal representative's fees in respect of those services; and

'legal representative' means the person providing the advocacy or litigation services to which the conditional fee agreement relates.

2 REQUIREMENTS FOR CONTENTS OF CONDITIONAL FEE AGREEMENTS: GENERAL

(1) A conditional fee agreement must specify—
- (a) the particular proceedings or parts of them to which it relates (including whether it relates to any appeal, counterclaim or proceedings to enforce a judgement or order),
- (b) the circumstances in which the legal representative's fees and expenses, or part of them, are payable,
- (c) what payment, if any, is due—
  - (i) if those circumstances only partly occur,
  - (ii) irrespective of whether those circumstances occur, and
  - (iii) on the termination of the agreement for any reason, and
- (d) the amounts which are payable in all the circumstances and cases specified or the method to be used to calculate them and, in particular, whether the amounts are limited by reference to the damages which may be recovered on behalf of the client.

(2) A conditional fee agreement to which regulation 4 applies must contain a statement that the requirements of that regulation which apply in the case of that agreement have been complied with.

3 REQUIREMENTS FOR CONTENTS OF CONDITIONAL FEE AGREEMENTS PROVIDING FOR SUCCESS FEES

(1) A conditional fee agreement which provides for a success fee—
- (a) must briefly specify the reasons for setting the percentage increase at the level stated in the agreement, and
- (b) must specify how much of the percentage increase, if any, relates to the cost to the legal representative of the postponement of the payment of his fees and expenses.

(2) If the agreement relates to court proceedings, it must provide that where the percentage increase becomes payable as a result of those proceedings, then—
- (a) if—
  - (i) any fees subject to the increase are assessed, and

(ii) the legal representative or the client is required by the court to disclose to the court or any other person the reasons for setting the percentage increase at the level stated in the agreement,

he may do so,

(b) if—

(i) any such fees are assessed, and

(ii) any amount in respect of the percentage increase is disallowed on the assessment on the ground that the level at which the increase was set was unreasonable in view of facts which were or should have been known to the legal representative at the time it was set,

that amount ceases to be payable under the agreement, unless the court is satisfied that it should continue to be so payable, and

(c) if—

(i) sub-paragraph (b) does not apply, and

(ii) the legal representative agrees with any person liable as a result of the proceedings to pay fees subject to the percentage increase that a lower amount than the amount payable in accordance with the conditional fee agreement is to be paid instead,

the amount payable under the conditional fee agreement in respect of those fees shall be reduced accordingly, unless the court is satisfied that the full amount should continue to be payable under it.

(3) In this regulation 'percentage increase' means the percentage by which the amount of the fees which would be payable if the agreement were not a conditional fee agreement is to be increased under the agreement.

4 INFORMATION TO BE GIVEN BEFORE CONDITIONAL FEE AGREEMENTS MADE

(1) Before a conditional fee agreement is made the legal representative must—

(a) inform the client about the following matters, and

(b) if the client requires any further explanation, advice or other information about any of those matters, provide such further explanation, advice or other information about them as the client may reasonably require.

(2) Those matters are—

(a) the circumstances in which the client may be liable to pay the costs of the legal representative in accordance with the agreement,

(b) the circumstances in which the client may seek assessment of the fees and expenses of the legal representative and the procedure for doing so,

(c) whether the legal representative considers that the client's risk of incurring liability for costs in respect of the proceedings to which an agreement relates is insured against under an existing contract of insurance,

(d) whether other methods of financing those costs are available, and, if so, how they apply to the client and the proceedings in question,

(e) whether the legal representative considers that any particular method or methods of financing any or all of those costs is appropriate and, if he considers that a contract of insurance is appropriate or recommends a particular such contract—

(i) his reasons for doing so, and

(ii) whether he has an interest in doing so.

(3) Before a conditional fee agreement is made the legal representative must explain its effect to the client.

(4) In the case of an agreement where—

(a) the legal representative is a body to which section 30 of the Access to Justice Act 1999 (recovery where the body undertakes to meet costs liabilities) applies, and

(b) there are no circumstances in which the client may be liable to pay any costs in respect of the proceedings,

paragraph (1) does not apply.

(5) Information required to be given under paragraph (1) about the matters in paragraph (2)(a) to (d) must be given orally (whether or not it is also given in writing), but information required to be so given about the matters in paragraph (2)(e) and the explanation required by paragraph (3) must be given both orally and in writing.

(6) This regulation does not apply in the case of an agreement between a legal representative and an additional legal representative.

5 FORM OF AGREEMENT

(1) A conditional fee agreement must be signed by the client and the legal representative.

(2) This regulation does not apply in the case of an agreement between a legal representative and an additional legal representative.

6 AMENDMENT OF AGREEMENT

Where an agreement is amended to cover further proceedings or parts of them—

(a) regulations 2, 3 and 5 apply to the amended agreement as if it were a fresh agreement made at the time of the amendment, and

(b) the obligations under regulation 4 apply in relation to the amendments in so far as they affect the matters mentioned in that regulation.

1. REGULATION 1

Regulation 1 includes in the definition of 'client' a person who is liable to pay for litigation services under a conditional fee agreement, for example an insurance company or trade union. The same regulation specifies that a 'legal representative' is the person providing the advocacy or litigation services – a definition of considerable importance when applying the requirements to provide information to clients.

Section 58(1) of the Courts and Legal Services Act 1990 provides that a conditional fee agreement (of any kind) shall not be unenforceable if it satisfies certain conditions and regulations 2 and 3 set out those conditions.

2. REGULATION 2

Regulation 2 applies to all conditional fee agreements and requires each of them to specify:

(a) The proceedings, or parts of them, to which it relates and particularly whether it relates to any counterclaim or proceedings for enforcement.

(b) The circumstances in which the legal representative's fees and expenses, or part of them are payable. In other words, what is a 'win'?

It may be appropriate when engaging the services of a stallion to include a provision 'no foal, no fee', but can the equivalent be applied to the services of a lawyer? A foal can readily be identified, but what is a 'win'? It is rare for any litigant to realise his maximum expectation. The majority of actions are compromised at something less than the optimum and it is a fortunate claimant who recovers everything he is seeking at a trial. 'No-win, no-fee' is an attractive sound-bite, but it is too simplistic. In the House of Lords, the Lord Chancellor warned that 'it would be wise' for lawyers and clients to discuss at the outset the likely proceeds from the enterprise and that 'it might be possible to meet the point by putting in some requirement about the situation that should obtain with regard to the net amount that the client could expect to recover as a measure of success in terms of the agreement'. Quantifying a personal injury claim at the outset for the purposes of a conditional fee agreement is a daunting prospect but, in any event, a win (however defined) is surely not enough. What if none, or only part of, the damages awarded and between-the-parties costs are recovered because, for example, the defendant is, or becomes, insolvent? Unless the formula is 'no recovery, no pay' the empty-handed client will have nothing to pay with. The lawyers will be entitled to their costs and success fee, so the client will, in fact, be substantially worse off than if he had lost the action! And what effect is a successful counterclaim, perhaps arising out of an allegation of contributory negligence, to have on the specified circumstances? The Law Society's Model CFA for Personal Injury defines a win in terms only of a final decision on the claim in the client's favour. Until the indemnity principle is removed it is difficult to see how there can be a definition of 'win' in terms of actual recovery. Some argue that the lawyer is not a guarantor of the solvency of the client's opponent and is entitled to his success fee whether or not the judgment is paid. But surely the lawyer is being rewarded for taking the risk, which includes the risk of the client not recovering his award – if not where is the sharing of risk?

(c) What payment is due, if any, for only partial success; or on termination of the agreement for any reason, for example the failure of the client to co-operate, or if his evidence has been fabricated?

(d) The amount of the fees payable or the method used to calculate them, and whether they are capped with reference to the damages. It is surprising to find a reference to such a limit in respect of a non-success fee agreement. When conditional fee agreements were first introduced there was concern that a 100% success fee might swallow up most or all of the damages leading to a justifiable public outcry. To avoid this the Law Society recommended a cap on the uplift of 25% of the amount recovered, while the Bar suggested a modest 10%. Now that success fees are recoverable between the parties the cap has gone and the Law Society model agreement provides *'If you win your claim, you pay our basic charges, our disbursements, and a success fee. The amount of these is not based on or limited by the damages.'* Indeed the indemnity principle would again cause problems were a CFA to limit the success fee to a percentage of damages.

The agreement must also confirm that the information required by the regulation has been supplied to the client.

3. REGULATION 3

Regulation 3 contains the extra requirements for conditional fee agreements which provide for a success fee. These could be tricky. The agreement must give the reasons for setting the success fee at the agreed percentage, with a break-down showing what part relates to the risk and what, if any, to the solicitor funding the litigation, because the latter element is not recoverable between the parties. What if the reasons are that the client is extremely demanding or difficult, or that he and his witnesses are of doubtful credibility? That will require tactful wording, but you cannot afford to be too tactful because the reasons given will have to be relied upon if the percentage increase is challenged by the paying party. The client must consent in the agreement to the reasons being disclosed if required by the court, which, of course, it will do if there is a dispute. The agreement must also provide that any between-the-parties reduction of the success fee shall be binding on the solicitor unless the court orders otherwise. The court will only 'order otherwise' if the solicitor can show that there were exceptional circumstances. The conflict between a solicitor and his client could not be more starkly illustrated. The client is unlikely to have been separately advised before entering into the agreement; will he be separately advised when the solicitor seeks to recover the shortfall? For the procedure see CPR Rule 44.16 on p 529.

4. REGULATION 4

Regulation 4 contains the information to be given to clients before they enter into a conditional fee agreement. It is important to appreciate that this provision applies to all clients entering into a conditional fee agreement, including family, friends and employees. The temptation to avoid going to the trouble of doing this must be firmly resisted because on a dispute the solicitor must be able to prove compliance. The regulation contains the novel requirement that four elements of information, while they may be given in writing, must also be given *orally*: what is a win; the right to a detailed assessment; has the client pre-purchased legal expenses insurance and what other methods of financing the costs are available. All of this must be given by the 'legal representative' which means the 'person' providing the advocacy or litigation services. Can it be assumed that 'person' means the firm or is it to be taken literally to mean the physical being(s) who will conduct the case? It makes for difficulty in the use of agents, whether or not they are solicitors. The solicitor's views and advice on any particular method of funding and insurance together with an explanation of the effect of the agreement must be given to the client both *orally* and *in writing*. There must clearly be some careful drafting and record keeping (perhaps even literally an audio recording of the oral advice, or perhaps a tape recording to be played to each client?!) to ensure that compliance with these provisions can be proved when necessary.

5. REGULATION 5

Regulation 5 requires the agreement to be signed by both parties except between one legal representative and an additional legal representative. This usually means counsel although it includes any other person providing advocacy or litigation services such as a solicitor advocate.

6. THE LAW SOCIETY'S MODEL CONDITIONAL FEE AGREEMENT

I am grateful to the Law Society for permission to reproduce their model, or as they modestly describe it 'sample', conditional fee agreement for personal injury actions. It is not, of course, mandatory but it complies with all the statutory requirements and you deviate from it at your own risk. This was illustrated in *Woods v Chaleff* [2002] NLJR 1276 where Master Rogers held that failure to comply with regs 3(d) and 4(1) and (2) resulted in a CFA being unenforceable because they are mandatory. The provisions of CPR Rule 3.9 enabling a judge to grant relief from sanctions could not save it because the rule applied to the CPR and not to a statutory instrument. This is the new war zone. A district judge in Peterborough has held that solicitors on the Accident Group panel cannot recover under a CFA because the prescribed information was not given to the client by a solicitor but on a home visit by an employee of an associated company. In Middlesbrough a district judge has held that the pre-2000 Law Society model CFA (*not* the one on this page, below) was not binding because it failed to specify that all the costs, not just the success fee, were limited by reference to the amount awarded. Meanwhile in Macclesfield County Court it has been held that the prescribed written explanation of a CFA must be in a document separate from the CFA itself and, for good measure, that solicitors must make it clear when they do not have an interest in the ATE insurance premium, as well as when they do. All are going to appeal, and the senior costs judge is hearing urgent test cases, but be warned and beware.

CONDITIONAL FEE AGREEMENT

For use in personal injury cases, but not clinical negligence
This agreement is a binding legal contract between you and your solicitor/s. Before you sign, please read everything carefully.
Words like 'our disbursements', 'basic charges', 'win' and 'lose' are explained in condition 3 of the Law Society Conditions which you should also read carefully.
Agreement date
[..]
I/We, the solicitor/s [..]
You, the client [..]

WHAT IS COVERED BY THIS AGREEMENT

Your claim against [..] for damages for personal injury suffered on [..].
Any appeal by your opponent.
Any appeal you make against an interim order during the proceedings.
Any proceedings you take to enforce a judgment, order or agreement.

WHAT IS NOT COVERED BY THIS AGREEMENT

Any counterclaim against you.
Any appeal you make against the final judgment order.

Paying us

If you win your claim, you pay our basic charges, our disbursements and a success fee. The amount of these is not based on or limited by the damages. You are entitled to seek recovery from your opponent of part or all of our basic charges, our disbursements, a success fee and insurance premium. Please also see conditions 4 and 6.

It may be that your opponent makes a Part 36 offer or payment which you reject and, on our advice, your claim for damages goes ahead to trial where you recover damages that are less than that offer or payment. We will not add our success fee to the basic charges for the work done after we received notice of the offer or payment.

(Note that some insurers require an alternative clause for Part 36 which provides that no fee at all will be charged for the work after the time the offer could have been accepted. This protects the client's damages but arguably increases the pressure to settle.)

If you receive interim damages, we may require you to pay our disbursements at that point and a reasonable amount for our future disbursements.

If you receive provisional damages, we are entitled to payment of our basic charges our disbursements and success fee at that point.

If you win but on the way lose an interim hearing, you may be required to pay your opponent's charges of that hearing. Please see conditions 3(h) and 5.

If on the way to winning or losing you win an interim hearing, then we are entitled to payment of our basic charges and disbursements related to that hearing together with a success fee on those charges if you win overall.

If you lose, you pay your opponent's charges and disbursements. You may be able to take out an insurance policy against this risk. Please also see conditions 3(j) and 5. If you lose, you do not pay our charges but we may require you to pay our disbursements.

If you end this agreement before you win or lose, you pay our basic charges. If you go on to win, you pay a success fee. Please also see condition 7(a).

We may end this agreement before you win or lose. Please also see condition 7(b) for details.

Basic charges

These are for work done from now until this agreement ends.

HOW WE CALCULATE OUR BASIC CHARGES

These are calculated for each hour engaged on your matter [from now until the review date on [...] ...]. Routine letters and telephone calls will be charged as units of one tenth of an hour. Other letters and telephone calls will be charged on a time basis. The hourly rates are:
Solicitors with over four years' experience after qualification
£ [....................]
Other solicitors and legal executives and other staff of equivalent experience
£ [....................]
Trainee solicitors and other staff of equivalent experience
£ [....................]
[We will review the hourly rate on the review date and on each anniversary of the review date. We will not increase the rate by more than the rise in the Retail Prices Index and will notify you of the increased rate in writing.]

Success fee

This is [..........]% of our basic charges

The reasons for calculating the success fee at this level are set out in Schedule 1 to this agreement.

You cannot recover from your opponent the part of the success fee that relates to the cost to us of postponing receipt of our charges and disbursements (as set out at paragraphs (a) and (b) at Schedule 1). This part of the success fee remains payable by you.

Value added tax (VAT)

We add VAT, at the rate (now [...............]%) that applies when the work is done, to the total of the basic charges and success fee.

Law Society Conditions

The Law Society Conditions are attached because they are part of this agreement. Any amendments or additions to them will apply to you. You should read the conditions carefully and ask us about anything you find unclear.

Other points

Immediately before you signed this agreement, we verbally explained to you the effect of this agreement and in particular the following:

(a) the circumstances in which you may be liable to pay our disbursements and charges;

(b) the circumstances in which you may seek assessment of our charges and disbursements and the procedure for doing so;

(c) whether we consider that your risk of becoming liable for any costs in these proceedings is insured under an existing contract of insurance;

(d) other methods of financing those costs, including private funding, Community Legal Service funding, legal expenses insurance, trade union funding;

(e) (i) In all the circumstances, on the information currently available to us, we believe that a contract of insurance with [......................................] is appropriate. Detailed reasons for this are set out in Schedule 2.

(ii) In any event, we believe it is desirable for you to insure your opponent's charges and disbursements in case you lose.

(iii) We confirm that we do not have an interest in recommending this particular insurance agreement.

SIGNATURES

Signed for the solicitor/s
Signed by the client
I confirm that my solicitor has verbally explained to me the matters in paragraphs (a) to (e) under 'Other points' above.
Signed .... (Client)
I specifically confirm that I verbally explained to the client the matters in paragraphs (a) to (e) under 'Other points' and confirm the matters at (e) in writing in Schedule 2.
Signed .... (Solicitors)
This agreement complies with the Conditional Fee Agreements Regulations 2000 (SI 2000 No. 692).

Schedule 1 The Success Fee

The success fee is set at [..........]% of basic charges and cannot be more than 100% of the basic charges.
The percentage reflects the following:

(a) the fact that if you win we will not be paid our basic charges until the end of the claim;

(b) our arrangements with you about paying disbursements;

(c) the fact that if you lose, we will not earn anything;

(d) our assessment of the risks of your case. These include the following:

(e) any other appropriate matters.

The matters set out at paragraphs (a) and (b) above together make up [. ... ..]% of the increase on basic charges. The matters at paragraphs (c), (d) [and (e)] make up [..........]% of the increase on basic charges. So the total success fee is [..........]% as stated above.

Schedule 2 The Insurance Policy

In all the circumstances and on the information currently available to us, we believe, that a contract of insurance with [....................] is appropriate to cover your opponent's charges and disbursements in case you lose.
This is because
We are not, however, insurance brokers and cannot give advice on all products which may be available.

Law Society Conditions

1. Our responsibilities

We must:
always act in your best interests, subject to our duty to the court;
explain to you the risks and benefits of taking legal action;
give you our best advice about whether to accept any offer of settlement;
give you the best information possible about the likely costs of your claim for damages.

2. Your responsibilities

You must:
give us instructions that allow us to do our work properly;
not ask us to work in an improper or unreasonable way;
not deliberately mislead us;
co-operate with us;
go to any medical or expert examination or court hearing.

3. Explanation of words used

(a) Advocacy
Appearing for you at court hearings.

(b) Basic charges
Our charges for the legal work we do on your claim for damages.

(c) Claim
Your demand for damages for personal injury whether or not court proceedings are issued.

(d) Counterclaim
A claim that your opponent makes against you in response to your claim.

(e) Damages
Money that you win whether by a court decision or settlement.

(f) Our disbursements
Payment we make on your behalf such as:
court fees;
experts' fees;
accident report fees;
travelling expenses.

(g) Interim damages
Money that a court says your opponent must pay or your opponent agrees to pay while waiting for a settlement or the court's final decision.

(h) Interim hearing
A court hearing that is not final.

(i) Lien
Our right to keep all papers, documents, money or other property held on your behalf until all money due to us is paid. A lien may be applied after this agreement ends.

(j) Lose
The court has dismissed your claim or you have stopped it on our advice.

(k) Part 36 offers or payments
An offer to settle your claim made in accordance with Part 36 of the Civil Procedure Rules.

(l) Provisional damages
Money that a court says your opponent must pay or your opponent agrees to pay, on the basis that you will be able to go back to court at a future date for further damages if:
you develop a serious disease; or

your condition deteriorates;
in a way that has been proved or admitted to be linked to your personal injury claim.

(m) Success fee
The percentage of basic charges that we add to your bill if you win your claim for damages and that we will seek to recover from your opponent.

(n) Win
Your claim for damages is finally decided in your favour, whether by a court decision or an agreement to pay you damages. 'Finally' means that your opponent:
is not allowed to appeal against the court decision; or
has not appealed in time; or
has lost any appeal.

4. What happens if you win?

If you win:

You are then liable to pay all our basic charges, our disbursements and success fee – please see condition 3(n).

Normally, you will be entitled to recover part or all of our basic charges, our disbursements and success fee from your opponent.

If you and your opponent cannot agree the amount, the court will decide how much you can recover. If the amount agreed or allowed by the court does not cover all our basic charges and our disbursements, then you pay the difference.

You will not be entitled to recover from your opponent the part of the success fee that relates to the cost to us of postponing receipt of our charges and our disbursements. This remains payable by you.

You agree that after winning, the reasons for setting the success fee at the amount stated may be disclosed:
(i) to the court and any other person required by the court;
(ii) to your opponent in order to gain his or her agreement to pay the success fee.

If the court carries out an assessment and disallows any of the success fee percentage because it is unreasonable in view of what we knew or should have known when it was agreed, then that amount ceases to be payable unless the court is satisfied that it should continue to be payable.

If we agree with your opponent that the success fee is to be paid at a lower percentage than is set out in this agreement, then the success fee percentage will be reduced accordingly unless the court is satisfied that the full amount is payable.

It may happen that your opponent makes an offer that includes payment of our basic charges and a success fee. If so, unless we consent, you agree not to tell us to accept the offer if it includes payment of the success fee at a lower rate than is set out in this agreement.

If your opponent is receiving Community Legal Service funding, we are unlikely to get any money from him or her. So if this happens, you have to pay us our basic charges, disbursements and success fee.

You remain ultimately responsible for paying our success fee.

You agree to pay into a designated account any cheque received by you or by us from your opponent and made payable to you. Out of the money, you agree to let us take the balance of the basic charges; success fee; insurance premium; our remaining disbursements; and VAT. You take the rest.

We are allowed to keep any interest your opponent pays on the charges.

Payment for advocacy is explained in condition 6.

IF YOUR OPPONENT FAILS TO PAY

If your opponent does not pay any damages or charges owed to you, we have the right to take recovery action in your name to enforce a judgment, order or agreement. The charges of this action become part of the basic charges.

5. What happens if you lose?

If you lose, you do not have to pay any of our basic charges or success fee.
You do have to pay:
us for our disbursements;
your opponent's legal charges and disbursements.
If you are insured against payment of these amounts by your insurance policy, we will make a claim on your behalf and receive any resulting payment in your name. We will give you a statement of account for all money received and paid out.
If your opponent pays the charges of any hearing, they belong to us.
Payment for advocacy is dealt with in condition 6.

6. Payment for advocacy

The cost of advocacy and any other work by us, or by any solicitor agent on our behalf, forms part of our basic charges. We shall discuss with you the identity of any barrister instructed, and the arrangements made for payment.

BARRISTERS WHO HAVE A CONDITIONAL FEE AGREEMENT WITH US

If you win, you are normally entitled to recover their fee and success fee from your opponent. The barrister's success fee is shown in the separate conditional fee agreement we make with the barrister. We will discuss the barrister's success fee with you before we instruct him or her. If you lose, you pay the barrister nothing.

BARRISTERS WHO DO NOT HAVE A CONDITIONAL FEE AGREEMENT WITH US

If you win, then you will normally be entitled to recover all or part of their fee from your opponent. If you lose, then you must pay their fee.

7. What happens when this agreement ends before your claim for damages ends?

(A) PAYING US IF YOU END THIS AGREEMENT

You can end the agreement at any time. We then have the right to decide whether you must:

pay our basic charges and our disbursements including barristers' fees when we ask for them; or

pay our basic charges, and our disbursements including barristers' fees and success fees if you go on to win your claim for damages.

(B) PAYING US IF WE END THIS AGREEMENT

(i) We can end this agreement if you do not keep to your responsibilities in condition 2. We then have the right to decide whether you must:
pay our basic charges and our disbursements including barristers' fees when we ask for them; or
pay our basic charges and our disbursements including barristers' fees and success fees if you go on to win your claim for damages.

(ii) We can end this agreement if we believe you are unlikely to win. If this happens, you will only have to pay our disbursements. These will include barristers' fees if the barrister does not have a conditional fee agreement with us.

(iii) We can end this agreement if you reject our opinion about making a settlement with your opponent. You must then:
pay the basic charges and our disbursements, including barristers' fees;
pay the success fee if you go on to win your claim for damages.
If you ask us to get a second opinion from a specialist solicitor outside our firm, we will do so. You pay the cost of a second opinion.

(iv) We can end this agreement if you do not pay your insurance premium when asked to do so.

(c) *DEATH*

This agreement automatically ends if you die before your claim for damages is concluded. We will be entitled to recover our basic charges up to the date of your death from your estate.

If your personal representatives wish to continue your claim for damages, we may offer them a new conditional fee agreement, as long as they agree to pay the success fee on our basic charges from the beginning of the agreement with you.

8. What happens after this agreement ends?

After this agreement ends, we will apply to have our name removed from the record of any court proceedings in which we are acting unless you have another form of funding and ask us to work for you.

We have the right to preserve our lien unless another solicitor working for you undertakes to pay us what we are owed including a success fee if you win.

NOTES FOR ACCIDENT LINE PROTECT CASES

For Accident Line Protect cases, you need to annex the following clause to the agreement

'Accident Line Protect insurance (ALP)

Accident Line Protect is an insurance policy only made available to you by solicitors who have joined the Accident Line Protect scheme.

You agree to pay a premium of £[..............................] for Accident Line Protect Insurance when you sign this agreement. We undertake to send this to the broker on your behalf. If you lose after proceedings have been issued, Accident Line Protect will cover our disbursements and your opponent's charges and disbursements. It will not cover fees to your barristers or advocates. The maximum cover is £100,000.

If this agreement ends before your claim for damages ends, Accident Line Protect ends automatically at the same time.'

7. SEMANTIC NOTE

'The Conditional Fee Agreement Regulations 2000 require a solicitor to give certain information to the client "orally" (whether or not also in writing). I welcomed this appropriate use of the word "orally" and was dismayed when the Law Society replaced it with the word "verbally" in their model conditional fee agreement. When I remonstrated, they were unrepentant and said they had substituted the word in order to "receive Clear English accreditation". They referred to the Concise OED definition that

> "verbal meant not in writing", whilst my Shorter OED informs me that since at least 1637 "verbally" has meant "in speech, as contrasted with writing".
>
> I was surprised to discover that we now have two words doing the work of one. Is "oral" now to be used only in the context of food, drink, and medicine? Are we henceforth to have verbal examinations, or if the words are to be interchangeable, accusations that the police oralled the accused?'

Letter from me published in The Times, *26 July 2000*

This, I hasten to add, was not a criticism of the Law Society but of the verbal police who required the word 'oral' to be changed. The requirement of an oral explanation was no doubt influenced by the findings of the University of Westminster in their report 'Nothing to Lose'. The research found widespread confusion among clients on fundamental matters, such as a failure to understand that solicitors were only paid if they won; how solicitors calculated success fees and that 'no-win, no-fee' was a misnomer if the client had to pay the after-the-event insurance premium and disbursements, which could include experts' fees. Commenting on the report, David Lock, the then Parliamentary Secretary at the LCD, said the research showed it was 'absolutely crucial' that not only solicitors understood the intricacies of conditional fee agreements but their clients did as well. The clients approached solicitors not in a 'gentle, balanced and stable sense of mind', but when there was a crisis in their lives'. He commented that the reason why lawyers were paid more than bus drivers was their ability to put the interests of their clients above their own, although he did not explain the alleged conflict of interest between bus drivers and their passengers.

PART 5 THE RULES AND PRACTICE DIRECTIONS

Here are the provisions relating exclusively to conditional fee agreements with their supplementary practice directions:

1. DEFINITIONS

CPR Rule 43.2 had sub-paragraphs (k) to (o) added to the list of definitions. To save you looking in Chapter 9, here it is again:

CPR RULE 43.2 DEFINITIONS AND APPLICATION

(1) In Parts 44 to 48, unless the context otherwise requires—

(a) 'costs' includes fees, charges, disbursements, expenses, remuneration, reimbursement allowed to a litigant in person under rule 48.6 , any additional liability incurred under a funding arrangement and any fee or reward charged by a lay representative for acting on behalf of a party in proceedings allocated to the small claims track;

(b) 'costs judge' means a taxing master of the Supreme Court;

(c) 'costs officer' means—

(i) a costs judge;

(ii) a district judge; and

(iii) an authorised court officer;

(d) 'authorised court officer' means any officer of—

(i) a county court;

(ii) a district registry;

(iii) the Principal Registry of the Family Division; or
(iv) the Supreme Court Costs Office;
whom the Lord Chancellor has authorised to assess costs.

(e) 'fund' includes any estate or property held for the benefit of any person or class of person and any fund to which a trustee or personal representative is entitled in his capacity as such;
(f) 'receiving party' means a party entitled to be paid costs;
(g) 'paying party' means a party liable to pay costs;
(h) 'assisted person' means an assisted person within the statutory provisions relating to legal aid;
(i) 'LSC funded client' means an individual who receives services funded by the Legal Services Commission as part of the Community Legal Service within the meaning of Part I of the Access to Justice Act 1999;
(j) 'fixed costs' means the amounts which are to be allowed in respect of solicitors' charges in the circumstances set out in Part 45.
(k) 'funding arrangement' means an arrangement where a person has—
  (i) entered into a conditional fee agreement or a collective conditional fee agreement which provides for a success fee within the meaning of section 58(2) of the Courts and Legal Services Act 1990;
  (ii) taken out an insurance policy to which section 29 of the Access to Justice Act 1999 (recovery of insurance premiums by way of costs) applies; or
  (iii) made an agreement with a membership organisation to meet his legal costs;
(l) 'percentage increase' means the percentage by which the amount of a legal representative's fee can be increased in accordance with a conditional fee agreement which provides for a success fee;
(m) 'insurance premium' means a sum of money paid or payable for insurance against the risk of incurring a costs liability in the proceedings, taken out after the event that is the subject matter of the claim;
(n) 'membership organisation' means a body prescribed for the purposes of section 30 of the Access to Justice Act 1999 (recovery where body undertakes to meet costs liabilities); and
(o) 'additional liability' means the percentage increase, the insurance premium, or the additional amount in respect of provision made by a membership organisation, as the case may be.

(The Conditional Fee Agreements Regulations 2000, the Collective Conditional Fee Agreements 2000 and the Access to Justice (Membership Organisations) Regulations 2000 contain further provisions about conditional fee agreements and arrangements to meet costs liabilities)

(2) The costs to which Parts 44 to 48 apply include—
(a) the following costs where those costs may be assessed by the court—
  (i) costs of proceedings before an arbitrator or umpire;
  (ii) costs of proceedings before a tribunal or other statutory body; and
  (iii) costs payable by a client to his solicitor; and
(b) costs which are payable by one party to another party under the terms of a contract, where the court makes an order for an assessment of those costs.

SECTION 2: PRACTICE DIRECTION SUPPLEMENTING CPR RULE 43.2

2.1 Where the court makes an order for costs and the receiving party has entered into a funding arrangement as defined in rule 43.2, the costs payable by the paying party include any additional liability (also defined in rule 43.2) unless the court orders otherwise.

2.2 In the following paragraphs—

'funding arrangement', 'percentage increase', 'insurance premium', 'membership organisation' and 'additional liability' have the meanings given to them by rule 43.2 .

** A 'conditional fee agreement' is an agreement with a person providing advocacy or litigation services which provides for his fees and expenses, or part of them, to be payable only in specified circumstances, whether or not it provides for a success fee as mentioned in section 58(2)(b) of the Courts and Legal Services Act 1990.*

'base costs' means costs other than the amount of any additional liability.

2.3 Rule 44.3A(1) provides that the court will not assess any additional liability until the conclusion of the proceedings or the part of the proceedings to which the funding arrangement relates. (As to the time when detailed assessment may be carried out see paragraph 27.1 below).

2.4 For the purposes of the following paragraphs of this practice direction and rule 44.3A proceedings are concluded when the court has finally determined the matters in issue in the claim, whether or not there is an appeal. The making of an award of provisional damages under Part 41 will also be treated as a final determination of the matters in issue.

2.5 The court may order or the parties may agree in writing that, although the proceedings are continuing, they will nevertheless be treated as concluded.

'Additional liability' is the compendium description of a success fee, an after-the-event insurance premium, or both. Paragraph 2.2 defines costs other than the amount of any additional liability as 'base costs', while the Law Society model agreement refers to them as 'basic charges'. It is important not to confuse either definition with 'direct cost', which is the basic cost of doing the work before adding a profit mark-up.

2. ASSESSMENT

CPR RULE 44.3A COSTS ORDERS RELATING TO FUNDING ARRANGEMENTS

(1) The court will not assess any additional liability until the conclusion of the proceedings, or the part of the proceedings, to which the funding arrangement relates.

('Funding arrangement' and 'additional liability' are defined in rule 43.2)

(2) At the conclusion of the proceedings, or the part of the proceedings, to which the funding arrangement relates the court may—

- (a) make a summary assessment of all the costs, including any additional liability;
- (b) make an order for detailed assessment of the additional liability but make a summary assessment of the other costs; or
- (c) make an order for detailed assessment of all the costs.

(Part 47 sets out the procedure for the detailed assessment of costs)

SECTION 9: PRACTICE DIRECTION SUPPLEMENTING CPR RULE 44.3A

9.1 Under an order for payment of 'costs' the costs payable will include an additional liability incurred under a funding arrangement.

9.2

(1) If before the conclusion of the proceedings the court carries out a summary assessment of the base costs it may identify separately the amount allowed in respect of: solicitors' charges; counsels' fees; other

disbursements; and any value added tax (VAT). (Sections 13 and 14 of this Practice Direction deal with summary assessment.)

(2) If an order for the base costs of a previous application or hearing did not identify separately the amounts allowed for solicitor's charges, counsel's fees and other disbursements, a court which later makes an assessment of an additional liability may apportion the base costs previously ordered.

This provision is necessary because the barrister and the solicitor may have agreed different success fees. Even where there is not an additional liability it is good practice for the judge to separately assess the barrister's and solicitor's awards, so that it is clear what has been allowed to each.

3. RECOVERY

CPR RULE 44.3B LIMITS ON RECOVERY UNDER FUNDING ARRANGEMENTS

(1) A party may not recover as an additional liability—

(a) any proportion of the percentage increase relating to the cost to the legal representative of the postponement of the payment of his fees and expenses;

(b) any provision made by a membership organisation which exceeds the likely cost to that party of the premium of an insurance policy against the risk of incurring a liability to pay the costs of other parties to the proceedings;

(c) any additional liability for any period in the proceedings during which he failed to provide information about a funding arrangement in accordance with a rule, practice direction or court order;

(d) any percentage increase where a party has failed to comply with—

(i) a requirement in the costs practice direction; or

(ii) a court order,

to disclose in any assessment proceedings the reasons for setting the percentage increase at the level stated in the conditional fee agreement.

(2) This rule does not apply in an assessment under rule 48.9 (assessment of a solicitor's bill to his client).

(Rule 3.9 sets out the circumstances the court will consider on an application for relief from a sanction for failure to comply with any rule, practice direction or court order)

SECTION 10: PRACTICE DIRECTION SUPPLEMENTING CPR RULE 44.3B

10.1 In a case to which rule 44.3B(1)(c) or (d) applies the party in default may apply for relief from the sanction. He should do so as quickly as possible after he becomes aware of the default. An application, supported by evidence, should be made under Part 23 to a costs judge or district judge of the court which is dealing with the case. (Attention is drawn to rules 3.8 and 3.9 which deal with sanctions and relief from sanctions).

10.2 Where the amount of any percentage increase recoverable by counsel may be affected by the outcome of the application, the solicitor issuing the application must serve on counsel a copy of the application notice and notice of the hearing as soon as practicable and in any event at least 2 days before the hearing. Counsel may make written submissions or may attend and make oral submissions at the hearing. (Paragraph 1.4 contains definitions of the terms 'counsel' and 'solicitor'.)

Any element of a success fee which relates to the funding of the litigation by the solicitor because of his inability to receive payments on account is not recoverable between parties. It is recoverable from the client and must therefore be shown separately.

4. FACTORS TO BE TAKEN INTO ACCOUNT IN DECIDING THE AMOUNT OF COSTS

SECTION 11: PRACTICE DIRECTION SUPPLEMENTING CPR RULE 44.5

11.1 In applying the test of proportionality the court will have regard to rule 1.1(2)(c). The relationship between the total of the costs incurred and the financial value of the claim may not be a reliable guide. A fixed percentage cannot be applied in all cases to the value of the claim in order to ascertain whether or not the costs are proportionate.

11.2 In any proceedings there will be costs which will inevitably be incurred and which are necessary for the successful conduct of the case. Solicitors are not required to conduct litigation at rates which are uneconomic. Thus in a modest claim the proportion of costs is likely to be higher than in a large claim, and may even equal or possibly exceed the amount in dispute.

11.3 Where a trial takes place, the time taken by the court in dealing with a particular issue may not be an accurate guide to the amount of time properly spent by the legal or other representatives in preparation for the trial of that issue.

11.4 Where a party has entered into a funding arrangement the costs claimed may, subject to rule 44.3B include an additional liability.

11.5 In deciding whether the costs claimed are reasonable and (on a standard basis assessment) proportionate, the court will consider the amount of any additional liability separately from the base costs.

11.6 In deciding whether the base costs are reasonable and (if relevant) proportionate the court will consider the factors set out in rule 44.5.

11.7 Subject to paragraph 17.8(2), when the court is considering the factors to be taken into account in assessing an additional liability, it will have regard to the facts and circumstances as they reasonably appeared to the solicitor or counsel when the funding arrangement was entered into and at the time of any variation of the arrangement.

11.8

(1) In deciding whether a percentage increase is reasonable relevant factors to be taken into account may include:—
   - *(a) the risk that the circumstances in which the costs, fees or expenses would be payable might or might not occur;*
   - *(b) the legal representative's liability for any disbursements;*
   - *(c) what other methods of financing the costs were available to the receiving party.*

(2) The court has the power, when considering whether a percentage increase is reasonable, to allow different percentages for different items of costs or for different periods during which costs were incurred.

11.9 A percentage increase will not be reduced simply on the ground that, when added to base costs which are reasonable and (where relevant) proportionate, the total appears disproportionate.

11.10 In deciding whether the cost of insurance cover is reasonable, relevant factors to be taken into account include:

(1) where the insurance cover is not purchased in support of a conditional fee agreement with a success fee, how its cost compares with the likely cost of funding the case with a conditional fee agreement with a success fee and supporting insurance cover;

(2) the level and extent of the cover provided;
(3) the availability of any pre-existing insurance cover;
(4) whether any part of the premium would be rebated in the event of early settlement;
(5) the amount of commission payable to the receiving party or his legal representatives or other agents.

11.11 Where the court is considering a provision made by a membership organisation, rule 44.3B(1)(b) provides that any such provision which exceeds the likely cost to the receiving party of the premium of an insurance policy against the risk of incurring a liability to pay the costs of other parties to the proceedings is not recoverable. In such circumstances the court will, when assessing the additional liability, have regard to the factors set out in paragraph 11.10 above, in addition to the factors set out in rule 44.5.

The practice direction has been considerably simplified from the original draft, 14 factors having been reduced to five. Note that a late addition was the amount of any commission included in a premium.

5. INFORMATION

CPR RULE 44.15 PROVIDING INFORMATION ABOUT FUNDING ARRANGEMENTS

(1) A party who seeks to recover an additional liability must provide information about the funding arrangement to the court and to other parties as required by a rule, practice direction or court order.
(2) Where the funding arrangement has changed, and the information a party has previously provided in accordance with paragraph (1) is no longer accurate, that party must file notice of the change and serve it on all other parties within 7 days.
(3) Where paragraph (2) applies, and a party has already filed—
(a) an allocation questionnaire; or
(b) a pre-trial check list (listing questionnaire),
he must file and serve a new estimate of costs with the notice.
(The costs practice direction sets out—
the information to be provided when a party issues or responds to a claim form, files an allocation questionnaire, a pre-trial check list, and a claim for costs;
the meaning of estimate of costs and the information required in it) (Rule 44.3B sets out situations where a party will not recover a sum representing any additional liability)

SECTION 19: PRACTICE DIRECTION SUPPLEMENTING CPR RULE 44.15

19.1
(1) A party who wishes to claim an additional liability in respect of a funding arrangement must give any other party information about that claim if he is to recover the additional liability. There is no requirement to specify the amount of the additional liability separately nor to state how it is calculated until it falls to be assessed. That principle is reflected in rules 44.3A and 44.15, in the following paragraphs and in Sections 6, 13, 14 and 31 of this Practice Direction. Section 6 deals with estimates of costs, Sections 13 and 14 deal with summary assessment and Section 31 deals with detailed assessment.

(2) In the following paragraphs a party who has entered into a funding arrangement is treated as a person who intends to recover a sum representing an additional liability by way of costs.

(3) Attention is drawn to paragraph 57.9 of this Practice Direction which sets out time limits for the provision of information where a funding arrangement is entered into between 31 March and 2 July 2000 and proceedings relevant to that arrangement are commenced before 3 July 2000.

Method of giving information

19.2

(1) In this paragraph, 'claim form' includes petition and application notice, and the notice of funding to be filed or served is a notice containing the information set out in Form N251.

(2)

(a) A claimant who has entered into a funding arrangement before starting the proceedings to which it relates must provide information to the court by filing the notice when he issues the claim form.

(b) He must provide information to every other party by serving the notice. If he serves the claim form himself he must serve the notice with the claim form. If the court is to serve the claim form, the court will also serve the notice if the claimant provides it with sufficient copies for service.

(3) A defendant who has entered into a funding arrangement before filing any document

(a) must provide information to the court by filing notice with his first document. A 'first document' may be an acknowledgement of service, a defence, or any other document, such as an application to set aside a default judgment;

(b) must provide information to every party by serving notice. If he serves his first document himself he must serve the notice with that document. If the court is to serve his first document the court will also serve the notice if the defendant provides it with sufficient copies for service.

(4) In all other circumstances a party must file and serve notice within 7 days of entering into the funding arrangement concerned.

(5) There is no requirement in this Practice Direction for the provision of information about funding arrangements before the commencement of proceedings. Such provision is however recommended and may be required by a pre-action protocol.

Notice of change of information

19.3

(1) Rule 44.15 imposes a duty on a party to give notice of change if the information he has previously provided is no longer accurate. To comply he must file and serve notice containing the information set out in Form N251. Rule 44.15(3) may impose other duties in relation to new estimates of costs.

(2) Further notification need not be provided where a party has already given notice:

(a) that he has entered into a conditional fee agreement with a legal representative and during the currency of that agreement either of them enters into another such agreement with an additional legal representative; or

(b) of some insurance cover, unless that cover is cancelled or unless new cover is taken out with a different insurer.

(3) Part 6 applies to the service of notices.

(4) The notice must be signed by the party or by his legal representative.

Information which must be provided

19.4

(1) Unless the court otherwise orders, a party who is required to supply information about a funding arrangement must state whether he has— entered into a conditional fee agreement which provides for a success fee within the meaning of section 58(2) of the Courts and Legal Services Act 1990;
taken out an insurance policy to which section 29 of the Access to Justice Act 1999 applies;
made an arrangement with a body which is prescribed for the purpose of section 30 of that Act;
or more than one of these.

(2) Where the funding arrangement is a conditional fee agreement, the party must state the date of the agreement and identify the claim or claims to which it relates (including Part 20 claims if any).

(3) Where the funding arrangement is an insurance policy the party must state the name of the insurer, the date of the policy and must identify the claim or claims to which it relates (including Part 20 claims if any).

(4) Where the funding arrangement is by way of an arrangement with a relevant body the party must state the name of the body and set out the date and terms of the undertaking it has given and must identify the claim or claims to which it relates (including Part 20 claims if any).

(5) Where a party has entered into more than one funding arrangement in respect of a claim, for example a conditional fee agreement and an insurance policy, a single notice containing the information set out in Form N251 may contain the required information about both or all of them.

19.5 Where the court makes a Group Litigation Order, the court may give directions as to the extent to which individual parties should provide information in accordance with rule 44.15. (Part 19 deals with Group Litigation Orders.)

This is another section of the practice direction which was drastically altered from the original draft. The concern was that it could be prejudicial to a party if the success fee percentage and insurance premium were revealed to another party during the currency of the litigation. An early draft proposed that the success fee and insurance premium should be fixed at the outset by the court at a between-the-parties hearing. It disappeared after I pointed out the scenario would be the claimant explaining his case had little chance of success and was purely speculative, justifying a 100% success fee, with the defendant contending that the claim was cast iron and certain to succeed, that the defence was only a delaying tactic and therefore no success fee was warranted! The information to be provided has been reduced to a minimum: the date and existence of a conditional fee agreement; the date and existence of after-the-event insurance and the name of the insurer; the name of any trade union or other funding body and the terms of their undertaking together in all cases with an indication of the claim or claims to which the funding relates are all that must be revealed. The amount of the success fee percentage or of the insurance premium does not have to be disclosed until after the final order for costs and any appeal has been disposed of or the time for seeking permission to appeal has expired. Concern has been expressed that the paucity of information to be disclosed defeats the avowed aim of the CPR to provide transparency as to costs throughout the course of the litigation. It is an aspect which will certainly need to be re-addressed if benchmark costs and pre-trial fixed costs on the fast track are to be introduced. If after the time for appeal has expired details of the additional liabilities have been disclosed to the paying party, this would be strong grounds for resisting an application for permission to appeal out of time, and it may therefore be good tactics to pre-empt such an application by making voluntary disclosure as soon as the time for appeal has expired! The prescribed form of notice of funding is on p 557. It is important to note that no success fee is recoverable in respect of any period during which Rule 44.15 has not been complied with.

6. PRACTICE DIRECTION ON PROTOCOLS

INFORMATION ABOUT FUNDING ARRANGEMENTS

4A.1 Where a person enters into a funding arrangement within the meaning of rule 43.2(1)(k) he should inform other potential parties to the claim that he has done so.

4A.2 Paragraph 4A.1 applies to all proceedings whether proceedings to which a pre-action protocol applies or otherwise.

(Rule 44.3B(1)(c) provides that a party may not recover any additional liability for any period in the proceedings during which he failed to provide information about a funding arrangement in accordance with a rule, practice direction or court order.)

It is interesting to note that the practice direction states that it is to apply whether or not there is a relevant protocol. It also lays down a requirement to give notice which is not a requirement of any protocols themselves and it seemingly contradicts the Costs Practice Direction which recommends but expressly does not require pre-issue disclosure. The Civil Procedure Rules only make provision for disclosure at the time of issue. The Protocols Practice Direction applies even where there is no applicable protocol. CPR Rule 44.3B(1)(*c*) should mean early disclosure is made of funding arrangements and perhaps we will even reach the stage where disclosure of an intention to enter into such an arrangement becomes good practice.

7. DISALLOWANCE

CPR RULE 44.16 ADJOURNMENT WHERE LEGAL REPRESENTATIVE SEEKS TO CHALLENGE DISALLOWANCE OF ANY AMOUNT OF PERCENTAGE INCREASE

Where—

(a) the court disallows any amount of a legal representative's percentage increase in summary or detailed assessment proceedings; and

(b) the legal representative applies for an order that the disallowed amount should continue to be payable by his client,

the court may adjourn the hearing to allow the client to be—

(i) notified of the order sought; and

(ii) separately represented.

(Regulation 3(2)(b) of the Conditional Fee Agreements Regulations 2000 provides that a conditional fee agreement which provides for a success fee must state that any amount of a percentage increase disallowed on assessment ceases to be payable unless the court is satisfied that it should continue to be so payable. Regulation 5(2) of the Collective Conditional Fee Agreements Regulations 2000 makes similar provision in relation to collective conditional fee agreements).

SECTION 20: PRACTICE DIRECTION SUPPLEMENTING CPR RULE 44.16

20.1

(1) Attention is drawn to Regulation 3(2)(b) of the Conditional Fee Agreements Regulations 2000 and to Regulation 5(2)(b) of the Collective Conditional Fee Agreements Regulations 2000, which provide that some or all of a success fee ceases to be payable in certain circumstances.

(2) Rule 44.16 allows the court to adjourn a hearing at which the legal representative acting for the receiving party applies for an order that a disallowed amount should continue to be payable under the agreement.

20.2 In the following paragraphs 'counsel' means counsel who has acted in the case under a conditional fee agreement which provides for a success fee. A reference to counsel includes a reference to any person who appeared as an advocate in the case and who is not a partner or employee of the solicitor or firm which is conducting the claim or defence (as the case may be) on behalf of the receiving party.

Procedure following summary assessment

20.3

(1) If the court disallows any amount of a legal representative's percentage increase, the court will, unless sub-paragraph (2) applies, give directions to enable an application to be made by the legal representative for the disallowed amount to be payable by his client, including, if appropriate, a direction that the application will be determined by a costs judge or district judge of the court dealing with the case.

(2) The court that has made the summary assessment may then and there decide the issue whether the disallowed amount should continue to be payable, if:

- *(a) the receiving party and all parties to the relevant agreement consent to the court doing so;*
- *(b) the receiving party (or, if corporate, an officer) is present in court; and*
- *(c) the court is satisfied that the issue can be fairly decided then and there.*

Procedure following detailed assessment

20.4

(1) Where detailed assessment proceedings have been commenced, and the paying party serves points of dispute (as to which see Section 34 of this Practice Direction), which show that he is seeking a reduction in any percentage increase charged by counsel on his fees, the solicitor acting for the receiving party must within 3 days of service deliver to counsel a copy of the relevant points of dispute and the bill of costs or the relevant parts of the bill.

(2) Counsel must within 10 days thereafter inform the solicitor in writing whether or not he will accept the reduction sought or some other

reduction. Counsel may state any points he wishes to have made in a reply to the points of dispute, and the solicitor must serve them on the paying party as or as part of a reply.

(3) Counsel who fails to inform the solicitor within the time limits set out above will be taken to accept the reduction unless the court otherwise orders.

20.5 Where the paying party serves points of dispute seeking a reduction in any percentage increase charged by a legal representative acting for the receiving party, and that legal representative intends, if necessary, to apply for an order that any amount of the percentage disallowed as against the paying party shall continue to be payable by his client, the solicitor acting for the receiving party must, within 14 days of service of the points of dispute, give to his client a clear written explanation of the nature of the relevant point of dispute and the effect it will have if it is upheld in whole or in part by the court, and of the client's right to attend any subsequent hearings at court when the matter is raised.

20.6 Where the solicitor acting for a receiving party files a request for a detailed assessment hearing it must if appropriate, be accompanied by a certificate signed by him stating:

(1) that the amount of the percentage increase in respect of counsel's fees or solicitor's charges is disputed;

(2) whether an application will be made for an order that any amount of that increase which is disallowed should continue to be payable by his client;

(3) that he has given his client an explanation in accordance with paragraph 20.5; and,

(4) whether his client wishes to attend court when the amount of any relevant percentage increase may be decided.

20.7

(1) The solicitor acting for the receiving party must within 7 days of receiving from the court notice of the date of the assessment hearing, notify his client, and if appropriate, counsel in writing of the date, time and place of the hearing.

(2) Counsel may attend or be represented at the detailed assessment hearing and may make oral or written submissions.

20.8

(1) At the detailed assessment hearing, the court will deal with the assessment of the costs payable by one party to another, including the amount of the percentage increase, and give a certificate accordingly.

(2) The court may decide the issue whether the disallowed amount should continue to be payable under the relevant conditional fee agreement without an adjournment if:

(a) the receiving party and all parties to the relevant agreement consent to the court deciding the issue without an adjournment,

(b) the receiving party (or, if corporate, an officer or employee who has authority to consent on behalf of the receiving party) is present in court, and

(c) the court is satisfied that the issue can be fairly decided without an adjournment.

(3) In any other case the court will give directions and fix a date for the hearing of the application.

8. DETAILED ASSESSMENT

CPR RULE 48.8 BASIS OF DETAILED ASSESSMENT OF SOLICITOR AND CLIENT COSTS

(1) This rule applies to every assessment of a solicitor's bill to his client except a bill which is to be paid out of the Community Legal Service Fund under the Legal Aid Act 1988 or the Access to Justice Act 1999.
(1A) Section 74 (3) of the Solicitors Act 1974 applies unless the solicitor and client have entered into a written agreement which expressly permits payment to the solicitor of an amount of costs greater than that which the client could have recovered from another party to the proceedings.
(2) Subject to paragraph (1A), costs are to be assessed on the indemnity basis but are to be presumed—
- (a) to have been reasonably incurred if they were incurred with the express or implied approval of the client;
- (b) to be reasonable in amount if their amount was expressly or impliedly approved by the client;
- (c) to have been unreasonably incurred if—
  - (i) they are of an unusual nature or amount; and
  - (ii) the solicitor did not tell his client that as a result he might not recover all of them from the other party.

(3) Where the court is considering a percentage increase, whether on the application of the legal representative under rule 44.16 or on the application of the client, the court will have regard to all the relevant factors as they reasonably appeared to the solicitor or counsel when the conditional fee agreement was entered into or varied.
(4) In paragraph (3), 'conditional fee agreement' means an agreement enforceable under section 58 of the Courts and Legal Services Act 1990(a) at the date on which that agreement was entered into or varied.

CPR RULE 48.9 ASSESSMENT PROCEDURE

(1) This rule sets out the procedure to be followed where the court has made an order under Part III of the Solicitors Act 1974 for the assessment of costs payable to a solicitor by his client.
(2) The solicitor must serve a breakdown of costs within 28 days of the order for costs to be assessed.
(3) The client must serve points of dispute within 14 days after service on him of the breakdown of costs.
(4) If the solicitor wishes to serve a reply, he must do so within 14 days of service on him of the points of dispute.
(5) Either party may file a request for a hearing date—
- (a) after points of dispute have been served; but
- (b) no later than 3 months after the date of the order for the costs to be assessed.

(6) This procedure applies subject to any contrary order made by the court.

SECTION 54: BASIS OF DETAILED ASSESSMENT OF SOLICITOR AND CLIENT COSTS: RULE 48.8

54.1 A client and his solicitor may agree whatever terms they consider appropriate about the payment of the solicitor's charges for his services. If however, the costs are of an unusual nature (either in amount or in the type of costs incurred) those costs will be presumed to have been unreasonably incurred unless the solicitor satisfies the court that he informed the client that they were unusual and, where the costs relate to litigation, that he informed the client they might not be allowed on an assessment of costs between the parties. That information must have been given to the client before the costs were incurred.

54.2

(1) Costs as between a solicitor and client are assessed on the indemnity basis as defined by rule 44.4.

(2) Attention is drawn to the presumptions set out in rule 48.8(2). These presumptions may be rebutted by evidence to the contrary.

54.3 Rule 48.10 and Section 56 of this Practice Direction deal with the procedure to be followed for obtaining the assessment of a solicitor's bill pursuant to an order under Part III of the Solicitors Act 1974.

54.4 If a party fails to comply with the requirements of rule 48.10 concerning the service of a breakdown of costs or points of dispute, any other party may apply to the court in which the detailed assessment hearing should take place for an order requiring compliance with rule 48.10. If the court makes such an order, it may—

(a) make it subject to conditions including a condition to pay a sum of money into court; and

(b) specify the consequence of failure to comply with the order or a condition.

54.5

(1) Attention is drawn to rule 48.9(1) as amended by the Civil Procedure (Amendment No 3) Rules 2000 (SI 2000/1317) with effect from 3 July 2000. Rule 48.9 applies only where the solicitor and the client have entered into a conditional fee agreement as defined in section 58 of the Courts and Legal Services Act 1990 as it was in force before 1 April 2000. A client who has entered into a conditional fee agreement with a solicitor may apply for assessment of the base costs (which is carried out in accordance with rule 48.8(2) as if there were no conditional fee agreement) or for assessment of the percentage increase (success fee) or both.

(2) Where the court is to assess the percentage increase the court will have regard to all the relevant factors as they appeared to the solicitor or counsel when the conditional fee agreement was entered into.

54.6 Where the client applies to the court to reduce the percentage increase which the solicitor has charged the client under the conditional fee agreement, the client must set out in his application notice:

(a) the reasons why the percentage increase should be reduced; and

(b) what the percentage increase should be.

54.7 The factors relevant to assessing the percentage increase include—

(a) the risk that the circumstances in which the fees or expenses would be payable might not occur;

(b) the disadvantages relating to the absence of payment on account;

[c] [whether the amount which might be payable under the conditional fee agreement is limited to a certain proportion of any damages recovered by the client;] (c) whether there is a conditional fee agreement between the solicitor and counsel;

(d) the solicitor's liability for any disbursements.

54.8 When the court is considering the factors to be taken into account, it will have regard to the circumstances as they reasonably appeared to the solicitor or counsel when the conditional fee agreement was entered into.

9. COLLECTIVE CONDITIONAL FEES

Collective conditional fee agreements (CCFAs) are a response to concerns expressed during the passage of the Access to Justice Act 1999 that the individual CFA regime was not administratively suitable for the bulk purchase of legal services. In particular commercial organisations and membership organisations such as motoring associations and trade unions were not able to use the existing CFA provisions because of the practical and physical difficulties of administering the rules on an individual basis. A new consultation process was launched in June 2000 and the CCFA Regulations were published in November 2000. Those regulations and the use of CCFAs are however dependent upon either the amendment of the indemnity principle or its abolition, neither of which has happened. The statutory authority for the abrogation of the indemnity principle is s 31 of the Access to Justice Act 1999. That provision has yet to be commenced nearly two years after the Regulations were brought into force. Thus although the Collective Conditional Fee Agreements Regulations came into force on 30 November 2000, a CCFA made before the indemnity principle has been abolished must raise the question as to the effect of that abolition on any funding agreements entered before the commencement of s 31 of the 1999 Act. It could be argued that a reversal of case law by statute cannot be retrospective. However, the implementation of that reversal will be through the CPR which are applied at the time of a costs assessment. On this basis any lawful CCFA made after 30 November 2000 would not be cut down at an assessment hearing which takes place after the reversal of the indemnity principle. It remains to be seen whether the wording of the CPR will shed any light on the retrospective effect. In the meantime there are those who will be content that the CCFAs are intended to work and that no indemnity principle arguments should succeed, and there will be those who will point to s 31 and ask why it exists if it was not thought essential to remove the indemnity principle to make the system work.

COLLECTIVE CONDITIONAL FEE AGREEMENTS REGULATIONS 2000

1 CITATION, COMMENCEMENT AND INTERPRETATION

(1) These regulations may be cited as the Collective Conditional Fee Agreements Regulations 2000, and shall come into force on 30th November 2000.

(2) In these Regulations, except where the context requires otherwise—

'client' means a person who will receive advocacy or litigation services to which the agreement relates;

'collective conditional fee agreement' has the meaning given in regulation 3;

'conditional fee agreement' has the same meaning as in section 58 of the Courts and Legal Services Act 1990;

'funder' means the party to a collective conditional fee agreement who, under that agreement, is liable to pay the legal representative's fees;

'legal representative' means the person providing the advocacy or litigation services to which the agreement relates.

2 TRANSITIONAL PROVISIONS

These Regulations shall apply to agreements entered into on or after 30th November 2000, and agreements entered into before that date shall be treated as if these Regulations had not come into force.

3 DEFINITION OF 'COLLECTIVE CONDITIONAL FEE AGREEMENT'

(1) Subject to paragraph (2) of this regulation, a collective conditional fee agreement is an agreement which—

(a) disregarding section 58(3)(c) of the Courts and Legal Services Act 1990, would be a conditional fee agreement; and

(b) does not refer to specific proceedings, but provides for fees to be payable on a common basis in relation to a class of proceedings, or, if it refers to more than one class of proceedings, on a common basis in relation to each class.

(2) An agreement may be a collective conditional fee agreement whether or not—

(a) the funder is a client; or

(b) any clients are named in the agreement.

4 REQUIREMENTS FOR CONTENTS OF COLLECTIVE CONDITIONAL FEE AGREEMENTS: GENERAL

(1) A collective conditional fee agreement must specify the circumstances in which the legal representative's fees and expenses, or part of them, are payable.

(2) A collective conditional fee agreement must provide that, when accepting instructions in relation to any specific proceedings the legal representative must—

(a) inform the client as to the circumstances in which the client may be liable to pay the costs of the legal representative; and

(b) if the client requires any further explanation, advice or other information about the matter referred to in sub-paragraph (a), provide such further explanation, advice or other information about it as the client may reasonably require.

(3) Paragraph (2) does not apply in the case of an agreement between a legal representative and an additional legal representative.

(4) A collective conditional fee agreement must provide that, after accepting instructions in relation to any specific proceedings, the legal representative must confirm his acceptance of instructions in writing to the client.

5 REQUIREMENTS FOR CONTENTS OF COLLECTIVE CONDITIONAL FEE AGREEMENTS PROVIDING FOR SUCCESS FEES

(1) Where a collective conditional fee agreement provides for a success fee the agreement must provide that, when accepting instructions in relation to any specific proceedings the legal representative must prepare and retain a written statement containing—

(a) his assessment of the probability of the circumstances arising in which the percentage increase will become payable in relation to those proceedings ('the risk assessment');

(b) his assessment of the amount of the percentage increase in relation to those proceedings, having regard to the risk assessment; and

(c) the reasons, by reference to the risk assessment, for setting the percentage increase at that level.

(2) If the agreement relates to court proceedings it must provide that where the success fee becomes payable as a result of those proceedings, then—

(a) if—

(i) any fees subject to the increase are assessed, and

(ii) the legal representative or the client is required by the court to disclose to the court or any other person the reasons for setting the percentage increase at the level assessed by the legal representative,

he may do so,

(b) if—

(i) any such fees are assessed by the court, and

(ii) any amount in respect of the percentage increase is disallowed on the assessment on the ground that the level at which the increase was set was unreasonable in view of facts which were or should have been known to the legal representative at the time it was set that amount ceases to be payable under the agreement, unless the court is satisfied that it should continue to be so payable, and

(c) if—

(i) sub-paragraph (b) does not apply, and

(ii) the legal representative agrees with any person liable as a result of the proceedings to pay fees subject to the percentage increase that a lower amount than the amount payable in accordance with the conditional fee agreement is to be paid instead,

the amount payable under the collective conditional fee agreement in respect of those fees shall be reduced accordingly, unless the court is satisfied that the full amount should continue to be payable under it.

(3) In this regulation 'percentage increase' means the percentage by which the amount of the fees which would have been payable if the agreement were not a conditional fee agreement is to be increased under the agreement.

6 FORM AND AMENDMENT OF COLLECTIVE CONDITIONAL FEE AGREEMENT

(1) Subject to paragraph (2), a collective conditional fee agreement must be signed by the funder, and by the legal representative.

(2) Paragraph (1) does not apply in the case of an agreement between a legal representative and an additional legal representative.

(3) Where a collective conditional fee agreement is amended, regulations 4 and 5 apply to the amended agreement as if it were a fresh agreement made at the time of the amendment.

7 AMENDMENT TO THE CONDITIONAL FEE AGREEMENTS REGULATIONS 2000

After regulation 7 of the Conditional Fee Agreements Regulations 2000 there shall be inserted the following new regulation:—

'8 Exclusion of collective conditional fee agreements

These Regulations shall not apply to collective conditional fee agreements within the meaning of regulation 3 of the Collective Conditional Fee Agreements Regulations 2000.'.

The CCFA Regulations 2000 make provision for all CCFAs irrespective of the context in which they are to be used. The Regulations apply to bulk purchasers of legal services, such as the legal department of a multi-national company, and to bulk providers of legal services such as the legal representatives retained by a trade union to act for its members. There is a crucial difference between these two categories in that the bulk purchaser is also the client, whereas the bulk provider situation will involve numerous clients who are not funding the litigation. The Regulations, however, apply consumer protection provisions to all CCFAs, including those where the client is also the funder. The Regulations are not set out so as to have provisions applying according to whether the CCFA is for a bulk purchaser or not.

A CCFA is governed in the same way as an individual CFA in terms of the CPR and Costs Practice Direction. The CCFA Regulations define a CCFA as a CFA but for s 58(3)(*c*) and it is assumed that for the purposes of the CPR and Practice Direction a CFA includes a CCFA. A CCFA is therefore a 'funding arrangement' within the meaning of CPR Rule 43.2(1) which provides:

> 'In Parts 44 to 48, unless the context otherwise requires "funding arrangement" means an arrangement where a person has – (i) entered into a conditional fee agreement which provides for a success fee within the meaning of section 58(2) of the Courts and Legal Services Act 1990.'

It follows that the rules concerning the disclosure of funding arrangements apply to CCFAs in the same way as for individual CFAs, CPR 44.15(1) provides:

> 'A party who seeks to recover an additional liability must provide information about the funding arrangement to the court and to other parties as required by a rule, practice direction or court order.'

The Costs Practice Direction s 19 requires disclosure of the existence of a CCFA but not its terms and notice to be given at the time of issue of a claim form if the CCFA is already in place or where a CCFA is made after the issue of proceedings within seven days of the making of the agreement. The pre-issue disclosure required by the protocols Practice Direction also applies. Where the CCFA relates to a defendant, notice of it must be given when filing the first document. CCFAs made after the serving of the first document must be notified within seven days of the making of the agreement. All of these provisions are identical to those applying to individual CFAs. Form N 251 may be used for the giving of this information.

10. MEMBERSHIP ORGANISATIONS

The Lord Chancellor's Department issued a Consultation Paper in 1998 which encompassed the provision of legal services by membership organisations, such as trade unions, to their members as a benefit of membership. The maintenance of legal actions by a trade union has long been recognised as being in the public interest. Such organisations not only fund the action by the member but also indemnify the member against adverse costs. This was recognised as a service which contributed to access to justice but which at the same time was a financial burden on the organisation concerned. It was also recognised that such organisations did not use commercially available insurance products but effectively 'self-insured'. With the introduction of recoverable insurance premiums, the question addressed was whether some equivalent recoupment could be established for such organisations. By s 30 of the Access to Justice Act 1999 and the Access to Justice (Membership Organisations) Regulations 2000 provision is made for the recoupment of a sum no greater than the equivalent of the cost to a member of taking out a personal insurance policy covering adverse costs only. This still leaves to the organisation the administration of the litigation and of ensuring that an agreement with the member exists which can give rise to the recoupment of the costs. Trade unions and other organisations are likely to consider collective CFAs (CCFAs) rather than the membership organisations provisions. A CCFA would mean that the organisation could avoid the costs of administering its own scheme. The organisation would not then be left trying to recoup costs – it could instead transfer that risk to its lawyers who could approach the matter of costs in the usual manner under a CCFA where a success fee can be charged and recovered from the losing opponent. Whether any membership organisations will seek to make use of CCFAs rather than s 30 will however depend upon the interpretation which is given to s 29 Access to Justice Act 1999 dealing with the recovery of insurance premiums, and to the amendments to the CPR to abolish the indemnity principle. A statutory regime which permitted a membership organisation to use a CCFA with insurance for adverse costs and own disbursements in the case of failed proceedings, would need to overcome the wording of s 29 and the indemnity principle because the individual member in whose favour a costs order can be made is not a party to the CCFA and will generally be intended to not have a personal liability for any costs. Whilst admirably transparent, such an arrangement fits well with neither s 29 nor the indemnity principle.

(a) The statutory requirements

The regulations are based upon the individual CFA Regulations, a matter which itself may give rise to some difficulties. The basis of the recovery of the amount representing the 'self-insurance cost' to the organisation is a provision which enables the member to recover such an amount, not for the organisation to recover it directly. The regulations make no requirement that the member be under any liability to account to the organisation for such an amount. Provisions are made for the giving of a written statement to the member of the circumstances in which the member may be liable for costs, but the recovery of the sum intended to reflect the cost to the organisation is a recovery by the member. As to the costs actually incurred by the organisation in 'self-insuring', the relevant figure appears to be that at which an individual could have obtained insurance. Had the organisation itself purchased an insurance policy to cover its entire litigation activities on behalf of its members it is likely that the cost would be substantially lower than the cost to an individual member obtaining insurance for his or her own case alone.

ACCESS TO JUSTICE ACT 1999

30 RECOVERY WHERE BODY UNDERTAKES TO MEET COSTS LIABILITIES

(1) This section applies where a body of a prescribed description undertakes to meet (in accordance with arrangements satisfying prescribed conditions) liabilities which members of the body or other persons who are parties to proceedings may incur to pay the costs of other parties to the proceedings.
(2) If in any of the proceedings a costs order is made in favour of any of the members or other persons, the costs payable to him may, subject to subsection (3) and (in the case of court proceedings) to rules of court, include an additional amount in respect of any provision made by or on behalf of the body in connection with the proceedings against the risk of having to meet such liabilities.
(3) But the additional amount shall not exceed a sum determined in a prescribed manner; and there may, in particular, be prescribed as a manner of determination one which takes into account the likely cost to the member or

other person of the premium of an insurance policy against the risk of incurring a liability to pay the costs of other parties to the proceedings.
(4) In this section 'prescribed' means prescribed by regulations made by the Lord Chancellor by statutory instrument; and a statutory instrument containing such regulations shall be subject to annulment in pursuance of a resolution of either House of Parliament.
(5) Regulations under subsection (1) may, in particular, prescribe as a description of body one which is for the time being approved by the Lord Chancellor or by a prescribed person.

Sub-section (1) makes it clear that the provision which can lead to the recovery of an additional amount is a provision to meet a member's liability for opponent's costs, not his own costs. The 'provision' made by the organisation is therefore an 'additional liability' which can be claimed by the individual and may be included in a costs order. Section 30(2) can be taken to mean that there has to be evidence of the making of such a provision. The assumption will be made that where a body such as a trade union or motoring organisation is providing an indemnity to its membership for own and opponent's costs (ie costs liability should the case lose), there is a clear provision in the accounts to enable such indemnity to be financed. By sub-section (3) the amount claimed cannot exceed the 'likely' cost to an individual in purchasing an insurance policy to provide cover only for opponent's costs. That is more restrictive than the provisions of s 29 which permit the recovery by an individual of a premium paid in respect not only of opponent's costs but own disbursements and costs.

ACCESS TO JUSTICE (MEMBERSHIP ORGANISATIONS) REGULATIONS 2000

1 CITATION, COMMENCEMENT AND INTERPRETATION

(1) These Regulations may be cited as the Access to Justice (Membership Organisations) Regulations 2000.
(2) These Regulations come into force on 1st April 2000.

2 BODIES OF A PRESCRIBED DESCRIPTION

The bodies which are prescribed for the purpose of section 30 of the Access to Justice Act 1999 (recovery where body undertakes to meet costs liabilities) are those bodies which are for the time being approved by the Lord Chancellor for that purpose.

3 REQUIREMENTS FOR ARRANGEMENTS TO MEET COSTS LIABILITIES

(1) Section 30(1) of the Access to Justice Act 1999 applies to arrangements which satisfy the following conditions.
(2) The arrangements must be in writing.
(3) The arrangements must contain a statement specifying—
- (a) the circumstances in which the member or other party may be liable to pay costs of the proceedings,
- (b) whether such a liability arises—
  - (i) if those circumstances only partly occur,
  - (ii) irrespective of whether those circumstances occur, and
  - (iii) on the termination of the arrangements for any reason,
- (c) the basis on which the amount of the liability is calculated, and
- (d) the procedure for seeking assessment of costs.

(4) A copy of the part of the arrangements containing the statement must be given to the member or other party to the proceedings whose liabilities the body is undertaking to meet as soon as possible after the undertaking is given.

4 RECOVERY OF ADDITIONAL AMOUNT FOR INSURANCE COSTS

(1) Where an additional amount is included in costs by virtue of section 30(2) of the Access to Justice Act 1999 (costs payable to a member of a body or other person party to the proceedings to include an additional amount in respect of provision made by the body against the risk of having to meet the member's or other person's liabilities to pay other parties' costs), that additional amount must not exceed the following sum.
(2) That sum is the likely cost to the member of the body or, as the case may be, the other person who is a party to the proceedings in which the costs order is made of the premium of an insurance policy against the risk of incurring a liability to pay the costs of other parties to the proceedings.

(b) Complying with regulation 3

Until CCFAs are fully operational with the removal of the indemnity principle, it is highly likely that membership organisations will continue to provide legal services to members by the use of an indemnity agreement under which the member is indemnified for own and opponents costs and the member's appointed legal representative will not be acting under a CFA. In these circumstances compliance with reg 3 is required but presents problems. The difficulty arises because the wording of reg 3 has been transferred directly from the individual CFA regulations. Accordingly there is a reference to the circumstances in which fees will be payable and a further reference to the failure in part of those circumstances. Such wording is relevant and meaningful where there is a CFA because there will be circumstances in which fees will be payable and others when fees will not be payable. In most membership organisation cases this will not be the case but to obtain an arrangement satisfying s 30 and leading to a recoupment of the provision made for meeting this liability, that arrangement must comply with reg 3. Of course if the fees payable are different in different circumstances there will be a CFA and the whole of the CFA Regulations would have to be complied with in addition to the Membership Organisation Regulations. Section 30 and the indemnity principle require that the member has a primary legal liability to pay fees, albeit that there is an arrangement whereby that liability is to be indemnified by the organisation. The arrangement must accordingly make this primary liability clear. It must also make reference to the terms of the indemnity, in particular when the indemnity will not be given, such as for any period in which membership has lapsed. An arrangement which referred only to the primary liability and omitted explanation of the indemnity would be unlikely to satisfy reg 3. It should be borne in mind that Practice Rule 15 and the Client Care Code will require this information to be given in any event. It could be argued that these requirements are unnecessarily cumbersome and of no real benefit to the member who in nearly all circumstances will be indemnified against all costs. However, there will always be circumstances in which such an indemnity will not apply and those circumstances need to be explained.

Suggested wordings to comply with regulation 3

(i) You [the member] are ultimately responsible for paying the fees and disbursements of your legal representative, whether you win your case or not.

If you win you are entitled to seek recovery of your costs from your opponent. Your legal representative's own costs are calculated as follows: [insert charging rate(s) of the legal representative who will act for the member].

(ii) If you lose you are ultimately responsible for paying the fees and disbursements of your opponent, in addition to your own costs.

(iii) The [Name of membership organisation] has agreed to indemnify you for the liability for costs mentioned in (i) and (ii) above.

(iv) This arrangement between you and [name of membership organisation] may be ended by [set out any terms in the Membership organisation's rules under which it or the member can terminate the indemnity arrangement.].

(v) If this arrangement is ended you will be ultimately liable for all the costs referred to in (i) and (ii) above but you will not be entitled to an indemnity for that liability from the [name of membership organisation].

(vi) You are entitled to apply to the court for a detailed assessment of the costs of your legal representative which means that the court will check the bill. There are strict time limits for doing this. If you apply to the court within one month of receiving the bill the court will order that the bill be assessed. If you apply after that time but within 12 months of receiving the bill the court may, but does not have to, order an assessment. If 12 months have passed since you received the bill, or you have paid the bill and 12 months have not passed since you paid it, you will have to show special circumstances to the court if it is to order an assessment. If 12 months have passed since you have paid the bill you cannot obtain an assessment. An application for an assessment and the assessment itself can be an expensive process if you lose.

There has here been no attempt to incorporate the language of the regulation. The wording of the regulation is inappropriate for a non-CFA funded case, particularly reg 3(3)(*b*)(ii) and (iii) – clearly the member's primary liability will not differ according to circumstances in a non CFA funded case.

(c) Application of Access to Justice Act 1999, s 29 to membership organisations

Section 29 provides for a costs order to include the premium of an insurance policy but it refers only to such a policy taken out by a 'party'. A membership organisation which uses a CCFA will not be a party in whose favour a costs order can be made. Such an organisation can only recover the costs of insurance by the indirect method of the Membership Organisation Regulations discussed above. Alternatively, the membership organisation can fund the individual member to purchase an insurance policy and then the member can seek to recover that cost under section 29. Given that the basis of the CCFA is that the membership organisation is the funder of the litigation and as such has a direct liability for adverse costs, the body will be seeking to insure its liability as well as any potential liability of the individual. Whether such a policy would be recognised as being within section 29 is unclear. The administrative costs of operating such a method may well also be unattractive.

(d) Disclosure of the existence of a section 30 arrangement

A section 30 arrangement is a 'funding arrangement' within the meaning of CPR Rule 43.2(1). It follows that the rules concerning the disclosure of funding arrangements apply to section 30 arrangements.

PART 6 GATE-KEEPERS TO JUSTICE

The gate-keepers to justice are now the lawyers and the insurers. They decide not only who is to be admitted through the portals of justice, but the price of admission. There are two – often three – gates to pass through. First, the solicitors backed by their risk assessment panel, then the barrister if he too is invited to act under a conditional fee agreement in consultation with the members of his chambers, and then the insurers and their risk assessors; all three decide not only if they are willing to act, but the profit they wish to make out of the transaction. The lay client, of course, plays no part in these deliberations nor receives any independent advice. Do I hear murmurs about conflict of interest? You will have to shout louder than that, because no one wants to hear you. Intentionally or unintentionally, one of the benefits conferred on clients by the provision that additional liabilities are recoverable between the parties is that in every case which results in an order for costs the court must now assess the amount of the additional liability, not only between the parties, but also between the solicitor and the client. This, unfortunately, is no protection for the great majority of clients because they settle without any input from the court or independent advice. The protection for the client only extends to the risk element of the success fee, because the court is not concerned with that part of the success fee which relates to funding the litigation which is not recoverable between the parties. The client is still on his own in respect of this fee.

It is ironic that, by reducing the availability of state funding and encouraging the use of conditional fee agreements, a Labour government should have, in effect, privatised civil litigation.

PART 7 LEGAL EXPENSES INSURANCE

A client does not have to enter into a conditional fee agreement to benefit from litigation insurance. There is of course the traditional legal expenses insurance – known now as before-the-event insurance. Premiums for before-the-event policies are not recoverable, but neither are they significant. Most people do not take out before-the-event insurance because they do not expect to be involved in litigation and most policies are simply add-ons to other policies such as car and house insurance. It is also true to say that many who do have before-the-event insurance do not even know that they have it, a fact which has caused difficulties with recoverability of the after-the-event premium and which was dealt with by the Court of Appeal in *Sarwar v Alam* (see p 554). A client who does not wish to enter into a conditional fee agreement could still insure himself against paying between-the-parties costs if he loses by taking out an after-the-event insurance policy. Indeed he could insure himself against his own legal costs as well. Many of the after-the-event providers have just such a policy (see p 506). The decision of the Court of Appeal in *Callery v Gray* (see p 546) does not deal with the recoverability of the after-the-event of premium in respect of insurance against solicitor and client costs.

PART 8 THE BAR

The Bar has never been comfortable with conditional fee agreements. A former chairman said:

> 'There is a very real danger of abuse. There is a conflict of interest at the very heart of these conditional fee agreements which could lead to the public being ripped-off. Ordinary people have no way of knowing whether the risk assessment on which lawyers

> increase their fees was accurate. The blunt truth is that people will end up paying more to lawyers and we do not think that is a satisfactory arrangement in the public interest.'

Paul Shrubsall, a Vice-President of the Institute of Barristers' Clerks, speaking at the Bar Conference 1999 asked: 'Would any barrister take a CFA by choice?' and answered his own question: 'No'. His reply to his next question, 'Is there a choice?', was: 'Ultimately, no'. The Bar had advocated a Contingency Legal Aid Fund – CLAF to its friends – a self-financing fund into which litigants put a slice of their winnings. This is what is envisaged in the provision for litigation funders in the Access to Justice Act 1999, s 28, a section of the Act still not in force. Barristers are also concerned at what role they will play in risk assessment – and whether they will be paid for reading papers and evaluating the prospects of success. What if there is a dispute between the barrister, the solicitor and the client about how a case is to be conducted and funded or over whether or not an offer is to be made or accepted? The bar is also concerned about the problem of returned briefs – if a barrister who has entered into a conditional fee agreement cannot appear at the hearing, will another barrister be willing to take over on the same terms? Some chambers have now made arrangements to ensure that there will be another barrister available for returned briefs. With barristers being less than enthusiastic about entering into conditional fee agreements, solicitors will have to grasp the problem of who is to pay counsel's fees. Or is this where solicitor High Court advocates will come into their own?

PART 9 EXPERTS

I once saw an advertisement by an expert in an American law journal proclaiming 'Never been on the losing side'. I was only slightly less horrified when I read recently a justification for expert witnesses in this country entering into conditional fee agreements. That would be an end to their role as independent advisers to the court and would seriously undermine and devalue their written and oral evidence. The Court of Appeal has made this very point in *Factortame v Secretary of State for Transport (No 2)* [2002] EWCA Civ 932, [2002] 4 All ER 97. It is also likely that the professional body to which the expert belongs prohibits such arrangements. An expert entering into such an agreement would have no protection against charges of maintenance and champerty and could well be personally liable for any unpaid costs as maintainers of litigation. But there is still the question of how experts are to be financed under a conditional fee agreement, some are not willing to wait until the end of the case for payment or to limit their fees to the amount allowed on assessment between the parties. The *Factortame* case involved professional services in support of litigation but not the provision of expert evidence. The fee agreement was a contingency fee, being a direct share of the proceeds. The Court held that to be valid at common law, however the question of liability for costs if the case had failed did not arise. If such arrangements become common we shall no doubt have the benefit of yet another Court of Appeal decision.

PART 10 SOLICITORS

1. SUCCESS FEES

(a) Warning

I cannot stress too strongly that the funding of conditional fee agreements is now a growth industry with many new players using highly sophisticated techniques of risk assessment and cash-flow monitoring, way beyond the concept of the non-specialist lawyer and virtually all members of the judiciary. I include myself in that latter category and what follows is no more than a general outline. Rules and practice directions to protect the naive and the innocent are given in Parts 4 and 5 above. If you enter into CFAs or make ATE insurance arrangements without studying those rules you are inviting catastrophe.

(b) Calculating the odds

(i) Prospects of success

When betting at the racecourse the search is for value for money, a horse at 6/1 or 7/1 may give better value than either an odds-on favourite or a 100/1 outsider. The search for value may be helpful on a racecourse but it is a disastrous guide to deciding whether or not to act under a conditional fee agreement. That decision must be on the merits alone. There must be a sophisticated system for evaluating the prospects of success. You cannot increase the prospects of success by increasing the success fee. Another sure-fire way of losing money is to act for the client who has shopped around and tells you that unless you reduce your proposed success fee he is going elsewhere. Do not let fear of losing work cloud your judgement. And do not take on a no-hoper on the grounds that the case is bound to settle as soon as the other side learn that it is you who is acting against them. It is a matter of risk assessment. There was little risk to either the solicitor or the client, when virtually all conditional fee agreement were entered into in relation to personal injury actions, where the prospect of success is high and the insurance premium low. But the picture changes dramatically in respect of other forms of litigation. How may firms of solicitors keep records of their success rate in different types of litigation? For example, in commercial actions, actions involving estate agents, boundary disputes, building contracts, etc. How many solicitors record the amount of their solicitor and client and between-the-parties profit costs in the different categories? What are the average profit costs and average disbursement in a personal injury action and a medical negligence action? There are various formulae for assessing the risk and calculating the appropriate success fee based on that risk. It requires information experience and expertise to evaluate the prospects of success. The success fee must be expressed in terms of percentage and so should the prospect of success.

On p 512 I say an aspect of success fees to which not enough attention is given, is the prospect of recovery. This was not usually a problem where the other party was backed by an insurance company, but as conditional fee agreements spread to all forms of litigation there are going to be cases where the victory will prove to be Pyrrhic because the loser cannot pay the damages or costs. Defendants as well as claimants can enter into conditional fee agreements, and they may obtain judgment against a claimant who is a man of straw, or has the protection of a funding certificate. For the reasons I give on pp 511–512, the agreement should not be, but at the moment has to be, 'no win, no fee'. It should be 'no recovery, no fee', and the risk of not recovering the amount that has been awarded and the between-the-parties costs should surely, in appropriate cases, be reflected in the risk assessment. Because of the indemnity principle the Law Society Model CFA does not take this approach. It is also relevant when calculating the after-the-event insurance premium to keep in mind that the other party may also have entered into a conditional fee agreement, perhaps with a 100% success fee.

(ii) Calculating the fee

The fee must be calculated in two parts, one to reflect the risk of losing the litigation and one to cover the cost of funding it. The former is recoverable between the parties, the latter is not.

The first step must be to estimate the costs if the action goes to trial and is lost. That is the amount you will lose, both in the actual cost of doing the work and the lost profit.

The next step is to consider the additional profit you wish to make if the proceedings are successful, expressed in percentage terms. The Law Society's publication *Conditional Fees – A Survival Guide* (2nd edn, 2001) by Michael Napier, Fiona Bawdon and Gordon Wignall provides the following method of calculating a success fee:

F divided by S multiplied by 100 equals SF, where:
F = chances of failure
S = chances of success
SF = success fee

For example:
You assess the chances of success in a particular case as 75%. This gives you a success fee of 33.3%. In other words, out of every 4 cases, 1 is going to lose. In order to pay for that losing case the costs on the other 3 must each yield an additional 1/3 in costs.

The calculation comes out as follows:
A case with a 75% chance of success has a 25% chance of failure so: 25 divided by 75 equals 0.333 multiplied by 100 equals 33.3%.

Ready Reckoner

Prospects of success %	Success fee %
100	0
90	11
80	25
75	33.3
70	43
65	54
60	67
50	100

The authors express a caveat about the assumption made in the ready reckoner that costs earned in won cases will be at the same level as those in lost cases. David Chalk in *Risk Assessment in Litigation* (Butterworths, 2001), illustrates the effect on success fees of assuming different costs ratios in won to lost cases. I am grateful to him for permission to reproduce it here.

Costs ratio	1	1.25	1.5	2	2.5	3
Chance of winning			Success Fee			
50	100%	125%	150%	200%	250%	300%
51	96%	120%	144%	192%	240%	288%
52	92%	115%	138%	185%	231%	277%
53	89%	111%	133%	177%	222%	266%
54	85%	106%	128%	170%	213%	256%
55	82%	102%	123%	164%	205%	245%
56	79%	98%	118%	157%	196%	236%
57	75%	94%	113%	151%	189%	226%
58	72%	91%	109%	145%	181%	217%
59	69%	87%	104%	139%	174%	208%
60	67%	83%	100%	133%	167%	200%
61	64%	80%	96%	128%	160%	192%
62	61%	77%	92%	123%	153%	184%
63	59%	73%	88%	117%	147%	176%
64	56%	70%	84%	113%	141%	169%
65	54%	67%	81%	108%	135%	162%
66	52%	64%	77%	103%	129%	155%
67	49%	62%	74%	99%	123%	148%
68	47%	59%	71%	94%	118%	141%
69	45%	56%	67%	90%	112%	135%
70	43%	54%	64%	86%	107%	129%
71	41%	51%	61%	82%	102%	123%
72	39%	49%	58%	78%	97%	117%
73	37%	46%	55%	74%	92%	111%
74	35%	44%	53%	70%	88%	105%
75	33%	42%	50%	67%	83%	100%
76	32%	40%	47%	63%	79%	95%

(c) Assessment of success fees

Callery v Gray [2001] EWCA Civ 1117, [2001] 3 All ER 833 and [2001] EWCA Civ 1246, [2001] 4 All ER 1

(i) The Court of Appeal

The long-awaited judgment of the Court of Appeal was delivered in two parts on 17 and 31 July 2001. The Court emphasised that the information before it was sketchy and it was dealing only with a routine road traffic accident (RTA) case.

THE FACTS

The claimant was a passenger in a vehicle struck side-on by the defendant's vehicle. The claimant's solicitors acted under a conditional fee agreement (CFA) with a 40% success fee (plus 20% for postponement of the payment of their fees). The claimant took out after-the-event insurance. Both the conditional fee agreement and the insurance were arranged before any letter was sent to the defendant. The case settled without the issue of proceedings and with the defendant agreeing to pay reasonable costs. The parties failed to agree the amount of the costs, so the claimants issued costs-only proceedings. The district judge allowed both the 40% success fee and the after-the-event insurance premium of £350.

THE QUESTIONS

1. Is it reasonable to enter into a CFA with a success fee before contacting the other side in the dispute?
2. What principles govern the reasonableness of success fees?

THE ANSWERS

1. Yes.
2. The Court of Appeal identified three categories of CFA with different principles applying to the success fees of each category, as follows:
   (a) *Category A – Off the peg:* In RTA cases the success fee should not exceed 20% of the costs. This is based upon the overall success rate being in the region of 90%. No guidance was given on cases other than RTA cases. The Court allowed 20% on these facts on the grounds of a global success fee for all RTA cases undertaken by firms of solicitors handling bulk quantities of RTA cases. Therefore, 20% does not mean that one-off passenger claims warrant that figure – it means that bulk RTA case loads do, even though these include some claims by innocent passengers. This approach also has the advantage that individual cases need not be assessed before setting the success fee.
   (b) *Category B – Bespoke:* Where there are at the outset factors suggesting the case may fail, then a higher success fee than the standard 20% is reasonable but it is likely that the figure cannot be set until a response has been obtained to a letter before action.
   (c) *Category C – Two-stages:* Where it is expected that the case will not settle until at least the end of the protocol period, it would be reasonable to set a higher success fee, but to provide for a significant rebate if the case unexpectedly settles within the protocol period. The Court gave no guidance as to how the two figures should be calculated but it envisaged both figures being set at the outset. If the case settled in the protocol period the lower fee would apply to the whole case; if the case does not settle, the higher figure applies to the whole case. The court gave an example of a 100% fee rebated to 5% if the claim settled within the protocol period.

(ii) The House of Lords

The costs industry held its collective breath and 150,000 cases were put on hold awaiting the certainty of an authoritative ruling by the House of Lords on appeal from the decisions of the Court of Appeal ([2002] 3 All ER 417). They did not get one. In the view of the House the appropriate forum to monitor the new funding regime and resolve its teething problems was the Court of Appeal, not the House of Lords, so they dismissed the appeal. If that were so, enquired the *Law Society's Gazette*, why did the House of Lords grant leave to appeal to itself and then spend a year in saying the subject matter of the appeal was not appropriate for it to deal with? Although the year's delay and the uncertainty it caused were regrettable the judgments of the five law lords are treasures of lucidity and perspective, which well repay reading in full. Their Lordships expressed concerns about abuses arising out of the amount of costs charged, over-generous success fees, excessive ATE premiums and the fact that there is no incentive for the client to keep solicitor and client costs down, because the client will not be liable for those costs, whatever the outcome. Lord Scott dissented from the majority decision to allow the ATE premium, because in his view it was far too early to take out ATE insurance when the prospect of litigation was remote.

(iii) The Court of Appeal – again

In *Halloran v Delaney* ([2002] EWCA Civ 1258, [2002] All ER (D) 30) the Court of Appeal held that in cases involving Conditional Fee Agreements entered into after 1 August 2001 where simple claims were settled without court proceedings judges should ordinarily allow an uplift of only 5% on the claimant's lawyers' costs, including the costs of any costs-only proceedings, unless the judge was persuaded that a higher uplift was appropriate in the particular circumstances of the case. This policy should be adopted in relation to all CFAs however they were structured, entered into on or after 1 August 2001, by which date both the *Callery* judgments had been published, removing the main uncertainties about costs recovery.

The court approved the approach to success fees in costs-only cases adopted in *Bensusan v Freedman* [2001] All ER (D) 212. On its proper construction this CFA (based on the Law Society Model) included the costs of costs-only proceedings within the meaning of 'claim', for which the CFA provided coverage, even though it could not be said that the costs-only proceedings constituted proceedings taken to 'enforce' an agreement, because liability under the agreement still had to be quantified before it could be enforced. Any future re-draft of the Law Society's model agreement should make this point transparently clear. The CFA under consideration in *Halloran* was made very soon after the coming into force of the Conditional Fee Agreement Regulations 2000 and before *Callery v Gray* had been decided. Accordingly, because at that time there was uncertainty about a number of matters concerning the recoverability of costs, the costs judge was not wrong to hold that an uplift of 20% was reasonable, given her wide discretion in a case like this. Even at the present time the court would reject a submission that there was no risk in costs-only proceedings, against which a lawyer acting under a CFA was entitled to seek protection on the principles in *Callery*. However, following *Callery* it was time to reappraise the appropriate level of success fee that should be recoverable on these simple claims when they were settled without the need for court proceedings.

(iv) Life after Halloran

Although the Court in *Halloran* drew particular attention to the contemplation of a two-stage success fee by Lord Woolf in his judgment in *Callery*, it did not explain its own guidance in terms of the *Callery* categories of success fee. The Court in *Halloran* was addressing what it referred to as 'simple claims'. It seems clear enough, therefore, that for Category A CFAs ('off-the-peg') the figure from 1 August 2001 is 5%, unless the court is persuaded that a higher figure is appropriate in the particular circumstances. For Category B ('bespoke') the standard figure is also 5% after *Halloran*, but it is likely that a higher figure will be more easily justified if it has been set in the light of a response from the opponent (although the Court did not specifically say this). As for Category C ('two-stage'), the Court, after referring to Lord Woolf's example, concluded that the standard figure for cases which settle without proceedings should also be 5%. It seems therefore, that the two-stage CFA has survived *Halloran*, although it appears the 5% cap may apply to any settlement without proceedings, and not merely to one within the protocol period. Further, if the higher success fee is triggered by the commencement of proceedings, the question may then arise of whether the institution of proceedings was reasonable.

There is never a dull or a predictable moment in costs. In *Callery* the various interests of the costs industry were represented and taken into account, but not so here. No sooner was the ink dry on the House of Lords decision not to interfere with *Callery*, than the Court of Appeal not only replaced the 20% success fee benchmark with 5%, but back-dated its effect to 1 August 2001. How can anyone run a business among such shifting sands? How will it work? It has been suggested that in future all CFAs will contain a two-stage success fee of 100% and 5% on the basis that cases rarely settle within the protocol period (even more rarely in future, we suggest) and thereafter proceedings will be instituted triggering a 100% fee instead of the present 20% under *Callery*. Thus over all the decision could result in a total increase in success fees. Practitioners must also take into account the Claims Direct decision that where liability is admitted before an ATE premium is paid the premium will not usually be justified or recoverable.

(d) *Callery* in action

In *Bensusan v Freedman* ([2001] All ER (D) 212, SCCO, 20 September) the Senior Costs Judge, Master Peter Hurst, equated a simple clinical negligence case, which involved a dental tool being dropped in the claimant's mouth who then swallowed it, with a personal injury action arising out of a rear-end shunt. (The analogy escaped me!) While accepting that the risk of failure in a clinical negligence action can be greater than in a PI case, this particular case was 'simple and straightforward'. Costs Practice Direction s 11.7 provides that, subject to para 17.2, the court when considering the factors to be taken into account will have regard to the circumstances as they reasonably appear to the solicitor or counsel when the funding arrangement was entered into and at the time of any variation of the arrangement. Paragraph 18.8(2) provides that in cases in which an additional liability is claimed, the costs judge should have regard to the time when and the extent to which the claim has been settled and to the fact that the claim has been settled without the need to commence proceedings. In *Callery v Gray* the Court of Appeal indicated that in a routine road traffic accident action the success fee should not exceed 20% and the Senior Costs Judge took the same view in this case, reducing a success fee of 50% to 20%. Using *Callery* as 'no more than a starting point', he said the effect of the Costs Practice Direction was to prevent excessive claims for success fees in cases which settle without the need for proceedings when it was clear, or ought to have been clear, from the outset that the risk of having to commence proceedings was minimal.

(e) Cash-flow

It is not merely a question of risk assessment but also one of cash-flow. Conditional fee agreements are about funding litigation as well as the risks of not being paid at all. Conditional fee agreements have an adverse effect on cash-flow in a number of ways. First, solicitors cannot require interim payments during the litigation, which of course they may do if the litigation is either privately or state funded. Second, there is the question of disbursements. For example, who is to pay the after-the-event insurance premium? There have been various suggestions including the state, the solicitors, trade unions or the clients themselves. Many insurers now arrange loans for the client or defer payment of the premium until the conclusion of the case. If the solicitors pay the premiums or lend the client money with which to pay them, this will certainly adversely affect their cash-flow. Then there are all the court fees and other disbursements during the currency of the litigation – who is to pay these? Research by the Institute for the Study of the Legal Profession at Sheffield University revealed that a medium-sized firm of between five and eleven partners doing a significant volume of personal injury work would have to find £450,000 a year to carry the cost of disbursements and clients' insurance. If solicitors are to pay counsel or experts during the currency of the litigation this too will affect their cash-flow, but some recompense may be built into the final success fee if the litigation is successful, even though this is not recoverable between the parties. If the litigation is lost and the solicitors are to pay these disbursements out of their own pockets, this will seriously affect not only their cash-flow but also their profit. The value of the claim is also a relevant factor in deciding whether to undertake it or not. The value may be too low, as with a claim in the small claims court or on the fast track, or it may be too high, involving millions of pounds lasting for several years. There are decisions to be made at both ends of the financial spectrum.

(f) Waiting for payment

The standard practice for a CFA is for payment of fees to be postponed until the (successful) outcome of the case. The payment of disbursements is less standard, with some CFAs providing for payment before the conclusion of the case and others postponing this also. The cost of this delay is carried by the solicitor and if a charge for this is to be included in the success fee then the percentage relating to waiting for payment must be separately stated in the CFA (CFA Regulations 2000, reg 3(1)(*b*)) because it cannot form part of the additional liability to be recovered from an unsuccessful opponent (CPR Rule 44.3B (inserted by Civil Procedure (Amendment No 3) Rules 2000). It remains the liability of the client if the case is successful and is lost to the firm if the case fails.

The client can challenge the percentage of the success fee in the usual way under Rule 48. The percentage of the success fee relating to waiting for payment will on the face of the CFA apply to the base costs actually incurred in the litigation. Those costs will have been incurred over a period of time accumulating to a total to which the percentage of the success fee is then applied. Using the success fee as the mechanism for this recovery of cost will, therefore, have a tendency to inflate the amount recovered because the success fee in effect assumes all the costs were incurred form day one. This tendency can be accounted for when setting the percentage figure. The difficulty in an individual case is accurately to predict the length of time during which the solicitor is waiting for payment.

The use of the success fee as the mechanism for recovering the cost of waiting for payment calls for an accurate prediction of the length of time which will elapse before the conclusion of the case. The following table illustrates the percentage of a success fee which would be called for to obtain the annual interest rates in the table but remember that the costs to which it applies will not have been outstanding for the whole of the time that the case runs.

Interest Rate (%)	**6.0**	**8.0**	**10.0**	**Interest Rate (%)**	**6.0**	**8.0**	**10.0**
Month				**Month**			
9	4.5	6.0	7.5	**23**	11.5	15.3	19.2
10	5.0	6.7	8.3	**24**	12.0	16.0	20.0
11	5.5	7.3	9.2	**25**	12.5	16.7	20.8
12	6.0	8.0	10.0	**26**	13.0	17.3	21.7
13	6.5	8.7	10.8	**27**	13.5	18.0	22.5
14	7.0	9.3	11.7	**28**	14.0	18.7	23.3
15	7.5	10.0	12.5	**29**	14.5	19.3	24.2
16	8.0	10.7	13.3	**30**	15.0	20.0	25.0
17	8.5	11.3	14.2	**31**	15.5	20.7	25.8
18	9.0	12.0	15.0	**32**	16.0	21.3	26.7
19	9.5	12.7	15.8	**33**	16.5	22.0	27.5
20	10.0	13.3	16.7	**34**	17.0	22.7	28.3
21	10.5	14.0	17.5	**35**	17.5	23.3	29.2
22	11.0	14.7	18.3	**36**	18.0	24.0	30.0

(g) Disbursement liability

Section 11.8(1)(*b*) of the Costs Practice Direction expressly refers to the legal representative's liability for any disbursements as being a factor to be taken into account in assessing the reasonableness of the success fee. The success fee is applied to the fees charged and is not applied to disbursements. If the solicitor is carrying the liability for disbursements in the event that the case is unsuccessful, the only mechanism for reflecting that risk lies in increasing the percentage of the success fee. The increase attributable to this liability will be recoverable from a losing opponent and can therefore be challenged as being set at an unreasonable level. The test is whether the percentage increase was reasonable having regard to the circumstances as they reasonably appeared at the time the percentage was set (section 11.7).

As with the percentage for waiting for payment the difficulty is in accurately predicting the level of disbursements to be reflected in a percentage of the success fee which is a multiplier to the fees incurred throughout the life of the case. In order to calculate the percentage success fee to recover disbursement liability it is first necessary to express the disbursements as a percentage of costs. That percentage is then multiplied by the percentage figure representing the risk of the case losing since that is also the risk value in relation to losing the disbursements. This element of the success fee is vulnerable to inaccuracy in predicting the level of costs and/or disbursements with a risk of over or underestimating.

Illustration of the calculation of the disbursement element of a success fee

A	B	C	D	E
Disbursements	Costs	Ratio D to C	% Confidence success fee	Disbursement success fee %
£500	£10000	5%	33.3%	1.66

The formula:
A ÷ B × 100 = C
C × D ÷ 100 = E
E is then added to the success fee (D).

2. AFTER-THE-EVENT INSURANCE

(a) Collateral benefits

The Court of Appeal in *Callery* held that s 29 of the Access to Justice Act 1999 should be interpreted so as to treat the words 'insurance against the risk of incurring a costs liability' as meaning 'insurance against the risk of incurring a costs liability that cannot be passed on to the opposing party'. This dealt with any argument about allowing a premium in costs-only proceedings, a pint not pursued in the House of Lords.

Accordingly, cover which included some own costs liabilities was within s 29. The court left open however the extent of own costs cover which a court might consider to be reasonable. In *Callery* itself the cover was for own disbursements (not including counsel), premium and un-recovered premium. The court considered the last item to be insignificant in terms of the attributable premium in this case. The recoverability of a premium for a full, both sides' costs policy was left open.

Reference is made to collateral benefits provided by insurers. No such benefits were given in the case and the court thus left open the question of the recovery of premium which pays for such benefits. Examples of collateral benefits are case handling and negotiation and practical assistance such as counselling or arranging business matters. These kinds of benefit were considered in the Claims Direct Test Cases (2002), in the context of a claims management company and were not allowable as part of the premium.

On the facts the Court in *Callery* held that the premium of £350 was reasonable.

(b) Master O'Hare's Report

Before giving judgment on the insurance questions the Court in *Callery* adjourned for a report to be prepared by Costs Judge Master John O'Hare. That Report was annexed to the 31 July judgment but does not have the status of a Court of Appeal judgment. It was made available by the court to give some assistance in assessing additional liabilities. The court did not accept all of his suggestions, including his proposal that an insurance premium should be presumed reasonable unless the paying party proved otherwise.

Guidance for assessment

I am indebted to David Chalk for the following tables. Table I is a summary of the Report's analysis of premiums based upon a list of benefits additional to adverse costs cover. Master O'Hare was giving guidance as to the percentage of premium which could be attributed to these items, information which will be needed only where on assessment it is considered that that part of the premium ought not to be recovered. The effect of the court's judgment on each item is therefore given since not all items can be treated in the same way as to recoverability.

Table II sets out Master O'Hare's guidance for the conduct of detailed assessments in RTA cases. Again the effect of the court's judgment is given alongside the Report's conclusions.

Table I

What does the premium cover?

Item	Court of Appeal – recoverable*	Report
Own counsel's fees	Yes	Allow in full
Other disbursements	Yes	Allow in full
Cover for appeals	Not considered	Negligible
Costs of Part 36	Yes	Substantial but not quantified
Top up cover option	Not considered	Not quantified
Interest foregone on deferred premiums	No decision, see [65]**	Allow in full
Premium cover in event case losses	Yes	Allow in full
Un-recovered	Doubted, see [54]** and [62]**	Not quantified premium
Claims record of solicitor	Not considered	Not quantified
Interest on disbursement loans if claim fails	Not considered	Consider: likely rate of interest, size of loan, likely duration of proceedings, risk of loss
Advice and assistance of claims managers	Arguably not	Not quantified

* The court's decision is as to recoverability and not the question of the cost of that cover which might be found nonetheless to be unreasonable.

** All paragraph numbers are references to the judgment of Lord Phillips MR.

Table II

Guidance for detailed assessment – RTA

	Guidance	Court of Appeal
(a)	No benchmarking – develop benchmarks through experience	
(b)	High limit of indemnity does not itself indicate unreasonable premium	
(c)	Block risk policies not unreasonable	May be difficult to justify see [23]** There is no presumption that the premium is reasonable
(d)	[rejected by Court]	
(e)	Allowed premium is total not the pure underwriting risk premium	Do not look to how the premium is used by the insurer.
(f)	Assessment fees and profit costs of complying with policy recoverable	Not considered
(g)	Receiving party need not have made the best choice – must be reasonable choice	Premium actually allowed was not lowest available.
(h)	Paying party to provide evidence from 'Litigation Funding' or similar source	ATE insurer to provide evidence of reasonableness – see [16]**
(i)	Can be reasonable to insure before sending letter to opponent	Yes
	Also reasonable to wait until defendant's reaction known	Not considered
(j)	If premium at or above top of range of other policies – purchaser must explain	Not specifically addressed but judgment generally consistent
(k)	High cost premium easier to justify where high success fee has been allowed	Not considered
(l)	Consider reductions for irrecoverable elements [Table I]	See Table I
(m)	Value deductions by broad brush	Not considered

** All paragraph numbers are references to the judgment of Lord Phillips MR.

(c) Challenging the premium

There are two challenges which can be made to premiums: first, that not all of the sum paid is in fact premium and, second, that the premium paid is unreasonably high. In the Claims Direct Test Cases (SCCO, Senior Costs Judge Hurst, *Law Society Gazette*, 25 July 2002) the former was the main argument. The Court of Appeal in *Callery* had made it clear that this was a legitimate enquiry where there was evidence that what was being purchased was not merely insurance. In the case of the Claims Direct scheme £621 of the £1,312 was found to be attributable to insurance and was allowed as premium. An additional premium, taking the total to £1,569.75, giving protection to the first £1,000 of damages was disallowed as falling outside of s 29. This was an off-the-peg 'block rated' policy so the same premium applied to RTA cases as it does to complex personal injury claims involving employer's liability. In *Ashworth v Peterborough United Football Club* ([2002] SCCO 0201106) the challenge came in the form of the premium paid of £45,937.50 being too high. The policy covered the costs of both parties. There was no CFA. The entire amount was allowed on assessment. It was found that the insurer would not have provided cover for less and that it was unlikely that any other insurer would have done so. The claimant had acted reasonably in accepting the quote having previously been refused cover by a different insurer. The policy gave retrospective cover, a matter which was found to be legitimate in principle. Significantly the premium was seen as proportionate to the complexity and risk involved in the case and was not judged simply in terms of the limit of indemnity.

To sum up:

1. Is it all premium?
2. To the extent that it is, did it purchase collateral benefits? If so deduct from premium (unless already deducted at 1.).
3. Is what is left reasonable and proportionate?

The provisions of CPR 44.4(1) and (2) (p 99) and 44.5(3) (the seven pillars of wisdom, p 100) and ss 11.1, 11.5, 11.7 and 11.10 of the Costs Practice Direction (p 525) are especially relevant to the assessment of premiums. CPR 44.12A (p 110) applies to costs-only proceedings.

3. BTE OR ATE?

Sarwar v Alam [2001] EWCA Civ 1401, [2001] 4 All ER 541
Lord Justice Brooke, a member of the court, provided the following helpful summary.

This is another appeal concerned with the new arrangements for financing the costs of personal injury litigation which came into effect last year. Legal Aid is now no longer available for most litigation of this type. In *Callery v Gray*, the Court of Appeal was concerned two months ago with issues relating to the appropriate size of a success fee in a conditional fee agreement made in connection with a small claim for personal injuries suffered in a road traffic accident which was settled quite quickly without any need to bring court proceedings. In that case a passenger in a car had made a claim against the driver of the car involved in an accident. The court was also concerned with the appropriateness of taking out 'after the event' ('ATE') insurance in connection with such a claim, and the reasonableness of the ATE premium claimed in that case.

The present appeal is concerned with a similar claim brought by a passenger against the driver of the car in which he was travelling. The court below had disallowed the recovery of an ATE premium on the grounds that the claimant ought to have enquired into the availability of 'before the event' ('BTE') legal expenses insurance which formed part of the cover provided by the driver's insurance policy, and then made use of that cover. This policy covered the costs and expenses of both sides in a claim brought by a passenger in the car against the insured driver himself up to a limit of £50,000.

The Court of Appeal allowed the appeal on the grounds that the policy did not provide the claimant with appropriate cover in the circumstances of this case. Representation arranged by the insurer of the opposing party, to which the claimant had never been a party, and of which he had no knowledge of the time it was entered into and where the opposing insurer through its chosen representative reserved to itself the full conduct and control of the claim, was not a reasonable alternative to representation by a lawyer of the claimant's own choice, backed by an ATE policy.

The court suggested that the position might be different if BTE insurers financed some transparently independent organisation to handle such claims, and made it clear in the policy that this is what they were doing.

The court said, however, that if a claimant making a relatively small (ie under about £5,000) claim in a road traffic accident had access to pre-existing BTE cover which appeared to be satisfactory for a claim of that size, that in the ordinary course of things he/she should be referred to the relevant BTE insurer. The court gave guidance as to the nature of the inquiries a solicitor should make in this class of case into the availability of BTE cover and the insurance policies and other documents the solicitor should ask the client to produce. It stressed, however, that this guidance should not be treated as an inflexible code, and that the overriding principle was that the claimant, assisted by his/her solicitor, should act in a manner that was reasonable.

4. BTE GUIDANCE

The Law Society was disappointed that in *Sarwar v Alam* the Court of Appeal did not accept the Society's contention that there is a strong public interest in maintaining the client's freedom of choice, which should prevail over any implied requirement to use before-the-event insurance even if held in the claimant's name, at least unless certain minimum conditions were met. It has not generally been the case hitherto that a method of funding is rendered unreasonable by the fact that individual claimants may have an alternative available. In the view of the Law Society the availability of a BTE policy should be taken into account only in limited circumstances and cannot be regarded as a suitable alternative unless:

- the claimant has a reasonable choice of solicitor (for example, any Law Society personal injury panel member);
- the BTE insurer pays reasonable fees (that is, normal between the party rates); and
- the policy provides for the freedom for the instructed solicitor to conduct the litigation on its merits rather than being subject to direction by the BTE insurer.

The Law Society accepts that the court in *Sarwar* did not give great weight to these considerations in the context of low-value RTA claims. It remains to be seen how future courts will deal with these issues. In the meantime solicitors will obviously wish to follow the guidance set by the court.

Jeremy Fleming of the Law Society advised:

> 'Solicitors should ask clients to bring copies of their major insurance policies to their first meetings – if these policies reveal that the client is already covered by before-the-event insurance, the solicitor should refer the client to that insurer. Where an injured client was a passenger in an accident, the client should obtain a copy of the driver's insurance policies, and if the driver's consent is required, the solicitor should ask the client to obtain consent. Although solicitors should make proportionate inquiries into the existence of before-the-event insurance, the court found they were not obliged to embark on a treasure hunt and that it was not proportionate for solicitors to inquire into details of insurance policies connected to credit cards held by clients and policies which seek to reserve full control of conduct of the claim might be unreasonable.'

5. QUESTIONNAIRE

Here is a check for the existence of valid and acceptable BTE insurance in the form of a questionnaire from the supplement to *Risk Assessment in Litigation* by David Chalk, to whom I am again indebted for permission to publish it.

	Yes	No	Not known
1. Do you, or a partner living with you, own (with or without a mortgage) your home?			
2. Do you, or a partner living with you, have home contents insurance?			
3. Have you, or a partner living with you, purchased Legal Expenses insurance?			
4. Are you, or a partner living with you, employed?			
5. Are you, or a partner living with you, a member of a trade union?			
6. Were you driving a car when the accident occurred?			
7. If you were a passenger, do you know the name of the driver of the car you were in?			
8. If you were a passenger, is the driver related to you?			
9. In your opinion, was the accident the fault of the driver?			
10. Are you likely to be able to find any insurance policies that you have?			

Those are the questions, here are the answers:

1. YES = Likely to be buildings insurance which may have an add-on BTE cover (but may exclude road traffic claims).
   NO = No buildings insurance is likely to exist giving cover to the client.
2. YES = BTE may exist as an add-on to the contents policy (but may exclude road traffic claims).
   NO = Not a source for BTE.
3. YES = This is specifically purchased as a stand-alone BTE policy.
   NO = No stand-alone likely to exist.
4. YES = Possible that the employer provides BTE.
   NO = Not a source of BTE.
5. YES = May provide legal assistance though not BTE.
   NO = Not a source of funding.
6. YES = Client ought to have liability insurance – it may include a BTE add-on.
   NO = Client's own motor policy BTE add-on will not provide cover.
7. YES = Client to request copy of driver's BTE policy and seek consent to use it.
   NO = Unlikely to be cost effective to pursue this source.
8. YES = Potential conflict of interest may make this BTE unsuitable.
   NO = No conflict of interest arising from family relationship.
9. YES = Likely conflict of interest may make this BTE unsuitable.
   NO = Need to assess nonetheless the possibility that blame will eventually attach to own driver.
10. YES = Indicates information provided will be accurate.
    NO = indicates that information will be incomplete and some unavailable.

FORM N251

NOTICE OF FUNDING OF CASE OR CLAIM **N251**

Notice of Funding of Case or Claim

In the	
Claim No.	
Claimant (include Ref.)	
Defendant (include Ref.)	

Notice of funding by means of a conditional fee agreement, insurance policy or undertaking given by a prescribed body should be given to the court and all other parties to the case:

- on commencement of proceedings
- on filing an acknowledgment of service, defence or other first document; and
- at any later time that such an arrangement is entered into, changed or terminated

Take notice that in respect of [all claims herein] [the following claims . . . .] . the case of . . . . *(specify name of party)*

[is now] [was] being funded by:
(Please tick those boxes which apply)

- ☐ a conditional fee agreement dated . . . . which provides for a success fee;
- ☐ an insurance policy issued on *(date)* . . . . by *(name of insurers)* . . . . ;
- ☐ an undertaking given on *(date)* . . . . by *(name of prescribed body)* . . . . in the following terms . . . .

The funding of the case has now changed:

- ☐ the above funding has now ceased
- ☐ the conditional fee agreement has been terminated
- ☐ a conditional agreement dated . . . . which provides for a success fee has been entered into
- ☐ the insurance policy dated . . . . has been cancelled
- ☐ an insurance policy has been issued by *(name of insurer)* . . . . on *(date)* . . . .
- ☐ the undertaking given on *(date)* . . . . has been terminated
- ☐ an undertaking has been given on *(date)* . . . . by *(name of prescribed body)* . . . . in the following terms . . . .

Signed . . . . **Date** . . . .
Solicitor for the (claimant) (defendant) (Part 20 defendant) (respondent) (appellant)

The court office at

is open between 10 am and 4 pm Monday to Friday. When corresponding with the court, please address forms or letters to the Court Manager and quote the claim number.

INDEX